THE Enduring Vision

A HISTORY OF THE AMERICAN PEOPLE

VOLUME TWO: FROM 1865

Concise Sixth Edition

PAUL S. BOYER
University of Wisconsin, Madison

CLIFFORD E. CLARK, JR.
Carleton College

SANDRA MCNAIR HAWLEY
San Jacinto College

JOSEPH F. KETT
University of Virginia

ANDREW RIESER
State University of New York, Dutchess Community College

NEAL SALISBURY
Smith College

HARVARD SITKOFF
University of New Hampshire

NANCY WOLOCH
Barnard College

WADSWORTH
CENGAGE Learning

Australia • Brazil • Japan • Korea • Mexico • Singapore • Spain • United Kingdom • United States

Editor-in-Chief: P. J. Boardman

Publisher: Suzanne Jeans

Senior Sponsoring Editor: Ann West

Senior Developmental Editor: Lisa Kalner Williams

Assistant Editor: Megan Curry

Senior Marketing Manager: Katherine Bates

Marketing Communications Manager: Christine Dobberpuhl

Senior Content Project Manager: Jane Lee

Art and Design Manager: Jill Haber

Cover Design Director: Tony Saizon

Senior Photo Editor: Jennifer Meyer Dare

Composition Buyer: Chuck Dutton

Print Buyer: Paula Vang

Permissions Manager, Images: Jennifer Meyer Dare

Permissions Manager, Text: Katie Huha

Editorial Assistant: Laura Collins

Cover image: Mary Helmreich, *San Francisco Tiburon Ferry*, 2006. Watercolor. Credit: © 2006 Mary Helmreich

© 2010 Wadsworth, Cengage Learning

For product information and technology assistance, contact us at **Cengage Learning Academic Resource Center, 1-800-354-9706**
For permission to use material from this text or product, submit all requests online at **www.cengage.com/permissions**. Further permissions questions can be emailed to **permissionrequest@cengage.com**

Library of Congress Control Number: 2008939229

ISBN-13: 978-0-547-22278-3

ISBN-10: 0-547-22278-5

Wadsworth
25 Thomson Place
Boston, MA 02210
USA

Cengage Learning products are represented in Canada by Nelson Education, Ltd.

For your course and learning solutions, visit **academic.cengage.com**

Purchase any of our products at your local college store or at our preferred online store **www.ichapters.com**

Printed in Canada
1 2 3 4 5 6 7 12 11 10 09 08

The Enduring Vision

Contents

19

Immigration, Urbanization, and Everyday Life, 1860–1900   426

20

Politics and Expansion in an Industrializing Age, 1877–1900   451

21
The Progressive Era, 1900–1917   476

22
Global Involvements and World War I, 1902–1920   505

23
The 1920s: Coping with Change, 1920–1929   532

24

The Great Depression and the New Deal, 1929–1939   557

25

Americans and a World in Crisis, 1933–1945   587

26

The Cold War Abroad and at Home, 1945–1952   616

27

America at Mid-Century, 1952–1960   638

28

The Liberal Era, 1960–1968   662

29

A Time of Upheaval, 1968–1974   685

30

Conservative Resurgence, Economic Woes, Foreign Challenges, 1974–1989   709

Maps

Charts, Graphs, and Tables

Much has changed in America and the world since we began planning *The Enduring Vision* more than two decades ago. Some of these developments have been welcome and positive; others deeply unsettling. This new Concise Sixth Edition fully documents all of these changes, as well as the continuities that offer reassurance for the future.

The Concise Sixth Edition builds on the underlying strategy that has guided us from the beginning. We want our history to be not only comprehensive and illuminating, but also lively, readable, and true to the lived experience of earlier generations of Americans. Within a clear political and chronological framework, we integrate the best recent scholarship in all areas of American history. Our interest in social and cultural history, which shapes our own teaching and scholarship, has suffused *The Enduring Vision* from the outset, and it remains central. We integrate the historical experience of women and men of all regions, ethnic groups, and social classes who make up the American mosaic.

New Interpretations, Expanded Coverage

In recent years, American historians have emphasized how deeply our history is embedded within a larger global context. In the Concise Sixth Edition we have underscored the wider context of American history throughout the narrative. From the origins of agriculture two millennia ago to the impact of globalization today, we have emphasized how the social, economic, and political developments central to our historical experience emerge with fresh new clarity when viewed within a broader world framework.

As in earlier editions, coverage of environmental history, the land, and the West is fully integrated into the narrative, and treated analytically, not simply "tacked on" to a traditional account. We also incorporate the best of the new political history, stressing the social, cultural, and economic issues at stake in political decisions and debates.

We again offer extensive coverage of medicine and disease, from the epidemics brought by European explorers and settlers to today's AIDS crisis, bioethics debates, and controversies over health-care financing. We also give careful attention to religious history, from the spiritual values of pre-Columbian communities to the political activism of contemporary conservative Christian groups.

Visual Resources and Aids to the Student

The layout of this edition has changed from previous editions. A new one-column format allows for more seamless integration of images and a smoother narrative flow. Each chapter begins with Focus Questions that correspond to the major sections of the chapter to give students a preview of the key topics to be covered. These questions are briefly answered at the end of the chapter in the "Chapter Summary." Throughout the chapters, students get assistance from key terms that are boldfaced in the text and defined in the margins; "Checking In" boxes at the end of each section summarize the key points in that section.

SUPPLEMENTARY RESOURCES

A wide array of supplements accompanies this text to help students master the material and guide instructors in teaching from *The Enduring Vision, Concise Sixth Edition.* For details on viewing or ordering these materials, please consult your Cengage Learning sales representative.

Instructor Tools

The **Instructor Website** (found at **www.cengage.com/ history/boyer/enduringconcise6e**) offers the *Instructor's Guide,* an online manual including Instructional Techniques and Resources, Historical Investigations for students, and for each chapter, chapter themes, lecture suggestions, print and nonprint resources, and a guide to using the Enduring Voices document sets. Also available on the Instructor Website are primary sources with instructor notes, PowerPoint slides for classroom presentation, and personal response system slides. A computerized testing program, available on CD-ROM, provides flexible test-editing capabilities.

Instructors who adopt *The Enduring Vision, Concise Sixth Edition* also receive access to **HistoryFinder**, a powerful search engine and primary source repository that helps instructors create rich and exciting classroom presentations. This online tool offers thousands of online resources, including art, photographs, maps, primary sources, multimedia content, and Associated Press interactive modules. HistoryFinder's assets can easily be searched by keyword or from pull-down menus by topic, media type, or by Wadsworth/Cengage Learning textbook. Instructors can then browse, preview, and download resources straight from the website.

Student Tools

The **Student Website** (found at **www.cengage.com/ history/boyer/enduringconcise6e**) contains a variety of tutorial resources including ACE quizzes with practice feedback, interactive maps, primary sources, chronology exercises, flashcards, and MP3 chapter summaries.

The **American History Resource Center** offers hundreds of primary sources such as speeches, letters, legal documents and transcripts, poems, maps, simulations, timelines, and additional images that bring history to life—along with interactive assignable exercises. A map feature using Google Earth coordinates helps students learn geography by comparing traditional textbook maps with an aerial view of the location today.

ACKNOWLEDGMENTS

Any book, and this one in particular, is the result of the hard work of many people. As always, the editorial staff at Houghton Mifflin has been outstanding. Particularly deserving of thanks are Ann West, Lisa Kalner Williams, and Bob Greiner.

Sandra Hawley thanks her daughter, Lee Anne Hawley, who as ever, has been invaluable in multiple ways. Great thanks are owed as well to Lisa LaDay Morris, Patricia Piper, Dorothy White, Larry Kallus, Eric Johnson, Melanie Welavir, and Tony Sisk for their continuing support.

Andrew Rieser acknowledges Sandra McNair Hawley and the co-authors for handing him a superb text from which to whittle down the second volume; and he thanks Paul S. Boyer for his support and friendship.

CHAPTER 16

The Crisis of Reconstruction

1865–1877

The Devastated South

CHAPTER PREVIEW

Reconstruction Politics, 1865–1868
On what major issues did Radical Republicans and President Johnson struggle over Reconstruction policy?

Reconstruction Governments
What impact did federal Reconstruction policy have on the former Confederacy and ex-Confederates?

The Impact of Emancipation
In what ways did newly freed slaves reshape their lives after emancipation?

New Concerns in the North, 1868–1876
Why did northern concern about Reconstruction begin to wane?

Reconstruction Abandoned, 1876–1877
What led the North to abandon Reconstruction?

The end of the Civil War was a time of uncharted possibilities—and unresolved conflicts. While former slaves exulted over their freedom, their former owners were often as grim as the ravaged southern landscape. Several thousand fled to Brazil, Mexico, or Europe, but most remained.

After most wars, victors care little for the mood of the vanquished, but the Civil War was different. The Union had sought not merely victory but the return of national unity. The federal government faced unprecedented questions. How could the Union be restored and the South reintegrated? Who would control the process—Congress or the president? Should Confederate leaders be tried for treason? Most important, what would happen to the

3.5 million former slaves? The freedmen's future was *the* crucial postwar issue, for emancipation had set in motion the most profound upheaval in the nation's history. Slavery had been both a labor system and a means of racial control; it had determined the South's social, economic, and political structure. The end of the Civil War, in short, posed two huge challenges that had to be addressed simultaneously: readmitting the Confederate states to the Union and defining the status of free blacks in society.

Between 1865 and 1877 the nation faced major and often divisive challenges and crises. Conflict characterized congressional debates, the former Confederacy, and the industrializing postwar North. These crises of Reconstruction—the restoration of the former Confederate states and the fate of the former slaves—reshaped the legacy of the Civil War.

RECONSTRUCTION POLITICS, 1865–1868

On what major issues did Radical Republicans and President Johnson struggle over Reconstruction policy?

The end of the Civil War offered multiple possibilities for chaos and vengeance. The federal government could have imprisoned Confederate leaders; former rebel troops could have become guerrillas; freed slaves could have waged a racial war against their former masters. None of this happened. Instead, intense *political* conflict dominated the immediate postwar period. The political upheaval, sometimes attended by violence, produced new constitutional amendments, an impeachment crisis, and some of the most ambitious domestic legislation ever enacted by Congress, the Reconstruction Acts of 1867–1868. It culminated in something that few expected, the enfranchisement of African-American men.

Radical Republicans Former abolitionists who controlled Congress and Reconstruction in late 1860s

In 1865 only a handful of **Radical Republicans** advocated African-American suffrage. But in the complex political battles of Reconstruction, the Radicals won broad support for their program, including African-American male enfranchisement. Just as the Civil War had led to emancipation, so Reconstruction led to African-American suffrage.

Lincoln's Plan

Conflict over Reconstruction began even before the war ended. In December 1863, President Lincoln issued the Proclamation of Amnesty and Reconstruction, which allowed southern states to form new governments if at least 10 percent of those who had voted in the 1860 elections swore an oath of allegiance to the Union and accepted emancipation. This plan excluded most Confederate officials and military officers, who would have had to apply for presidential pardons, as well as African-Americans, who had not voted in 1860. Lincoln hoped both to undermine the Confederacy and to build a southern Republican party.

Radical Republicans in Congress wanted a slower readmission process that would exclude even more ex-Confederates from political life. The Wade-Davis Bill, passed by Congress in July 1864, provided that a military government would rule

Chronology

1863	President Abraham Lincoln issues Proclamation of Amnesty and Reconstruction
1864	Wade-Davis Bill passed by Congress and pocket-vetoed by Lincoln
1865	Freedmen's Bureau established; Civil War ends; Lincoln assassinated; Andrew Johnson becomes president; Johnson issues Proclamation of Amnesty and Reconstruction; Ex-Confederate states hold constitutional conventions (May–December); Thirteenth Amendment added to the Constitution; Presidential Reconstruction completed
	Civil Rights Act of 1866 and the Supplementary Freedmen's Bureau Act over Johnson's vetoes; Ku Klux Klan founded in Tennessee; Race riots in southern cities; Republicans win congressional elections; Howard University founded
	Reconstruction Act of 1867; William Seward negotiates the purchase of Alaska; Constitutional conventions meet in the ex-Confederate states
	Andrew Johnson impeached, tried, and acquitted; Fourteenth Amendment added to the Constitution; Ulysses S. Grant elected president
1869	Transcontinental railroad completed
1870	Congress readmits the four remaining southern states to the Union; Fifteenth Amendment added to the Constitution; Enforcement Act of 1870
	Second Enforcement Act; Ku Klux Klan Act
	Liberal Republican party formed; Amnesty Act; Alabama claims settled; Grant reelected president
1873	Panic of 1873 begins (September–October), setting off five-year depression
1874	Democrats gain control of the House of Representatives
1875	Civil Rights Act of 1875; Specie Resumption Act
1876	Disputed presidential election: Rutherford B. Hayes versus Samuel J. Tilden
1877	Electoral commission decides election in favor of Hayes; the last Republican-controlled state governments fall in Florida, South Carolina, and Louisiana
1879	"Exodus" movement spreads through several southern states

each former Confederate state and that at least half of the eligible voters would have to swear allegiance before they could choose a convention to repeal secession and abolish slavery. In addition, to qualify as a voter or a delegate, a southerner would have to take the "ironclad" oath, swearing that he had never voluntarily supported the Confederacy. The Wade-Davis Bill would have delayed readmission of southern states almost indefinitely.

Lincoln pocket-vetoed* the Wade-Davis Bill, and an impasse followed. Arkansas, Louisiana, Tennessee, and parts of Virginia moved toward readmission under variants of Lincoln's plan, but Congress refused to seat their delegates. Lincoln hinted that he might be moving toward a more rigorous policy than his original one, a program that would include African-American suffrage. But his death foreclosed the possibility that he and Congress might draw closer to agreement, and Radicals now looked with hope to the new president, Andrew Johnson.

---

* Pocket-vetoed: failed to sign the bill within ten days of Congress's adjournment.

Presidential Reconstruction Under Johnson

At first glance, Andrew Johnson seemed a likely ally for the Radicals. The only southern senator to remain in Congress when his state seceded, Johnson had taken a strong anti-Confederate stance, proclaiming that "treason is a crime and must be made odious," and had served as military governor of Tennessee for two years. Self-educated, an ardent Jacksonian, a foe of the planter class, a supporter of emancipation—Johnson carried impeccable credentials. However, as a lifelong Democrat he had his own political agenda, sharply different from that of the Radicals. He neither adopted abolitionist ideals nor challenged racist sentiments. He hoped mainly that the fall of slavery would cripple southern aristocrats.

In May 1865, with Congress out of session, Johnson shocked Republicans by announcing his own program, A Proclamation of Amnesty and Reconstruction, to bring the southern states still without Reconstruction governments—Alabama, Florida, Georgia, Mississippi, North Carolina, South Carolina, and Texas—back into the Union. Virtually all southerners who took an oath of allegiance would receive pardon and amnesty, and all their property except slaves would be restored to them. Confederate civil and military officers would still be disqualified, as would well-to-do former Confederates (anyone owning taxable property worth $20,000 or more). This purge of the plantation aristocracy, Johnson said, would benefit "humble men, the peasantry of the South, who have been decoyed . . . into rebellion." Poorer whites would now be in control, oath takers could elect delegates to state conventions, which would call regular elections, proclaim secession illegal, repudiate debts incurred under the Confederacy, and ratify the Thirteenth Amendment, which abolished slavery.

Presidential Reconstruction began in summer 1865 with unforeseen results. Johnson handed out pardons liberally (some thirteen thousand) and dropped his plans for the punishment of treason. By the end of 1865 all seven states had created new civil governments that in effect restored the *status quo ante bellum* (state of affairs before the war). Confederate officers and large planters resumed state offices, and former Confederate congressmen and generals won election to Congress. Because many of these new representatives were former Whigs who had not supported secession, southerners believed that they genuinely had elected "Union" men. Some states refused to repudiate their Confederate debts or to ratify the Thirteenth Amendment.

Most infuriating to the Radicals, every state passed **"black codes"** intended to ensure a landless, dependent black labor force—to "secure the services of the negroes, teach them their place," in the words of one Alabamian. These codes, which replaced earlier slave codes, guaranteed the freedmen some basic rights—marriage, ownership of property, the right to testify in court against other blacks—but also restricted freedmen's behavior. Some states established segregation, and most prohibited racial intermarriage, jury service by blacks, and court testimony by blacks against whites. Most harmful, black codes included economic restrictions to prevent blacks from leaving the plantation, usually through labor contracts stipulating that anyone who had not signed a labor contract was a vagrant and subject to arrest.

These codes left freedmen no longer slaves but not really liberated. Although many of their provisions never actually took effect—for example, the Union army and the **Freedmen's Bureau** suspended the enforcement of the racially discriminatory laws—the black codes reflected white southern attitudes and showed what "home rule" would have been like without federal intervention.

"black codes" Laws passed by southern states to limit the rights of freedmen

Freedmen's Bureau Agency established by federal government to aid former slaves

To many northerners, both the black codes and the election of former Confederates to high office reeked of southern defiance. When the Thirty-ninth Congress convened in December 1865, it refused to seat the southern delegates and prepared to dismantle the black codes and to lock ex-Confederates out of power.

Primary Source: Louisiana Black Code

Congress Versus Johnson

Southern blacks' status became the major issue in Congress. With Congress split into four blocs—Democrats, and Radical, moderate, and conservative Republicans—a politically adroit president could have protected his program. Ineptly, Johnson alienated the moderates and pushed them into the Radicals' arms by vetoing some key moderate measures.

In late 1865 Congress voted to extend the life of the Freedmen's Bureau for three more years. Staffed mainly by army officers, the bureau provided relief, rations, and medical care; built schools for former slaves; put them to work on abandoned or confiscated lands; and tried to protect their rights as laborers. To strengthen the bureau, Congress had voted to allow it to run special military courts that would settle labor disputes and invalidate labor contracts forced on African-Americans under the black codes. In February 1866 Johnson vetoed the bill; the Constitution, he declared, neither sanctioned military trials of civilians in peacetime nor supported a system to care for "indigent persons." Then in March 1866 Congress passed the Civil Rights Act of 1866, which made African-Americans U.S. citizens with the same civil rights as other citizens and authorized federal intervention to ensure African-Americans' rights in court. Johnson vetoed this measure as well, arguing that it would "operate in favor of the colored and against the white race." In April Congress overrode his veto, and in July it enacted the Supplementary Freedmen's Bureau Act over another presidential veto.

These vetoes puzzled many Republicans, for the new laws did not undercut the basic structure of presidential Reconstruction. Although the vetoes gained support for Johnson among northern Democrats, they cost him dearly among moderate Republicans, who began to ally with the Radicals. Was Johnson a political incompetent, or was he merely trying, unsuccessfully, to forge a centrist coalition? Whatever the case, he drove moderate and Radical Republicans together toward their next step: the passage of a constitutional amendment to protect the new Civil Rights Act.

The Fourteenth Amendment, 1866

In April 1866 Congress adopted the **Fourteenth Amendment,** its most ambitious attempt to deal with the problems of Reconstruction and the freed slaves. In the first clause, the amendment proclaimed that all persons born or naturalized in the United States were citizens and that no state could abridge their rights without due process of law or deny them equal protection under the law. Second, the amendment guaranteed that, if a state denied suffrage to any male citizen, its representation in Congress would be proportionally reduced. Third, the amendment disqualified from state and national offices *all* prewar officeholders who had supported the Confederacy. Finally, it repudiated the Confederate debt and maintained the validity of the federal debt. In effect, the Fourteenth Amendment nullified the *Dred Scott* decision, threatened southern states that deprived African-American men of the right to vote, and invalidated most of the pardons that President Johnson had ladled out.

Fourteenth Amendment
Amendment that defines citizenship and guarantees equal protection under the law

Passage of the amendment created a fire-storm. Abolitionists said that it did not go far enough to protect African-American voting rights, southerners blasted it as vengeful, and President Johnson denounced it. The president's unwillingness to compromise solidified the new alliance between moderate and Radical Republicans, and transformed the congressional elections of 1866 into a referendum on the Fourteenth Amendment.

Over the summer Johnson set off on a whistle-stop train tour campaigning against the amendment. Humorless and defensive, the president made fresh enemies, however, and doomed his hope of creating a new political party, the National Union party, opposed to the amendment. Meanwhile, the moderate and Radical Republicans defended the amendment, condemned President Johnson, and branded the Democratic party "a common sewer . . . into which is emptied every element of treason, North and South."

Republicans carried the congressional elections of 1866 in a landslide, winning nearly two-thirds of the House and three-fourths of the Senate. They had secured a mandate for the Fourteenth Amendment and their own Reconstruction program.

Congressional Reconstruction, 1866–1867

The congressional debate over reconstructing the South began in December 1866 and lasted three months. Radical leaders, anxious to stifle a resurgence of Confederate power, called for African-American suffrage, federal support for public schools, confiscation of Confederate estates, and extended military occupation of the South. Moderate Republicans accepted part of this plan, and in February 1867, after complex political maneuvers, Congress passed the Reconstruction Act of 1867. Johnson vetoed it, and on March 2, Congress passed the law over his veto. Three more Reconstruction acts—passed in 1867 and 1868 over presidential vetoes—refined and enforced the first act.

The Reconstruction Act of 1867 invalidated the state governments formed under the Lincoln and Johnson plans; only Tennessee, which had already ratified the Fourteenth Amendment and had been readmitted to the Union, escaped further Reconstruction. The new law divided the other ten former Confederate states into five military districts. It provided that voters—all black men, plus whites not disqualified by the Fourteenth Amendment—could elect delegates who would write a new state constitution granting African-American suffrage. After congressional approval of the state constitution, and after the state legislature's ratification of the Fourteenth Amendment, Congress would readmit the state into the Union. The enfranchisement of African-Americans and disfranchisement of so many ex-Confederates made the Reconstruction Act of 1867 far more radical than Johnson's program. Even then, however, it provided only temporary military rule, made no provisions to prosecute Confederate leaders for treason, and neither confiscated nor redistributed property.

Radical Republican leader Thaddeus Stevens had proposed confiscation of large Confederate estates to "humble the proud traitors" and to provide land for the former slaves. Because political independence rested on economic independence, he contended, land grants would be far more valuable to African-Americans than the vote. But moderate Republicans and others backed away from Stevens's proposal.

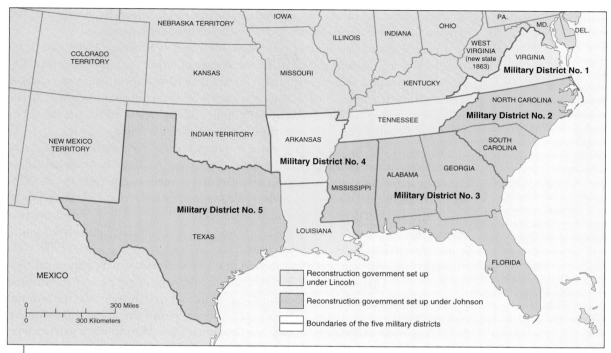

Map 16.1   The Reconstruction of the South

The Reconstruction Act of 1867 divided the former Confederate states, except Tennessee, into five military districts and set forth the steps by which new state governments could be created.

Tampering with property rights in the South might well jeopardize them in the North, they argued, and could endanger the entire Reconstruction program. Thus Congress rejected the most radical parts of the Radical Republican program.

Congressional Reconstruction took effect in spring 1867, but Johnson impeded its implementation by replacing pro-Radical military officers with conservative ones because Reconstruction could not be enforced without military power. Furious and more suspicious than ever of the president, congressional moderates and Radicals again joined forces to block Johnson from further hampering Reconstruction.

Interactive Map:
The Reconstruction

congressional Reconstruction
The four Reconstruction acts that Congress imposed on the South in 1867

The Impeachment Crisis, 1867–1868

In March 1867, responding to Johnson's obstructionist tactics, Republicans in Congress passed two laws to restrict presidential power. The Tenure of Office Act prohibited the president from removing civil officers without Senate consent. Its purpose was to protect Secretary of War Edwin Stanton, a Radical ally needed to enforce the Reconstruction acts. The other law banned the president from issuing military orders except through the commanding general, Ulysses S. Grant, who could not be removed without the Senate's consent. Not satisfied with clipping the president's wings, Radicals also began to look for grounds for **impeachment** and conviction to remove all possible obstacles to Reconstruction. Intense investigations by the House

impeachment Process to remove a president from office; attempted but failed in case of Andrew Johnson

Judiciary Committee and private detectives turned up no impeachable offenses, but Johnson himself soon provided the charges that his opponents needed.

In August 1867 Johnson suspended Stanton and in February 1868 tried to remove him. The president's defiance of the Tenure of Office Act drove moderate Republicans back into alliance with the Radicals. The House approved eleven charges of impeachment, nine of them based on violation of the Tenure of Office Act and the other two accusing Johnson of being "unmindful of the high duties of the office," of seeking to disgrace Congress, and of not enforcing the Reconstruction acts.

Johnson's trial by the Senate, which began in March 1868, riveted public attention for eleven weeks. Seven congressmen, including leading Radicals, served as prosecutors, or "managers." Johnson's lawyers maintained that by violating the Tenure of Office Act, he was merely seeking a court test of a law that he believed to be unconstitutional. They also contended that the law did not protect Stanton, because Lincoln, not Johnson, had appointed him. And they asserted that Johnson was guilty of no crime indictable in a regular court.

Congressional "managers" countered that impeachment was a political process, not a criminal trial, and that Johnson's "abuse of discretionary power" constituted an impeachable offense. Some Senate Republicans wavered, fearful that the removal of a president would destroy the balance of power within the federal government. They also distrusted Radical Republican Benjamin Wade, the president pro tempore of the Senate, who, since there was no vice president, would become president if Johnson were thrown out.

Ultimately, despite intense pressure, seven Republicans risked political suicide by voting with the Democrats against removal, and the Senate failed by one vote to convict Johnson. In so doing, the legislators set two critical precedents: in the future, no president would be impeached on political grounds, nor would he be impeached because two-thirds of Congress disagreed with him. In the short term, nonetheless, the anti-Johnson forces achieved their goals, for Andrew Johnson had no future as president. Republicans in Congress could now pursue their last major Reconstruction objective: guaranteeing African-American male suffrage.

The Fifteenth Amendment and the Question of Woman Suffrage, 1869–1870

African-American suffrage was the linchpin of congressional Reconstruction. Only with the support of African-American voters could Republicans secure control of the southern states. The Reconstruction Act of 1867 had forced southern states to enfranchise black men in order to reenter the Union, but most northern states still refused to grant suffrage to African-Americans. The **Fifteenth Amendment,** drawn up by Republicans and approved by Congress in 1869, aimed to protect black suffrage in the South and to extend it to the northern and border states on the assumption that newly enfranchised African-Americans would gratefully vote Republican. The amendment prohibited the denial of suffrage by the states to anyone on account of "race, color, or previous condition of servitude."

Democrats opposed the amendment on the grounds that it violated states' rights, but they did not control enough states to prevent its ratification. However, to some southerners, the amendment's omissions made it acceptable; as a Richmond

Fifteenth Amendment
Amendment guaranteeing men the right to vote

THE RECONSTRUCTION AMENDMENTS

AMENDMENT AND DATE OF CONGRESSIONAL PASSAGE	PROVISIONS	RATIFICATION
Thirteenth (January 1865)	Prohibited slavery in the United States	December 1865
Fourteenth (June 1866)	Defined citizenship to include all persons born or naturalized in the United States	July 1868, after Congress made ratification a prerequisite for readmission of ex-Confederate states to the Union
	Provided proportional loss of congressional representation for any state that denied suffrage to any of its male citizens	
	Disqualified prewar officeholders who supported the Confederacy from state or national office	
	Repudiated the Confederate debt	
Fifteenth (February 1869)	Prohibited the denial of suffrage because of race, color, or previous condition of servitude	March 1870; ratification required of Virginia, Texas, Mississippi, and Georgia for readmission to the Union

newspaper pointed out, it had "loopholes through which a coach and four horses can be driven." Indeed, the new amendment did not guarantee African-American office-holding, nor did it prohibit restrictions on suffrage, such as property requirements and literacy tests, both of which might be used to deny African-Americans the vote.

The debate over black suffrage drew new participants into the fray. Women's rights advocates had tried to promote both black suffrage and woman suffrage, but Radical Republicans rejected any linkage between the two, preferring to concentrate on black suffrage. Supporters of women's rights were themselves divided. Frederick Douglass argued that black suffrage had to receive priority. "If the elective franchise is not extended to the Negro, he is dead," explained Douglass. "Woman has a thousand ways by which she can attach herself to the ruling power of the land that we have not." Women's rights leaders Elizabeth Cady Stanton and Susan B. Anthony disagreed. If the Fifteenth Amendment did not include women, they emphasized, it would establish an "aristocracy of sex" and increase the disabilities under which women already labored.

The battle over black suffrage and the Fifteenth Amendment split women's rights advocates into two rival suffrage associations, both founded in 1869. The Boston-based American Woman Suffrage Association sought state-by-state suffrage, whereas the more radical National Woman Suffrage Association, based in New York and led by Stanton and Anthony, promoted a constitutional amendment for woman suffrage.

Throughout the 1870s the two groups competed for support. Two western states, Wyoming and Utah, extended the vote to women, but the

CHECKING IN

- Lincoln's somewhat lenient plan for Reconstruction died with him.

- President Johnson's even more tolerant plan for Reconstruction infuriated Radical Republicans.

- Congress overrode presidential vetoes of Reconstruction measures such as the Freedmen's Bureau and passed its own harsher version of Reconstruction legislation.

- The Fourteenth Amendment defined citizenship and guaranteed equal protection under the law, and the Fifteenth Amendment guaranteed the right of freedmen, but not of women, to vote.

- The attempt to impeach Johnson on political grounds failed by a narrow margin.

suffrage movement had little to do with it. In 1872 Susan B. Anthony mobilized about seventy women to try to vote nationwide; she was indicted, convicted, and fined. In 1875 the Supreme Court ruled that a state could deny women the right to vote. Woman suffrage advocates braced for a long struggle.

By the time the Fifteenth Amendment was ratified in 1870, Congress could look back on five years of momentous achievement. Three constitutional amendments had broadened the scope of democracy by abolishing slavery, affirming the rights of citizens, and prohibiting the denial of suffrage on the basis of race. Congress had re-admitted the former Confederate states into the Union. At the same time, momentum had slowed at the federal level. In 1869 the center of action shifted to the South, where tumultuous change was under way.

RECONSTRUCTION GOVERNMENTS

What impact did federal Reconstruction policy have on the former Confederacy and ex-Confederates?

During the years of presidential Reconstruction, 1865–1867, the southern states faced formidable tasks: creating new governments, reviving war-torn econo-mies, and dealing with the impact of emancipation. Racial tensions flared as freed-men organized political meetings to protest ill treatment and demand equal rights, and deadly race riots erupted in major southern cities. In May 1866 white crowds at-tacked African-American veterans in Memphis and rampaged through African-American neighborhoods, killing forty-six people.

Congressional Reconstruction, supervised by federal troops, began in spring 1867 with the dismantling of existing governments and the formation of new state governments dominated by Republicans. By 1868 most former Confederate states had rejoined the Union, and within two years the process was complete.

But Republican rule did not long endure in the South. Opposition from south-ern Democrats, the landowning elite, vigilantes, and most white voters proved insur-mountable. Nevertheless, these Reconstruction governments were unique because African-American men, including former slaves, participated in them. Slavery had ended in other societies, too, but only in the United States had freedmen gained dem-ocratic political rights.

A New Electorate

The Reconstruction laws of 1867–1868 transformed the southern electorate by temporarily disfranchising 15 per-cent of potential white voters and by enfranchising more than 700,000 freed slaves. Black voters outnumbered whites by 100,000 overall and held voting majorities in five states.

This new electorate provided a base for the Republican party, which had never existed in the South. To scornful Democrats, the Republicans comprised three types of scoundrels: northern **"carpetbaggers"** who had come south for wealth and power; southern **scalawags,** poor and ignorant, who sought to profit by supporting Repub-lican rule; and hordes of uneducated freedmen, who were easily manipulated. In

"carpetbagger" Northerner who moved south after Civil War, supported Republicans and Reconstruction

scalawag Southerner who supported Reconstruction

fact, the hastily assembled Republican party, crossing racial and class lines, constituted a loose coalition of diverse factions with often-contradictory goals.

To northerners who moved south after the war, the former Confederacy was an undeveloped region, ripe with possibilities. The carpetbaggers included many former Union soldiers who hoped to buy land, open factories, build railroads, or simply enjoy the warmer climate. Holding almost one in three state offices, they wielded disproportionate political power.

A handful of scalawags were old Whigs, but most were small farmers from the mountain regions of North Carolina, Georgia, Alabama, and Arkansas. Former Unionists who had owned no slaves and who felt no loyalty to the old plantation elite, they wanted to improve their economic position and lacked commitment to black rights or suffrage. Most came from regions with small black populations and cared little whether blacks voted or not. Scalawags held the most political offices during Reconstruction, but they proved the least stable element of the southern Republican coalition; eventually, many drifted back to the Democratic fold.

Freedmen, the backbone of southern Republicanism, provided eight out of ten Republican votes. They sought land, education, civil rights, and political equality, and remained loyal Republicans. "We know our friends," an elderly freedman said. Although Reconstruction governments depended on African-American votes, freedmen held at most one in five political offices and constituted a legislative majority only in South Carolina, whose population was more than 60 percent black. No African-Americans won the office of governor, and only two served in the U.S. Senate—the same number as served during the twentieth century. A mere 6 percent of southern members of the House were African-American, and almost 50 percent came from South Carolina.

Black officeholders on the state level formed a political elite. They often differed from black voters in background, education, wealth, and complexion. Many were literate blacks who had been free before the Civil War. In the South Carolina legislature, for example, most black members came from large towns and cities; many had spent time in the North; and some were well-off property owners or even former slave owners themselves. Color differences were evident as well; 43 percent of South Carolina's black legislators were of mixed race, compared to just 7 percent of the state's black population.

Black officials and black voters often had different priorities. Most freedmen cared mainly about their economic future, especially about acquiring land, while black officeholders cared most about attaining equal rights. Still, both groups shared high expectations and prized enfranchisement. "We'd walk fifteen miles in wartime to find out about the battle," a Georgia freedman declared. "We can walk fifteen miles and more to find how to vote."

Republican Rule

Large numbers of African-Americans participated in government for the first time in the state constitutional conventions of 1867–1868. The South Carolina convention had an African-American majority, and in Louisiana half the delegates were freedmen. In general, these conventions instituted democratic changes, such as universal manhood suffrage and public-school systems, almost nonexistent in the antebellum South, but they failed to provide either integrated schools or land reform.

When proposals for land confiscation and redistribution arose in the state conventions, they fell to defeat, as they had in Congress. Southern Republicans hoping to attract northern investment hesitated to threaten property rights or to adopt land-reform measures that northern Republicans had rejected. South Carolina did set up a commission to buy land and make it available to freedmen, and several states changed their tax structures to force uncultivated land onto the market, but in no case was ex-Confederate land confiscated.

Once civil power shifted to the new state governments, Republican administrations began ambitious public-works programs. They built roads and bridges, promoted railroad development, and funded institutions to care for orphans, the insane, and the disabled. Republican regimes also expanded state government and formed state militias in which African-Americans often were heavily represented. These reforms cost millions, and state debts and taxes skyrocketed. During the 1860s, taxes rose 400 percent. Although northern tax rates still exceeded southern tax rates, southerners, particularly landowners, resented the new levies.

Opponents of Reconstruction viewed Republican rule as wasteful and corrupt, the "most stupendous system of organized robbery in history." Indeed, corruption did permeate some state governments, as in Louisiana and South Carolina. The main profiteers were government officials who accepted bribes and railroad promoters who doled them out. But neither group was exclusively Republican. In fact, corruption increasingly characterized government *nationally* in these years and was both more flagrant and more lucrative in the North.

Counterattacks

For ex-Confederates, African-American enfranchisement and the "horror of Negro domination" created nightmares. As soon as congressional Reconstruction began, it fell under attack. Democratic newspapers assailed delegates to the North Carolina constitutional convention as an "Ethiopian minstrelsy . . . baboons, monkeys, mules . . . and other jackasses."

But Democrats delayed any political mobilization until the readmission of the southern states was completed. Then they swung into action, often calling themselves Conservatives to attract former Whigs. At first, they pursued African-American votes, but when that initiative failed, they switched tactics. In every southern state the Democrats contested elections, backed dissident Republican factions, elected some Democratic legislators, and lured scalawags away from the Republican party.

Vigilante efforts to reduce black votes bolstered Democratic campaigns to win white ones. Antagonism toward free blacks, long present in southern life, grew increasingly violent. As early as 1865, Freedmen's Bureau agents itemized a variety of outrages against blacks, including shooting, murder, rape, arson, roasting, and "severe and inhuman beating." White vigilante groups sprang up in all parts of the former Confederacy, but one organization became dominant. In spring 1866, six young Confederate war veterans in Tennessee formed a social club, the **Ku Klux Klan,** distinguished by elaborate rituals, hooded costumes, and secret passwords. New Klan dens spread rapidly. By the election of 1868, when African-American suffrage

Primary Source:
Mr. Solid South

Ku Klux Klan Organization that used terrorism to prevent freedmen from voting and to reestablish white supremacy

had become a reality, the Klan had become a terrorist movement directed against potential African-American voters.

The Klan sought to suppress black voting, reestablish white supremacy, and topple the Reconstruction governments. It targeted Union League officers, Freedmen's Bureau officials, white Republicans, black militia units, economically successful blacks, and African-American voters. Concentrated in areas where white and black populations were nearly even and racial tensions greatest, Klan dens adapted their tactics to local conditions. In Mississippi, the Klan targeted black schools; in Alabama it concentrated on Republican office holders. In Arkansas terror reigned in 1868, while it peaked in Georgia and Florida in 1870. Some Democrats denounced Klan members as "cutthroats and riff-raff," but some prominent Confederate leaders, including General Nathan Bedford Forrest, who had commanded Confederate troops at the Fort Pillow massacre, (see p. 340) were active Klansmen. Vigilantism united southern whites of different social classes and drew on the energy of many Confederate veterans.

Republican legislatures tried to outlaw vigilantism, but when state militias could not enforce the laws, state officials turned to the federal government for help. In response, between May 1870 and February 1871 Congress passed three **Enforcement Acts,** each progressively more stringent. The First Enforcement Act protected African-American voters. The Second Enforcement Act provided for federal supervision of southern elections, and the Third Enforcement Act (also known as the Ku Klux Klan Act) authorized the use of federal troops and the suspension of habeas corpus (HAY-bee-us KORP-us), the requirement that cause for detaining a prisoner be shown in court. Although thousands were arrested under the Enforcement Acts, most terrorists escaped conviction.

By 1872 the federal government had effectively suppressed the Klan, but vigilantism had served its purpose. A large military presence in the South could have protected black rights, but instead federal troop levels fell steadily. Congress allowed the Freedmen's Bureau to die in 1869, and the Enforcement Acts became dead letters.

Klan Member in Disguise
The menacing disguise characterized the Ku Klux Klan's campaign of intimidation during Reconstruction. The Klan strove to end Republican rule, restore white supremacy, and obliterate, in a southern editor's words, "the preposterous and wicked dogma of negro equality."

Enforcement Acts Series of laws to protect African-American voters; banned the Klan and similar groups

CHECKING IN

- The Republican party, with a large bloc of freedmen, temporarily dominated the South.

- Reconstruction governments instituted such reforms as public-school systems.

- To many southerners, such reforms seemed a costly waste of money, aggravated by government corruption.

- The Ku Klux Klan and other groups used terrorism against freedmen and their white supporters in an effort to prevent black voting and restore white supremacy.

- The federal government passed laws against such activities but left too few troops in place to protect freedmen.

THE IMPACT OF EMANCIPATION

In what ways did newly freed slaves reshape their lives after emancipation?

"The master he says we are all free," a South Carolina slave declared in 1865. "But it don't mean we is white. And it don't mean we is equal." Yet despite the daunting handicaps they faced—illiteracy, lack of property, meager skills—most former slaves found the exhilaration of freedom overwhelming. Emancipation had given them the right to their own labor and a sense of autonomy, and during Reconstruction they asserted their independence by casting off white control and shedding the vestiges of slavery.

Confronting Freedom

For the ex-slaves, mobility was often liberty's first fruit. Some left the slave quarters; others fled the plantation completely. Emancipation stirred waves of migration within the former Confederacy. Some slaves headed to the Deep South, where desperate planters would pay higher wages for labor, but more moved to towns and cities. Urban African-American populations doubled and tripled after emancipation. The desire to find lost family members drove some migrations. Parents sought children who had been sold; husbands and wives who had been separated reunited; and families reclaimed children who were being raised in masters' homes. The Freedmen's Bureau helped former slaves to get information about missing relatives and to travel to find them, and bureau agents also tried to resolve entanglements over the multiple alliances of spouses who had been separated under slavery.

Once reunited, freed blacks quickly legalized unions formed under slavery, sometimes in mass ceremonies of up to seventy couples. Legal marriage had a tangible impact on family life. In 1870 eight out of ten African-American families in the cotton-producing South were two-parent families, about the same proportion as white families. Men asserted themselves as household heads, and their wives often withdrew from the work force to care for homes and families. "When I married my wife, I married her to wait on me and she has got all she can do right here for me and the children," a Tennessee freedman explained.

Severe labor shortages followed immediately after the war because women had made up half of all field workers. However, by Reconstruction's end, many African-American women had rejoined the work force out of economic necessity, either in the fields or as cooks, laundresses, and domestic servants. (White women often sought employment as well, for the war had incapacitated many white breadwinners, reduced the supply of future husbands, and left families destitute.) Former slaves continued to view stable, independent domestic life, especially the right to rear their own children, as a major blessing of freedom.

African-American Institutions

The freed blacks' desire for independence also led to the growth of African-American churches. The African Methodist Episcopal Church, founded by Philadelphia blacks in the 1790s, gained thousands of new southern members. Negro Baptist churches, their roots often in plantation "praise meetings" organized by slaves, sprouted everywhere.

The Freedmen's School
Supported by the Freedmen's Bureau, northern freedmen's aid societies, and African-American denominations, freedmen's schools reached about 12 percent of school-age African-American children in the South by 1870. Here a northern teacher poses with her students at a school in rural North Carolina.

The influence of African-American churches extended far beyond religion. They provided relief, raised funds for schools, and supported Republican policies. African-American ministers assumed leading political roles until Reconstruction's end and then remained the main pillars of authority within African-American communities.

Schools, too, played a crucial role for freedmen as the ex-slaves sought literacy for themselves and above all for their children. At emancipation, African-Americans organized their own schools, which the Freedmen's Bureau soon supervised. Northern philanthropic organizations paid the wages of instructors, half of whom were women. In 1869 the bureau reported more than four thousand African-American schools in the former Confederacy. Within three more years each southern state had a public-school system, at least in principle, generally with separate schools for blacks and whites. The Freedmen's Bureau and others also helped to establish Howard, Atlanta, and Fisk Universities in 1866–1867 and Hampton Institute in 1868. Nonetheless, African-American education remained limited. Few rural blacks could reach the schools, and those who tried were sometimes the targets of vigilante attacks. Thus, by the end of Reconstruction, more than 80 percent of the African-American population remained illiterate, although literacy was rising among children.

Not only school segregation but also other forms of racial separation were taken for granted. Whether by law or by custom, segregation continued on streetcars and trains as well as in churches, theaters, and restaurants. In 1875 Congress passed the Civil Rights Act, banning segregation except in schools, but in the **1883 *Civil Rights Cases,*** the Supreme Court threw the law out. The Fourteenth Amendment did not prohibit discrimination by individuals, the Court ruled, only that perpetrated by the state.

1883 *Civil Rights Cases*
Decisions in which the Supreme Court threw out major laws designed to protect freedmen

White southerners adamantly rejected the prospect of racial integration, which they insisted would lead to racial amalgamation. "If we have social equality, we shall have intermarriage," one white southerner contended, "and if we have intermarriage, we shall degenerate." Urban blacks occasionally protested segregation, but most freed blacks were less interested in "social equality" than in African-American liberty and community. Moreover, the new black elite—teachers, ministers, and politicians—served African-American constituencies and thus had a vested interest in separate black institutions. In addition, rural blacks had little desire to mix with whites; rather, they sought freedom from white control. Above all, they wanted to secure personal independence by acquiring land.

Land, Labor, and Sharecropping

"The sole ambition of the freedman," a New Englander wrote from South Carolina in 1865, "appears to be to become the owner of a little piece of land, there to erect a humble home, and to dwell in peace and security, at his own free will and pleasure." Indeed, to free blacks everywhere, "forty acres and a mule" (a phrase that originated during the war as General William T. Sherman set aside land on the South Carolina sea islands for black settlement) promised emancipation from plantation labor, white domination, and cotton, the "slave crop."

But the freedmen's visions of landownership failed to materialize, for large-scale land reform never occurred. A few slaves did obtain land, with the help of the Freedmen's Bureau or sometimes by pooling resources. The federal government also sought to provide former slaves with land; in 1866 Congress passed the Southern Homestead Act, which set aside 44 million acres of public land in five southern states for freedmen and poor whites. But the soil was poor, and few former slaves had the resources to survive until their first harvest. About four thousand blacks settled on homesteads under the law, but most were unable to establish farms—and poor whites fared little better. By the end of Reconstruction, only a small minority of former slaves in each state owned working farms. In Georgia in 1876, for example, blacks controlled a mere 1.3 percent of total acreage. Without large-scale land reform, barriers to African-American landownership remained overwhelming.

Three obstacles impeded African-American landownership. Freedmen lacked capital to buy land or tools. Furthermore, white southerners generally opposed selling land to blacks. Most important, planters sought to preserve a cheap labor force and forged laws to ensure that black labor would remain available on the plantations.

The black codes written during presidential Reconstruction were designed to preserve a captive labor force. Under labor contracts in effect in 1865–1866, freedmen received wages, housing, food, and clothing in exchange for field work. But cash was scarce, and wages often became a small share of the crop, typically one-eighth or less, to be divided among the entire work force. Freedmen's Bureau agents encouraged African-Americans to sign the contracts, seeing wage labor as a step toward economic independence. "You must begin at the bottom of the ladder and climb up," the head of the Freedman's Bureau told Louisiana freedmen in 1865.

Problems arose immediately. Freedmen disliked the new wage system, especially the use of gang labor, which resembled the work pattern under slavery. Moreover, postwar planters had to compete for labor even as many scorned African-American workers as lazy or inefficient. One landowner estimated that workers accomplished only "two-fifths of what they did under the old system." As productivity fell, so did land values. Plummeting cotton prices and poor harvests in 1866 and 1867 combined with these other factors to create an impasse: landowners lacked labor, and freedmen lacked land.

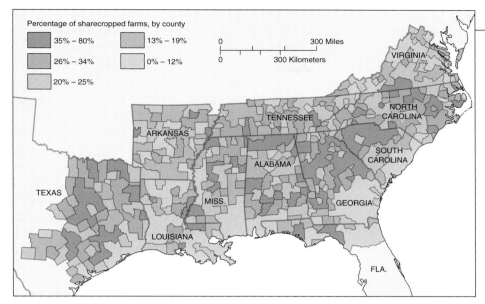

Percentage of sharecropped farms, by county

- 35% – 80%
- 26% – 34%
- 20% – 25%
- 13% – 19%
- 0% – 12%

Map 16.2   Southern Sharecropping, 1880
The depressed economy of the late 1870s caused poverty and debt, increased tenancy among white farmers, and forced many renters, black and white, into sharecropping. By 1880 the sharecropping system pervaded most southern counties, with highest concentrations in the Cotton Belt from South Carolina to eastern Texas. *Source:* U.S. Census Office, Tenth Census, 1880, Report of the Production of Agriculture (Washington, D.C.: Government Printing Office, 1883), Table 5.

Southerners began experimenting with new labor schemes, including the division of plantations into small tenancies. **Sharecropping** was the most widespread arrangement. Under this system, landowners subdivided large plantations into farms of thirty to fifty acres and rented them to freedmen under annual leases for a share of the crop, usually one-half. Freedmen liked this decentralized system, which let them use the labor of family members and represented a step toward independence. Planters, meanwhile, retained control of their land. The most productive land thus remained in the hands of a small group of owners; in effect sharecropping helped to preserve the planter elite.

Although the wage system continued on sugar and rice plantations, by 1870 the plantation tradition had yielded to sharecropping in the cotton South. A severe depression in 1873 drove many blacks and independent white farmers into sharecropping. By 1880, sharecroppers, white and black, farmed 80 percent of the land in cotton-producing states. In fact, white sharecroppers outnumbered black, although a higher proportion of southern blacks, almost 75 percent, were involved in the system. Changes in marketing and finance, meanwhile, made the sharecroppers' lot increasingly precarious.

sharecropping System in which tenant farmer paid a share of the crop as rent to the landowner

Primary Source:
Barrow Plantation

Toward a Crop-Lien Economy

The postwar South's hundreds of thousands of tenant farmers and sharecroppers needed a local credit system to see them through the growing season until they could harvest their crops. Rural merchants advanced supplies to tenants and sharecroppers on credit and sold their crops to wholesalers. Because renters had no property to serve as collateral, merchants secured their loans with a lien (leen), or claim, on each farmer's next crop. Exorbitant interest rates, 50 percent or more, quickly forced many tenants and sharecroppers into a cycle of indebtedness. The sharecropper might well owe part of his crop to the landowner and another part (the rest of his

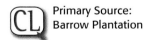

crop lien Borrowing against future crops; often created a cycle of debt that tied tenants to sharecropping

crop, or more) to the merchant. Illiterate tenants who could not keep track of their financial arrangements were at the mercy of sometimes-unscrupulous merchants. Once a tenant's real or alleged debts exceeded the value of his crop, he was tied to the land, to cotton, and to sharecropping.

By the end of Reconstruction, sharecropping and **crop liens** had bound the South to easily marketable cash crops, such as cotton, and prevented crop diversification. Soil depletion, land erosion, and outmoded equipment stranded capital-short planters in a cycle of poverty. Trapped in perpetual debt, tenant farmers became the chief victims of the new agricultural order. Cotton remained the only survival route open to poor farmers, regardless of race, but low income from cotton locked them into sharecropping and crop liens. African-American tenants, for whom neither landownership nor economic independence ever materialized, saw their political rights dwindle as rapidly as their hopes for economic freedom. When Reconstruction ended, neither state governments nor the national government offered them protection, for northern politicians were preoccupied with their own problems.

CHECKING IN

- Tens of thousands of freedmen sought missing family members, and former slaves hastened to legalize the marriages they had made under slavery.

- Blacks formed their own communities, churches, and schools as segregation became firmly established in the South.

- Few former slaves achieved land ownership, and sharecropping became the dominant form of agricultural labor for blacks and many poor whites.

- Without economic status, blacks quickly saw their political rights erode.

NEW CONCERNS IN THE NORTH, 1868–1876

Why did northern concern about Reconstruction begin to wane?

The nomination of Ulysses S. Grant for president in 1868 launched a chaotic era in national politics. His eight years in office featured political scandals, a party revolt, a massive depression, and a steady retreat from Reconstruction. By the mid-1870s northern voters cared more about economics, unemployment, labor unrest, and currency problems than about the "southern question." Eager to end sectional conflict, Republicans turned their backs on the freedmen.

Grantism

Republicans had good reason to nominate General Grant. A war hero, he was endorsed by veterans, admired throughout the North, and unscathed by the bitter feuds of Reconstruction politics. To oppose Grant, the Democrats nominated Horatio Seymour, arch-critic of the Lincoln administration and an opponent of Reconstruction and greenbacks. Grant ran on his personal popularity more than on issues. Although he carried all but eight states, the popular vote was close; newly enfranchised freedmen provided Grant's margin in the South.

Grant's presidential leadership proved as weak as his war leadership had been strong, although he lacked Johnson's instinct for disaster. He had little political skill; his cabinet appointments were at best mediocre; and a string of scandals plagued his administration. In 1869 financier Jay Gould and his partner Jim Fisk attempted to corner the gold market with the help of Grant's brother-in-law. When gold prices tumbled, investors were ruined, and Grant's reputation was tarnished. Near the end of Grant's first term, his vice president, Schuyler Colfax, got caught up in the **Crédit Mobilier** (CRAY-dee MOH-bill-yay) scandal, an elaborate scheme to

Crédit Mobilier Scheme to skim profits from the Union Pacific Railroad; one of several scandals to engulf Grant administration

skim off the profits of the Union Pacific Railroad. Then in 1875 Grant's personal secretary, Orville Babcock, was found guilty of accepting bribes from the "whiskey ring," distillers who preferred bribery to payment of federal taxes. And in 1876 voters learned that Grant's secretary of war, William E. Belknap, had taken bribes to sell lucrative Indian trading posts in Oklahoma.

Although Grant was not personally involved in the scandals, he did little to restrain such activities, and "Grantism" came to stand for fraud, bribery, and corruption in office. Such evils, however, spread far beyond Washington. The New York City press in 1872 revealed that Democrat boss William M. Tweed led a ring that had looted the city treasury and collected some $200 million in kickbacks and bribes. When Mark Twain and Charles Dudley Warner published their satiric novel *The Gilded Age* in 1873, readers recognized the book's speculators, self-promoters, and opportunists as familiar figures in public life. (The term "Gilded Age" has subsequently been used to refer to the decades from the 1870s to the 1890s.)

Grant did enjoy some foreign policy successes. In 1872 his administration engineered the settlement of the *Alabama* claims with England: an international tribunal ordered Britain to pay $15.5 million to the United States in compensation for damage inflicted by Confederate-owned but British-built raiders. But the administration went astray when it tried to add nonadjacent territory to the Union. In 1867 the Johnson administration had purchased Alaska from Russia at the bargain price of $7.2 million. The purchase had rekindled expansionists' hope, and in 1870 Grant decided to annex the Caribbean island nation of Santo Domingo (the modern Dominican Republic). The president believed that annexation would promote Caribbean trade and provide a haven for persecuted southern blacks. Despite speculators' hopes for windfall profits, the Senate rejected the annexation treaty and further diminished Grant's reputation.

As the election of 1872 approached, dissident Republicans feared that "Grantism" would ruin the party. Former Radicals and other Republicans left out of Grant's "Great Barbecue" formed their own party, the Liberal Republicans.

Boss Tweed

Thomas Nast's cartoons in *Harper's Weekly* helped topple New York Democratic boss William M. Tweed, who, with his associates, embodied corruption on a large scale. The Tweed Ring had granted lucrative franchises to companies they controlled, padded construction bills, practiced graft and extortion, and exploited every opportunity to plunder the city's funds.

The Liberals' Revolt

The Liberal Republican revolt split the party and undermined Reconstruction. Liberals demanded civil service reform to bring the "best men" into government. In the South they demanded an end to "bayonet rule" and argued that African-Americans, now enfranchised, could fend for themselves. Corruption in government posed a greater threat than Confederate resurgence, the Liberals claimed, and they demanded that the "best men" in the South, ex-Confederates barred from holding office, be returned to government.

New York Tribune editor Horace Greeley, inconsistently supporting both a stringent Reconstruction policy and leniency toward the ex-Confederates, received the Liberal Republican nomination, and the Democrats endorsed Greeley as well. Republican reformers found themselves allied with the party that they had recently castigated as a "sewer" of treasonable sentiments.

Despite Greeley's arduous campaigning (he literally worked himself to death on the campaign trail and died a few weeks after the election), Grant carried 56 percent of the popular vote and won the electoral vote handily. But to nullify the Liberals' issues, "regular" Republicans had passed an amnesty act allowing all but a few hundred ex-Confederates to resume office. And during Grant's second term, Republicans' desire to discard the "southern question" grew as a depression gripped the nation.

The Panic of 1873

The postwar years brought accelerated industrialization, rapid economic expansion, and frantic speculation as investors rushed to take advantage of seemingly unlimited opportunities. Railroads led the speculative boom. The transcontinental line reached completion in 1869 (see Chapter 17), and by 1873 almost four hundred railroads crisscrossed the Northeast. But in addition to transforming the northern economy, the railroad boom led entrepreneurs to overspeculate, with drastic results.

In 1869 Philadelphia banker Jay Cooke took over a new transcontinental line, the Northern Pacific. For four years Northern Pacific securities sold briskly, but in 1873 construction costs outran bond sales. In September, Cooke, his bank vaults stuffed with unsalable bonds, defaulted on his obligations. His bank, the largest in the nation, shut down. Then the stock market collapsed, and smaller banks and other firms followed; the Panic of 1873 plunged the nation into a devastating five-year depression. Thousands of businesses went bankrupt. By 1878 unemployment had risen to more than 3 million. Labor protests mounted, and industrial violence spread (see Chapter 18). The depression of the 1870s demonstrated ruthlessly that conflicts born of industrialization had replaced sectional divisions.

The depression also fed a dispute over currency that had begun in 1865. During the Civil War, Americans had used greenbacks, a paper currency not backed by a specific weight in gold. "Sound-money" supporters demanded the withdrawal of greenbacks from circulation as a means of stabilizing the currency. Their opponents, "easy-money" advocates, such as farmers and manufacturers dependent on easy credit, wanted to expand the currency by issuing additional greenbacks. The deepening depression created even more demand for easy money, and the issue split both major parties.

Controversy over the type of currency was compounded by the question of how to repay the federal debt. In wartime the Union government had borrowed astronomical sums through the sale of war bonds. Bond holders wanted repayment in "coin," gold or silver, even though many of them had paid for the bonds in greenbacks. The Public Credit Act of 1869 promised payment in coin.

Senator John Sherman, the author of the Public Credit Act, put together a series of compromises to satisfy both "sound-money" and "easy-money" advocates. Sherman's measures, exchanging Civil War bonds for new ones payable over a longer period of time and defining "coin" as gold only, preserved the public credit, the currency, and Republican unity. His Specie Resumption Act of 1875 promised to put the nation back on the gold standard by 1879.

But Sherman's measures, however ingenious, did not placate the Democrats, who gained control of the House in 1875. Many Democrats, and a few Republicans, were "free-silver" advocates who wanted the silver dollar restored in order to expand the currency and end the depression. The Bland-Allison Act of 1878 partially restored silver coinage by requiring the government to buy and coin several million dollars' worth of silver each month. In 1876 other expansionists formed the Greenback party to keep the paper money in circulation for the sake of debtors, but they enjoyed little success. As the depression receded, the clamor for "easy money" subsided, only to return in the 1890s (see Chapter 20). Although never settled, the controversial "money question" diverted attention away from Reconstruction and thus contributed to its demise.

Reconstruction and the Constitution

During the 1870s the Supreme Court also played a role in weakening northern support for Reconstruction as new constitutional questions surfaced. Would the Court support laws to protect freedmen's rights? The decision in *Ex Parte Milligan* (1866) had suggested not. In *Milligan,* the Court had ruled that a military commission could not try civilians in areas where civilian courts were functioning, thus dooming the special military courts that had been established to enforce the Supplementary Freedmen's Bureau Act. Would the Court sabotage the congressional Reconstruction plan? In 1869, in *Texas* v. *White,* the Court had let Reconstruction stand, ruling that Congress had the power to ensure each state a republican form of government.

However, during the 1870s the Supreme Court backed away from Reconstruction. In the *Slaughterhouse* decision of 1873, the Court ruled that the Fourteenth Amendment protected the rights of *national* citizenship, such as the right to interstate travel, but that the federal government did not have to safeguard such rights against violation by the *states.* The *Slaughterhouse* decision effectively gutted the Fourteenth Amendment, which was intended to secure freedmen's rights against state encroachment.

The Supreme Court retreated even further from Reconstruction in two cases involving the Enforcement Act of 1870. In *United States* v. *Reese* (1876), the Court threw out the indictment of Kentucky officials who had barred African-Americans from voting. Another decision that same year, *United States* v. *Cruikshank,* again weakened the Fourteenth Amendment. In the *Cruikshank* case, the Court ruled that the amendment barred *states,* but not *individuals,* from encroaching on individual rights.

Continuing this retreat from Reconstruction, the Supreme Court in 1883 invalidated both the Civil Rights Act of 1875 and the Ku Klux Klan Act of 1871. Taken cumulatively, these decisions dismantled Republican Reconstruction and confirmed rising northern sentiment that Reconstruction's egalitarian goals were unenforceable.

Republicans in Retreat

The Republicans gradually disengaged from Reconstruction, beginning with the election of Grant as president in 1868. Grant, like most Americans, hesitated to approve the use of federal authority in state or local affairs.

> ## CHECKING IN
>
> - Grant's administration was riddled by corruption, mirroring politics in much of the country.
> - The Panic of 1873 devastated the northern economy, plunging the nation into a deep depression.
> - Through the 1870s the Supreme Court struck down basic legislation protecting freedmen's rights.
> - Most Radical Republican leaders had died by the early 1870s, and commercial and industrial interests began to dominate the Republican party.

MAJOR RECONSTRUCTION LEGISLATION

LAW AND DATE OF CONGRESSIONAL PASSAGE	PROVISIONS	PURPOSE
Civil Rights Act of 1866 (April 1866)*	Declared blacks citizens and guaranteed them equal protection of the laws.	To invalidate the black codes.
Supplementary Freedmen's Bureau Act (July 1866)*	Extended the life of the Freedmen's Aid Bureau and expanded its powers.	To invalidate the black codes.
Reconstruction Act of 1867 (March 1867)*	Invalidated state governments formed under Lincoln and Johnson. Divided the former Confederacy into five military districts. Set forth requirements for readmission of ex-Confederate states to the Union.	To replace presidential Reconstruction with a more stringent plan.
Supplementary Reconstruction Acts		To enforce the First Reconstruction Act.
Second Reconstruction Act (March 1867)*	Required military commanders to initiate voter enrollment.	
Third Reconstruction Act (July 1867)*	Expanded military commanders' powers.	
Fourth Reconstruction Act (March 1868)*	Provided that a majority of voters, however few, could put a new state constitution into force.	
Army Appropriations Act (March 1867)*	Declared in a rider that only the general of the army could issue military orders.	To prevent President Johnson from obstructing Reconstruction.
Tenure of Office Act (March 1867)*	Prohibited the president from removing any federal official without the Senate's consent.	To prevent President Johnson from obstructing Reconstruction.
Omnibus Act (June 1868)†	Readmitted seven ex-Confederate states to the Union.	To restore the Union, under the term of the First Reconstruction Act.
Enforcement Act of 1870 (May 1870)‡	Provided for the protection of black voters.	To enforce the Fifteenth Amendment.
Second Enforcement Act (February 1871)	Provided for federal supervision of southern elections.	To enforce the Fifteenth Amendment.
Third Enforcement Act (Ku Klux Klan Act) (April 1871)	Strengthened sanctions against those who impeded black suffrage.	To combat the Ku Klux Klan and enforce the Fourteenth Amendment.
Amnesty Act (May 1872)	Restored the franchise to almost all ex-Confederates.	Effort by Grant Republicans to deprive Liberal Republicans of a campaign issue.
Civil Rights Act of 1875 (March 1875)§	Outlawed racial segregation in transportation and public accommodations and prevented exclusion of blacks from jury service.	To honor the late senator Charles Sumner.

*Passed over Johnson's veto.
†Georgia was soon returned to military rule. The last four states were readmitted in 1870.
‡Sections of the law declared unconstitutional in 1876.
§Invalidated by the Supreme Court in 1883.

In the 1870s Republican idealism waned. Instead, commercial and industrial interests dominated both the Liberal and "regular" wings of the party, and few wanted any further sectional strife. By 1875, moreover, the Radical Republicans had virtually disappeared. The Radical leaders Chase, Stevens, and Sumner had died, and others had grown tired of "waving the bloody shirt," or defaming Democratic opponents by reviving wartime animosity. It seemed pointless to prop up southern Republican regimes that even President Grant found corrupt. Finally, Republicans generally agreed with southern Democrats that African-Americans were inferior and that to insist on black equality would quash any hope of reunion between North and South. The Republican retreat set the stage for Reconstruction's end in 1877.

RECONSTRUCTION ABANDONED, 1876–1877

What events led the North to abandon Reconstruction?

"We are in a very hot political contest just now," a Mississippi planter wrote his daughter in 1875, "with a good prospect of turning out the carpetbag thieves by whom we have been robbed for the past six to ten years." Indeed, an angry white majority had led a Democratic resurgence throughout the South in the 1870s, and by 1876 Republican rule survived in only three southern states. Democratic victories in state elections that year and political bargaining in Washington in 1877 ended what little remained of Reconstruction.

THE DURATION OF REPUBLICAN RULE IN THE EX-CONFEDERATE STATES

FORMER CONFEDERATE STATES	READMISSION TO THE UNION UNDER CONGRESSIONAL RECONSTRUCTION	DEMOCRATS (CONSERVATIVES) GAIN CONTROL	DURATION OF REPUBLICAN RULE
Alabama	June 25, 1868	November 14, 1874	6½ years
Arkansas	June 22, 1868	November 10, 1874	6½ years
Florida	June 25, 1868	January 2, 1877	8½ years
Georgia	July 15, 1870	November 1, 1871	1 year
Louisiana	June 25, 1868	January 2, 1877	8½ years
Mississippi	February 23, 1870	November 3, 1875	5½ years
North Carolina	June 25, 1868	November 3, 1870	2 years
South Carolina	June 25, 1868	November 12, 1876	8 years
Tennessee	July 24, 1866*	October 4, 1869	3 years
Texas	March 30, 1870	January 14, 1873	3 years
Virginia	January 26, 1870	October 5, 1869[†]	0 years

Source: Reprinted by permission from John Hope Franklin, Reconstruction After the Civil War (Chicago: University of Chicago Press, 1962), 231.
*Admitted before the start of Congressional Reconstruction.
[†]Democrats gained control before readmission.

"Redeeming" the South

After 1872 the Republican collapse in the South accelerated. Congressional amnesty enabled virtually all ex-Confederate officials to regain office, divided Republicans lost their grip on the southern electorate, and attrition diminished Republican ranks. Carpetbaggers returned north or joined the Democrats, and scalawags deserted the Republicans in large numbers. Tired of northern interference and seeing the possibility of "home rule," scalawags decided that staying Republican meant going down with a sinking ship. Unable to win new white votes or retain the old ones, the fragile Republican coalition crumbled.

Bourbons Southern elite who returned to power as Reconstruction wound down

Meanwhile, the Democrats mobilized formerly apathetic white voters. Although still faction-ridden—businessmen who dreamed of an industrialized "New South" had little in common with the old planter elite, the so-called **Bourbons**—the Democrats shared one goal: kicking the Republicans out. The Democrats' tactics varied. In several Deep South states Democrats resorted to violence. In Vicksburg in 1874 rampaging whites slaughtered about three hundred blacks and terrorized thousands of potential voters. Vigilante groups in several southern states disrupted Republican meetings and threatened blacks who had registered to vote. In 1875, the "Mississippi plan" took effect; local Democratic clubs armed their members who broke up Republican meetings, patrolled registration locations, and marched through black areas. "The Republicans are paralyzed through fear and will not act," the anguished carpetbag governor of Mississippi wrote to his wife. "Why should I fight a hopeless battle?" In 1876 South Carolina's "Rifle Clubs" and "Red Shirts," armed groups that threatened Republicans, continued the terrorist tactics that had worked so well in Mississippi.

Terrorism did not completely squelch black voting, but it did deprive Republicans of enough African-American votes to win state elections. Throughout the South, economic pressures reinforced intimidation; labor contracts included clauses barring attendance at political meetings, and planters threatened to evict sharecroppers who stepped out of line.

redemption Bourbon term for regaining control of South

Redemption, the word that Democrats used to describe their return to power, introduced sweeping changes. States rewrote constitutions, cut expenses, lowered taxes, eliminated social programs, limited the rights of tenants and sharecroppers, and shaped laws to ensure a stable African-American labor force. Legislatures restored vagrancy laws, strengthened crop-lien statutes, and remade criminal law. Local ordinances in heavily black counties often restricted hunting, fishing, gun carrying, and even dog ownership, drastically curtailing the ability of freedmen to live off the land. New criminal codes directed at African-Americans imposed severe penalties for what formerly were misdemeanors: stealing livestock or wrongly taking part of a crop became grand larceny, punishable by five years at hard labor. By Reconstruction's end, a large African-American convict work force had been leased out to private contractors. Freedmen whose hopes had been raised by Republicans saw their prospects destroyed by the redeemers. The new laws, Tennessee blacks stated at an 1875 convention, imposed "a condition of servitude scarcely less degrading than that endured before the late civil war." In the late 1870s an increasingly oppressive political climate gave rise to an "exodus" movement among African-Americans. Nearly fifteen thousand African-American "exodusters" from the Deep South moved to Kansas and set up homesteads. But scarce resources left most of the freed slaves stranded. Not until the twentieth century would the mass migration of southern blacks to the Midwest and North gain momentum.

The Election of 1876

By autumn 1876, with redemption almost complete, both parties moved to discard the animosity left by the war and Reconstruction. The Republicans nominated Rutherford B. Hayes, the governor of Ohio, for president. Popular with all factions and untainted by the Grant scandals, Hayes, a "moderate," favored "home rule" in the South and civil and political rights for all—clearly contradictory goals. The Democrats nominated Governor Samuel J. Tilden of New York, a political reformer known for his assaults on the Tweed Ring that had plundered New York City's treasury. Both candidates were fiscal conservatives, favored sound money, endorsed civil service reform, and decried corruption.

Tilden won the popular vote by a small margin, but the Republicans challenged pro-Tilden electoral votes from South Carolina, Florida, and Louisiana, and the Democrats challenged one electoral vote from Oregon. Southern Republicans managed to throw out enough Democratic ballots in the contested states to proclaim Hayes the winner.

The nation now faced an unprecedented dilemma. Each party claimed victory, and each accused the other of fraud. In fact, both sets of southern votes were fraudulent: Republicans had discarded legitimate Democratic ballots, and Democrats had illegally prevented freedmen from voting. In January 1877, Congress created a special electoral commission to resolve the conflict. The commission originally consisted of seven Republicans, seven Democrats, and one independent, but when the independent resigned, a Republican replaced him. The commission gave the Republican Hayes the election by an 8-to-7 vote.

Congress now had to certify the new electoral vote. But the Democrats controlled the House, and some planned to forestall approval of the electoral vote. For many southern Democrats, regaining control of their states was far more important than preventing the election of a Republican president—*if* the new Republican administration would leave the South alone. Republican leaders, for their part, were willing to bargain, for Hayes wanted not just victory but also southern approval. Informal negotiations followed, with both parties exchanging promises. Ohio Republicans and southern Democrats agreed that, if Hayes won the election, he would remove federal troops from all southern states. Other negotiations led to the understanding that southerners would receive federal patronage, federal aid to railroads, and federal support for internal improvements. In turn, southerners promised to accept Hayes as president and to treat the freedmen fairly.

Congress thus ratified Hayes's election. Once in office, Hayes fulfilled many of the agreements made by his colleagues. Republican rule toppled in Louisiana, South Carolina, and Florida. But some of the bargains struck in the so-called **Compromise of 1877** fell apart, particularly Democratic promises to treat the freedmen fairly and Hayes's pledges to ensure the freed slaves' rights. "When you turned us loose, you turned us loose to the sky, to the storm, to the whirlwind, and worst of all . . . to the wrath of our infuriated masters," Frederick Douglass had charged at the 1876 Republican convention. "The question now is, do you mean to make good to us the promises in your Constitution?" By 1877 the answer was clear: "No."

Compromise of 1877 Deal that gave northern Republicans the presidency and restored southern Democrats to power, ending Reconstruction

CHECKING IN

- The Republican collapse in the South accelerated after 1872.
- Democrats regained control of southern states.
- "Redeemers" ended reforms and limited or eliminated black rights.
- The election of 1876 resulted in challenges to some electoral votes and charges of fraud on both sides.
- The price of Republican victory in the election was the end of Reconstruction and the virtual abandonment of the freedmen.

Chapter Summary

 DOWNLOAD THE MP3 AUDIO FILE OF THE CHAPTER SUMMARY, AND LISTEN TO IT ON THE GO.

On what major issues did Radical Republicans and President Johnson struggle over Reconstruction policy? (page 354)

Radical Republicans saw Johnson as too lenient on Reconstruction and passed a stringent congressional Reconstruction program over his veto. They even attempted to impeach the president for political reasons, but failed. The Fourteenth and Fifteenth Amendments, which Johnson opposed, were major triumphs for the Radicals.

What impact did federal Reconstruction policy have on the former Confederacy and ex-Confederates? (page 362)

Democrats and ex-Confederates were largely excluded from political power in the South, which fell to Republicans and freedmen. The Reconstruction governments passed costly reform measures, most of which were later abandoned or scaled back. Terrorist organizations such as the Ku Klux Klan flourished briefly. They were outlawed by the federal government but had already intimidated freedmen.

In what ways did newly freed slaves reshape their lives after emancipation? (page 366)

Former slaves sought missing family members, legalized marriages made under slavery, and created schools and churches in large numbers. But without land reform most remained poor and ultimately were caught in the pernicious sharecropping system; their rights were soon eroded.

Why did northern concern about Reconstruction begin to wane? (page 370)

Other concerns soon began to preoccupy Republicans. Corruption, epitomized by the Grant administration, permeated the nation. The Panic of 1873 led to a major depression. The Supreme Court threw out most important measures intended to protect freedmen's rights. Finally, with most Radical Republican leaders gone by the early 1870s, commercial and industrial interests began to dominate the Republican party.

What led the North to abandon Reconstruction? (page 375)

Republican control of the South began to collapse in the early 1870s. As Democrats "redeemed" southern states, they curtailed reforms and eliminated black rights. The price of the Republican victory in the disputed presidential election of 1876 was the end of Reconstruction and the return of the South to Democratic control.

KEY TERMS

Radical Republicans *(p. 354)*

"black codes" *(p. 356)*

Freedmen's Bureau *(p. 356)*

Fourteenth Amendment *(p. 357)*

congressional Reconstruction *(p. 359)*

impeachment *(p. 359)*

Fifteenth Amendment *(p. 360)*

"carpetbagger" *(p. 362)*

scalawag *(p. 362)*

Ku Klux Klan *(p. 364)*

Enforcement Acts *(p. 365)*

1883 *Civil Rights Cases (p. 367)*

sharecropping *(p. 369)*

crop lien *(p. 370)*

Crédit Mobilier *(p. 370)*

Bourbons *(p. 376)*

redemption *(p. 376)*

Compromise of 1877 *(p. 377)*

The Transformation of the Trans-Mississippi West

CHAPTER 17

1860–1900

Fire Canoe at Fort Berthold,
by William de la Montagne Cary

CHAPTER PREVIEW

Native Americans and the Trans-Mississippi West
How was Indian life on the Great Plains transformed in the second half of the nineteenth century?

Settling the West
What roles did the federal government, the army, and the railroads play in the settlement of the West?

Southwestern Borderlands
How did ranchers and settlers displace Spanish-speaking Americans in the Southwest?

Exploiting the Western Landscape
How did mining, ranching, and farming shape the West?

The West of Life and Legend
How was the Wild West image of cowboys and Indians created, and what developments prompted the establishment of national parks?

The buffaloes and the black-tail deer are gone, and our Indian ways are almost gone," reminisced Maxidiwiac (mah-chee-dee-WEE-ahsh), or Buffalo Bird Woman, in 1920. A Hidatsa Indian born about 1843 in present-day North Dakota, she found the changes overwhelming. "Sometimes I find it hard to believe I ever lived them [her Indian ways]," she continued. "My little son grew up in the white man's school. He can read books, and he owns cattle and has a farm. . . . But for me, I cannot forget our old ways." In her own lifetime, Buffalo Bird Woman had moved from a traditional native existence into the modern world.

President Jefferson's emissaries Meriwether Lewis and William Clark had wintered among the Hidatsas in 1804 and had been impressed by their horsemanship and hunting ability. The Hidatsas in the 1840s had joined with two neighboring tribes to build a new village called Like-A-Fishhook. Initially the new settlement prospered. But, after the Civil War, as white settlers crowded onto their lands, Buffalo Bird Woman and her tribe were pressured by a nearby military garrison into signing away more and more of their territory and forced to scatter onto small farms. Buffalo Bird Woman and her tribe abandoned their village in 1885.

Buffalo Bird Woman's experience was all too common. The settlement of the trans-Mississippi West began with the removal of native peoples. This peaceful or, more commonly, brutal relocation of the Indians onto reservations opened up vast tracts of land for settlement and development. Miners, farmers, land speculators, and railroad developers in the 1850s flooded onto the fertile prairies of Iowa, Minnesota, and Kansas, carving the land into farms and communities. Then, in the 1860s, drawn by the earlier discovery of gold in the Rocky Mountains, these same settlers swarmed onto the Great Plains and the semiarid regions beyond them. Scarcely a decade later, the trans-Mississippi West became a contested terrain as Native peoples fought to protect their homeland from these newcomers.

The transformation of the West left a mixed legacy. Although many white families prospered on the High Plains, the heedless pursuit of land and profit threatened not only the Native Americans, but the environment, and sometimes the settlers themselves. Unscrupulous westerners exploited white, Native American, Chinese, and Mexican laborers alike. Hunters slaughtered millions of bison for their hides, and farmers plowed up the prairie sod to build farms. Although westerners attributed their economic achievements to American individualism and self-reliance, the development of the trans-Mississippi West depended heavily on the federal government. The government sent troops, fresh from their victories in the Civil War, to subjugate the Indians. It promoted the acquisition of farm land through the Homestead Act (1862) and subsidized the construction of transcontinental railroad lines. Eastern banks and foreign capitalists provided investment capital. In their scramble for new economic opportunities, many Americans chose to view the destruction of the Indian ways of life as the necessary price of civilization and progress.

NATIVE AMERICANS AND THE TRANS-MISSISSIPPI WEST

How was Indian life on the Great Plains transformed in the second half of the nineteenth century?

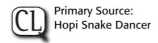

Primary Source:
Hopi Snake Dancer

No aspect of the transformation of the West was more visible and dramatic than the assault on the traditional Indian way of life. Caught between a stampede of miners and settlers who took their land and the federal government that sought to force them onto reservations, Native Americans resisted and fought back. By the 1890s confinement on inferior reservations had become the fate of almost every Indian nation. Undaunted, Native Americans struggled to preserve their customs and rebuild their numbers.

Chronology

1862	Homestead Act; Morrill Anti-Bigamy Act; Pacific Railroad Act
1864	Nevada admitted to the Union; Massacre of Cheyennes at Sand Creek, Colorado; George Perkins Marsh, *Man and Nature*
1867	Joseph McCoy organizes cattle drives to Abilene, Kansas; New Indian policy of smaller reservations adopted; Medicine Lodge Treaty; Purchase of Alaska
1868	Fort Laramie Treaty
1869	Board of Indian Commissioners established to reform Indian reservation life; Wyoming gives women the vote
1872	Yellowstone National Park established
1873	Panic allows speculators to purchase thousands of acres in the Red River valley of North Dakota cheaply; Timber Culture Act; Biggest strike on Nevada's Comstock Lode
1874	Invention of barbed wire; Gold discovered in the Black Hills of South Dakota; Red River War
1875	John Wesley Powell, *The Exploration of the Colorado River*
1876	Colorado admitted to the Union, gives women the right to vote in school elections; Little Bighorn massacre
1877	Desert Land Act
1878	John Wesley Powell, *Report on the Lands of the Arid Regions of the United States*
1879	*United States* v. *Reynolds*
1881	Helen Hunt Jackson, *A Century of Dishonor*
1883	Women's National Indian Rights Association founded; William ("Buffalo Bill") Cody organizes Wild West Show
1884	Helen Hunt Jackson, *Ramona*
1886	Severe drought on the Plains destroys cattle and grain
1887	Dawes Severalty Act; Edmunds-Tucker Act
1888	White Caps raid ranches in northern New Mexico
1889	Oklahoma Territory opened for settlement
1890	Ghost Dance movement spreads to the Black Hills; Massacre of Teton Sioux at Wounded Knee, South Dakota
1892	John Muir organizes Sierra Club
1898	Curtis Act

The Plains Indians

The Indians of the Great Plains inhabited three major subregions. The northern Plains, from the Dakotas and Montana southward to Nebraska, were home to several large tribes, most notably the Lakota as well as Flat-heads, Blackfeet, Assiniboins (ah-SIN-ih-bwans), northern Cheyennes (shy-ANNS), Arapahos (a-RAP-a-hose), Crows, Hidatsas, and Mandans. Some of these were allies, but others were bitter enemies. In the Central Plains, the so-called Five Civilized Tribes, driven there from the Southeast in the 1830s, pursued an agricultural life in the Indian Territory (present-day Oklahoma). Farther west, the Pawnees of Nebraska maintained the older, more settled tradition characteristic of Plains river valley culture. On the southern Plains of western Kansas, Colorado, eastern New Mexico, and Texas, the Comanches, Kiowas, Cheyennes, southern Arapahos, and Apaches still maintained a migratory life appropriate to the arid environment.

Considerable diversity flourished among the Plains peoples, and customs varied even within subdivisions of the same tribe. For example, the Dakota Sioux (soo) of Minnesota led a semisedentary life based on small-scale agriculture, deer and bison hunting, and wild rice harvesting. In contrast, many Plains tribes—the Lakota Sioux, Blackfeet, Crows, and Cheyennes—using horses obtained from the Spanish and guns obtained from traders, roamed the High Plains to the west and followed the bison migrations.

Plains Indians Diverse Native American societies inhabiting the region from the Dakotas to Texas

For all the **Plains Indians,** life revolved around extended family ties and tribal cooperation. Families and clans joined forces to hunt and farm, and reached decisions by consensus. Religious and harvest celebrations provided the cement for village and camp life. Sioux religion was complex. The Lakota Sioux thought of life as a series of circles. Living within the daily cycles of the sun and moon, Lakotas were born into a circle of relatives, which broadened to the band, the tribe, the Sioux Nation, and on to animals and plants. The Lakotas also believed in a hierarchy of spirits whose help could be invoked in ceremonies like the Sun Dance. On the semiarid High Plains, where rainfall averaged less than twenty inches a year, both the bison and the Native peoples adapted to the environment. The huge bison herds, which at their peak contained an estimated 30 million animals, broke into small groups in the winter and dispersed into river valleys. In the summer, they returned to the High Plains in vast herds to mate and feed on the nutritious short grasses. Like the bison, the Indians dispersed across the landscape to minimize their impact on any one place, wintering in the river valleys and returning to the High Plains in summer.

The movement of miners and settlers onto the eastern High Plains in the 1850s threatened the Native American way of life. In the 1860s, the whites began systematically to hunt the animals to supply the eastern market with carriage robes and industrial belting. **William F. "Buffalo Bill" Cody,** a famous scout and Indian fighter, killed nearly forty-three hundred bison in 1867–1868 to feed construction crews building the Union Pacific Railroad. Army commanders also encouraged the slaughter of buffalo to undermine Indian resistance. The carnage that resulted was almost inconceivable in its scale. Between 1872 and 1875, hunters killed 9 million buffalo, taking only the skin and leaving the carcasses to rot. By the 1880s, the once-thundering herds had been reduced to a few thousand animals, and the Native American way of life dependent on the buffalo had been ruined.

William F. "Buffalo Bill" Cody Renowned scout, Indian fighter, and showman who symbolized the "Wild West" mythos

The Assault on Nomadic Indian Life

In the 1850s, Indians who felt pressure from the declining bison herds and deteriorating grasslands faced the onslaught of thousands of pioneers lured by the discovery of gold and silver in the Rocky Mountains. The federal government's response was to reexamine its Indian policies. Abandoning the previous position, which had treated much of the West as a vast Indian reserve, the federal government sought to introduce a system of smaller tribal reservations where the Indians were to be concentrated, by force if necessary.

Indian Mother and Son, c. 1890s
Indian children were taught to ride horses at an early age. Horses were a form of wealth for migratory Plains peoples and made hunting buffalo (depicted on the tipi) considerably easier.

Some Native Americans peacefully adjusted to their new life. Others, among them the Navajos (NAH-vuh-hohs) of Arizona and New Mexico and the eastern Dakota Sioux, opposed the new policy to no avail. By 1860, eight western reservations had been established. Significant segments of the remaining tribes on the Great Plains, more than a hundred thousand people, fought against removal for decades. Between 1860 and 1890, the western Sioux, Cheyennes, Arapahos, Kiowas, and Comanches on the Great Plains; the Nez Percés (nez per-SAY) and Bannocks in the northern Rockies; and the Apaches in the Southwest—faced the U.S. army, toughened by its experiences in the Civil War, in a series of final battles for the West (see Map 17.1).

Misunderstandings, unfulfilled promises, brutality, and butchery marked the conflict. Near Sand Creek, Colorado in 1864, soldiers from the local militia who had replaced regular army troops fighting in the Civil War, destroyed Cheyenne and Arapaho camps. The Indians retaliated with a flurry of attacks on travelers. The governor, in a panic, authorized Colorado's white citizenry to kill hostile Indians on sight. He then activated a regiment of troops under Colonel John M. Chivington, a Methodist minister. At dawn on November 29, Chivington's troops massacred a peaceful band of Indians, including terrified women and children, camped at Sand Creek.

This massacre and others that followed rekindled public debate over federal Indian policy. In response, in 1867 Congress sent a peace commission to end the fighting and set aside two large land reserves, one north of Nebraska, the other south of Kansas. Behind the federal government's persuasion lay the threat of force. Any Native Americans who refused to relocate, warned Commissioner of Indian Affairs Ely S. Parker, himself a Seneca Indian, "would be . . . treated as friendly or hostile as circumstances might justify." At first the plan appeared to work. Representatives of

CL Primary Source: Helen Hunt Jackson's Account of Sand Creek

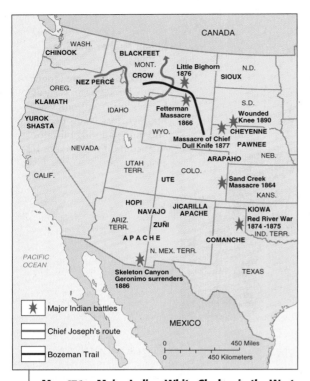

Map 17.1   Major Indian-White Clashes in the West

Although never recognized as such in the popular press, the battles between Native Americans and the U.S. Army on the Great Plains amounted to a major undeclared war.

Fort Laramie Treaty Agreement that moved thousands of Plains Indians to reservations in South Dakota in 1867

sixty-eight thousand southern Kiowas, Comanches, Cheyennes, and Arapahos signed the Medicine Lodge Treaty of 1867 and pledged to live on land in present-day Oklahoma. The following year, scattered bands of Sioux, representing nearly fifty-four thousand northern Plains Indians, signed the **Fort Laramie Treaty** and agreed to move to reservations in what is now South Dakota in return for money and provisions.

Indian dissatisfaction with the treaties ran deep. In August 1868, war parties of defiant Cheyennes, Arapahos, and Sioux raided frontier settlements in Kansas and Colorado, burning homes and killing whites. In retaliation, army troops attacked Indians, even peaceful ones, who refused confinement. That autumn, Lieutenant Colonel George Armstrong Custer's raiding party attacked a sleeping Cheyenne village, killing more than one hundred warriors. Other Cheyennes and Arapahos were pursued, captured, and returned to reservations.

In 1869, spurred on by Christian reformers, Congress established a Board of Indian Commissioners to reform abuses on the reservations by Indian agents. But the new and inexperienced church-appointed Indian agents quickly encountered problems. As conditions on the reservations deteriorated, Indians left in large numbers. Other agents were unable to restrain scheming whites who fraudulently purchased reservation lands from the Indians. Frustrated by the manipulation of Indian treaties and irritated by the ineptness of the Indian agents, Congress in 1871 abolished treaty making and replaced treaties with executive orders and acts of Congress. In the 1880s, the federal government ignored the churches' nominations for Indian agents and made its own appointments. Caught in the sticky web of an ambiguous and deceptive federal policy, defiant Native Americans struck back in the 1870s. On the southern Plains, Kiowa, Comanche, and Cheyenne raids in the Texas Panhandle in 1874 set off the so-called Red River War. In a fierce winter campaign, regular army troops slaughtered a hundred Cheyenne fugitives in Kansas. With the exile of seventy-four "ringleaders" to reservations in Florida, Native American independence on the southern Plains came to an end. In the Southwest, the Apaches fought an intermittent guerrilla war until their leader, Geronimo (jer-RON-eh-moe), surrendered in 1886.

Custer's Last Stand, 1876

Of all the acts of Indian resistance against the new reservation policy, none aroused more passion or caused more bloodshed than the battles waged by the western Sioux tribes in the Dakotas, Montana, and Wyoming. The 1868 Treaty of Fort Laramie had set aside the Great Sioux Reserve "in perpetuity." But not all the Sioux bands had fought in the war or signed the treaty.

In 1873, skillfully playing local officials against the federal government, Chief Red Cloud's Oglala band and Chief Spotted Tail's Brulé (BROO-lay) band won the concession of staying on their traditional lands. To protect their hunting grounds, they raided encroaching non-Indian settlements in Nebraska and Wyoming, intimidated federal agents, and harassed anyone who ventured onto their lands.

Non-treaty Sioux found a powerful leader in the Lakota Sioux chief and holy man **Sitting Bull.** Broad-shouldered and powerfully built, Sitting Bull led by example and had considerable fighting experience. In 1874, General William Tecumseh Sherman sent a force under Colonel George Armstrong Custer into the Black Hills of South Dakota, near the western edge of the Great Sioux Reserve. Lean and mustachioed, the thirty-four-year-old Custer had been a celebrity since his days as an impetuous young Civil War officer.

Custer's original mission was to extract concessions from the Sioux. But when negotiations broke down in November 1875, Custer now sought to drive the Indians out of the Black Hills. In June 1876, leading 600 troops of the Seventh Cavalry, Custer proceeded to the Little Bighorn River area of present-day Montana, a hub of Indian resistance. On the morning of June 25, underestimating the Indian enemy and unwisely dividing his force, Custer, with 209 men, recklessly advanced against a large company of Cheyenne and Sioux warriors led by Chief Sitting Bull, who had encamped along the Little Bighorn. Custer and his outnumbered troops were wiped out.

Americans reeled from this unexpected Indian victory. Newspaper columnists groped to assess the meaning of "Custer's last stand." Some questioned the wisdom of current federal policy toward the Indians. Others worried that an outraged public would demand retaliation. Most, however, endorsed the federal government's determination to quash the Native American rebellion.

Defeat at Little Bighorn made the army more determined. In Montana, troops harassed various Sioux bands for more than five years, attacking Indian camps in the dead of winter and destroying all supplies. Even Sitting Bull, who had led his band to Canada to escape the army, surrendered in 1881 for lack of provisions. The slaughter of the buffalo had wiped out his tribe's major food source.

Similar measures were used elsewhere in the West against Chief Joseph and his Nez Percés of Oregon and against the northern Cheyennes. Chief Dull Knife led the remnants of his tribe north to join the Sioux in September 1878. But the army chased them down and imprisoned them in Fort Robinson, Nebraska. On a frigid night in January 1879, Dull Knife and his followers shot the guards and broke for freedom. Soldiers fired and gunned down half of them in the snow, including women and children as well as Dull Knife himself. These brutal tactics sapped the Indians' will to resist.

Sitting Bull Leader of the Sioux warriors who wiped out George Armstrong Custer's force at the Little Bighorn in 1876

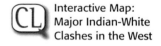

Interactive Map: Major Indian-White Clashes in the West

"Saving" the Indians

A growing number of Americans were outraged by the federal government's flagrant violation of its Indian treaties. The Women's National Indian Rights Association, founded in 1883, and other groups took up the cause. **Helen Hunt Jackson** of Colorado published *A Century of Dishonor* in 1881 to rally public opinion against the government's record of broken treaty obligations. "It makes little difference . . . where one opens the record of the history of the Indians," she wrote; "every page and every year has its dark stain."

Helen Hunt Jackson Humanitarian who popularized wrongs done to Indians

To help Indians abandon hunting and nomadic life, reformers like Jackson advocated the creation of Indian boarding schools. Richard Henry Pratt, a retired military officer, opened such a school in Carlisle, Pennsylvania, in 1879. Pratt believed that the Indians' customs and languages had halted their progress toward white civilization. His motto therefore became "Kill the Indian and save the man." Modeled after Carlisle, other Indian boarding schools taught farming, carpentry, dressmaking, and nursing. Despite the reformers' best efforts, the attempt to stamp out Indian identity in the boarding schools often backfired. Forming friendships with Indians from many different tribes, boarding school students forged their own sense of Indian identity.

In addition to their advocacy of boarding schools, well-intentioned humanitarians concluded that the Indians' interests would be best served by breaking up the reservations and gradually incorporating individual Native Americans into mainstream society by giving them the rights of citizens. In short, they proposed to eliminate the "Indian problem" by eliminating the Indians as a culturally distinct entity. Inspired by this vision, they supported the **Dawes Severalty Act,** passed in 1887.

Dawes Severalty Act Law intended to "civilize" Indians by distributing tribal lands to individuals

The Dawes Act was designed to turn Indians into landowners and farmers. The law emphasized severalty, or the treatment of Indians as individuals rather than as members of tribes, and called for the distribution of reservation land plots to each head of an Indian family who accepted the law's provisions. The remaining reservation lands (often the richest) were to be sold to speculators and settlers, and the income thus obtained would go toward purchase of farm tools. After twenty-five years, those Indians who had accepted allotments would also be declared citizens of the United States.

The Dawes Act proved to be a boon to speculators, who commonly evaded its safeguards and obtained the Indians' best land. By 1934, the act had slashed Indian acreage by 65 percent. Much of what remained in Indian hands was too dry and gravelly for farming. Although some Native Americans who received land under the Dawes Act prospered enough to expand their holdings, countless others struggled just to survive. Alcoholism, a continuing problem exacerbated by the prevalence of whiskey as a trade item, became more prevalent as Native Americans strove to adapt to the constraints of reservation life.

The Ghost Dance and the End of Indian Resistance on the Great Plains, 1890

Living conditions for the Sioux worsened in the late 1880s. The federal government reduced their meat rations and restricted hunting. When disease killed a third of their cattle, they became desperate. The Sioux turned to Wovoka, a new visionary prophet popular among the Great Basin Indians in Nevada. Wovoka foresaw a catastrophic event that would bring the return of dead relatives, the restoration of the bison herds, and the renewal of traditional life. Some versions of his vision included the destruction of European-Americans. To bring on this new day, the prophet preached a return to traditional ethics, and taught his followers a cycle of ritual songs and dance steps known as the **Ghost Dance.**

Ghost Dance Ritual that the prophet Wovoka promised would restore Indians to control of their lands

In the fall of 1890, as the Ghost Dance movement spread among the Sioux in the Dakota Territory, Indian officials and military authorities grew alarmed. The local reservation agent decided that Chief Sitting Bull, whose cabin on the reservation had become a rallying point for the Ghost Dance movement, must be arrested. When

Wounded Knee, Pine Ridge Reservation, South Dakota, 1890

Thrown into an open trench, the frozen bodies of the Sioux slaughtered at Wounded Knee were a grim reminder that the U.S. army would brook no opposition to its control of Indian reservations.

two policemen pulled the chief from his cabin, a scuffle ensued, shots rang out, and Sitting Bull was mortally wounded.

Two weeks later, one of the bloodiest episodes of Indian-white strife on the Plains occurred. On December 29, the Seventh Cavalry was rounding up 340 starving and freezing Sioux at **Wounded Knee,** South Dakota, when someone fired a gun. The soldiers retaliated with cannon fire. Within minutes 300 Indians, including 7 infants, were slaughtered. As the frozen corpses at Wounded Knee were dumped into mass graves, a generation of Indian-white conflict on the Great Plains shuddered to a close.

Many Natives did try to adapt to non-Indian ways, and some succeeded fully. Goodbird, the son of Buffalo Bird Woman, became a Congregational minister, a prosperous farmer, and a leader of the Hidatsa tribe. Others did less well economically. Driven onto reservations, many Plains Indians became dependent on governmental support. By 1900, the Plains Indian population had shrunk from nearly a quarter-million to just over a hundred thousand. Nevertheless, the population began to increase slowly after 1900. Against overwhelming odds, the pride, religious traditions, and cultural identities of the Plains Indians survived all efforts at eradication.

Unlike the nomadic western Sioux, the more settled Navajos of the Southwest adjusted more successfully to the reservation system, preserving traditional ways while incorporating elements of the new order. By 1900, the Navajos had tripled their reservation land, dramatically increased their numbers and their herds, and carved out for themselves a distinct place in Arizona and New Mexico.

These extraordinary changes were forced on the Indian population by the advance of non-Indian settlement. In the name of civilization and progress, non-Indians in the generation after the Civil War pursued a course that involved a mixture of sincere (if misguided) benevolence and outbursts

Wounded Knee Massacre of three hundred Indians by U.S. Army; last chapter of battle for Great Plains

CHECKING IN

- The destruction of the Great Plains buffalo herds opened the way for the destruction of the Plains Indians.
- The battle for control of the Plains pitted nomadic Indians who rejected reservation life against the U.S. Army.
- Custer's Last Stand, in which Indians wiped out 209 cavalry troops, infuriated Americans and increased support for violence against the Plains tribes.
- The Dawes Act sought to "civilize" Plains Indians by dissolving tribal bonds and distributing tribal lands among individual Indians and speculators.
- The massacre of 300 starving Indians at Wounded Knee signaled the end of armed conflict on the Great Plains and the end of Plains Indian culture.

of naked violence. Many white Americans felt toward the Indians only contempt, hatred, and greed for their land. Others viewed themselves as divinely chosen instruments for uplifting and Christianizing Native peoples. Both groups, however, were blind to the value of Native American life and traditions. And both were unsuccessful in their attempts to shatter proud peoples and their ancient cultures.

SETTLING THE WEST

What roles did the federal government, the army, and the railroads play in the settlement of the West?

The successive defeats of the Native Americans opened a vast territory for settlement. After 1870, railroad expansion made the trip from the East to Oregon and California faster and considerably easier than ever before. In the next three decades, more land was parceled out into farms than in the previous 250 years of American history combined, and agricultural production doubled.

The First Transcontinental Railroad

Passed in 1862, the Pacific Railroad Act authorized the construction of a new transcontinental link. The act provided grants of land and other subsidies to the railroads for each mile of track laid, which made them the largest landholders in the West. More than any other factor, the expansion of these railroads accelerated the transformation of everyday life west of the Mississippi.

Building the railroad took backbreaking work. Searching for inexpensive labor, the railroads turned to immigrants. The Central Pacific employed Chinese workers to chip and blast rail bed out of solid rock in the Sierra Nevada. Nearly twelve thousand Chinese graded the roadbed while Irish, Mexican-American, and black workers put down the track.

On May 10, 1869, Americans celebrated the completion of the first railroad spanning North America. As the two sets of tracks—the Union Pacific's, stretching westward from Omaha, Nebraska, and the Central Pacific's, reaching eastward from Sacramento, California—met at Promontory Point, Utah, beaming officials drove in a final ceremonial golden spike. The nation's vast midsection was now far more accessible than it had ever been.

The railroads quickly proved their usefulness. In the battles against Native Americans, the army shipped horses and men west in the dead of winter to attack the Indians when they were most vulnerable. From the same trains, hunters gained quick access to the bison ranges and increased their harvest of the animals. Once Indian resistance had been broken, the railroads hastened the arrival of new settlers and provided access for the shipment of cattle and grain to eastern urban markets. In short, the railroads accelerated the development of the West.

Settlers and the Railroad

During the decade after the passage of the Pacific Railroad Act, Congress awarded the railroads 170 million acres, worth over half a billion dollars. By 1893, Minnesota and Washington had also deeded to railroad companies a quarter of their state lands. As

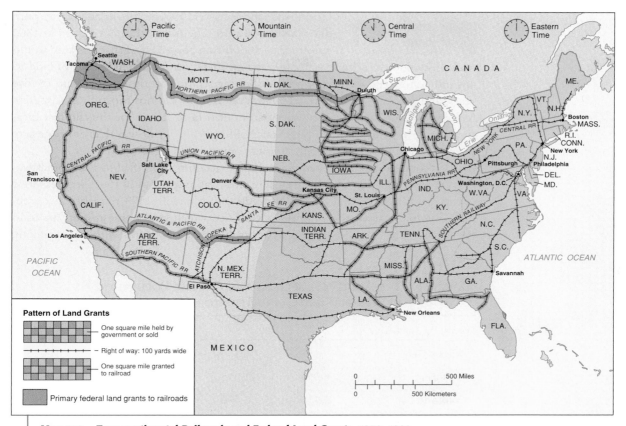

Map 17.2   Transcontinental Railroads and Federal Land Grants, 1850–1900

Despite the laissez-faire ideology that argued against government interference in business, Congress heavily subsidized American railroads and gave them millions of acres of land. As illustrated in the box, belts of land were reserved on either side of a railroad's right of way. Until the railroad claimed the exact one-mile-square sections it chose to possess, all such sections within the belt remained closed to settlement.

mighty landowners, the railroads had a unique opportunity to shape settlement in the region—and to reap enormous profits (see Map 17.2).

The railroads set up land sales offices and sent agents to the East Coast and Europe to recruit settlers. The land bureaus offered prospective buyers long-term loans and free transportation. Acknowledging that life on the Great Plains could be lonely, the promoters advised young men to bring their wives (because "maidens are scarce") and to emigrate as entire families and with friends. The railroads also helped bring nearly 2.2 million foreign-born settlers to the trans-Mississippi West between 1870 and 1900. Some agents recruited whole villages of Germans and eastern Europeans to relocate to the North Dakota plains.

The railroads influenced agriculture as well. To ensure quick repayment of the money owed to them, the railroads urged new immigrants to specialize in cash crops—wheat on the northern Plains, corn in Iowa and Kansas, cotton and tobacco in Texas. Although these crops initially brought in high revenues, many farmers grew dependent on income from a single crop and became vulnerable to fluctuating market forces.

Homesteading on the Great Plains

Liberalized land laws were another powerful magnet pulling settlers westward. The Homestead Act passed in 1862 reflected the Republican party's belief that free land would enable the poor to achieve economic independence. It offered 160 acres of land to any individual who would pay a ten-dollar registration fee, live on the land for five years, and cultivate and improve it. However, the law did not function as Congress had envisioned. Unscrupulous speculators filed false claims for the choicest locations, and railroads acquired huge landholdings. The result was that only one acre in every nine went to the pioneers for whom it was intended.

A second problem resulted from the 160-acre limit specified by the Homestead Act. On the rich soils of Iowa, a 160-acre farm was ample, but in the drier areas west of the hundredth meridian, a farmer needed more land. In 1873, to rectify this problem, Congress passed the Timber Culture Act, which gave homesteaders an additional 160 acres if they planted trees on 40 acres. For states with little rainfall,

TABLE 17.1 | THE AFRICAN-AMERICAN AND CHINESE POPULATION IN WESTERN STATES AND TERRITORIES, 1880–1900

STATE OR TERRITORY	BLACKS		CHINESE	
Arizona Terr.	155	1,846	1,630	1,419
California	6,018	11,045	75,132	45,753
Colorado	2,435	8,570	612	599
Idaho	53	293	3,379	1,467
Kansas	43,107	52,003	19	39
Montana	346	1,523	1,765	1,739
Nebraska	2,385	6,269	18	180
Nevada	488	134	5,416	1,352
New Mexico Terr.	1,015	1,610	57	341
North Dakota	113	286	NA	32
Oklahoma Indian Terr.	NA	56,684*	NA	31
Oregon	487	1,105	9,510	10,397
South Dakota	288	465	NA	165
Texas	393,384	620,722	136	836
Utah	232	672	510	572
Washington	325	2,514	3,186	3,629

Source: U.S. Bureau of the Census, Negro Population in the United States, 1790–1915 (Washington, D.C.: U.S. Government Printing Office, 1918), 43, 44; Michael Doran, "Population Statistics of Nineteenth Century Indian Territory," *Chronicles of Oklahoma* 53 No. 4 (Winter 1975), 501; and *The Tenth Census, 1880, Population, and Twelfth Census, 1900, Population* (Washington, D.C.: U.S. Government Printing Office, 1883 &1901).

*Combined total for Indian and Oklahoma territories.

Congress enacted the Desert Land Act in 1877, which made 640 acres available at $1.25 an acre on condition that the owner irrigate part of it within three years. However, this act was abused by grasping speculators. Even though families did not receive as much land as Congress had intended, federal laws kept alive the dream of the West as a place for new beginnings.

In addition to problems faced by those who chose property in areas that lacked sufficient rainfall to grow crops, almost all settlers faced difficult psychological adjustments to frontier life. The first years of settlement were the most difficult. Toiling to build a house, plow the fields, and plant the first crop, the pioneers put in an average of sixty-eight hours of back-breaking work a week. For blacks who emigrated from the South to Kansas and other parts of the Plains after the Civil War, prejudice compounded the burdens of adjusting to a different life (see Chapter 16).

Many women found adaptation to Plains frontier life especially difficult. At least initially, some were enchanted by the landscape. But far more were struck by the "horrible tribes of Mosquitoes" and the crude sod huts that served as their early homes because of the scarcity of timber. One woman burst into tears upon first seeing her new sod house. The young bride angrily informed her husband that her father had built a better house for his hogs.

The high transience rate on the frontier in these years reflected the difficulty that newcomers faced in adjusting to life on the Great Plains. Nearly half of those who staked homestead claims in Kansas between 1862 and 1890 relinquished their rights to the land and moved on. Those who stayed eventually came to identify deeply with the land. Within a decade, the typical Plains family that had "stuck it out" had moved into a new wood-framed house and had fixed up the front parlor. There were just enough of these success stories to sustain the popular ideal of the West as a place of hope and opportunity.

 Interactive Map: Settlement of the Trans-Mississippi West, 1860–1890

New Farms, New Markets

Farmers on the Plains took advantage of advances in farm mechanization and the development of improved strains of wheat and corn to boost production dramatically. Efficient steel plows; specially designed wheat planters; and improved grain binders, threshers, and windmills all allowed the typical Great Plains farmer of the late nineteenth century to increase the land's yield tenfold.

Barbed wire, patented in 1874, was another crucial invention that permitted farmers to keep roving livestock out of their crops. But fencing the land touched off violent clashes between farmers and cattle ranchers, who demanded the right to let their herds roam freely until the roundup. Generally the farmers won.

The invention of labor-saving machinery together with increased demand for wheat, milk, and other farm products created the impression that farming was entering a period of unparalleled prosperity. But few fully understood the perils of pursuing agriculture as a livelihood. Faced with huge start-up costs and substantial mortgage payments, many farmers had to specialize in a crop such as wheat or corn that would fetch high prices. This specialization made them dependent on the railroads for shipping and put them at the mercy of the international grain market's shifting prices. High demand could bring prosperity, but when world overproduction forced grain prices down, the heavily indebted grower faced ruin. Confronted with these realities, many Plains farmers quickly abandoned the illusion of frontier independence and easy wealth.

Unpredictable rainfall and weather conditions further exacerbated homesteaders' difficulties west of the hundredth meridian, where rainfall averaged less than twenty inches a year. Farmers in such places used specialized "dry farming" techniques, built windmills, and diverted creeks for irrigation. But the onset of unusually dry years in the 1870s, together with grasshopper infestations and the major economic depression that struck the United States between 1873 and 1878 (see Chapter 16), made the plight of some midwesterners desperate.

Building a Society and Achieving Statehood

Despite the hardships, many remote farm settlements blossomed into thriving communities. Among the first institutions to appear, churches and Sunday schools became humming centers of social activity as well as of worship. Neighbors readily lent a hand to the farmer whose barn had burned or whose family was sick. Cooperation was a practical necessity and a form of insurance in a rugged environment where everyone was vulnerable to instant misfortune or even disaster.

When the population increased, local boosters lobbied to turn the territory into a state. Kansas entered the Union in 1861, followed by Nevada in 1864 and Nebraska in 1867. Colorado joined in 1876. Not until 1889 did North Dakota, South Dakota, Montana, and Washington gain statehood. Wyoming and Idaho came into the Union the following year. Utah finally entered in 1896. With Oklahoma's admission in 1907 and Arizona's and New Mexico's in 1912, the process of creating permanent political institutions in the trans-Mississippi West was complete.

Although generally socially conservative, the new state governments supported woman suffrage. As territories became states, pioneer women battled for the vote. Success came first in the Wyoming Territory, where men outnumbered women 6 to 1. The tiny legislature enfranchised women in 1869 in the hope that it would attract women, families, and economic growth. The Utah Territory followed in 1870. Nebraska in 1867 and Colorado in 1876 permitted women to vote in school elections. Although these successes were significant, by 1910 only four states—Idaho, Wyoming, Utah, and Colorado—had granted women full voting rights.

The Spread of Mormonism

Persecuted in Illinois, members of the Church of Jesus Christ of Latter-day Saints, known as Mormons, had moved to the Great Salt Lake Valley in 1847. Led by Brigham Young, their prophet-president, they sought to create the independent country of Deseret. Their faith emphasized self-sufficiency and commitment to family. In the next two decades, recruitment boosted their numbers to more than 100,000. Increasingly, these Mormon communities conflicted with non-Mormons and with the U.S. government, which disapproved of the church's involvement in politics, its communal business practices, and its support of polygamy.

CHECKING IN

- The completion of the first transcontinental railroad in 1869 opened the Great Plains for white settlement.
- Railroad companies encouraged the settlement of the Plains, recruiting settlers and offering loans and free transportation.
- The Homestead Act, offering free land to people who would farm it, lured tens of thousands of would-be settlers to the Plains.
- Homesteaders persevered in the face of such major obstacles as isolation, drought, and the perils of the commercial market.
- The Mormons, persecuted elsewhere, found a home in the West and helped Utah achieve statehood in 1896. By 1912 all western territories had been brought into the Union as states.

The Mormons sought at first to be economically independent. In 1869, they developed their own railroad lines out of Salt Lake City. But a series of federal acts and court decisions, starting with the Morrill Anti-Bigamy Act in 1862, challenged the authority of their church and their practice of polygamy or plural marriage. In *United States v. Reynolds* (1879), the Supreme Court declared plural marriages unlawful. Then, in 1887, the **Edmunds-Tucker Act** dissolved the church corporation and put its properties and funds into receivership (control by the courts).

Edmunds-Tucker Act Federal confiscation of Mormon church property to pressure it to abandon practice of polygamy

In response, in 1890 the church president publicly announced the official end of polygamy. The church supported the application for statehood (Utah), which was granted in 1896. Confiscated church properties were returned, and jailed polygamists were pardoned, but the balance between sacred and secular had permanently shifted. Mormon settlements would continue in the twentieth century to draw new members and to influence development in western communities.

SOUTHWESTERN BORDERLANDS

How did ranchers and settlers displace Spanish-speaking Americans in the Southwest?

The treaty that ended the Mexican-American War in 1848 ceded to the United States an immense territory, part of which became Texas, California, Arizona, and New Mexico. At the time, Mexicans had controlled vast expanses of the Southwest. They had built their own churches, had maintained large ranching operations, and had traded with the Indians. Although the United States had pledged to protect the liberty and property of Mexicans who remained on American soil, over the next three decades American ranchers and settlers took control of the territorial governments and forced much of the Spanish-speaking population off the land. Mexicans who stayed in the region adapted to the new Anglo society with varying degrees of success.

In Texas, the struggle for independence from Mexico had left a legacy of bitterness and misunderstanding. After 1848, Texas cotton planters confiscated Mexican lands and began a racist campaign that labeled Mexicans as nonwhite. Mexican bandits retaliated by raiding American communities. In 1859, a Mexican rancher named Juan Cortina attacked the border community of Brownsville, Texas. He continued to harass the U.S. army for years until the Mexican government, fearing a U.S. invasion, imprisoned him in 1875.

Mexican-Americans in California in the 1850s and 1860s faced similar pressures. A cycle of flood and drought, together with a slumping cattle industry, had ruined many of the large southern California ranches owned by the *californios,* Spanish-speaking descendants of the original Spanish settlers. The collapse of the ranch economy forced many of them to retreat into segregated urban neighborhoods called barrios. Maintaining a tenacious hold on their traditions, many Spanish-speaking people in Santa Barbara and other towns survived by working as day laborers.

In California, the pattern was similar. At first, the number of new "Anglos" was small. As the number of whites increased, they identified minority racial, cultural, and language differences as marks of inferiority. White state legislators passed laws

Santa Fe Plaza, New Mexico, in the 1880s, by Francis X. Grosshenney

After the railroad went through in 1878, Santa Fe became a popular tourist attraction known for its historic adobe buildings.

White Caps Mexican-American vigilante group in northern New Mexico that protested the enclosure of grazing lands

CHECKING IN

- Violence frequently flared between Anglos and Mexicans in Texas and California.
- In California, thousands of Mexicans, deprived of their land, ended up in urban barrios.
- The Spanish-speaking population adapted more smoothly in New Mexico and Arizona, where their numbers were smaller.
- After losing their land, many Mexican-Americans became laborers.
- Women often held Mexican-American communities together, emphasizing culture and kinship.

that made ownership of property difficult for non-Anglos. Relegated to a migratory labor force, non-Anglos were tagged as shiftless and irresponsible. Yet their labor made possible increased prosperity for the farmers, railroads, and households that hired them.

The cultural adaptation of Spanish-speaking Americans to Anglo society initially unfolded more smoothly in Arizona and New Mexico, where Spanish settlement had been sparse, and a small class of wealthy Mexican landowners had long dominated a poor, illiterate peasantry. Moreover, since the 1820s, well-to-do Mexicans in Tucson, Arizona, had educated their children in the United States and had formed trading partnerships and business alliances with Americans.

Such examples of successful cooperation between Hispanic and white Americans helped moderate American settlers' antagonistic attitudes. So, too, did the work of popular writers like Helen Hunt Jackson. By sentimentalizing the gracious colonial Spanish past, Jackson increased public sympathy for Spanish-speaking Americans. Jackson's 1884 romance *Ramona*, a tale of the doomed love of a Hispanicized mixed-blood (Irish-Indian) woman set on a California ranch overwhelmed by the onrushing tide of Anglo civilization, was enormously popular.

Still, conflicts over property persisted in Arizona and New Mexico. In the 1880s, Mexican-American ranchers organized themselves into a self-protection vigilante group called Las Gorras Blancas (the **White Caps**). In 1888, they tore up railroad tracks and attacked both Anglo newcomers and those upper-class Hispanics who had fenced acreage in northern New Mexico that had previously been considered public grazing land. But this vigilante action did not help, as Anglo-dominated corporate ranchers steadily increased their land holdings. Meanwhile, the Spanish-speaking population living in the cities became more impoverished. In Tucson, 80 percent of the Mexican-Americans in the work force were laborers in 1880, taking jobs as butchers, barbers, cowboys, and railroad workers.

Violence and discrimination against Spanish-speaking citizens of the Southwest escalated in the 1890s, a time of rising racism in the United States. Rioters in Beeville and Laredo, Texas, in 1894 and 1899 attacked and beat up Mexican-Americans. Whites increasingly labeled Mexican-Americans as violent and lazy. For Spanish-speaking citizens, the battle for fair treatment and respect would continue into the twentieth century

EXPLOITING THE WESTERN LANDSCAPE

How did mining, ranching, and farming shape the West?

The displacement of Mexican-American and Native peoples from their lands opened the way for the exploitation of the natural environment in the trans-Mississippi West. White boosters had long promoted the region as a land of boundless opportunity. Between 1860 and 1900, a generation of Americans sought to strike it rich by joining the ranks of miners, ranchers, and farmers intent on making a fortune. Some succeeded; but others went bankrupt or barely survived. Of all the groups that surged into the nation's midcontinent in the late nineteenth century, none had to revise their expectations more radically than the speculators and adventurers looking for quick fortunes.

Interactive Map: Natural Resources and the Development of the West

The Mining Frontier

In the half-century that began with the California gold rush in 1849, a series of mining booms swept from the Southwest northward into Canada and Alaska. In 1853, a year after gold was discovered in California's Sierra Nevada, prospector Henry Comstock stumbled on the rich **Comstock Lode** along Nevada's Carson River. Later in the same decade, prospectors uncovered deep veins of gold and silver near present-day Denver. Over the next five decades, gold was discovered in Idaho, Montana, Wyoming, South Dakota, and, in 1896, in the Canadian Klondike. By 1900 more than a billion dollars' worth of gold had been mined in California alone.

Comstock Lode Fabulously rich silver discovery that opened mining bonanza in West

The early discoveries of "placer" gold, panned from streams, attracted a young male population thirsting for wealth and reinforced the myth of mining country as "a poor man's paradise." In contrast to the Great Plains, where ethnic groups recreated their own ethnic enclaves, western mining camps became ethnic melting pots. In the California census of 1860, more than thirty-three thousand Irish and thirty-four thousand Chinese had staked out early claims.

Although a few prospectors became fabulously wealthy, the experience of Henry Comstock, who sold out one claim for eleven thousand dollars and another for two mules, was more typical. Because the larger gold and silver deposits lay embedded in veins of quartz deep within the earth, extracting them required huge investments in workers and expensive equipment. No sooner had the major discoveries been made, therefore, than large mining companies backed by eastern or British capital bought them out and took them over.

Life in the new mining towns was vibrant but unpredictable. During the heyday of the Comstock Lode in the 1860s and 1870s, Virginia City, Nevada, erupted in an orgy of speculation and building. Men outnumbered women three to one. Money quickly earned was even more rapidly lost. The gold rush mania also spurred the growth of settlement in Alaska. Small strikes were made there in 1869, two years after the United States had purchased the territory from Russia. But it was the discovery of gold in the Canadian Klondike in 1897 that brought thousands of prospectors into the area and eventually enabled Alaska to establish its own territorial government in 1912.

Word of new ore deposits like the ones in Alaska lured transient populations salivating to get rich. Miners who worked deep within the earth for large corporations typically earned about $2,000 a year at a time when teachers made $450 to $650 and domestic help $250 to $350. But most prospectors at best earned only enough to go elsewhere, perhaps buy some land, and try again.

Progress came at a price. The long-term cost to the environment to extract these metals was high. Hydraulic mining turned creeks brown, and flushed millions of tons of silt into valleys. The scarred landscape that remained was littered with rock and gravel filled with traces of mercury and cyanide, and nothing would grow on it. Smelters spewed dense smoke containing lead, arsenic, and other carcinogenic chemicals on those who lived nearby. The destruction to the environment is still evident today.

Cowboys and the Cattle Frontier

Like the feverish expansion of the mining frontier during the 1860s and 1870s, open-range cattle ranching boomed in these same decades. In this case, astute businessmen and railroad entrepreneurs, eager to fund their new investments in miles of track, promoted cattle herding as the new route to fame and fortune. The cowboy, once scorned as a ne'er-do-well and drifter, was now glorified as a man of rough-hewn integrity and self-reliant strength.

In 1868, Joseph G. McCoy, a young cattle dealer from Springfield, Illinois, shrewdly transformed the cattle industry into a new money-maker. With the forced relocation of the Plains Indians onto reservations and the extension of the railroads into Kansas, McCoy realized that cattle dealers could now amass enormous fortunes by raising steers cheaply in Texas and bringing them north for shipment to eastern urban markets.

McCoy built a new stockyard in Abilene, Kansas. To make the overland cattle drives from Texas to Abilene easier, McCoy also helped survey and shorten the Chisholm Trail in Kansas. At the end of his first year in business, thirty-five thousand steers were sold in Abilene; the following year the number more than doubled. The great **cattle drives** of the 1860s and 1870s turned into a bonanza for herd owners. Steers purchased in Texas at nine dollars a head could be sold in Abilene for twenty-eight dollars. But the cattlemen, like the grain growers farther north on the Great Plains, lived at the mercy of high interest rates and an unstable market. During the financial panic of 1873, cattle drovers fell into bankruptcy by the hundreds.

Little of the money made by the large-scale cattle ranchers found its way into the pockets of the cowboys themselves. The typical cowpuncher endured long hours, low pay, and hazardous work, all for a mere thirty dollars a month, about the same as common laborers. They also braved the gangs of cattle thieves—most notably

cattle drives Millions of head of cattle moved from Texas grazing lands to the railroad terminals in Kansas in the 1870s and 1880s

William H. Bonney, better known as Billy the Kid—that operated along the trails. Most cowboys were men in their teens and twenties who worked for a year or two and then pursued different livelihoods. Of the estimated 35,000 to 55,000 men who rode the trails in these years, nearly one-fifth were black or Mexican. Barred by discrimination from many other trades, blacks enjoyed the freedom of life on the trail.

The cattle bonanza, which peaked between 1880 and 1885, produced more than 4.5 million head of cattle for eastern markets. Prices began to sag as early as 1882, however, and many ranchers plunged heavily into debt. In 1885 and 1886, two of the coldest winters on record combined with summer droughts and Texas fever to destroy nearly 90 percent of the cattle in some regions, pushing thousands of ranchers into bankruptcy. The cattle industry lived on, but railroad expansion brought the days of the open range and the great cattle drives to an end.

Cattle Towns and Prostitutes

One legacy of the cattle boom was the growth of cities like Abilene, Kansas, which shipped steers to Chicago and eastern markets. Like other cattle towns, Abilene went through an early period of violence that saw cowboys pulling down the walls of the jail as it was being built. But the town quickly established a police force to maintain law and order. City ordinances—enforced by the legendary town marshal James B. "Wild Bill" Hickok—forbade carrying firearms and regulated saloons, gambling, and prostitution. Transient, unruly types certainly gave a distinctive flavor to cattle towns like Abilene, Wichita, and Dodge City, but the overall homicide rates there were not unusually high.

If cattle towns were neither as violent nor as lawless as legend would have it, they did still experience a lively business in prostitution. Given the large numbers of unattached young men and numerous saloons, prostitution thrived. Some became prostitutes as an escape from domestic violence or because of economic hardship. Others, like the Chinese, were forced into the trade. But whatever the reasons for entering the business, prostitutes risked venereal disease, physical abuse, and drug and alcohol addiction. As western towns became more settled, the numbers of women in other occupations increased.

Bonanza Farms

The enthusiasm that permeated mining and ranching in the 1870s and 1880s also percolated into agriculture. Like the gold rushes and cattle bonanzas, the wheat boom in the Dakota Territory started small but rapidly attracted large capital investments that produced the nation's first agribusinesses.

The boom began during the Panic of 1873, when the failure of numerous banks caused the price of Northern Pacific Railroad bonds to plummet. The railroad responded by exchanging land for its depreciated bonds. Speculators, including the railroad's own president, George W. Cass, jumped at the opportunity and purchased more than three hundred thousand acres in the fertile Red River Valley of North Dakota for between fifty cents and a dollar an acre.

Operating singly or in groups, the speculators established factory-like ten-thousand-acre farms, each run by a hired manager, and invested heavily in labor and

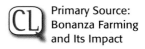
Primary Source: Bonanza Farming and Its Impact

equipment. On the Cass-Cheney-Dalrymple farm near Fargo, North Dakota, fifty or sixty plows rumbled across the flat landscape on a typical spring day. Cass's first harvest earned a huge profit. The publicity generated by the tremendous success of a few large investors like Cass and Oliver Dalrymple led to an unprecedented wheat boom. North Dakota's population tripled in the 1880s, and wheat production sky-rocketed. But the profits soon evaporated. By 1890, some Red River valley farmers were destitute.

The wheat boom collapsed for a variety of reasons. Overproduction, high invest-ment costs, too little or too much rain, excessive reliance on one crop, and depressed grain prices on the international market all undercut farmers' earnings. Large-scale farmers who had invested in hopes of getting rich felt lucky just to survive.

Large-scale farms proved most successful in California's Central Valley. Using canals and other irrigation systems to water their crops, farmers were growing higher-priced specialty crops and had created new cooperative marketing associa-tions for cherries, apricots, grapes, and oranges by the mid-1880s. Led by the Cali-fornia Citrus Growers' Association, which used the "Sunkist" trademark for their oranges, large-scale agribusinesses in California were shipping a variety of fruits and vegetables in refrigerated train cars to midwestern and eastern markets by 1900.

The Oklahoma Land Rush, 1889

As farmers in the Dakotas and Minnesota endured hard times, would-be homesteaders greedily eyed the Indian Territory, as present-day Oklahoma was then known. The federal government, considering much of this land virtually worthless, had reserved it for the Five Civilized Tribes since the 1830s. Because these tribes (except for some Cherokees) had sided with the Confederacy during the Civil War, Washington had punished them by settling thousands of Indians from other tribes on lands in the western part of the territory. Citing this past betrayal, non-Indians in the 1880s de-manded more land.

Map 17.3   The Oklahoma Land Rush, 1889-1906

Lands in Oklahoma not settled by "Sooners" were sold by lotteries, allotments, and sealed-bid auctions. By 1907, the major reservations had been broken up, and each Native American family had been given a small farm.

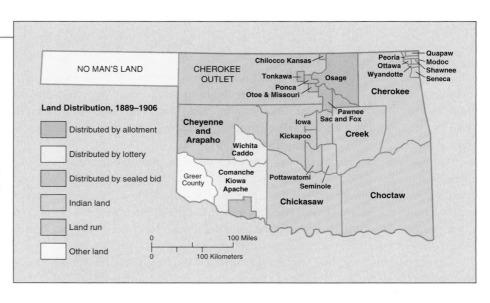

In 1889, over the Native Americans' protests, Congress transferred to the federally owned public domain nearly 2 million acres in the central part of the Oklahoma Territory that had not been specifically assigned to any Indian tribe. At noon on April 22, 1889, thousands of men, women, and children in buggies and wagons stampeded into the new lands to stake out homesteads. (Other settlers, the so-called Sooners, had illegally arrived earlier and were already plowing the fields.) Nine weeks later, six thousand homestead claims had been filed. In the next decade, the Dawes Severalty Act broke up the Indian reservations into individual allotments and opened the surplus to non-Indian settlement (see Map 17.3). The **Curtis Act** in 1898 dissolved the Indian Territory and abolished tribal governments.

The Oklahoma land rush demonstrated the continuing power of the frontier myth, which tied "free" land to the ideal of economic opportunity. Still, within two generations a combination of exploitative farming, poor land management, and sporadic drought would place Oklahoma at the desolate center of what in the 1930s would be called the dust bowl (see Chapter 24).

CHECKING IN

- Mining booms periodically flared in the West, producing a boom-and-bust cycle that enriched a few.
- The fabled era of the great cattle drives lasted a scant twenty years.
- The real-life low pay and hazardous work of cowboys and the settled monotony of cow towns were much less exciting than the fictionalized and romanticized version.
- Wheat farming became "agribusiness" in North Dakota, but weather and market forces deflated the boom in factory farms.
- The Oklahoma land rush, in which homesteaders staked claims to 2 million acres of free land, epitomized the power of the frontier myth.

THE WEST OF LIFE AND LEGEND

How was the Wild West image of cowboys and Indians created, and what developments prompted the establishment of national parks?

Curtis Act Dissolved the Indian Territory and abolished tribal governments in 1898

In 1893, a young Wisconsin historian, Frederick Jackson Turner, delivered a lecture entitled "The Significance of the Frontier in American History." "[T]he frontier has gone," declared Turner, "and with its going has closed the first period of American history." Although Turner's assertion that the frontier was closed was based on a Census Bureau announcement, it was inaccurate (more western land would be settled in the twentieth century than in the nineteenth). But his linking of economic opportunity with the transformation of the trans-Mississippi West caught the popular imagination and launched a new school of historical inquiry into the effects of the frontier on U.S. history.

Scholars now recognize that many parts of Turner's "frontier thesis," particularly its ethnocentric omission of Native Americans' claims to the land, were inaccurate. Yet his idealized view of the West did reflect ideas popular among his contemporaries in the 1890s. A legendary West had taken deep root in the American imagination. In the nineteenth century, this mythic West was a product of novels, songs, and paintings. In the twentieth century, it would be perpetuated by movies, radio programs, and television shows. The legend merits attention, for its evolution is fascinating and its influence has been far-reaching.

The American Adam and the Dime-Novel Hero

Mid-nineteenth-century writers, presented the frontiersman as a kind of mythic American Adam—simple, virtuous, and innocent—untainted by a corrupt social order. For example, at the end of Mark Twain's *Huckleberry Finn,* Huck rejects the constraints of settled society as represented by Aunt Sally and heads west with the declaration, "I reckon I got to light out for the territory ahead of the rest, because Aunt Sally she's going to adopt me and sivilize me, and I can't stand it. I been there before." In this version of the legend, the West is a place of adventure, romance, or contemplation where one can escape from society and its pressures.

But even as this conception of the myth was being popularized, another powerful theme had emerged as well. The authors of the dime novels of the 1860s and 1870s offered the image of the western frontiersman as a new masculine ideal, the tough guy who fights for truth and honor. In *Buffalo Bill: King of the Border Men* (1869), a dime novel loosely based on real-life William F. "Buffalo Bill" Cody, Edward Judson (pen-named Ned Buntline) created an idealized hero who is a powerful moral force as he drives off treacherous Indians and rounds up villainous cattle rustlers.

Cody himself, playing upon the public fascination with cowboys, organized his own **Wild West Show** in 1883. In the show, which toured the East Coast and Europe, cowboys engaged in mock battles with Indians, reinforcing the dime-novel image of the West as an arena of moral encounter where virtue always triumphed.

Wild West Show William F. "Buffalo Bill" Cody's extravagant Western-themed traveling show

Revitalizing the Frontier Legend

Eastern writers and artists eagerly embraced both versions of the myth—the West as a place of escape from society and the West as a stage on which the moral conflicts confronting society were played out. Three young members of the eastern establishment, Theodore Roosevelt, Frederic Remington, and Owen Wister, spent much time in the West in the 1880s, and each was intensely affected by the adventure.

Each man found precisely what he was looking for. The frontier that Roosevelt glorified in such books as *The Winning of the West* (four volumes, 1889–1896), and that Remington portrayed in his statues and paintings, was a stark physical and moral environment that stripped away all social artifice and tested each individual's character. Roosevelt and Remington exalted the disappearing frontier as the proving ground for a new kind of virile manhood and the last outpost of an honest and true social order.

This version of the frontier myth reached its apogee in **Owen Wister's** enormously popular novel *The Virginian* (1902). In Wister's tale, the environment of the Great Plains produces individuals like his unnamed cowboy hero, "the Virginian." The Virginian is one of nature's aristocrats—ill-educated and unsophisticated but tough, steady, and deeply moral. The Virginian sums up his own moral code in describing his view of God's justice: "He plays a square game with us." For Wister, as for Roosevelt and Remington, the cowboy was the Christian knight on the Plains, indifferent to material gain as he upheld virtue, pursued justice, and attacked evil.

Owen Wister Author of *The Virginian,* which portrayed the cowboy as a moral force

Needless to say, the western myth was far removed from the reality of the West. The idealized version of the West also glossed over the darker underside of frontier expansion—the hard physical labor of the cattle range, the forced removal of the Indians to reservations, the racist discrimination against Mexican-Americans and blacks, and the boom-and-bust mentality rooted in the selfish exploitation of natural resources.

Further, the myth obscured the complex links between the settlement of the frontier and the emergence of the United States as a major industrialized nation increasingly tied to a global economy. Eastern and foreign capitalists controlled large-scale mining, cattle, and agricultural operations in the West. Without the railroad—the brainchild of well-financed inventors, not rough-and-tumble cowboys—the transformation of the West would have been far slower.

Grand Canyon of Yellowstone, by Thomas Moran
Dazzled by the monumental beauty of the scene, painters strove to portray the western landscape as one of God's wonders. In the process, they stimulated a new popular interest in preserving the spectacular features of the land.

Beginning a National Parks Movement

Despite its one-sided and idealized vision, Owen Wister's celebration of the western experience reinforced a growing recognition that many unique features of the western landscape were being threatened by overeager entrepreneurs. One important by-product of the western legend was a surge of public support for creating national parks and the beginning of an organized conservation movement.

Those who went west in the 1860s and 1870s to map the rugged terrain of the High Plains and the Rocky Mountains were often awed by the natural beauty of the landscape. Major **John Wesley Powell,** the one-armed veteran of the Civil War who charted the Colorado River through the Grand Canyon in 1869, waxed euphoric about its towering rock formations and powerful cataracts. "On coming nearer," he wrote, "we find fountains bursting from the rock, high overhead, and the spray in the sunshine forms the gems which bedeck the way." In his important study, *Report on the Lands of the Arid Regions of the United States* (1878), Powell called for public ownership and governmental control of watersheds, irrigation, and public lands, a request that went largely unheeded.

John Wesley Powell Explorer who wrote eloquently about beauty of West, necessity for environmental conservation

Around the time Powell was educating Congress about the arid nature of the far West, a group of adventurers led by General Henry D. Washburn visited the hot springs and geysers near the Yellowstone River in northwestern Wyoming and eastern Montana. Overwhelmed by the view, the Washburn explorers abandoned their plan to claim the area for the Northern Pacific Railroad and instead petitioned Congress to protect it from settlement, occupancy, and sale. Congress responded in 1872 by creating **Yellowstone National Park** to "provide for the preservation . . . for all time, [of] mineral deposits, natural curiosities, or wonders within said park . . . in their natural condition." In doing so, they excluded the Native Americans who had long considered the area a prime hunting range.

Yellowstone National Park First national park founded as a result of conservation movement

These first steps to conserve a few of the West's unique natural sites reflected the beginning of a changed awareness of the environment. In his influential study *Man and Nature* in 1864, **George Perkins Marsh,** an architect and politician from

George Perkins Marsh Architect and politician from Vermont who challenged the notion that nature existed merely to be exploited

Vermont, had attacked the view that nature existed to be tamed and conquered. "Man," he wrote, "is everywhere a disturbing agent. Wherever he plants his foot, the harmonies of nature are turned to discords."

Marsh's plea for conservation found its most eloquent support in the work of **John Muir,** a Scottish immigrant who had grown up in Wisconsin. Temporarily blinded by an accident, Muir left for San Francisco in 1869 and quickly fell in love with the redwood forests. For the next forty years, he tramped the rugged mountains of the West and campaigned for their preservation. A romantic at heart, he yearned to experience the wilderness at its most elemental level. Once trekking high in the Rockies during a summer storm, he climbed the tallest pine he could find and swayed back and forth in the raging wind.

Muir became the late nineteenth century's most articulate publicist for wilderness protection. "Climb the mountains and get their good tidings," he advised city-dwellers. "Nature's peace will flow into you as the sunshine into the trees." Muir's spirited campaign to protect the wilderness contributed strongly to the establishment of Yosemite National Park in 1890. Two years later, the Sierra Club, an organization created to encourage the enjoyment and protection of the wilderness in the mountain regions of the Pacific coast, made Muir its first president.

Ironically, despite the crusades of Muir, Powell, and Marsh to educate the public about conservation, the campaign for wilderness preservation reaffirmed the image of the West as a unique region whose magnificent landscape produced tough individuals of superior ability. Overlooking the senseless violence and ruthless exploitation of the land, contemporary writers proclaimed that the settlement of the final frontier marked a new stage in the history of civilization, and they kept alive the legend of the western frontier as a seedbed of American virtues.

John Muir Conservationist who played a major role in wilderness preservation

CHECKING IN

- Historian Frederick Jackson Turner linked the frontier to economic opportunity but ignored the land's native occupants.
- Dime novels and Wild West shows reinforced the myth of the West as a moral arena where virtue always triumphed.
- Writers like Theodore Roosevelt and Owen Wister exalted the cowboy as a Christian knight on a pinto pony.
- John Wesley Powell led the way in extolling the western landscape, while stressing the need to conserve its resources.
- John Muir played a major role in encouraging preservation of the western wilderness and the creation of national parks.

Chapter Summary

DOWNLOAD THE MP3 AUDIO FILE OF THE CHAPTER SUMMARY, AND LISTEN TO IT ON THE GO.

How was Indian life on the Great Plains transformed in the second half of the nineteenth century? (page 380)

After the Civil War, the Great Plains became a battleground between the nomadic Plains Indians and the U.S. Army. The destruction of the buffalo herds on which they depended for subsistence opened the way for the destruction of the Indians. Well-intentioned Americans tried to "civilize" the Indians through measures such as the Dawes Act, but it was the massacre at Wounded Knee that finally marked the end of conflict on the Plains.

KEY TERMS

Plains Indians *(p. 382)*

William F. "Buffalo Bill" Cody *(p. 382)*

Fort Laramie Treaty *(p. 384)*

Sitting Bull *(p. 385)*

Helen Hunt Jackson *(p. 385)*

Dawes Severalty Act *(p. 386)*

Ghost Dance *(p. 386)*

What roles did the federal government, the army, and the railroads play in the settlement of the West? *(page 388)*

Aided by federal subsidies and the protection of the U.S. Army, the transcontinental railroad was completed in 1869. The railroad companies actively recruited settlers. Homesteaders faced obstacles they had not foreseen—isolation, drought, the perils of the commercial agricultural market—but many persevered. The Mormons, persecuted elsewhere, found a home in the West and helped Utah achieve statehood in 1896. By 1912 all of the western lands had been brought into the Union.

How did ranchers and settlers displace Spanish-speaking Americans in the Southwest? *(page 393)*

In California and Texas there were frequent clashes between Anglo and Mexican populations as the Mexicans gradually lost control of their lands; many Spanish-speakers ended up in urban barrios. In New Mexico and Arizona, adaptation went somewhat more smoothly. Nonetheless, Mexicans gradually lost status, and most became laborers.

How did mining, ranching, and farming shape the West? *(page 395)*

All three of these sectors of the economy enjoyed periodic booms in the West, from the Comstock Lode to the great cattle drives to the bonanza wheat farms of North Dakota. However, these booms often led to busts, and they did serious harm to the environment.

How was the Wild West image of cowboys and Indians created, and what developments prompted the establishment of national parks? *(page 399)*

Dime novels and Wild West shows reinforced the idea of the West as a moral arena in which good triumphed; Theodore Roosevelt, Owen Wister, and other writers portrayed the cowboy as a heroic figure. John Wesley Powell and John Muir powerfully described the western landscape and urged its conservation, leading to the creation of a national park system.

KEY TERMS continued

Wounded Knee *(p. 387)*

Edmunds-Tucker Act *(p. 393)*

White Caps *(p. 394)*

Comstock Lode *(p. 395)*

cattle drives *(p. 396)*

Curtis Act *(p. 399)*

Wild West Show *(p. 400)*

Owen Wister *(p. 400)*

John Wesley Powell *(p. 401)*

Yellowstone National Park *(p. 401)*

George Perkins Marsh *(p. 401)*

John Muir *(p. 402)*

CHAPTER 18

The Rise of Industrial America

1865–1900

Night Pageant, the Grand Columbian Carnival

CHAPTER PREVIEW

The Rise of Corporate America
How did Carnegie, Rockefeller, and other corporate leaders consolidate control over their industries?

Stimulating Economic Growth
What innovations in technology and business drove increases in industrial production after 1865?

The New South
Why did the South's experience with industrialization differ from that of the North and the Midwest?

Factories and the Work Force
How did factory workers respond to the changing nature of work?

Labor Unions and Industrial Conflict
In the 1890s how did corporate executives undercut labor's bargaining power?

On October 21, 1892, before two hundred thousand onlookers, presidential candidate Grover Cleveland proudly opened the World's Columbian Exposition in Chicago. The Chicago world's fair represented the triumph of fifty years of industrial development. The country's largest corporations displayed their newest products, including Westinghouse Company's dynamos, American Bell Telephone's connections to the East Coast, and Thomas A. Edison's phonograph. The fair dazzled its more than 25 million visitors.

Many late-nineteenth-century Americans found themselves both unsettled and exhilarated as the nation was transformed by industrialization. At mid century, the United States had played a minor role in the world economy. Five decades later, the United States now produced 35 percent of the world's manufactured goods—more than England, Germany, and France combined. It had become one of the world's greatest industrial powers. By 1900, new enterprises both large and small, supported by investment bankers and using a nationwide railroad distribution system, offered a vast array of goods.

This stunning industrial growth came at a high cost. New manufacturing processes transformed the nature of work, undercut skilled labor, and created mind-numbing assembly-line routines. Large-scale manufacturing companies often polluted the environment. The challenges of new business practices made the American economy difficult to control. Rather than smoothly rolling forward, it lurched between booms and busts in business cycles that produced labor unrest and crippling depressions in 1873–1879 and 1893–1897.

▌THE RISE OF CORPORATE AMERICA

How did Carnegie, Rockefeller, and other corporate leaders consolidate control over their industries?

In the early nineteenth century, the corporate form of business organization had been used to raise large amounts of start-up capital for transportation enterprises such as turnpikes and canals. By selling stocks and bonds to raise money, the corporation separated the company's managers, who guided its day-to-day operation, from its owners. After the Civil War, American business leaders pioneered new forms of corporate organization that combined innovative technologies, creative management structures, and limited liability should the enterprise fail. The rise of the giant corporation is a story of risk-taking and innovation as well as of conspiracy and corruption.

The Character of Industrial Change

Six features dominated the world of large-scale manufacturing after the Civil War: the exploitation of immense coal deposits as a source of cheap energy; the rapid spread of technological innovation in transportation, communication, and factory systems; the need for enormous numbers of new workers who could be carefully controlled; the constant pressure on firms to compete tooth-and-nail by cutting costs and prices; the relentless drop in prices; and finally, the failure of the money supply to keep pace with productivity.

All six factors were closely related. The great coal deposits in Pennsylvania, West Virginia, and Kentucky provided cheap energy to fuel railroad and factory growth. New technologies stimulated productivity and catalyzed breathtaking industrial expansion. Technology also enabled manufacturers to cut costs and hire cheap unskilled or semiskilled labor. Cost cutting enabled firms to undersell one another, destroy weaker competitors, and consolidate themselves into stronger, more efficient and more ruthless firms. Cheap energy, cost reduction, new technology, and fierce competition forced down overall price levels.

Out of the new industrial system poured clouds of haze and soot, as well as the first tantalizing trickle of what would become an avalanche of consumer goods. In

Abusive Monopoly Power

This Puck cartoon depicts financiers Jay Gould (left) and Cornelius Vanderbilt (right) and suggests that their manipulation of markets and their ownership of railroads, telegraph companies, and newspapers is powerful enough to strangle Uncle Sam.

Jay Gould Captain of industry and owner of the Union Pacific Railroad

turn, mounting demands for consumer goods stimulated heavy industry's production of capital goods—machines to boost farm and factory output even further. Together with the railroads, the corporations that manufactured capital goods, refined petroleum, and made steel became driving forces in the nation's economic growth.

Railroad Innovations

Competition among the aggressive and innovative capitalists who headed American heavy industry was intense, especially among the nation's railroads. By 1900, 193,000 miles of railroad track crisscrossed the United States—more than in all of Europe including Russia. These rail lines connected every state in the Union and opened up an immense new internal market.

Railroad entrepreneurs such as Collis P. Huntington of the Central Pacific Railroad and **Jay Gould** of the Union Pacific faced enormous financial and organizational problems. To raise the staggering sums necessary, railroads obtained generous land and loan subsidies from the government and borrowed money from the public (in the form of stocks and bonds). By 1900, the yearly interest repayments required by the combined debt of all U.S. railroads (which stood at an astounding $5.1 billion—nearly five times that of the federal government) cut heavily into their earnings.

In addition to developing ways to raise large amounts of capital, the railroads created new systems for collecting and using information. Railroads relied heavily on the magnetic telegraph, invented in 1837. To improve efficiency, the railroads set up clearly defined, hierarchical organizational structures and used elaborate accounting systems. Railroad officials could set rates and accurately predict profits as early as the 1860s, a time when most businesses had no idea of their total profit until they closed their books at year's end. Railroad management innovations thus became a model for many other businesses seeking a national market.

Consolidating the Railroad Industry

The expansion and consolidation of railroading reflected both the ingenuity and the dishonesty flourishing on the corporate management scene. Despite advances in organizational technique, the industry remained chaotic. Hundreds of small companies used different standards for rails, track width, and engine size. Huntington, Gould, and others devoured these smaller lines to create large, integrated track networks. West of the Mississippi five companies controlled most of the track by 1893.

Huntington, Gould, and the other larger-than-life figures who reorganized the railroad industry in the 1870s and 1880s were often depicted by their contempo-

Chronology

1859	First oil well drilled in Titusville, Pennsylvania
1866	National Labor Union founded
1869	Transcontinental railroad completed; Knights of Labor organized
1870	John D. Rockefeller establishes Standard Oil Company
1873	Panic of 1873 triggers a depression lasting until 1879
1876	Alexander Graham Bell patents the telephone
1877	Edison invents phonograph; Railway workers stage first nationwide strike
1879	Henry George, *Progress and Poverty*; Edison perfects incandescent lamp
1882	Standard Oil Trust established; Edison opens first electric power station in New York City; Chinese Exclusion Act
1883	William Graham Sumner, *What Social Classes Owe to Each Other*; Lester Frank Ward, *Dynamic Sociology*
1886	American Federation of Labor (AFL) formed; Haymarket riot in Chicago
1887	Interstate Commerce Act establishes Interstate Commerce Commission
1888	Edward Bellamy, *Looking Backward*
1889	Andrew Carnegie, "The Gospel of Wealth"
1890	Sherman Anti-Trust Act; United Mine Workers formed
1892	Standard Oil of New Jersey and General Electric formed; Homestead Strike; Columbian Exposition in Chicago
1893	Panic of 1893 triggers a depression lasting until 1897
1894	Pullman Palace Car workers strike
1901	J. Pierpont Morgan organizes United States Steel

raries as villains who manipulated stock markets and company policies to line their own pockets. Recent historians, however, have pointed out that the great industrialists were a diverse group. Although some were ironfisted pirates who engaged in fraudulent practices, others were upstanding businessmen who managed their companies with sophistication, originality, and inventiveness.

The massive systems created by these entrepreneurs became the largest business enterprises in the world. They standardized all basic equipment and facilities. In 1883, independently of the federal government, the railroads corrected scheduling problems by dividing the country into four time zones. In May 1886 all railroads shifted simultaneously to the new standard 4' 8½" gauge track. Finally, cooperative billing arrangements enabled the railroads to ship cars from other roads at uniform rates nationwide.

But the systemization and consolidation of the railroads had its costs. Heavy indebtedness, overextended systems, and crooked business practices forced the railroads to compete recklessly with each other for traffic. Competition and expansion drove some overbuilt lines into bankruptcy.

They also faced opposition from unlikely quarters. Stung by exorbitant rates and secret kickbacks, farmers turned to state governments for help. In the 1870s many midwestern state legislatures responded by outlawing rate discrimination. Initially upheld by the Supreme Court, these and other decisions were negated in the 1880s when the Court ruled that states could not regulate interstate commerce. In response in 1887, Congress passed the **Interstate Commerce Act.** A five-member Interstate Commerce Commission (ICC) was established to oversee the practices of interstate railroads. Although the law was supposed to ban monopolistic activity, it went largely unenforced until the Progressive Era of the early twentieth century (see Chapter 21).

In 1893 a national depression forced a number of railroads into the hands of **J. Pierpont Morgan,** who reorganized their administration, refinanced their debts, and built intersystem alliances. By 1906, thanks to the bankers' centralized management, seven giant networks controlled two-thirds of the nation's rail mileage.

Interstate Commerce Act
First federal attempt to control unfair practices by railroads

J. Pierpont Morgan
Investment banker who helped create U.S. Steel, other huge corporations

Andrew Carnegie Scottish immigration who build enormous steel company

vertical integration Technique of controlling all phases of production, extracting maximum profit

Applying the Lessons of the Railroads to Steel

The close connections between railroad expansion and the growth of corporate organization and management are well illustrated in the career of **Andrew Carnegie** (CAR-neh-gee). Born in Scotland, Carnegie immigrated to America in 1848 at the age of twelve. His first job as a bobbin boy in a Pittsburgh textile mill paid only $1.20 a week. After enrolling in a night course to learn bookkeeping, Carnegie became a Western Union messenger boy. He soon became the city's fastest telegraph operator. The job gave Carnegie an insider's view of railroad operations.

Carnegie's big break came in 1852 when Tom Scott, superintendent of the Pennsylvania Railroad's western division, hired him as his secretary and personal telegrapher. Later promoted to division chief, Carnegie cut costs while doubling the road's mileage and quadrupling its traffic. By 1868 Carnegie was earning more than $56,000 a year from his investments, a substantial fortune in that era.

In the early 1870s Carnegie decided to build his own steel mill. Carnegie's philosophy was deceptively simple: "Watch the costs, and the profits will take care of themselves." Using rigorous cost accounting and limiting wage increases to his workers, he lowered his production costs and prices below those of his competitors. His adoption of a new production technique named after its English inventor, Henry Bessemer, ensured a high quality product.

As output climbed, Carnegie discovered the benefits of **vertical integration**—that is, controlling all aspects of manufacturing, from extracting raw materials to selling the finished product. By 1900, Carnegie Steel had become the world's largest industrial corporation. Carnegie's competitors, worried about his domination of the market, decided to buy him out. In 1901, J. Pierpont Morgan purchased Carnegie Steel for nearly half a billion dollars and consolidated it with Federal Steel to form the United States Steel Corporation, the first business capitalized at more than $1 billion (see Figure 18.1).

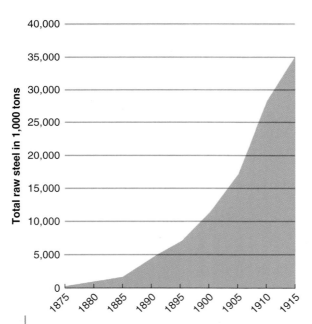

Figure 18.1   Iron and Steel Production, 1875–1915
New technologies, improved plant organization, economies of scale, and the vertical integration of production brought a dramatic spurt in iron and steel production.
Note: short ton = 2,000 pounds.
Source: Historical Statistics of the United States.

Carnegie consistently portrayed his success as the result of self-discipline and hard work. He also cultivated a reputation as a philanthropist, giving away more than $300 million to libraries, universities, and international-peace causes. However, the full story was more complex. Carnegie's success came not just from his work-ethic, but also from his opportunistic temperament and callousness in keeping wages for his workers as low as possible. To a public unaware of corporate management techniques, however, Carnegie's success leant credence to the idea that anyone might rise from rags to riches.

Primary Source: Carnegie Steel and Black Diamond Steel Companies Mills

The Trust: Creating New Forms of Corporate Organization

Between 1870 and 1900, the same fierce competition that had stimulated consolidation in the railroad and steel industries also swept the oil, salt, sugar, tobacco, and meat packing industries. The evolution of the oil industry illustrates the process by which new corporate structures evolved. After Edwin L. Drake drilled the first successful petroleum (or "crude-oil") well in 1859 near Titusville, Pennsylvania, competitors rushed into the business. Petroleum was distilled into oil, which soon replaced animal tallow as the major lubricant, and into kerosene, which became the leading fuel for household and public lighting.

By the 1870s the landscape near Pittsburgh and Cleveland was littered with rickety drilling rigs. In this rush for riches, **John D. Rockefeller,** a young Cleveland merchant, gradually achieved dominance. Rockefeller opened his first refinery in 1863. Like Carnegie, Rockefeller had a passion for cost cutting and understood the benefits of vertical integration. In 1872 he purchased his own tanker cars and obtained a 10 percent rebate from the railroads for hauling his oil shipments. When new pipeline technology became available, Rockefeller set up his own massive interregional pipeline network.

John D. Rockefeller Creator of Standard Oil and master of the use of pools and trusts to monopolize an industry

Like Carnegie, Rockefeller aggressively forced out his competitors. When local refineries rejected his offers to buy them out, he priced his products below cost and strangled their businesses. When rival firms teamed up against him, Rockefeller set up a pool—an agreement among several companies—that established production quotas and fixed prices. By 1879 Rockefeller had seized control of 90 percent of the country's oil-refining capacity.

Worried about competition, Rockefeller in 1882 decided to eliminate it by establishing a new form of corporate organization, the **Standard Oil Trust.** In place of the "pool," which lacked legal status, the trust created an umbrella corporation that ran them all. Within three years the Standard Oil Trust had consolidated crude-oil buying throughout its member firms. In this way Rockefeller integrated the petroleum industry both *vertically* and *horizontally,* by merging the competing oil companies into one giant system.

Standard Oil Trust An umbrella organization of forty companies that controlled the U.S. oil industry

Taking a leaf from Rockefeller's book, companies in the copper, sugar, whiskey, lead, and other industries established their own trust arrangements. Their unscrupulous tactics, semimonopolistic control, and sky-high earnings provoked a public outcry. Both major political parties denounced them in the presidential election of 1888.

Fearful that the trusts would stamp out all competition, Congress passed the **Sherman Anti-Trust Act** in 1890. The Sherman Act outlawed trusts and any other

Sherman Anti-Trust Act Law against trusts; initially unsuccessful

monopolies that fixed prices in restraint of trade. But the act failed to define clearly either *trust* or *restraint of trade*. When Standard Oil's structure was challenged in 1892, its lawyers simply reorganized the trust as a giant holding company, which simply owned a controlling share of the stock of one or more firms. The new board of directors for Standard Oil (New Jersey), the new holding company, made more money than ever.

The Supreme Court further hamstrung congressional antitrust efforts by interpreting the Sherman Act in ways sympathetic to big business. In 1895, for example, the federal government brought suit against the sugar trust in *United States* v. *E. C. Knight Company*—and lost. Thus vindicated, corporate mergers and consolidations surged ahead. By 1900, these mammoth firms accounted for nearly two-fifths of the capital invested in the nation's manufacturing sector.

STIMULATING ECONOMIC GROWTH

What innovations in technology and business drove increases in industrial production after 1865?

Large-scale corporate enterprise was not the only cause of the colossal growth of the U.S. economy. Other factors proved equally important, including new inventions, specialty production, and innovations in advertising and marketing.

The Triumph of Technology

New inventions not only streamlined the manufacture of traditional products but also stimulated consumer demand by creating entirely new product lines. The development of a safe, practical way to generate electricity, for example, made possible a vast number of electrical motors, household appliances, and lighting systems.

Many of these inventions were intended for use in factory production. However, three new domestic technologies had a dramatic impact on the patterns of everyday life. The sewing machine, mass-produced by the Singer Sewing Machine Company beginning in the 1860s (see Chapter 16); the telephone, developed by Alexander Graham Bell in 1876; and the light bulb, perfected by **Thomas A. Edison** in 1879, eased household drudgery and reshaped social interactions. The advent of inexpensive mass-produced clothing thus led to a considerable expansion in personal wardrobes. Meanwhile, the spread of telephones transformed communication while the light bulb made it possible to shop after work.

In the eyes of many, Thomas A. Edison epitomized the inventive impulse. Born in 1847 in Milan, Ohio, Edison, like Andrew Carnegie, had little formal education and got his start in the telegraphic industry. He also was a born salesman and self-promoter. Edison, moreover, shared Carnegie's vision of a large, interconnected industrial system resting on a foundation of technological innovation.

Edison's first major invention, a stock-quotation printer, in 1868, earned enough money to set up his first "invention factory" in Newark, New Jersey, a research facility

Thomas A. Edison Inventor, founder of the first industrial research laboratory

Thomas Edison's Laboratories in Menlo Park, New Jersey, c. 1881
Always a self-promoter, Edison used this depiction of his "invention factory" to suggest that his development of a durable light bulb in 1879 would have an impact on life around the globe.

that he moved to nearby Menlo Park in 1876. Edison boastfully predicted "a minor invention every ten days, and a big one every six months."

Buoyed by the success and popularity of his invention in 1877 of a phonograph, or "sound writer" (*phono*: "sound"; *graph*: "writer"), Edison set out to develop a new filament for incandescent (in-can-DESS-ent) light bulbs. Edison realized that practical electrical lighting had to be part of a complete system containing generators, regulators, and wiring. In 1882, the Edison Illuminating Company opened a power plant in the heart of New York City's financial district.

In the following years, Edison and his researchers pumped out invention after invention, including the mimeograph machine, the microphone, the motion picture camera and film, and the storage battery. By the time of his death in 1931, he had patented 1,093 inventions and amassed an estate worth more than $6 million. Edison's Menlo Park laboratory demonstrated that the systematic use of science in support of industrial technology paid large dividends. Invention had become big business.

Specialized Production

Along with inventors, manufacturers of custom and specialized products such as machinery, jewelry, furniture, and women's clothes dramatically expanded economic output. Keenly attuned to innovations in technology and design, they constantly created new products tailored to the needs of individual buyers.

Until the turn of the twentieth century, when ready to-wear clothes came to dominate the market, most women's apparel was custom produced in small shops run by women proprietors. Unlike the tenement sweatshops that produced men's shirts and pants, dressmakers and milliners paid good wages to highly skilled seamstresses. The small size of the shops together with the skill of the workers enabled them to shift styles quickly to follow the latest fashions.

Thus, alongside of the increasingly rationalized and bureaucratic big businesses like steel and oil in the late nineteenth century, American productivity was also stimulated by small producers who provided a variety of goods that supplemented the bulk-manufactured staples of everyday life.

Advertising and Marketing

As small and large factories alike spewed out an amazing array of new products, business leaders often discovered that their output exceeded what the market could absorb. Strategies for whetting consumer demand represented a critical component of industrial expansion in the post–Civil War era.

The growth of the flour industry illustrates both the spread of mass production and the emergence of new marketing concepts. In the 1870s, the nation's flour mills installed continuous-process machines that graded, cleaned, hulled, ground, and packaged the product in one rapid operation. These companies, however, soon produced more flour than they could sell. To unload this excess, the mills thought up new product lines such as cake flours and breakfast cereals and sold them using easy-to-remember brand names like Quaker Oats.

Through the use of brand names, slogans, endorsements, and other gimmicks, manufacturers built demand for their products and won enduring consumer loyalty. For instance, Americans bought Ivory Soap, first made in 1879 by Procter and Gamble of Cincinnati, because of the absurdly overprecise but impressive pledge that it was "99 and percent pure."

In the 1880s, George Eastman developed a paper-based photographic film as an alternative to the bulky, fragile glass plates then in use. Manufacturing a cheap camera for the masses, the Kodak, Eastman introduced a system whereby customers returned the film and the camera to his Rochester factory. There, the film was developed and printed, the camera reloaded, and everything shipped back. Eastman had revolutionized an industry and democratized a visual medium previously confined to a few.

Primary Source:
The Genius of
Advertising

Economic Growth: Costs and Benefits

By 1900, the chaos of early industrial competition, when thousands of companies had struggled to enter a national market, had given way to the most productive economy in the world. An industrial transformation that had originated in railroading and expanded to steel and petroleum had spread to every nook and cranny of American business.

The vast expansion of economic output brought social benefits, in the form of labor-saving products, lower prices, and advances in transportation and communications. At the same time, industrial growth often devastated the environment. Rivers fouled by

Industrial Pollution
Although some Americans celebrated factory smoke as a sign of industrial growth, those who lived downwind, such as the longshoreman in this Thomas Nast cartoon, often suffered from respiratory diseases and other ailments. For him as well as for other Americans, the price of industrial progress was often pollution.

oil or chemical waste, skies filled with clouds of soot, and a landscape littered with reeking garbage and toxic materials bore mute witness to the relentless drive for efficiency and profit.

For those who fell by the wayside, the cost could be measured in bankrupted companies and shattered dreams. John D. Rockefeller put things with characteristic bluntness when he said he wanted "only the big ones, only those who have already proved they can do a big business" in the Standard Oil Trust. "As for the others, unfortunately they will have to die." The cost was high, too, for millions of American workers, immigrant and native-born alike. The vast expansion of new products was built on the backs of an army of laborers who were paid subsistence wages and who could be fired on a moment's notice.

Whatever the final balance sheet of social gains and costs, one thing was clear: the United States had muscled its way onto the world stage as an industrial titan. The ambition and drive of countless inventors, financiers, managerial innovators, and marketing wizards had combined to lay the groundwork for a new social and economic order in the twentieth century.

▌THE NEW SOUTH

Why did the South's experience with industrialization differ from that of the North and the Midwest?

The South entered the industrial era far more slowly than the Northeast. As late as 1900, total southern cotton-mill output, for example, remained little more than half that of the mills within a thirty-mile radius of Providence, Rhode Island.

The reasons for the South's late economic blossoming are not hard to discern. The Civil War's physical devastation, racism, the scarcity of southern towns and cities, lack of capital, illiteracy, northern control of financial markets, and a low rate of technological innovation crippled efforts by southern business leaders to promote industrialization. Economic progress was also impeded by the myth of the Lost Cause, which, through its nostalgic portrayal of pre-Civil War society, perpetuated an image of the South as traditional and unchanging. As a result, southern industrialization inched forward haltingly.

Obstacles to Economic Development

Much of the South's difficulty in industrializing arose from its lack of capital and the devastation of the Civil War. During the war, the federal government required anyone wishing to start a bank to have fifty thousand dollars in capital. Few southerners could meet this standard. With capital in short supply, country merchants leant supplies rather than cash to local farmers in return for a mortgage on their crops. The burden of paying those mortgages trapped farmers on their own land and created a shortage of the labor needed for industrial expansion.

The South's chronic shortage of funds also limited the resources available for education. During Reconstruction northern philanthropists together with various relief agencies had begun a modest expansion of public schooling for both blacks and whites. But Georgia and many other southern states operated segregated schools and refused to tax property for school support until 1889. As a result, school attendance remained low, severely limiting the number of educated people able to staff technical and managerial positions in business and industry.

Southern states, like those in the North, often contributed the modest funds they had to war veterans' pensions. In this way, southern state governments built a white patronage system for Confederate veterans. As late as 1911, veterans' pensions in Georgia ate up 22 percent of the state's entire budget, leaving little for economic or educational development.

Henry W. Grady Editor of the *Atlanta Constitution* and tireless booster of his city and region

The New South Creed and Southern Industrialization

Despite these obstacles, energetic southern newspaper editors such as **Henry W. Grady** of the *Atlanta Constitution* championed the doctrine that became known as the New South creed. The South's rich coal and timber resources and cheap labor, they proclaimed in their papers, made it a natural site for industrial development.

The movement to industrialize the South gained momentum in the 1880s. To attract northern capital, southern states offered tax exemptions for new businesses, set up industrial and agricultural expositions, and leased prison convicts to serve as cheap labor. Florida, Texas, and other states gave huge tracts of lands to railroads, which expanded dramatically throughout the South and in turn stimulated the birth of new towns and villages.

Following the lead of their northern counterparts, the southern iron and steel industries expanded as well. Birmingham, Alabama, founded in 1871 in the heart of a region blessed with rich deposits of coal, limestone, and iron ore, grew in less than three decades to a bustling city with noisy railroad yards and roaring blast furnaces. By 1900 it was the nation's largest pig-iron shipper.

As large-scale recruiters of black workers, the southern iron and steel mills contributed to the migration of blacks to the cities. By 1900, 20 percent of the southern black population was urban. Southern industry reflected the patterns of racial segregation in southern life. Tobacco companies used black workers, particularly women, to clean the tobacco leaves while white women, at a different location, ran the machines that made cigarettes. The burgeoning textile mills were lilywhite. In the iron and steel industry, blacks, who comprised 60 percent of the unskilled work force by 1900, had practically no chance of advancement.

Black miners were also recruited by the West Virginia coal industry that lured them with free transportation, high wages, and company housing. Still, economic opportunities for blacks remained severely limited. In the lumbering industry, wages for black workers could be better than those offered to farm laborers. However, during economic downturns workers were laid off or confined to work camps by vagrancy laws and armed guards.

The Southern Mill Economy

Unlike the urban-based southern iron and steel industry, the textile mills that mushroomed in the southern countryside in the 1880s often became catalysts for the formation of new towns and villages. In the mill towns, country ways and values suffused the new industrial workplace.

The cotton-mill economy grew largely in the Piedmont, the highland country of central Virginia and northern Georgia and Alabama. The Piedmont had long been the South's backcountry. But postwar railroad construction opened the region to textile-mill expansion. By 1920 the South was the nation's leading textile-mill center. Augusta, Georgia, with 2,800 mill workers, became known as the Lowell of the South, named after the mill town in Massachusetts where industrialization had flourished earlier.

Sharecroppers and tenant farmers at first hailed the new cotton mills as a way out of rural poverty. But appearances were deceptive. The chief cotton-mill promoters were drawn from the same ranks of merchants, lawyers, doctors, and bankers who had profited from the commercialization of southern agriculture. Cotton-mill entrepreneurs shamelessly exploited their workers, paying just seven to eleven cents an hour, 30 percent to 50 percent less than what comparable mill workers in New England were paid.

The mills dominated most Piedmont textile communities. The mill operator not only built and owned the workers' housing and the company store but also supported the village church, financed the local elementary school, and pried into the morals and behavior of the mill hands. Because they were often paid in scrip—a certificate redeemable only in goods from the company store—workers frequently were drawn into a cycle of indebtedness very much like that faced by sharecroppers.

Since farm families shared responsibilities as a unit, southern mill superintendents accommodated themselves to local customs and hired whole families, including the children. Mothers commonly brought babies into the mills and kept them in baskets nearby while tending their machines.

As northern cotton mills did before the Civil War, southern textile companies exploited the cheap rural labor around them, settling transplanted farm people in paternalistic company-run villages. Using these tactics, the industry underwent a period of steady growth.

The Southern Industrial Lag

Industrialization occurred on a smaller scale and at a slower rate in the South than in the North and also depended far more on outside financing, technology, and expertise. The late-nineteenth-century southern economy remained essentially in a colonial status, subject to domination by northern industries and financial syndicates.

An array of factors thus combined to retard industrialization in the South. Banking regulations requiring large reserves, scarce capital, absentee ownership, unfavorable railroad rates, cautious state governments, wartime debts, lack of industrial experience, a segregated labor force, discrimination against blacks, and control by profit-hungry northern enterprises all hampered the region's economic development. Dragged down by a poorly educated white population and by a largely unskilled black population, southern industry languished.

As in the North, industrialization brought significant environmental damage, including polluted rivers and streams, decimated forests, grimy coal-mining towns, and soot-infested steel-making cities. Although Henry Grady's vision of a New South may have inspired many southerners to work

CHECKING IN

- Lack of capital proved a major obstacle to southern industrialization.

- An underfunded, poorly attended public education system became another impediment to the industrialization of the South.

- Proponents of the New South creed urged industrialization, with some success.

- Cotton textile mills blossomed across the South from the 1880s onward.

- Despite such advances, the South lagged far behind the rest of the nation in industrialization and economic development.

toward industrialization, economic growth in the South, limited as it was by outside forces, progressed in its own distinctly regional way.

FACTORIES AND THE WORK FORCE

How did factory workers respond to the changing nature of work?

Industrialization proceeded unevenly nationwide, and most late-nineteenth-century Americans still worked in small shops. But as the century unfolded, large factories with armies of workers sprang onto the industrial scene in more and more locales. The pattern of change was evident. Between 1860 and 1900, the number of industrial workers jumped from 885,000 to 3.2 million, and the trend toward large-scale production became unmistakable.

From Workshop to Factory

The transition to a factory economy came not as an earthquake but rather as a series of seismic jolts varying in strength and duration. Changes in factory production had a profound impact on artisans and unskilled laborers alike. The impact of these changes can be seen by examining the shoe industry. As late as the 1840s, almost every shoe was custom-made by a skilled artisan who worked in a small, independent shop. Shoemakers were aristocrats in the world of labor. They took pride in their work and controlled the quality of their products.

A distinctive working-class culture subdivided along ethnic lines evolved among these shoemakers. Foreign-born English, German, and Irish workers set up ethnic trade organizations and joined affiliated benevolent associations. Bound together by religious and ethnic ties, they observed weddings and funerals according to old-country traditions and relaxed together at the local saloon after work.

As early as the 1850s, changes in the ready-made shoe trade had eroded the status of skilled labor. The manufacturing process was broken down into a sequence of repetitive, easily mastered tasks. Thus instead of crafting a pair of shoes from start to finish, each team member specialized in only one part of the process, such as attaching the heel or polishing the leather.

In the 1880s, shoe factories became larger and more mechanized, and traditional skills largely vanished. Shoe companies replaced skilled operatives with lower-paid, less-skilled women and children. By 1890 women made up more than 35 percent of the work force. Like the laborer whose machine nailed heels on 4,800 shoes a day, even "skilled" workers in the new factories found themselves performing numbingly repetitive tasks.

The Hardships of Industrial Labor

The expansion of the factory system spawned an unprecedented demand for unskilled labor. By the 1880s nearly one-third of the 750,000 workers employed in the railroad and steel industries, for example, were common laborers. In the construction trades and the garment-making industries, the services of unskilled laborers were procured under the so-called contract system. Large companies negotiated an agreement with a subcontractor who supervised gangs of unskilled day laborers, who were hired in times of need and laid off in slack periods.

Notoriously transient, unskilled laborers drifted from city to city and from industry to industry. In the late 1870s unskilled laborers earned $1.30 a day, while bricklayers and blacksmiths earned more than $3. Only unskilled southern mill workers, whose wages averaged a meager eighty-four cents a day, earned less.

Unskilled and skilled workers alike not only worked up to twelve-hour shifts but also faced grave hazards to their health and safety. The alarming incidence of industrial accidents stemmed from a variety of circumstances, including dangerous factory conditions, workers' inexperience, and the rapid pace of the production process.

In the coal mines and cotton mills, child laborers typically entered the work force at age eight or nine. These youngsters not only faced the same environmental hazards as adults but were especially prone to injury. In the cotton mills, children could be injured by the unprotected pulley belts that powered the machines. In the coal industry, children were commonly employed as slate pickers, a job that exposed them to swirling clouds of coal dust. Coal dust gave them black lung disease—a disorder that leads to emphysema and heart failure.

For adult workers, the railroad industry was one of the most perilous. In 1889, the first year that the Interstate Commerce Commission compiled reliable statistics, almost two thousand rail workers were killed on the job and more than twenty thousand injured. Disabled workers and widows received minimal financial aid from employers. When a worker was killed or maimed in an accident, the family depended on minimal payouts from their fraternal organizations—or more commonly, the kindness of relatives or friends—for support.

Immigrant Labor

As we shall see in more detail in Chapter 19, factory owners turned to unskilled immigrant workers for the muscle they needed. Despite the hazardous conditions they found in the factories, those immigrants who were disposed to work an eighty-four-hour week could save fifteen dollars a month, far more than they could have earned in their homeland.

Although most immigrants worked hard, few adjusted easily to the fast pace of the factory. Peasants from southern and eastern Europe found it difficult to abandon their seasonal work habits for factory schedules. Factory operations were relentless, dictated by the unvarying speed of the machines. Employers used a variety of tactics to enforce discipline. Some sponsored temperance societies and Sunday schools to teach punctuality and sobriety. Employers sometimes also provided low-cost housing to gain leverage against work stoppages; if workers went on strike, the boss could simply evict them.

In the case of immigrants from southern Europe whose skin colors were often darker than northern Europeans', employers asserted that the workers were non-white and thus did not deserve the same compensation as native-born Americans. Rather than being a fixed category based on biological differences, the concept of "whiteness" was thus used to justify the harsh treatment of foreign-born labor.

Women and Work in Industrial America

Women's work experiences, like those of men, were shaped by marital status, social class, and race. Upper-class white married women widely accepted an ideology of "separate spheres" (see Chapter 19) and remained at home, raised children, and looked after the household. The well-to-do hired maids and cooks to ease their burdens.

Working-class married women, in contrast, not only lacked such assistance but also often had to contribute to the financial support of the family. In fact, working for wages at home by sewing, button-making, taking in boarders, or doing laundry had predated industrialization. In the late nineteenth century, unscrupulous urban entrepreneurs exploited this captive work force. In the clothing industry, manufacturers hired out finishing tasks to lower-class married women and their children, who labored long hours in crowded apartments.

Young, working-class single women often viewed factory work as an opportunity. In 1870, 13 percent of all women worked outside the home, the majority as cooks, maids, cleaning ladies, and laundresses. But most working women intensely disliked the long hours, low pay, and social stigma of being a "servant." Between 1870 and 1900, the number of women working outside the home nearly tripled.

A variety of factors propelled the rise in the employment of single women. Changes in agriculture prompted many young farm women to seek employment in the industrial sector (see Chapter 19). Plant managers welcomed young immigrant women as a ready source of inexpensive unskilled labor. But factory owners treated them as temporary help and kept their wages low. In 1890, young women operating sewing machines earned as little as four dollars for seventy hours of work while their male counterparts made eight. Far from ensuring economic independence, therefore, industrial work more commonly tied women more deeply to a family economy that depended on their earnings.

When the typewriter and the telephone came into general use in the 1890s, office work provided new employment opportunities. Women were attracted by the clean, safe working conditions and relatively good pay. First-rate typists could earn six to eight dollars a week, which compared favorably with factory wages. Office work carried higher prestige and was generally steadier than work in the factory or shop.

Despite the growing number of women workers, the late-nineteenth-century popular press portrayed women's work outside the home as temporary. Few people even considered the possibility that a woman could attain local or even national prominence in the emerging corporate order.

Hard Work and the Gospel of Success

Although women were generally excluded from the equation, influential opinion molders in these years preached that any man could achieve success in the new industrial era. In *Ragged Dick* (1867) and scores of later tales, **Horatio Alger**, a Unitarian minister turned dime novelist, recounted the adventures of poor but honest lads who rose through initiative and self discipline. The career of Andrew Carnegie was often offered as proof that the United States remained the land of opportunity and "rags to riches."

Horatio Alger Author of more than one hundred "rags to riches" books for boys

Some critics did not accept this belief. In an 1871 essay, Mark Twain chided the public for its naïveté and suggested that business success was more likely to come to those who lied and cheated. What are the facts? Carnegie's rise from abject poverty to colossal wealth was the rare exception, as studies of nearly two hundred of the largest corporations reveal. Ninety-five percent of the industrial leaders came from middle- and upper-class backgrounds. The best chance of success for immigrants and native-born working class Americans was in mastering a skill and rising to the top of a small company. Although only a few reaped immense fortunes, many attained substantial incomes.

The opportunities for advancement for unskilled immigrant workers were considerably more limited. Some did move to semiskilled or skilled positions. Yet most immigrants, particularly the Irish, Italians, and Chinese, moved far more slowly than the sons of middle-and upper-class Americans who began with greater educational advantages and family financial backing. The upward mobility possible for such unskilled workers was generally mobility within the working class. Immigrants who got ahead in the late nineteenth century went from rags to respectability, not rags to riches.

One positive economic trend in these years was the rise in real wages, representing gains in actual buying power. Average real wages climbed 31 percent for unskilled workers and 74 percent for skilled workers between 1860 and 1900. Overall gains in purchasing power, however, were often undercut by injuries and unemployment during slack times or economic slumps. During the depressions of the 1870s and 1890s, wage cuts, extended layoffs, and irregular employment pushed those at the bottom of the industrial work force to the brink of starvation.

Thus the overall picture of late-nineteenth-century economic mobility is complex. At the top of the scale, a mere 10 percent of American families owned 73 percent of the nation's wealth in 1890, while less than half of industrial laborers earned more than the five-hundred dollar poverty line annually. In between the very rich and the very poor, skilled immigrants and small shopkeepers improved their economic position significantly. So although the standard of living for millions of Americans rose, the gap between the poor and the well-off remained a yawning abyss.

LABOR UNIONS AND INDUSTRIAL CONFLICT

In the 1890s how did corporate executives undercut labor's bargaining power?

Aware that the growth of large corporations gave industrial leaders unprecedented power to control the workplace, labor leaders searched for ways to protect their members. But the drive to create a nationwide labor movement faced many problems. Employers deliberately accentuated ethnic and racial divisions within the work force. Skilled crafts workers, moreover, felt little kinship with low-paid common laborers. Because of these divisions, unionization efforts moved forward slowly and experienced setbacks.

Two groups, the National Labor Union and the Knights of Labor, struggled to build a mass labor movement that would unite skilled and unskilled workers. After impressive initial growth, however, both efforts collapsed. Far more effective was the

American Federation of Labor (AFL), which represented skilled workers in powerful independent craft unions. The AFL survived and grew, but it represented only a small portion of the total labor force.

With unions weak, labor unrest during economic downturns reached crisis proportions. When pay rates were cut or working conditions became intolerable, laborers walked off the job without union authorization. These actions, called **wildcat strikes,** often exploded into violence. The bloody labor clashes of the 1890s would increase the demand for state regulation and eventually contribute to a movement for progressive reform.

wildcat strikes Spontaneous strikes not authorized by a labor union; some turned violent

Organizing Workers

From the eighteenth century on, skilled workers had organized trade unions to fight wage reductions and provide benefits for their members in times of illness or accident. But the effectiveness of these organizations was limited. The challenge that labor leaders faced in the postwar period was how to boost the unions' clout. Some believed that this goal could be achieved by forming one big association that would transcend craft lines and pull in the mass of unskilled workers.

In 1866, Philadelphia labor leader William H. Sylvis called a convention in Baltimore to form a new organization, the **National Labor Union** (NLU). The NLU endorsed the eight-hour-day movement, which insisted that labor deserved eight hours for work, eight hours for sleep, and eight hours for personal affairs. It also endorsed immigration restriction, especially of Chinese migrants, whom native-born workers blamed for undercutting prevailing wage levels. The NLU supported the cause of working women and urged black workers to organize as well, though in racially separate unions.

National Labor Union (NLU) Early attempt to establish a single national union

After a failed strike against iron foundry owners in the winter of 1866–1867, Sylvis turned to national political reform. He invited a number of reformers to the 1868 NLU convention, including woman suffrage advocates Susan B. Anthony and Elizabeth Cady Stanton. But when Sylvis suddenly died in 1869, the NLU faded quickly.

The dream of a labor movement that combined skilled and unskilled workers lived on in a new organization, the **Knights of Labor,** founded in 1869. Led by Uriah H. Stephens of Philadelphia, the Knights welcomed all wage earners. The Knights demanded equal pay for women, an end to child labor and convict labor, and the cooperative employer-employee ownership of factories, mines, and other businesses. At a time when no federal income tax existed, they called for a progressive tax on all earnings, graduated so that higher-income earners would pay more.

Knights of Labor Organization that took up where the NLU left off; enjoyed considerable success for a while

The Knights grew slowly at first. But membership rocketed in the 1880s after the eloquent Terence V. Powderly replaced Stephens as the organization's head. During its growth years in the early 1880s, the Knights of Labor reflected both its idealistic origins and Powderly's collaborative vision. Powderly opposed strikes and urged temperance upon the membership. Powderly advocated the admission of blacks into local Knights of Labor assemblies, although he allowed southern local assemblies to be segregated. The Knights welcomed women members; by 1886, women made up an estimated 10 percent of the union's membership.

Powderly supported restrictions on immigration and a total ban on Chinese immigration. In 1877, San Francisco workers demonstrating for an eight-hour workday destroyed twenty-five Chinese-run laundries. In 1880 both major party platforms included anti-Chinese immigration plans. Two years later, Congress passed the Chinese Exclusion Act, placing a ten-year moratorium on Chinese immigration. The ban was extended in 1902 and not repealed until 1943.

Powderly's greatest triumph came in 1885. In that year, Jay Gould tried to get rid of the Knights of Labor on his Wabash railroad by firing active union members. Powderly instructed all Knights on the Wabash line to walk off the job and those on other lines to refuse to handle Wabash cars. This action crippled the Wabash's operations. To the nation's amazement, Gould met with Powderly and canceled his campaign against the Knights of Labor.

Membership in the Knights of Labor soared. By 1886, more than seven hundred thousand workers were organized in nearly six thousand locals. The Knights mounted campaigns in nearly two hundred towns and cities nationwide that fall, electing several mayors and judges. Business executives warned that the Knights could cripple the economy and take over the country if they chose.

But the organization's strength soon waned. Workers became disillusioned when a series of unauthorized strikes failed in 1886. By the late 1880s, the Knights of Labor was a shadow of its former self. Nevertheless, the organization had served as a major impetus to the labor movement and had awakened in thousands of workers a sense of group solidarity and potential strength.

As the Knights of Labor weakened, another national labor organization was gaining strength. The skilled craft unions had long been uncomfortable with labor organizations like the Knights that welcomed skilled and unskilled alike. They were also concerned that the Knights' broad reform goals would undercut the interests of their particular crafts. The break came in May 1886 when the craft unions left the Knights of Labor to form the **American Federation of Labor** (AFL).

The AFL replaced the Knights' grand visions with practical tactics aimed at bread-and-butter issues. This philosophy was vigorously pursued by **Samuel Gompers** the immigrant cigar maker who became head of the AFL in 1886 and led it until his death in 1924. Gompers believed in "trade unionism, pure and simple." Gompers argued that if labor were to stand up to the corporations, it would have to harness the bargaining power of skilled workers and concentrate on the practical goals of raising wages and reducing hours.

To persuade workers from the various trades to join forces without violating their sense of craft autonomy, Gompers organized the AFL as a federation of trade unions, each retaining control of its own members but all linked by an executive council that coordinated strategy during boycotts and strike actions.

Gompers at first sidestepped divisive political issues. The new organization's platform did, however, demand an eight-hour workday, employers' liability for

Ethnic and Racial Hatred
Conservative business owners used racist advertising, such as this trade card stigmatizing Chinese laundry workers, to promote their own products and to associate their company with patriotism.

 History in Focus: Ethnic and Racial Hatred

American Federation of Labor Skilled craft unions united under leadership of Samuel Gompers

Samuel Gompers AFL leader who focused on practical goals like wages, hours, and working conditions

workers' injuries, and mine safety laws. The AFL did little to recruit women workers after 1894 because Gompers and others believed that women workers undercut men's wages. By 1904, the AFL had grown to more than 1.6 million strong.

Despite these advances, labor organizations before 1900 remained weak. Less than 5 percent of the work force joined union ranks. Split between skilled artisans and common laborers, separated along ethnic and religious lines, and divided over tactics, the unions battled with only occasional effectiveness against the growing power of corporate enterprise. They typically watched from the sidelines when unorganized workers launched wildcat strikes that sometimes turned violent.

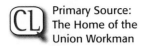

Primary Source: The Home of the Union Workman

Strikes and Labor Violence

Americans had lived with a high level of violence from the nation's beginnings. Terrible labor clashes toward the end of the century were part of this continuing pattern, but they nevertheless shocked and dismayed contemporaries. From 1881 to 1905, close to 37,000 strikes erupted, in which nearly 7 million workers participated.

The first major wave of strikes began in 1873 when a Wall Street crash triggered a major depression. The tension turned deadly in 1877 during a wildcat railroad strike. Ignited by a wage reduction on the Baltimore and Ohio Railroad in July, the strike spread across the country. Rioters in Pittsburgh torched Union Depot. By the time troops could arrive to quell the strike two weeks later, nearly one hundred people had died.

The railroad strike stunned middle-class America. The same middle-class Americans who worried about Jay Gould and the corporate abuse of power grew terrified of mob violence from the bottom ranks of society. Employers capitalized on the public hysteria to crack down on labor. Many required their workers to sign "yellow dog" contracts in which they promised not to strike or join a union. Some hired Pinkerton agents, a private police force, to defend their factories and turned to the U.S. army to suppress labor unrest.

Although the economy recovered, more strikes and violence followed in the 1880s. On May 4, 1886, Chicago police shot and killed four strikers at the McCormick Harvester plant. At a protest rally the next evening in the city's Haymarket Square, someone threw a bomb from a nearby building, killing or fatally wounding seven policemen. In response, the police fired wildly into the crowd and killed four demonstrators.

Public reaction was immediate. Business leaders and middle-class citizens lashed out at labor activists and particularly at the sponsors of the Haymarket meeting, most of whom were associated with a German-language anarchist newspaper. Eight men were arrested. Although no evidence connected them directly to the bomb throwing, all were convicted of murder, and four were executed. In Haymarket's aftermath, animosity toward labor unions intensified.

The events of 1892 intensified this trend. In one incident at a mine along Idaho's Coeur d'Alene (coor dah-LEEN) River, miners blew up a mill and captured the guards sent to defend it. Back east that same year, armed conflict broke out during the **Homestead Strike** at the Carnegie Steel Company plant in Homestead, Pennsylvania. To destroy the union, managers had cut wages and locked out the workers. When workers fired on the armed men from the Pinkerton Detective Agency who

Homestead Strike Company lock-out that sparked a strike and violence at a Carnegie steel plant in 1892

came to protect the plant, a battle broke out. Seven union members and three Pinkertons died. A week later the governor sent eight thousand National Guardsmen to restore order. The union crushed, the mills resumed full operation a month later.

The most systematic use of troops to smash union power came in 1894 during a strike against the Pullman Palace Car Company. In 1880 railroad car manufacturer George Pullman had constructed a factory and town, called Pullman, ten miles south of Chicago. When the depression of 1893 hit, he slashed workers' wages without reducing their rents. In reaction thousands of workers went on strike. Led by their fiery young organizer, **Eugene V. Debs,** union members working for the nation's largest railroads refused to switch Pullman cars, paralyzing rail traffic in and out of Chicago.

In response, top railroad executives set out to break the union. They imported strikebreakers and asked U.S. attorney general Richard Olney, who sat on the board of directors of three major railroad networks, for a federal injunction (court order) against the strikers for allegedly refusing to move railroad cars carrying U.S. mail. Olney, citing the Sherman Anti-Trust Act, secured an injunction against the union, arrested Debs, and sent federal troops in. During the ensuing riot, workers burned seven hundred freight cars and thirteen people died. By July 18 the strike had been crushed. In 1895, the U.S. Supreme court upheld Debs's prison sentence and legalized the use of injunctions against labor unions (*In re Debs*).

There were some successes. In 1897, the feisty Irish-born Mary Harris Jones, known as Mother Jones, succeeded in persuading coal miners in Pennsylvania to join the United Mine Workers of America. By 1900, their numbers had climbed to 300,000. However, despite the achievements of the United Mine Workers, the successive attempts by the National Labor Union, Knights of Labor, American Federation of Labor, and American Railway Union to build a national working-class labor movement achieved only limited success. Ineffective in the political arena, blocked by state officials, divided by ethnic differences, harassed by employers, and frustrated by court decisions, American unions failed to expand their base of support. Post-Civil War labor turmoil had given it a negative public image that it would not shed until the 1930s.

Eugene V. Debs Union organizer, arrested as leader of striking National Railway Union; would become Socialist leader

Social Thinkers Probe for Alternatives

Widespread violence sparked a new debate over the social meaning of the new industrial order. At stake was a fraught issue: should government become the mechanism for helping the poor and regulating big business?

Defenders of capitalism preached the laissez-faire (LESS-ay fare), or "hands-off" argument, insisting that government should never attempt to control business. In his essay "The Gospel of Wealth" (1889), Andrew Carnegie justified laissez-faire by applying the evolutionary theories of British social scientist Herbert Spencer to human society. "The law of competition," Carnegie argued, "may be sometimes hard for the individual, [but] it is best for the race, because it insures the survival of the fittest in every department."

Yale professor **William Graham Sumner** shared Carnegie's disapproval of government interference. His combative book *What Social Classes Owe to Each Other* (1883) applied the evolutionary theories of British naturalist Charles Darwin to human

William Graham Sumner Tough-minded Yale professor and theorist of Social Darwinism

Social Darwinism Theory that "survival of the fittest" competition benefits society by weeding out the unfit

society. In an early statement of what became known as **Social Darwinism,** Sumner asserted that inexorable natural laws controlled the social order. The state, declared Sumner, owed its citizens nothing but law, order, and basic political rights. As to the question of whether society should help the less fortunate, Sumner wrote famously: "A drunkard in the gutter is just where he ought to be."

Sumner's argument did not go unchallenged. In *Dynamic Sociology* (1883), Lester Frank Ward, a geologist, argued that contrary to Sumner's claim, the supposed "laws" of nature could be circumvented by human will. Just as scientists had applied their knowledge to breeding superior livestock, government experts could use the power of the state to protect society's weaker members and prevent the heedless exploitation of natural resources.

Other social theorists offered more utopian solutions to the problems of poverty and social unrest. Henry George, a self-taught San Francisco newspaper editor and economic theorist, proposed to solve the nation's uneven distribution of wealth through what he called the single tax. In *Progress and Poverty* (1879), he argued that land should be taxed and the funds used to mitigate the misery caused by industrialization. George's program was so popular that he only narrowly missed being elected mayor of New York in 1886.

The vision of a harmonious industrialized society was vividly expressed in the utopian novel *Looking Backward* (1888) by the Massachusetts newspaper editor Edward Bellamy. Cast as a glimpse into the future, Bellamy's novel envisioned a completely centralized, state-run economy and a society in which everyone works for the common welfare. Bellamy's vision so inspired middle-class Americans fearful of corporate power and working-class violence that nearly five hundred local Bellamyite organizations, called Nationalist clubs, sprang up to try to turn his dream into reality.

Marxism Belief that capitalism would inevitable destroy itself in a violent class struggle, thus paving way for classless, communist utopia

Ward, George, and Bellamy did not deny the benefits of the existing industrial order; they simply sought to humanize it. These utopian reformers envisioned a harmonious society whose members all worked together.

Marxist socialists advanced a different view. Elaborated by the German philosopher and radical agitator Karl Marx (1818–1883) in *Das Kapital* (dass cop-ee-TALL) (1867) and other works, **Marxism** rested on the labor theory of value: a proposition that the labor required to produce a commodity was the only true measure of that commodity's value. Any profit made by the capitalist employer was "surplus value" appropriated from the exploited workers. The essence of modern history, according to Marx, was the class struggle between the bourgeoisie (capitalists) and the impoverished proletariat (the workers). The eventual victors of this revolutionary struggle, according to Marx, would be the workers. Their triumph would usher in a classless, communist utopia in which all exploitation would cease.

Despite Marx's keen interest in the United States, Marxism proved to have little appeal in late-nineteenth-century America other than for a tiny group of primarily German-born immigrants. More alarming to the public at large was the handful of anarchists, again mostly immigrants, who rejected Marxist discipline and preached the destruction of capitalism, the violent overthrow of the state, and the immediate introduction of a stateless utopia. In 1892 an anarchist attempted to assassinate Henry Clay Frick, the manager of Andrew Carnegie's Homestead Steel Works. His act confirmed the business stereotype of "labor agitators" as lawless and violent.

CHECKING IN

- Early organizers attempted to create all-encompassing unions, such as the National Labor Union, with grand political aims.
- The Knights of Labor, which welcomed all workers, enjoyed considerable success but eventually fizzled.
- The more tightly focused craft union movement under AFL leader Samuel Gompers prospered by concentrating on lunchbox issues like wages.
- Violence, such as the Haymarket Square riot, turned many Americans against labor unions and made the use of violence against them seem acceptable.
- Ideas like Social Darwinism and the Gospel of Wealth clashed with the beliefs of those who criticized industrial society's excesses.

Chapter Summary

 DOWNLOAD THE MP3 AUDIO FILE OF THE CHAPTER SUMMARY, AND LISTEN TO IT ON THE GO.

How did Carnegie, Rockefeller, and other corporate leaders consolidate control over their industries? (page 405)

Abundant resources and technological innovation combined with other factors to fuel industrial growth. Railroads pioneered new business techniques; Carnegie, Rockefeller, and others successfully transferred these techniques to other industries, such as steel and oil. Pools were created to limit competition but were replaced by more efficient trusts and, ultimately, holding companies, leading to huge corporations.

What innovations in technology and business drove increases in industrial production after 1865? (page 410)

Technology contributed new ways of manufacturing as well as new products to stimulate growth. Many inventions, such as the telephone and electric light bulb, changed daily life. Advertising and marketing stimulated demand for the growing output of products.

Why did the South's experience with industrialization differ from that of the North and the Midwest? (page 413)

Lack of capital and a poor education system hamstrung southern development. Major growth came with the establishment of cotton textile mills and a handful of heavy industries, such as steel, but the South lagged far behind the rest of the nation.

How did factory workers respond to the changing nature of work? (page 416)

Factory work depended on unskilled workers who performed mind-numbing routine tasks, often hazardous, for low pay. Immigrants became the mainstay of the industrial work force, but children as young as eight worked in coal mines and cotton mills. Women worked out of their homes and entered both the factory and the office work force.

In the 1890s how did corporate executives undercut labor's bargaining power? (page 419)

Workers tried to create all-encompassing structures, such as the National Labor Union and the Knights of Labor, to protect workers' rights, but these attempts failed. The American Federation of Labor, focusing on skilled workers and practical issues, was far more successful. Violence flared, used by strikers and strikebreakers alike; governments generally were willing to use violence against strikes. Social Darwinism and the Gospel of Wealth were attempts to explain and justify the harshness of the new industrial order, although a number of utopian thinkers, notably Marxists and anarchists, protested.

KEY TERMS

Jay Gould *(p. 406)*
Interstate Commerce Act *(p. 408)*
J. Pierpont Morgan *(p. 408)*
Andrew Carnegie *(p. 408)*
vertical integration *(p. 408)*
John D. Rockefeller *(p. 409)*
Standard Oil Trust *(p. 409)*
Sherman Anti-Trust Act *(p. 409)*
Thomas A. Edison *(p. 410)*
Henry W. Grady *(p. 414)*
Horatio Alger *(p. 418)*
wildcat strikes *(p. 420)*
National Labor Union (NLU) *(p. 420)*
Knights of Labor *(p. 420)*
American Federation of Labor *(p. 421)*
Samuel Gompers *(p. 421)*
Homestead Strike *(p. 422)*
Eugene V. Debs *(p. 423)*
William Graham Sumner *(p. 423)*
Social Darwinism *(p. 424)*
Marxism *(p. 424)*

Immigration, Urbanization, and Everyday Life

Backyard Baseball, Boston, 1906,
by Lewis Hine

Scott Joplin Black composer who gained great popularity with ragtime, a jazzy, syncopated dance music

This icon will direct you to the website where you can Prepare for Class, Improve Your Grade, and Ace the Test:
www.cengage.com/history/boyer/ enduringconcise6e

CHAPTER PREVIEW

The New American City
How did the influx of immigrants before 1900 create an awareness of ethnic and class differences?

Middle- and Upper-Class Society and Culture
How did Victorian morality shape middle-class society and culture?

Working-Class Politics and Reform
How did political machines and social and religious reformers address urban poverty?

Working-Class Leisure in the Immigrant City
How did the urban working class change attitudes toward leisure and recreation by 1900?

Cultures in Conflict
How did writers, artists, and educational reformers address issues of cultural conflict?

In the early twentieth century, the jazzy, syncopated dance music known as ragtime became a national sensation, and **Scott Joplin,** a young black composer and pianist, became the king of ragtime. Joplin's rise from unknown saloon piano player to renowned composer sheds light not only on the extraordinary expansion of the entertainment industry at the turn of the nineteenth century but also on the class and racial tensions that pervaded popular culture.

Despite Joplin's enormous success, white competitors stereotyped his compositions as "Negro music" and "Coon songs." His publishers refused to accept his classical compositions, including his opera *Treemonisha.* Opera was considered a high art form for the upper classes; blacks, even those with Joplin's talent, could not enter the field. As Joplin's experience revealed, racial discrimination could reinforce the barriers of social class.

Joplin's thwarted dreams were similar to countless others who tried to move up the economic ladder. American society was slowly shifting from a rural producer economy that stressed work and thrift to an urban consumer economy in which new forms of entertainment, leisure activities, and material possessions were becoming the hallmarks of personal identity. These changes, together with the expansion of salaried, white-collar occupations such as teaching and accounting, fostered growing class awareness.

Nowhere was the class awareness more pronounced than in the cities crowded with immigrants. The working class in America's bustling cities created its own vigorous culture of dance halls, saloons, vaudeville theaters, social clubs, and amusement parks. Middle-class reformers who strove to remake this working-class culture into their own image of propriety were soon frustrated. In the long run, the culture of the masses would prove more influential in shaping modern America.

THE NEW AMERICAN CITY

How did the influx of immigrants before 1900 create an awareness of ethnic and class differences?

Everyday life was transformed most dramatically and visibly in cities. Between 1870 and 1900 New Orleans's population nearly doubled, Buffalo's tripled, and Chicago's increased more than fivefold. By 1900, Philadelphia, New York, and Chicago all had more than a million residents, and 40 percent of all Americans lived in cities (see Table 19.1).

TABLE 19.1 | URBAN GROWTH: 1870–1900

CITY	1870 POPULATION	1900 POPULATION	PERCENT INCREASE
Boston	250,525	560,892	123.88
Chicago	298,977	1,698,575	468.12
Cincinnati	216,239	325,902	50.71
Los Angeles	5,728	102,479	1,689.08
Milwaukee	71,440	285,315	299.37
New Orleans	191,418	287,104	49.98
New York	1,478,103	3,437,202	132.54
Philadelphia	647,022	1,293,697	99.94
Pittsburgh	86,076	321,616	273.64
Portland, Oregon	8,293	90,426	990.38
Richmond	51,038	85,050	66.64
San Francisco	149,473	342,782	129.32
Seattle	1,107	237,194	21326.73

Source: Thirteenth Census of the United States (Washington, D.C.: U.S. Government Printing Office, 1913).

This spectacular urban growth, fueled by the influx of nearly 11 million immigrants, stimulated economic development. Mushrooming cities created new jobs and markets that in turn dramatically stimulated national economic expansion. Like the frontier, the city symbolized opportunity for all comers.

The city's unprecedented scale and diversity threatened traditional expectations of community life and stability. A medley of immigrant groups contended with one another and with native-born Americans for jobs, power, and influence. Rapid growth strained city services, generating terrible housing and sanitation problems.

Native-born American city dwellers complained about the noise, stench, and congestion of this transformed cityscape. They fretted about the newcomers' squalid tenements, fondness for drink, and strange social customs. When native-born reformers set about cleaning up the city, they sought not only to improve the physical environment but also to destroy the distinctive customs that made immigrant cultures different from their own. The late nineteenth century thus witnessed an intense struggle to control the city and to benefit from its economic and cultural potential.

CL Interactive Map: Percentage of Foreign-born Whites and Native Whites of Foreign or Mixed Parentage in Total Populations, 1910

Migrants and Immigrants

Because the new industries that were concentrated in urban settings required thousands of new workers, the promise of good wages and plentiful jobs attracted many rural and small-town dwellers to the cities.

Young farmwomen led the exodus to the cities. With the growing mechanization of farming in the late nineteenth century, farming was increasingly male work.

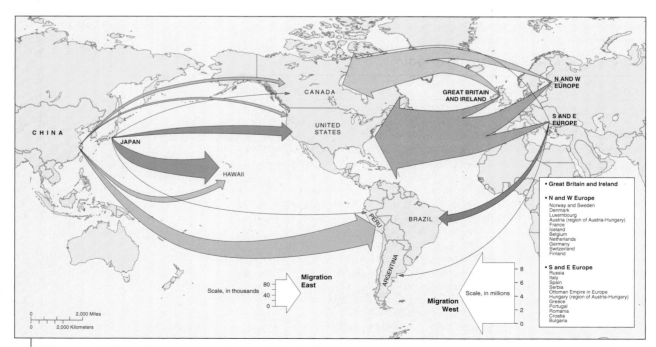

Map 19.1   Asian and European Immigrants Living in the Western Hemisphere and Hawaii in 1900

Chronology

1865	Vassar College founded
1869	Boss William Marcy Tweed gains control of New York's Tammany Hall political machine; first intercollegiate football game
1872	Anthony Comstock founds New York Society for the Suppression of Vice
1873	John Wanamaker opens his Philadelphia department store
1875	Smith and Wellesley colleges founded
1876	National League of baseball organized
1880	William Booth's followers establish an American branch of the Salvation Army
1881	Josephine Shaw Lowell founds New York Charity Organization Society (COS)
1884	Mark Twain, *Huckleberry Finn*
1885	Stanford University founded
1889	Jane Addams and Ellen Gates Starr open Hull House
1891	University of Chicago founded; Basketball invented at Springfield College, Massachusetts
1892	Ellis Island Immigration Center opened; General Federation of Women's Clubs organized
1895	Coney Island amusement parks open in Brooklyn, New York.
1899	Scott Joplin, "Maple Leaf Rag"; Kate Chopin, *The Awakening*; Thorstein Veblen, *The Theory of the Leisure Class*
1900	Theodore Dreiser, *Sister Carrie*; National Association of Colored Women's Clubs organized
1910	Angel Island Immigration Center opens in San Francisco

Mail-order sales of factory-made goods meanwhile reduced the need for women's work on subsistence tasks. So, young farmwomen flocked to the cities, where they competed for jobs with immigrant, African-American, and city-born women.

From 1860 to 1890, the prospect of a better life also attracted nearly 10 million northern European immigrants to American cities. Their numbers included 3 million Germans; 2 million English, Scottish, and Welsh; and 1.5 million Irish. Moreover, by 1900 more than 800,000 French-Canadians had migrated southward to work in the New England mills, and close to a million Scandinavians newcomers had put down roots in the rich farmlands of Wisconsin and Minnesota (see Map 19.1).

In the 1890s, these earlier immigrants from northern and western Europe were joined by swelling numbers of "**new immigrants**"—Italians, Slavs, Greeks, and Jews from southern and eastern Europe, Armenians from the Middle East, and, in Hawaii, Japanese from Asia (see Map 19.2). In the next three decades, these new immigrants, many from peasant backgrounds, would boost America's foreign-born population by more than 18 million.

new immigrants Wave of immigrants after 1880 coming mainly southern and eastern Europe

The overwhelming majority of both old and new immigrants settled in cities in the northeastern and north-central states. The effect of their numbers was staggering. In 1890 New York City contained twice as many Irish as Dublin, as many Germans as Hamburg, half as many Italians as Naples, and two and a half times the Jewish population of Warsaw. Four out of five people in New York City had been born abroad or were children of foreign-born parents. Overpopulation, crop failure,

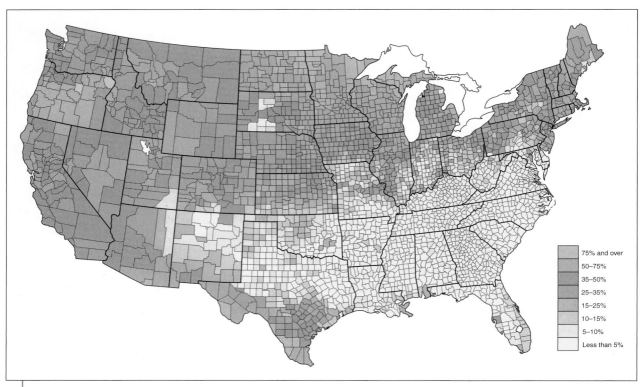

Map 19.2   Percent of Foreign-born Whites and Native Whites of Foreign or Mixed Parentage in Total Population, by Counties, 1910

As this map indicates, new immigrants rarely settled in the South.

Source: D. W. Meinig, *The Shaping of America—A Geographical Perspective of 500 Years of History.* New Haven: Yale University Press, 1986. Volume 3.

famine, and industrial depression had driven some of these immigrants from their homelands. At the same time, the promise of high wages lured more than 100,000 Japanese to work on Hawaiian sugar plantations. Many people, especially single young men, immigrated in the belief that the United States held a better future than their homeland. Wives and children waited in the old country until the family breadwinner had secured a job and saved enough money to pay for their passage to America.

The transatlantic journey, cramped and often stormy, featured poor food, little privacy, and rudimentary sanitary facilities. Immigrants arrived tired, fearful, and in some cases sick. Then customs officials examined them for physical handicaps and contagious diseases. After 1891 those with a "loathsome" infection, such as leprosy, or a sexually transmitted disease were deported. Immigrants who passed the physical examination had their names recorded. If a customs official had difficulty pronouncing a foreign name, he anglicized it. One German Jew became flustered when asked for his name and mumbled, "Schoyn vergessen [I forget]." The inspector, who did not know Yiddish, wrote, "Sean Ferguson."

Ellis Island   Immigrant processing center in New York City harbor through which millions passed

In 1892 the federal government established a facility for admitting immigrants on **Ellis Island,** replacing a nearby facility run by the state of New York on Castle Garden. Angel Island in San Francisco Bay on the West Coast served a similar purpose after

1910. At the immigrant processing centers, America's newest residents exchanged foreign currency for U.S. dollars, purchased railroad tickets, and arranged lodgings. Those who arrived with enough cash, including many Germans and Scandinavians, commonly traveled west to Chicago, Milwaukee, and the prairies beyond. But most of the Irish and Italians, largely from poor peasant backgrounds, stayed in eastern cities, such as Boston, New York, and Philadelphia, where they filled the lowest-paying jobs.

Adjusting to an Urban Society

Immigrants tended to cluster together to ease the transition to life in a new society. In 1890 a reporter observed that, if a map of New York City's streets were colored in by nationality, it "would show more stripes than on the skin of a zebra, and more colors than any rainbow."

Late-nineteenth-century social commentators often assumed that each nationality clumped together for reasons of national clannishness. But settlement patterns were far more complex. Most newcomers preferred to live near others not merely of their own nationality but from their own region or village. New York City held not a single "Little Italy" but dozens of them, inhabited by Neapolitans and Calabrians at Mulberry Bend, Genoese on Baxter Street, northern Italians west of Broadway, and Tyrolese Italians on Sixty-ninth Street near the Hudson River.

Some immigrant groups adjusted more easily than others. Skilled workers and those familiar with Anglo-American customs had relatively few problems. Ethnic groups that formed a substantial percentage of a city's population also had a major advantage. The Irish of Boston, New York, and Chicago, as well as the Germans of Milwaukee, dominated local government and church organizations. This eased the path for their fellow immigrants and made adjustment to American society more difficult for members of smaller groups. English and German dominance of the building trades, for example, enabled those nationalities to limit the numbers of Italians hired. Not all immigrants intended to remain in the United States. Expecting only a brief stay, they made little effort to learn English or understand American customs. Of the Italians who immigrated to New York before 1914, nearly 50 percent went back to Italy.

However, most immigrants stayed. As the number of foreigners in U.S. cities ballooned toward the turn of the century, all immigrant groups faced increasing hostility from white native-born Americans who disliked the newcomers' social customs and worried about their growing influence. Fearing the loss of the privileges and status that were associated with their white skin color, native-born whites often stigmatized immigrants as racially different and inferior. The experience of discrimination helped to create a new common ethnic identity for many groups. Immigrants from the same home country forged a new sense of ethnic distinctiveness as Irish-American, German-American, or Jewish-American that helped them compete for political power and eventually assimilate into mainstream society.

Slums and Ghettos

Every major city had run-down, overcrowded slum neighborhoods, created when landlords subdivided old buildings and packed in too many residents. The poorer the renters, the worse the slums. Slums became ghettos when laws, prejudice, and community

Primary Source:
The Tenement
Question—Inside
and Out!

W. E. B. Du Bois Black sociologist, later one of founders of NAACP

pressure prevented inhabitants from moving out. During the 1890s, Italians in New York City, African-Americans in Philadelphia and Chicago, Mexicans in Los Angeles, and Chinese in San Francisco increasingly became locked into segregated ghettos.

Life in the slums was particularly difficult for children. Juvenile diseases, such as whooping cough, measles, and scarlet fever, took a fearful toll, and infant mortality was high. In one immigrant ward in Chicago in 1900, 20 percent of infants died in their first year.

Because tenements often bordered industrial districts, residents had to put up with the noise, pollution, and foul odors of tanneries, foundries, factories, and packing houses. Reliance on coal for steam engines and heating released vast quantities of soot and coal dust to drift over the slums. As smoke tinged the atmosphere a hazy gray, buildings took on a dingy, grimy patina.

Most immigrants stayed in the shabbiest tenements only until they could afford better housing. Blacks, in contrast, were trapped in segregated districts. Driven out of the skilled trades and excluded from most factory work, blacks took menial jobs whose low pay left them little income for housing (see Chapter 18). Racist city dwellers used high rents, real estate covenants (agreements not to rent or sell to blacks), and neighborhood pressure to exclude them from areas inhabited by whites. Nevertheless, as **W. E. B. Du Bois,** a black sociologist, pointed out in *The Philadelphia Negro* (1899), wealthy black entrepreneurs within these neighborhoods built their own churches, ran successful businesses, and established charitable organizations to help their people.

Fashionable Avenues and Suburbs

The same cities that harbored slums, suffering, and violence also boasted neighborhoods of dazzling opulence. The wealthy built monumental residences on exclusive thoroughfares just outside the downtown, among them Fifth Avenue in New York, Commonwealth Avenue in Boston, and Euclid (YOO-clid) Avenue in Cleveland.

Middle-class city dwellers followed the wealthy, moving to new suburbs. In the 1890s, Chicago developer Samuel Eberly Gross created entire low-cost subdivisions north and west of the city, and advertised homes for as little as ten dollars a month. Lawyers, doctors, small businessmen, and other professionals moved farther out along the main thoroughfares served by the street railway and purchased homes with large lots.

A pattern of informal residential segregation by income took shape in the cities and suburbs. Built for families of a particular income level, certain city neighborhoods and suburbs developed remarkably similar internal standards for lot size and house design. Commuters who rode the new street railways out from the city center could identify the changing neighborhoods along the way as readily as a geologist might distinguish different strata on a washed-out riverbank. And with the physical change in American cities came a new awareness of class and cultural disparities.

CHECKING IN

- From 1890 to 1920, 18 million immigrants flooded into American cities.
- Native-born Americans disliked and feared these "new immigrants."
- The majority of immigrants crammed into tenements and slums.
- Wealthy city dwellers created fashionable avenues as havens, while the middle class moved to the suburbs.
- These physical changes in cities created a new awareness of cultural and class differences.

MIDDLE- AND UPPER-CLASS SOCIETY AND CULTURE

How did Victorian morality shape middle-class society and culture?

Spared the struggle for survival that confronted most Americans, the middle and upper classes faced a different challenge: explaining and rationalizing the material benefits of the emerging consumer society. To justify the achievements of society's wealthiest members, ministers, advice-book writers, and other commentators appealed to **Victorian morality,** a set of social ideas influential among the privileged classes of England and the United States during the reign (1837–1901) of Britain's Queen Victoria.

Proponents of Victorian morality argued that the success of the middle and upper classes rested on their superior talent, intelligence, morality, and self-control. Women were identified as the driving force for moral improvement. While men engaged in the world's work, women provided the gentle, elevating influence that would lead society in its upward march.

Victorian morality Strict code of gentility that permeated late-nineteenth-century society

Manners and Morals

Several fundamental assumptions shaped the Victorian world view. First, human nature was malleable; people could improve themselves. Thus Americans in the Victorian era pursued reform with intense moralism. Second, hard work developed personal self-discipline and also fostered national progress. Finally, good manners and "culture" in the form of literature and the fine arts were hallmarks of a truly civilized society.

Victorian morality after the Civil War was marked by a preoccupation with manners and social rituals. Behavior as well as income defined social standing. Good manners, including a knowledge of proper etiquette in all social occasions, especially dining and entertaining, became a badge of status. Meals evolved into rituals that differentiated the social classes. They presented occasions for displaying the elaborate silver and china that middle- and upper-class families exclusively possessed, and they provided telltale clues to a family's level of refinement and sophistication.

The Victorian code, with its emphasis on morals, manners, and behavior, heightened class differences and created visible distinctions among social groups. Prominent Victorians might claim their sincere interest in helping others to improve themselves, but more often than not their self-righteous, intensely moralistic outlook simply widened the gap created by income disparities.

The Cult of Domesticity

Victorian views on morality and culture, coupled with rising pressures on consumers to make decisions about a mountain of domestic products, had a subtle but important impact on middle-class expectations about a woman's role within the home. From the 1840s onward, the home had been idealized as "the woman's sphere," a protected retreat where she could express her special maternal gifts, including a sensitivity toward children and an aptitude for religion.

Victorian advocates of the cult of domesticity added a new obligation for women: to foster an artistic environment that would nurture the family's cultural improvement. Houses became statements of cultural aspirations, with rarely used front parlors that were cluttered with ornate furnishings and curios, and elaborately ornamented architectural styles gained popularity. Excluded from the world of business and commerce, women directed their energy to transforming their homes into "a place of repose, a refuge from the excitement and distractions of outside. . . , provided with every attainable means of rest and recreation."

Not all middle-class women pursued this domestic ideal. For some, the drudgery of housework and of running the family overwhelmed any concern for artistic accomplishment. For others, the artistic ideal itself was not to their taste. In the 1880s and 1890s, women increasingly sought other outlets for their creative energies in settlement-house work, social reform, and women's club activities.

Department Stores

Although Victorian thought justified the privileges of the well-to-do, many people found it difficult to shake the thriftiness of their early years and accept the new preoccupation with accumulation and display. In the 1880s merchandisers encouraged Americans to loosen their purse strings and enjoy prosperity by emphasizing the high quality and low cost of their goods.

Key to changing attitudes about consumption was the **department store.** In the final quarter of the nineteenth century, entrepreneurs like Roland Macy, John

department store Emporium dedicated to convincing middle- and upper-class women that consumption was attractive and respectable

Marshall Field's Department Store, Chicago, 1890

Department stores set the standard for men's and women's fashions. Brightly lit store windows drew crowds of onlookers eager to discover the latest fabrics and styles.

Wanamaker, and Marshall Field made the department store an urban institution and transformed the shopping experience for their middle- and upper-class patrons. Merchants like Macy and Wanamaker overcame middle- and upper-class reluctance to spend by advertising products at "rock-bottom" prices and by waging price wars to validate their claims.

They also tried to make shopping an exciting activity. The stores became more and more ornate, with stained-glass skylights, marble staircases, brilliant chandeliers, and plush carpets. The large urban department store functioned as a workplace for the lower classes and as a kind of social club for comfortably fixed women. For those who could afford it, shopping became an adventure, a form of entertainment, and a way to affirm their place in society.

The Transformation of Higher Education

At a time when relatively few Americans possessed even a high-school education, colleges and universities represented another stronghold of the business and professional elite and of the moderately well-to-do middle class. Wealthy capitalists gained stature and a measure of immortality by endowing colleges and universities. In 1885 Leland Stanford and his wife launched Stanford University with a bequest of $24 million; in 1891 John D. Rockefeller donated $34 million to found the University of Chicago. Industrialists and businessmen dominated the boards of trustees of many educational institutions, and colleges were viewed as a training ground for future business and professional leaders.

The athletic field as well as the classroom prepared affluent young men for business and the professions. Football, adapted from English rugby, became an elite sport played by college teams. Because Social Darwinism emphasized struggle, football seemed an ideal arena for improving the strength, courage, and self-discipline of youth. Some defenders of the sport insisted that football could function as a surrogate frontier experience in an increasingly urban society. By 1900 football had become a popular fall sport, stimulating alumni giving and building goodwill for those elite institutions that otherwise remained far outside the experience of the average American.

More than 150 new colleges and universities appeared between 1880 and 1900, and enrollments more than doubled. This expansion of college education led to the expansion of women's roles. Coeducational private colleges and public universities enrolled increasing numbers of women. Some colleges—for instance, Vassar (1865) and Bryn Mawr (1884)—were founded solely for women. At these institutions, participation in college organizations, athletics, and dramatics enabled female students to learn traditionally "masculine" strategies for gaining power. By the turn of the century, women made up more than one-third of the total college-student population.

Cigar-Box Label, c. 1910
Vassar College, founded in 1865, promoted the new image of womanhood by stressing the interconnections among education, athletics, and ethics.

CHECKING IN

- The Victorian middle class had upper-class attitudes that focused on morality and social convention.
- The "cult of domesticity" shaped the lives of middle-class women, who were expected to focus on the home and its cultural refinement.
- Department stores catered to the middle and upper classes, and made shopping attractive and respectable.
- Football became the dominant college sport because it was thought to build character.
- Higher education flourished; new co-educational policies allowed women to acquire college education as never before; the research university emerged.

research university New type of school offering wide variety of subjects, encouraging research

"boss" Urban political leader; headed the machine, often corrupt

political machine Urban political organization that controlled patronage, manipulated immigrants

Innovative presidents such as Cornell's Andrew D. White and Harvard's Charles W. Eliot sought to change the focus of higher education. The change was most evident in medical education. Using the experimental method developed by German scientists, American medical professors insisted that all medical students be trained in biology, chemistry, and physics, including working in a laboratory. New educational and professional standards, similarly, were established for architects, engineers, and lawyers.

These changes were part of a larger transformation in higher education that produced a new institution, the **research university.** Unlike antebellum colleges, which taught little beyond classical languages, theology, logic, and mathematics, the new research universities offered courses in a wide variety of subjects, established professional schools, and encouraged faculty members to pursue basic research. Cornell, the University of Wisconsin at Madison, Johns Hopkins, Harvard, and others laid the groundwork for the central role that U.S. universities would play in the intellectual, cultural, and scientific life of the twentieth century.

WORKING-CLASS POLITICS AND REFORM

How did political machines and social and religious reformers address urban poverty?

The contrast between the affluent world of the college-educated middle and upper classes and the gritty lives of the working class was graphically displayed in the nation's growing urban centers, where immigrant newcomers reshaped political and social institutions to meet their needs. If department stores furnished new social spaces for the middle and upper classes, saloons became the poor man's club, and dance halls became single women's home away from home. While the rich and the well-born looked askance at lower-class recreational activities and sought to force the poor to change their ways, working-class Americans, the immigrant newcomers in particular, fought to preserve their own way of life. Indeed, the late nineteenth century witnessed an ongoing battle to eradicate social drinking, reform **"boss"** politics, and curb lower-class recreational activities.

Political Bosses and Machine Politics

Earlier in the century, the swelling numbers of urban poor had given rise to a new kind of politician, the "boss," who presided over the city's **political machine**—an unofficial political organization designed to keep a particular party or faction in office. Whether officially serving as mayor or not, the boss, assisted by local ward or precinct captains, wielded enormous influence in city government.

For better or worse, the political machine was America's unique contribution to municipal government in an era of pell-mell urban growth. Typified by Tammany Hall, the Democratic organization that dominated New York City politics from the 1830s to the 1930s, machines emerged in a host of cities during the late nineteenth century.

By the turn of the century, many cities had experienced machine rule. Working through the local ward captains to turn out unusually high numbers of voters, the machine rode herd on the tangle of municipal bureaucracies, controlling who was hired for the police and fire departments. It rewarded its friends and punished its enemies through its control of taxes, licenses, and inspections.

At the neighborhood level, the ward boss often acted as a welfare agent, helping the needy and protecting the troubled. Apparent generosity enhanced the bosses' image, at little cost: ten dollars to pay a tenement dweller's rent meant a lot to the poor but was small change to bosses who raked in millions from public contracts and land deals. Although the machine helped alleviate some suffering, it entangled urban social services with corrupt politics and often prevented city government from responding to the real problems of the city's neediest inhabitants.

Under New York City's boss **William "Magear" Tweed,** the Tammany Hall machine sank to new depths of corruption. Between 1869 and 1871, Tweed dispensed 60,000 patronage positions and pumped up the city's debt by $70 million through graft and inflated contracts. The details of the Tweed ring's massive fraud and corruption were brilliantly satirized in *Harper's Weekly* by German immigrant cartoonist Thomas Nast. Convicted of fraud and extortion, Tweed was sentenced to jail in 1873, served two years, escaped to Spain, was reapprehended and reincarcerated, and died in jail in 1878.

William "Magear" Tweed
Corrupt boss of the Tammany Hall organization that ran New York City

By the turn of the century, the bosses were facing well-organized assaults on their power, led by an urban elite whose members sought to restore "good government" (see Chapter 21). In this atmosphere the bosses increasingly forged alliances with civic organizations and reform leagues. The results, although never entirely satisfactory to any of the parties involved, paved the way for new sewer and transportation systems, expanded parklands, and improved public services—a record of considerable accomplishment, given the magnitude of the problems created by urban growth.

Battling Poverty

In contrast to the bosses' piecemeal attempts to aid the urban poor, middle-class reformers sought comprehensive solutions. Jacob Riis and other reformers believed that immigrants' lack of self-control led to their miseries. Thus reformers often focused on the moral improvement of the poor while ignoring the crippling effect of low wages and dangerous working conditions. Humanitarian campaigns to help the destitute often turned into crusades to Americanize the immigrants and eliminate their "offensive" and "self-destructive" behaviors.

Poverty relief workers first targeted the young, considered the most malleable. Early Protestant social reformers started charitable societies to help transient youths and street waifs. In 1843 Robert M. Hartley, a former employee of the New York Temperance Society, founded the New York Association for Improving the Condition of the Poor to urge poor families to change their ways.

Hartley's voluntaristic approach was supplemented by the more coercive tactics of Charles Loring Brace, who founded the New York Children's Aid Society in 1853. Worried that they might join the city's "dangerous classes," Brace swept orphaned children off the streets, shipped them to the country, and placed them with families to work as farm hands. Where Brace gave adolescents an alternative to living in the slums, the Young Men's Christian Association (YMCA) and Young Women's Christian Association (YWCA) provided housing and wholesome recreation for country boys and young women who had migrated to the city. Both organizations subjected their members to curfews and expelled them for drinking and other forbidden behavior.

By 1900, more than fifteen hundred YMCAs and YWCAs served as havens for nearly a quarter-million young men and women. But YMCA and YWCA leaders reached only a small portion of the young adult population. The strategy was too narrowly focused to stem the rising tide of urban problems.

New Approaches to Social Reform

The inability of relief organizations to cope with the explosive growth of the urban poor in the 1870s and 1880s convinced many middle-class Americans that urban poverty had reached dangerous proportions. Social reformers began to develop new strategies to fight poverty. One of the earliest and most effective agencies was the **Salvation Army.** A church established along paramilitary lines in England in 1865 by Methodist minister "General" William Booth, the Salvation Army sent its uniformed volunteers to the United States in 1880 to provide food, shelter, and temporary employment for families. The army's strategy was simple: attract the poor with marching bands and lively preaching; follow up with offers of food, assistance, and employment; and then teach them the solid, middle-class virtues of temperance, hard work, and self-discipline.

| **Salvation Army** Religious group established to aid the poor

New York's Charity Organization Society (COS), founded in 1882 by Josephine Shaw Lowell, implemented a similar approach, attempting to make the poor more honest and efficient. The society sent "friendly visitors" into the tenements to counsel families on how to improve their lives. Convinced that moral deficiencies lay at the root of poverty, and that the "promiscuous charity" of overlapping welfare agencies undermined the desire to work, the COS tried to foster self-sufficiency in its charges.

Critics justly accused the COS and similar groups of seeking more to control than to help the poor. More often than not, the friendly visitors wore cultural blinders, misunderstanding the real source of the difficulties faced by the poor and expecting to effect change by imposing middle-class standards. Unable to see slum problems from the vantage point of the poor, the organizations ultimately failed to convert the poor to their own codes of morality and decorum.

The Moral Purity Campaign

Other reformers pushed for tougher measures against sin and immorality. In 1872 **Anthony Comstock,** a pious young dry-goods clerk, founded the New York Society for the Suppression of Vice and demanded that municipal authorities close down gambling and lottery operations and censor obscene publications.

| **Anthony Comstock** Leader of Moral Purity crusade against urban vice, corruption

Nothing symbolized the contested terrain between middle- and lower-class culture better than the fight over prostitution, socially degenerate to some and a source of recreation to others. Brothels—houses of prostitution—expanded rapidly from the time of the Civil War until the 1880s, when saloons and cabarets, often controlled by political machines, replaced them. Reformers assumed, incorrectly, that immigrant women made up the majority of urban prostitutes.

In 1892 Charles Parkhurst, a Presbyterian minister and New York reformer, founded the City Vigilance League to clean up prostitution, gambling dens, and saloons. Parkhurst blamed the "slimy, oozy soil of Tammany Hall" and the New York City police for the city's rampant evil and pressured city officials to enforce the laws against prostitution, gambling, and Sunday liquor sales.

The purity campaign lasted scarcely three years. The reform coalition quickly fell apart. New York's population was too large and its ethnic constituencies too diverse for the middle and upper classes to curb all the illegal activities flourishing within the sprawling metropolis.

The Social Gospel

Meanwhile, in the 1870s and 1880s a handful of Protestant ministers explored radical alternatives for aiding impoverished city dwellers. Appalled by slum conditions, they argued that the rich and well-born deserved part of the blame for poverty and thus had a responsibility to do something about it.

William S. Rainsford, the minister of New York City's St. George's Episcopal Church, pioneered the so-called institutional church movement, whereby large downtown churches in once-elite districts now overrun by immigrants provided their new neighbors with social services as well as a place to worship. Supported by his wealthy church warden, J. Pierpont Morgan, Rainsford organized a boys' club, built recreational facilities on the Lower East Side, and established an industrial training program.

Another effort within Protestantism to right contemporary wrongs was the **Social Gospel** movement, launched in the 1870s by Congregational minister Washington Gladden of Columbus, Ohio. Gladden insisted that true Christianity commits men and women to fight social injustice. If Gladden set the tone for the Social Gospel, Walter Rauschenbusch, a minister in New York City's notorious Hell's Kitchen neighborhood, articulated its philosophy. Educated in Germany, Rauschenbusch argued that a truly Christian society would unite all churches, reorganize the industrial system, and work for international peace. Although the Social Gospel attracted only a handful of Protestants, their earnest voices blended with a growing chorus of critics bemoaning the nation's urban woes.

Social Gospel Protestant doctrine that wealthy must aid the poor

The Settlement-House Movement

By the 1880s many concerned citizens had become convinced that reform pressure applied from the top down, however well intentioned, was ineffective and wrong-headed. A new approach to social work was needed. A younger generation of charity workers, led by **Jane Addams,** developed a new weapon against destitution: the settlement house. Like the Social Gospelers, these reformers recognized that the hardships of slum life were often beyond individuals' control. Stressing the environmental causes of crime and poverty, settlement-house relief workers themselves moved into poor neighborhoods, where, in Addams's words, they could see firsthand "the struggle for existence, which is so much harsher among people near the edge of pauperism."

Jane Addams Leader in settlement-house movement; later won Nobel Peace Prize

Garbage Box, First Ward, Chicago, c. 1900

Lacking space for recreation, immigrant children play atop garbage boxes in crowded alleys. Concerned for their health, Jane Addams wrote that "this slaughter of innocents, this infliction of suffering on the newborn, is so gratuitous and so unfair, that it is only a question of time until an outraged sense of justice shall be aroused on behalf of these children."

The youngest daughter of a successful Illinois businessman, Jane Addams purchased a dilapidated mansion in Chicago in 1889. After overseeing extensive repairs, she and her coworkers opened it as Hull House, the first experiment in the settlement-house approach. Drawing on the middle-class ideal of true womanhood as supportive and self-sacrificing, Addams turned Hull House into a social center for recent immigrants. She invited newly arrived Italian immigrants to plays; held classes in English, civics, cooking, and dressmaking; and encouraged them to preserve their traditional crafts. She set up a kindergarten, a laundry, an employment bureau, and a day nursery for working mothers. Addams and her coworkers made studies of city housing conditions and pressured politicians to enforce sanitation regulations.

By 1895 at least fifty settlement houses had opened around the nation. Their leaders trained a generation of young college students, mostly women, many of whom would later serve as state and local government officials. Florence Kelley, for example, who had worked at Hull House, became the chief factory inspector for Illinois in 1893. Through their sympathetic attitudes toward the immigrants and their systematic publication of data about slum conditions, settlement-house workers gave Americans new hope that the cities' problems could be overcome.

But in their attempt to promote class cooperation and social harmony, settlement houses had mixed success. Although immigrants appreciated the settlement houses' resources and activity, they widely felt that the reformers cared little for increasing immigrant political power.

CHECKING IN

- Urban politics was often dominated by corrupt bosses and the machines they ran.

- Reformers blamed weak moral discipline for the plight of the poor; with this focus, reformers ignored the issues of low wages and dangerous working conditions.

- The Salvation Army and other reform groups provided needed aid and tried to improve moral character by instilling middle-class values.

- The Social Gospel taught the responsibility of the rich and well-born to help the poor.

- Settlement houses brought middle-class women into the slums to provide services and attack urban problems.

WORKING-CLASS LEISURE IN THE IMMIGRANT CITY

How did the urban working class change attitudes toward leisure and recreation by 1900?

In colonial America the subject of leisure time had generally arisen only when ministers condemned "idleness" as the first step toward sin. In the rural culture of the early nineteenth century, the unremitting routines of farm labor had left little time for relaxation. Family picnics, horse races, county fairs, revivals, and holidays like the Fourth of July and Christmas had provided permissible diversion, but even in relaxation earlier generations had guarded against "laziness."

As urban populations and factories multiplied after the Civil War, new patterns of leisure and amusement emerged, especially among the urban working class. After long hours in factories and mills or behind department store counters, working-class Americans craved relaxation and diversion. They thronged the streets, patronized saloons and dance halls, cheered at boxing matches and baseball games, and organized boisterous group picnics and holiday celebrations. Amusement parks, vaudeville theaters, sporting clubs, and racetracks provided further entertainment for workers, and mass leisure became a big business.

Streets and Saloons

No segment of the populace had a greater need for recreation than the urban working class. Hours of tedious, highly disciplined, and physically exhausting labor left workers tired but thirsty for excitement and escape from their cramped living quarters. In 1889 a banner carried by a carpenters' union summed up their needs: "eight hours for work, eight hours for rest, and eight hours for what we will."

City streets provided some recreation. Relaxing after a day's work, shop girls and laborers clustered on busy corners, watching shouting pushcart peddlers and listening to organ grinders play familiar melodies. For a penny or a nickel, they could buy a bagel, a baked potato, or a soda. In the summer, when the heat and humidity within the tenements reached unbearable levels, the streets became the center of neighborhood life.

The streets were open to all, but other leisure institutions drew mainly a male clientele. Saloons offered men companionship, conviviality, and five-cent beer, often with a free lunch thrown in. By 1900 New York City had an estimated ten thousand saloons. As gathering places in ethnic neighborhoods, saloons reinforced group identity and became centers for immigrant politics. Saloonkeepers often doubled as local ward bosses who performed small services for their patrons. With rich mahogany bars, shiny brass rails, and elegant mirrors, saloons provided a taste of luxury for their factory-worker clientele.

The saloon provided an antidote to the socially isolating routines of factory labor and the increasingly private and family-centered social life of the middle class. And saloons often served as bases for prostitution and criminal activity. Moreover, drinking too much at the saloon frequently led to family violence, and "treating"—buying drinks for friends—and cut deeply into already meager paychecks.

The Rise of Professional Sports

As an English game called rounders, baseball had existed since the seventeenth century. If Americans did not create baseball, they nevertheless took this informal children's game and turned it into a major professional sport. In 1845 the New York Knickerbockers, the first organized baseball team, was established. In the 1860s, rules were codified, and the sport assumed its present form, featuring overhand pitching, fielders' gloves, nine-inning games, and bases spaced ninety feet apart. In 1869 the Cincinnati Red Stockings, the first team to put its players under contract for the whole season, toured the country and ended the season with fifty-seven wins and no losses.

Team owners organized the National League in 1876 and took control of the game. Crowds of ten thousand to twelve thousand fans flooded into ballparks each game, creating enormous profits for the owners. Newspapers thrived on baseball. Joseph Pulitzer introduced the first separate sports page when he bought the *New York World* in 1883, and baseball dominated the paper's sports reporting. By the 1890s baseball was big business.

The working class in particular took baseball to heart. The most profitable teams came from industrial cities with large working-class populations. However, if baseball helped build solidarity among some ethnic groups, it also fostered discrimination against blacks. At least fifty-five blacks played on integrated teams between 1883 and 1898. Increasingly thereafter, blacks were banned from playing on professional teams and banished to their own league.

Although no other organized sport attracted as large a following as baseball, horse racing and boxing also drew large crowds of spectators and received wide press coverage. But whereas races such as Louisville's Kentucky Derby became social events for the rich, professional boxing aroused passionate devotion in the working class. Bare-knuckle prizefighting was already a popular amusement for working-class men. The boxing rings became an arena where lower-class men could assert their individuality and physical prowess.

John L. Sullivan Heavyweight boxing champion

The hero of nineteenth-century professional sports was heavyweight fighter **John L. Sullivan**. Of Irish-immigrant stock, Sullivan began boxing in 1877 at age nineteen. With his massive physique, handlebar mustache, and arrogant swagger, Sullivan was enormously popular. Barnstorming across the country, he vanquished a succession of local strong men, invariably wearing his trademark green tights with an American flag wrapped around his middle. Sullivan already refused to fight blacks, supposedly in deference to the wishes of his fans. This policy conveniently allowed him to avoid facing the finest boxer of the 1880s, the Australian black, Peter Jackson.

Vaudeville, Amusement Parks, and Dance Halls

In contrast to the male preserve of saloons and prizefights, the world of vaudeville shows, amusement parks, and neighborhood dance halls welcomed all comers, regardless of gender, and proved particularly congenial to working-class women.

Vaudeville (VAWD-vill), with roots in antebellum minstrel shows that featured white comedians made up as blacks (see Chapter 11), offered a succession of acts designed for mass appeal. The vaudeville show typically opened with an animal act or a dance number, followed by a musical interlude. Then came comic skits ridiculing the trials of urban life, satirizing police and municipal ineptitude, poking fun at the different accents in the immigrant city, and mining a rich vein of ethnic humor and stereotypes. After more musical numbers and acts by ventriloquists and magicians, the program ended with a "flash" finale featuring flying-trapeze artists or the like. By the 1880s vaudeville was drawing larger crowds than any other form of theater. It provided an evening of inexpensive, lighthearted entertainment and let immigrants laugh at their own experiences, as translated into slapstick and caricature.

Whereas vaudeville offered psychological release from the stresses of working-class life, amusement parks provided physical escape. The fun houses, thrill rides, and games of New York's Coney Island opened in 1895 as the prototype of urban amusement parks, sprawled along the Brooklyn waterfront. By 1900 as many as 500,000 people would throng the beach, the boardwalk, and the amusement parks on a summer Saturday. Young couples rode through the dark Tunnel of Love, sped down the dizzying roller coaster, and watched belly dancers in the sideshows, momentarily surrendering to the spirit of exuberant play and losing themselves in fantasy. For immigrant women, in particular, the exciting music and the warm spell of a summer night could seem like a magical release from the drudgery of daily life.

Primary Source:
Vaudeville Poster,
Majestic Theater

Ragtime

Nothing more vividly illustrates the differences between the cultures of the middle class and the working class than the contrasting styles of popular music that each favored. Whereas the middle class preferred hymns or songs with a moral message, the working class embraced ragtime, the product of African-American musicians in the saloons of the South.

Ragtime developed out of the rich tradition of songs through which black Americans had eased the burdens of their life. Like spirituals, ragtime used syncopated rhythms and complex harmonies, but it blended them with marching-band musical structures to create a distinctive style. A favorite of "honky-tonk" piano players, ragtime was introduced to the broader public in the 1890s and became a national sensation.

The reasons for the sudden ragtime craze were complex. Inventive, playful, with catchy syncopations and an infectious rhythm in the bass clef, the music displayed an originality that had an appeal all its own. Part of ragtime's popularity also came from its origin in brothels and its association with blacks, who were widely stereotyped in the 1890s as sexual, sensual, and uninhibited by the rigid Victorian social conventions that restricted whites. Hence, ragtime's great popularity proved a mixed blessing for blacks. While it helped break down the barriers faced by blacks in the music industry, it also confirmed some whites' stereotype of blacks as primitive and sensual, a bias that underlay the racism of the period and helped justify segregation and discrimination.

CHECKING IN

- Saloons became political as well as social centers for immigrant men.
- Professional sports, such as baseball, appealed strongly to urban immigrants.
- Boxing produced heroes like John L. Sullivan.
- Vaudeville and dance halls provided cheap popular entertainment, and urban amusement parks like Coney Island attracted huge crowds.
- Ragtime brought African-American music into white communities even as it confirmed racial stereotypes.

CULTURES IN CONFLICT

How did writers, artists, and educational reformers address issues of cultural conflict?

Even within the elite and middle classes, Victorian morality and genteel cultural standards were never totally accepted. As 1900 dawned, questions about Victorian morality and new cultural stirrings intensified. At the center of the cultural turbulence stood women, increasingly dissatisfied with the restrictive code of feminine propriety. The growth of women's clubs and women's colleges, and even the bicycle fad of the 1890s, all contributed to the emergence of what some began to call the "new woman."

At the same time, a widening chasm divided the well-to-do from the mass of immigrant laborers. In no period of American history have class conflicts been as open and raw. Nervously eyeing the noisy culture of city streets, saloons, boxing clubs, dance halls, and amusement parks, middle-class leaders perceived a massive, if unconscious, challenge to their own cultural and social standing. Some middle-class reformers promoted public schools as a means to impose middle-class values on the urban masses, and others battled urban "vice" and "immorality." By 1900 the Victorian social and moral ethos was crumbling on every front.

The Genteel Tradition and Its Critics

What was this genteel culture that aroused such opposition? In the 1870s and 1880s, a group of upper-class writers and editors, led by Charles Eliot Norton of Harvard and E. L. Godkin of *The Nation,* codified standards for writing and design, and tried to create a coherent national artistic culture. Joining forces with allies in Boston and New York, these elites lobbied to "improve" American taste in interior furnishings, textiles, ceramics, wallpaper, and books. Godkin and editors of other "quality" periodicals created an important forum for serious writers in *The Nation* and *The Atlantic Monthly.* Novelist Henry James, who published virtually all of his work in the *Atlantic,* reflected the views of this elite literary establishment. "It is art that *makes* life," he wrote. Although these genteel magazines provided an important forum for new authors, their editors' strident elitism and imperialistic desire to control national literary standards bred opposition. Samuel Langhorne Clemens, better known as **Mark Twain,** spoke for many young writers when he declared as early as 1869 that he was through with "literature and all that bosh." Attacking aristocratic literary conventions, Twain and others who shared his concerns worked to broaden literature's appeal to the general public.

Mark Twain Writer, humorist, critic of genteel tradition

These efforts by a younger generation of writers to chart new directions for American literature rested on sweeping changes within the publishing industry. New magazines like *Ladies' Home Journal, Cosmopolitan,* and *McClure's* competed with the elite publications. The new magazines slashed their prices and tripled their circulation. Supported by advertising rather than subscriptions, they provided an outlet for younger authors who wanted to write about real people in the "whirlpool of real life."

Some of these writers were labeled regionalists because they captured the distinctive dialects and details of their featured locale, whether New England or the

South. Others, among them William Dean Howells, focused on a truthful, if optimistic, depiction of the commonplace. Another group, called naturalists, stressed economic and psychological determinants and often examined the dark underside of life. In *Maggie: A Girl of the Streets* (1893), a bleak story of an innocent girl's exploitation and suicide in an urban slum, Stephen Crane wrote what is generally considered the first naturalist American novel. Labels aside, all these writers shared a skepticism about literary conventions and an intense desire to understand the society around them.

The careers of Mark Twain and Theodore Dreiser highlight the changes in the publishing industry and the evolution of new forms of writing. Both were products of the Midwest, outsiders to the East Coast literary establishment—Twain from Missouri and Dreiser from Indiana. As young men, both worked as newspaper reporters and traveled widely.

Mark Twain

Twain not only broke from highbred literary standards but also created a unique personal style through his studied prose and distinctive attire.

Twain and Dreiser called on their own experiences to write about the human impact of the wrenching social changes that surrounded them: the flow of people to the expanding cities and the relentless scramble for power, wealth, and fame. In *Adventures of Huckleberry Finn* (1884), Twain uses the river journey of two runaways, the rebellious Huck and the slave Jim, to explore the nature of contemporary American society by contrasting the idyllic life on the raft with the tawdry, fraudulent world of the small riverfront towns. Dreiser's *Sister Carrie* (1900) traces the journey of Carrie Meeber, an innocent and attractive girl, from her Wisconsin farm home to Chicago. Seduced by a traveling salesman, Carrie moves in with Hurstwood, the married proprietor of a fancy saloon. Driven by her desire for expensive department-store clothes and lavish entertainment, Carrie follows Hurstwood to New York, abandons him when his money runs out, and pursues her own career in the theater.

Twain and Dreiser broke sharply with the genteel tradition's emphasis on manners and decorum. *Century* magazine readers complained that *Huckleberry Finn* was "destitute of a single redeeming quality." The publisher of *Sister Carrie* found the novel so repugnant that he printed only one thousand copies to fulfill his contract—and then stored them in a warehouse.

Similarly, growing numbers of scholars and critics challenged the elite's self-serving beliefs, including assumptions that moral worth and economic standing were closely linked and that the status quo represented a social order decreed by God and nature alike. Economist Thorstein Veblen's *The Theory of the Leisure Class* (1899) caustically critiqued the lifestyle of the new capitalist elite. The product of a poor Norwegian farm community in Minnesota, Veblen looked at the captains of industry and their families with a jaundiced eye. He mercilessly documented their "conspicuous consumption" and lamented the widening economic gap between "those who worked without profit" and "those who profited without working."

Within the new discipline of sociology, Annie MacLean exposed the exploitation of department-store clerks, Walter Wyckoff uncovered the hand-to-mouth existence of unskilled laborers, and W. E. B. Du Bois documented the hardships of African-Americans in Philadelphia. The publication of these writings, coupled with the economic depression and seething labor agitation of the 1890s, made it increasingly difficult for turn-of-the-century middle-class Americans to accept the smug, self-satisfied belief in progress and genteel culture that had been a hallmark of the Victorian outlook.

Modernism in Architecture and Painting

The challenge to the genteel tradition also found support among architects and painters. Architects followed the lead of Louis Sullivan, who argued that a building's form should follow its function. In their view, banks, for example, should look like financial institutions, not Greek temples. Rejecting elite pretensions, architects looked to the future—to **modernism,** a quest for new modes of expression—for inspiration.

modernism Trend in early twentieth-century thought and aesthetics that rejected Victorian formalism in favor of new modes of experience and expression

Frank Lloyd Wright Architect who rejected Victorian fussiness

Frank Lloyd Wright's "prairie-school" houses, first built in the Chicago suburb of Oak Park in the 1890s, represented a typical modernist break with the past. Wright scorned the bulky Victorian house, with its large attics and basements; his designs, featuring broad, sheltering roofs and low silhouettes harmonious with the flat prairie landscape, used open, interconnecting rooms to create a sense of spaciousness.

Modernism's rejection of Victorian gentility influenced late-nineteenth-century painting as well. Winslow Homer's watercolors pictured nature as brutally tough and unsentimental; in his grim, elemental seascapes, lone men struggle against massive waves that threaten to overwhelm them. Thomas Eakins's canvases of swimmers, boxers, and rowers (such as his well-known *The Champion Single Sculls,* 1871) captured moments of vigorous physical exertion. Mary Cassatt shared Eakins's interest in everyday life, but she often took as her subject the bond between mother and child, as in her painting *The Bath* (c. 1891). The architects' and painters' revolt was symptomatic of a larger shift in middle-class thought that resulted from fundamental economic changes. As one minister observed in 1898, the transition from muscle to mechanical power had "separated, as by an impassable gulf, the simple, homespun, individualistic world of the . . . past, from the complex, closely associated life of the present." Victorian platitudes about proper manners and graceful arts seemed out of place in the big, glittering, electrified cities of iron and glass.

Distrusting idealistic Victorian assumptions about social progress, the middle class nevertheless disagreed over how to replace them. Not until the Progressive Era would social reformers draw on new expertise in social research with an enlarged conception of the federal government's regulatory power to break sharply with their Victorian predecessors' social outlook.

From Victorian Lady to New Woman

The role of middle-class women in the revolt against Victorian refinement was complex and ambiguous. Women's dissatisfaction with the cult of domesticity did not necessarily lead to their open rebellion. Although they chafed against the constraints of the genteel code and the assumption that they should limit their activities to the home, many women remained committed to playing a supportive role within the family. In fact, early advocates of a "widened sphere" for women often fused the traditional Victorian ideal of womanhood with a firm commitment to political action.

The career of temperance leader **Frances Willard** illustrates how the cult of domesticity could evolve into a broader view of women's social and political responsibilities. Willard believed that by nature women were compassionate, nurturing, and sensitive to others; she was equally convinced that drinking encouraged men to squander their earnings and profoundly threatened family life. In 1874 Willard resigned her positions as dean of women and professor of English at Northwestern University to devote her energies completely to the temperance cause. Five years later, she became president of the recently formed Woman's Christian Temperance Union (WCTU).

Willard took the traditional belief that women had unique moral virtues and transformed it into a rationale for political action. The domestication of politics, she asserted, would protect the family and improve public morality. Choosing as her badge a white ribbon, symbolizing the purity of the home, in 1880 Frances Willard launched a crusade to win women's right to vote so that they could outlaw liquor. Willard also expanded the WCTU's activities to include welfare work, prison reform, labor arbitration, and public health. By 1890 the WCTU, with a membership of 150,000, had become the nation's first mass organization of women. Its members gained experience as lobbyists, organizers, and lecturers, undercutting the assumption of "separate spheres."

An expanding network of women's clubs offered another means by which middle- and upper-class women could hone their skills in civic affairs, public speaking, and intellectual analysis. Club women became involved in social-welfare projects, public-library expansion, and tenement reform. By 1892, the General Federation of Women's Clubs boasted 495 affiliates and a hundred thousand members. Middle-class black women, excluded from many white clubs, formed their own National Association of Colored Women's Clubs in 1900.

A bicycling vogue that swept urban America at the end of the century further loosened Victorian constraints on women. Fearful of waning vitality, middle- and upper-class Americans sought new means of improving their vigor, ranging from such health products as cod-liver oil and sarsaparilla to enthusiastic participation in basketball (invented in 1891 by a physical education instructor at Springfield College in Massachusetts). Bicycling, which could be enjoyed individually or in groups, quickly became the most popular sport for those who wished to combine exercise with recreation.

Bicycling especially appealed to young women uncomfortable with restrictive Victorian ideas, which included the views that proper young ladies must never sweat, the female body must be fully covered at all times, and physical exertion should take place in private. Pedaling along without corsets or padded clothing, the woman bicyclist implicitly broke with genteel conventions.

Changing attitudes about femininity also found expression in shifting ideas about marriage. Charlotte Perkins Gilman, a suffrage advocate and speaker for women's rights, asserted that women would make an effective contribution to society only when they won economic independence from men through work outside the home. The climbing divorce rate between 1880 and 1900 testified to women's changing relationship to men; in 1880 one in twenty-one marriages ended in divorce, but by 1900 the rate had shot up to one in twelve. Women who sued for divorce increasingly cited their husbands' failure to act responsibly and to respect their autonomy.

Frances Willard Activist in temperance, women's issues

Accepting such arguments, courts frequently awarded wives alimony, a monetary settlement payable by ex-husbands to support their former spouses.

Women writers generally welcomed the new female commitment to self-sufficiency and independence. Mary Wilkins Freeman's short stories, for example, compare women's expanding role to the frontier ideal of freedom. Her characters fight for their beliefs without concern for society's reaction. Feminist **Kate Chopin** pushed the debate to the extreme by having the married heroine of her 1899 novel *The Awakening* violate social conventions by falling in love with another man and then taking her life when his ideas about women prove as narrow and traditional as those of her husband.

Nonetheless, attitudes changed slowly. The enlarged concept of women's role in society had its greatest influence on middle-class women who enjoyed the privilege of higher education, possessed some leisure time, and could hope for success in journalism, education, social work, and nursing. For shop girls who worked sixty hours a week to make ends meet, such opportunities remained a distant goal.

Kate Chopin Feminist author; plotlines of her novel *The Awakening* violated social conventions

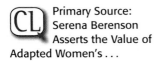 **Primary Source: Serena Berenson Asserts the Value of Adapted Women's . . .**

Public Education as an Arena of Class Conflict

Controversy over the scope and function of public education engaged Americans of all socioeconomic levels and highlighted class and cultural divisions in late-nineteenth-century society. Viewing public schools as an instrument for indoctrinating and controlling the lower ranks, middle-class educators and civic leaders campaigned to expand and centralize public schooling. Not surprisingly, the reformers' efforts aroused considerable opposition from ethnic and religious groups whose outlook and interests differed sharply from theirs.

Thanks to the crusade for universal public education started by Horace Mann, most northern states had public-school systems by the Civil War. More than half the nation's children received some formal education, but most attended only a few years, and few went to high school. In the 1870s, middle-class activists, concerned that many Americans lacked sufficient knowledge to participate wisely in public affairs or function effectively in the labor force, worked to raise the overall educational level and to increase the number of years spent in school.

One such reformer was federal commissioner of education William Torrey Harris. Harris urged teachers to instill in their students a sense of order, decorum, self-discipline, and civic loyalty. Believing that modern industrial society depended on citizens' conforming to the timetables of the factory and the train, he envisioned the schools as models of precise scheduling: "The pupil must have his lessons ready at the appointed time, must rise at the tap of the bell, move to the line, return; in short, go through all the evolutions with equal precision."

To achieve these goals, reform-minded educators like Harris wrested control of schools from neighborhood leaders and ward politicians by stressing punctuality and order, compulsory-attendance laws, and a tenure system to insulate teachers from political favoritism and parental pressure. By 1900 thirty-one states required all children from eight to fourteen years of age to attend school. But the steamroller methods of Harris and others to systematize public education prompted protests. New York pediatrician Joseph Mayer Rice, after interviewing twelve hundred teachers, lashed out at the schools' singsong memorization and prisonlike discipline.

Rice overlooked real advances; for example, the national illiteracy rate dropped from 17 percent in 1880 to 13 percent by 1900, despite the influx of immigrants. He was on target, however, in assailing many teachers' rigid emphasis on silence, docility, and unquestioning obedience to rules.

By the 1880s several different groups were opposing the centralized urban public-school bureaucracies. Working-class families that depended on their children's meager wages for survival, for example, resisted attempts to force their sons and daughters to attend school past the elementary grades. Although some immigrant families sacrificed to give their children an education, many withdrew their offspring from school as soon as they had learned the rudiments of reading and writing, and sent them to work. Catholic immigrants, moreover, objected to the public schools' overwhelmingly Protestant orientation. The Catholic church thus established separate parochial systems and rejected federal aid to public schools as a ploy to "form one homogeneous American people after the New England Evangelical type." Meanwhile, upper-class parents, especially in the Northeast, commonly did not wish to send their children to the immigrant-thronged public schools. Many therefore enrolled their children in private seminaries and boarding schools, like St. Paul's in Concord, New Hampshire. These institutions reinforced the elite belief that higher education should be the preserve of the well-to-do.

The proliferation of private and parochial schools, along with controversies over compulsory education, public funding, and classroom decorum, reveals the extent to which public education had become entangled in ethnic and class differences. Unlike Germany and Japan, which standardized and centralized their national educational systems in the nineteenth century, the United States created a diverse system of locally run public and private institutions, a system that allowed each segment of society some influence over its schools. Amid the disputes, school enrollments expanded dramatically. In 1870 fewer than 72,000 students attended the nation's 1,026 high schools. By 1900 the number of high schools had jumped to more than 5,000 and the number of students to more than 500,000.

CHECKING IN

- Cultural conflict pitted Victorian gentility against rowdier immigrant life.
- Mark Twain and Theodore Dreiser led the attack on "genteel" literature.
- Louis Sullivan, Frank Lloyd Wright, and other architects and artists created "modernism."
- Women struggled against the bonds of genteel tradition.
- Public schools were increasingly seen as a way to inculcate middle-class values.

Chapter Summary

 DOWNLOAD THE MP3 AUDIO FILE OF THE CHAPTER SUMMARY, AND LISTEN TO IT ON THE GO.

How did the influx of immigrants before 1900 create an awareness of ethnic and class differences? (page 427)

A flood of immigrants jostled against native-born Americans who feared and disliked them; the immigrants were crowded into ghettos. The wealthy created fashionable enclaves, the middle class moved to the suburbs, and the physical

KEY TERMS

Scott Joplin *(p. 426)*
new immigrants *(p. 429)*
Ellis Island *(p. 430)*
W. E. B. Du Bois *(p. 432)*
Victorian morality *(p. 433)*

changes in cities sharpened class awareness. To further distinguish themselves from these newcomers, native-born Americans stressed their commitment to Victorian morality.

How did Victorian morality shape middle-class society and culture? (page 433)

Victorian morality and its emphasis on gentility, manners, decorum, and self-control shaped the middle class. The cult of domesticity demanded that women maintain culturally refined homes. Lavish department stores and artistically designed houses reflected the middle-and upper-class faith that the consumption of material goods indicated good taste. To raise standards, the prosperous classes expanded the number of high schools and created a new research university system for training educators, lawyers, doctors, and other professionals.

How did political machines and social and religious reformers address urban poverty? (page 436)

In contrast to the upper classes, immigrant newcomers created their own political machines. Political bosses, at times supported by graft and corruption, handed out jobs and helped many constituents face problems of sickness and misfortune. While Jacob Riis, Jane Addams, and other reformers worked to improve overcrowded housing and dangerous working conditions, Anthony Comstock and other less sympathetic reformers attacked immigrant values and cultures in an effort to uplift and Americanize them.

How did the urban working class change attitudes toward leisure and recreation by 1900? (page 441)

Urban immigrants thronged saloons, dance halls, vaudeville theaters, and amusement parks. They listened avidly to ragtime and cheered on professional baseball teams and sports heroes such as boxer John L. Sullivan. The elite vision of sport as a vehicle for instilling self-discipline and self-control was transformed into a new commitment to sports as spectacle and entertainment. Sports had become big business and an important part of the new consumerism.

How did writers, artists, and educational reformers address issues of cultural conflict? (page 444)

Genteel Victorianism found itself pitted against immigrant rowdiness and spirit. Mark Twain and others challenged the "genteel tradition" in literature, while architects like Louis Sullivan and Frank Lloyd Wright reshaped the urban landscape. Women struggled to escape the bonds of Victorian gentility. Public schools were seen as a place to inculcate middle-class values and overthrow immigrant patterns. Despite these efforts, the raucous working-class culture of the late-nineteenth-century city can be seen as the seedbed of twentieth-century mass culture.

KEY TERMS continued

department store *(p. 434)*
research university *(p. 436)*
"boss" *(p. 436)*
political machine *(p. 436)*
William "Magear" Tweed *(p. 437)*
Salvation Army *(p. 438)*
Anthony Comstock *(p. 438)*
Social Gospel *(p. 439)*
Jane Addams *(p. 439)*
John L. Sullivan *(p. 442)*
Mark Twain *(p. 444)*
modernism *(p. 446)*
Frank Lloyd Wright *(p. 446)*
Frances Willard *(p. 447)*
Kate Chopin *(p. 448)*

CHAPTER 20

Politics and Expansion in an Industrializing Age

1877–1900

The Politics of Industrialization

(CL) This icon will direct you to the website where you can Prepare for Class, Improve Your Grade, and Ace the Test:
www.cengage.com/history/boyer/ enduringconcise6e

CHAPTER PREVIEW

Party Politics in an Era of Upheaval, 1877–1884
How did political parties build coalitions out of their diverse ethnic and regional constituencies?

Politics of Privilege, Politics of Exclusion, 1884–1892
What factors prompted the rise of the Grange and the Farmers' Alliance movements?

The 1890s: Politics in a Depression Decade
Why did William Jennings Bryan fail to win the presidency in 1896?

Expansionist Stirrings and War with Spain, 1878–1901
Why did the United States go to war with Spain and become an imperial power?

July 2, 1881, was a muggy summer day in Washington, D.C., and President James A. Garfield was leaving town for a visit to western Massachusetts. At 9:30 A.M., as he strolled through the railroad station, shots rang out. Garfield fell, a bullet in his back. The shooter, Charles Guiteau, immediately surrendered. At first, doctors thought the president would recover. But as the doctors probed the wound with bare hands and unsterilized instruments, blood poisoning set in. On September 19, Garfield died.

The nation mourned. Garfield embodied the American dream of the self-made man. Born in a log cabin in Ohio, he fought in the Civil War, went to Congress in 1863, and was elected president in 1880.

Garfield also embodied a political generation that seemed more preoccupied with the spoils of office than with the problems of

451

ordinary people. The obscure Guiteau, a loyal party member who had supported Garfield, expected to be rewarded with a high diplomatic post. When this failed to materialize, his delusionary mental state worsened. Viewing Garfield's death as "a political necessity," he believed that the public would hail him as a hero. The jury rejected Guiteau's insanity plea, and in June 1882 he was hanged.

While contemporary critics like Henry Adams viewed Garfield's assassination as an example of the absurdity of late-nineteenth-century politics, historians today see it as a sign of how closely contested political battles were. The expansion of large corporations, the settlement of the trans-Mississippi West, and the surge in urban growth put intense pressure on the political process. At stake was the government's proper role in the stimulation and regulation of America's explosive industrial growth.

This intense debate involved nothing less than contending visions of how industrial growth should or should not be regulated and who should benefit financially. The struggle to control economic expansion reached its peak in the 1890s when a new third party, the Populists, joined with the Democrats to challenge corporate control of the economy. Representing the opposite position, the Republican Party's support for high tariffs and the gold standard represented a commitment to encouraging the growth of large corporations, to freeing industry to expand without regulation, and to developing new markets.

From the mid-1870s to the mid-1890s, no party was able to control the political process. But in 1896, the election of President William F. McKinley ushered in a generation of Republican domination of national politics. Elected in a campaign focused on the restoration of prosperity, McKinley stumbled into war with Spain, substantially increased U.S. territory, and established new outposts from which American corporations could gain access to overseas markets.

PARTY POLITICS IN AN ERA OF UPHEAVAL, 1877–1884

How did political parties build coalitions out of their diverse ethnic and regional constituencies?

Between 1877 and 1894, four presidents squeezed into office by the narrowest of margins; control of the House of Representatives changed hands five times; and seven new western states were admitted into the Union. Amid intense competition, no party could muster a working majority. Republicans, Democrats, and third-party leaders sought desperately to reshape their political organizations to win over and cement the loyalty of their followers. Not until 1896, in the aftermath of a massive depression that hit when their opponents were in office, did the Republicans build a coalition that would control Congress and the presidency for the next fifteen years.

Contested Political Visions

Between 1876 and 1896, the intense competition between parties produced an incredible turnout of voters. At the same time that voter turnout shot up, however, political parties sidestepped many of the issues created by industrialization, such as taxation

Chronology

1878	Congress requires U.S. Treasury to purchase silver
1880	James Garfield elected president
1881	Assassination of Garfield; Chester A. Arthur becomes president
1883	Pendleton Civil Service Act
1884	Grover Cleveland elected president
1886	*Wabash* v. *Illinois*
1887	Interstate Commerce Act
1888	Benjamin Harrison elected president
1889	National Farmers' Alliance formed
1890	Sherman Silver Purchase Act; Sherman Anti-Trust Act; McKinley Tariff pushes tariffs to all-time high
1893	Panic of 1893; start of depression of 1893–1897; repeal of the Sherman Silver Purchase Act
1894	Coxey's "army" marches on Washington; Pullman strike; Wilson-Gorman Tariff
1895	Supreme Court declares federal income tax unconstitutional
1896	Free-silver forces capture Democratic Party and nominate William Jennings Bryan; William McKinley elected president
1898	Acquisition of Hawaii; Spanish-American War
1898–1902	Guerrilla uprising in Philippines
1900	Currency Act officially places United States on gold standard
1901	Platt Amendment retains U.S. role in Cuba; Regular Army Nursing Corps founded
1902	Philippine Government Act

of corporations, support for those injured in factory accidents, and poverty relief. Except for the Interstate Commerce Act of 1887 and the largely symbolic Sherman Anti-Trust Act of 1890, Washington generally ignored the social consequences of industrialization and focused instead on encouraging economic growth.

How can we explain this refusal and, at the same time, account for the enormous popular support for parties? The answer lies in the political ideology of the period and the two major symbolic and economic issues that preoccupied lawmakers nationally: tariffs and civil service reform.

Political parties in the late nineteenth century energized voters not only by appealing to economic self-interest, as in support for industrialization and pensions for Civil War veterans and their widows, but also by linking their programs to deeply held beliefs about the nature of the family and the proper role of government. In its prewar years, the Republican party had enhanced economic opportunities for common people by using governmental authority to expand railroads, increase tariff protection for industry, and provide land subsidies to farmers. It had also espoused a belief in female moral superiority and a willingness to use government as an instrument to protect family life.

After the Civil War, these positions hardened into political ideologies. Republicans justified their support for the tariff and defended their commitment to Union widows' pensions as ways to protect the family home and female wage earners. Men in particular associated loyalty to party with a sense of masculinity. Democrats countered, using metaphors of the seduction and rape of white women by external forces and labeling Republican programs as classic examples of the perils of excessive government force. High tariffs imperiled the family and threatened economic disaster.

Despite their differences, neither Republicans nor Democrats believed that the national government had any right to regulate corporations or to protect the social welfare of workers. Members of both parties, particularly among the middle and upper classes, embraced the doctrine of **laissez-faire**—the belief that unregulated competition represented the best path to progress. According to this view, the federal government should promote economic development but not regulate the industries that it subsidized.

laissez-faire Belief that government should not interfere with the workings of the free market

Rather than looking to Washington, people turned to local or state authorities. On the Great Plains, angry farmers demanded that their state legislatures regulate railroad rates. In the cities, immigrant groups competed for political power while native-born reformers periodically attempted to oust the political machines and clean up corruption (see Chapter 19). Meanwhile, city and state governments vied with each other for control. When Chicago wanted to issue permits to street popcorn vendors, for example, the Illinois legislature had to pass a special act.

Both parties in the North and the South engaged in election fraud by rigging elections, throwing out opposition votes, and paying for "floaters" who moved from precinct to precinct to vote. Accusations of fraud invigorated party loyalty as members of each party developed a sense of moral outrage at the other's behavior that invigorated party spirit.

By linking economic policy to family values, both national parties encouraged the active role that women played in politics in this period, although most could not vote. Frances Willard and her followers in the Woman's Christian Temperance Union (WCTU), for example, helped create a Prohibition and Home Protection Party in the 1880s. A decade later, western women Populists won full suffrage in Colorado, Idaho, and Utah.

Patterns of Party Strength

In the 1870s and 1880s, each party had its own ideological appeal and centers of regional strength. The Democrats ruled the South, southern sections of border states like Ohio, and northern cities with large immigrant populations. They campaigned for minimal government expenditures, opposed tariff increases, and attacked "governmental interference in the economy." In addition, Democrats staunchly defended their immigrant followers. On state and local levels, they fiercely opposed attempts to limit alcohol use, advocated support for parochial schools, and opposed attempts to require English-only schooling.

The Republicans reigned in rural and small-town New England, Pennsylvania, and the upper Midwest, and drew support from the **Grand Army of the Republic (GAR),** a social and political organization of northern Civil War veterans. Republicans often "waved the bloody shirt," invoking the South's responsibility for starting

Grand Army of the Republic (GAR) Union veterans' group that sought to broaden pensions and exercised political power by "waving the bloody shirt"

the Civil War as the reason to keep Democrats out of power. The Republicans ran a series of former Union army generals for president and voted generous veterans' benefits.

Although issues of governmental authority dominated on the federal level, family tradition, ethnic ties, religious affiliation, and local issues often determined an individual's vote. Outside the South, ethnicity and religion were the most reliable predictors of party affiliation. Catholics, especially Irish Catholics, and Americans of German ancestry tended to vote Democratic. Old-stock Protestant northerners and immigrants from northern Europe, in contrast, voted Republican, as did African-Americans, North and South. Although intolerant of racial differences, the Democrats were generally more accepting of religious diversity than were the Republicans. Electoral skirmishes often centered on cultural differences, notably the perennial Republican attempt to force prohibition on Irish whiskey drinkers, German beer drinkers, and Italian wine drinkers.

In this era of locally based politics and a diminished presidency, the state leaders who controlled both major parties tended to favor appealing but pliable presidential candidates. Rutherford B. Hayes (1877–1881) fit the mold perfectly. Hayes, a Civil War general, had won admiration as an honest Ohio governor, and his major presidential achievement was restoration of respect for the office after the Grant scandals. The benevolent, bearded Hayes brought dignity to the White House. His wife, Lucy, a highly intelligent, college-educated woman of great moral earnestness, actively supported the Woman's Christian Temperance Union (WCTU), and Hayes banished alcohol from the White House. After one presidential dinner, the secretary of state grumbled, "It was a brilliant affair. The water flowed like champagne."

Poster Announcing GAR Encampment, Chicago, 1900

In addition to their nostalgic annual reunions, Union army veterans, organized as the Grand Army of the Republic, were a potent force in Republican party politics, lobbying for pensions and other benefits.

Regulating the Money Supply

In the 1870s, politicians confronted a tough problem of economic policy: how to create a money supply adequate for a growing economy without producing inflation. Americans' almost superstitious reverence for gold and silver added to the difficulty of establishing a coherent monetary policy. Many believed that the only trustworthy money was gold, silver, or certificates exchangeable for these scarce metals. All antebellum federal currency consisted of gold or silver coins or U.S. Treasury notes redeemable in gold or silver.

There were other issues. Bankers, business leaders, and politicians believed that economic stability required a strictly limited currency supply, which would drive interest rates up and prices down. Debtors, especially manufacturers and southern and western farmers, wanted to expand the money supply, a policy that would help them to pay off their debts. The monetary debate focused on a specific question: Should the Civil War paper "greenbacks" still in circulation be retained, or should they be eliminated to leave a currency backed by gold (see Chapter 15)? The hard times associated with the Panic of 1873 sharpened this dispute.

Greenback party Sought to maintain inflationary currency through printing of money not backed by gold

The **Greenback party** (founded in 1877) called for an expanded money supply and other measures to benefit workers and farmers. In the 1878 midterm elections, Greenback candidates received more than 1 million votes and won fourteen seats in Congress.

As prosperity returned, the Greenback party faded, but the money issue did not. An even longer-lasting controversy surged over the coinage of silver. In 1873 Congress instructed the U.S. Mint to cease making silver coins, thus "demonetizing" silver. But new discoveries in Nevada (see Chapter 17) soon increased the silver supply, and debtor groups now demanded that the government resume coining silver.

Enthusiastically backed by the silver-mine owners, silver forces won a partial victory in 1878, when Congress required the treasury to buy and mint up to $4 million worth of silver each month. But the treasury, dominated by monetary conservatives, sabotaged the law's intent by refusing to circulate the silver dollars that it minted.

Sherman Silver Purchase Act Law passed in 1890 in response to farmers' calls for inflationary monetary policies

Frustrated silver advocates tried a new approach in the **Sherman Silver Purchase Act** of 1890. This measure instructed the treasury to buy 4.5 million ounces of silver monthly and issue treasury notes, redeemable in gold or silver, equivalent to the cost of these silver purchases. The money supply increased, but only slightly. The controversy over silver dragged on.

Civil-Service Reform

For decades, successful candidates had rewarded supporters and contributors with jobs ranging from cabinet seats to lowly municipal posts. Defenders called the system "rotation in office" and claimed that it was a democratic way of filling government positions. Critics, however, dubbed it the spoils system after the old expression "To the victor belong the spoils." Too often, the new officeholders were ill prepared or just incompetent, and once in office they had to continue making campaign contributions to their patrons to keep their jobs.

For years, a small but influential group of reformers had campaigned for a merit-based civil service. Well-bred, well-educated, and well-heeled, these reformers called for a civil service staffed by "gentlemen." They had a point. A professional civil service was needed as the government's functions grew more complex.

Cautiously embracing the civil service cause, President Hayes in 1877 launched an investigation of the corrupt New York City customs office and demanded the resignation of two high officials. One, Chester A. Arthur, had played a key role in passing out jobs. Hayes's willingness to confront factions within his own party won praise from civil-service reformers, but critics ridiculed "snivel service" and "Rutherfraud B. Hayes."

When Congressman James A. Garfield won the 1880 Republican presidential nomination, the delegates, to appease the opposing New York faction, chose Chester A. Arthur, the loyalist Hayes had recently fired, as Garfield's running mate. Since Garfield enjoyed excellent health, the choice of the totally unqualified Arthur seemed safe. The Democrats nominated a career army officer, Winfield Scott Hancock, and the Greenbackers gave the nod to Congressman James B. Weaver of Iowa. Garfield edged out Hancock by a razor-thin margin; Weaver trailed far behind.

CHECKING IN

- Late-nineteenth-century Republicans stressed probusiness measures, such as the tariff, and claimed they were protecting American families.

- Democrats decried government interference, such as the tariff, and said they were the ones protecting families.

- Republicans flourished in New England and the Midwest, whereas Democrats dominated the South and urban areas.

- Battles over greenbacks and the coinage of silver—measures that would favor debtors, especially farmers—played a major role in national politics.

- Civil service reform became a major issue, especially after Garfield's death at the hands of an assassin who seemed motivated by the spoils system.

Garfield's assassination in 1881—which brought to the White House Chester A. Arthur, the very symbol of the corrupt patronage system—gave a powerful emotional boost to civil service reform, as reformers painted Garfield as a martyr to the spoils system. In 1883 Congress enacted the **Pendleton Civil Service Act,** drafted by the Civil Service Reform League that had been created two years earlier. The act set up a commission to prepare competitive examinations and establish standards of merit for a variety of federal jobs; it also forbade political candidates from soliciting contributions from government workers. The creation of a professional civil service thus helped bring the federal government in step with the modernizing trends transforming society. As for Chester A. Arthur, the fact that he proved to be a mediocre president pleasantly surprised those who had expected him to be an utter disaster. Arthur supported civil-service reform and proved quite independent. Fed up with the feuding Republicans, in 1882 the voters gave the Democrats a strong majority in the House of Representatives. In 1884, for the first time since 1856, they would put a Democrat in the White House: Grover Cleveland.

Pendleton Civil Service Act
Attempt to end spoils system and create a professional civil service

Politics of Privilege, Politics of Exclusion, 1884–1892

What factors prompted the rise of the Grange and the Farmers' Alliance movements?

▌The stalemate between the two major parties in their battle to establish the standards for economic growth continued under President Cleveland. Although no radical, Grover Cleveland challenged powerful interests by calling for cuts in the tariff and veterans' pensions. After Cleveland served a single term (1885–1889), one of the most corrupt elections in American history put Republican Benjamin Harrison (1889–1893) in the White House—and restored big business and the veterans' lobby to the driver's seat. Simultaneously, debt-ridden farmers mounted a spirited protest movement. And in the South, the white majority used the machinery of politics to strip black citizens of their basic rights.

A Democrat in the White House: Grover Cleveland, 1885–1889

At a tumultuous Chicago convention in 1884, the Republicans nominated their best-known leader, James G. Blaine. Blaine was a gifted orator; but his name had been stained by the revelation that he, as Speaker of the House, had offered political favors to a railroad company in exchange for stock. For reformers, Blaine epitomized the hated patronage system. To E. L. Godkin, he "wallowed in spoils like a rhinoceros in an African pool."

Sensing Blaine's vulnerability, the Democrats chose a sharply contrasting nominee, Grover Cleveland of New York. In a meteoric rise from reform mayor of Buffalo to governor, Cleveland had fought the bosses and spoils men. The shrewdness of the Democrats' choice became apparent when a number of prominent Republican reformers bolted to Cleveland. They were promptly nicknamed **Mugwumps,** an Algonquian term for a renegade chief.

Mugwumps Reformers, including E. L. Godkin and Carl Schurz, who switched from the Republican to the Democratic Party in 1884

Unfortunately, as a young man Cleveland had fathered an illegitimate child. He admitted the indiscretion, but the Republicans still jeered at rallies: "Ma, Ma, where's my pa?" (to which Democrats responded, "Gone to the White House ha ha ha"). Facing opposition from the New York City Democratic machine that he had fought as governor, Cleveland risked losing his own state. The tide turned in November when Blaine alienated Catholic voters by failing to rebuke a New York City Protestant clergyman who denounced the Democrats as the party of "Rum, Romanism, and Rebellion." Cleveland carried New York State by 1,200 votes and with it the election.

The corpulent Cleveland settled comfortably into the shadowy role expected of Gilded Age presidents. Embracing the belief that government must not meddle in the economy, he asserted the power of the presidency mostly through his vetoes and displayed a limited grasp of industrialization's impact. Vetoing a bill that would have provided seeds to drought-stricken farmers in Texas, he warned that people should not expect the government to solve their problems.

One matter did arouse Cleveland: the tariff, an issue entangled in conflicting economic and political interests. Since it was a major source of revenue in the era before a federal income tax, the tariff was really a form of taxation. But which imported goods should be taxed, and how much? Opinions differed radically. Producers of commodities like coal and wool demanded tariff protection against foreign competition, as did many manufacturers, joined by workers in these industries. Other manufacturers, however, while seeking protection for their finished products, wanted low tariffs on the raw materials they required. Most farmers hated all tariffs for inflating farm-equipment prices and making it hard to sell American farm products abroad.

Initially, Cleveland called for tariff reform largely because the high protective tariffs of the era were creating huge federal budget surpluses. In his 1887 annual message to Congress, Cleveland argued that lower tariffs not only would cut the federal surplus but also would reduce prices and slow the development of trusts. Although politicians paid little attention, corporate leaders found Cleveland's talk of lower tariffs threatening.

Cleveland stirred up another hornet's nest by opposing the routine payment of veterans' disability pensions. No one opposed pensions for the deserving, but fraudulent claims proliferated; one veteran collected a disability pension for poor eyesight caused, he said, by wartime diarrhea. Cleveland, unlike his predecessors, personally investigated these claims and rejected many. He also vetoed a bill that would have pensioned all disabled veterans and their dependents, whether or not the disability occurred in military service. The pension roll should be an honor roll, he stressed, not a refuge for frauds.

Big Business Strikes Back: Benjamin Harrison, 1889–1893

By 1888 some influential groups had concluded that Cleveland had to go. Republican kingmakers nominated Benjamin Harrison, a corporate lawyer and former senator. In a new style of electioneering, instead of sending the candidate around the country, his managers brought delegations to his Indiana home, where he hammered at the tariff issue. Harrison warned that only a high tariff could ensure business prosperity, decent wages, and a healthy home market for farmers. The Republicans amassed a $4 million campaign fund from worried business leaders. This war chest purchased not only posters and buttons but also votes.

Despite such fraud, Cleveland received almost 100,000 more votes than Harrison. But Harrison won the key states of New York and Indiana and won the electoral vote. Once in office, Harrison swiftly rewarded his supporters. He appointed as commissioner of pensions a GAR official who, on taking office, declared "God help the surplus!" The pension rolls soon ballooned from 676,000 to nearly a million. This massive pension system, coupled with a network of veterans' hospitals, became America's first large public-welfare program. In 1890 the triumphant Republicans also passed the McKinley Tariff, which pushed rates to an all-time high.

Rarely has the federal government been so subservient to entrenched economic interests and so out of touch with the plight of the disadvantaged as during the 1880s. But inaction bred discontent. The 1890 election awakened the nation to a tide of political activism in the agrarian South and West, spawned by chronic problems in rural America.

Agrarian Protest and the Rise of the People's Party

Plains farming had long been a risky venture (see Chapter 17). Between 1873 and 1877, terrible grasshopper infestations consumed half the midwestern wheat crop. After 1870, production rose and prices fell. Wheat tumbled from $2.95 a bushel in 1866 to $1.06 in 1880. Farmers who had borrowed to finance their homesteads and machinery went bankrupt or barely survived.

In 1867, midwestern farmers formed the **Grange,** or "Patrons of Husbandry." Membership climbed to more than 1.5 million by the early 1870s. Offering education, emotional support, and fellowship, the Grange maintained a library of information on planting and livestock, and organized covered-dish dinners and songfests. The

Grange First major farmers' political movement

Grange's central concern was farmers' economic plight. Grangers shared the Jacksonian belief that the products of the soil formed the basis of all honorable wealth and that the producer classes—people who worked with their hands—formed the true backbone of society. The Grange negotiated discounts from farm-machinery dealers and established "cash-only" cooperative stores and grain elevators to eliminate the "middlemen"—bankers, grain brokers, and merchants who grew rich at the farmers' expense. And the Grangers attacked the railroads, which gave discounts to large shippers, bribed state legislators, and charged higher rates for short runs than for long hauls. Midwestern Grangers lobbied state legislatures for laws setting maximum rates for freight shipments.

The railroads appealed these "Granger laws" to the Supreme Court. But in *Munn* v. *Illinois* (1877), the Court ruled against the railroads and upheld an Illinois law fixing a maximum rate for grain storage. The case of *Wabash* v. *Illinois* (1886), however, prohibited states from regulating *interstate* railroad rates. Then in 1887 Congress passed the Interstate Commerce Act, establishing a new agency, the Interstate Commerce Commission, to investigate and oversee railroad operations. The commission did little to curb the railroads, but it did establish the principle of federal regulation of interstate transportation.

Despite promising beginnings, the Grange movement soon faltered. By 1878, through lobbying at the state level, railroads had won repeal of most state regulations. The cash-only cooperatives failed because few farmers had cash. The Grange ideal of financial independence proved unrealistic because conditions prevailing on the Plains made it impossible to farm without borrowing money. When the prices of corn, wheat, and cotton briefly revived after 1878, many farmers deserted the Grange.

For all its weaknesses, however, the Grange laid the groundwork for an even more powerful wave of agrarian protest. The problems that drove midwestern and Great Plains farmers to form the Grange drove southern and western farmers to begin the alliance movement. The **Farmers' Alliance** movement began in the 1870s when Texas farmers gathered to discuss their problems, and it spread eastward across the lower South. Like Grangers, alliance members initially advocated farmers' cooperatives to purchase equipment and supplies and to market their cotton. And, as had the Grange cooperatives, these generally failed for lack of capital.

In 1887 a farsighted Texan, Charles W. Macune, assumed leadership of the alliance movement. By 1889 Macune had merged several regional groups into the National Farmers' Alliance and Industrial Union, or the Southern Alliance. A parallel organization of black farmers emerged, the National Colored Farmers' Alliance. By 1890 the Southern Alliance boasted 3 million members and its black counterpart another 1.2 million. As they attended alliance rallies and picnics, read the alliance newspaper, and listened to alliance speakers, hard-hit farm families became increasingly aware of their political potential. An Arkansas member wrote in 1889, "Reform never begins with the leaders, it comes from the people."

Meanwhile, alliance fever also hit the Great Plains, where alliances sprang up in Kansas, Nebraska, Iowa, and Minnesota in the drought-plagued years of 1880 and 1881. After renewed rainfall nourished a brief boom, drought returned to rekindle the alliance spirit in 1886–1887. From 1887 to 1897, only two Great Plains wheat crops were worth harvesting. To make matters worse, wheat prices fell as world production increased. Innumerable Midwestern families packed up and returned East.

Primary Source: The Farmers' Movement in the West

Farmers' Alliance Successful farm protest movement; spawned Populist party

Some departing families scrawled a sad refrain on their wagons: "In God we trusted, in Kansas we busted."

Reformers at first tried to create a biracial movement. Southern Alliance leaders Tom Watson of Georgia and Leonidas Polk of North Carolina urged southern farmers, black and white, to act together. For a time, this message of racial cooperation in the interest of reform offered promise. Women were involved in the movement as well. Mary E. Lease, a Wichita lawyer, burst on the scene in 1890 as a fiery alliance orator. Other women rallied to the new cause, founding the National Women's Alliance (NWA) in 1891.

As the movement swelled, the opposition turned nasty. Jerry Simpson, a Kansas alliance leader, mentioned the silk stockings of a conservative politician in his district and noted that he had no such finery. In response, a hostile newspaper editor labeled him "Sockless Jerry" Simpson, the nickname he carried to his grave. When Mary Lease advised Kansans to "raise less corn and more hell," a conservative newspaper sneered, "[Kansas] has started to raise hell, as Mrs. Lease advised, and [the state] seems to have an overproduction."

All this activity helped shape a new political agenda. In 1889 the Southern and Northwestern alliances arranged a loose merger and supported candidates who agreed with them. They focused on increasing government action on behalf of farmers and workers, and sought tariff reduction, a graduated income tax, public ownership of railroads, federal funding for irrigation research, a prohibition on landownership by aliens, and "the free and unlimited coinage of silver."

The 1890 elections revealed the strength of agrarian discontent. Southern Democrats who endorsed alliance goals won four governorships and control of eight state legislatures. On the Great Plains, alliance-endorsed candidates controlled Kansas and Nebraska and gained the balance of power in Minnesota and South Dakota. Three alliance-backed senators and fifty congressmen went to Washington in 1890 as angry winds from the hinterlands buffeted the political system.

Regional differences, which threatened to divide the movement, were soon overcome by shared economic grievance. In February 1892, alliance leaders organized the People's Party of the United States, generally called the **Populist Party.** At the party convention in Omaha, Nebraska, that August, cheering delegates nominated for president the former Civil War general James B. Weaver of Iowa. The Populist platform called for the direct popular election of senators and other electoral reforms. It also endorsed a **subtreasury plan** by which farmers could store their nonperishable commodities in government warehouses and then sell the stored commodities when market prices rose. Ignatius Donnelly's ringing preamble called for a return of the government "to the hands of 'the plain people' with which class it originated."

Populist Party Agrarian-based third-party challenge to Republicans and Democrats

subtreasury plan Charles Macune's plan to bring government aid to struggling farmers

African-Americans After Reconstruction

As populists geared up, a group of citizens with far more profound grievances suffered renewed oppression. With the end of Reconstruction in 1877 and the restoration of power to white elites, southern whites sought an end to "Negro rule" and tried to suppress the black vote (see Chapter 16). Initially, whites relied on intimidation, terror, and fraud to limit black voting rights, but in 1890 Mississippi amended its state constitution to exclude most African-American voters, and other southern states followed suit.

Because the Fifteenth Amendment (1870) had guaranteed all male citizens' right to vote, white southerners used indirect means, such as literacy tests, poll taxes, and property requirements, to disfranchise African-Americans. To ensure that these measures excluded only blacks, whites employed such devices as the grandfather clause, which exempted anyone whose ancestor had voted in 1860. African-American disfranchisement proceeded erratically, but by the early twentieth century it was effectively complete.

Disfranchisement was the keystone of an arch of white supremacy that stretched across the South as state after state passed laws strictly segregating many realms of life by race (see Chapter 21). African-American caterers, barbers, contractors, bricklayers, carpenters, and other artisans lost their white clientele. Blacks who went to prison—sometimes for minor offenses—faced the convict-lease system, which allowed cotton planters and others to "lease" prison gangs and to put them to work under slave-labor conditions. Thousands died under the brutal convict-labor system. It survived in to the early decades of the twentieth century, ultimately succumbing to humanitarian protest and to economic changes that made it unprofitable.

lynching Vigilante hanging of those accused of crimes; used primarily against blacks

Lynching became the ultimate enforcer of white supremacy. Through the 1880s and 1890s, about a hundred African-Americans were lynched annually in the United States, mainly in the South. Rumors and unsubstantiated accusations, frequently of raping a white woman, unleashed this mob violence. (The vague charge of "attempted rape" could mean a wide range of behavior unacceptable to whites, such as questioning authority or talking back.)

The lynch mob demonstrated whites' absolute power. In the South, more than 80 percent of the lynchings involved black victims. Lynchings most commonly occurred in the Cotton Belt, and they tended to rise at times of economic distress when cotton prices were falling and competition between poor whites and poor blacks was most intense. Not surprisingly, lynching reached its highest point in 1892 as many poor African-Americans joined the agrarian protest and rallied to the Populist party banner.

The relationship between southern agrarian protest and white racism was complex. Some Populists, among them Georgia's Tom Watson, tried to build a genuinely interracial movement and denounced both lynching and the convict-lease system. When an African-American Populist leader pursued by a lynch mob took refuge in Watson's house during the 1892 campaign, he summoned two thousand armed white Populists to defend him. But most white Populists, encouraged by such rabble-rousers as "Pitchfork Ben" Tillman of South Carolina, held fast to racism. And the white ruling elite, eager to drive a wedge in the protest movement, inflamed lower-class white racism. On balance, the rise of southern agrarian protest deepened racial hatred and worsened blacks' situation. Meanwhile, the federal government did nothing. A generation of northern politicians paid lip service to egalitarian principles and failed to apply them to African-Americans.

Plessy v. Ferguson Supreme Court ruling validating "separate but equal"

The Supreme Court similarly abandoned African-Americans. The Court ripped gaping holes in the Fourteenth Amendment, which guaranteed equal protection of the law, and the Civil Rights Act of 1875, which outlawed racial discrimination. In the *Civil Rights Cases* (1883), the Court ruled that the Fourteenth Amendment prevented governments, but not individuals, from infringing on civil rights. In **Plessy v. Ferguson** (1896), the Court upheld a Louisiana law requiring segregated railroad cars. Racial segregation was legal, the justices ruled, provided that equal facilities were made available to each race. With the Supreme Court's blessing, the South also segregated its public schools, ignoring the caveat that separate facilities must be equal. White children studied in nicer buildings, used newer equipment, and were taught by better-paid teachers than black children. Not until 1954 would the Court abandon the "separate but equal" doctrine. Rounding out a dismal record, the justices in 1898 upheld the poll tax and literacy tests. Such racist and separatist policies affected blacks nationwide, Mexicans in Texas, and Asians in California among other groups.

Few northerners protested the South's white-supremacist society. The restoration of sectional harmony came at a high price: northern acquiescence in the utter debasement of a people whose freedom had cost the lives of thousands of northern men.

Blacks responded to their plight in various ways. The nation's foremost African-American leader from the 1890s until his death in 1915 was **Booker T. Washington.** Born into slavery in Virginia in 1856, the son of a slave woman and her white master, Washington enrolled at a freedman's school in Hampton, Virginia, and in 1881 organized a state vocational school in Tuskegee (tuss-KEE-ghee), Alabama, which became Tuskegee University. Washington attained prominence in 1895 when he gave an address in Atlanta insisting that the first task of African-Americans must be to acquire vocational skills. Once blacks proved their economic value, he predicted, racism would ebb; meanwhile, they must accept their lot. Washington lectured widely, and his autobiography, *Up From Slavery* (1901), recounted his rise from poverty thanks to honesty, hard work, and kindly patrons—themes familiar from Horatio Alger's books.

Booker T. Washington
Leading black figure of late nineteenth century; stressed education and accommodation

Other blacks responded resourcefully to racism. Black churches provided emotional support, as did black fraternal lodges. And a handful of African-Americans established banks and successful businesses, such as insurance companies and barbershops.

Meanwhile, voices of black protest never wholly died out. Frederick Douglass urged that blacks press on for full equality. "Who would be free, themselves must strike the first blow," he proclaimed in 1883. But for others, the solution was to leave the South. In 1879 several thousand moved to Kansas, and ten thousand migrated to Chicago between 1870 and 1890. Blacks who went north, however, discovered that public opinion sanctioned many forms of de facto discrimination.

The rise of the so-called solid South, firmly established on racist foundations, had important political implications. The Republican Party had practically no presence in the South. For nearly a century, the only important election in most southern states was the Democratic primary. Furthermore, the large bloc of southern Democrats in Congress accumulated seniority and power, and helped shape public policy. Finally, southern Democrats wielded enormous clout in the national party. No Democratic contender for national office who was unacceptable to them stood a chance.

Above all, the rigid caste system of the post-Reconstruction South shaped the consciousness of those caught up in it, black and white alike.

CHECKING IN

- Grover Cleveland attempted tariff reforms and tried to gain control of the pension system.

- Big business and the GAR combined to defeat Cleveland in 1888.

- The Grange movement rose as an attempt by farmers to reassert control over their lives, which seemed to be at the mercy of railroads, middlemen, and bankers.

- The Alliance superseded the Grange and ultimately organized the Populist party in 1892.

- African-Americans were increasingly shut out of political life; they turned to accommodationist leaders like Booker T. Washington.

Describing her girlhood in the turn-of-the-century South, white novelist Lillian Smith wrote, "I learned it is possible to pray at night and ride a Jim Crow car the next morning; . . . to glow when the word democracy was used, and to practice slavery from morning to night."

THE 1890S: POLITICS IN A DEPRESSION DECADE

Why did William Jennings Bryan fail to win the presidency in 1896?

In the 1890s smoldering discontent with the major parties and their support for unrestricted business enterprise burst into flames. As banks failed and railroads went bankrupt, the nation slid into a grinding depression. The crises of the 1890s laid bare the paralysis of the federal government—dominated by a business elite—when confronted by the new social realities of factories, urban slums, immigrant workers, and desperate farmers. In response, irate farmers, laborers, and their supporters joined a new party, the Populists, to change the system.

1892: Populists Challenge the Status Quo

The Populist Party platform adopted in July 1892 offered a broad vision of national reform. That same month, thirteen people died in a gun battle between strikers and strikebreakers at the Homestead steel plant near Pittsburgh, and President Harrison sent federal troops to Idaho, where a silver-mine strike had turned violent. Events seemed to justify the Populists' warnings of chaos ahead.

The 1892 campaign for the White House was a replay of 1888, Harrison versus Cleveland, but this time Cleveland won by more than 360,000 votes, a decisive margin in an age of close elections. A public reaction against labor violence and the McKinley Tariff hurt Harrison. Meanwhile, a solid showing by Populist candidates sparked great hopes for the future. Their presidential candidate, James B. Weaver, got more than 1 million votes, 8.5 percent of the total, and the Populists elected five senators, ten congressmen, and three governors. But the party's strength was spotty; it made no dent in New England or the urban East and little in the Midwest.

In the South, racism, Democratic loyalty, distaste for the former Union general Weaver, and widespread intimidation and voter fraud kept the Populist tally under 25 percent. The party's failure killed the prospects for interracial agrarian reform. After 1892 southern politicians seeking to appeal to poor whites—including a disillusioned Tom Watson—stayed within the Democratic fold and laced their populism with racism.

Capitalism in Crisis: The Depression of 1893–1897

Cleveland soon confronted a major crisis: an economic collapse in the railroad industry that quickly spread. Railroads had led the awesome industrial growth of the 1880s, triggering both investment and speculation. In the early 1890s railroad growth slowed, affecting other industries, including iron and steel. The first hint of trouble flared up in February 1893 when the Philadelphia and Reading Railroad failed.

This bankruptcy occurred at a moment of weakened confidence in the government's ability to redeem paper money with gold on demand. Economic problems in London in 1890 had forced British investors to unload millions of dollars in American stocks; $68 million in U.S. gold reserves flowed across the Atlantic to Britain. At the same time, heavy spending on pensions and pork-barrel projects had substantially reduced the federal surplus, while paying for silver purchases under the Sherman Silver Purchase Act was straining the gold reserve. From January 1892 to March 1893 (the month Cleveland was inaugurated), the gold reserve had fallen to $100 million, the minimum considered necessary to support the dollar. This decline alarmed those who viewed the gold standard as the only sure evidence of the government's financial stability.

With the collapse of the Philadelphia and Reading, fear fed on itself as panicky investors converted their stock holdings to gold. Stock prices plunged, the gold reserve plummeted, and by the end of the year seventy-four railroads, six hundred banks, and fifteen thousand businesses had failed. The **Panic of 1893** set off four years of hard times. By 1897 one-third of the nation's railroad mileage was in bankruptcy. The railroad boom had spurred the prosperity of the 1880s, and the railroad collapse of the 1890s battered the economy into a full-scale depression.

Panic of 1893 Wall Street collapse that touched off a nationwide economic depression

The crisis took a heavy human toll. Industrial unemployment soared to as much as 25 percent. Millions of factory workers had no money to buy food or heat their homes, and jobless men tramped the streets looking for work. Unusually harsh winters in 1893 and 1894 aggravated the misery, especially in major cities. In New York City, where the crisis quickly swamped local relief agencies, a minister reported actual starvation.

Rural America, already hard hit by declining agricultural prices, faced ruin. Corn plummeted from 50¢ to 21¢ a bushel and wheat from 84¢ to 51¢. Cotton fell to 5¢ a pound.

Some desperate Americans turned to protest. In Massillon, Ohio, self-taught monetary expert Jacob Coxey proposed as a solution to unemployment a $500 million public-works program funded with paper money. Coxey organized a march on Washington to lobby for his scheme. Thousands joined him en route, and several hundred actually reached Washington in late April 1894. Police arrested Coxey and other leaders when they attempted to enter the Capitol grounds, and his "army" broke up. Although some considered Coxey eccentric, his proposal closely resembled programs that the government would adopt during the depression of the 1930s.

As unrest intensified, fear clutched middle-class Americans. A church magazine demanded that troops put "a pitiless stop" to outbreaks of unrest. To some observers, a bloody upheaval seemed imminent.

Business Leaders Respond

In the face of suffering and turmoil, Cleveland retreated into a laissez-faire fortress. Boom-and-bust economic cycles were inevitable, he insisted, and government could do nothing. Missing the larger picture, Cleveland focused on a single peripheral issue, the gold standard. In August 1893 he persuaded Congress to repeal the Sherman Silver Purchase Act, which he blamed for the dwindling gold reserve.

Nevertheless, the gold drain continued. In early 1895, with the gold reserve down to $41 million, Cleveland turned to Wall Street. Bankers J. P. Morgan and

August Belmont agreed to lend the government $62 million in exchange for discounted U.S. bonds. The government then purchased gold to replenish the reserve, and Morgan and Belmont resold their bonds for a substantial profit. The deal helped to restore confidence in the government's economic stability. However, Cleveland's gambit to save the gold standard came at a high price. His deal with Morgan and Belmont, and the handsome profits they made, confirmed radicals' suspicions of an unholy alliance between Washington and Wall Street.

As the tariff battle made clear, corporate interests held the whip hand. Although Cleveland favored tariff reform, the Democrat-controlled Congress of 1892–1893 generally yielded to high-tariff lobbyists. The Wilson-Gorman Tariff of 1894 made so many concessions to special interests that a disgusted president allowed it to become law without his signature.

One feature of the Wilson-Gorman Tariff suggested an enlarging vision of government's role in an age of towering fortunes: an income tax of 2 percent on all income over $4,000 (roughly $40,000 in present-day purchasing power). But in 1895 the Supreme Court declared the tax unconstitutional. Thus, whether one looked at the executive, the legislature, or the judiciary, Washington's subordination to the corporate elite seemed nearly complete.

The depression also helped reorient social thought. Middle-class charitable workers, long convinced that individual character flaws caused poverty, now realized that even sober, hard-working people could succumb to economic forces beyond their control. Laissez-faire ideology weakened in the 1890s, as depression-worn Americans adopted a broader conception of government's proper role in dealing with the social consequences of industrialization. This new perspective would activate powerful political energies. The depression, in short, not only brought suffering; it also taught lessons.

1894: Protest Grows Louder

Republican gains in the 1894 midterm elections revealed popular revulsion against Cleveland and the Democrats, who were blamed for the hard times. As 1896 approached, the monetary question became the overriding symbolic issue. Conservatives clung to the gold standard, but advocates of "free silver" triumphed at the Democratic convention when a young champion of silver, **William Jennings Bryan,** secured the nomination. Despite Bryan's eloquence, Republican William McKinley emerged victorious. His triumph laid the groundwork for a major political realignment that would influence American politics for a generation.

The midterm election of 1894 spelled Democratic disaster. Immigrants, who were battered by the depression, abandoned their traditional Democratic allegiance, and Republicans gained control of Congress and several key states. Populist candidates won nearly 1.5 million votes, 40 percent over their 1892 total. Most Populist gains came in the South.

The serious economic conflict that split Americans focused on a symbolic issue: free silver. Cleveland's rigid defense of the gold standard forced his opponents into an exaggerated obsession with silver, obscuring the genuine issues dividing rich and poor, creditor and debtor, and farmer and city dweller. Conservatives tirelessly upheld the gold standard, and agrarian radicals—urged on and sometimes financed by western silver-mine owners—extolled silver as a universal cure-all.

William Jennings Bryan
Orator, champion of farm interests, anti-imperialist, three-time Democratic presidential candidate

Silver Advocates Capture the Democratic Party

At the 1896 Democratic convention in Chicago, western and southern delegates adopted a platform demanding the free and unlimited coinage of silver—in effect, repudiating the Cleveland administration. An ardent advocate of the silver cause captured the party's nomination: William Jennings Bryan of Nebraska. Only thirty-six, the young lawyer had already served western agrarian interests during two terms in Congress.

Joining Christian imagery with economic analysis, Bryan gave his major convention speech during the debate over the platform. His booming voice carried his rousing words to the highest galleries of the convention hall. Praising farmers as the nation's bedrock, Bryan roared to the cheering delegates, "You shall not press down upon the brow of labor this crown of thorns, you shall not crucify mankind upon a cross of gold."

The silverites' capture of the Democratic party left the Populists with a dilemma. Free silver was only one reform among many that they advocated. If they jumped aboard the Bryan bandwagon, they would abandon their own program. But a separate Populist ticket would siphon votes from Bryan and guarantee a Republican victory. Reluctantly, the Populists endorsed Bryan. Meanwhile, the Republicans nominated former Ohio governor William McKinley on a platform endorsing the high protective tariff and the gold standard.

Primary Source: The Sacrilegious Candidate

1896: Republicans Triumphant

Bryan did his best to sustain the momentum of the Chicago convention, crisscrossing the country by train to deliver his free-silver campaign speech. One skeptical editor compared him to Nebraska's notoriously shallow Platte River: six inches deep and a mile wide at the mouth.

Mark Hanna, a Cleveland industrialist, managed the Republican McKinley's campaign. Dignified and aloof, McKinley could not match Bryan's popular touch.

William McKinley's "Front-Porch" Campaign, 1896

McKinley (front row, sixth from left) poses with an Italian-American brass band from Buffalo, New York, in front of his home in Canton, Ohio.

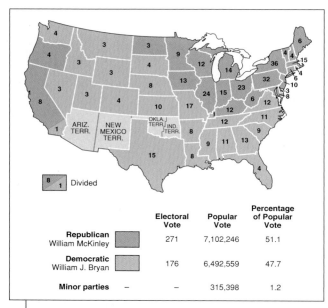

	Electoral Vote	Popular Vote	Percentage of Popular Vote
Republican William McKinley	271	7,102,246	51.1
Democratic William J. Bryan	176	6,492,559	47.7
Minor parties	–	315,398	1.2

Map 20.1   The Election of 1896

CHECKING IN

- Populists polled more than a million votes in the 1892 presidential election.

- The Panic of 1893 hardened into a deep depression; want and suffering were widespread.

- Coxey's Army showed the depth of discontent with the political system; nevertheless, corporate interests continued to dominate national politics.

- The midterm elections of 1894 showed revulsion against the Democrats, whom voters blamed for the depression following the panic of 1893.

- In 1896 the Democrats bowed to free-silver interests and nominated William Jennings Bryan after he electrified the convention with his "cross of gold" speech.

- Republican William McKinley defeated Bryan on a conservative platform. Populism collapsed, paving the way for a Republican majority that would dominate national politics for the next fifteen years.

Accordingly, Hanna built the campaign not around the candidate but around posters, pamphlets, and newspaper editorials. These publications warned of the dangers of free silver, caricatured Bryan as a radical, and portrayed McKinley and the gold standard as twin pillars of prosperity.

Drawing on a war chest possibly as large as $7 million, Hanna spent lavishly. J. P. Morgan and John D. Rockefeller together contributed $500,000 to the McKinley campaign, more than Bryan's total campaign contributions. McKinley himself stayed home in Canton, Ohio, emerging occasionally to read speeches to visiting delegations. All told, some 750,000 people trekked to Canton to take part in McKinley's cleverly organized "front-porch campaign."

On election day, McKinley beat Bryan by over six hundred thousand votes (see Map 20.1). He swept the Northeast and the Midwest and even carried three farm states beyond the Mississippi as well as California and Oregon. Bryan's strength was limited to the South and the Great Plains and mountain states.

Why did Bryan lose despite protest spirit abroad in the land? His core constituency, while passionately loyal, was limited. Seduced by free silver, the Democrats had upheld a platform and a candidate with little appeal for factory workers. Urban voters, realizing that higher farm prices also meant higher food prices, went heavily for McKinley. Cultural differences were also in play. To urban Catholics and Jews, this teetotaling Nebraskan thundering like a Protestant revival preacher seemed utterly alien. Finally, the Populists' effort to define a democratic alternative relied heavily on visions of a premodern economic order of independent farmers and entrepreneurs. Although appealing, this vision bore little relationship to the new corporate order taking shape in America.

The McKinley administration translated its conservative platform into law. The Dingley Tariff (1897) pushed rates to all-time highs, and the Currency Act of 1900 committed the United States to the gold standard. Because of returning prosperity, rising farm prices, and the discovery of gold in Alaska, these measures roused little opposition, and McKinley easily defeated Bryan again in 1900.

The elections of 1894 and 1896 produced a Republican majority that, except for Woodrow Wilson's presidency (1913–1921), would dominate national politics until the election of Franklin D. Roosevelt in 1932. Populism collapsed, but an emerging new reform movement, progressivism, would bring many populist reform proposals to fruition.

EXPANSIONIST STIRRINGS AND WAR WITH SPAIN, 1878–1901

Why did the United States go to war with Spain and become an imperial power?

The same corporate elite that dominated late-nineteenth-century domestic politics influenced U.S. foreign policy as well, contributing to surging expansionist pressures. Business leaders, politicians, statesmen, and editorial writers insisted that national greatness required that America match Europe's imperial expansion. Fanned by sensationalistic newspaper coverage of a Cuban struggle for independence and by elite calls for greater American international assertiveness, war between the United States and Spain broke out in 1898.

Roots of Expansionist Sentiment

Ever since the first European settlers had colonized North America's Atlantic coast, the newcomers had been an expansionist people. By the 1840s the push westward had acquired a name: Manifest Destiny. Directed inward after 1865 toward the settlement of the trans-Mississippi West (see Chapter 17), this impulse turned outward in the 1880s as Americans followed the imperial example set by Great Britain, France, Belgium, Italy, Germany, and Japan. Furthermore, many business leaders believed that continued domestic prosperity required overseas markets. Foreign markets offered a safety valve for potentially explosive pressures in the U.S. economy. National greatness, it appeared, demanded an empire.

Proponents of a strong navy contributed to the expansionist mood. In *The Influence of Sea Power upon History* (1890), **Alfred Thayer Mahan** equated sea power with national greatness and urged a rapid U.S. naval buildup, which required overseas bases. Meanwhile, some religious leaders proclaimed America's mission to spread Christianity, an argument with racist tinges. One minister averred that "God is training the Anglo-Saxon race for its mission"—a mission of bringing Christianity and civilization to the world's "weaker races."

Alfred Thayer Mahan Leading proponent of imperialism, sea power

A group of Republican expansionists, led by Senator Henry Cabot Lodge, diplomat John Hay, and Theodore Roosevelt of New York, preached imperial greatness and military might. "I should welcome almost any war," declared Roosevelt in 1897; ". . . this country needs one" (see Map 20.2). Such advocates of expansionism applied Social Darwinist rhetoric of the day to argue that war, as a vehicle for natural selection, would test and refurbish American manhood, honor, and civic commitment. This gendered appeal both counterbalanced concerns about women's political activism and helped forge the disparate arguments for expansionism into a simple, visceral plea that had a broad appeal.

A series of diplomatic skirmishes in the mid-1890s revealed the newly assertive American mood. In the mid-1880s, quarrels between the United States and Great Britain had flared over fishing rights in the North Atlantic and North Pacific, reawakening latent anti-British feelings and the old dream of acquiring Canada.

In 1898 a compromise settled the fishing rights dispute, but by then attention had shifted to Latin America. In 1891 tensions had flared between the United States

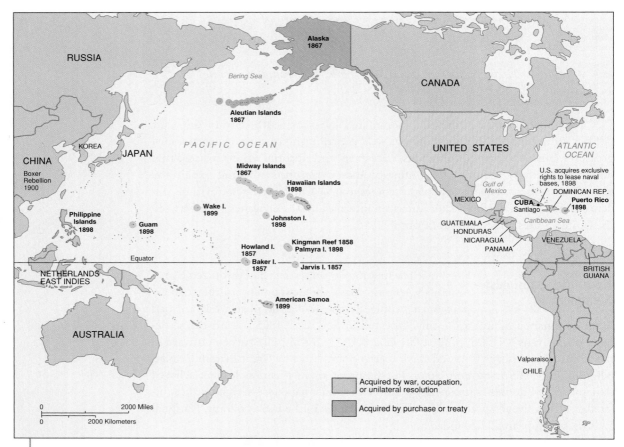

Map 20.2   U.S. Territorial Expansion in the Late Nineteenth Century

The major period of U.S. territorial expansion abroad came in a short burst of activity in the late 1890s, when newspapers and some politicians beat the drums for empire.

Interactive Map: U.S. Territorial Expansion in the Late 19th Century

and Chile after a mob in Valparaiso (val-puh-RYE-zoh) killed two American sailors on shore leave. War fever subsided after Chile apologized and paid an indemnity of $75,000.

Another Latin American conflict arose from a boundary dispute between Venezuela and British Guiana (ghee-AHN-uh) in 1895. When the British rejected a U.S. arbitration offer, a livid Grover Cleveland asked Congress to set up a commission to settle the dispute even without Britain's approval. As patriotic fervor pulsed through the nation, the British in 1897 accepted the commission's findings.

Pacific Expansion

Meanwhile, the U.S. Navy focused on the Samoan (suh-MOH-un) Islands in the South Pacific, where it sought the port of Pago Pago (PON-go PON-go) as a refueling station. In March 1889 the United States narrowly avoided a naval clash with Germany over the islands when a timely hurricane wrecked both fleets. Ultimately, America established a three-way protectorate over the islands with Germany and Great Britain.

The **Hawaiian Islands,** with their economic and strategic significance, also beckoned U.S. imperialists. American missionaries and merchants had been active in the islands since the end of the eighteenth century. American-owned sugar plantations worked by Chinese and Japanese laborers dominated the Hawaiian economy. Under an 1887 treaty, the United States built a naval base at Pearl Harbor, near Honolulu. Then in 1891, angered by American economic domination, islanders welcomed Liliuokalani (lil-ee-oo-oh-ka-LAW-nee) to the Hawaiian throne. Strong-willed and hostile toward Americans, she became queen amid a crisis set off by a U.S. decision in 1890 to tax Hawaiian sugar. Hawaiian sugar prices plunged 40 percent as a result. Facing ruin, the planters deposed the queen in January 1893, proclaimed the independent Republic of Hawaii, and requested U.S. annexation.

The grab for Hawaii troubled Cleveland, especially when an emissary whom he sent cast doubt on whether the Hawaiians desired annexation. But when McKinley succeeded Cleveland, annexation moved rapidly forward, and in 1898 Congress proclaimed Hawaii an American territory. Sixty-one years later, it joined the Union as the fiftieth state.

Hawaiian Islands Independent island nation in Pacific Ocean annexed by U.S. in 1898

Crisis over Cuba

In 1898 American attention shifted to Cuba, where a rebellion against Spanish rule had erupted in 1895. American businessmen had $50 million invested in the island and annually imported $100 million in sugar and other products from Cuba. Revolutionary turmoil would jeopardize these interests. Neither the Cleveland nor the McKinley administration supported the rebellion.

But the rebels' cause aroused popular sympathy in the United States. This support increased with revelations that the Spanish commander in Cuba, Valeriano Weyler (vah-lair-ee-AH-no WAY-ler), was herding vast numbers of Cubans into squalid camps. Malnutrition and disease turned these camps into hellholes in which perhaps two hundred thousand Cubans died.

Fueling American anger were sensational stories published by two competing New York newspapers, William Randolph Hearst's *Journal* and Joseph Pulitzer's *World*. The *Journal*'s color comic strip "The Yellow Kid" provided a term for Hearst's debased editorial approach: yellow journalism. In the cutthroat battle for readers, both editors exploited the Cuban crisis, turning rumor into fact and detailing "Butcher" Weyler's atrocities.

In 1897 a new, more liberal Spanish government sought a peaceful solution to the Cuban crisis. But Hearst and Pulitzer continued to inflame public opinion. On February 8, 1898, Hearst's *Journal* published a private letter from a Spanish diplomat describing McKinley as "weak" and "a bidder for the admiration of the crowd." Irritation over this incident turned to outrage on February 15, 1898, when an explosion rocked the battleship *Maine* in Havana harbor, killing 226 American crewmen. Scholarly opinion about what caused the explosion is still divided, but a careful review of the evidence in 1998 concluded that a mine most likely set off the ammunition explosion that sank the ship. Newspaper headlines at the time blamed the same cause and war spirit flared high.

Despite further Spanish concessions, on April 11 McKinley sent a war message to Congress, and legislators passed a joint resolution recognizing Cuba's independence and authorizing force to expel the Spanish. The Teller amendment introduced by Senator Henry M. Teller of Colorado declared that the United States had no desire for "sovereignty, jurisdiction, or control" in Cuba and pledged that America would leave the island alone once independence was assured.

The Spanish-American War, 1898

The war with Spain involved only a few days of actual combat. Action began on May 1, 1898, when a U.S. fleet under Admiral George Dewey steamed into Manila (muh-NILL-uh) Bay in the Philippines and destroyed or captured all ten Spanish ships anchored there, at the cost of 1 American and 381 Spanish lives. In mid-August, U.S. troops occupied the capital, Manila.

In Cuba, the war's only significant land engagement took place on July 1 when American troops seized two strongly defended Spanish garrisons on El Caney Hill and San Juan (sahn wahn) Hill overlooking the Spanish military stronghold of Santiago de Cuba (sahn-tee-AH-go day cue-bah). Leading the volunteer "Rough Riders" at San Juan Hill was Theodore Roosevelt, getting his taste of war—and abundant publicity—at last. Two days later, the Spanish fleet at Santiago de Cuba made a gallant but doomed break for the open sea. Blockading American ships sank the seven ancient vessels, killing 474 Spaniards and ending four hundred years of Spanish empire in America.

John Hay thought that it had all been "a splendid little war," but many who served in Cuba found it far from splendid. They went into battle in the tropical midsummer wearing heavy wool uniforms, received abysmal medical care, and died in droves from yellow fever, food poisoning, and malaria. The United States lost more than 5,000 men in Cuba, only 379 of them in combat.

The thousands of black troops who fought in Cuba encountered Jim Crow racism at assembly points in Georgia and their embarkation port in Tampa, Florida. In

Primary Source: War Dead

African-American Soldiers of the Tenth U.S. Cavalry in Cuba, July 1898

These men posed shortly after the capture of San Juan Hill. Black troops, known as buffalo soldiers, played an important role in the Spanish-American War, but they were subject to harassment and discrimination.

Tampa, taunted by whites and refused service at restaurants and bars, some black troops exploded in riotous rage on June 6; white troops from Georgia restored order. The transport ships that carried troops to Cuba were segregated, with black troops often confined to the lowest quarters in stifling heat and denied permission to mingle on deck with other units. Despite such encounters with racism, African-American troops served with honor in Cuba, playing key roles in the battles of San Juan Hill and El Caney Hill.

The Spanish sought an armistice on July 17. In the peace treaty signed that December in Paris, Spain recognized Cuba's independence and, after a U.S. payment of $20 million, ceded the Philippines, Puerto Rico, and the Pacific island of Guam to the United States. Americans now possessed an island empire stretching from the Caribbean to the Pacific.

From 1898 to 1902 the U.S. Army governed Cuba under the command of General Leonard Wood. Wood's administration improved public health, education, and sanitation but violated the spirit of the 1898 Teller Amendment. The troops eventually withdrew, although the so-called **Platt Amendment** (1901), requested by the War Department, authorized the withdrawal only after Cuba agreed not to make any treaty with a foreign power limiting its independence and not to borrow beyond its means. The United States also reserved the right to intervene in Cuba and to establish a naval base there, Guantánamo (gwan-TAHN-uh-moh) Bay, near Santiago de Cuba, which it still maintains. The Platt Amendment remained in force until 1934. U.S. investments in Cuba, some $50 million in 1898, soared to $500 million by 1920.

Platt Amendment Agreement to withdraw U.S. troops from Cuba; U.S. maintained a naval base

Critics of Empire

Some Americans had opposed imperialism for more than a decade, and the victories in Cuba and the Philippines did not bring universal praise. Although few in number, the critics were influential. Some of them, like Carl Schurz and E. L. Godkin, were former Mugwumps. Other anti-imperialists included William Jennings Bryan, settlement-house founder Jane Addams, novelist Mark Twain, and Harvard philosopher William James. Steel king Andrew Carnegie gave thousands of dollars to the cause. In 1898 these critics of empire had formed the **Anti-Imperialist League.**

Anti-Imperialist League Small but influential group that opposed imperialism

For the United States to rule other peoples, the anti-imperialists believed, was to violate the principles of the Declaration of Independence and the Constitution. The military fever that accompanied expansionism also dismayed the anti-imperialists.

In February 1899 the anti-imperialists failed by one vote to prevent Senate ratification of the expansionist peace treaty with Spain, and McKinley's overwhelming victory in 1900 over anti-imperialist Bryan eroded the cause. Nevertheless, at a time of jingoistic rhetoric and militaristic posturing, the opponents of expansion had upheld an older, finer vision of America.

Guerrilla War in the Philippines, 1898–1902

Events in the Philippines confirmed the anti-imperialists' worst fears. When the Spanish-American War began, few Americans knew what or where the Philippine Islands were. American business, though, saw them as a stepping-stone to the rich China market.

McKinley, reflecting the prevailing mood as always, reasoned that the Filipinos were unready for self-government and would be gobbled up if set adrift in a world of imperial rivalries. He further persuaded himself that American rule would enormously benefit a people he called "our little brown brothers." A devout Methodist, he explained that America's mission was "to educate the Filipinos, and to uplift and civilize and Christianize them, and by God's grace do the very best we could by them." (Most Filipinos were already Christian, a legacy of centuries of Spanish rule.) Having prayerfully reached his decision, McKinley instructed the American peace negotiators in Paris to insist on U.S. acquisition of the Philippines.

"Uplifting" the Philippines proved difficult. In 1896 young **Emilio Aguinaldo** (eh-MEEL-ee-oh ah-gwin-ALL-doh) had organized a Filipino independence movement to drive out the Spanish. In the summer of 1898, with arms supplied by Admiral Dewey, Aguinaldo's forces captured most of Luzon (loo-ZAHN), the Philippines' main island. Aguinaldo proclaimed Filipino independence and drafted a democratic constitution. In 1899, feeling betrayed by the U.S. decision to take possession of his country, Aguinaldo ordered his troops to fight the occupying American army.

It took the United States four years to crush the Filipino independence movement, which waged a guerrilla war against the U.S. forces. More than 125,000 American troops ultimately served in the Philippine jungles, and 4,000 died. As many as 20,000 Filipino independence fighters perished. As in the later Vietnam and Iraq Wars, casualties and suffering ravaged the civilian population as well. Historians estimate that at least 200,000 civilians died in the conflict. Aguinaldo was captured in March 1901, but large-scale guerrilla fighting continued through the summer of 1902.

In 1902 a special Senate committee heard testimony from veterans of the Philippines war about executing prisoners, torturing suspects, and burning villages. The humanitarian mood of 1898, when Americans had rushed to save Cuba from the cruel Spaniards, seemed remote indeed. In retrospect, the American troops' attitude toward the Filipinos, although deplorable, is not hard to understand. The cauldron of immigration, imperialism, and the "winning of the West" intermixed racist concerns over "backward" and "useless" peoples with rhetorical pleas for supervision and stewardship. In the process, as was evident in the treatment of American Indians, well-meaning paternalism often degenerated into deadly domination.

The years of expansionism and the subjugation of the Philippines had proclaimed America's debut on the world stage. Nevertheless, most Americans remained ambivalent about the acquisition of territory. While anti-imperialist Mark Twain acidly condemned "the Blessings of Civilization Trust," labor leader Samuel Gompers warned that "an inundation of Mongolians" might steal jobs from white labor. White Americans recoiled from making the "barbarian peoples" of these territories a part of the United States. Not fit to manage their own affairs, Filipinos were placed in a protective status that denied their independence but kept them under U.S. control.

In 1902 Congress passed the Philippine Organic Act, under which a presidentially appointed governor would rule the islands and a Filipino assembly would be elected. The law also promised eventual self-government. Progress toward this goal inched forward, with intervals of semimilitary rule. In 1946, nearly half a century after Admiral Dewey's guns had boomed in Manila Bay, independence finally came to the Philippines.

Emilio Aguinaldo Nationalist leader of Filipino war against American occupation

CHECKING IN

- Expansionist, even warlike sentiment flared in the 1890s.
- The United States took over Hawaii after American planters deposed the rightful queen.
- The Spanish-American War was a popular assertion of rising American power.
- A small but vocal group criticized imperialism as a betrayal of American values.
- Acquisition of the Philippines from Spain led to a guerrilla war and the expansion of American empire into the western Pacific.

Chapter Summary

 DOWNLOAD THE MP3 AUDIO FILE OF THE CHAPTER SUMMARY, AND LISTEN TO IT ON THE GO.

How did political parties build coalitions out of their diverse ethnic and regional constituencies? (page 452)

Both major national parties pursued centrist courses, with Republicans supporting big business and Democrats warning against government interference. Greenbacks and the coinage of silver were major issues, and Civil Service reform emerged. As the parties struggled to achieve political dominance, they were forced to deal with ethnic, cultural, and racial issues that included prohibition, church schools, and segregation.

What factors prompted the rise of the Grange and the Farmers' Alliance movements? (page 457)

In the competition for new voters, the needs of rural Americans were often overlooked. Farmers formed a succession of movements, including the Grange and the Alliance, to try to reassert control over their lives; these led to the Populist party in 1892. African-Americans were increasingly excluded from political life.

Why did William Jennings Bryan fail to win the presidency in 1896? (page 464)

Corporate interests continued to dominate politics. Populists won more than a million votes in the 1892 election, reflecting deep dissatisfaction among western and southern farmers. The Panic of 1893 and the subsequent depression devastated individuals and led to political unrest, such as Coxey's Army. The victory of Republican William McKinley over William Jennings Bryan in the 1896 presidential election undermined Populism as an organized movement. Many of ideas were incorporated into the two larger parties. The Republican coalition that put McKinley in the White House would control national politics for the next fifteen years.

Why did the United States go to war with Spain and become an imperial power? (page 469)

The 1890s saw a surge of expansionist and warlike (jingoistic) sentiment. The Spanish-American War gave the United States control in the Caribbean and expanded American power far into the western Pacific with the acquisition of the Philippines. A bitter guerrilla war in the Philippines showed American determination to keep the new U.S. empire, despite angry criticism from a vocal group of anti-imperialists.

KEY TERMS

laissez-faire *(p. 454)*
Grand Army of the Republic (GAR) *(p. 454)*
Greenback party *(p. 456)*
Sherman Silver Purchase Act *(p. 456)*
Pendleton Civil Service Act *(p. 457)*
Mugwumps *(p. 458)*
Grange *(p. 459)*
Farmers' Alliance *(p. 460)*
Populist Party *(p. 461)*
subtreasury plan *(p. 461)*
lynching *(p. 462)*
Plessy v. *Ferguson (p. 462)*
Booker T. Washington *(p. 463)*
Panic of 1893 *(p. 465)*
William Jennings Bryan *(p. 466)*
Alfred Thayer Mahan *(p. 469)*
Hawaiian Islands *(p. 471)*
Platt Amendment *(p. 473)*
Anti-Imperialist League *(p. 473)*
Emilio Aguinaldo *(p. 474)*

CHAPTER 21

The Progressive Era 1900–1917

Mulberry Street on New York City's
Lower East Side, Around 1900

CHAPTER PREVIEW

Progressives and Their Ideas
*How did intellectuals, novelists, and journalists
inspire the progressive movement?*

State and Local Progressivism
*How did state and local progressives seek to reform
cities and the new industrial order?*

Blacks, Women, and Workers Organize
*How did progressives try to control morality, and
how did they view immigrants and blacks?*

**National Progressivism Phase I: Roosevelt and
Taft, 1901–1913**
*What strategies did African-Americans, women,
and industrial workers use to improve their lot?*

**National Progressivism Phase II: Woodrow
Wilson, 1913–1917**
*As progressivism became a national movement,
what issues proved most important?*

I t was late Saturday afternoon on March 25, 1911, but at the Triangle Shirtwaist factory in New York City, hundreds of young
women and a few men remained at work at their clattering sewing
machines. Suddenly fire broke out. Feeding on bolts of cloth, the fire
soon turned the upper floors into an inferno. Panicked workers
found some of the doors locked. Other doors that opened inward (a
fire-law violation) were jammed shut by the crush of people trying to
get out.

A few escaped. Young Pauline Grossman crawled to safety across
a narrow alleyway when three male employees formed a human
bridge. As others tried to cross, however, the weight became too great,

and the three men fell to their deaths. Dozens of workers leaped from the windows to certain death below. Sunday's headlines summed up the grim count: 141 dead.

The Triangle fire offered horrifying evidence of what many citizens had long recognized. Industrialization, for all its benefits, had taken a heavy toll on American life. Immigrants in unsafe factories often endured a desperate cycle of poverty, exhausting labor, and early death. After the Triangle tragedy, New York passed a series of laws regulating factories and protecting workers.

Growing concerns about industrialization, urban growth, and the rise of great corporations prompted a wave of reform that came to be called the progressive movement. The progressive movement was a response to vast changes that had erased the familiar contours of an older America. In contrast to the rural Populists (see Chapter 20), progressives concentrated on the social effects of the new urban-industrial order.

Emerging in the 1890s at the city and state levels, an array of organizations, many led by women, pursued varied reform objectives. As journalists, novelists, religious leaders, social thinkers, and politicians joined in, these grass-roots efforts evolved into a national movement. By 1917, when reform gave way to war, America's political and social landscape had been transformed. New laws, organizations, and regulatory agencies had arisen to address the consequences of helter-skelter urbanization, industrial expansion, and corporate growth. The progressives could be maddeningly moralistic. They had their blind spots (especially on such subjects as immigration and race), and their reforms didn't always work as planned. But, on balance, their achievements left a powerful legacy for future generations.

▌PROGRESSIVES AND THEIR IDEAS

How did intellectuals, novelists, and journalists inspire the progressive movement?

▌As the twentieth century dawned, local groups across the nation, from workers to women's clubs to expert investigative commissions, grappled with the problems of the new urban-industrial order. Workers protested unsafe and exhausting jobs. Experts investigated social conditions. Women's clubs embraced reform. Intellectuals challenged the ideological foundations of a business-dominated social order, and journalists publicized municipal corruption and industrialism's human toll. Activists tried to make government more democratic, eradicate dangerous conditions in cities and factories, and curb corporate power.

Although historians group all these efforts under a single label, "progressivism" was in fact never a single movement. It is perhaps best understood as a widespread yearning for reform and an exciting sense of new social possibilities.

The Many Faces of Progressivism

Who were the progressives, and what reforms did they pursue? To answer these questions, we need to look at the pattern of urban growth in the early twentieth century. Along with immigration, a rapidly growing middle class transformed U.S. cities. From the men and women of this class—most of them native-born, white, and Protestant—came many of the progressive movement's leaders and foot soldiers.

From 1900 to 1920, the white-collar work force jumped from 5.1 million to 10.5 million, twice the growth rate for the work force as a whole. This new middle class included such diverse groups as skilled technicians and desk workers, bureaucrats, local business owners and managers, lawyers, physicians, and teachers. Ambitious, well educated, and valuing self-discipline and social stability, members of the new middle class were eager to make their influence felt.

For middle-class women, the city offered both opportunities and frustrations. Some became public-school teachers, secretaries, clerks, and telephone operators, pushing the number of women in white-collar jobs from 949,000 in 1900 to 3.4 million in 1920. The ranks of college-educated women, although still small, more than tripled in this twenty-year period. But married urban middle-class women, hedged in by the demands of home and children, typically faced isolation and limited opportunity. The divorce rate rose from one in twelve marriages in 1900 to one in nine by 1916. Many middle-class women mired in domestic routines joined white-collar and college-educated women in a resurgent women's movement, and cultural commentators wrote nervously of the "New Woman."

This urban middle class rallied to the banner of reform. The initial reform impetus came not from political parties but from women's clubs, settlement houses, and private groups with names like the Playground Association of America and the American League for Civic Improvement.

The native-born middle class was not the only force behind progressivism. On issues affecting factory workers and slum dwellers, the urban-immigrant political machines—and workers themselves—often took the initiative. Some corporate leaders helped shape regulatory measures in ways to serve their interests.

The Gendering of Labor in Corporate America

Male bookkeepers and female "typewriters" at the headquarters of the Metropolitan Life Insurance Company in New York City.

Chronology

1900	International Ladies' Garment Workers' Union (ILGWU) founded; Carrie Chapman Catt becomes president of the National American Woman Suffrage Association (NAWSA)
1901	Assassination of McKinley; Theodore Roosevelt becomes president; J.P. Morgan forms United States Steel Company
1902	Jane Addams, *Democracy and Social Ethics*
1903	W. E. B. Du Bois, *The Souls of Black Folk*; Wright brothers' flight
1904	Theodore Roosevelt elected president in his own right; Lincoln Steffens, *The Shame of the Cities*
1905	Industrial Workers of the World (IWW) organized
1906	Upton Sinclair, *The Jungle*
1907	William James, *Pragmatism*
1908	William Howard Taft elected president; Model T Ford introduced
1909	Ballinger-Pinchot controversy; National Association for the Advancement of Colored People (NAACP) founded; Herbert Croly, *The Promise of American Life*; Daniel Burnham, *Plan of Chicago*
1910	Insurgents curb power of House Speaker Joseph Cannon
1911	Triangle Shirtwaist Company fire
1912	Republican Party split; Progressive (Bull Moose) Party founded; Woodrow Wilson elected president; International Opium Treaty
1913	Sixteenth Amendment (Congress empowered to tax incomes); Seventeenth Amendment (direct election of U.S. senators)
1914	American Social Hygiene Association founded; Narcotics Act
1915	D.W. Griffith, *The Birth of a Nation*
1916	Margaret Sanger opens nation's first birth-control clinic in Brooklyn, New York; National Park Service created; Louis Brandeis appointed to Supreme Court
1919	Eighteenth Amendment (national prohibition)
1920	Nineteenth Amendment (woman suffrage)

At the most basic level, then, progressivism was a series of political and cultural responses to industrialization and its by-products. In contrast to populism, progressivism's strength lay in the cities. Finally, most progressives were *reformers,* not radicals. They wished to make the new urban-industrial order more humane, not overturn it entirely.

But which parts of the urban-industrial order most needed attention, and what remedies were required? Reaching different answers to these key questions, progressive reformers spawned an array of activities that sometimes overlapped, sometimes diverged. Many reformers wanted stricter regulation of business, from local transit companies to the almighty trusts. Others focused on protecting workers and the urban poor. Still others tried to reform the structure of government, especially at the municipal level. Finally, some reformers fought for immigration restriction or various social-control strategies to combat urban immorality and disorder.

Progressives had a high regard for science and expert knowledge, and tended to believe that, when channeled through organized effort, such expertise, which had produced the new industrial order, would solve the social problems spawned by industrialism. Progressives marshaled research data, expert opinion, and statistics to support their various causes.

Intellectuals Offer New Social Views
A group of turn-of-the-century thinkers helped to reorient American social thought and laid the ideological foundation for progressivism. As we have seen, some Gilded Age intellectuals had argued that Charles Darwin's theory of evolution justified unrestrained economic competition. In the 1880s and 1890s, sociologist Lester Ward, utopian novelist Edward Bellamy, and leaders of the settlement-house and Social Gospel movements had all attacked this harsh version of Social Darwinism (see Chapters 18 and 19). This attack intensified after 1900.

Economist Thorstein Veblen was among the sharpest critics of the new business order, satirizing the lifestyles of the captains of industry and their "conspicuous consumption" (see Chapter 19). In later writings he argued that engineers, molded by the stern discipline of the machine, were better fitted than the business class to lead society.

Harvard philosopher William James, in an influential 1907 book called *Pragmatism*, argued that truth emerges not from abstract theorizing but from the experience of coping with life. By emphasizing the importance of practical action, James's philosophy of pragmatism deepened the reformers' skepticism toward the older generation's entrenched ideas and strengthened their belief in the necessity of social change.

Herbert Croly shared this faith that new ideas could transform society. In *The Promise of American Life* (1909), he called for an activist government of the kind advocated by Alexander Hamilton, the first secretary of the treasury. But rather than serving the interests of the business class, as Hamilton had proposed, Croly argued that this activist government should promote the welfare of all. In 1914, Croly founded the *New Republic* magazine to promote progressive ideas. Few argued those ideas more effectively than settlement-house leader Jane Addams. In her books *Democracy and Social Ethics* (1902) and *Twenty Years at Hull House* (1910), Addams rejected the claim that unrestrained competition offered the best path to social progress. Instead, she argued, in a modern industrial society, each individual's well-being depends on the well-being of all. Teaching by example, Addams made her Chicago social settlement, Hull House, a center of social activism and legislative-reform initiatives.

With public-school enrollment growing from about 7 million in 1870 to more than 23 million in 1920, philosopher John Dewey saw schools as potent engines of social change. Banishing bolted-down chairs and desks from his model school at the University of Chicago, Dewey encouraged pupils to interact. The ideal school, he said in *Democracy and Education* (1916), would be an "embryonic community" where children would learn to live as members of a social group.

Oliver Wendell Holmes, Jr., of Harvard Law School focused on changing judicial thinking. In these years, most judges interpreted the law in ways that protected corporate interests and struck down reform legislation. In *The Common Law* (1881), however, Holmes had insisted that law must evolve as society changes. "The life of the law has not been logic; it has been experience," he argued. Appointed to the United States Supreme Court in 1902, Holmes often dissented from the conservative Court majority. As the new social thinking took hold, the courts slowly grew more open to reform legislation.

Novelists, Journalists, and Artists Spotlight Social Problems

While intellectuals reoriented American social thought, novelists and journalists roused the reform spirit by chronicling corporate wrongdoing, municipal corruption, and slum conditions. Advances in printing and photo reproduction ensured a mass audience and sharpened the emotional impact of the message.

In his novel *The Octopus* (1901), Frank Norris of San Francisco portrayed the epic struggle between California railroad barons and the state's wheat growers. Theodore Dreiser's novel *The Financier* (1912) featured a hard-driving business tycoon utterly lacking a social conscience. Like Veblen's *Theory of the Leisure Class,* such works aroused sentiment against the industrial elite and in favor of tougher regulation of business.

Mass-circulation magazines such as *McClure's* and *Collier's* published articles exposing urban corruption and corporate wrongdoing. President Theodore Roosevelt criticized the authors as **"muckrakers"** obsessed with the seamier side of American life, but the name became a badge of honor, and the circulation of *McClure's* and *Collier's* soared.

The muckrakers emphasized facts rather than abstractions; some actually worked as factory laborers or lived in slum tenements. In a 1903 series, journalist Maria Van Vorst described her experiences working in a Massachusetts shoe factory where women's fingernails rotted away from repeated immersion in caustic dyes. Some magazine exposés later appeared in book form, including Lincoln Steffens's *The Shame of the Cities* (1904), Ida Tarbell's damning *History of the Standard Oil Company* (1904), and David Graham Phillips's *Treason of the Senate* (1906).

Artists and photographers played a role as well. A group of New York painters dubbed the Ashcan School portrayed the harshness of life in the city's crowded slums. Wisconsin-born photographer Lewis Hine captured images of immigrants and factory laborers. His photos of child workers, with their stunted bodies and worn expressions, helped build support for national laws against child labor.

Primary Source: Muckrakers

"muckrakers" Journalists and novelists who wrote about urban corruption and wrongdoing

CHECKING IN

- The new middle class was an important part of the progressive movement; so, too, were urban workers and, occasionally, political machines and corporate leaders.

- Progressivism was a response to the massive changes spawned by industrialization, urbanization, and immigration.

- The progressives were reformers who wanted to save, not to overthrow, the existing capitalist system.

- Intellectuals like William James, Herbert Croly, and John Dewey provided the foundation for progressive reforms, emphasizing the power of new ideas and purposeful effort in bettering society.

- Muckraking authors and journalists played a major role in unveiling problems and stirring the public to demand solutions.

STATE AND LOCAL PROGRESSIVISM

How did state and local progressives seek to reform cities and the new industrial order?

Middle-class readers also observed firsthand, in their own communities, the problems besetting urban-industrial America. In fact, the progressive movement began with grass-roots campaigns at the local level from New York to San Francisco.

Reforming the Political Process

Beginning in the 1890s, native-born elites and middle-class reformers battled corrupt city governments (see Chapter 19). New York City experienced a succession of reform spasms in which Protestant clergy rallied against Tammany Hall, the city's entrenched Democratic organization. In Detroit, the reform mayor Hazen Pingree (served 1890–1897) brought honesty to city hall, lowered transit fares, adopted a fairer tax structure, and provided public baths and other services for the poor.

In San Francisco in 1907, the original prosecutor in a case against the city's corrupt boss, Abe Reuf, was gunned down in court. Attorney Hiram Johnson took over the case, and Reuf and his cronies were convicted. Full of reform zeal—one observer called him "a volcano in perpetual eruption"—Johnson rode his newly won fame to the California governorship and the U.S. Senate. In Toledo, Ohio, the colorful eccentric Samuel M. "Golden Rule" Jones led the reform campaign. A self-made businessman converted to the Social Gospel (see Chapter 19), Jones introduced profit sharing in his factory; as mayor, he established playgrounds, free kindergartens, and lodging houses for homeless transients.

The political reformers soon moved beyond simply "throwing the rascals out" to probing the roots of urban misgovernment, including the private monopolies that ran municipal water, gas, electricity, and transit systems. Reformers passed laws regulating the rates that utilities could charge, taxing them more equitably, and curbing their political influence. Some advocated public ownership of utilities.

Reflecting the Progressive Era vogue of expertise and efficiency, a number of municipal reformers sought to substitute professional managers and administrators, chosen in citywide elections, for mayors and aldermen elected on a ward-by-ward basis. Supposedly above politics, these experts were to run the city like an efficient business.

Municipal reform attracted different groups depending on the issue. The native-born middle class provided the initial impetus for urban beautification and political reform. Business leaders often supported city-manager systems and citywide elections, which diminished the power of the ward bosses and increased that of the corporate elite. On practical matters, such as municipal services, immigrants and even political bosses supported reform.

The movement for electoral reform soon expanded to the state level. By 1910 all states had instituted secret ballots, making it much harder than before to rig elections. Another widely adopted reform was the direct primary, in which party members, rather than leaders, selected candidates for public office. And some western states inaugurated the initiative, referendum, and recall. By an initiative, voters can instruct the legislature to consider a specific bill. In a referendum, they can actually enact a law or, in a *nonbinding* referendum, express their views on a measure. By a recall petition, voters can remove an official from office by gathering enough signatures.

While these reforms aimed to democratize voting, party leaders and interest groups soon learned to manipulate the new electoral machinery. Ironically, the new procedures may have weakened party loyalty and reduced voter interest. Voter-participation rates dropped steeply in these years, while political activity by organized interest groups increased.

Regulating Business, Protecting Workers

The late-nineteenth-century corporate consolidation that produced giants like Carnegie Steel and Standard Oil continued after 1900 (see Chapter 18). Following the U.S. Steel pattern, J. P. Morgan in 1902 combined six competing companies into the International Harvester Company, which dominated the farm-implement business. The General Motors Company, formed in 1908 by William C. Durant, bought up various independent automobile manufacturers, from the inexpensive Chevrolet to the luxury Cadillac.

Many workers benefited from this corporate growth. Industrial workers' average annual real wages (defined, that is, in terms of actual purchasing power) rose from $532 in the late nineteenth century to $687 by 1915. In railroading and other unionized industries, wages climbed still higher. Still, such wages could barely support a family.

To survive, entire families went to work. Two-thirds of young immigrant women entered the labor force in the early 1900s, working in factories, laundries, or bakeries, or as domestics. Even children worked. In 1910 the nonfarm labor force probably included at least 1.6 million children aged ten to fifteen employed in factories, mills, tenement sweatshops, and street trades such as shoe shining and newspaper vending.

Most laborers faced long hours and great hazards. Despite the 8-hour movement of the 1880s, in 1900 the average worker still toiled 9½ hours a day. Some southern textile mills required workdays of 12 or 13 hours. In one typical year (1907), 4,534 railroad workers and more than 3,000 miners were killed on the job. Few employers accepted responsibility for work-related accidents and illnesses.

Factory workers accustomed to the rhythms of farm labor faced the discipline of the time clock and the machine. Efficiency experts used time-and-motion studies to increase production and make human workers as predictable as machines. In *Principles of Scientific Management* (1911), Frederick W. Taylor explained how to increase output by standardizing job routines and rewarding the fastest workers. Most workers deeply resented the drive for "efficiency."

For Americans troubled by the social implications of industrialization, the drive to regulate big business, inherited from the populists, became vitally important. Because corporations had benefited from such government policies as high protective tariffs, reformers reasoned, they should also be subject to government supervision.

Of the many states that passed laws regulating railroads, mines, and other businesses, none did so more avidly than Wisconsin under Governor **Robert La Follette** (lah FALL-ett). As a Republican congressman, La Follette had feuded with the state's conservative party leadership, and in 1900 he won the governorship as an independent. Challenging the state's long-dominant business interests, La Follette and his administration adopted the direct-primary system, set up a railroad regulatory commission, increased corporate taxes, and limited campaign spending. Reflecting progressivism's faith in experts, La Follette met regularly with reform-minded professors at the University of Wisconsin and set up a legislative reference library so lawmakers would not have to rely on corporate lobbyists for factual information.

Robert La Follette Progressive politician; won Wisconsin governorship as independent and oversaw several reforms; later a U.S. Senator

If electoral reform and corporate regulation represented the brain of progressivism, the impulse to improve conditions in factories and mills represented its heart. This movement, too, began at the local and state level. By 1907, for example, thirty

The Triangle Fire
The bodies of Triangle Shirtwaist factory workers lie on the sidewalk after they jumped from the burning building.

states had outlawed child labor. A 1903 Oregon law limited women in industry to a ten-hour workday.

Campaigns to improve industrial safety and otherwise better conditions for the laboring masses won support from political bosses in cities with large immigrant populations. New York state senator Robert F. Wagner, a leader of Tammany Hall, headed the investigation of the 1911 Triangle fire. Thanks to his committee's efforts, New York passed fifty-six worker-protection laws, including required fire-safety inspections of factories. By 1914, spurred by the Triangle disaster, twenty-five states had made employers liable for job-related injuries or deaths.

Florence Kelley, a Hull House resident and the daughter of a conservative Republican congressman, helped launch the drive to remedy industrial abuses. In 1893, Kelley persuaded the Illinois legislature to outlaw child labor and limit working hours for women. In 1899, she became general secretary of the National Consumers' League, which mobilized consumer pressure for improved factory conditions. Campaigning for a federal child-labor law, Kelley asked, "Why are seals, bears, reindeer, fish, wild game in the national parks, buffalo, [and] migratory birds all found suitable for federal protection, but not children?"

Like many progressive reforms, the crusade for workplace safety relied on expert research. Alice Hamilton, for example, a pioneer in the new field of "industrial hygiene," taught bacteriology at Northwestern University while also working at Hull House. In 1910 she conducted a major study of lead poisoning among industrial workers. Appointed an investigator by the U.S. Bureau of Labor in 1911, Hamilton became an expert on and campaigned against work-related medical hazards.

Workers themselves provided further pressure for reform. For example, when new power drills created a fine dust that granite workers inhaled, the *Granite Cutters' Journal* warned of "stone cutters' consumption" and called the new drills "widow makers." Sure enough, investigators soon linked the dust to a deadly respiratory disease, silicosis—another industrial hazard that worker-safety advocates sought to remedy.

Making Cities More Livable

In the early twentieth century, America became an urban nation. By 1920 the urban population passed the 50 percent mark, and sixty-eight U.S. cities boasted more than 100,000 inhabitants. New York City grew by 2.2 million from 1900 to 1920, and Chicago by 1 million.

As manufacturing and businesses grew, a surging tide of immigrants and native-born newcomers engulfed the cities. Overwhelmed by this rapid growth, many cities became dreary, sprawling human warehouses lacking such basic civic amenities as parks, municipal services, and public-health resources. Unsurprisingly, as the progressive movement took shape, urban problems loomed large.

Building on the achievements of Frederick Law Olmsted and others (see Chapter 11), reformers campaigned for parks, boulevards, and street lights, and proposed laws against billboards and unsightly overhead electrical wires. These crusaders had faith that beautiful cities and imposing public buildings would ensure a law-abiding and civic-minded urban populace. An influential voice for city planning and beautification was Daniel Burnham, chief architect of the 1893 Chicago world's fair. Burnham developed beautification plans for Washington, D.C., Cleveland, San Francisco, and other cities. Many Progressive Era urban planners shared Burnham's faith that more beautiful cities and imposing public buildings would produce orderly, law-abiding citizens.

Beyond urban beautification, reformers worked for such practical goals as decent housing and better garbage collection and street cleaning. Providing a model for other cities and states, the New York legislature passed laws imposing strict health and safety regulations on tenements in 1911. The discovery in the 1880s that germs cause diseases like cholera and typhoid fever made municipal hygiene and sanitation high priorities. Progressive reformers called for improved water and sewer systems, regulation of milk suppliers and food handlers, school medical examinations and vaccination programs, and campaigns to spread public-health information to the urban masses.

These efforts bore fruit. From 1900 to 1920, infant mortality (defined as death in the first year of life) dropped from 165 per 1,000 population to around 75, and the tuberculosis death rate fell by nearly half. The municipal health crusades had a social-class dimension. Middle-class reformers set the "sanitary agenda," and the campaigns often targeted immigrants and the poor as the sources of contagion. When Mary Mallon, an Irish-immigrant cook in New York, was found to be a healthy carrier of the typhoid bacillus in 1907, she was confined for years by city health authorities and demonized in the press as "Typhoid Mary."

Urban reformers also shared the heightened environmental consciousness of these years (see Chapter 17). The battle against air pollution illustrates both the promise and the frustrations of municipal environmentalism. Coal-fueled steam boilers in factories produced massive amounts of soot and smoke, which by the early 1900s physicians had linked to respiratory problems.

As with other progressive reforms, the resulting antismoke campaign combined expertise with activism. Civil engineers formed the Smoke Prevention Association in 1906, and researchers at the University of Pittsburgh documented the hazards and costs of air pollution. As women's clubs and other civic groups embraced the cause, many cities passed smoke abatement laws. But coal still provided 70 percent of the nation's energy as late as 1920, and railroads and corporations fought back in the courts and often won. Not until years later, with the shift to other energy sources, did municipal air pollution significantly diminish.

Progressivism and Social Control

Progressives' belief that they could improve society through research, legislation, and aroused public opinion sprang from their confidence that they knew what was best for other people. While municipal corruption, unsafe factories, and corporate abuses captured their attention, so, too, did issues of personal behavior, particularly the behavior of immigrants. The problems they addressed deserved attention, but their self-righteous rhetoric and the remedies they proposed also betrayed an impulse to impose their own moral standards by force of law.

Moral Control in the Cities

Early twentieth-century urban life was more than crowded slums and exhausting labor. For all their problems, cities also offered fun and diversion. Department stores, vaudeville, music halls, and amusement parks (see Chapter 19) continued to flourish. Although some vaudeville owners strove for respectability, raucous and bawdy routines full of sexual innuendo were popular with working-class audiences. New York City's amusement park, Coney Island, was drawing as many as a million visitors a day by 1914.

For families, amusement parks provided escape from tenements. For female garment workers or department store clerks, they provided an opportunity to spend time with friends, meet young men, and show off new outfits. With electrification, simply riding the streetcars or taking an evening stroll on well-lit downtown streets became leisure activities in themselves. The introduction of Henry Ford's Model T in 1908, which transformed the automobile from a toy of the rich to a vehicle for the masses, heightened the sense of exciting changes ahead, with cities at the heart of the action.

Jaunty popular songs were introduced in the music halls and produced in a district of lower Manhattan called Tin Pan Alley. Joining ragtime (see Chapter 19), the blues, rooted in the chants of southern black sharecroppers, reached a broader public with such songs as W. C. Handy's classic "St. Louis Blues" (1914).

These years also brought a new medium of mass entertainment—the movies. Five-cent halls called "nickelodeons" appeared in immigrant neighborhoods with *The Great Train Robbery* (1903) and *A Fool There Was* (1914), which with its famous line "Kiss me, my fool!" made Theda Bara the first female movie star. The British music-hall performer Charlie Chaplin emigrated to America in 1913 and appeared in some sixty short comedies between 1914 and 1917. Like amusement parks, the movies allowed immigrant youth to briefly escape parental supervision.

The diversions that eased city life for the poor struck some middle-class reformers as moral traps. Fearful of immorality and social disorder, reformers campaigned to regulate amusement parks, dance halls, and the movies. The darkened nickelodeons struck many middle-class men and women as potential dens of vice. Warning of "nickel madness," reformers demanded film censorship. Several states and cities set up censorship boards, and the Supreme Court upheld such measures in 1915.

Building on the moral purity crusade of the Woman's Christian Temperance Union (WCTU) and other groups in the 1890s (see Chapter 19), reformers also targeted prostitution, a major urban problem. The paltry wages paid women for factory work or domestic service diverted many to this more lucrative occupation.

As prostitution came to symbolize the larger moral dangers of cities, a "white slave" hysteria gripped the nation amid warnings of farm girls' being kidnapped and forced into urban brothels. In the usual progressive fashion, investigators gathered statistics on what they called "the social evil." The American Social Hygiene Association (1914), financed by John D. Rockefeller, Jr., sponsored medical research on sexually transmitted diseases, paid for "vice investigations" in various cities, and drafted model municipal statutes against prostitution. The federal Mann Act (1910) made it illegal to transport a woman across a state line "for immoral purposes." Amid much fanfare, reformers shut down the red-light districts of New Orleans, Chicago, and other cities.

Battling Alcohol and Drugs

Temperance had long been part of the American reform agenda, but reformers' tactics and objectives changed in the Progressive Era. Most earlier campaigns had urged individuals to give up drink. The powerful **Anti-Saloon League,** founded in 1895, shifted the emphasis to legislating a ban on the sale of alcoholic beverages, and its presses produced propaganda touting prohibition. As the ASL added its efforts to those of the WCTU and various church bodies, many localities banned the sale of alcoholic beverages, and the campaign for national prohibition gained strength.

Anti-Saloon League Political advocacy group founded in 1895; signaled a new phase in the movement to ban the sale of alcohol

This was a heavy-drinking era, and alcohol abuse did indeed contribute to domestic abuse, health problems, and work injuries. But like the antiprostitution crusade, the prohibition campaign pitted native-born citizens against new immigrants. Although it raised legitimate issues, the ASL also embodied Protestant America's impulse to control the immigrant city.

These years also saw the first sustained campaign against drug abuse—and for good reason. Many easily obtained medicines contained opium and its derivatives, morphine and heroin. Cocaine was widely used as well. Coca-Cola contained cocaine until about 1900.

As reformers focused on the problem, the federal government backed a 1912 treaty aimed at halting the international opium trade. The Narcotics Act of 1914 strictly regulated opiates and cocaine. In their battle against drugs, as in their environmental concerns, the progressives anticipated an issue that would remain important into the twenty-first century. But here, too, racist undertones colored antidrug crusaders' warnings about Chinese "opium dens" and "drug-crazed Negroes" who imperiled white womanhood.

Immigration Restriction and Eugenics

Although many of the new city dwellers came from farms and small towns, the main source of urban growth continued to be immigration. More than 17 million newcomers arrived from 1900 to 1917, and most settled in cities. As in the 1890s (see Chapter 19), the influx came mainly from southern and eastern Europe, but some 200,000 Japanese, 40,000 Chinese, and thousands of Mexicans also arrived between 1900 and 1920.

The obvious answer to the threats posed by the immigrant city, some reformers concluded, lay in excluding immigrants (see Figure 21.1). The many progressives who supported immigration restriction documented their case with alleged scientific expertise. In 1911 a congressional commission produced a statistical study "proving" the new immigrants' innate degeneracy. In 1914 the progressive sociologist Edward A. Ross described recent immigrants as "hirsute, low-browed, big-faced persons of obviously low mentality." In 1896, 1913, and 1915, Congress passed literacy-test bills aimed at slowing immigration, but they fell victim to veto by a succession of presidents. In 1917, however, such a bill became law over President Wilson's veto.

Figure 21.1   Immigration to the United States, 1870–1930

With the end of the depression of the 1890s, immigrants from southern and eastern Europe poured into America's cities, spurring an immigration restriction movement, urban moral-control campaigns, and efforts to improve the physical and social conditions of immigrant life.

Sources: Statistical History of the United States from Colonial Times to the Present (Stamford, Conn.: Fairfield Publishers, 1965); and report presented by Senator William P. Dillingham, Senate document 742, 61st Congress, 3rd session, December 5, 1910: Abstracts of Reports to the Immigration Commission.

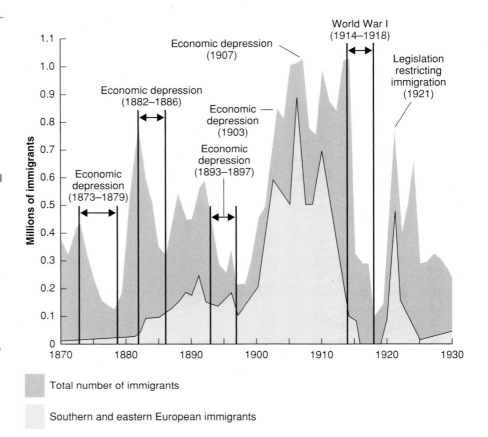

Total number of immigrants

Southern and eastern European immigrants

Anti-immigrant fears helped fuel the eugenics (you-JEN-icks) movement. Eugenics is the control of reproduction to alter a plant or animal species, which some U.S. eugenicists believed could be used to improve human society. A leading eugenicist, the zoologist Charles B. Davenport, urged immigration restriction to keep America from pollution by "inferior" genetic stock.

In *The Passing of the Great Race* (1916), Madison Grant, a prominent progressive and eugenics advocate, used bogus data to denounce immigrants from southern and eastern Europe, especially Jews. He also viewed African-Americans as inferior. Anticipating the program of Adolf Hitler in the 1930s (see Chapter 25), Grant called for racial segregation, immigration restriction, and the forced sterilization of the "unfit," including "worthless race types." The vogue of eugenics gave "scientific" respectability to anti-immigrant sentiment, as well as the racism that pervaded white America in these years. Inspired by eugenics, many states legalized the sterilization of criminals, sex offenders, and persons adjudged mentally deficient.

Racism and Progressivism

Progressivism arose at a time of significant changes in African-American life—and also one of intense racism in white America. These racial realities are crucial to a full understanding of the movement.

In 1900 more than two-thirds of the nation's 10 million blacks lived in the South as sharecroppers and tenant farmers. By 1910 the cotton boll weevil and ruinous floods had driven 20 percent of these southern blacks into cities. Urban African-American men took jobs in factories, mines, docks, and railroads or became carpenters or bricklayers, and African-American women became domestic servants, seamstresses, and laundry or tobacco workers. By 1910, 54 percent of America's black women held jobs.

Across the South, legally enforced racism peaked in the early twentieth century. Local "Jim Crow" laws segregated streetcars, schools, parks, and even cemeteries. The facilities for blacks, including the schools, were invariably inferior. Many southern cities imposed residential segregation by law until the Supreme Court restricted such measures in 1917. Most labor unions excluded black workers. Disfranchised and trapped in a cycle of poverty, poor education, and discrimination, southern blacks faced bleak prospects.

Fleeing poverty and racism, and drawn by job opportunities, 200,000 African-Americans migrated north between 1890 and 1910. World War I drew still more (see Chapter 22), and by 1920, 1.4 million African-Americans lived in the North. Northern blacks encountered conditions similar to those in the South. Segregation, although not legally imposed, existed everywhere and was supported by social pressure and occasional violence. Blacks lived in run-down "colored districts," attended dilapidated schools, and took low-paying jobs. Even the movies preached racism. D. W. Griffith's 1915 film classic *The Birth of a Nation* glorified the Ku Klux Klan and vilified and ridiculed African-Americans.

Smoldering racism sometimes exploded in violence. Antiblack rioters in Atlanta in 1906 murdered twenty-five blacks and burned many black homes. Lynchings continued, an average of about seventy-five yearly from 1900 to 1920, often as reprisal for assertive behavior or economic aspirations that angered whites. Some lynchings involved incredible sadism: with large crowds on hand, the victim's body was mutilated, and graphic postcards were sold later. Authorities rarely intervened. At a 1916 lynching in Texas, the mayor warned the mob not to damage the hanging tree, as it was on city property.

In the face of such hostility, African-Americans developed strong social institutions and a vigorous culture. Black religious life, centered in the African Methodist Episcopal church, provided a bulwark of support for many. Black colleges and universities, among them Fisk in Nashville and Howard in Washington, D.C., survived against heavy odds. The urban African-American community included black-owned insurance companies and banks, and boasted a small elite of entrepreneurs, teachers, ministers, and sports figures, including Texan Jack Johnson, who won the heavyweight boxing championship in 1908. Although major league baseball excluded blacks, a thriving Negro League attracted many black fans.

In this racist age, progressives compiled a mixed record on racial issues. Muckraker Ray Stannard Baker documented racism in his 1908 book *Following the Color Line*. Settlement-house worker Mary White Ovington helped found the National Association for the Advancement of Colored People in 1909 and wrote *Half a Man* (1911) about the emotional scars of racism.

But most progressives kept silent as blacks' rights were trampled, viewing blacks as inferior and prone to immorality and social disorder. White progressives generally supported segregation and the strict moral oversight of African-American communities, occasionally advocating, at best, paternalistic efforts to "uplift" this supposedly backward and childlike people. Viciously racist southern politicians like Governor James K. Vardaman of Mississippi and Senator Ben Tillman of South Carolina also supported progressive reforms.

At the national level, President Theodore Roosevelt's record on race was marginally better than that of other politicians in this racist age. In a symbolically important gesture, he dined with Booker T. Washington at the White House. In 1906, however, he approved the dishonorable discharge of an entire regiment of black soldiers, including Congressional Medal of Honor winners, in Brownsville, Texas, because some members of the unit, goaded by racist taunts, had killed a local civilian. The "Brownsville Incident" incensed black Americans.

Under President Woodrow Wilson, racism became rampant in Washington. A Virginia native reared in Georgia, Wilson displayed at best a patronizing attitude toward blacks, praised the racist movie *The Birth of a Nation*, appointed southerners to his cabinet, and allowed racial segregation in all levels of the government.

BLACKS, WOMEN, AND WORKERS ORGANIZE

How did progressives try to control morality, and how did they view immigrants and blacks?

The organizational impulse so important to progressivism generally also proved a useful strategy for groups that found themselves discriminated against or exploited, such as African-Americans, middle-class women, and wage workers. All three groups organized to address their grievances in these years.

African-American Leaders Organize Against Racism

With racism on the rise, Booker T. Washington's accommodationist message (see Chapter 20) seemed increasingly unrealistic, particularly to educated northern blacks. In 1902 one editor of a black newspaper called Washington's go-slow policies "a fatal blow . . . to the Negro's political rights and liberty." Another opponent was the black journalist and activist **Ida Wells-Barnett.** Moving to Chicago from Memphis in 1892 after a white mob destroyed her offices, Wells-Barnett mounted a national antilynching campaign.

Washington's most potent challenger was **W. E. B. Du Bois** (1868–1963). After earning a Ph.D. in history from Harvard in 1895, Du Bois taught at Atlanta University. Openly criticizing Washington in *The Souls of Black Folk* (1903), he rejected Washington's emphasis on patience and manual skills. Instead, Du Bois demanded full racial equality and called on blacks to resist all forms of racism.

Du Bois's militancy signaled a new era of African-American activism. Beginning in 1905 in Niagara Falls, under his leadership, blacks who favored vigorous resistance to racism held annual conferences for the next few years. In 1909 a group of

Ida Wells-Barnett Eloquent speaker, writer, and civil rights activist who championed antilynching legislation

W. E. B. Du Bois African-American scholar and civil rights leader; author of *The Souls of Black Folk*

white reformers who also rejected Washington's cautiousness joined Du Bois and other blacks from the Niagara Movement to form the **National Association for the Advancement of Colored People (NAACP).** This new organization called for vigorous activism, including legal challenges, to achieve political equality for blacks and full integration into American life. Attracting the urban black middle class, by 1914 the NAACP had six thousand members in fifty branches.

National Association for the Advancement of Colored People (NAACP) Major civil rights organization founded during the Progressive Era

Revival of the Woman-Suffrage Movement

By 1910, following six failed state referenda on woman suffrage in 1896, women could vote in only four thinly populated western states: Wyoming, Utah, Colorado, and Idaho (see Map 21.1). But the active role of women in the progressive reform movement revitalized the suffrage cause. That recently arrived immigrant men could vote and they could not especially galled middle-class women. A vigorous suffrage movement in Great Britain reverberated in America as well.

The suffrage campaign in California illustrates both the strengths and the limitations of the revived movement. By the early 1900s California's women's clubs had evolved into a potent statewide organization active in municipal reform and public-school issues. This activism convinced many members that full citizenship meant the right to vote. A state woman-suffrage referendum lost in 1896. The leaders bounced back to form alliances with labor leaders and male progressives, built on a shared commitment to "good government." But while joining forces with male reformers, these woman-suffrage strategists—mostly elite white women who marginalized or excluded women of color—insisted on the unique role of "organized

Map 21.1 Woman Suffrage Before the Nineteenth Amendment

Beginning with Wyoming in 1869, woman suffrage made steady gains in western states before 1920. Farther east, key victories came in New York (1917) and Michigan (1918). But much of the East remained an antiwoman suffrage bastion throughout the period.

Full voting rights for women with effective date

Women voting in primaries

Women voting in presidential elections

No voting by women

Parading for Woman Suffrage
Suffrage leaders built support for the cause by using modern advertising and publicity techniques, including automobiles festooned with flags, banners, and—in this case—smiling little girls.

Carrie Chapman Catt Leader of women's movement; drive for woman suffrage in early twentieth century

Primary Source: Give Mother the Vote

womanhood" in building a better society. Success came in 1911 when California voters approved woman suffrage.

New leaders built the momentum in California and other states into a revitalized national movement. When Susan B. Anthony retired from the presidency of the National American Woman Suffrage Association (NAWSA) in 1900, **Carrie Chapman Catt** of Iowa succeeded her. Under Catt's shrewd direction, NAWSA adopted the so-called Winning Plan: grass-roots organization with tight central coordination.

Suffragists shrewdly deployed techniques drawn from the new urban consumer culture. They not only lobbied legislators, but they also organized parades in open cars, held photo opportunities, and devised catchy slogans that they used in newspaper ads and posters; they distributed fans, playing cards, and other items emblazoned with the suffrage message. Gradually, state after state fell into the suffrage column. A key victory came in 1917 when New York voters approved a woman-suffrage referendum.

As in California (and like progressive organizations generally), NAWSA's membership remained largely white, native born, and middle class. Some upper-class women opposed the reform. The leader of the "Antis," wealthy Josephine Dodge of New York, argued that women already had behind-the-scenes influence and that to invade the male realm of electoral politics would tarnish their moral and spiritual role.

Not all suffragists accepted Catt's strategy. Alice Paul, who had observed the British suffragists' militant tactics while studying in England, grew impatient with NAWSA's state-by-state approach. In 1913 Paul founded the Congressional Union for Woman Suffrage, renamed the National Woman's party in 1917, to pressure Congress for a woman-suffrage amendment. In 1917–1918, with the United States at war, the suffrage cause won key victories in New York and Michigan and advanced toward final success (see Chapter 22).

Enlarging "Woman's Sphere"   The suffrage movement did not exhaust American women's talents or organizational energies. Women's club members, settlement-house leaders, and individual female activists joined in various campaigns: to bring playgrounds and day nurseries to the slums, to abolish child labor, to improve conditions for women workers, and to ban unsafe foods and quack remedies.

Cultural assumptions about "woman's sphere" crumbled as women became active on many fronts. Katherine Bement Davis served as the innovative superintendent of a woman's reformatory before becoming New York City's commissioner of corrections. Anarchist Emma Goldman crisscrossed the country delivering riveting lectures on politics, feminism, and modern drama while coediting a radical monthly, *Mother Earth.* A vanguard of pioneering women in higher education included Marion Talbot, first dean of women at the University of Chicago.

In *Women and Economics* (1898) and other works, feminist intellectual Charlotte Perkins Gilman explored the historical and cultural roots of female subordination, and linked women's inferior status to their economic dependence on men. Confining women to the domestic sphere, Gilman argued, was an evolutionary throwback that had become outdated and inefficient. She advocated economic independence for women through equality in the workplace; the collectivization of domestic chores; and state-run day-care centers.

Some Progressive Era reformers challenged federal and state laws banning the distribution of contraceptives and birth-control information. Although countless women, particularly the poor, suffered health problems from frequent pregnancies, artificial contraception was widely denounced as immoral. In 1914 **Margaret Sanger** of New York, a practical nurse and socialist whose mother had died after bearing eleven children, began her crusade for birth control, a term she coined. When the authorities proscribed her journal *The Woman Rebel* on obscenity charges, Sanger fled to England. She returned in 1916 to open the nation's first birth-control clinic in Brooklyn. In 1918 she founded a new journal, the *Birth Control Review,* and three years later she founded the American Birth Control League, the ancestor of today's Planned Parenthood Federation.

Meanwhile, another New Yorker, Mary Ware Dennett, a feminist and activist, had also emerged as an advocate of birth control and sex education. Her 1919 pamphlet for youth, *The Sex Side of Life,* discussing human reproduction in clear, straightforward terms, was long banned as obscene. Dennett founded the National Birth Control League (later the Voluntary Parenthood League) in 1915. While Sanger championed direct action to promote the cause, Dennett urged lobbying efforts to change the law. Sanger insisted that only physicians should supply contraceptives; Dennett argued for widespread distribution.

The emergence of the birth-control movement stands as one of progressivism's most important legacies. At the time, however, it stirred bitter resistance among conservatives and many religious leaders. Indeed, not until 1965 did the Supreme Court fully legalize the dissemination of contraceptive materials and information.

Interactive Map: Woman Suffrage Before 1920

Margaret Sanger Founder of birth-control movement; leading feminist

Workers Organize; Socialism Advances

In this age of organization, labor unions continued to expand. The American Federation of Labor (AFL) grew from less than half a million members in 1897 to 4 million by 1920—but this was only 20 percent of the nonfarm labor force. With immigrants hungry for jobs, union activities could be risky; bosses could easily fire an "agitator" and hire a newcomer. Judicial hostility also plagued the labor movement. In the 1908 *Danbury Hatters* case, a unanimous Supreme Court ruled that boycotts in support of strikes violated the Sherman Anti-Trust Act. The AFL's strength remained in the skilled trades, not in the factories and mills where most immigrants and women worked.

A few unions did try to reach these laborers. In 1900 immigrants in New York City founded the International Ladies' Garment Workers' Union (ILGWU), which conducted successful strikes in 1909 and 1911. The women on the picket lines found these strikes both exhilarating and frightening.

The **Industrial Workers of the World (IWW),** or Wobblies, founded in Chicago in 1905, also targeted the most exploited workers. Led by the colorful and compelling William D. "Big Bill" Haywood, the IWW was never large and was torn by dissent. It peaked at around 30,000 members, mainly western miners, lumbermen, fruit pickers, and itinerant laborers.

The IWW led some mass strikes of miners and timber workers, but its greatest success came in 1912 when it won a rancorous textile strike in Lawrence, Massachusetts. The victory owed much to Elizabeth Gurley Flynn, a fervent Irish-American orator, and Margaret Sanger, who publicized the cause by sending strikers' children to New York sympathizers for temporary care.

The Wobblies had a reputation, much exaggerated, for violence and sabotage, and they faced unremitting government harassment, especially during World War I. By 1920 the IWW's strength was broken.

Others appalled by capitalism's human toll, including some in the middle class, turned to socialism. Socialists advocated an end to capitalism and demanded public ownership of factories, utilities, railroads, and communications systems. But American workers generally rejected the revolutionary ideology of German social theorist Karl Marx in favor of democratic socialism achieved at the ballot box. In 1900 democratic socialists formed the Socialist Party of America (SPA). **Eugene V. Debs,** the Indiana labor leader, became the SPA's most popular spokesman and its candidate for president five times between 1900 and 1920.

The pinnacle of socialist strength came in 1912 when the SPA counted 118,000 members, Debs received over 900,000 (about 6 percent) of the votes for president, and the Socialists elected a congressman along with hundreds of municipal officials.

Industrial Workers of the World (IWW) Occasionally radical union discredited by use of violence

Eugene V. Debs Socialist labor leader whose surprising showing in the 1912 presidential election illustrated the growing frustrations of many workers

CHECKING IN

- In pursuit of political rights, some African-Americans, led by W. E. B. Du Bois, rejected Booker T. Washington's gradualism and became activists.
- The woman-suffrage movement emerged as a major component of progressivism.
- Women like Emma Goldman and Margaret Sanger pushed beyond the boundaries of the traditional "woman's sphere," promoting economic independence and birth control.
- The AFL grew larger and stronger but remained focused on the skilled trades; the more radical IWW blossomed, bloomed, and faded.
- Socialists gained strength, even among the middle class.

NATIONAL PROGRESSIVISM PHASE I: ROOSEVELT AND TAFT, 1901–1913

What strategies did African-Americans, women, and industrial workers use to improve their lot?

By 1905 localized reform movements had coalesced into a national effort. Symbolically, in 1906 Robert La Follette became a U.S. senator. Five years earlier, progressivism had found its first national leader, **Theodore Roosevelt.**

Bombastic, self-righteous, and jingoistic—but also brilliant, politically masterful, and endlessly interesting—Roosevelt, "TR," became president in 1901. He made the White House a cauldron of political activism. Skillfully orchestrating public opinion, the popular young president pursued his goals: labor mediation, consumer protection, conservation, business virtue, and activism abroad.

Roosevelt's activist approach permanently enlarged the powers of the presidency. TR's hand-picked successor, **William Howard Taft,** lacked his master's political genius, however, and his administration floundered amid sniping among former allies. With the Republican Party split, the Democrat Woodrow Wilson, holding a somewhat different vision of progressive reform, won the presidency in 1912.

Theodore Roosevelt Youthful successor to William McKinley in 1901; pushed an agenda of progressive reform

William Howard Taft Roosevelt's hand-picked successor for president; later served as Supreme Court justice

Roosevelt's Path to the White House

On September 6, 1901, in Buffalo, an anarchist shot President William McKinley. On September 14 McKinley died, and forty-two-year-old Vice President Theodore Roosevelt became president. Reflecting the view of many politicians, Republican kingmaker Mark Hanna exclaimed, "My God, that damned cowboy is in the White House!" Roosevelt was the son of an aristocratic New York family and sickly as a child, but he had used a body-building program and active summers in Wyoming to become a model of physical fitness. Later, two years on a Dakota ranch helped him to struggle past grief over his young wife's death in 1884 and nurtured the physical and mental toughness that he would later extol as "the strenuous life."

Plunging into politics when most of his social class considered it unbefitting gentlemen, Roosevelt held various posts in New York State before leading the Rough Riders in Cuba (see Chapter 20). He was elected New York's governor in 1898. Two years later, Republican bosses, eager to be rid of him, arranged for his nomination as vice president.

Unexpectedly thrust into the White House, TR energized the presidency. Roosevelt enjoyed public life and loved the limelight. As a relative wryly observed, he wanted to be the bride at every wedding and the corpse at every funeral. Americans were fascinated by their rambunctious young president, with his toothy grin, machine-gun speech, and passion for the outdoors.

Labor Disputes, Trustbusting, Railroad Regulation

The new president's political skills were quickly tested. In May 1902 the United Mine Workers Union (UMW) called a strike to gain higher wages, shorter hours, and recognition as a union. The mine owners refused to talk to UMW leaders. After five months, with coal reserves dwindling, TR summoned the deadlocked parties to the White House. Threatening to take over the mines, he won reluctant acceptance of an arbitration commission to settle the dispute. In 1903 the commission granted miners a 10 percent wage hike and reduced their workday from ten to nine hours.

TR approached such labor disputes very differently from his predecessors, who had called out federal troops to break strikes. Although not consistently prolabor, he defended labor's right to organize and derided as "arrogant stupidity" business owners' resistance to arbitration.

With his elite background, TR neither feared nor much liked business tycoons. Conservative at heart, he had no desire to abolish big corporations, but he embraced the progressive philosophy that corporate behavior must be carefully regulated. A strict moralist, he believed that corporations, like individuals, must meet a high standard of virtue.

J. P. Morgan's formation in 1901 of the U.S. Steel Company, the nation's first billion-dollar corporation, deepened public uneasiness over business consolidation. His 1902 State of the Union message gave high priority to breaking up business monopolies, or "trustbusting." Roosevelt's attorney general soon filed suit against the Northern Securities Company, a mammoth holding company formed to control railroading in the Northwest, for violating the Sherman Anti-Trust Act. TR called for a "square deal" for all Americans and denounced special treatment for capitalists. "We don't wish to destroy corporations," he insisted, "but we do wish to make them serve the public good." In 1904, by a 5 to 4 vote, the Supreme Court ordered the Northern Securities Company dissolved.

The Roosevelt administration filed forty-three other antitrust lawsuits. In two key cases in 1911, the Court ordered the breakup of the Standard Oil Company and the reorganization of the American Tobacco Company to make it less monopolistic.

As the 1904 presidential election approached, Roosevelt made peace with the Republicans' big-business wing. When the convention that unanimously nominated Roosevelt adopted a conservative, probusiness platform, $2 million in corporate campaign contributions poured in. The conservative-dominated Democrats meanwhile nominated New York judge Alton B. Parker and wrote a platform firmly embracing the gold standard.

Hepburn Act Legislation that strengthened government power to regulate railroads

Winning easily, Roosevelt turned to one of his major goals: railroad regulation. He saw regulation, rather than antitrust lawsuits, as the most promising long-term strategy. His work for passage of the **Hepburn Act** (1906) reflected this shift in outlook. This measure empowered the Interstate Commerce Commission to set maximum railroad rates and to examine railroads' financial records. Although the Hepburn Act did not fully satisfy reformers, it did increase the government's regulatory powers.

Consumer Protection

No progressive reform proved more popular than the fight against unsafe and falsely labeled food, drugs, and medicine. Upton Sinclair's stomach-turning *The Jungle* (1906) described the foul conditions under which sausages and cold cuts were produced. In a vivid passage, Sinclair wrote, "[A] man could run his hand over these piles of meat and sweep off handfuls of dried dung of rats. These rats were nuisances, and the packers would put poisoned bread out for them, they would die, and then rats, bread, and meat would go into the hoppers together." Women's organizations and consumer groups rallied public opinion on this issue. Other muckrakers exposed useless or dangerous patent medicines, many laced with cocaine, opium, or alcohol. One tonic "for treatment of the alcohol habit" contained 26.5 percent alcohol. Peddlers of these nostrums freely claimed that they could cure cancer, grow hair, and restore sexual vigor.

Sensing the public mood, Roosevelt supported the Pure Food and Drug Act and the Meat Inspection Act, both passed in 1906. The former outlawed the sale of adulterated food and drugs, and required accurate ingredient labels; the latter imposed strict sanitary rules on meatpackers, set up a quality-rating system, and created a program of federal meat inspection.

CL Primary Source:
The Patent Medicine
Fraud

On racial matters, Roosevelt's record was marginally better than that of other politicians in this racist age. He appointed an African-American as the head of the Charleston customhouse and closed a Mississippi post office rather than yield to demands that he dismiss the black postmistress. In a gesture of symbolic import, he dined with Booker T. Washington at the White House. The worst blot on his record came in 1906 with the aforementioned "Brownsville Incident," when he approved the dishonorable discharge of an entire regiment of black soldiers in Brownsville, Texas for the crimes of a few. (In 1972, when most of the men were long dead, Congress removed the dishonorable discharges from their records.)

Environmentalism Progressive-Style

In his first State of the Union message, Roosevelt singled out conservation as "the most vital internal question." By 1900 decades of urban-industrial growth and western expansion had taken a heavy toll on the land. In the West, land use disputes raged as mining and timber interests, farmers, ranchers, sheep growers, and preservationists advanced competing claims.

Western business interests and boosters preached exploitation of the region's resources, and farmers pushed for irrigation projects, but organizations like the Sierra Club battled to preserve large wild areas for their pristine beauty. After Congress in 1891 authorized the president to designate public lands as forest reserves, Presidents Harrison and Cleveland set aside 35 million acres.

A wilderness vogue swept the United States in the early twentieth century. From congested cities and clanging factories, Americans looked to the wilderness for tranquility and spiritual solace. Popular writers evoked the lure of the primitive, and the Boy Scouts (1910) and Girl Scouts (1912) gave city children a taste of the outdoors.

Between the wilderness enthusiasts and the developers stood government professionals like Gifford Pinchot, who saw the public domain as a resource to be managed wisely. Named by Roosevelt to head the new U.S. Forest Service in 1905, Pinchot campaigned not for preservation but for conservation—the planned, regulated use of forests for public and commercial purposes.

At heart Roosevelt was a preservationist, a champion of wilderness and wildlife preservation. However, Roosevelt the politician backed the conservationists' call for planned development. He supported the **National Reclamation Act** of 1902, which earmarked the proceeds of public-land sales for water management in the arid western regions and established the Reclamation Service to plan dams and irrigation projects.

National Reclamation Act
Sold public land and used the revenues for water management and dam projects

President Theodore Roosevelt and Friends Commune with Nature, 1903

Dwarfed by an ancient sequoia, the Grizzly Giant, in the Mariposa Grove of California's Yosemite National Park, TR's party includes California governor George Pardee (third from left), the naturalist and Sierra Club founder John Muir (fourth from right) and the presidents of Columbia University (third from right) and the University of California (far right). The Grizzly Giant still stands, and remains a favorite with tourists.

The Reclamation Act, according to some historians, ranks with the Northwest Ordinance for promoting the development of a vast region of North America. For example, the Roosevelt Dam spurred the growth of Phoenix, Arizona, and the Snake River project converted thousands of barren Idaho acres into fertile farmland. The law required those who benefited from reclamation projects to repay the government for construction costs, thus establishing a revolving fund for other projects. It made possible the transition of the West from a series of isolated "island settlements" into a thriving, interconnected region.

The competition for scarce water resources in the West sparked bitter political battles. The Los Angeles basin, for example, with 40 percent of California's population in 1900, found itself with only 2 percent of the state's surface water. In 1907, the City of Los Angeles derailed a Reclamation Service project intended for the farmers of California's Owens Valley, more than 230 miles to the north, and diverted the precious water to Los Angeles.

Meanwhile, President Roosevelt backed Pinchot's program of multiuse land management and set aside more than 200 million acres of public land as national forests, mineral reserves, and potential water-power sites. But because of opposition in the West, Congress in 1907 rescinded the president's power to create national forests in six timber-rich states. Roosevelt signed the bill—only, however, after designating twenty-one new national forests totaling 16 million acres in those six states. Congress established the National Park Service in 1916 to manage them.

With Roosevelt's blessing, Pinchot organized a White House conservation conference for the nation's governors in 1908, but John Muir and other wilderness preservationists were not invited. However, preservationists won key victories in this era. Initiatives by private citizens saved a large grove of California's giant redwoods and a lovely stretch of the Maine coastline.

The Sierra Club lost a major battle to save the Hetch Hetchy Valley in Yosemite National Park when Congress in 1913 approved a dam on the Tuolumne River to provide water and hydroelectric power for San Francisco. The controversy focused attention and publicized the environmentalist cause, as Americans for the first time weighed the aesthetic implications of a major public-works project.

Taft in the White House, 1909–1913

Roosevelt had pledged not to run for a third term in 1908, and to the disappointment of millions, he kept his promise. The Republicans' most conservative wing regained control. Although they nominated Roosevelt's choice, William Howard Taft, for president, they selected a conservative vice presidential candidate and drafted an extremely conservative platform. The Democrats, meanwhile, nominated William Jennings Bryan for a third and final time. The Democratic platform called for a lower tariff, denounced the trusts, and embraced the cause of labor.

With Roosevelt's endorsement, Taft coasted to victory. But the Democrats made gains, and progressive Republican state candidates outran the national ticket. Overall, the outcome suggested a lull in the reform movement, not its end.

Taft differed markedly from Roosevelt. Whereas TR kept in fighting trim and loved boxing, Taft was grossly overweight and played golf. TR loved dramatic public donnybrooks against the forces of evil and greed, but Taft disliked controversy. His happiest days would come later, as chief justice of the Supreme Court.

Pledged to carry on TR's program, Taft supported the Mann-Elkins Act (1910), which strengthened the Interstate Commerce Commission's rate-setting powers and extended its authority to telephone and telegraph companies. The Taft White House filed more antitrust suits than the Roosevelt administration had, but its lack of fanfare left most people considering TR the quintessential "trustbuster."

The reform spotlight, meanwhile, shifted to Congress. During the Roosevelt administration, a small group of reform-minded Republican legislators, nicknamed the Insurgents, had challenged their party's conservative congressional leadership. The Insurgents, who included senators La Follette of Wisconsin and Albert Beveridge of Indiana and congressman George Norris of Nebraska turned against President Taft in 1909 after a tariff struggle.

Taft had originally believed that the tariff should be lowered, but in 1909 he signed the high Payne-Aldrich Tariff, praising it as "the best tariff bill that the Republican party ever passed." The battle between conservative and progressive Republicans was on.

The so-called Ballinger-Pinchot affair widened the rift. Richard A. Ballinger, Taft's secretary of the interior, was a Seattle lawyer who favored the unregulated private development of natural resources. Ballinger approved the sale of several million acres of public land in Alaska in 1909 to some Seattle businessmen, who promptly sold it to a banking consortium that included J. P. Morgan. When a Department of

Interior official protested, he was fired. In true muckraking style, he immediately published an article in *Collier's* blasting Ballinger's actions. When Gifford Pinchot of the Forestry Service publicly criticized Ballinger, he, too, got the ax. TR's supporters seethed.

When Roosevelt returned to the United States from an African safari in June 1910, Pinchot met the boat. In the 1910 midterm elections, Roosevelt campaigned for Insurgent candidates. In a speech that alarmed conservatives, he attacked judges who struck down progressive laws and endorsed the radical idea of reversing judicial rulings by popular vote. Borrowing a term from Herbert Croly's *The Promise of American Life,* TR proposed a "New Nationalism" that would powerfully engage the federal government in reform.

Democrats captured the House of Representatives in 1910, and a coalition of Democrats and Insurgents controlled the Senate. As fervor for reform rose, Roosevelt sounded more and more like a presidential candidate.

Progressive Party National third party formed around TR's presidential candidacy in 1912

Woodrow Wilson Democratic president whose election in 1912 ushered in a second wave of progressive reforms on the national level

The Four-Way Election of 1912

In February 1912 Roosevelt announced his candidacy for the Republican nomination. In state primaries and conventions, Roosevelt beat Taft handily. But Taft controlled the party machinery. At the Republican convention in Chicago, Taft's forces disqualified many of Roosevelt's delegates. Outraged, TR's backers left the convention and formed the **Progressive Party.** What had been a general term for a broad reform movement now became the official name of a political party.

"I feel fit as a bull moose," Roosevelt trumpeted, thereby giving his organization its nickname, the Bull Moose Party. The convention platform endorsed virtually every reform cause of the day. The charismatic Roosevelt attracted a diverse following to the new party.

Meanwhile, the reform spirit had infused the Democratic party at state and local levels. In New Jersey, voters elected a political novice, **Woodrow Wilson,** as governor in 1910. A "Wilson for President" boom soon arose, and when the Democrats assembled in Baltimore in June 1912, Wilson won the nomination, defeating several established party leaders.

The Republican Taft essentially gave up. Eugene V. Debs ran on the Socialist platform, demanding an end to capitalism, and Roosevelt and Wilson vied for the moderate reform vote. TR preached his New Nationalism: governmental regulation of big business in the public interest. Wilson called for a "New Freedom," evoking an earlier era of small government, small businesses, and free competition. The divided Republicans proved no match for the united Democrats. Wilson prevailed, and the Democrats took both houses of Congress (see Map 21.2).

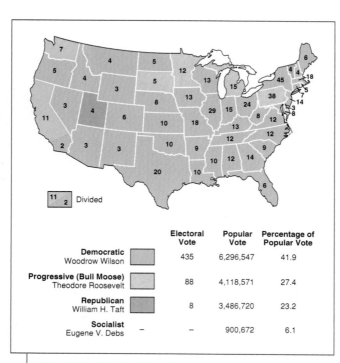

	Electoral Vote	Popular Vote	Percentage of Popular Vote
Democratic Woodrow Wilson	435	6,296,547	41.9
Progressive (Bull Moose) Theodore Roosevelt	88	4,118,571	27.4
Republican William H. Taft	8	3,486,720	23.2
Socialist Eugene V. Debs	–	–	900,672	6.1

Map 21.2   The Election of 1912

The 1912 election identified the triumphant Democrats with reform (except on the issue of race), launching a tradition on which Franklin D. Roosevelt would build in the 1930s. The breakaway Progressive party demonstrated the support for reform among grass-roots Republicans while leaving the Republican party in the grip of conservatives.

NATIONAL PROGRESSIVISM PHASE II: WOODROW WILSON, 1913–1917

As progressivism became a national movement, what issues proved most important?

The son and grandson of Presbyterian ministers, Wilson grew up in southern towns in a churchly atmosphere that shaped his oratory and moral outlook. He graduated from Princeton, earned a Ph.D. in political science from Johns Hopkins University, taught at Princeton, and became president there in 1902. He lost support at Princeton because of his unwillingness to compromise and left the academic world for the political arena in 1910. Three years later, he was president of the United States.

Wilson was an eloquent orator who excelled at political deal making. But he could also retreat into a fortress of absolute certitude that tolerated no opposition. During his years as president, all these facets of his personality would come into play. Wilson proved ready to use government to address the problems of the new corporate order, and the national progressive movement gained powerful new momentum.

Tariff and Banking Reform

Tariff reform—long a goal of southern and agrarian Democrats—headed Wilson's agenda. A low-tariff bill passed the House but bogged down in the Senate. Showing his flair for drama, Wilson denounced tariff lobbyists, and his censure led to a Senate investigation of lobbyists and of senators who profited from high tariffs. Stung by the publicity, the Senate slashed tariff rates even more than the House had done. The Underwood-Simmons Tariff reduced rates an average of 15 percent.

In June 1913 Wilson called for banking and currency reform. The nation's totally decentralized banking system clearly needed overhauling. But no consensus existed on specifics. Many reformers wanted a publicly controlled central banking system, but the nation's bankers favored private control. Some opposed any central banking authority, public or private.

No banking expert, Wilson insisted that the monetary system ultimately be publicly controlled. As the bargaining went on, Wilson played a crucial behind-the-scenes role. The result was the **Federal Reserve Act** of December 1913. A compromise measure, this law created twelve regional Federal Reserve banks under mixed public and private control. Each regional bank could issue U.S. dollars, called Federal Reserve notes, to the banks in its district to make loans. Overall control of the system was assigned to the heads of the twelve regional banks and a Washington-based

Federal Reserve Act Major step toward establishing solid national banking system

Federal Reserve Board (FRB), whose members were appointed by the president for fourteen-year terms. (The secretary of the treasury and the comptroller of the currency were made ex officio members.)

The Federal Reserve Act stands as Wilson's greatest legislative achievement. In time the FRB, nicknamed "the Fed," grew into the strong central monetary institution it remains today, adopting fiscal policies to prevent financial panics, promote economic growth, and dampen inflationary pressures.

Regulating Business; Aiding Workers and Farmers

Federal Trade Commission
Agency to ensure fair trade and practices

In 1914 Wilson and his congressional allies turned to that perennial progressive cause, business regulation. Two key regulatory laws resulted, embodying different approaches. The **Federal Trade Commission** Act (1914) reflected an administrative approach by creating a "watchdog" agency, the FTC, with power to investigate suspected violations, require regular reports from corporations, and issue cease-and-desist orders against unfair methods of competition. The Clayton Antitrust Act (1914) took a legal approach. It remedied the Sherman Anti-Trust Act's vagueness by spelling out a series of illegal practices, such as selling at a loss to undercut competitors. With the added clout of the Clayton Act, the Wilson administration filed antitrust suits against close to a hundred corporations.

The Democrats historically identified with workers, and Wilson supported the American Federation of Labor, defended workers' right to organize, and endorsed a Clayton Act clause that exempted strikes, boycotts, and peaceful picketing from "restraint of trade" injunctions. In 1916 (a campaign year), Wilson and congressional Democrats enacted three important worker-protection laws. The Keating-Owen Act barred from interstate commerce products manufactured by child labor (later declared unconstitutional). The Adamson Act established an eight-hour workday for interstate railway workers. The Workmen's Compensation Act provided accident and injury protection to federal workers.

Wilson also championed the Federal Farm Loan Act and the Federal Warehouse Act (1916), which allowed farmers to secure long-term, low-interest federal loans using land or crops as security. The Federal Highway Act (1916) matched federal funds with state appropriations for highway construction, benefiting the new automobile industry as well as farmers plagued by bad roads.

Progressivism and the Constitution

Louis Brandeis Jurist who pioneered use of sociology and other social sciences in arguing legal cases

The late-nineteenth-century probusiness bias of the courts moderated in the Progressive Era. In 1908 the Supreme Court in *Muller* v. *Oregon* upheld an Oregon law setting maximum hours for women laundry workers at ten hours. To defend the constitutionality of the Oregon law, Boston attorney **Louis Brandeis** had offered economic, medical, and sociological evidence of how long hours harmed women workers. The Court's acceptance of the "Brandeis brief" marked a breakthrough in the legal system's responsiveness to new social realities.

In 1916 Wilson nominated Brandeis to the Supreme Court. Many conservatives, including Republican leaders in Congress, disapproved of Brandeis's innovative approach to the law and protested. Anti-Semites opposed him because he was a Jew. But Wilson stood by his nominee, and after a fierce battle, the Senate confirmed him.

These years also produced four constitutional amendments. The Sixteenth Amendment (ratified in 1913) granted Congress the authority to tax income. An earlier income tax measure had been declared unconstitutional, spurring advocates to campaign for an amendment. Quickly exercising its new authority, Congress in 1913 imposed a graduated federal income tax with a maximum rate of 7 percent on incomes in excess of $500,000. Income tax revenues helped pay for the government's regulatory activities under Progressive Era legislation. The Seventeenth Amendment (1913) completed a Populist crusade by mandating the direct popular election of U.S. senators. The Eighteenth Amendment (1919) established prohibition of "intoxicating liquors." The Nineteenth Amendment (1920) granted women the vote. This array of amendments demonstrated how profoundly progressivism had transformed the political landscape.

1916: Wilson Edges out Hughes

In 1916 Wilson easily won renomination. The Republicans nominated Charles Evans Hughes, Supreme Court justice and former New York governor. Urged by Roosevelt, who was obsessed with drawing the United States into the war that had broken out in Europe in 1914 (see Chapter 22), the Progressive party endorsed Hughes. With the Republicans more or less reunited, the election was extremely close. Wilson won the popular vote, but the Electoral College outcome remained in doubt for weeks as the California tally seesawed back and forth. Ultimately, Wilson carried the state by less than four thousand votes and, with it, the election.

The progressive movement lost momentum as attention turned from reform to war. Final success for the prohibition and woman-suffrage campaigns came later, in 1919–1920, and Congress enacted a few reform measures in the 1920s. But, overall, the movement's zest and drive clearly waned as America went to war in 1917.

CHECKING IN

- Wilson achieved the long-sought Democratic goal of tariff reduction.
- The Federal Reserve Act, which gave the nation a central banking system, was Wilson's most important legislative achievement.
- The Clayton Anti-Trust Act strengthened government's regulatory powers.
- Wilson helped shepherd four constitutional amendments to ratification: direct popular election of senators, the income tax, prohibition, and woman suffrage.
- The outbreak of World War I curtailed and eventually ended the first great surge of progressivism.

Chapter Summary

 DOWNLOAD THE MP3 AUDIO FILE OF THE CHAPTER SUMMARY, AND LISTEN TO IT ON THE GO.

How did intellectuals, novelists, and journalists inspire the progressive movement? (page 477)

The progressive movement began as preachers, novelists, journalists, photographers, and painters highlighted appalling conditions in America's cities and factories. Intellectuals offered ideas for reform through the creative use of government. Primarily middle class, progressives sought to improve urban life and working conditions, eliminate political corruption, and curb the excesses of the new urban, industrial society.

KEY TERMS

"muckrakers" *(p. 481)*
Robert La Follette *(p. 483)*
Anti-Saloon League *(p. 487)*
Ida Wells-Barnett *(p. 490)*
W. E. B. Du Bois *(p. 490)*
National Association for the Advancement of Colored People (NAACP) *(p. 491)*

How did state and local progressives seek to reform cities and the new industrial order? (page 481)

At the local and state level, reformers like Mayor Hazen Pingree of Detroit and Wisconsin governor Robert M. La Follette, together with a host of reform organizations, worked to combat political corruption, make cities safer and more beautiful, regulate corporations, and improve conditions for workers.

How did progressives try to control morality, and how did they view immigrants and blacks? (page 490)

Progressivism had its coercive side. Some reformers concentrated on regulating urban amusements and banning alcohol consumption. Racism and hostility to immigrants comprise a part of the progressive legacy as well. Because of the refusal of progressive reformers to substantively address the problem of racial injustice, African-Americans became more politically active, founding the National Association for the Advancement of Colored People.

What strategies did African-Americans, women, and industrial workers use to improve their lot? (page 495)

The women's movement focused on the achievement of suffrage. A handful of women, like birth-control advocate Margaret Sanger, pushed far beyond the accepted "woman's sphere." The labor movement grew stronger, especially the AFL; more radical movements like the IWW flared, but few had long-term impact. Meanwhile, Roosevelt's activist presidency captivated the American public; he was committed to a multitude of progressive reforms. Under TR, Congress strengthened railroad regulation, established the Food and Drug Administration, and enormously increased the amount of land set aside for conservation and preservation. TR became known as "the great trustbuster." However, President Taft alienated TR and progressive Republicans, who formed the Bull Moose (Progressive) party. With Republicans divided, Democrat Woodrow Wilson won the presidency in 1912.

As progressivism became a national movement, what issues proved most important? (page 501)

Wilson's presidency saw enormous strides in increasing government's regulatory powers. For example, the Clayton Act strengthened antitrust law, and the Federal Reserve Act centralized banking. Four amendments to the Constitution embodied many progressive goals: direct popular election of senators, the income tax, prohibition, and woman suffrage. However, progressivism began to wane as attention turned to World War I. The next great reform movement, the New Deal of the 1930s, would draw on progressivism's legacy.

KEY TERMS continued

Carrie Chapman Catt *(p. 492)*

Margaret Sanger *(p. 493)*

Industrial Workers of the World (IWW) *(p. 494)*

Eugene V. Debs *(p. 494)*

Theodore Roosevelt *(p. 495)*

William Howard Taft *(p. 495)*

Hepburn Act *(p. 496)*

National Reclamation Act *(p. 497)*

Progressive Party *(p. 500)*

Woodrow Wilson *(p. 501)*

Federal Reserve Act *(p. 501)*

Federal Trade Commission *(p. 502)*

Louis Brandeis *(p. 502)*

CHAPTER 22

Global Involvements and World War I

1902–1920

Sow the seeds *of* Victory!
plant &
raise
your own
vegetables

World War I Poster Urging Food
Conservation, by the Illustrator
James Montgomery Flagg

This icon will direct you to the website
where you can Prepare for Class,
Improve Your Grade, and Ace the Test:
www.cengage.com/history/boyer/
enduringconcise6e

CHAPTER PREVIEW

Defining America's World Role, 1902–1914
What goals underlay America's early-twentieth-century involvements in Asia and Latin America?

War in Europe, 1914–1917
Considering both immediate and long-term factors, why did the United States go to war in 1917?

Mobilizing at Home, Fighting in France, 1917–1918
How did Washington mobilize the nation for war, and what role did U.S. troops play in the war?

Promoting the War and Suppressing Dissent
How did Americans respond to propaganda and suppression of dissent?

Economic and Social Trends in Wartime America
What was the war's economic, political, and social impact on the American home front?

Joyous Armistice, Bitter Aftermath, 1918–1920
How did the League of Nations begin, and why did the Senate reject U.S. membership in the League?

It was April 6, 1917, and Jane Addams was troubled. Congress had just supported President Woodrow Wilson's call for a declaration of war on Germany. Addams had deep patriotic roots, but she believed in peace and deplored her nation's decision for war. As the founder of Hull House, a Chicago settlement house, Addams had worked to overcome tensions among different ethnic groups. When war broke out in Europe in 1914, Addams worked to end the conflict. A founder of the Woman's Peace Party in 1915, she attended an International Congress of Women that called on the warring nations to submit their differences to arbitration. Addams met with President Wilson to enlist his support for arbitration, but with no success.

Now America had entered the war, and Addams had to take a stand. Many of her friends, including John Dewey, were lining up behind Wilson. Despite the pressures, Addams heeded her conscience and opposed the war. The reaction was swift. Editorial writers who had earlier praised her settlement-house work now criticized her. For years after, the American Legion and other patriotic organizations attacked Addams for her "disloyalty" in 1917.

Addams did not sit out the war on the sidelines, however. She gave speeches across America urging increased food production to aid refugees. In 1919, she was elected first president of the Women's International League for Peace and Freedom. In 1931, she won the Nobel Peace Prize.

Addams's experience underscores how deeply World War I affected American life. Beyond its immediate effects, the war had long-lasting social, economic, and political ramifications. In the late nineteenth century, America had become an industrial powerhouse seeking markets and raw materials worldwide. In the early twentieth century, these broadening economic interests helped give rise to a new international role for the nation. This expanded role influenced home-front developments, and it has continued to shape American history to the present. These broader global realities, culminating in World War I, are the focus of this chapter.

DEFINING AMERICA'S WORLD ROLE, 1902–1914

What goals underlay America's early-twentieth-century involvements in Asia and Latin America?

As we saw in Chapter 20, the annexation of Hawaii, the Spanish-American War, the occupation of the Philippines, and other developments in the 1890s signaled America's growing involvement abroad. These foreign engagements reflected a desire to assert American power in an age of imperial expansion. This process of foreign engagement continued under Presidents Theodore Roosevelt, William Howard Taft, and Woodrow Wilson. America's dealings with Asian and Latin American nations in these years were shaped by both economic and ideological considerations.

The "Open Door": Competing for the China Market

As the campaign to suppress the Philippines insurrection dragged on (see Chapter 20), Americans shifted their focus to China. Their aim was not territorial expansion but rather protection of U.S. commercial opportunities. Textile producers dreamed of clothing China's millions of people; investors envisioned Chinese railroad construction. As China's 250-year-old Manchu Ch'ing empire grew weaker, U.S. businesspeople watched carefully.

China's weakness had drawn other imperialists—including Russia, Germany, and Great Britain—who had won major concessions of land and trading rights. In September 1899, fearful of American businesses being shut out of China, Secretary of State John Hay sent notes to the imperialist powers in China requesting that they open the ports within their spheres of influence to all comers and not grant special privileges to traders of their own nations. Although the six nations gave noncom-

Interactive Map: Imperialism in Asia

Chronology

1899	First U.S. Open Door note seeking access to China market; Boxer Rebellion erupts in China
1900	Second U.S. Open Door note
1904	President Theodore Roosevelt proclaims" Roosevelt Corollary" to Monroe Doctrine
1905	Roosevelt mediates the end of the Russo-Japanese War
1906	San Francisco ends segregation of Asian schoolchildren; Panama Canal construction begins
1911	U.S.-backed revolution in Nicaragua
1912	U.S. Marines occupy Nicaragua
1914	U.S. troops occupy Veracruz, Mexico; Panama Canal opens; World War I begins; President Wilson proclaims American neutrality
1915	U.S. Marines occupy Haiti and the Dominican Republic; Woman's Peace Party organized; British liner *Lusitania* sunk by German U-boat; Wilson permits U.S. bank loans to Allies
1916	U.S. punitive expedition invades Mexico, seeking Pancho Villa; Germany pledges not to attack merchant ships without warning; Wilson reelected
1917	U.S. troops withdraw from Mexico; Germany resumes unrestricted U-boat warfare; United States declares war; Selective Service Act sets up national draft; War Industries Board, Committee on Public Information, and Food Administration created; Espionage Act passed; War Risk Insurance Act authorizes payments to servicemen's dependents; NAACP march in New York City protests upsurge in lynchings; Bolsheviks seize power in Russia; Russia leaves the war; New York State passes woman-suffrage referendum; U.S. government operates the nation's railroads
1918	Wilson outlines Fourteen Points; Sedition Amendment passed; Global influenza pandemic takes heavy toll in United States; National War Labor Board created; American forces see action at Château-Thierry; Belleau Wood, St. Mihiel, and Meuse-Argonne campaign; Republicans win control of both houses of Congress (November 5); Armistice signed (November 11)
1919	Eighteenth Amendment added to the Constitution (prohibition); Peace treaty, including League of Nations covenant, signed at Versailles; Supreme Court upholds silencing of war critics in *Schenck* v. *United States*; Upsurge of lynchings; Racial violence in Chicago; Wilson suffers paralyzing stroke; Versailles treaty, with League covenant, rejected by Senate
1920	"Red raids" organized by Justice Department; Nineteenth Amendment added to the Constitution (woman suffrage); Warren G. Harding elected president

mittal answers, Hay blithely announced that they had accepted the principle of an "Open Door" to American business in China.

Hay's Open Door note showed how commercial considerations were increasingly influencing American foreign policy. It reflected a quest for what has been called "informal empire," in contrast to the formal acquisition of overseas territories.

In 1899, even as the Open Door notes were circulating, an antiforeign secret society known as the Harmonious Righteous Fists (called "Boxers" by Western journalists) killed thousands of foreigners and Chinese Christians. In June 1900 the Boxers occupied Beijing (BAY-jing), China's capital, and besieged the district housing the foreign legations. The United States contributed twenty-five hundred soldiers to an international army that marched on Beijing, quashed the **Boxer Rebellion,** and rescued the occupants of the threatened legations.

Boxer Rebellion Fanatical Chinese insurgency against Christians and foreigners, defeated by an international force

Open Door notes John Hay's statement of American policy to keep trade open in China

The defeat of the Boxer uprising further weakened China's government. Fearing that the regime's collapse would allow European powers to carve up China, John Hay issued a second, more important, series of **Open Door notes** in 1900. He reaffirmed the principle of open trade in China for all nations and announced America's determination to preserve China's territorial and administrative integrity. In general, China remained open to U.S. business interests and Christian missionaries. In the 1930s, when Japanese expansionism menaced China, Hay's policy helped shape the American response.

Along with U.S. economic expansion in China came missionary activity. American Protestant missionaries had come to Asia as early as the 1820s. By 1900 some five thousand U.S. missionaries were active in China, Africa, India, and elsewhere. As they preached their religious message, the missionaries also spread American influence globally and blazed the way for U.S. economic expansion.

The Panama Canal: Hardball Diplomacy

 Primary Source: Panama Canal

Dreams of a canal across the ribbon of land joining North and South America dated back to the Spanish conquest. Yellow fever and mismanagement brought a French company's late-nineteenth-century attempt to build a canal to disaster and left a half-completed waterway. To recoup some of the $400 million loss, the company offered to sell its assets, including a concession from Colombia, which then controlled the isthmus, to the United States for $109 million.

America was in an expansionist mood. In 1902, after the French lowered their price to $40 million, Congress authorized President Theodore Roosevelt to accept the offer. The U.S. negotiated an agreement with Colombian diplomat for a ninety-nine-year lease on the proposed canal. But when the Colombian Senate rejected the deal, seeking a better offer, Roosevelt privately denounced the Colombians as "greedy little anthropoids."

Roosevelt found a willing collaborator in Philippe Bunau-Varilla (fih-LEEP boo-NAW vah-REE-yuh), an official of the bankrupt French company. Dismayed that his company might lose its $40 million, Bunau-Varilla organized a "revolution" in Panama from a New York hotel room. While his wife stitched a flag, he wrote a declaration of independence and a constitution for the new nation. On November 3, 1903, the "revolution" erupted on schedule, with a U.S. warship anchored offshore. In short order, Bunau-Varilla gained American recognition of the newly hatched nation and signed a treaty guaranteeing the United States a ten-mile-wide strip of land across Panama "in perpetuity" in return for $10 million and an annual payment of $250,000. Roosevelt later summarized the episode: "I took the Canal Zone, and let Congress debate, and while the debate goes on, the canal does also."

Before completing the canal, the United States first had to conquer yellow fever. After Dr. Walter Reed recognized the mosquito as its carrier, the U.S. Army carried out a prodigious drainage project that eradicated the disease-bearing pest. Construction began in 1906, and in August 1914 the first ship sailed through the **Panama Canal.**

Panama Canal Waterway between the Pacific and Atlantic Oceans, completed by the U.S. in 1914

A technical wonder, the canal also symbolized an arrogant American imperialism. The ill feeling generated by Theodore Roosevelt's actions, combined with other instances of U.S. interventionism, would long shadow U.S.-Latin American relations.

Roosevelt and Taft Assert U.S. Power in Latin America and Asia

While the Panama Canal remains this era's best-known foreign-policy achievement, other U.S. actions underscored Washington's growing determination to assert U.S. power and protect U.S. business interests in Latin America (see Map 22.1) and Asia. Theodore Roosevelt believed that the United States must strengthen its world role, protect U.S. interests in Latin America, and preserve the balance of power in Asia. In 1904, when several European nations threatened to invade the Dominican Republic, a small Caribbean island nation that had defaulted on its debts, Roosevelt reacted swiftly. If any nation intervened, he believed, it should be the United States. In December 1904 Roosevelt declared that "chronic wrongdoing" by any Latin American nation would justify U.S. intervention.

This pronouncement became known as the Roosevelt Corollary to the Monroe Doctrine. (The original "doctrine," issued in 1823, had warned European powers

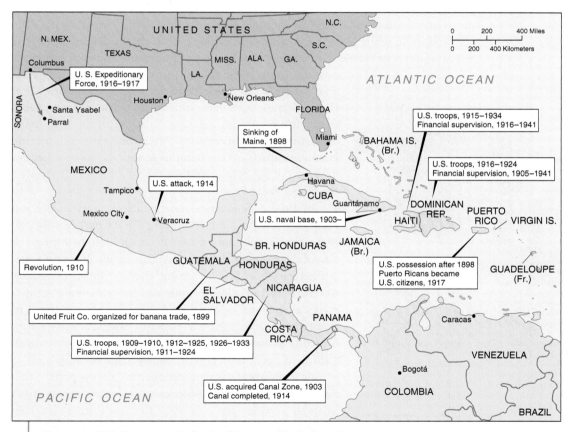

Map 22.1   U.S. Hegemony in the Caribbean and Latin America, 1900–1941

Through many interventions, territorial acquisitions, and robust economic expansion, the United States became the predominant power in Latin America in the early twentieth century. Acting on Theodore Roosevelt's assertion of a U.S. right to combat "wrongdoing" in Latin America and the Caribbean, the United States dispatched troops to the region, where they met nationalist opposition.

against meddling in Latin America.) The Roosevelt Corollary announced that in some circumstances the United States had the *right* to meddle. Suiting actions to words, the United States ran the Dominican Republic's customs service for two years and took over the management of the country's foreign debt. Roosevelt summed up his foreign-policy approach in a 1901 speech quoting what he said was an old African proverb, "Speak softly and carry a big stick."

In 1911 a U.S.-supported revolution in Nicaragua brought to power Adolfo Díaz, an officer of an American-owned Nicaraguan mining property. U.S. bankers loaned the Díaz government $1.5 million in exchange for control of the Nicaraguan national bank, the customs service, and the national railroad. When a revolt against Díaz broke out in 1912, Taft sent in the marines to protect the bankers' investment. Except for one brief interval, they remained until 1933.

In Asia, too, both Roosevelt and Taft sought to project U.S. power and advance the interests of American business. In 1900 Russia exploited the chaos unleashed by the Boxer uprising by sending troops to occupy Manchuria (man-CHOO-ree-uh), China's northeastern province. In February 1904 a surprise Japanese attack destroyed Russian ships anchored at Port Arthur, Manchuria. Japan completely dominated in the Russo-Japanese War that followed.

Roosevelt, while pleased to see Russian expansionism challenged, believed that a Japanese victory would disrupt the Asian balance of power and threaten America's position in the Philippines. Accordingly, he invited Japan and Russia to a peace conference at Portsmouth, New Hampshire. In September 1905 the two rivals signed a peace treaty. Russia recognized Japan's rule in Korea and made other territorial concessions. After this outcome, curbing Japanese expansionism became America's major objective in Asia. For his role in ending the war, Roosevelt received the Nobel Peace Prize.

In 1906, U.S.-Japanese relations soured when the San Francisco school board, reflecting West Coast hostility to Asian immigrants, assigned all Asian children to segregated schools. Japan angrily protested this insult. Roosevelt persuaded the school board to reverse this discriminatory policy. In return, in 1908 the administration negotiated a "gentlemen's agreement" with Japan by which Tokyo pledged to halt Japanese emigration to America. Racist attitudes continued to poison U.S.-Japanese relations, however. In 1913, California prohibited Japanese aliens from owning land.

As Californians worried about the "yellow peril," Japanese journalists watching America's growing military strength wrote of a "white peril." In 1907 Roosevelt ordered sixteen gleaming white battleships on a "training operation" to Japan. Although officially treated as friendly, this "Great White Fleet" underscored America's growing naval might.

Under President Taft, U.S. foreign policy in Asia continued to focus on promoting U.S. commercial interests. A plan for a U.S.-financed railroad in Manchuria did not work

Woodrow Wilson, Schoolteacher
This 1914 cartoon captures the patronizing self-righteousness of Wilson's approach to Latin America that planted the seeds of long-term resentments.

out, however. Not only did U.S. bankers find the project too risky, but Russia and Japan signed a treaty carving up Manchuria for commercial purposes, freezing out the Americans.

| **Wilson and Latin America** | In 1913 the Democrat Woodrow Wilson repudiated his Republican predecessors' expansionism and pledged that the United States would "never again seek one additional |

foot of territory by conquest." But he, too, intervened in Latin America. In 1915, after bloody upheavals in Haiti (HAY-tee) and the Dominican Republic, Wilson ordered in the marines. A Haitian (HAY-shun) constitution favorable to American commercial interests was ratified in 1918 by a vote of 69,377 to 355—in a marine-supervised election—and marines brutally suppressed Haitian resistance to American rule. They remained in the Dominican Republic until 1924 and in Haiti until 1934.

The most serious crisis Wilson faced in Latin America was the Mexican Revolution. Mexico had won independence from Spain in 1820, but the nation remained divided between a landowning elite and an impoverished peasantry. In 1911, rebels led by the democratic reformer Francisco Madero had ended the thirty-year rule of President Porfirio Díaz, who had defended the interests of the wealthy elite. Early in 1913, just as Wilson took office, Mexican troops loyal to General Victoriano Huerta, a full-blooded Indian, overthrew and murdered Madero.

Amid the chaos, Wilson tried to promote good government, protect U.S. investments, and safeguard U.S. citizens living in Mexico or along its border. Reversing the long-standing U.S. policy of recognizing all governments, Wilson refused to recognize Huerta's regime, which he called "a government of butchers." Wilson authorized arms sales to Venustiano Carranza (kuh-RON-zuh), a Huerta foe, and blockaded Vera Cruz (VAIR-uh krooz) to prevent weapons from reaching Huerta. Announced Wilson, "I am going to teach the South American republics to elect good men." In April 1914 seven thousand U.S. troops occupied Veracruz and engaged Huerta's forces. Sixty-five Americans and approximately five hundred Mexicans were killed or wounded. Bowing to U.S. might, Huerta abdicated; Carranza took power; and the U.S. troops withdrew.

But the turmoil continued. In January 1916 a bandit chieftain in northern Mexico, Pancho Villa (PAN-choh VEE-yuh), murdered 16 American mining engineers and then crossed the border; burned Columbus, New Mexico; and killed 19 of its inhabitants. Sharing the public's outrage, Wilson sent into Mexico a punitive expedition that eventually totaled 12,000 U.S. troops. When Villa brazenly staged another raid across the Rio Grande (REE-oh GRAN-day) into Texas, Wilson ordered 150,000 National Guardsmen into duty along the border—a massive response that stirred anti-American feelings among Mexico's poor, for whom Villa was a folk hero.

Although soon overshadowed by World War I, these involvements in Asia and Latin America illuminate the U.S. foreign-policy goal, which was, essentially, to achieve a global order that would welcome both American political values and American business. They also illustrate the underlying world view of the old-stock, upper-class men who directed U.S. foreign policy. Convinced of their ethnic, gender, and social superiority,

CHECKING IN

- The Open Door notes, asserting that trade with China must be open to all nations, represented an important part of the American quest for "informal empire."

- The Panama Canal was both a major accomplishment and a symbol of American imperialism.

- The Roosevelt Corollary, announcing that the United States would act as an international policeman in Latin America, was meant to guarantee American preeminence in the Caribbean.

- Wilson intervened in the Mexican Revolution to try to enforce American ideals.

- The Wilsonian view of a world based on American principles shaped American policy during and after World War I.

they confidently promoted America's global interests while viewing with patronizing condescension the "backward" societies they sought to manipulate. The vision of a world order based on U.S. ideals would soon find expression in Woodrow Wilson's response to the crisis in Europe.

WAR IN EUROPE, 1914–1917

Considering both immediate and long-term factors, why did the United States go to war in 1917?

When war engulfed Europe in 1914, most Americans wished only to remain aloof. For nearly three years, the United States officially stayed neutral. But by April 1917 cultural ties to England and France, economic considerations, visions of a world remade in America's image, and German violations of Wilson's definition of neutral rights all combined to draw the United States into the maelstrom.

The Coming of War

With Europe at peace through much of the nineteenth century, some concluded that war was a thing of the past. However, a series of ominous developments suggested otherwise. Germany, Austria-Hungary, and Italy signed a mutual-defense treaty in 1882. In 1904 and 1907, Great Britain signed treaties with France and Russia. Meanwhile, the slow-motion collapse of the once-powerful Ottoman Empire, centered in Turkey, left in its wake such newly independent nations as Romania, Bulgaria, and Serbia.

Serbian patriots dreamed of expanding their boundaries into Bosnia-Herzegovina, Serbia's neighbor to the west. Russia supported these ambitions. Meanwhile, the Austro-Hungarian Empire also saw opportunities for expansion as Ottoman power faded. In 1908, Austria-Hungary annexed (took over) Bosnia-Herzegovina, alarming Russia and Serbia. Germany, ruled by Kaiser Wilhelm II, also displayed expansionist impulses. Germany had achieved national unification only in 1871, and many Germans believed that their nation had lagged in the race for empire.

Such was the context when Archduke Franz Ferdinand of Austria made a state visit to Bosnia in June 1914. As he and his wife rode in an open car through Sarajevo, the Bosnian capital, a young Bosnian Serb gunned them down. In response, Austria declared war on Serbia. Russia, aligned with Serbia by a secret treaty, mobilized for war. Germany declared war on Russia and France. Great Britain, linked by treaty to France, declared war on Germany. An assassin's bullets had plunged Europe into war.

Thus began what contemporaries called the Great War, which we know as World War I. On one side were Great Britain, Russia, and France, called the Allies. On the other side were the Central Powers: Germany and Austria-Hungary. Italy, initially neutral despite its alliance with the Central Powers, joined the Allies in 1915.

The Perils of Neutrality

Proclaiming U.S. neutrality, President Wilson urged the nation to be neutral "in thought as well as in action." Most Americans fervently agreed. A popular song summed up the mood: "I Didn't Raise My Boy to Be a Soldier."

Neutrality proved difficult, however. Not only economic ties but also a common language, ancestry, and culture linked many Americans to Britain by strong emotional bonds. Still, not all Americans shared these ties. Because millions were of German origin, many sided with Germany. Irish-Americans speculated that a German victory might free Ireland from British rule, while some Scandinavian immigrants identified more with Germany than with England.

Neutral in 1914, America went to war in 1917. What caused this turnabout? Fundamentally, Wilson's vision of a world order in America's image conflicted with his neutrality. An international system based on democracy and capitalism would be impossible, he believed, in a world dominated by imperial Germany. To shape the peace, America would have to fight the war.

These underlying ideas influenced Wilson's handling of the immediate issue that dragged the United States into the conflict: neutral nations' rights on the high seas. When the war began, Britain intercepted U.S. merchant ships bound for Germany. Wilson's protests intensified in late 1914 and early 1915 when Britain declared the North Sea a war zone and planted it with explosive mines. Britain was determined to exploit its naval advantage, even if it meant alienating America.

But Germany, not England, ultimately pushed the United States into war. If Britannia ruled the waves, Germany controlled the ocean depths with its torpedo-equipped submarines, or U-boats. In February 1915 Berlin proclaimed the waters around Great Britain a war zone and warned off all ships. Wilson responded: Germany would be held to "strict accountability" for any loss of U.S. ships or lives.

On May 1, 1915, in a small ad in U.S. newspapers, the German embassy cautioned Americans against travel on British or French vessels. Six days later, a U-boat sank the British liner *Lusitania* off the Irish coast, with the loss of 1,198 lives, including 128 Americans. (The *Lusitania,* historians later discovered, had carried munitions destined for England, a secret traffic in weapons known to British officials.)

The Sinking of the Cunard Liner *Lusitania,* May 7, 1915, off the Irish Coast

The destruction of the *Lusitania* by a German U-boat, portrayed here in an illustration from an English newspaper, took nearly 1,200 lives, including 128 Americans. This event outraged U.S. public opinion and led to build-up in military preparedness. But as President Wilson pursued diplomatic exchanges with Germany, nearly two more years would pass before the United States entered the war.

The *Lusitania* disaster exposed deep divisions in U.S. public opinion. Many Americans were ready for war. Theodore Roosevelt, strongly pro-British, condemned Wilson—who had counseled patience after the attack—for "abject cowardice and weakness." The National Security League, a lobby of bankers and industrialists, led a "preparedness" movement, stirring up patriotism and promoting an arms buildup and military training. By late 1915, Wilson himself called for a military buildup.

Other citizens, however, deplored the drift toward war. Some progressives warned that war fever was eroding support for reforms. Jane Addams lamented that the international movements to reduce infant mortality and improve care for the aged had been "scattered to the winds by the war." Divisions surfaced even within the Wilson administration. Secretary of State William Jennings Bryan, believing that Wilson's *Lusitania* notes were too hostile, resigned in June 1915. Early in 1916, Congress considered a bill to ban travel on belligerent ships, but President Wilson successfully opposed it, insisting that the principle of neutral rights must be upheld.

For a time, Wilson's approach seemed to work. Germany ordered U-boats to spare passenger ships, and offered compensation for the Americans lost in the *Lusitania* sinking. In March 1916, however, a German submarine sank a French passenger ship, the *Sussex,* in the English Channel, injuring several Americans. Wilson threatened to break diplomatic relations—a step toward war. In response, Berlin pledged not to attack merchant vessels without warning, and the crisis eased.

Meanwhile, U.S. banks' support for the Allies eroded the principle of neutrality. In August 1915, Wilson's advisors urged him to allow Allies to purchase American munitions and farm products and to authorize substantial loans to England. Only these measures, they argued, could prevent serious financial problems in the United States. Swayed by such arguments and personally sympathetic to the Allies, Wilson permitted bank loans of $500 million to the British and French governments. By April 1917, U.S. banks had lent $2.3 billion to the Allies, in contrast to $27 million to Germany.

While Americans concentrated on neutral rights, the land war settled into a grim stalemate. A September 1914 German drive into France had bogged down and the two sides had dug in, constructing trenches across France from the English Channel to the Swiss border. For more than three years, this line scarcely changed. Occasional offensives devastated the countryside and took a horrendous cost in human life. Trench warfare was a nightmare of mud, lice, rats, artillery bursts, poison gas, and random death.

The war dominated the 1916 presidential election. Wilson faced Republican Charles Evans Hughes, a former New York governor. Wilson campaigned on his success in keeping the country out of the war. Hughes criticized Wilson's lack of aggressiveness while rebuking him for policies that risked war. Wilson held the Democratic base and won support from women voters in western states that had adopted woman suffrage. Wilson's victory, although close, revealed the strength of the popular longing for peace as late as November 1916.

The United States Enters the War

In January 1917, facing stalemate on the ground, Germany resumed unrestricted submarine warfare. Germany's military leaders believed that even if the United States declared war as a result, full-scale U-boat warfare could bring victory before American troops reached the front.

Events now rushed forward. Wilson broke diplomatic relations on February 3. During February and March, U-boats sank five American ships. A coded telegram from the German foreign secretary, Arthur Zimmermann, to Germany's ambassador to Mexico promised that if Mexico would declare war on the United States, Germany would help restore Mexico's "lost territories" of Texas, Arizona, and New Mexico. Intercepted and decoded by the British, the "Zimmermann telegram" further inflamed the war spirit in America.

Events in distant Russia also helped create favorable conditions for America's entry into the war. In March 1917 liberal reformers and communist revolutionaries joined in an uprising that overthrew the repressive government of Tsar Nicholas II. A provisional government seemed to promise a democratic Russia, making it easier for President Wilson to portray the war as a battle for democracy.

On April 2, Wilson appeared before a joint session of Congress and called for a declaration of war. Applause rang out as Wilson described his vision of America's role in creating a postwar international order to make the world "safe for democracy." After a short but bitter debate, the Senate voted 82 to 6 for war. The House agreed, 373 to 50. Three key factors— German attacks on American shipping, U.S. economic investment in the Allied cause, and American cultural links to the Allies, especially England— had propelled the United States into the war.

CHECKING IN

- When World War I erupted, Wilson asked Americans to remain neutral in both thought and action.
- The question of neutral rights on the high seas was a point of dispute with both Great Britain and Germany.
- Americans loaned billions to the Allies, a few million to the Central Powers.
- Wilson was reelected in 1916 on the slogan "He kept us out of war."
- Renewed unrestricted submarine warfare and the Zimmermann telegram, suggesting a German-Mexican alliance, gave the United States the final push into World War I.

MOBILIZING AT HOME, FIGHTING IN FRANCE, 1917–1918

How did Washington mobilize the nation for war, and what role did U.S. troops play in the war?

Compared to its effects on Europe, the war only grazed the United States. Russia, ill-prepared for war, suffered heavily. France, Great Britain, and Germany fought for more than four years and suffered casualties of 70 percent or more; the U.S. casualty rate was 8 percent. The fighting left parts of France and Belgium brutally scarred; North America was physically untouched. Nevertheless, the war profoundly affected America.

Raising, Training, and Testing an Army

A woefully unprepared American military faced war in April 1917. The regular army of 120,000 enlisted men had virtually no combat experience. An aging officer corps was dozing away the years until retirement. There was enough ammunition for only two days of fighting, and the War Department was a snakepit of jealous bureaucrats.

Raising an army and imposing order on the War Department posed a daunting challenge. Wilson's secretary of war, Newton D. Baker, skillfully implemented the **Selective Service Act,** passed in May 1917. Baker cleverly made the first draft registration day a "festival and patriotic occasion." Thanks to a carefully orchestrated public-relations campaign and local civilian draft boards' deft handling of the draft, 24 million men registered by November 1918, of whom nearly 3 million were drafted.

Selective Service Act Draft act to raise army during World War I

African-Americans at the Front

Black troops of the 369th Infantry Regiment in the trenches near Maffrecourt, France in 1918. Most African-American soldiers were assigned to noncombat duty, such as unloading supplies and equipment.

In addition, following a precedent-breaking decision by the secretary of the navy, 11,000 women served in the navy during the war. Although not assigned to combat, they performed crucial support functions as nurses, clerical workers, and telephone operators.

Some twelve thousand Native Americans served in the **American Expeditionary Force** (AEF). While some reformers eager to preserve Indian culture argued for all-Indian units, military officials integrated Native Americans into the general army. Some observers predicted that the wartime experience would hasten the assimilation of Indians into mainstream American life.

The War Department monitored the off-duty behavior of young men cut off from family and community. The Commission on Training Camp Activities presented films, lectures, and posters on the dangers of alcohol and prostitution. Beginning in December 1917, all recruits also underwent intelligence testing. Psychologists eager to demonstrate the usefulness of their new profession claimed that tests measuring recruits' "intelligence quotient" (IQ) could help in assigning their duties. In fact, the tests mostly revealed that many recruits lacked formal education and cultural sophistication, while reinforcing racial and ethnic stereotypes.

American Expeditionary Force
Three million American men were drafted into a force to fight in Europe during WWI

In April 1917 W. E. B. Du Bois urged African-Americans to support the war. Most did. More than 260,000 blacks volunteered or were drafted, and 50,000 went to France. However, racism pervaded the military; the navy assigned blacks only to menial positions, and the marines excluded them completely.

Blacks in training camps endured crude racial abuse. One racist senator from Mississippi warned that the sight of "arrogant, strutting" African-American soldiers would trigger race riots in the United States. Tensions reached the breaking point in Houston in August 1917, when some black soldiers, endlessly goaded by local whites, seized weapons from the armory and killed seventeen whites. After a hasty trial with no opportunity for an appeal, thirteen African-American soldiers were hanged, and forty-one went to jail for life.

Organizing the Economy for War

The war years of 1917–1918 helped shape modern America. The war's administrative innovations sped up longer-term processes of social reorganization. The war furthered many key developments of the 1920s and beyond—including the spread of mass production; the collaboration between government, business, and labor; and the growth of new professional and managerial elites.

War Industries Board (WIB)
Major federal agency created to regulate wartime production, allocation of materials

The war led to unprecedented government oversight of the economy and the regulation of corporations, something progressives had long urged. The **War Industries Board (WIB)** was established in 1917 to coordinate military purchasing, to fight waste, and to ensure that the military received the weapons, equipment, and supplies it needed. Especially under the wealthy Wall Street speculator Bernard Baruch (bah-ROOK), whom Wilson appointed to run the WIB in March 1918, the agency exercised enormous control over the industrial sector. In addition to allocating raw materials, the board established production priorities and introduced all kinds of efficiencies. The Fuel Administration controlled coal output, regulated fuel prices and consumption, and in March 1918 introduced daylight savings time as a wartime conservation measure.

Baruch's counterpart on the agricultural front was Herbert Hoover, the head of the Food Administration. A mining engineer who had amassed a fortune in Asia, Hoover oversaw the production and allocation of wheat, meat, and sugar to ensure supplies for the army and the food-short Allies.

The War Industries Board and the Food Administration represented only the tip of the regulatory iceberg. Nearly five thousand government agencies supervised home-front activities. When a railroad tie-up during the winter of 1917–1918 threatened the flow of supplies to Europe, the Railroad Administration stepped in and transformed the thousands of miles of track operated by competing companies into an efficient national transportation system.

The war accelerated corporate consolidation and economic integration. In place of trustbusting, the government now encouraged cooperation among businesses. Overall, the war was good for business. Despite added taxes imposed by Congress, profits soared. After-tax profits in the copper industry, for example, jumped from 12 percent in 1913 to 24 percent in 1917.

The old laissez-faire suspicion of government, which was already eroded, now suffered further blows in 1917–1918. In the 1930s, when the nation faced a different kind of crisis, the government activism of World War I would be remembered.

With the American Expeditionary Force in France

American troops first saw action in the campaign to throw back Germany's spring 1918 offensive in the Somme and Aisne-Marne sectors. The next heavy American engagement came that autumn as part of the Allies' Meuse-Argonne offensive that ended the war.

When the United States entered the war, Allied prospects had looked bleak. German U-boat attacks had taken a horrendous toll on Allied shipping. A failed French offensive in the spring led to an army mutiny, and an almost equally disastrous British-French offensive in November cost 400,000 casualties to gain just four miles.

Russia had suffered serious setbacks, contributing to the revolutionary upheaval. The communist faction of the revolution, the Bolsheviks, gained strength when its top leaders, including Vladimir Lenin and Leon Trotsky, returned from exile abroad. On November 6, 1917, a Bolshevik coup overthrew Alexander Kerensky's provisional government and effectively removed Russia from the war. Early in 1918, the Bolsheviks signed an armistice with Germany, the Treaty of Brest-Litovsk, freeing thousands of German troops on the Russian front for fighting in France.

The first U.S. troops reached France in October 1917. Eventually about 2 million American soldiers served in France as members of the American Expeditionary Force (AEF) under General **John J. Pershing.** Most men of the AEF at first found the war

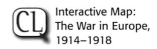
Interactive Map: The War in Europe, 1914–1918

John J. Pershing Commander of American Expeditionary Force that fought in Europe

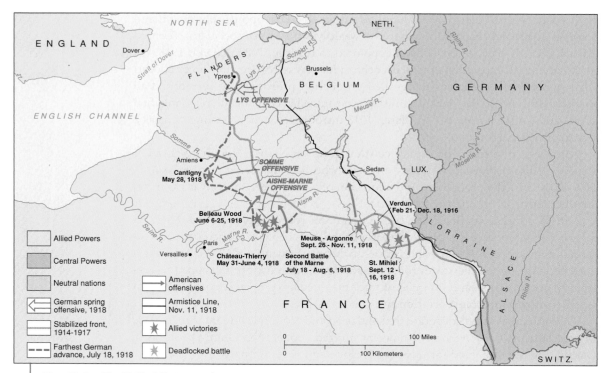

Map 22.2   The United States on the Western Front, 1918

American troops first saw action in the campaign to throw back Germany's spring 1918 offensive in the Somme and Aisne-Marne sectors. The next heavy American engagement came that autumn as part of the Allies' Meuse-Argonne offensive that ended the war.

a great adventure. Plucked from towns and farms, they sailed for Europe on crowded freighters; a lucky few traveled on captured German passenger liners.

The African-Americans with the AEF in France worked mainly as mess-boys (mealtime aides), laborers, and stevedores (ship-cargo handlers). The latter assignments, though they were discriminatory, vitally aided the war effort. Except for two segregated divisions, African-Americans did not engage in combat. Only in death was the AEF integrated: graves in military cemeteries were not segregated by race.

In desperate circumstances, French and British commanders wanted to incorporate AEF troops into Allied units already at the front. But Pershing and his superiors in Washington insisted that the AEF be "distinct and separate," in part because he scorned the defensive mentality of the Allied commanders and in part because separate combat would strengthen the U.S. voice at the peace table.

American forces saw their first real combat in March 1918 when a German offensive threatened France's English Channel ports. The Allies created a unified command under French general Ferdinand Foch (fohsh), and American troops were thrown into the fighting around Amiens (AH-mee-ehn) and Armentières (are-men-TEE-air) that stemmed the German advance. In May 1918 Germany launched the second phase of its spring offensive. By the end of the month, the Germans had broken through the Allied lines and had secured a nearly open road to Paris, only fifty miles away. At this critical moment, Americans spearheaded the forces that finally stopped the German advance at the town of Château-Thierry (shah-TOE tee-AIR-ee) and nearby Belleau (BELL-oh) Wood (see Map 22.2). Eighty-five thousand American troops helped to staunch the final German offensive of the war, a thrust at the ancient cathedral city of Rheims (reems). Germany's desperate attempt to take the offensive had failed. Now it was the Allies' turn.

Turning the Tide

On July 18, 1918, the Allies launched their counteroffensive, and the war's last great battle began on September 26 as 1.2 million Americans joined the struggle to drive the Germans from the Meuse River and the dense Argonne Forest north of Verdun. Poison gas hung in the air, and rats scurried through the mud, gorging on human remains. Americans now endured the filth, vermin, and dysentery familiar to veterans of the trenches. Some welcomed injuries as a ticket out of the battle zone. Others collapsed emotionally and were hospitalized for "shell shock."

Four black infantry regiments served with distinction under French command. One entire regiment, the 369th, was honored with the French Croix de Guerre (crwah duh gair), and several hundred individual black soldiers won French decorations for bravery.

Theodore Roosevelt's "great adventure" seemed remote indeed in the Meuse-Argonne campaign. Death came in many forms and without ceremony. Bodies, packs, rifles, photos, and letters from home sank indiscriminately into the all-consuming mud. Influenza killed thousands of AEF troops at the front and in training camps back home. The war's brutality would shape the literature of the 1920s, as writers like Ernest Hemingway stripped away the illusions obscuring the reality of mass slaughter. By early November, the AEF had fulfilled its assignment, at a cost of 26,277 dead.

CHECKING IN

- The U.S. government instituted the draft to fill manpower needs.
- Government regulation of the economy, oversight of resources, and collaboration with business reached into American households and became accepted facts of life during the war.
- The Allied cause looked grim when America entered the war, but the 2 million American soldiers who served in France would play a key role in halting the last German offensive.
- American troops then spearheaded the Allied counteroffensive that led to the Armistice in November 1918.

PROMOTING THE WAR AND SUPPRESSING DISSENT

How did Americans respond to propaganda and suppression of dissent?

In their own way, the war's domestic effects were as important as its battles. Spurred by government propaganda, patriotic fervor gripped America. The war fever, in turn, encouraged intellectual conformity and intolerance of dissent. Fueling the repressive spirit, government authorities and private vigilante groups hounded socialists, pacifists, and other dissidents, trampling citizens' constitutional rights.

Advertising the War

To President Wilson, selling the war at home was crucial to success in France. "It is not an army we must shape and train for war, it is a nation," he declared. The administration drew on the new professions of advertising and public relations to pursue this goal. Treasury Secretary McAdoo orchestrated a series of government bond drives, called Liberty Loans, that financed about two-thirds of the $35.5 billion (including loans to the Allies) that the war cost the United States.

Posters exhorted citizens to "Fight or Buy Bonds." Parades, rallies, and appearances by movie starts all aided the cause. Patriotic war songs reached a large public through phonograph recordings. Beneath the ballyhoo ran a note of coercion. Only "a friend of Germany," McAdoo warned, would refuse to buy bonds. The balance of the government's war costs came from taxes. Using the power granted it by the Sixteenth Amendment, Congress imposed wartime income taxes that reached 70 percent at the top levels.

Committee on Public Information Wartime propaganda agency established in April 1917; led by journalist George Creel

Journalist George Creel headed the key wartime propaganda agency, the **Committee on Public Information** (CPI). While claiming merely to combat rumors with facts, the Creel committee in reality publicized the government's version of events and discredited all who questioned that version. Posters, news releases, advertisements, and movies all trumpeted the government's sanitized version of events. The CPI poured foreign-language publications into the cities to ensure the loyalty of recent immigrants. Creel also organized the "four-minute men": a network of 75,000 speakers throughout the nation who gave patriotic talks to audiences of all kinds. Teachers, writers, religious leaders, and magazine editors overwhelmingly supported the war. These custodians of culture viewed the conflict as a struggle to defend threatened values and standards. Alan Seeger, a young Harvard graduate who volunteered to fight for France in 1916, wrote highly popular poems romanticizing the war. An artillery barrage became "the magnificent orchestra of war." The "sense of being the instrument of Destiny," wrote Seeger, represented the "supreme experience" of combat. He was killed in action in 1916.

Progressive reformers who had applauded Wilson's domestic program now cheered his war. Herbert Croly, Walter Lippmann, and other intellectuals associated with the *New Republic* magazine zealously backed the war. According to educator John Dewey, the war presented exciting "social possibilities." The government's wartime activism, he argued, could be channeled to reform purposes when peace returned.

Wartime Intolerance and Dissent

Responding to this drumfire of propaganda, some Americans became almost hysterical in their hatred of all things German, their hostility to aliens and dissenters, and their strident patriotism. Isolated actions by German saboteurs, including the blowing-up of a New Jersey munitions dump, fanned the flames. In Collinsville, Illinois, a mob of 500 lynched a young German-born man in April 1918. When a jury exonerated the mob leaders, a jury member shouted, "Nobody can say we aren't loyal now."

German books vanished from libraries, towns with German names changed them, and "liberty sandwich" and "liberty cabbage" replaced "hamburgers" and "sauerkraut" on restaurant menus. The Philadelphia Orchestra banned all German music except for Bach (bahkh), Beethoven (BAIT-hoh-vun), Mozart (MOATS-art), and Brahms (brawms). Popular evangelist Billy Sunday proclaimed, "If you turn hell upside down you will find 'Made in Germany' stamped on the bottom." The zealots also targeted war critics and radicals. A Cincinnati mob horsewhipped a pacifist minister. Theodore Roosevelt branded antiwar Senator Robert La Follette "an unhung traitor."

Despite the persecution, many Americans persisted in opposing the war. Some were immigrants with ancestral ties to Germany. Others were religious pacifists, including Quakers, Mennonites, and Jehovah's Witnesses. Of some sixty-five thousand men who registered as conscientious objectors (COs), twenty-one thousand were drafted. The army assigned most to noncombat duty, such as cleaning latrines. Those who rejected this alternative were sent to military prisons.

Socialist leaders such as Eugene Debs denounced the war as a capitalist struggle for markets, with the soldiers as cannon fodder. The U.S. declaration of war, they insisted, mainly reflected Wall Street's desire to protect its loans to England and France. But other socialists supported the war, dividing the party. The war split the women's movement as well. While some leaders joined Jane Addams in opposition, others endorsed the war while keeping their own goals in view.

Draft resistance extended beyond the ranks of conscientious objectors. An estimated 2.4 to 3.6 million young men failed to register for the draft, and of those that did, about 12 percent did not appear when drafted or deserted from training camp. The rural South saw high levels of draft resistance, especially because the urban elites who ran draft boards were more likely to defer young men of their own class than poor farmers, white or black.

Of southern blacks who registered, one-third were drafted, compared to one-fourth of whites. White draft boards argued that low-income black families could more easily spare a male breadwinner. But the dynamics of race worked in complex ways: some southern whites, fearful of arming black men even for military service, favored drafting only whites.

The war's most incisive critic was Randolph Bourne, a young journalist. Although Bourne much admired John Dewey, he rejected his hero's prowar position. He dismissed the contention that reformers could direct the war to their own purposes. "If the war is too strong for you to prevent," he asked, "how is it going to be weak enough for you to . . . mould to your liberal purposes?" Eventually, many prowar intellectuals came to agree. By 1919, Dewey conceded that the war, far from promoting reform, had encouraged reaction and intolerance.

Suppressing Dissent by Law

Wartime intolerance also surfaced in federal laws and official actions. The **Espionage Act** of June 1917 set fines and prison sentences for a variety of loosely defined antiwar activities. The **Sedition Amendment** to the Espionage Act (May 1918) imposed stiff penalties on anyone convicted of using "disloyal, profane, scurrilous, or abusive language" about the government, the Constitution, the flag, or the military.

Espionage Act Criminalized virtually any antiwar activity

Sedition Amendment Curtailed First Amendment rights in criticizing war or government

Wilson's attorney general, Thomas W. Gregory, used these laws to stamp out dissent. Opponents of the war should expect no mercy "from an outraged people and an avenging government," he said. Under this sweeping legislation and similar state laws, some fifteen hundred pacifists, socialists, and war opponents were arrested. Kate Richards O'Hare, a midwestern socialist organizer, spent more than a year in jail for declaring, "The women of the United States are nothing more than brood sows, to raise children to get into the army and be made into fertilizer." Eugene

Debs was imprisoned for three years (1918–1921) for a speech discussing the economic causes of the war.

The Espionage Act also authorized the postmaster general to bar suspect materials from the mail—a provision enthusiastically enforced by Wilson's postmaster general, Albert S. Burleson, a reactionary superpatriot. Upton Sinclair protested to President Wilson that no one of Burleson's "childish ignorance" should wield such power; but Wilson did little to restrain Burleson's excesses. The 1917 Bolshevik takeover in Russia sharpened the attacks on domestic radicals.

In 1919, the U.S. Supreme Court upheld Espionage Act convictions of war critics. In *Schenck* v. *United States,* Justice Oliver Wendell Holmes, Jr., writing for a unanimous court, justified such repression in cases where a person's exercise of the First Amendment right of free speech posed a "clear and present danger" to the nation. It also upheld Debs's conviction. Although the war was over, a vindictive Wilson refused to commute Debs's sentence.

The early wartime mood of idealism had degenerated into persecution of all who failed to meet the zealots' notions of "100 percent Americanism." This climate of conformity and suspicion would linger long after the war's end.

ECONOMIC AND SOCIAL TRENDS IN WARTIME AMERICA

What was the war's economic, political, and social impact on the American home front?

While the war affected the lives of millions of Americans—including industrial workers, farmers, women, and blacks—another of the war's byproducts, a deadly influenza pandemic, took a grievous toll. Some Progressive Era reforms advanced in 1917–1918, but overall the war and its aftermath weakened the reform movement.

Boom Times in Industry and Agriculture

For all its horrendous human toll, World War I brought glowing prosperity to the American economy. Factory production climbed about 35 percent from 1914 to 1918, and the civilian work force grew by 1.3 million from 1916 to 1918. Prices rose, but so did wages. Even unskilled workers enjoyed wartime wage increases averaging nearly 20 percent. Samuel Gompers, head of the American Federation of Labor, urged workers not to strike during the war. With the economy booming, most workers observed the no-strike request.

The war's social impact took many forms. Job seekers pouring into industrial centers strained housing, schools, and municipal services. The consumption of cigarettes more than tripled. Reflecting wartime prosperity, automobile production jumped from 460,000 in 1914 to 1.8 million in 1917. Farmers profited, too. With European farm production disrupted, U.S. agricultural prices more than doubled between 1913 and 1918, and farmers' real income rose significantly.

This agricultural boom proved a mixed blessing. Farmers who borrowed heavily to expand production faced a credit squeeze when farm prices fell after the war. In the 1920s and 1930s, hard-pressed farmers would look back to the war years as a golden age of prosperity.

Blacks Migrate Northward

The war sped the exodus of southern blacks. An estimated half-million African-Americans moved north during the war, and most settled in cities. Chicago's black population swelled from 44,000 in 1910 to 110,000 in 1920 and Cleveland's from 8,000 to 34,000.

With European immigration disrupted by the war, booming industries hired more black workers. Labor agents along with African-American newspapers like the *Chicago Defender* spread the word. One southern black, newly settled near Chicago, wrote home, "Nothing here but money, and it is not hard to get." Impoverished southern blacks welcomed the prospect of earning three dollars a day or more in a region where racism seemed less intense. By 1920, 1.5 million African-Americans were working in northern industry.

This vast population movement had widespread social ramifications. New city churches and storefront missions met the spiritual needs of deeply religious migrants from the South. The National Association for the Advancement of Colored People (NAACP) grew from 9,000 members before the war to nearly 100,000 by the early 1920s. Heightened race consciousness and activism of the war years helped create the groundwork for the civil-rights movement that lay ahead. The concentration of blacks in New York City also prepared the way for the cultural flowering known as the Harlem Renaissance (see Chapter 23).

Still, these African-American newcomers in northern cities faced severe challenges. White workers resented the labor competition, and white homeowners lashed

***During the World War,* by Jacob Lawrence, 1940–1941**

Lawrence (1917–2000), a leading African-American artist, lived in Harlem. This vivid painting, part of his "Migration of the Negro" series, captures the eager intensity of the black migration northward during World War I.

out as jammed black neighborhoods spilled over into surrounding areas. Tensions sometimes sparked deadly riots. An outbreak on July 2, 1917, in East St. Louis, Illinois, led to the deaths of thirty-nine blacks. A few weeks later, an NAACP protest in New York City included one banner that echoed Wilson's phrase justifying U.S. involvement in the war: "Mr. President, Why Not Make AMERICA Safe for Democracy?"

Women in Wartime

The war affected women profoundly. Feminist leaders like Carrie Chapman Catt hoped that the war would lead to full equality and greater opportunity for women. For a time, these goals seemed attainable. In addition to the women in the AEF and in wartime volunteer agencies, about 1 million women worked in industry. Thousands more held other jobs, from streetcar conductors to bricklayers.

As the woman-suffrage movement gained momentum, a key victory came in November 1917 when New York voters amended the state constitution to permit women to vote. In Washington, Alice Paul and members of her National Woman's Party (see Chapter 21) picketed the White House. Several protesters were jailed and, when they went on a hunger strike, they were force-fed. Under growing pressure, Wilson declared that women's war service had earned them the right to vote. In 1919, the House and Senate overwhelmingly passed the **Nineteenth Amendment** granting women the vote. Ratification followed in 1920.

Beyond this victory, however, the war did little to better women's status permanently. Relatively few women actually entered the work force for the first time in 1917–1918; most simply moved to better-paying jobs. As for the women in the AEF, the War Department refused their requests for military rank and benefits. At the war's end, many women lost their jobs to returning veterans. In 1920, the percentage of U.S. women in the paid labor force was actually slightly lower than it had been in 1910.

Public Health Crisis: The 1918 Influenza Pandemic

Amid battlefield casualties and home-front social changes, the nation in 1918 coped with global outbreak of influenza, a highly contagious viral infection. The **influenza pandemic** killed as many as 50 million people worldwide.

Moving northward from its origins in southern Africa, the epidemic spread from the war zone in France to U.S. military camps and quickly advanced to the urban population. The flu hit the cities hard. In Philadelphia on September 19, the day after 200,000 people had turned out for a Liberty Loan rally, 635 new influenza cases were reported. Many cities forbade all public gatherings. The worst came in October, when the flu killed 195,000 Americans. The total U.S. death toll was about 550,000, more than six times the total of AEF battle deaths in France. In more recent times, researchers have found alarming similarities between the 1918 flu virus and the avian (bird) virus of the late 1990s and early twenty-first century. The discovery prompted public-health agencies worldwide to take measures to prevent another global pandemic.

The War and Progressivism

The war had mixed effects on Progressive Era reform movements. The war strengthened the coercive, moral-control aspect of progressivism, including the drive for the prohibition of alcohol. When the **Eighteenth Amendment** establishing na-

Primary Source: Women in Various Occupations

Nineteenth Amendment
Wilson rewarded women for their wartime service and supported the amendment granting women the vote; ratified in 1920

influenza pandemic On the heels of the devastation of World War I, more than a half million Americans died of influenza in 1918

Eighteenth Amendment
Established national prohibition to encourage and regulate morality during wartime

tional prohibition passed Congress in December 1917, it was widely seen as a war measure. Ratified in 1919, it went into effect on January 1, 1920. Similarly, the war strengthened the Progressive Era antiprostitution campaign. The War Department closed red-light districts near military bases, including New Orleans's famed Story-ville. (As Storyville's jazz musicians moved north, jazz reached a national audience.) Meanwhile, "protective bureaus" urged women to uphold standards of sexual morality.

Along with woman suffrage, other reforms advanced as well. The **War Labor Board** (WLB) pressured factory owners to introduce the eight-hour workday and recognize unions' right to bargain with management. Under these favorable conditions, union membership rose from 2.7 million in 1916 to more than 5 million by 1920. Another wartime agency, the United States Housing Corporation, built housing projects for workers. The Bureau of War Risk Insurance (BWRI) provided direct aid to soldiers' families. By the war's end, the BWRI was sending regular checks to 2.1 million families.

Overall, however, the war weakened the progressive social-justice impulse. While the war brought increased regulation of the economy—a key progressive goal—business interests often dominated the regulatory agencies, and they were quickly dismantled after the war. In addition, the government's repression of radicals and antiwar dissenters fractured the progressive coalition and ushered in a decade of reaction. The 1918 midterm election signaled the shift: the Democrats lost both houses of Congress to a deeply conservative Republican party.

Reform energies, after diminishing in the 1920s, would reemerge in the depression decade of the 1930s. And as Franklin D. Roosevelt's New Deal took shape (see Chapter 24), the memory of such World War I agencies as the War Labor Board, the United States Housing Corporation, and the Bureau of War Risk Insurance provided ideas and inspiration.

War Labor Board Wartime agency that encouraged unionization and collective bargaining as a means of avoiding labor discord

CHECKING IN

- The war produced boom times for farmers and manufacturers but left farmers in a credit squeeze later.
- Black migration to northern cities accelerated, but racial tensions also traveled north.
- Women advanced in the work force in large numbers but were seen only as temporary replacements for men.
- The war bolstered some progressive goals: greater government regulation of the economy, woman suffrage, and labor laws.
- In spite of the progressive advances, the war undermined the social-justice movement, as conservatives gained ground amid the wartime repression.

JOYOUS ARMISTICE, BITTER AFTERMATH, 1918–1920

How did the League of Nations begin, and why did the Senate reject U.S. membership in the League?

In November 1918, the war finally ended. The peace conference that followed stands as a high point of America's growing internationalist involvement, but it also triggered a sharp domestic reaction against that involvement. Woodrow Wilson dominated the peace conference but failed in his most cherished objective—American membership in the League of Nations. At home, the electorate repudiated Wilsonianism and in 1920 sent a conservative Republican to the White House.

Wilson's Fourteen Points; The Armistice

President Wilson planned to put his personal stamp on the peace. American involvement, he believed, could transform a sordid power conflict into something higher and finer—a crusade for a new, more democratic world order.

In a speech to Congress in January 1918, Wilson summed up U.S. war aims in fourteen points. Nine of these spelled out Wilson's belief that the subject peoples of the Austro-Hungarian and Ottoman empires should have the freedom to choose their own political futures. The remaining five points offered Wilson's larger postwar vision: a world of free navigation, free trade, reduced armaments, openly negotiated treaties, and "a general association of nations" to resolve conflicts peacefully. The **Fourteen Points** helped solidify American support for the war, especially among liberals. They seemed proof that the United States had entered the war not for selfish reasons but out of noble motives.

Fourteen Points Wilson's blueprint for a better world; emphasized self-determination

In early October 1918, reeling from the Allies' advances, Germany proposed an armistice based on Wilson's Fourteen Points. The British and French hesitated, but when Wilson threatened to negotiate a separate peace, they agreed. Meanwhile, in Berlin, Kaiser Wilhelm II had abdicated and a German republic had been proclaimed.

In the early morning of November 11, 1918, the Allied commander Marshal Foch and his German counterparts signed an armistice ending hostilities at 11:00 A.M. Rockets burst over the front that night, not in anger but in relief and celebration. Back home, cheering throngs filled the streets. "Everything for which America has fought has been accomplished," Wilson proclaimed.

The Versailles Peace Conference, 1919

The challenge of forging a peace treaty remained. Wilson opted personally to lead the U.S. delegation to the peace conference. This decision was probably a mistake, for Wilson's oratorical skills outstripped his talent for negotiation and compromise. The president compounded his mistake by selecting only one Republican peace commissioner, an elderly diplomat. In the November 1918 congressional elections, Republicans gained control of both houses of Congress, an ominous sign for Wilson.

Wilson received a hero's welcome in Europe. Shouts of "Voodrow Veelson" rang out in Paris, in Britain children spread flowers in his path, and in Italy an exuberant official compared him to Jesus Christ.

The euphoria faded when the peace conference began on January 18, 1919, at the palace of Versailles (verh-SIGH) near Paris. A Council of Four, comprising the heads of state of the Allied powers: Italy, France, Great Britain, and the United States. (Japan participated as well.) The European statesmen at the **Versailles Peace Conference** were determined to avenge their nations' horrendous wartime losses, which they blamed directly on German aggression. Their goals bore little relation to Wilson's liberal vision. As the French leader Georges Clemenceau remarked, "God gave us the Ten Commandments and we broke them. Mr. Wilson has given us the Fourteen Points. We shall see."

Versailles Peace Conference Negotiations for a peace settlement in France; the resulting settlement harshly punished Germany, laying the seeds of future conflict

Differences surfaced quickly. Italy demanded a port on the eastern Adriatic Sea. Japan insisted on keeping the trading rights it had seized from Germany in China. Clemenceau was obsessed with revenge. At one point, an appalled Wilson threatened to leave the conference.

Reflecting this toxic climate, the peace treaty signed by a sullen German delegation in June 1919 was harshly punitive. Germany was disarmed, stripped of its colonies, forced to admit sole blame for the war, and saddled with reparation payments of $56 billion. France regained the provinces of Alsace and Lorraine and took control for fifteen years of Germany's coal-rich Saar Basin. The treaty demilitarized Germany's western border and transferred a slice of eastern Germany to Poland. Italy received land; Japan got the economic concessions it wanted. All told, the treaty cost Germany one-tenth of its population and one-eighth of its territory. These harsh terms, bitterly resented in Germany, planted the seeds of an even more devastating future war.

Some treaty provisions did reflect Wilson's themes of democracy and self-determination. The treaty recognized the independence of Poland and the Baltic states of Estonia, Latvia, and Lithuania. Separate treaties provided for the independence of Czechoslovakia and Yugoslavia, new nations carved from the Austro-Hungarian and Ottoman empires. Palestine, a part of Turkey's collapsed Ottoman Empire, went to Great Britain under a mandate arrangement. In 1917, the British had issued the Balfour Declaration supporting a Jewish "national home" in the region while also acknowledging the rights of the non-Jewish Palestinians.

Nor did the peacemakers come to terms with revolutionary Russia. In August 1918 a fourteen-nation Allied army, including some seven thousand U.S. troops, had landed at various Russian ports, ostensibly to secure them from German attack and to protect Allied war equipment. In fact, the aim was to overthrow the new Bolshevik regime, whose communist ideology stirred deep fear in the capitals of Europe and America. Wilson and the other Allied leaders agreed to support a Russian military leader waging a last-ditch struggle against the Bolsheviks. Not until 1933 would the United States recognize the Soviet Union.

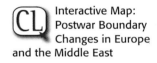

Interactive Map: Postwar Boundary Changes in Europe and the Middle East

The Fight over the League of Nations

Wilson focused on his one shining achievement at Versailles—the creation of a new international organization, the **League of Nations.** The agreement to establish the League, written into the treaty, embodied Wilson's vision of a new world order of peace and justice. But Wilson's League faced major hurdles. A warning sign had come in February 1919 when thirty-nine Republican senators signed a letter rejecting the League in its present form.

League of Nations Wilson's plan for an international deliberative body, viewed as necessary to keep the peace; rejected by the U.S. Senate; the U.S. never joined

When Wilson sent the treaty to the Senate for ratification in July 1919, Henry Cabot Lodge bottled it up in the Foreign Relations Committee. Convinced that he could rally popular opinion to his cause, Wilson left Washington on September 3 for a speaking tour. Covering more than nine thousand miles by train, Wilson defended the League in thirty-seven speeches in twenty-two days. People wept as Wilson described his visits to American war cemeteries in France and cheered his vision of a new world order.

But the trip exhausted Wilson, and on October 2. He suffered a stroke that for a time left him near death. He spent the rest of his term mostly in bed or in a wheelchair, a reclusive invalid, his mind clouded, his fragile emotions betraying him into vindictive actions and tearful outbursts. He broke with close advisers and dismissed Secretary of State Lansing, accusing him of disloyalty. In January 1920, his physician advised him to resign, but Wilson refused.

Wilson's first wife, Ellen, had died in 1914. His strong-willed second wife, Edith Galt, played a crucial role behind the scenes during this crisis. She hid Wilson's condition from the public and decided who could see him. Cabinet members, diplomats, and congressional leaders were barred from the White House. Because the Twenty-fifth Amendment, dealing with issues of presidential disability, was not adopted until 1967, the impasse continued.

The League drama unfolded against this grim backdrop. On September 10, 1919, the Foreign Relations Committee at last sent the treaty to the Senate, but with a series of amendments. The Senate split into three groups. First were Democrats who supported the League covenant without changes. Second were Republican "Irreconcilables," who opposed the League absolutely. They feared that League membership would dangerously restrict U.S. freedom of action and entangle America with foreign powers they viewed as corrupt. Finally, a group of Republican "Reservationists," led by Lodge, demanded amendments as a condition of their support.

Had Wilson accepted compromise, the Senate would probably have ratified the Versailles treaty. But Wilson's illness aggravated his tendency toward rigidity. Isolated in the White House, he instructed Senate Democrats to vote against the treaty, which now included Lodge's reservations. Although international-law specialists argued that these reservations would not significantly weaken U.S. participation in the League, Wilson rejected them as "a knife thrust at the heart of the treaty."

Despite Wilson's speaking tour, the public did not rally behind the League. On November 19, 1919, pro-League Democrats obeying Wilson's instructions and anti-League Irreconcilables joined forces to defeat the version of the Versailles treaty that included Lodge's reservations. A second vote in March 1920 produced the same result. The United States would not join the League. A president who had been elected amid high hopes in 1912, cheered when he called for war in 1917, and adulated in Europe in 1918 now lay embittered and impotent. What might have been Wilson's crowning achievement had turned to ashes.

Racism and Red Scare, 1919–1920

The wartime spirit of "100 percent Americanism" left an acrid aftertaste as 1919–1920 saw racial violence and fresh antiradical hysteria. Lynch mobs murdered seventy-six African-Americans in 1919, including ten military veterans, several still in uniform. The bloodiest disorder occurred in 1919 in Chicago, where an influx of southern African-Americans had intensified tensions. On a hot July afternoon, whites at a Lake Michigan beach threw stones at a black youth swimming offshore. He sank and drowned. A thirteen-day reign of terror followed, as white and black marauders roamed the streets, randomly attacked innocent victims, and torched buildings. The violence left fifteen whites and twenty-three blacks dead, and more than five hundred injured.

Wartime antiradical panic, reinforced by the fear and hatred of bolshevism, crested in the Red Scare of 1919–1920. Such emotions deepened as a rash of strikes broke out, representing an accumulation of grievances. When Seattle's labor unions organized an orderly general work stoppage early in 1919, the mayor accused the strikers of trying to "duplicate the anarchy of Russia" and called for federal troops. In April, mail bombs were sent to various public officials. One blew off the hands of a senator's maid, and another damaged the home of Attorney General A. Mitchell Palmer.

The mounting frenzy over supposed radicals took political form. In November 1919 the House of Representatives refused to seat Milwaukee socialist Victor Berger. The New York legislature expelled several socialist members. The Justice Department established a countersubversive division under young J. Edgar Hoover, the future head of the Federal Bureau of Investigation, who arrested hundreds of suspected communists and radicals. In December 1919, the government deported 249 Russian-born aliens, including Emma Goldman, a prominent radical and leader of the birth-control movement.

On January 2, 1920, in a Justice Department dragnet, federal marshals and local police raided the homes of suspected radicals and the headquarters of radical organizations in thirty-two cities. Without search or arrest warrants, authorities arrested more than four thousand people and ransacked homes and offices. These lightning raids grossly violated civil rights and simple decency. Marshals barged into one woman's bedroom to arrest her. In Lynn, Massachusetts, police arrested thirty-nine men and women who were meeting to discuss forming a cooperative bakery. The rabidly antiradical and politically ambitious attorney general, A. Mitchell Palmer, coordinated these "Red raids." Palmer had succumbed to the anticommunist hysteria of the early postwar period. He ominously predicted a "blaze of revolution . . . burning up the foundations of society."

The Red Scare subsided as Palmer's irrational predictions failed to materialize. When a bomb exploded in New York City's financial district in September 1920, killing thirty-eight people, most Americans saw the deed as the work of an isolated fanatic, not evidence of approaching revolution.

Warren G. Harding Elected in 1920; the well-meaning but conservative and undistinguished successor to Woodrow Wilson

The Election of 1920

In this unsettled climate, the election of 1920 approached. Wilson, out of touch with political reality, considered seeking a third term, but was persuaded otherwise. Few heeded his call to make the election a "solemn referendum" on the League. When the Democrats convened in San Francisco, the delegates nominated James M. Cox, the mildly progressive governor of Ohio. As Cox's running mate they chose the young assistant secretary of the navy, Franklin D. Roosevelt, who possessed a potent political name.

The confident Republicans, meeting in Chicago, nominated Senator **Warren G. Harding** of Ohio, an amiable politician of little distinction. For vice president, they chose Massachusetts governor Calvin Coolidge, who had won attention in 1919 with his denunciation of a Boston policemen's strike. Harding's vacuous campaign speeches reminded one critic of "an army of pompous phrases moving over the landscape in search of an idea." But his reassuring promise of a return to "normalcy" resonated with many voters, and he won by a landslide—16 million votes against 9 million for Cox.

The election dashed all hope for American entry into the League of Nations. During the campaign, Harding vaguely endorsed some form of "international organization," but once elected he bluntly declared the League question "dead." The sense of high purpose that Wilson had evoked so eloquently in April 1917 seemed remote indeed as Americans turned to a new president and a new era.

CHECKING IN

- Wilson saw the war as an opportunity to spread democracy globally.
- The Fourteen Points speech summed up Wilsonian ideals; European leaders were skeptical.
- Wilson was hailed by the European public but could not control the Versailles negotiations.
- Although it established the League of Nations, the Versailles treaty solved none of the problems that had led to World War I; instead, it laid the groundwork for World War II.
- The Senate ultimately refused to ratify the treaty, and the United States did not join the League.
- The election of 1920 was interpreted as a rejection of the crusading spirit, both at home and overseas.

Chapter Summary

 DOWNLOAD THE MP3 AUDIO FILE OF THE CHAPTER SUMMARY, AND LISTEN TO IT ON THE GO.

What goals underlay America's early-twentieth-century involvements in Asia and Latin America? (page 506)

The early twentieth century saw intensifying U.S. involvement abroad. This new globalism arose from a desire to promote U.S. business interests internationally while exporting American values to other societies. Americans demanded an "Open Door" to the China trade. Theodore Roosevelt seized Panama and built the canal, then declared the Caribbean to be under American domination. Wilson intervened in the Mexican Revolution in an attempt to shoehorn Mexican politics into an American mold.

Considering both immediate and long-term factors, why did the United States go to war in 1917? (page 512)

Wilson attempted to maintain neutrality, but issues of neutral rights on the high seas and loans to the Allies made neutrality almost impossible to attain. The deaths of Americans on British ships, such as *Lusitania,* poisoned U.S. relations with Germany, and the Zimmermann telegram, suggesting a German-Mexican alliance, ultimately pushed the United States into the war.

How did Washington mobilize the nation for war, and what role did U.S. troops play in the war? (page 515)

During the war, the federal government influenced the lives of Americans as never before. The United States initiated the draft and called 3 million men into service. Government regulation of the economy and the nation's resources, exemplified by the War Industries Board and the Food Administration, greatly increased, as did government-business collaboration. Two million Americans fought in France, arriving just in time to stop Germany's 1918 summer offensive and lead the Allies' counteroffensive.

How did Americans respond to propaganda and suppression of dissent? (page 519)

The Wilson administration drew successfully on the techniques of modern advertising to "sell" the war and conducted massive campaigns to sell war bonds. The all-too-effective anti-German propaganda led to intolerance and distrust of almost everything German, including frankfurters (hot dogs), sauerkraut, and German-Americans. Some Americans criticized the war, but to do so was risky. The Espionage Act and the Sedition Amendment intensified the climate of intolerance and were used to jail hundreds of dissenters.

KEY TERMS

Boxer Rebellion *(p. 507)*
Open Door notes *(p. 508)*
Panama Canal *(p. 508)*
Selective Service Act *(p. 515)*
American Expeditionary Force *(p. 516)*
War Industries Board (WIB) *(p. 516)*
John J. Pershing *(p. 517)*
Committee on Public Information *(p. 520)*
Espionage Act *(p. 521)*
Sedition Amendment *(p. 521)*
Nineteenth Amendment *(p. 524)*
influenza pandemic *(p. 524)*
Eighteenth Amendment *(p. 524)*
War Labor Board *(p. 525)*
Fourteen Points *(p. 526)*
Versailles Peace Conference *(p. 526)*
League of Nations *(p. 527)*
Warren G. Harding *(p. 529)*

What was the war's economic, political, and social impact on the American home front? (page 522)

World War I had a profound impact on the United States. Farm production and prosperity soared, as did industry, but farmers faced a credit squeeze after the war. Large numbers of blacks left the South to live in northern cities; racism followed them. Women advanced in the work force in large numbers, but most lost their positions to returning troops. Some progressive goals benefited from the war—government regulation, woman suffrage, and labor laws—but the war ultimately revived conservative attitudes and extinguished the progressive spirit for a generation.

How did the League of Nations begin, and why did the Senate reject U.S. membership in the League? (page 525)

Wilson's goals, expressed in the Fourteen Points, included spreading democracy and reforming the international political system. Essentially, he wanted to Americanize the world. However, he never achieved most of these goals. Negotiations at Versailles were dominated by European leaders' thirsty for vengeance, and the Versailles Treaty guaranteed future conflict. Even participation in the League of Nations, which Wilson saw as the centerpiece of his new world order, eluded his grasp because of Republican opposition and the president's own stubbornness.

The Dunes Beaches

By the SOUTH SHORE LINE

Trains from Chicago operated over Illinois Central R.R. from Randolph, VanBuren, 12 TH, 43 RD, 53 RD & 63 RD St. Stations.

A Pleasure-Mad Decade

Among the thousands of immigrants who arrived at Ellis Island in 1913 seeking a better life was the eighteen-year-old Rodolfo Alfonso Raffaello Piero Filiberto Guglielmi di Valentina d'Antoguolla. After moving to Hollywood—and wisely shortening his name to "Rudolph Valentino"—he appeared in fifteen short films in 1919–1920. For the next six years, Valentino reigned as Hollywood's most popular male star. With his smoldering good looks and piercing dark eyes, he exuded sex appeal. In August 1926, at only thirty-one, Valentino died after surgery for a perforated ulcer. Lines of female fans stretched for blocks around the funeral home.

The popularity of the movies and their larger-than-life stars was only one novelty in a turbulent decade. These years also saw a rising tide of consumerism, changing cultural values, creativity in the arts, and bitter social conflicts. The decade soon acquired a nickname, "the Roaring Twenties." Many features of contemporary American life first became clearly evident in the 1920s. This chapter explores how different groups of Americans responded to technological, social, and cultural changes that could be both exciting and deeply threatening.

A NEW ECONOMIC ORDER

What economic innovations came in the 1920s, and what was their effect on different social groups?

With consumer products aplenty, sophisticated advertising, and innovative forms of corporate organization, the economy raced forward in the 1920s. Some key industries declined, and farmers relapsed into chronic economic problems. Still, the overall picture seemed rosy, and most Americans celebrated the nation's thriving business culture.

Booming Business, Ailing Agriculture

A recession struck in 1920 after the government canceled wartime defense contracts and returning veterans reentered the job market. Recovery came in 1922, however, and for the next few years the nonfarm economy hummed. Unemployment fell to as low as 3 percent, prices held steady, and the gross national product (GNP) grew by 43 percent from 1922 to 1929.

With the growth of cities, new consumer goods, including home electrical products, fed the prosperity. Many factories already ran on electricity, but now many urban households joined the grid as well. By the mid-1920s, with more than 60 percent of the nation's homes electrified, new appliances, from refrigerators and vacuum cleaners to fans and razors, filled the stores. Their manufacture provided a potent economic stimulus.

The automobile helped fuel the boom. Introduced before the war (see Chapter 21), the automobile came into its own in the 1920s. By 1930, some 60 percent of U.S. families owned cars. The Ford Motor Company led the market until mid-decade, when General Motors (GM) spurted ahead by touting greater comfort and a range of colors. GM's lowest-priced car, named for French automotive designer Louis Chevrolet, proved especially popular. Meeting the challenge, in 1927 **Henry Ford** introduced the stylish Model A. By the end of the decade, the automobile industry accounted for about 9 percent of all wages in manufacturing and had stimulated such industries as rubber, gasoline and motor oil, advertising, and highway construction.

Henry Ford Perfected assembly-line manufacturing techniques and democratized the automobile

The business boom had a global impact. To supply overseas markets, Ford, GM, and other corporations built production facilities abroad. U.S. meatpackers built plants in Argentina; Anaconda Copper acquired Chile's biggest copper mine; the mammoth United Fruit Company established plants across Latin America. U.S. private investment abroad also increased as American investment firms loaned European nations money to repay war debts and modernize their economies.

CL Primary Source:
Model T Ford

"Honey, Where Did You Park the Car?"

Hundreds of identical Fords jam Nantasket Beach near Boston on a Fourth of July in the early 1920s.

But the era of economic globalization still lay far in the future. Economic nationalism prevailed in the 1920s, as the industrialized nations, including the United States, erected high tariff barriers. The Fordney-McCumber Tariff (1922) and the Smoot-Hawley Tariff (1930) pushed U.S. import duties to all-time highs, benefiting domestic manufacturers but stifling foreign trade. The percentage of the GNP represented by exports actually fell between 1913 and 1929. Manufactured goods increasingly replaced agricultural commodities in U.S. exports, however, rising to 61 percent of the total by 1930.

While prosperity lifted overall wage rates, workers benefited unequally. The variation between North and South loomed largest. In 1928, unskilled laborers in New England earned an average of forty-seven cents an hour, in contrast to twenty-eight cents in the South. African-Americans faced special difficulties. "Last hired and first fired," they generally held the most menial jobs.

For farmers, wartime prosperity gave way to hard times. Grain prices plummeted when European agriculture revived and America's high tariffs depressed agricultural exports. Ironically, when new machinery increased farm production, the resulting surpluses further weakened prices. Farmers who had bought land and equipment on credit during the war now felt the squeeze as payments came due.

New Modes of Producing, Managing, and Selling

The 1920s saw striking increases in productivity. New assembly-line techniques boosted the per capita output of industrial workers by some 40 percent. At the Ford plants near Detroit, workers stood in place and performed repetitive tasks as chains conveyed the partly assembled vehicles past them. To keep workers on task, managers discouraged initiative and forbade talking or laughter. *Fordism* became a synonym for American industrial might and efficient assembly-line methods. Business consolidation, spurred by the war, continued. By the late 1920s, over a thousand companies a year vanished through merger. Corporate giants dominated the major industries: Ford, GM, and Chrysler in automobiles; General Electric and Westinghouse in electricity; and so forth. Samuel Insull presided over a multibillion-dollar empire of local and regional power companies and electric railroads. By 1930, one hundred corporations controlled nearly half the nation's business.

As U.S. capitalism matured, management structures evolved. Giant corporations set up separate divisions for product development, market research, economic forecasting, and employee relations. The modernization of business also affected wage policies. Rejecting the old view that employers should pay the lowest wages possible, business leaders now concluded that higher wages would improve productivity and increase consumer buying power. Henry Ford had led the way in 1914 by paying

Chronology

1920	Postwar recession; Warren G. Harding elected president; Radio station KDKA, Pittsburgh, broadcasts election returns; Sinclair Lewis, *Main Street*
1921	Economic boom begins; agriculture remains depressed; Sheppard-Towner Act; *Shuffle Along*, all-black musical review
1921–1922	Washington Naval Arms Conference
1922	Supreme Court declares child-labor law unconstitutional; Fordney-McCumber Tariff restores high rates; Herbert Hoover, *American Individualism*
1923	Harding dies; Calvin Coolidge becomes president; Teapot Dome scandals investigated; National Origins Act (immigration restriction)
1924	Calvin Coolidge elected president
1925	Scopes Trial; Ku Klux Klan scandal in Indiana; Alain Locke, *The New Negro*; DuBose Heyward, *Porgy*; F. Scott Fitzgerald, *The Great Gatsby*
1926	Book-of-the-Month Club founded; National Broadcasting Company founded; Langston Hughes, *The Weary Blues*
1927	*The Jazz Singer,* first sound movie; Coolidge vetoes the McNary-Haugen farm bill; Henry Ford introduces the Model A; Ford apologizes for anti-Semitic publications; Execution of Sacco and Vanzetti; Charles A. Lindbergh's transatlantic flight; Marcus Garvey deported; Mississippi River flood
1928	Herbert Hoover elected president
1929	Federal Farm Board created; Sheppard-Towner program terminated; Textile strike in Gastonia, North Carolina; Ernest Hemingway, *A Farewell to Arms;* Claude McKay, *Home to Harlem*

his workers five dollars a day, well above the average for factory workers. Other companies soon followed suit.

New systems for distributing goods emerged as well. Automobiles reached consumers through dealer networks. By 1926, nearly ten thousand Ford dealerships dotted the nation. The A&P grocery chain boasted 17,500 stores by 1928. Chain stores accounted for about a quarter of all retail sales by 1930. Department stores grew more inviting, with remodeled interiors and attractive display windows. Air conditioning, an early-twentieth-century invention, made department stores (as well as movie theaters and restaurants) welcome havens on summer days.

Advertising and credit sales further strengthened the new consumer economy. In 1929, corporations spent nearly $2 billion on radio, billboard, newspaper, and magazine ads, and advertising companies employed some six hundred thousand people.

Advertisers offered a seductive vision of the new era of abundance. Portraying a fantasy world of elegance, grace, and pleasure, ads aroused desires that the new consumer oriented capitalist system happily fulfilled. One critic in 1925 described the "dream world" created by advertising:

> [S]miling faces, shining teeth, schoolgirl complexions, cornless feet, perfect fitting [underwear], distinguished collars, wrinkleless pants, odorless breath, regularized bowels, . . . charging motors, punctureless tires, perfect busts, shimmering shanks, self-washing dishes, backs behind which the moon was meant to rise.

Participation in this fantasy world came at a price. Americans of the 1920s increasingly bought major purchases on credit. By 1929, credit purchases accounted for 75 percent of automobile sales.

What some have called "the cult of business" saturated 1920s' U.S. culture. "America stands for one idea: Business. . . ," proclaimed the *Independent* magazine in 1921; "Thru business, . . . the human race is finally to be redeemed." Presidents Harding and Coolidge praised business values and hobnobbed with corporate leaders. A 1923 opinion poll ranked Henry Ford as a leading presidential prospect. In *The Man Nobody Knows* (1925), ad man Bruce Barton described Jesus Christ as a managerial genius who "picked up twelve men from the bottom ranks of business and forged them into an organization that conquered the world."

Women in the New Economic Era

Although the ranks of women employed outside the home increased in the 1920s, their share as a proportion of the total female population hardly changed, hovering at about 24 percent. Male workers dominated the auto plants and other assembly-line factories. Women who did enter the workplace faced wage discrimination. In 1929, for example, a male trimmer in the meatpacking industry received fifty-two cents an hour; a female trimmer, thirty-seven cents.

Most women workers held low-paying, unskilled positions. By 1930, however, some 2 million women were working in corporate offices as secretaries, typists, or filing clerks, although rarely at higher ranks.

As for higher education, nearly fifty thousand women received college degrees in 1930, almost triple the 1920 figure. Of those who entered the workplace, most took clerical jobs or entered such traditional "women's professions" as nursing, librarianship, and school teaching. With medical schools imposing a 5 percent quota on female admissions, the number of women physicians actually declined from 1910 to 1930. A handful of women, however, following the lead of Progressive Era feminist trailblazers, pursued postgraduate education to become faculty members in colleges and universities.

While marginalized in the workplace, women were courted as consumers. In the decade's advertising, glamorous women smiled behind the steering wheel, swooned over new appliances, and smoked cigarettes in romantic settings. One ad man promoted cigarettes for women as "torches of freedom." In the advertisers' dream world, housework became an exciting challenge. As one ad put it, "Men are judged . . . according to their power to delegate work. Similarly the wise woman delegates to electricity all that electricity can do."

Struggling Labor Unions in a Business Age

Organized labor faced tough sledding in the 1920s. Union membership fell from 5 million in 1920 to 3.4 million in 1929. Several factors underlay this decline. For one thing, despite inequities and regional variations, overall wage rates rose in the decade, reducing the incentive to join a union. Further, the union movement's strength lay in older industries like printing, railroading, mining, and construction. These unions were ill suited to the new mass-production factories.

Management hostility further weakened organized labor. Henry Ford hired thugs to intimidate union organizers. In 1929, anti-union violence flared in North Carolina, where textile workers faced low wages, long hours, and appalling work conditions. In Marion, deputy sheriffs shot and killed six striking workers. In Gastonia, a sniper shot and killed strike leader and balladeer Ella May Wiggins en route to a union rally. In the end, these strikes failed, and the textile industry remained nonunion.

As the wartime antiradical mood continued, opponents of labor unions often smeared them with the "communist" label, whether accurate or not. The anti-union campaign took subtler forms as well. Manufacturers' associations renamed the nonunion shop the "open shop" and dubbed it the "American Plan" of labor relations. Some corporations provided cafeterias and recreational facilities for employees. Corporate publicists praised "welfare capitalism" (the term for this antiunion strategy) as evidence of employers' benevolent concern for their workers.

Black membership in labor unions stood at only about eighty-two thousand by 1929, mostly miners, dockworkers, and railroad porters. The American Federation of Labor officially prohibited racial discrimination, but most AFL unions in fact barred African-Americans. Corporations often hired jobless blacks as strikebreakers, increasing organized labor's hostility toward them.

CHECKING IN

- Automobiles were at the root of the economic boom in the twenties; farmers were left out.
- Mass production and the assembly line came of age.
- Advertising played a major role in stimulating consumption.
- More women graduated from college and entered the office work force, but few were in high-wage industrial jobs.
- Labor unions struggled, in part because of general prosperity, in part because of management measures to undermine them.

THE HARDING AND COOLIDGE ADMINISTRATIONS

What political and social ideas shaped the administrations of Presidents Harding and Coolidge?

Politics in the 1920s reflected the decade's business orientation. Republicans controlled Congress and supplied presidents who mirrored the prevailing corporate outlook. In this climate, former progressives, would-be reformers, and exploited groups had few political options.

Standpat Politics in a Decade of Change

While the white South and the immigrant cities remained heavily Democratic, the Republican party continued to attract northern farmers, businesspeople, native-born white-collar workers and professionals, and some skilled blue-collar workers. The GOP also benefited from the antiradical mood that had produced the early postwar Red Scare (see Chapter 22) and fed the decade's anti-union sentiment.

With Republican progressives having weakened their influence in the party by bolting to Theodore Roosevelt in 1912, GOP conservatives controlled the 1920 convention and nominated Senator Warren G. Harding of Marion, Ohio, for president. A genial backslapper, Harding enjoyed good liquor, a good poker game, and at least one long-term extramarital relationship. In the election, Harding swamped his Democratic opponent James M. Cox. Harding made some notable cabinet selections:

Charles Evans Hughes, former New York governor and 1916 presidential candidate, secretary of state; Andrew Mellon, a Pittsburgh financier, treasury secretary; and Herbert Hoover, the wartime food czar, secretary of commerce.

Harding also made some disastrous appointments, including a wartime draft dodger, Charles Forbes, as Veterans' Bureau head. Such men set the low ethical tone of Harding's presidency. By 1922, Washington rumor hinted at corruption in high places. "I have no trouble with my enemies. . . ," Harding told an associate; "[b]ut . . . my goddamn friends . . . keep me walking the floor nights." In July 1923, vacationing in the West, Harding suffered a heart attack; on August 2 he died in a San Francisco hotel.

In 1924 a Senate investigation exposed the full scope of the scandals. Charles Forbes, convicted of stealing Veterans' Bureau funds, evaded prison by fleeing abroad. The bureau's general counsel committed suicide, as did an associate of Attorney General Daugherty who had been accused of influence peddling. Daugherty himself, forced from office in 1924, escaped conviction in two criminal trials. The seamiest scandal, known as **Teapot Dome,** involved interior secretary Albert Fall, who went to jail for secretly leasing government oil reserves in Elk Hills, California, and Teapot Dome, Wyoming, to two oilmen while accepting "loans" from them totaling $400,000. Like "Watergate" in the 1970s, "Teapot Dome" became a shorthand label for a tangle of scandals.

With Harding's death, Vice President **Calvin Coolidge,** on a family visit in Vermont, took the presidential oath by lantern light from his father, a local magistrate. Elected Massachusetts governor in 1918, he secured the Republican vice-presidential nomination in 1920. Coolidge's image as "Silent Cal," a prim Yankee embodiment of old-fashioned virtues, was carefully crafted. The advertising executive Bruce Barton guided Coolidge's bid for national office in 1919–1920. Barton marketed his candidate as one would a soap or an automobile. Wrote an admirer of Barton: "No man is his equal in [analyzing] the middle-class mind and directing an appeal to it."

Teapot Dome Scandal of Harding administration

Calvin Coolidge Former Massachusetts governor; soft-spoken, dour successor to Warren Harding

Republican Policy Making in a Probusiness Era

Other than in style, Coolidge's advent meant little change. Tariff rates reached all-time highs, income taxes for the rich fell, and the Supreme Court overturned several progressive measures. Coolidge rejected a request for aid from Mississippi flood victims with the reminder that government had no duty to protect citizens "against the hazards of the elements."

Another test of Coolidge's views came when hard-pressed farmers rallied behind the **McNary-Haugen Bill,** a price-support plan under which the government would annually purchase the surplus of basic farm commodities. Coolidge twice vetoed the McNary-Haugen Bill, in 1927 and 1928, warning of "the tyranny of bureaucratic regulation and control." These vetoes led many angry farmers to vote Democratic in 1928. In the 1930s, New Deal planners would draw upon the McNary-Haugen approach in shaping farm policy (see Chapter 24).

McNary-Haugen Bill Popular legislation to help farmers, vetoed by Coolidge

Independent Internationalism

Although the United States participated informally in some League of Nations activities in the 1920s, the country refused to join the League or the World Court. Nonetheless, the United States remained a world power, and Republican presidents

The 1927 Mississippi River Flood

A few of the 700,000 people displaced by the raging waters of the Mississippi await rescue, their partially submerged homes in the background. President Calvin Coolidge resisted calls for federal aid, insisting that the government had no obligation to help citizens suffering from "the hazards of the elements."

pursued what they saw as the national interest—an approach historians have called independent internationalism.

President Harding's most notable achievement was the **Washington Naval Arms Conference.** After the war ended, the United States, Great Britain, and Japan edged toward a dangerous (and costly) naval-arms race. In 1921, Secretary of State Hughes called for a conference in Washington and outlined a specific ratio of warships among the world's naval powers. Great Britain and Japan, together with Italy and France, accepted Hughes's plan and agreed to halt all battleship construction for ten years. Although this treaty ultimately failed to prevent war, it did represent an early arms-control effort.

Washington Naval Arms Conference Attempt to limit weapons, arms spending among major nations

Another U.S. peace initiative was mainly symbolic. In 1928, the United States and France, eventually joined by sixty other nations, signed the Kellogg-Briand Pact renouncing aggression and calling for the outlawing of war. Lacking enforcement mechanisms, this high-sounding document accomplished little.

The Republican administrations of these years used diplomacy to promote U.S. economic interests. For example, they vigorously sought repayment of $22 billion in Allied war debts and German reparation payments. A study commission in 1924 sharply reduced these claims, but high U.S. tariffs and Europe's economic problems, including runaway inflation in Germany, made repayment of even the reduced claims unrealistic. Meanwhile, the Harding and Coolidge administrations aggressively promoted American business interests around the world.

Progressive Stirrings, Democratic Party Divisions

The reform spirit survived feebly in the legislative branch. Congress staved off Andrew Mellon's proposals for even deeper tax cuts for the rich. And in 1927, Congress created the Federal Radio Commission, extending the regulatory principle to this new industry. In the 1922 midterm election, an alliance of labor and farm groups helped defeat some conservative Republicans. In 1924, this alliance revived the Progressive Party and nominated Senator Robert La Follette—who also received the endorsement of the Socialist Party—for president.

The 1924 Democratic convention in New York City split evenly between urban and rural wings. By one vote, the delegates defeated a resolution condemning the **Ku Klux Klan.** While the party's rural, Protestant, southern wing favored former Treasury Secretary William G. McAdoo, the big-city delegates rallied behind New York's Catholic governor **Alfred E. Smith.** The Democratic split mirrored deep divisions in the nation. After 102 ballots, the exhausted delegates nominated an obscure New York corporation lawyer, John W. Davis.

Calvin Coolidge, aided by his media adviser Bruce Barton, easily won the Republican nomination. The GOP platform praised the high protective tariff and urged tax cuts and reduced government spending. Coolidge polled nearly 16 million votes, about twice Davis's total. La Follette's 4.8 million votes cut into the Democratic total, contributing to the Coolidge landslide.

Ku Klux Klan Anti-modern reactionary group; wielded substantial political power in the 1920s

Alfred E. Smith Former Tammany Hall machine politician; Democratic nominee for president in 1928

Women and Politics in the 1920s: A Dream Deferred

Suffragists' hope that votes for women would transform politics survived briefly after the war. Polling places shifted from saloons to schools and churches. The 1920 major-party platforms endorsed several measures proposed by the League of Women Voters. The Women's Joint Congressional Committee, a coalition of activist groups, backed the **Sheppard-Towner Act,** which funded rural prenatal and baby-care centers staffed by public-health nurses.

Overall, however, the Nineteenth Amendment, though a historic achievement, had little short-term political effect. As former suffrage advocates scattered across the political spectrum, the women's movement lost focus. The League of Women Voters, drawing middle-class and professional women, abandoned feminist activism and instead conducted nonpartisan studies of civic issues. Alice Paul's National Woman's Party proposed a constitutional amendment guaranteeing women equal rights, but other reformers argued that such an amendment could jeopardize gender-based laws protecting women workers. The proposed amendment got nowhere. Politically active African-American women battled racial discrimination rather than addressing feminist issues; Hispanic women in the Southwest put their energies into labor-union organizing.

The reactionary political climate intensified this retreat from feminism. Patriotic groups accused Jane Addams and other women's-rights leaders of communist sympathies. Younger women, bombarded by ads that defined liberation in terms of consumption, rejected the prewar feminists' civic idealism.

The few reforms women's groups did achieve proved short-lived. The Supreme Court in 1922–1923 struck down child-labor and women's-protective

Sheppard-Towner Act Appropriated $1.2 million for rural prenatal and baby-care centers in 1921

CHECKING IN

- Corruption damaged the Harding administration.
- The Coolidge administration remained staunchly probusiness.
- The United States remained fundamentally isolationist but pursued its national interest through "independent internationalism."
- The Democratic party split between its urban and rural wings, and lost badly in 1924.
- Woman suffrage produced few changes as women splintered across the political spectrum.

laws. A 1924 constitutional amendment banning child labor passed Congress, but few states ratified it. The Sheppard-Towner Act, denounced by the American Medical Association as a threat to physicians' monopoly of health care, expired in 1929.

▌MASS SOCIETY, MASS CULTURE

What developments underlay 1920s' mass culture, and how did they affect American life and leisure?

▌As a conservative reaction dominated U.S. politics, major transformations were reshaping society. Assembly lines, new consumer products, advertising, the spread of mass entertainment, and innovations in corporate organization all signaled profound changes in American life. Some citizens found these changes exciting; others recoiled in fear and apprehension.

Cities, Cars, Consumer Goods

In the 1920 census, for the first time, the urban population (defined as persons living in communities of twenty-five hundred or more) surpassed the rural (see Figure 23.1). The United States had become an urban nation.

Urbanization affected different groups of Americans in different ways. African-Americans, for example, migrated cityward in massive numbers, especially after the 1927 Mississippi River floods. By 1930, more than 40 percent of the nation's 12 million blacks lived in cities. The first black congressman since Reconstruction, Oscar De Priest of Chicago, won election in 1928.

For many women, city life meant eased housework thanks to laborsaving appliances: gas stoves, electric irons, refrigerators, washing machines, and vacuum cleaners. Store-bought clothes replaced hand-sewn apparel. Home baking and canning declined as commercial bakeries arose and supermarkets offered canned fruit and vegetables.

For social impact, however, nothing matched the automobile. In *Middletown* (1929), a study of Muncie, Indiana, Robert and Helen Lynd reported one resident's

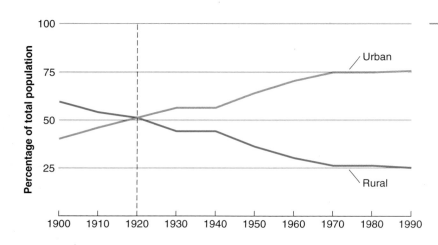

Figure 23.1   The Urban and Rural Population of the United States, 1900–2000

The urbanization of America in the twentieth century had profound political, economic, and social consequences. *Source:* Census Bureau, *Historical Statistics of the United States,* updated by relevant *Statistical Abstracts of the United States.*

comment: "Why . . . do you need to study what's changing this country? I can tell you . . . in just four letters: A-U-T-O."

The A-U-T-O's social impact was decidedly mixed, including traffic jams, parking problems, and highway fatalities (more than twenty-six thousand in 1924). In some ways, the automobile brought families together. Family vacations, rare a generation earlier, became more common. Tourist cabins and roadside restaurants served vacationing families. But the automobile also eroded family cohesion and parental authority. Young people could borrow the car to go to the movies, attend a distant dance, or simply park in a secluded lovers' lane.

Middle- and upper-class women welcomed the automobile. They could now drive to work, attend meetings, visit friends, and gain a sense of personal empowerment. Stereotypes of feminine delicacy faded as women mastered this new technology. As the editor of an automotive magazine wrote in 1927, "[E]very time a woman learns to drive, . . . it is a threat to yesterday's order of things."

For farm families, the automobile offered easier access to neighbors and to the city, lessening rural isolation. The automobile's country cousin, the tractor, proved instantly popular, with nearly a million in use in America by 1930. Yet increased productivity did not always mean increased profits. And as farmers bought tractors on credit, the rural debt crisis worsened.

Ads celebrated the freedom the automobile offered, in contrast to the fixed routes and schedules of trains and streetcars. Yet the automobile and other forms of motor transport in many ways further standardized American life. Neighborhood grocery stores declined as people drove to supermarkets served by trucks bringing commercial foods from distant facilities. With the automobile came the first suburban shopping center (in Kansas City), and the first fast-food chain (A & W Root Beer).

Even at $300 or $400, the automobile remained too expensive for many. The "automobile suburbs" that sprang up beyond the streetcar lines attracted mainly the well-to-do, widening class divisions in American society.

Soaring Energy Consumption and a Threatened Environment

Electrification and the spread of motorized vehicles placed heavy demands on the nation's natural resources and the environment. As electrical use soared, generating plants consumed growing quantities of coal. In 1929, with 20 million cars on the road, U.S. refineries used over a billion barrels of petroleum to meet the demand for gasoline and lubricating oil.

Rising gasoline consumption underlay Washington's efforts to ensure U.S. access to Mexican oil; played a role in the Teapot Dome scandal; and triggered fevered activity in the oilfields of Texas and Oklahoma. In short, heavy fossil-fuel consumption, though small by later standards, already characterized America in the 1920s.

The wilderness that had inspired nineteenth-century artists and writers became more accessible as cars, improved roads, and tourist facilities gave vacationers easier access to the national parks and once-pristine regions. This development, too, had mixed effects. On one hand, it created a broader constituency for wilderness preservation. On the other, it subjected the nation's parks and wilderness areas to heavy pressures as visitors expected good highways, service stations, restaurants, and hotels.

The Sierra Club and other groups worked to protect wilderness and wildlife. In 1923, a group of recreational fishermen persuaded Congress to halt a private-development scheme to drain a vast stretch of wetlands on the upper Mississippi. Instead, Congress declared this beautiful waterway a wildlife preserve. Aldo Leopold of the U.S. Forest Service warned of technology run amok. For too long, Leopold wrote in 1925, "a stump was our symbol of progress." However, few Americans in the expansive 1920s worried about the environmental issues that would occupy future generations.

Christmas in Consumerland

Giving a modern twist to an ancient symbol, this advertising catalog of the 1920s offered an enticing array of new electric products for the home.

Mass-Produced Entertainment

Growing prosperity and routinized work stimulated interest in leisure activities in the 1920s. In their free hours, Americans sought the fulfillment many found missing in the workplace.

Mass-circulation magazines provided diversion. By 1922, ten U.S. magazines boasted circulation of more than 2.5 million. The venerable *Saturday Evening Post,* with its Norman Rockwell covers, specialized in nostalgia. *Reader's Digest,* founded in 1921, offered condensed versions of articles first published elsewhere. A journalistic equivalent of the Model T, the *Digest* offered standardized fare for mass consumption.

Book publishers broadened their market by selling through department stores or directly to the public via the Book-of-the-Month Club, launched in 1926. While critics accused such mass-market ventures of debasing literary taste, they did help sustain a common national culture in an increasingly diverse society.

In an age of standardized consumer goods, radio and the movies offered standardized cultural fare. The radio era began on November 2, 1920, when Pittsburgh station KDKA reported Warren Harding's election. In 1922, five hundred new stations began operations, as radio fever gripped America. The first radio network, the National Broadcasting Company (NBC), formed four years later; the Columbia Broadcasting System (CBS) followed in 1927. Testing popular taste through market research, the networks soon ruled broadcasting. Americans everywhere laughed at the same jokes, heard the same news, and absorbed the same commercials.

Some commentators advocated preserving radio as a public educational and cultural medium, free of advertising, but commercial sponsorship soon won out. The first network comedy show, *Amos 'n' Andy* (1928)—which included stereotyped caricatures of African-American life—enriched its sponsor, Pepsodent toothpaste.

Featuring stars like Valentino, the movies expanded from the nickelodeons of the immigrant wards into elegant uptown pleasure palaces with names like Majestic, Ritz, and Orpheum. In deference to the conservatism of this new audience, in 1922 Hollywood enacted a new code of standards for movie content. Charlie Chaplin, who had played anarchic, anti-authority figures in his prewar comedies, now softened his character in such feature-length films as *The Gold Rush* (1925). *The Ten Commandments*

(1923), directed by Cecil B. De Mille, warned of the consequences of breaking moral taboos.

Technical innovations kept moviegoers coming. Al Jolson's *The Jazz Singer* (1927) introduced sound. Walt Disney's cartoon *Steamboat Willy* (1928) not only marked the debut of Mickey Mouse but also showed the potential of animation. Like advertising, the movies created a dream world only loosely tethered to reality. One ad promised "all the adventure, . . . romance, . . . [and] excitement you lack in your daily life." The movies also stimulated consumption with alluring images of the good life. Along with department stores, mass magazines, and advertising, they opened new vistas of consumer abundance.

For all its influence, the new mass culture penetrated society unevenly. It had less impact in rural America, especially among evangelical Christians. Mexican-Americans generally preferred traditional festivals and leisure activities. Local radio stations broadcast not only network shows, but also farm reports, local news, and religious programs, community announcements, and ethnic or regional music. In short, despite the new mass culture, America still had room for diversity in the 1920s.

Celebrity Culture

Professional sports and media-promoted spectacles provided diversion as well. In 1921, Atlantic City promoters launched a bathing-beauty contest they grandly called the Miss America Pageant. Celebrities dominated professional sports. Few Americans were more famous than Babe Ruth of the New York Yankees or Ty Cobb, the Detroit Tigers' player/manager. Ruth was a heavy-drinking womanizer; Cobb, a borderline psychotic racist. Yet the alchemy of publicity transformed them into heroes with contrived nicknames: "the Sultan of Swat" (Ruth) and "the Georgia Peach" (Cobb).

This celebrity culture illuminates the stresses facing ordinary Americans in these years of social change. For young women uncertain about society's shifting expectations, the beauty pageants offered one ideal to which they could aspire. For men grappling with unsettling developments from feminism to Fordism, the exploits of sports heroes like Ruth could help restore damaged self-esteem.

Celebrity worship reached a crescendo in the response to **Charles Lindbergh,** a daredevil stunt pilot who flew solo across the Atlantic in his small single-engine plane, *The Spirit of St. Louis,* on May 20–21, 1927. His success gripped the public's imagination. In New York, thousands turned out for a ticker-tape parade. Radio, newspapers, magazines, and movie newsreels offered saturation coverage. President Coolidge praised the flight as a triumph of American business and corporate technology. Others saw Lindbergh as proof that despite mechanization, the individual still counted. To conservatives, Lindbergh's solid virtues proved that the old verities survived. Overall, the new mass media had mixed social effects. Certainly, they promoted cultural standardization and uniformity of thought. But mass magazines, radio, and movies also introduced new viewpoints and conveyed a potent message: a person's immediate surroundings need not limit his or her horizons. If the larger world they opened for ordinary Americans was often superficial or tawdry, it could also be exciting and liberating.

Charles A. Lindbergh Celebrity hero; first to fly solo across the Atlantic

CHECKING IN

- The automobile had a major impact in every sector of American life.
- Energy consumption soared with little concern about environmental impact.
- The development of radio networks, large-circulation magazines, and national movie distribution created a shared mass culture.
- The 1920s were the first decade in which celebrity culture flourished; Babe Ruth and Charles Lindbergh were two noted celebrities of the time.
- Professional sports and athletes became highly popular.

CULTURAL FERMENT AND CREATIVITY

What social developments contributed to the cultural creativity of the 1920s?

▌ American life in the 1920s involved more than politics, assembly lines, and celebrity worship. As writers, artists, and musicians contributed to the modernist spirit of cultural innovation, African-Americans created a cultural flowering known as the Harlem Renaissance.

The Jazz Age and the Postwar Crisis of Values

The war and its sour aftermath sharpened the cultural restlessness of the twenties. The postwar crisis of values took many forms. The younger generation, especially college students, boisterously assailed older conventions of behavior. Seizing the freedom offered by the automobile, they threw parties, drank bootleg liquor, flocked to jazz clubs, and danced the Charleston.

Young people also discussed sex more freely than their elders had. Sigmund Freud, the Viennese physician who explored the sexual aspects of human psychology, enjoyed a popular vogue in a postwar climate that encouraged challenges to old taboos.

Despite much talk about sex and charges of rampant immorality, however, the 1920s' "sexual revolution" is hard to pin down. Premarital intercourse remained exceptional and widely disapproved. What *can* be documented are changing courtship patterns. "Courting" had once been a formal prelude to marriage. The 1920s brought the more casual practice of "dating," through which young people gained social confidence and a degree of sexual experience without necessarily contemplating marriage.

For women, these postwar changes in some ways proved liberating. Female sexuality was more openly acknowledged. Skirt lengths crept up; makeup became more acceptable; and the elaborate armor of petticoats and corsets fell away. The so-called flapper, with her bobbed hair, defiant cigarette, lipstick, and short skirt, similarly epitomized youthful rejection of entrenched stereotypes.

But this image also objectified young women as decorative sexual objects. Further, the double standard, which held women to a stricter code of conduct, remained in force. Young men could boast of sexual exploits, but young women reputed to be "fast" risked damaged reputations. In some ways, in short, 1920s' popular culture worked against full gender equality nearly as effectively as had the older Victorian stereotypes.

Around 1922, according to F. Scott Fitzgerald, adults embraced the rebelliousness of the young and "the orgy began." But such sweeping generalizations can mislead. During the years of Fitzgerald's alleged national orgy, the divorce rate remained constant, and many Americans adhered to traditional standards, rejecting alcohol and wild parties. Most farmers, industrial workers, blacks, Hispanics, and recent immigrants found economic survival more pressing than the latest fads and fashions.

But if the Jazz Age stereotype obscured the complexity of the 1920s, it did capture a part of the postwar scene, especially the brassy new mass culture and the hedonism and materialism of the well-to-do as they basked in the era's prosperity.

Alienated Writers

Like Fitzgerald, many other young writers found the cultural turbulence of the 1920s stimulating. They forged a remarkable body of work equally hostile to the moralistic pieties of the old order and the business pieties of the new. In *Main Street* (1920), the novelist Sinclair Lewis satirized the smugness and cultural barrenness of Gopher Prairie, a fictional mid-western town based on his native Sauk Centre, Minnesota. In *Babbitt* (1922), Lewis skewered a mythic larger city, Zenith, and the title character George F. Babbitt, a real-estate agent trapped in middle-class conformity.

H. L. Mencken, a journalist, editor, and critic, in 1924 launched the iconoclastic *American Mercury* magazine, an instant success with the decade's alienated intellectuals and young people. Mencken championed writers like Lewis and Theodore Dreiser while ridiculing politicians, small-town America, Protestant fundamentalism, and the middle-class "Booboisie." Asked why he stayed in America, Mencken replied, "Why do people visit zoos?"

For the novelist Ernest Hemingway, seriously wounded in 1918 while serving as a Red Cross volunteer in northern Italy, World War I was a watershed experience. In 1926, now an expatriate in Paris, Hemingway published *The Sun Also Rises,* portraying a group of American and English young people, variously damaged by the war, as they drift around Spain. His *A Farewell to Arms* (1929), loosely based on his own experiences, depicts the war's futility and politicians' empty rhetoric.

Although writers like Lewis and Hemingway deplored the inflated rhetoric of the war and the vulgarity of postwar culture, they remained American at heart, striving to create a more authentic national culture. Even F. Scott Fitzgerald, himself caught up in Jazz Age excesses, was fundamentally a moralist. Fitzgerald's masterpiece, *The Great Gatsby* (1925), portrayed not only the party-filled lives of the decade's moneyed class, but also their decadence, selfishness, and heedless disregard for the less fortunate.

H. L. Mencken Master of satire; journalist who pilloried narrow-minded thinking

Architects, Painters, and Musicians Celebrate Modern America

The creative energies of the 1920s found many outlets. A burst of architectural activity, for example, transformed the skylines of larger cities. By the end of the decade, New York City boasted four buildings more than fifty stories tall.

The decade's leading painters took America as their subject—either the real nation around them or an imagined one. While Thomas Hart Benton evoked a past of cowboys, pioneers, and riverboat gamblers, Edward Hopper portrayed faded towns and lonely cities of the present. Hopper's painting *Sunday* (1926), picturing a man slumped on the curb of an empty street of abandoned stores, conveyed both the bleakness and potential beauty of urban America. A similar fascination with the industrial city pervaded the work of artists Georgia O'Keeffe and Charles Sheeler. Though O'Keeffe is stereotyped as a painter of New Mexico, she earlier painted significant urban scenes in her New York days.

The creative ferment of the 1920s inspired composers as well. Of all the musical innovations, jazz best captured the modernist spirit. The white bandleader Paul Whiteman offered watered-down "jazz" versions of standard tunes. Aaron Copland's

Music for Theatre (1925) and George Gershwin's *Rhapsody in Blue* (1924) and *An American in Paris* (1928) revealed strong jazz influences.

Meanwhile, black musicians preserved authentic jazz and explored its potential. The 1920s recordings of trumpeter Louis Armstrong decisively influenced the future of jazz. The composer and bandleader Duke Ellington performed to sellout audiences at Harlem's Cotton Club. Meanwhile, the piano's jazz potential was demonstrated by Fats Waller and Ferdinand "Jelly Roll" Morton. Although much of 1920s' popular culture faded quickly, jazz endured.

Interactive Map: Urbanization, 1890 & 1929

The Harlem Renaissance

Jazz was only one of many black contributions to 1920s' American culture. The social changes of these years energized African-American cultural life, especially in New York City's Harlem. An elite white suburb before World War I, Harlem attracted many African-Americans during and after the war, and by 1930 most of New York's 327,000 blacks lived within its boundaries. This concentration, plus the proximity of Broadway theaters, record companies, book publishers, and the NAACP's national headquarters, all contributed to the Harlem Renaissance.

This cultural flowering took varied forms. The Mississippi-born black composer William Grant Still, moving to Harlem in 1922, produced many works, including *Afro American Symphony* (1931). The painter Aaron Douglas and the sculptor Augusta Savage worked in the visual arts. The multitalented Paul Robeson gave vocal concerts; made films; and appeared on Broadway in Eugene O'Neill's *The Emperor Jones* and other plays.

Among a host of writers, poet Langston Hughes drew upon southern black oral traditions in *The Weary Blues* (1926), and the Jamaican-born poet and novelist Claude McKay evoked Harlem's vibrant, sometimes sinister nightlife in *Home to Harlem* (1928). Nella Larsen, from the Danish West Indies, told of a mulatto woman's struggle with her mixed ethnicity in the 1928 novel *Quicksand*. In *The New Negro* (1925), Alain Locke, a philosophy professor at Howard University, assembled essays, poems, short stories, and reproductions of artworks to convey Harlem's rich cultural life.

The white cultural establishment took notice. Book publishers and magazine editors courted black writers. Broadway producers mounted black shows. Whites crowded Harlem's jazz clubs. DuBose Heyward's 1925 novel *Porgy* offered a sympathetic picture of Charleston's African-American community. George Gershwin's musical version, *Porgy and Bess,* premiered in 1935.

The Harlem Renaissance reached beyond America's borders. Jazz won a following in Europe. Langston Hughes and Claude McKay were admired in Africa, Latin America, and Europe. The dancer and singer Josephine Baker, after debuting in Harlem, moved to Paris in 1925, where her highly erotic performances created a sensation.

Along with white support came misunderstanding and attempts at control. Rebellious young whites romanticized Harlem nightlife, idealizing the spiritual or "primitive" qualities of black culture while ignoring the community's social problems. Nor did it bother them that the popular

CHECKING IN

- The Jazz Age, symbolized by the bold behavior of "flaming youth" and the flamboyant sexuality of flappers, shocked traditionalists.
- Appalled by World War I, alienated writers criticized American society; many fled to Paris and elsewhere abroad.
- Architects and artists created a national visual culture; jazz, with its frenetic rhythms and sexual overtones, dominated the era's music among whites as well as blacks.
- The Harlem Renaissance was primarily a literary movement that ignored politics and racism.

Cotton Club, controlled by gangsters, featured black performers but barred most blacks from the audience. When Langston Hughes's poems confronted the gritty realities of black life in America, his wealthy white patron angrily withdrew her support.

The hard times of the 1930s ended the Harlem Renaissance. Nevertheless, this burst of creativity stands as a memorable achievement. Future black writers, artists, musicians, and performers would owe a great debt to their predecessors of the 1920s.

A SOCIETY IN CONFLICT

What events or movements reveal the major social and cultural conflicts of the twenties?

The social changes of the 1920s produced a backlash, as a series of divisive episodes and social movements highlighted the era's tensions. While Congress restricted immigration, highly publicized court cases in Massachusetts and Tennessee underscored the nation's social and cultural divisions. Millions of whites embraced the racist bigotry and moralistic rhetoric of a revived Ku Klux Klan, and many newly urbanized African-Americans rallied to Marcus Garvey, a magnetic black leader with a riveting message of racial pride. Prohibition stirred further controversy in this conflict-ridden decade.

Immigration Restriction

Fed by wartime efforts to enforce patriotism, the old impulse to remake America into a nation of like-minded, culturally homogeneous people revived in the 1920s.

National Origins Act Limitation of immigrants to keep out the "wrong sort"

The **National Origins Act** of 1924, a revision of the immigration law, restricted annual immigration from any foreign country to 2 percent of the number of persons of that "national origin" in the United States in 1890. Since the great influx of southern and eastern Europeans had come after 1890, the intent of this provision was clear: to reduce the immigration of these nationalities. As Calvin Coolidge observed on signing the law, "America must be kept American."

This quota system, which survived to 1965, represented a strong counterattack by native-born Protestant America against the immigrant cities. Total immigration fell from 1.2 million in 1914 to 280,000 in 1929. The law excluded Asians and South Asians entirely.

Court rulings underscored the nativist message. In *Ozawa* v. *United States* (1922), the U.S. Supreme Court rejected a citizenship request by a Japanese-born student at the University of California. In 1923, the Supreme Court upheld a California law limiting the right of Japanese immigrants to own or lease farmland. That same year, the Supreme Court rejected an immigration application by a man from India who claimed that he was "Caucasian" and thus eligible for entry. Only those "from the British Isles and northwestern Europe" would be so classified, according to the court.

Needed Workers/ Unwelcome Aliens: Hispanic Newcomers

Most proponents of restriction regarded Asia and southern and eastern Europe as sources of "undesirables," and the laws reflected this bias. No restrictions, however, were placed on immigration from the Western Hemisphere; consequently, immigration from French Canada and Latin America soared during the 1920s. By 1930 at least 2 million Mexican-born people lived in the United States. California's Mexican-American population quadrupled, from 90,000 to nearly 360,000, in the decade.

Many of these newcomers became migratory workers in large-scale agribusiness. Mexican migrant labor sustained California's citrus industry. Cooperatives like the Southern California Fruit Growers Exchange (Sunkist) hired workers on a seasonal basis and provided substandard housing in isolated settlements that the workers called *colonias* (ko-lo-NEE-as). The growers bitterly opposed attempts to form labor unions.

Not all Mexican immigrants were migratory workers; many settled into U.S. communities. Although still emotionally linked to "*México Lindo*" ("Beautiful Mexico"), they formed local support networks and cultural institutions.

Deeply religious, Mexican-Americans found little support from the U.S. Catholic church. Earlier Catholic immigrants had attended ethnic parishes and worshipped in their own languages, but by the 1920s church policy had changed. In "Anglo" parishes with non-Hispanic priests, the Spanish-speaking newcomers faced discrimination and pressure to abandon their language and culture.

Attitudes toward Mexican immigrants were deeply ambivalent. Their labor was needed, but their presence disturbed nativists eager to preserve a "white" and Protestant nation. Would-be Mexican immigrants faced strict literacy and means tests. The Border Patrol was created in 1925, deportations increased, and in 1929 Congress made illegal entry a criminal offense. Nevertheless, an estimated 100,000 illegal Mexican newcomers arrived annually to fill pressing demands in the U.S. labor market.

Nativism, Antiradicalism, and the Sacco-Vanzetti Case

The immigration-restriction movement reflected deep strains of ethnic, racial, and religious prejudice in 1920s' America. Anti-Semitic propaganda filled the *Dearborn Independent,* a weekly newspaper owned by Henry Ford. At its peak, the *Dearborn Independent* reached 600,000 readers. Sued for defamation by a California Jewish attorney, Ford in 1927 issued an evasive apology (drafted by a prominent Jewish leader in New York) blaming subordinates.

Nativist, antiradical prejudices emerged starkly in the Sacco-Vanzetti case, a Massachusetts murder case that began in April 1920, when robbers shot and killed the paymaster and guard of a shoe factory in South Braintree, Massachusetts, and stole two cash boxes. In 1921, a jury found two Italian immigrants, Nicola Sacco and Bartolomeo Vanzetti, guilty of the crime. After many appeals and a review by a commission of notable citizens, they were electrocuted on August 23, 1927.

These bare facts hardly convey the passions the case aroused. **Sacco and Vanzetti** were anarchists, and the prosecution harped on their radicalism. The judge barely concealed his hostility to the pair, whom he privately called "those anarchist bastards." While many conservatives supported the death sentence, liberals and socialists rallied to their cause.

Sacco and Vanzetti Anarchists accused and convicted of murder

Later research on Boston's anarchist community and ballistics tests on Sacco's gun pointed to their guilt. But the prejudices that tainted the trial remain indisputable, as does the case's symbolic importance in exposing the deep fault lines in 1920s' American society.

Fundamentalism and the Scopes Trial

Meanwhile, an equally celebrated case in Tennessee highlighted another front in the cultural wars of the 1920s: the growing prestige of science. While many Americans welcomed the advance of science, some religious believers found it threatening. Their fears had deepened as scholars had subjected the Bible to critical scrutiny, psychologists and sociologists had studied supernatural belief systems as human social constructs and expressions of emotional needs, and biologists had embraced Charles Darwin's naturalistic explanation for the variety of life forms on Earth advanced in *Origin of Species* (1859).

While liberal Protestants had generally accepted the findings of science, evangelical believers had resisted. This gave rise to a movement called **Fundamentalism,** after *The Fundamentals,* a series of essays published in 1909–1914. Fundamentalists insisted on the Bible's literal truth, including the Genesis account of Creation.

In the early 1920s, fundamentalists targeted Darwin's theory of evolution as a threat to their faith. Many states considered legislation to bar public schools from teaching evolution, and several southern states enacted such laws. The former Democratic presidential candidate and secretary of state William Jennings Bryan, still widely admired in the American heartland, endorsed the antievolution cause.

When Tennessee's legislature barred the teaching of evolution in the state's public schools in 1925, the American Civil Liberties Union (ACLU) offered to defend any teacher willing to challenge this law. A high-school teacher in Dayton, Tennessee, John T. Scopes, encouraged by local businessmen eager to promote their town, accepted the offer. Scopes summarized Darwin's theory to a science class and was arrested. Famed criminal lawyer Clarence Darrow headed the defense, while Bryan assisted the prosecution. Journalists poured into Dayton; a Chicago radio station broadcast the proceedings live; and the **Scopes Trial** became a media sensation.

Cross-examined by Darrow, Bryan embraced the fundamentalist view of the Bible and dismissed evolutionary theory. Although the jury found Scopes guilty (in a decision later reversed on a technicality), the trial exposed Fundamentalism to ridicule. When Bryan died of a heart attack soon after, H. L. Mencken wrote a column mercilessly deriding him and his fundamentalist admirers.

Despite the setback in Dayton, Fundamentalism remained alive and well. Mainstream Protestant denominations grew more liberal, but many local congregations, radio preachers, Bible schools, and new conservative denominations upheld the traditional faith. So, too, did the flamboyant evangelist Billy Sunday, who remained popular in the 1920s. Southern and western states continued to pass antievolution laws, and textbook publishers deleted or modified their treatment of evolution to appease local school boards.

In Los Angeles, Aimee Semple McPherson, anticipating later TV evangelists, filled her cavernous Angelus Temple and reached thousands more by radio. The charismatic McPherson entranced audiences with theatrical sermons. She once used

Fundamentalism Evangelical movement that taught literal interpretation of the Bible

Primary Source: The Scopes Trial

Scopes Trial Trial of John T. Scopes, the Tennessee teacher accused of violating the state's anti-evolution law

a gigantic electric score-board to illustrate the triumph of good over evil. Her followers, mainly transplanted midwesterners, embraced her fundamentalist theology while enjoying her mass-entertainment techniques. At her death in 1944, her International Church of the Foursquare Gospel had more than six hundred branches in the United States and abroad.

The Ku Klux Klan

The tensions gnawing at American society of the 1920s also emerged in a resurrected Ku Klux Klan (KKK). The original Klan of the post-Civil War South had faded by the 1870s (see Chapter 16), but in 1915 hooded men who had gathered at Stone Mountain, Georgia, revived it. D. W. Griffith's glorification of the Klan in his 1915 movie *The Birth of a Nation* provided further inspiration.

The movement remained obscure until 1920, when two Atlanta entrepreneurs organized a national membership drive to exploit the appeal of the Klan's ritual and its nativist, white-supremacist ideology. Their wildly successful scheme involved a ten-dollar membership fee divided among the salesman and their managers at the state and national level—with a rake-off to themselves. The sale of Klan robes, masks, horse blankets, and the bottled Chattahoochee River water used in initiation rites added to the take.

Under the umbrella term "100 percent Americanism," the Klan demonized not only African-Americans but also Catholics, Jews, and aliens. Some Klan groups targeted whites suspected of sexual immorality or prohibition-law violations. Membership estimates for the KKK and its women's auxiliary in the early 1920s range as high as 5 million. From its southern base, the Klan spread through the Midwest and across the country from Long Island to the West Coast. Most of its members came from blue-collar ranks.

Although corrupt at the top and basically a money-making scam, the Klan was not a haven for criminals or fanatics. Observers commented on members' ordinariness. The Klan's promise to restore the nation's lost purity appealed to many economically marginal old-stock Protestants disoriented by social change. Some citizens upset by changing sexual mores welcomed the Klan's defense of "the purity of white womanhood." Klan membership, in short, gave a sense of empowerment to people who felt adrift in a new social order of great corporations; a raucous mass culture; and immigrant-filled cities. The rituals, parades, and cross burnings added drama and a sense of camaraderie to lonely, unfulfilling lives.

The Ku Klux Klan in Washington, D.C.
In a brazen display of power, the Ku Klux Klan organized a march in the nation's capital in 1926. By this time, however, the Klan was already in decline.

But the Klan's menace as a mass movement was real. Some KKK groups employed threats, beatings, and lynching in their quest to purify America. In several states, the Klan won political power. In Oregon, the Klan elected a governor and pushed through legislation requiring all children to attend public school, an attempt to destroy the state's Catholic schools.

The Klan collapsed with shocking suddenness. In March 1925, Indiana's Grand Dragon, David Stephenson, brutally raped his young secretary. When she swallowed poison, Stephenson panicked and refused to call a physician. The woman died several weeks later, and Stephenson went to prison, where he revealed sordid details of political corruption in Indiana. Its moral pretensions in shreds, the KKK faded. It did not disappear, however, and when African-Americans demanded equal rights in the 1950s, the Klan again reared its head.

The Garvey Movement

Marcus Garvey Founder of "Back to Africa" movement

Among African-Americans who had fled southern rural poverty and racism only to experience discrimination and racism in the urban North, the decade's social strains produced a different kind of mass movement, led by the spellbinding **Marcus Garvey** and his Universal Negro Improvement Association (UNIA). Born in Jamaica in 1887, Garvey founded UNIA in 1914 and two years later moved to Harlem, which became the movement's headquarters. In a white-dominated society, Garvey glorified all things black. Urging black economic solidarity, he founded UNIA grocery stores and other businesses. He summoned blacks to return to "Motherland Africa" and established the Black Star Steamship Line to help them get there.

An estimated eighty thousand blacks joined UNIA, drawn by the appeal of the vision of economic self-sufficiency and a glorious future in Africa. Garvey's popularity unsettled the NAACP's middle-class leaders, who advocated racial integration rather than separation. W. E. B. Du Bois was among Garvey's sharpest critics.

In 1923, a federal court convicted Garvey of fraud in the management of his Black Star Steamship Line. In 1927, after two years' imprisonment, he was deported to Jamaica, and the UNIA collapsed. But this first mass movement in black America had revealed both the social aspirations and the activist potential of African-Americans in the urban North. The NAACP, meanwhile, remained active even in a reactionary decade with racism rampant. In some 300 branches nationwide, members kept the civil-rights cause alive and patiently laid the groundwork for legal challenges to segregation.

Prohibition: Cultures in Conflict

prohibition Ban on alcohol consumption by the Eighteenth Amendment, effective 1920; failure; repealed in 1933

A bitter controversy over alcohol further exposed the fissures in American society. As noted in Chapter 21, the Progressive Era **prohibition** campaign was both a legitimate effort to address social problems associated with alcohol abuse and a weapon in the struggle of native-born Americans to control the immigrant cities. These tensions persisted in the 1920s.

When the Eighteenth Amendment took effect in 1920, prohibitionists rejoiced. Saloons closed, liquor advertising vanished, and arrests for drunkenness declined. In 1921, alcohol consumption stood at about one-third the prewar level. Yet prohibition gradually lost support, and in 1933 it ended.

Primary Source:
The Bootleggers

What went wrong? Essentially, prohibition's failure illustrates the difficulty in an open society of enforcing a widely opposed law. The Volstead Act, the 1919 prohibition law, was underfunded and weakly enforced. Would-be drinkers grew bolder as enforcement faltered. For rebellious youths, alcohol's illegality increased its appeal. Challenging the prohibition law, declared one college student, represented "the natural reaction of youth to rules and regulations."

Every city harbored speakeasies where customers could buy drinks. People concocted home brew and sacramental wine sales soared. By 1929, alcohol consumption reached about 70 percent of prewar levels.

Organized crime helped circumvent the law. Chicago, where rival gangs battled to control the liquor business, witnessed 550 gangland killings in the 1920s. Speakeasies controlled by Chicago gangster Al Capone generated annual profits of $60 million. Although not typical, Chicago's crime wave underscored prohibition's failure. A reform designed to improve the nation's morality was turning citizens into lawbreakers and mobsters into celebrities.

Thus prohibition, too, became a battleground in the decade's cultural wars and politics. The "drys"—usually native-born Protestants—praised it. The "wets"—liberals, Jazz Age rebels, big-city immigrants—condemned it as moralistic meddling. Prohibition influenced the 1928 presidential campaign. While Democratic candidate Al Smith advocated repeal of the Eighteenth Amendment, Republican Herbert Hoover praised it. When the Eighteenth Amendment was finally repealed in 1933, prohibition seemed little more than a relic of another age.

CHECKING IN

- Many Americans found rapid change disorienting and frightening, which led to reaction and protest.
- Immigration restriction was an attempt to keep out the "wrong sort" of people.
- The Sacco-Vanzetti case highlighted a resurgence of nativism and the cultural divide between the country's conservatives and liberals.
- The Scopes trial showed the enormous gap between religious fundamentalists and Americans who accepted modern science.
- The Ku Klux Klan attracted millions of ill-educated, deeply religious, and economically marginal Americans, and functioned as an all-purpose hate group.
- Prohibition, although it failed, represented the triumph of traditional morality over urban, immigrant culture.

HOOVER AT THE HELM

How did Herbert Hoover's social and political thought differ from that of Harding and Coolidge?

Herbert Hoover, elected president in 1928, appeared well fitted to sustain the nation's prosperity. No stubborn conservative like Harding and Coolidge, his social and political philosophy reflected his engineering background. In some ways, he seemed the ideal president for the new technological age.

The Election of 1928   A Hollywood casting agent could not have chosen two individuals who better personified America's divisions than the 1928 presidential candidates. New York governor Al Smith easily won the Democratic nomination. A Catholic and a "wet," his brown derby perpetually askew, Smith exuded the flavor of immigrant New York. Originally a machine politician, he had impressed reformers by backing social-welfare measures. Herbert Hoover won the Republican nomination with equal ease. An Iowan orphaned early in life, Hoover had put himself through Stanford University and made a fortune as a mining engineer in China and Australia. His service as wartime food administrator saved millions of lives in Europe and earned him a place in the Harding and Coolidge cabinets.

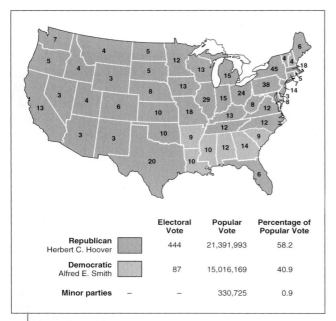

	Electoral Vote	Popular Vote	Percentage of Popular Vote
Republican Herbert C. Hoover	444	21,391,993	58.2
Democratic Alfred E. Smith	87	15,016,169	40.9
Minor parties	—	—	330,725	0.9

Map 23.1   The Election of 1928

Eschewing the handshaking and baby kissing of the campaign trail, Hoover delivered radio speeches in a boring monotone. Smith campaigned spiritedly throughout the country—a strategy that may have harmed him, for his big-city wisecracking and New York accent put off many voters.

How Smith's Catholicism affected his candidacy remains debatable. Hoover urged tolerance, and Smith denied any conflict between his faith and the duties of the presidency, but anti-Catholic prejudice played a role. Rumors circulated that Smith would follow the Vatican's orders if he won. The decisive issue was probably not popery but prosperity. Republican orators pointed to the booming economy and warned of "soup kitchens instead of busy factories" if Smith won. In his nomination-acceptance speech, Hoover grandly predicted "the final triumph over poverty."

Hoover won in a landslide, grabbing 58 percent of the vote and even making deep inroads in the Democratic "solid South" (see Map 23.1). However, the outcome also hinted at an emerging political realignment. Smith did well in the rural Midwest, where hard-pressed farmers, angered by Coolidge's insensitivity to their plight, abandoned their normal Republican allegiance. In northern cities, Catholic and Jewish wards voted heavily Democratic. Smith carried the nation's twelve largest cities, all of which had gone Republican in 1924. Should prosperity falter, these portents suggested, the Republican Party faced trouble.

Herbert Hoover's Social Thought

Americans looked hopefully to their new president, whom admirers dubbed "the Great Engineer." Although a self-made man himself, he did not uncritically praise big business. His Quakerism, humanitarian activities, engineering experience, and Republican loyalties combined to produce a unique social outlook.

Like Theodore Roosevelt, Hoover opposed cutthroat capitalist competition. Rational economic development, he insisted, demanded corporate cooperation in marketing, wage policy, raw-material allocation, and product standardization. The economy, in short, should operate like an efficient machine. But above all, he advocated voluntarism. The smoothly functioning, socially responsible economic order he envisioned must arise from the voluntary action of capitalist leaders, not government coercion.

Hoover as secretary of commerce had convened more than 250 conferences with business leaders. He urged higher wages to increase consumer purchasing power. During the 1927 Mississippi River floods, as President Coolidge remained in Washington, Hoover had rushed to the stricken area to mobilize private relief efforts.

Hoover as secretary of commerce had pushed for a number of environmental laws. Pollution, he warned in 1924, "is destroying . . . our fisheries . . . [and] beaches and endangering our harbors." In 1922, he negotiated a compact among Western states for a division of Colorado River water. This agreement, implemented in 1929, opened the way for a dam on the Colorado to provide hydroelectric power and water for irrigation. Construction began on Hoover Dam in 1930. (In an act of petty politics, Democrats changed the name to Boulder Dam in 1933, but Congress restored the original name in 1947.)

Hoover's ideology had limitations. He showed more enthusiasm for cooperation among capitalists than among consumers or workers. His belief that capitalists would voluntarily embrace enlightened labor policies overestimated the role of altruism in business decision making. And his opposition to government economic intervention brought him grief when such intervention became urgently necessary.

Hoover's presidency began promisingly. Responding to the farm problem, he persuaded Congress to create a Federal Farm Board to promote cooperative marketing. This, he hoped, would raise farm prices while preserving the voluntarist principle. But while Hoover applied his social philosophy to the business of government, a crisis was approaching that would overwhelm and ultimately destroy his presidency.

CHECKING IN

- The election of 1928 pitted urban immigrant champion Al Smith against self-made millionaire Herbert Hoover.
- Smith's Catholicism became a central issue in the campaign.
- Hoover's victory came with evidence of political realignment, as urban voters went heavily for Smith.
- Hoover believed strongly in voluntarism and welfare capitalism, but his ideas were limited by his opposition to direct government economic intervention.

Chapter Summary

 DOWNLOAD THE MP3 AUDIO FILE OF THE CHAPTER SUMMARY, AND LISTEN TO IT ON THE GO.

What economic innovations came in the 1920s, and what was their effect on different social groups? (page 533)

The assembly line and mass production created the consumer economy with the automobile at its center. Advertising flourished. Farmers were left out of the general prosperity. More women graduated from college, but few held high-wage industrial jobs. The labor union movement struggled.

What political and social ideas shaped the administrations of Presidents Harding and Coolidge? (page 537)

The Harding administration was stained by corruption. Both administrations were staunchly probusiness and wanted nothing to do with progressivism. Internationally, the United States followed an isolationist course but pursued its own national interest through independent internationalism. A split between rural and urban wings roiled the Democratic party, and the women's movement also splintered.

KEY TERMS

Henry Ford *(p. 533)*

Teapot Dome *(p. 538)*

Calvin Coolidge *(p. 538)*

McNary-Haugen Bill *(p. 538)*

Washington Naval Arms Conference *(p. 539)*

Ku Klux Klan *(p. 540)*

Alfred E. Smith *(p. 540)*

Sheppard-Towner Act *(p. 540)*

Charles Lindbergh *(p. 544)*

H.L. Mencken *(p. 546)*

National Origins Act *(p. 548)*

Sacco and Vanzetti *(p. 549)*

Fundamentalism *(p. 550)*

Scopes Trial *(p. 550)*

Marcus Garvey *(p. 552)*

prohibition *(p. 552)*

What developments underlay 1920s' mass culture, and how did they affect American life and leisure? (page 541)

The automobile had a major social as well as economic impact. Mass culture grew from the development of radio networks, large-circulation magazines, and movies. Celebrity culture celebrated heroes like Babe Ruth and Charles Lindbergh, and professional sports flourished. Skyscrapers, radio, the automobile, the movies, and electrical appliances—all familiar today—were exciting novelties in 1920s America.

What social developments contributed to the cultural creativity of the 1920s? (page 545)

The open sexuality of the Jazz Age, jazz music, and the flapper shocked many. Young people, freed from parental authority by the automobile, behaved in ways that seemed licentious to their elders. Alienated writers fled to Paris, and a literary renaissance among African-Americans flourished in Harlem.

What events or movements reveal the major social and cultural conflicts of the twenties? (page 548)

Rapid change itself was disorienting. Immigration restrictions sought to keep out the "wrong sort" of people; the Sacco-Vanzetti case demonstrated the resurgence of nativism and the cultural divide in the nation; and the Ku Klux Klan functioned as an all-purpose hate group. Prohibition represented an unsuccessful attack on urban, immigrant culture. The Scopes trial reflected the fundamentalist rejection of modern science.

How did Herbert Hoover's social and political thought differ from that of Harding and Coolidge? (page 553)

In many ways, the election summed up the conflicts of the 1920s. It pitted Al Smith, the epitome of urban immigrant culture, against Herbert Hoover, who seemed to be the embodiment of a Horatio Alger story. Smith's Catholicism dominated much of the political discussion. Hoover's victory represented a last hurrah for the rural traditionalism of the Republican party and put into the White House a man whose political philosophy proved inadequate to the demands of the Great Depression.

CHAPTER 24

The Great Depression and the New Deal

1929–1939

Young Farm Worker in Western Pennsylvania, 1930s, by Walker Evans

CL This icon will direct you to the website where you can Prepare for Class, Improve Your Grade, and Ace the Test: **www.cengage.com/history/boyer/ enduringconcise6e**

Franklin Delano Roosevelt seemed to have everything. Charming, handsome, and the scion of a well-to-do family, he had found life easy. Not yet forty, he had served as assistant secretary of the navy during World War I and had been the Democratic vice-presidential candidate in 1920. But in August 1921 an attack of polio left him paralyzed from the waist down and unable to walk. The illness seemed the end of his career, but after enduring years of therapy, he was ready to reenter politics in 1928.

By the time he nominated Al Smith at the 1928 Democratic convention, Franklin Roosevelt's long struggle had changed him from a superficial, even arrogant, man who relied on charm into a person of greater compassion and far more understanding of the disadvantaged. "If you had spent two years in bed trying to wiggle your big toe," he once said, "after that everything else would seem easy!" The charm remained, but it was now backed up by determination and fortitude. He was elected governor of New York in the fall of 1928.

Eleanor Roosevelt had devoted herself to her husband's care, ultimately encouraging him to return to politics. At the same time, already involved with social issues, she herself joined the executive board of the New York Democratic party and edited the women's division newsletter. Painfully shy, she forced herself to make public speeches.

The Roosevelts would soon need the qualities of character they had acquired. Elected president in 1932 amid the worst depression in U.S. history, Franklin Roosevelt dominated U.S. politics until his death in 1945. The early years of Roosevelt's long presidency spawned a dizzying array of laws, agencies, and programs. From 1933 to 1935, the first phase of the New Deal emphasized relief and recovery through a united national effort. In 1935 Roosevelt charted a more radical course. The so-called Second New Deal (1935 and after), placed less emphasis on unity and more on business regulation and on policies benefiting workers, small farmers, sharecroppers, migrant laborers, and others at the lower end of the scale.

This chapter develops two themes. The first is the New Deal's expansive view of the government's role in promoting economic and social welfare. The second is the response of the American people to the Depression. From factory workers, urban blacks, and Hispanic migrant laborers to moviemakers, artists, writers, and photographers, diverse groups met the crisis with resourcefulness, creativity, and organized social action.

CRASH AND DEPRESSION, 1929–1932

What caused the Great Depression, and how did President Hoover respond?

The prosperity of the 1920s collapsed in October 1929 with the stock-market crash. The crash, and the deeper economic problems that underlay it, launched a depression that reached into every household. President Hoover's commitment to private initiative and his horror of governmental coercion handcuffed him. In November 1932 a disillusioned nation gave an overwhelming electoral mandate to the Democratic party and Franklin D. Roosevelt. This election set the stage for a vast expansion in the federal government's role in social and economic issues.

Black Thursday and the Onset of the Depression

Stock prices had climbed throughout the 1920s. Beginning in 1928, optimism turned into frenzy as speculators plunged into the market. In 1925 the market value of all stocks stood at $27 billion; by October 1929 it had hit $87 billion. Nine million Americans "played the market," often with borrowed funds. Stockbrokers loaned speculators up to 75 percent of a stock's purchase price, and credit buying became the rule. Treasury Secretary Andrew Mellon's pressure for tax cuts increased the money available for speculation. In 1928–1929, construction declined by 25 percent, but few heeded the warning.

Chronology

1929	Stock market crash; onset of depression
1932	Reconstruction Finance Corporation; Veterans' bonus march; Franklin D. Roosevelt elected president
1933	Repeal of Eighteenth Amendment; Civilian Conservation Corps (CCC); Federal Emergency Relief Act (FERA); Tennessee Valley Authority (TVA); Agricultural Adjustment Administration (AAA); National Recovery Administration (NRA); Public Works Administration (PWA)
1934	Securities and Exchange Commission (SEC); Taylor Grazing Act; Indian Reorganization Act
1934–1936	Strikes by Mexican-American agricultural workers in the West
1935	Supreme Court declares NIRA unconstitutional; Works Progress Administration (WPA); Resettlement Administration; National Labor Relations Act (Wagner Act); Social Security Act; NAACP campaign for federal antilynching law; Huey Long assassinated; Revenue Act raises taxes on corporations and the wealthy; Supreme Court reverses conviction of the "Scottsboro Boys"; Harlem riot
1935–1939	Era of the Popular Front
1936	Supreme Court declares AAA unconstitutional; Roosevelt wins landslide reelection victory; Autoworkers' sit-down strike against General Motors begins (December)
1937	Roosevelt's "court-packing" plan defeated; Farm Security Administration; GM, U.S. Steel, and Chrysler sign union contracts
1937–1938	The "Roosevelt recession"
1938	Fair Labor Standards Act; Republicans gain heavily in midterm elections; Congress of Industrial Organizations (CIO) formed; Carnegie Hall concert by Benny Goodman Orchestra
1939	Hatch Act; Marian Anderson concert at Lincoln Memorial; John Steinbeck, *The Grapes of Wrath*
1940	Ernest Hemingway, *For Whom the Bell Tolls*

In July 1928, and again in September 1929, the Federal Reserve Board tried to dampen speculation by increasing interest rates. But with speculators paying up to 20 percent interest to buy more stock, lending institutions continued to loan money freely—an act akin to dumping gasoline on a raging fire.

The collapse came on October 24, 1929—"Black Thursday." As prices fell, some stocks found no buyers at all: they had become worthless. On Tuesday, October 29, a record 16 million stocks changed hands. In the ensuing weeks, feeble upswings alternated with further plunges. President Hoover, in the first of many optimistic statements, pronounced the economy "sound and prosperous." Indeed, a weak upswing early in 1930 suggested that the worst might be over. Instead, the economy went into a long tailspin, producing a full-scale depression.

What caused the depression? Structural weaknesses in the American economy made the 1920s' prosperity unstable. The agricultural sector remained depressed through the decade. Rises in productivity led not to higher wages but to high corporate profits. In 1929 the 40 percent of Americans at the lowest end of the economic scale received only 12 percent of the national income. This reduced consumer purchasing power. At the same time, assembly-line methods encouraged overproduction. By summer 1929 the automobile, housing, textile, tire, and other durable-goods industries were seriously overextended. Further, important sectors of industry—

including railroads, steel, textiles, and mining—lagged technologically in the 1930s and could not attract the investment needed to stimulate recovery.

All analysts link the U.S. depression to a global economic crisis. Enfeebled by massive war-debt payments and a huge trade imbalance with the United States, European economies crashed in 1931. This larger crisis depressed U.S. exports and fed panic.

Statistics tell the bleak story of depression America. The gross national product slumped from $104 billion in 1929 to $59 billion in 1932. Farm prices, already low, fell nearly 60 percent. More than 5,500 banks closed their doors by early 1933. Unemployment reached 25 percent in 1933; 13 million Americans had no jobs, and many who worked faced cuts in wages and hours. Some cities were far worse off. In Toledo in 1932, for example, unemployment hit 80 percent.

Hoover's Response

Historically, Americans had viewed depressions as acts of nature: little could be done other than ride out the storm. President Hoover, with his activist impulses, disagreed. Drawing upon his experience as U.S. food administrator in World War I and as secretary of commerce, Hoover initially responded boldly. But his belief in localism and in private initiative limited his options.

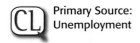
Primary Source: Unemployment

Business leaders whom Hoover summoned to the White House pledged to maintain wages and employment. Seeing unemployment as a local issue, Hoover called on municipal and state governments to create public-works projects. In October 1930 he established the Emergency Committee for Employment to coordinate voluntary relief efforts. In 1931, he persuaded the nation's largest banks to set up a private lending agency to help hard-pressed smaller banks make business loans.

The crisis only intensified, and public opinion turned against Hoover. In the 1930 midterm election, the Republicans lost eight Senate seats and control of the House of Representatives. Unemployment mounted, and in 1931 U.S. Steel, General Motors, and other large corporations broke their pledges and announced large wage cuts. Public charities and local welfare agencies faltered.

In 1932, a presidential election year, Hoover swallowed his principles and took a bold step. In January, at Hoover's recommendation, Congress set up a new agency, the **Reconstruction Finance Corporation (RFC),** to make loans to banks and other lending institutions. By July the RFC had pumped $1.2 billion into the economy. But Hoover gained little political benefit.

Reconstruction Finance Corporation (RFC) Agency established by Hoover to provide funds to banks and insurance companies

Hoover supported these measures reluctantly, warning of "socialism and collectivism." He blamed global forces for the depression and argued that only international measures would help. He advocated a one-year moratorium on war-debt and reparations repayments, a sensible plan but one that seemed irrelevant to hard-pressed Americans.

Mounting Discontent and Protest

An ominous mood spread as hordes of the jobless waited in breadlines, slept on park benches, trudged the streets, and rode freight trains seeking work. Americans reared on the ethic of hard work and self-reliance experienced chronic unemployment as a shattering emotional blow. The families of the jobless suffered as well.

Newspapers humanized the crisis. The *New York Times* described a section of Central Park where jobless men lived in boxes and packing crates. In winter they wrapped themselves in layers of newspapers, which they called Hoover blankets. Violence threatened in some cities when people unable to pay their rent were evicted from homes and apartments.

Hard times battered the nation's farms. Many farms underwent mortgage foreclosures or forced sales because of tax delinquency. At some forced farm auctions, neighbors bought the foreclosed farm for a trivial sum and returned it to the evicted family. In 1931, midwestern farmers organized the Farmers' Holiday Association to force prices up by withholding grain and livestock from the market, and dairy farmers dumped thousands of gallons of milk.

The most alarming protest came from World War I veterans. In 1924, Congress had voted veterans a bonus stretched over a twenty-year period. In June 1932, some ten thousand veterans, many jobless, descended on Washington to lobby for immediate payment. When Congress refused, most of the "bonus marchers" went home, but about two thousand stayed on, building makeshift shelters on the outskirts of Washington. President Hoover called in the army.

On July 28, one thousand armed soldiers under General Douglas MacArthur, equipped with tear gas, tanks, and machine guns, drove the veterans from their encampment and burned it to the ground. As a journalist described the aftermath, veterans and their families "wandered from street to street or sat in ragged groups, the men exhausted, the women with wet handkerchiefs laid over their smarting eyes, the children waking from sleep to cough and whimper from the tear gas in their lungs." For many, the incident symbolized the Hoover administration's utter bankruptcy.

Matching the mood of the time, American fiction of the early depression exuded disillusionment and despair. In *The 42nd Parallel* (1930), John Dos Passos drew a dark panorama of twentieth-century America as money-mad, exploitive, and lacking spiritual meaning. As one character says, "Everything you've wanted crumbles in your fingers as you grasp it."

The Election of 1932

Republicans renominated the unopposed Hoover at an intensely gloomy 1932 convention. The Democrats, in contrast, scented victory and drafted a platform to appeal to urban immigrants, farmers, and fiscal conservatives. Rejecting Al Smith, the delegates gave New York's governor, Franklin D. Roosevelt (FDR), the nomination.

Breaking precedent, FDR accepted the nomination in person, with a rousing speech promising "a new deal for the American people." But his campaign provided no clear program. He called for "bold, persistent experimentation" and promised more attention to "the forgotten man" while attacking Hoover's "reckless" spending.

But Roosevelt exuded confidence, and above all he was not Hoover. On November 8, FDR and his running mate, John Nance Garner of Texas, received nearly 23 million votes; the Republicans mustered fewer than 16 million. Both houses of Congress went heavily Democratic.

CHECKING IN

- A variety of economic problems, ranging from stock-market speculation to global economic problems, led to the crash and depression.

- Hoover turned to voluntarism to cope with the depression.

- The Reconstruction Finance Corporation was created to funnel money to banks and railroads, not directly to people.

- Americans grew increasingly angry at Hoover's failure to respond to their plight; the bonus march of 1932 illustrated the depth of despair.

- In the election of 1932, Americans rejected Hoover and gave the White House and Congress to Roosevelt and the Democrats.

THE NEW DEAL TAKES SHAPE, 1933–1935

What strategy guided the early New Deal, and what problems and challenges arose in 1934–1935?

The Roosevelt years began in a whirl of activity. An array of emergency measures proposed by Roosevelt and passed by Congress reflected three basic goals: industrial recovery through business-government cooperation and pump-priming federal spending; agricultural recovery through crop reduction; and short-term emergency relief distributed through state and local agencies when possible, but directly by the federal government if necessary. Presiding over this bustle, a confident FDR symbolized hope.

Roosevelt and His Circle

FDR's optimistic inaugural address dedicated his administration to helping a people in crisis. "The only thing we have to fear," he intoned, "is fear itself." In an outpouring of support, half a million letters deluged the White House.

Roosevelt seemed an unlikely popular hero. Like his distant cousin Theodore, he was of the social elite, from a long line of merchants and landed aristocrats. His Harvard-Columbia background highlighted his social status. But as a state senator and governor of New York, he had allied with the Democratic Party's urban-immigrant wing, and when the depression hit, he had introduced such innovative measures as unemployment insurance and a public-works program. Intent on reviving the economy while preserving capitalism and democracy, Roosevelt had no detailed agenda. He encouraged competing proposals, compromised (or papered over) differences, and then backed the measures he sensed could be sold to Congress and the public.

Roosevelt brought to Washington a circle of advisers nicknamed the brain trust, many of them from universities. But no single ideology or set of advisers controlled the New Deal, for FDR sought a broad range of opinions.

Eleanor Roosevelt Visits a West Virginia Coal Mine, 1933

A *New Yorker* cartoon of 1933 portrayed one coal miner exclaiming to another, "Oh migosh, here comes Mrs. Roosevelt." But reality soon caught up with humor as the First Lady immersed herself in the plight of the poor and exploited.

Eleanor Roosevelt played a key role. A niece of Theodore Roosevelt, she had expressed her keen social conscience in settlement-house work and Florence Kelley's National Consumers' League. Through her, FDR met reformers, social workers, and advocates of minority rights. Mrs. Roosevelt traveled ceaselessly, observing depression America firsthand for her wheelchair-bound husband.

Roosevelt's cabinet reflected the New Deal's diversity. Secretary of Labor **Frances Perkins,** the first woman cabinet member, had served as industrial commissioner of New York. Interior Secretary Harold Ickes had organized liberal Republicans for Roosevelt in 1932. Treasury Secretary Henry Morgenthau, Jr., FDR's neighbor and political ally, though a fiscal conservative, tolerated the spending necessary to finance New Deal anti-depression programs.

A host of newcomers poured into Washington in 1933—former progressives, liberal-minded professors, bright young lawyers—who drafted bills, competed for influence, and debated recovery strategies. From this pressure-cooker environment emerged the laws, programs, and agencies that became the New Deal.

Eleanor Roosevelt Wife of FDR; redefined the role of First Lady and influenced social policy during the New Deal

Frances Perkins Former Progressive reformer and first woman cabinet member; led the committee that wrote the Social Security Act

The Hundred Days

Between March 9 and June 16, 1933, a period labeled the "Hundred Days," Congress enacted more than a dozen major bills (see Table 24.1). Rooted in the Progressive Era, World War I, and the Hoover presidency, these measures sharply expanded federal involvement in the national economy.

The failure of thousands of banks by early 1933 had broken people's faith in the entire system, and the banking crisis was FDR's most urgent challenge. On March 5 he ordered all banks to close for four days. At the end of this so-called bank holiday, he proposed an Emergency Banking Act, which permitted healthy banks to reopen, set up procedures to manage failed banks, increased government oversight, and required that banks separate savings deposits from their investment funds. Congress also created the Federal Deposit Insurance Corporation (FDIC) to insure bank deposits up to $5,000. In the first of a series of radio talks dubbed "fireside chats," FDR assured Americans that they could again trust their banks.

 Primary Source: FDR's First Fireside Chat

TABLE 24.1 | MAJOR MEASURES ENACTED DURING THE "HUNDRED DAYS" (MARCH 9–JUNE 16, 1933)

March 9	Emergency Banking Relief Act
20	Economy Act
31	Unemployment Relief Act (Civilian Conservation Corps)
May 12	Agricultural Adjustment Act; Federal Emergency Relief Act
18	Tennessee Valley Authority
27	Federal Securities Act
June 13	Home Owners' Refinancing Act
16	Farm Credit Act; Banking Act of 1933 (Federal Deposit Insurance Corporation); National Industrial Recovery Act (National Recovery Administration; Public Works Administration)

Civilian Conservation Corps (CCC) Agency that employed millions of young men

Federal Emergency Relief Act Keystone of early New Deal that provided relief funds to cities and states

Agricultural Adjustment Administration Agency overseeing effort to help farmers by reducing production, raising prices

National Recovery Administration Attempt to gain cooperation in recovery efforts among government, business, labor leaders

Other Hundred Days measures dealt with relief—addressing the urgent plight of Americans struggling to survive. Two new agencies assisted those who were losing their homes. The Home Owners Loan Corporation helped city dwellers refinance their mortgages. The Farm Credit Administration provided loans to rural Americans to meet their farm payments. In another relief measure, on March 31 Congress created the **Civilian Conservation Corps** (core) **(CCC)** to employ jobless youths for reforestation, park maintenance, and erosion control. By 1935 half a million young men, some from families with no income at all, were earning $35 a month in CCC camps—a Godsend to desperate families. The principal relief measure of the Hundred Days, the **Federal Emergency Relief Act,** provided $500 million to fill the empty relief coffers of states and cities.

While supplying immediate relief, the early New Deal also faced the longer-term challenge of promoting recovery in the agricultural and industrial sectors. Some New Dealers advocated reduced production as a means of raising farm prices. As a first step to cutting production, the government paid southern cotton planters to plow under much of their crop and midwestern farmers to slaughter some 6 million piglets and pregnant sows. Killing pigs at a time of widespread hunger proved a public-relations nightmare. Pursuing the same goal more systematically, Congress passed the Agricultural Adjustment Act in May 1933. This law set up a program by which producers of the major agricultural commodities, such as hogs and wheat, received payments, called *subsidies,* in return for cutting production. A tax on food processors (a tax ultimately passed along to consumers) financed these subsidies. A new agency, the **Agricultural Adjustment Administration** (AAA), supervised the program.

The other key recovery measure of the Hundred Days, the National Industrial Recovery Act appropriated $3.3 billion for heavy-duty government public-works programs to provide jobs and stimulate the economy. Interior Secretary Harold Ickes headed the agency that ran this program, the Public Works Administration (PWA).

This law also set up the **National Recovery Administration,** which brought together business leaders to draft codes of "fair competition" for their industries. These codes set production limits, wages, and working conditions, and forbade price cutting and unfair competitive practices. The aim was to promote recovery by breaking the cycle of wage cuts, falling prices, and layoffs. But some New Dealers had further goals. Under pressure from Labor Secretary Frances Perkins, the NRA's textile-industry code banned child labor. And thanks to Senator Robert Wagner of New York, Section 7a of the NIRA affirmed workers' right to organize unions and to bargain collectively.

The NRA's success depended on voluntary support by both business and the public. The NRA's flamboyant head, Hugh Johnson, used parades, billboards, magazine ads, and celebrity events to persuade people to buy only from companies that subscribed to an NRA code and displayed the NRA symbol, a blue eagle, and its slogan, "We Do Our Part."

The Reconstruction Finance Corporation (RFC), dating from the Hoover years, remained active in the New Deal era. The RFC lent billions of dollars to banks, insurance companies, and even new business ventures, making it a potent financial resource for corporate America. The early New Deal thus had a strong probusiness flavor.

A few measures adopted during the Hundred Days, however, took a tougher approach to business. The 1929 crash had produced a strong antibusiness reaction. A Senate investigation of Wall Street in 1932–1934 discovered that none of the twenty partners of the Morgan Bank had paid any income tax in 1931 or 1932. People jeered when the president of the New York Stock Exchange told a Senate committee considering regulatory measures, "You gentlemen are making a big mistake. The Exchange is a perfect institution."

Reflecting the public mood, Congress in 1933 passed the Federal Securities Act requiring corporations to inform the government fully on all stock offerings. This law also made executives personally liable for any misrepresentation of securities their companies issued. (In 1934 Congress curbed the purchase of stock on credit—a practice that had contributed to the crash—and created the Securities and Exchange Commission [SEC] to enforce the new regulations.)

The most innovative program of the Hundred Days was the **Tennessee Valley Authority (TVA).** This program advanced the economic and social development of the entire Tennessee River valley, one of the nation's poorest regions. To help remedy substandard living conditions, a series of TVA dams supplied cheap hydroelectric power, bringing electricity, industry, and jobs to the region. The TVA also reduced flooding and soil erosion, and proved one of the New Deal's most popular and enduring achievements.

The mind-boggling burst of laws and the "alphabet-soup" of new agencies during the Hundred Days symbolized both the dynamism and the confusion of the New Deal. How these new programs and agencies would work in practice remained to be seen.

Tennessee Valley Authority (TVA) Ambitious plan of economic development; centered on dam building for poor Appalachian area

Interactive Map: The Tennessee Valley Authority

Problems and Controversies Plague the Early New Deal

As the depression persisted, several early New Deal programs faced difficulties. As the unity of the Hundred Days faded, corporate America chafed at NRA regulation. Small business objected that the codes favored big corporations. The agency itself bogged down in drafting trivial codes. Corporate trade associations used the codes to stifle competition and fix prices.

In May 1935 the Supreme Court unanimously declared the NRA unconstitutional. The Court ruled that the act gave the president regulatory powers that belonged to Congress and that it regulated commerce within states, violating the Constitution's limitation of federal regulation to commerce between or among states. As a recovery measure, the NRA had failed.

The AAA fared better but also generated controversy. Farm prices did rise as production declined; in 1933–1937 overall farm income increased by 50 percent. But the AAA's crop-reduction payments actually hurt southern tenants and sharecroppers because cotton growers removed acreage from production, evicted the sharecroppers, and banked the subsidy checks.

While some New Dealers focused on raising total agricultural income, others took a more class-based approach and urged attention to the poorest farmers. Their cause was strengthened as a parching drought centered in the Oklahoma panhandle region turned much of the Great Plains into a dust bowl (see Map 24.1). Each summer from 1934 through 1939, clouds of dust spread across the nation, darkening cities from Chicago to Boston and Savannah before blowing out to sea.

Map 24.1 The Dust Bowl

From the Dakotas southward to the Mexican border, farmers in the Great Plains suffered from a lack of rainfall and severe soil erosion in the 1930s, worsening the hardships of the Great Depression.

Battered farmers abandoned the land in droves. Some migrated to the cities; others packed their few belongings into old cars and headed west. Although from different states, they all bore the derisive nickname Okies.

Rivalries and policy differences also plagued the New Deal relief program. While Harold Ickes, head of the Public Works Administration, was supercautious, **Harry Hopkins** was impatient to get money circulating. As unemployment continued, Hopkins convinced Roosevelt to support direct federal relief programs, rather than channeling funds through state and local agencies. Late in 1933, FDR named Hopkins to head a temporary public-works agency, the Civil Works Administration (CWA), which through the winter expended nearly a billion dollars on short-term work projects for the jobless. When warm weather returned, FDR abolished the CWA. Like his conservative critics, he feared creating a permanent underclass living on relief. But persistent unemployment that swamped local relief agencies made further federal programs inevitable.

Harry Hopkins A former administrator of New York State charitable organizations; emerged as one of the most powerful figures in the New Deal

1934–1935: Challenges from Right and Left

Despite the New Deal's brave beginnings, the depression persisted. By 1934 national income stood 25 percent above 1933 levels but still far below 1929 figures. Millions had been jobless for three or four years. The rising frustration found expression in 1934 in nearly two thousand strikes, some of them communist-led. With the NRA under attack, conflict flaring over farm policy, and relief spending growing rather than declining, criticism mounted. Conservatives attacked the New Deal as socialistic. Anti-Roosevelt jokes circulated among the rich, many of whom denounced him as a traitor to his class.

But the New Deal remained popular, and FDR commanded the public stage. Pursuing the national-unity theme, he urged everyone to join the battle for economic recovery as they had united in 1917 against a foreign foe. Although Republican newspaper publishers remained hostile, FDR enjoyed good relations with the working press, and journalists responded with favorable stories. FDR also savored public appearances and took naturally to radio. His easy mastery of radio provided a model for his successors in the television era.

The 1934 midterm election ratified the New Deal's popularity as the Democrats increased their majorities in the House and Senate. Kansas journalist William Allen White observed of FDR that "he's been all but crowned by the people."

Still, the political scene was highly unstable. Conservatives criticized the New Deal for going too far, and critics on the left attacked it for not going far enough. Socialists and communists ridiculed Roosevelt's efforts to include big business in his "all-American team."

Demagogues peddled more radical social and economic programs. The Detroit Catholic priest and radio spellbinder Charles Coughlin attacked FDR as a "great betrayer and liar," made anti-Semitic allusions, and called for nationalization of the banks. For a time, Coughlin's followers, the mainly lower-middle-class National Union of Social Justice, seemed a potent force.

Meanwhile, California physician Francis E. Townsend proposed that the government pay $200 monthly to all retired citizens, requiring them to spend it within thirty days. This plan, Townsend insisted, would help elderly Americans, stimulate the economy, and create jobs by encouraging early retirement. Although the scheme would have quickly bankrupted the nation, many older citizens embraced it.

FDR's wiliest rival was Huey Long of Louisiana. A country lawyer elected governor in 1928, Long built highways, schools, and public housing. He roared into Washington as a senator in 1933 and preached his "Share Our Wealth" program: a 100 percent tax on annual incomes exceeding $1 million and appropriation of all fortunes over $5 million. Every American family, Long promised, could enjoy a comfortable income, a house, a car, old-age benefits, and a free college education. "Every man a king," proclaimed Long. By 1935 he boasted 7.5 million supporters and clearly had his eye on the White House. An assassin's bullet cut him down that September, but Share Our Wealth survived.

CHECKING IN

- FDR's own optimism, combined with his ability to convey it to the American people, was probably his single most important asset.

- The major goals of the New Deal were industrial recovery, agricultural recovery, and short-term relief.

- During the "Hundred Days," Congress rushed through major measures, such as the Federal Emergency Relief Act, the National Industrial Recovery Act, the Agricultural Adjustment Act, and the Civilian Conservation Corps.

- The New Deal also featured reforms, such as the establishment of the Securities and Exchange Commission and the Federal Deposit Insurance Corporation, and innovations, such as the Tennessee Valley Authority.

- Demagogues like Father Coughlin, Francis Townshend, and Huey Long peddled snake-oil alternatives to New Deal programs.

THE NEW DEAL CHANGES COURSE, 1935–1936

What key measures and setbacks marked the course of the New Deal from 1935 on?

Roosevelt responded vigorously to his challengers. With the spirit of national unity fading, he shelved the unity theme and veered leftward. His 1935 State of the Union address outlined six initiatives: expanded public-works programs, assistance to the rural poor, support for organized labor, benefits for retired workers, tougher business regulation, and heavier taxes on the well-to-do. These priorities translated into a bundle of reform measures some called "the Second New Deal." FDR's landslide victory in 1936 solidified a new Democratic coalition.

Expanding Federal Relief

With unemployment still high, Congress in April 1935 passed the Emergency Relief Appropriation Act. FDR swiftly established the **Works Progress Administration** (WPA). Like the CWA of the prior winter, the WPA funneled relief directly to individuals, and FDR insisted that the program provide work, not handouts. Over its eight-year life, the WPA employed more than 8 million Americans and constructed or improved vast numbers of bridges, roads, schools, post offices, and other public facilities.

Works Progress Administration Massive public works program during the Second New Deal; included programs to employ artists, writers, and actors

Primary Source: Memories of a Brutal Institution

The WPA also assisted writers, performers, and artists. The Federal Writers' Project employed out-of-work authors to produce state guides and histories of ethnic and immigrant groups. In the South they collected the reminiscences of ex-slaves. Under the Federal Music Project, unemployed musicians gave free concerts, often featuring American composers. By 1938 more than 30 million Americans had attended these events.

The Federal Theatre Project (FTP) employed actors. One FTP project, the Living Newspaper, dramatized contemporary social issues and was criticized as New Deal propaganda. FTP drama companies touring small-town America gave many their first taste of theater. Artists working for the Federal Arts Project designed posters, offered school courses, and decorated post offices and courthouses with murals.

Another 1935 agency, the National Youth Administration (NYA), provided job training for unemployed youth and part-time work to enable college students to remain in school. Eleanor Roosevelt, viewing young people as the hope of the future, took particular pride in the NYA. Harold Ickes's Public Works Administration now picked up steam, expending more than $4 billion over its life span. PWA workers completed some 34,000 construction projects, including New York City's Triborough Bridge and Lincoln Tunnel, and the awesome Grand Coulee Dam on the Columbia River.

Monumental relief spending brought monumental budget deficits, cresting at $4.4 billion in 1936. The government borrowed to cover the deficits. British economist John Maynard Keynes had advocated deficit spending on public works during a depression to increase purchasing power and stimulate recovery. However, the New Deal was not Keynesian. Because all the money spent on public-works programs was withdrawn from the economy by taxing or borrowing, the stimulus effect was zero.

Aiding Migrants, Supporting Unions, Regulating Business, Taxing the Wealthy

The second phase of the New Deal more frankly focused on the interests of workers, the poor, and the disadvantaged. Social-justice advocates like Frances Perkins and Eleanor Roosevelt helped shape this program, but so did hard-headed politics. Looking to 1936, FDR's political advisers feared that Coughlin, Townsend, and Long could siphon off enough votes to cost him the election.

The Second New Deal's agricultural policy addressed the plight of sharecroppers (worsened by the AAA) and other poor farmers. The Resettlement Administration (1935) made loans to help tenant farmers buy their own farms and to enable sharecroppers, tenants, and dust-bowl migrants to move to more productive areas. The Rural Electrification Administration, also started in 1935, made low-interest loans to utility companies and farmers' cooperatives, to extend electricity to the 90 percent of rural America that lacked it. By 1941, 40 percent of American farms enjoyed electricity.

The agricultural-recovery program suffered a setback in January 1936 when the Supreme Court declared the Agricultural Adjustment Act unconstitutional. The processing tax that funded the AAA's subsidies, the Court held, was an illegal use of the government's tax power. To replace the AAA, Congress passed a soil-conservation act that paid farmers to plant grasses and legumes instead of soil-depleting crops like wheat and cotton (which happened to be the major surplus commodities).

Organized labor won a key victory in 1935, again thanks to Senator Robert Wagner. Despite FDR's opposition during the New Deal's national-unity phase, Wagner built support for a prolabor law. In 1935 the Supreme Court ruled the NIRA unconstitutional, including Section 7a protecting union members' rights, and FDR called for a labor law that would stand up. The **National Labor Relations Act** of July 1935 guaranteed collective-bargaining rights, permitted closed shops (in which all employees must join a union), and outlawed such management tactics as blacklisting union organizers. The law created the National Labor Relations Board (NLRB) to supervise shop elections and deal with labor-law violations. A wave of unionization soon followed.

National Labor Relations Act Measure that furthered industrial unionization

The Second New Deal's more class-conscious thrust shaped other 1935 measures. The Banking Act strengthened the Federal Reserve Board's control over the nation's financial system. The Public Utilities Holding Company Act, targeting the public-utility empires of the 1920s, restricted gas and electric companies to one geographic region. Also in 1935, Roosevelt called for steeper taxes on the rich. With the Wealth Tax Act, Congress raised taxes on corporations and on the well-to-do to a maximum of 75 percent on incomes above $5 million. Although this law had many loopholes and was not quite the "soak the rich" measure some believed, it did express the Second New Deal's more radical spirit.

The Social Security Act of 1935: End of the Second New Deal

The **Social Security Act** of 1935 stands out among New Deal laws for its long-range significance. Drafted by a committee chaired by Frances Perkins, this measure established a mixed federal-state system of workers' pensions, survivors' benefits for victims of industrial accidents, unemployment insurance, and aid for disabled persons and dependent mothers and children. Taxes, paid in part by employers and in part by wages withheld from workers' paychecks, funded pensions and survivors' benefits. Payroll withholding made sense politically because workers would fight the repeal of a pension plan to which they had contributed. As FDR put it, "With those taxes in there, no damned politician can ever scrap my social security program."

Social Security Act Measure to establish old-age pensions, unemployment benefits, care for widows and orphans

The initial Social Security Act paid low benefits and bypassed farmers, domestic workers, and the self-employed. However, it established the principle of federal responsibility for social welfare and laid the foundation for a vastly expanded welfare system.

By September 1935, when Congress adjourned, the Second New Deal was complete. Without embracing the panaceas preached by Coughlin, Townsend, or Long, FDR had addressed the grievances they had exploited. Although conservatives called this phase of the New Deal "antibusiness," FDR always insisted that he had saved capitalism by addressing the social problems it spawned. Business remained influential in the 1930s, but as the New Deal evolved, the federal government acted increasingly as a broker for all organized interest groups, including organized labor, not just corporate America. And in 1935, with an election looming, New Deal strategists addressed the troubles of poor and needy Americans who had rarely concerned politicians of the past.

In the process, the New Deal vastly expanded the role of the federal government, as well as the power of the presidency. Americans began to expect presidents to offer national "programs" and shape the terms of public debate. This decisively altered the balance of power between the White House and Congress as the New Deal redefined the scope of the executive branch and, more broadly still, the social role of the state.

The 1936 Roosevelt Landslide and the New Democratic Coalition

With the Second New Deal in place and unemployment declining, FDR faced the 1936 election confidently. "There's one issue . . . ," he told an aide, "it's myself, and people must be either for me or against me."

The Republican party nominated progressive governor Alfred Landon of Kansas, who proved an inept campaigner. When Republicans lambasted Roosevelt's alleged dictatorial ambitions and charged that workers would soon have to wear metal dog tags engraved with their social security numbers, FDR struck back with typical zest. Only the forces of "selfishness and greed" opposed him, he told an election-eve rally in New York. "They are united in their hatred for me—and I welcome their hatred."

In the most crushing electoral victory since 1820, FDR carried every state but Maine and Vermont. The Democrats increased their already-large majorities in Congress. Roosevelt also buried candidates of the Socialist and Communist parties, as well as of the Union party (a coalition of Coughlin, Townsend, and Share Our Wealth enthusiasts).

FDR's 1936 landslide announced the emergence of a new Democratic coalition. Since Reconstruction, the Democrats had counted on three bases of support: the white South, parts of the West, and urban white ethnic voters mobilized by big-city Democratic machines. FDR retained these centers of strength. He rarely challenged state or local party leaders who produced the votes, whether they supported the New Deal or not.

FDR carried the nation's twelve largest cities. Not only did New Deal relief programs aid city dwellers, but Roosevelt wooed them persuasively. He appointed many from urban-immigrant groups, including Catholics and Jews, to New Deal positions.

Expanding the Democratic base, FDR reached out to four partially overlapping groups: farmers, union members, northern blacks, and women. Midwestern farmers, long rock-ribbed Republicans, liked the New Deal's agricultural program and switched to Roosevelt. The unions pumped money into Roosevelt's campaigns (although far less than business gave the Republicans), and union members voted overwhelmingly for FDR, whose reputation as a "friend of labor" proved unassailable.

Although most southern blacks remained disfranchised, northern blacks voted in growing numbers. As late as 1932, two-thirds of them went for Hoover, leading one exasperated African-American editor to advise his readers to "turn Lincoln's picture to the wall. That debt has been paid in full." The New Deal saw a historic shift. In 1936, 76 percent of black voters supported FDR. In economic terms, this shift made sense. Owing mainly to racial discrimination, blacks' unemployment rates in the 1930s surpassed those of the work force as a whole. Thus jobless blacks benefited heavily from New Deal relief programs.

On issues of racial justice, however, the New Deal's record was mixed at best. Racially discriminatory clauses in some NRA codes led African-American activists to dismiss the agency as "Negroes Ruined Again," and other New Deal agencies tolerated racism. Roosevelt kept aloof from an NAACP campaign to make lynching a federal crime. In 1935 and 1938 he remained passive as antilynching bills were narrowly defeated in Congress.

In limited ways, FDR did address racial issues. He worked cautiously to rid New Deal agencies of blatant racism. He appointed more than one hundred African-Americans to policy-level and judicial positions, including educator Mary McLeod Bethune as director of minority affairs in the National Youth Administration. Bethune led the "black cabinet" that served as a link between the New Deal and African-American organizations. In addition, the "Roosevelt Supreme Court" that took shape after 1936 issued antidiscrimination rulings on housing, voting rights, wage discrimination, jury selection, and real-estate transactions.

The New Deal also supported racial justice in symbolic ways. In 1938, when a meeting of an interracial welfare group in Birmingham, Alabama, was segregated in compliance with local statutes, Mrs. Roosevelt pointedly placed her chair halfway between the white and black delegates. In 1939, when the Daughters of the American Revolution barred a performance by black contralto Marian Anderson in Washington's Constitution Hall, Mrs. Roosevelt resigned from the organization, and Harold Ickes arranged for an Easter Sunday concert by Anderson at the Lincoln Memorial.

The Roosevelt administration also courted women voters. Molly Dewson led the effort as head of the Democratic party's women's division. In 1936 she mobilized fifteen thousand women who went door to door distributing flyers describing New Deal programs. Dewson did not push a specifically feminist agenda. New Deal programs of economic recovery and social welfare, in her view, served the best interests of both sexes. FDR appointed the first woman cabinet member, the first woman ambassador, and more female federal judges than any predecessor. Through Dewson's efforts, the 1936 Democratic platform committee had a fifty-fifty gender balance.

Despite such symbolic gestures and FDR's appointment of a few blacks and women, racism and sexism still pervaded American society in the 1930s. Roosevelt, preoccupied with the economic crisis, did relatively little to change things. That challenge would await a later time.

The Environment and the West

FDR's commitment to conservation ran deep. As early as 1910, he had tried to regulate logging that threatened wildlife in New York. Under his prodding, the Civilian Conservation Corps thinned forests, built hiking trails, and planted trees.

Soil conservation emerged as a major priority. The Great Plains dust storms resulted not only from drought but also from overgrazing and unwise farming practices. For decades settlers had used ever more powerful machines to cultivate more land on the Great Plains. They had plowed up the native grasses that anchored the soil, exposing the topsoil to parching winds when drought struck. By the 1930s erosion had destroyed 9 million acres of farmland, with more in jeopardy.

In response, the Department of Agriculture's Soil Conservation Service set up projects across the nation to demonstrate the value of contour plowing, terracing, crop rotation, and soil-strengthening grasses. The Taylor Grazing Act of 1934 restricted the grazing that had compounded the problem on public lands. The TVA helped control floods that worsened soil erosion.

New Deal planners promoted the national park movement. Washington state's Olympic, Virginia's Shenandoah, and California's Kings Canyon all became national parks in the 1930s. The administration also established some 160 new national wildlife refuges.

The wilderness-preservation movement kept pace. In 1935 Robert Marshall of the U.S. Forest Service and environmentalist Aldo Leopold helped found the Wilderness Society. Pressed by wilderness advocates, Congress set aside a large wilderness area in Kings Canyon National Park.

By later standards, the New Deal's environmental record was spotty. The decade's massive hydroelectric projects, while necessary at a time when many rural families still lacked electricity, had ecological consequences little noted at the time. The Grand Coulee Dam, for example, destroyed salmon spawning on much of the Columbia River's tributary system. Other New Deal dams disrupted fragile ecosystems and adversely affected local residents, particularly Native American communities, who depended on these ecosystems for their livelihood.

Viewed in context, however, the New Deal's environmental record remains impressive. While coping with a grave economic crisis, the Roosevelt administration focused on environmental issues in a way not seen since the Progressive Era, and not to be seen again for a generation.

In the American West, the depression profoundly affected hordes of hard-hit citizens, including dust-bowl refugees who sought a fresh start, especially in California. Continuing a long trend, the West Coast's share of the population spiked upward in the 1930s, and Los Angeles jumped from tenth to fifth among U.S. cities.

With the federal government owning a third or more of the land in eleven western states, the New Deal had an especially big impact. New Deal agencies and laws, such as the AAA, the Soil Conservation Service, and the Taylor Grazing Act, set new rules for western agriculture, from grain and cattle to citrus groves and truck farms dependent on migrant labor. Some of the largest PWA and WPA projects were built in the West, including thousands of public buildings.

Above all, the PWA in the West built dams—Grand Coulee (KOO-lee) and Bonneville (BAHN-eh-vill) on the Columbia, Shasta on the Sacramento, Glen Canyon on the Colorado, and others. Boulder (later Hoover) Dam on the Colorado, authorized by Congress in 1928, was completed by the PWA. Despite their ecological downside, these great undertakings—among the largest engineering projects in human history—supplied electric

Power to the People

The New Deal's massive hydroelectric projects were celebrated in this 1937 "Living Newspaper" production by the WPA's Federal Theatre Project.

power to vast regions while also contributing to flood control, irrigation, and soil conservation.

A New Deal initiative particularly important to the West was Harold Ickes's National Resources Planning Board, established in 1934. This agency facilitated state and regional planning for such natural resources as water, soil, timber, and minerals. Despite the West's celebrated "rugged individualism," New Deal planning, in tandem with the PWA's dams and infrastructure development, reshaped the public life of the region.

THE NEW DEAL'S END STAGE, 1937–1939

How did the New Deal end?

Buoyed by his enormous victory in the 1936 election, Roosevelt launched an abortive attack on the Supreme Court that weakened him politically. In the wake of this fight, FDR confronted both a stubborn recession and a newly energized conservative opposition; a few final measures in 1937–1938 brought the New Deal to a close.

FDR and the Supreme Court

In 1937 the Supreme Court comprised nine elderly men, four of them arch-conservatives who despised the New Deal. Joined by moderates, they had invalidated the NRA, the AAA, and progressive state laws. Roosevelt feared a similar fate for key measures of the Second New Deal.

In February 1937, FDR proposed a court-reform bill that would have allowed the president to appoint an additional Supreme Court member for each justice over seventy, up to a total of six. Roosevelt blandly insisted that he was concerned about the heavy workload of aging justices, but his political motivation escaped no one.

Congress and the public greeted the plan with hostility. The Supreme Court's size (although unspecified in the Constitution) had become almost sacrosanct. Conservatives blasted the "court-packing" scheme and the devious way FDR had presented it. Even many Democrats disapproved. When the Senate voted down the scheme in July, FDR quietly dropped it.

But was it a defeat? One conservative justice retired in May 1937, and others announced plans to step down. In April and May, the Court upheld several key New Deal measures, including the Wagner Act and a state minimum-wage law. This outcome may have been FDR's goal all along. He had sent a signal, and the justices heeded it. From 1937 to 1939, FDR appointed four new members to the Court, laying the groundwork for a liberal majority that would endure long after the 1930s.

The Roosevelt Recession

After showing signs of recovery, the economy dipped ominously in August 1937. Industrial production slumped. Soaring unemployment again dominated the headlines. This "Roosevelt recession" resulted in part from federal policies that reduced

CHECKING IN

- The focus of the Second New Deal shifted to include social justice concerns and attacks on, rather than cooperation with, business.
- Enormous relief projects like those undertaken by the Works Progress Administration characterized the Second New Deal.
- Organized labor won a major victory with the passage of the National Labor Relations Act, which guaranteed collective bargaining and permitted closed shops.
- The Social Security Act set the framework for an expanded social-welfare state.
- In the 1936 election, a new Democratic coalition emerged that would dominate national politics for decades.
- FDR and Congress continued to drag their feet on racial matters, such as lynching, but they promoted conservation and reformed Indian policy.

A Camera's-Eye View of Depression-Era America

This 1937 image by Dorothea Lange, a photographer with the Farm Security Administration, pictures migrants from the Texas dust bowl gathered at a roadside camp near Calipatria in southern California.

consumer income. Social-security payroll taxes withdrew some $2 billion from circulation. The Federal Reserve Board had raised interest rates to forestall inflation, further contracting the money supply. FDR, meanwhile, had seized on the signs of recovery to cut back the New Deal relief programs.

Echoing Hoover, FDR assured his cabinet, "Everything will work out all right if we just sit tight and keep quiet." Some New Dealers, though, took the Keynesian view that deficit spending was the key to recovery. Their warnings of a political backlash if breadlines and soup kitchens returned convinced FDR to authorize new relief spending in April 1938. WPA work-relief checks soon rained down on the parched economy, and the PWA received a new lease on life. By late 1938, unemployment declined and industrial output increased. As late as 1939, however, more than 17 percent of the labor force remained jobless.

Final Measures, Growing Opposition

Preoccupied by the Supreme Court fight, the recession, and menacing events abroad (see Chapter 25), FDR offered few domestic initiatives after 1936. Congress, however, enacted several significant measures. The Farm Tenancy Act of 1937 created the **Farm Security Administration** (FSA) to replace the Resettlement Administration. Although the FSA did little to help the poorest tenants and sharecroppers, whom it considered bad credit risks, its more than $1 billion in short-term loans by 1941 had enabled thousands of tenant farmers and sharecroppers to buy their own family farms.

The FSA operated camps offering clean, sanitary shelter and medical services to migrant farm workers living in wretched conditions. The FSA also commissioned

Farm Security Administration
Made low-interest loans to help tenant farmers and sharecroppers become more self-sufficient

gifted photographers to record the lives of tenants, migrants, and uprooted dust-bowl families. These FSA photographs helped shape a starkly realistic documentary style that pervaded 1930s popular culture.

Other late New Deal measures set precedents. The Housing Act of 1937 appropriated $500 million for urban slum clearance and public housing. The **Fair Labor Standards Act** of 1938 banned child labor and established a national minimum wage (initially 40 cents an hour) and a maximum workweek of forty hours. Despite many loopholes, the law improved conditions for some and underscored the government's role in regulating employers' abuses.

Fair Labor Standards Act
Federal regulation setting a national minimum wage and a maximum workweek

In a final stab at raising farm income, the Agricultural Adjustment Act of 1938 created a mechanism by which the government, in years of big harvests and low prices, would make loans to farmers and warehouse their surplus crops. When prices rose, farmers could repay their loans and sell their commodities. This complicated system set the framework of federal farm price support for decades. Overall, New Deal farm policy produced mixed results. Large-scale growers benefited from subsidy payments, but the cumbersome price-support mechanisms involved problems that would worsen with time.

The New Deal's slower pace after 1935 also reflected the rise of an anti-New Deal congressional coalition of Republicans and conservative southern Democrats. In 1937, this coalition rejected FDR's proposal to reorganize the executive branch. The conservative coalition also slashed relief appropriations, cut corporate taxes, and killed the Federal Theatre Project, a conservative target because of its radicalism. Suspecting that FDR used WPA staff members for political purposes, conservatives in 1939 passed the Hatch Act, forbidding federal workers from participating in electoral campaigns.

Although FDR campaigned actively in 1938's midterm election, the Republicans gained heavily in the House and Senate, and added thirteen governorships. Roosevelt also tried to purge several prominent anti–New Deal Democratic senators in 1938, but his major targets all won reelection. Focusing mainly on foreign affairs in his January 1939 State of the Union message, FDR proposed no new domestic measures and merely noted the need to "preserve our reforms." The New Deal was over.

CHECKING IN

- After reelection, FDR suffered a major setback in his "court-packing" scheme.
- Recession struck in 1937.
- A coalition of Republicans and conservative Democrats challenged the New Deal and blocked substantial measures.
- By 1939 the administration's focus had shifted to foreign affairs.

SOCIAL CHANGE AND SOCIAL ACTION IN THE 1930S

How did the depression and the New Deal affect specific social groups in the United States?

American life in the 1930s involved more than politics. The depression affected most Americans, including the jobless and their families; working women; and all age groups. For industrial workers, African-Americans, a growing Hispanic community, and Native Americans, the crisis brought hard times, but the activist climate of the era also encouraged organized resistance to exploitation and brought new legislative initiatives.

The Depression's Psychological and Social Impact

The depression brought untold human suffering. Unemployment never fell below about 14 percent, and for much of the decade it ran considerably higher. Those who were employed often had to take jobs below their qualifications. College alumni pumped gas; business-school graduates sold furniture. Bankruptcies, foreclosures, and abandoned farms multiplied. A quarter of all farm families had to accept public or private assistance during the 1930s.

Psychologists described "unemployment shock": jobless persons who walked the streets seeking work and then lay awake at night worrying. When shoes wore out, heel tacks pushed through, cutting the skin. "You pass . . . shoe-shops where a tack might be bent down," one young man recalled, "but you can't pull off a shoe and ask to have that done—for nothing."

Senator Robert Wagner called the working woman in the depression years "the first orphan in the storm." Indeed, for the 25 percent of women employed in 1930, the depression brought hard times. The female jobless rate hovered above 20 percent through much of the decade. Women desperate to continue working often had to take lower-paying, lower-status jobs. Competition from displaced male workers reduced the proportion of women even in such traditional "women's professions" as library work, social work, and school teaching.

Married women workers faced harsh criticism. Although most worked out of economic necessity, they were accused of stealing jobs from unemployed men. Many cities refused to hire married women as teachers and fired women teachers who married.

Women workers also faced wage discrimination. In 1939 the average woman teacher earned nearly 20 percent less than the average male with comparable experience. Most female office workers earned far less than male factory workers. A number of the NRA codes authorized lower pay for women. The minimum-wage clause of the Fair Labor Standards Act helped some but did not cover many, including the more than 2 million employed in private households.

A unionization drive of the later 1930s (discussed shortly) had mixed effects on women workers. Some in the mass-production industries benefited, but the most heavily female sectors—textiles, clerical, service, and sales—proved resistant to unionization. Despite the roadblocks, the percentage of wage-earning married women increased from under 12 percent to nearly 16 percent as married women took jobs to augment depressed family incomes.

The depression profoundly affected families, old and young alike. Bank failures wiped out the savings of many older Americans. By 1935 a million Americans over sixty-five were on relief. The birthrate fell in the early thirties as married couples postponed a family or limited its size. Family planning became easier with the spread of birth-control devices, such as condoms and diaphragms. A declining birthrate plus reduced immigration held population growth in the 1930s to a scant 7 percent, in contrast to an average of 20 percent per decade between 1900 and 1930.

Parents in the 1930s often struggled to make ends meet and hold the family together. They patched clothes, stretched food, and turned to public assistance when necessary. In homes with a tradition of strong male authority, the husband's loss of a job often eroded self-esteem with devastating psychological effect. "I would rather turn on the gas and put an end to the whole family than let my wife support me," one man told a social investigator. Desertions increased, and the divorce rate, after a dip in the early and mid-1930s, edged upward, hitting a then all-time high by 1940.

As for young people, one observer compared them to a team of runners waiting for a starting gun that never sounded. High-school enrollment increased sharply, because many youths, seeing no jobs in view, simply stayed in school. The marriage rate declined as young people facing bleak prospects postponed this step.

Out of necessity, many families rediscovered traditional skills. They painted their own houses and repaired their own cars. Home baking and canning revived. Many would look back on the 1930s as a time when adversity encouraged cooperation, savoring of simple pleasures, and sharing of scant resources.

For the neediest—among them blacks, Hispanics, and southern sharecroppers—the depression imposed added misery on poverty-blighted lives. In his novel *Native Son* (1940), Richard Wright vividly portrayed the desperate conditions of family life in Chicago's black slums. Yet not all was bleak. Emotional resilience and patterns of mutual aid and survival skills developed through years of oppression helped many black families cope.

Industrial Workers Unionize

Between 1900 and 1930, the ranks of factory workers had soared from 3.7 million to 7.7 million. Yet most of these workers remained unorganized. Major industries like steel, automobiles, and textiles had resisted attempts to unionize their workers. The prosperity and probusiness mood of the 1920s had further weakened the labor movement.

But hard times and a favorable government climate bred a new labor militancy in the 1930s. The Wagner Act's guarantee of workers' right to organize energized some American Federation of Labor (AFL) leaders. In November 1935 John L. Lewis of the United Mine Workers (UMW) and Sidney Hillman of the Amalgamated Clothing Workers, chafing at the AFL's slowness in organizing factory workers, started the Committee for Industrial Organization (CIO) within the AFL. CIO activists preached unionization in Pittsburgh's steel mills, Detroit's auto plants, and southern textile factories. Unlike the craft-based, racially exclusive AFL, the CIO unions welcomed all workers in a particular industry, regardless of race, gender, or degree of skill.

In 1936 a CIO-sponsored organizing committee geared up for a major strike to win union recognition by the steel industry. (In fact, Lewis had already secretly negotiated a settlement with the head of U.S. Steel, and in March 1937 U.S. Steel recognized the union, granted a wage increase, and accepted a forty-hour workweek.) Other steel companies followed, and soon 400,000 steelworkers had signed union cards.

Meanwhile, organizers led by the fiery, socialist-oriented Walter Reuther (ROOther), mapped a campaign to organize deeply antiunion General Motors. In December 1936 employees at GM's two body plants in Flint, Michigan, stopped work and peacefully occupied the factories, paralyzing GM's production by their "sit-down strike." GM's management responded by calling in local police to harass the sit-down strikers, sending spies to union meetings, and threatening to fire strikers. A January 1937 showdown with the police at one of the body plants led to the formation of the Women's Emergency Brigade, whose members, on twenty-four-hour alert for picket duty, played a key role during the rest of the strike.

GM asked the Roosevelt administration and the governor of Michigan to send troops to expel the strikers by force. Both officials declined. Although FDR disapproved of the sit-down tactic, he refused to intervene with troops. On February 11, GM signed a contract recognizing the United Automobile Workers (UAW). As Chrysler fell into line also, the UAW soon boasted more than 400,000 members. Unionization of the electrical and rubber industries moved forward as well.

In 1938 the Committee for Industrial Organization left the AFL to become the **Congress of Industrial Organizations,** a 2-million-member association of industrial unions. In response to the CIO challenge, the AFL began to adapt to the changed nature of the labor force. Union membership shot up from under 3 million in 1933 to more than 8 million in 1941.

Congress of Industrial Organizations Counterpart of AFL, but for unskilled industrial workers

Some big corporations fought on. Henry Ford hated unions, and his tough lieutenant, Harry Bennett, organized a squad of union-busting thugs to fight the UAW. In 1937 Bennett's men beat Walter Reuther and other UAW officials outside Ford's plant near Detroit. Not until 1941 did Ford yield to union pressure.

The Republic Steel Company, headed by union enemy Tom Girdler, also dug in. Even after U.S. Steel signed with the CIO in March 1937, Republic and other smaller companies, known collectively as "Little Steel," resisted. In May 1937, workers in twenty-seven Little Steel plants, including Republic's factory in South Chicago, walked off the job. On May 30, Memorial Day, strikers approached over 250 police officers guarding the plant. Someone threw a large stick at the police, who opened fire, killing four strikers and wounding scores. A blue-ribbon investigation found that the killings had been "clearly avoidable by the police." In 1941 the Little Steel companies finally signed union agreements with the CIO.

Another holdout was the textile industry, whose more than 600,000 workers, mostly in the South and 40 percent female, generally earned very low wages and had no recourse against autocratic bosses. In 1934 the CIO launched an organizing drive. Some 400,000 workers went on strike, but the mill owners fought back viciously. Several strikers were killed, many wounded, and thousands arrested. The strike failed, and the 1930s ended with most textile workers still unorganized.

The union movement bypassed low-paid workers—domestics, farm workers, department store clerks, restaurant and laundry workers—who tended to be women, blacks, or recent immigrants. More than three-quarters of all nonfarm workers remained unorganized in 1940. Nonetheless, the unionization of key sectors of the industrial work force represents one of the decade's most memorable achievements.

Why did powerful corporations yield to unions after years of resistance? Workers' militancy and the tactical skills of labor leaders like Reuther were crucial. But labor's successes also reflected the changed government climate. Corporations had once routinely called on the government to help break strikes. Although this still happened occasionally at the state level in the 1930s, the Wagner Act, the Fair Labor Standards Act, and the oversight of the NLRB made clear that Washington would no longer automatically back management in labor disputes. Once corporate managers realized this, unionization often followed.

Organized labor's successes in the later 1930s concealed complex tensions. A hard core of activists, some of them communists or socialists, led the unionizing drive. But most rank-and-file workers had no desire to overthrow the capitalist system. Indeed, many held back from striking, fearful for their jobs. But once the CIO's

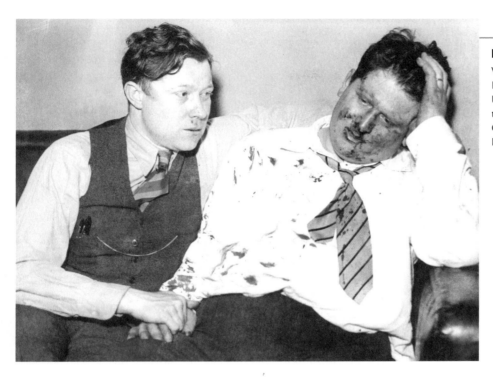

Labor Organizing, 1930s-Style
Walter Reuther (left) and Richard Frankensteen of the United Auto Workers, after their beating by Ford Motor Company security guards, Detroit, May 1937.

militant minority showed that picket lines and sit-down strikes could win union contracts and tangible gains, workers signed up by the thousands. As they did, the radical organizers lost influence, and the unions became more conservative.

Blacks and Hispanic-Americans Resist Racism and Exploitation

The depression also brought social changes and activism within the African-American and Hispanic communities. Black migration to northern cities continued in the 1930s, although at a slower rate than in the 1920s. Some 400,000 southern blacks moved to northern cities in the 1930s, and by 1940 nearly one quarter of the nation's 12 million blacks lived in the urban North.

Rural or urban, life was hard. Black tenant farmers and sharecroppers often faced eviction. Among black industrial workers, the depression-era jobless rate far outran the rate for whites, largely because of racism and discriminatory hiring policies. Although black workers in some industries benefited from the CIO's nondiscriminatory policy, workplace racism remained a fact of life.

Over one hundred blacks died by lynching in the 1930s, and other miscarriages of justice continued, especially in the South. In 1931 an all-white jury in Scottsboro, Alabama, sentenced eight black youths to death on highly dubious charges of rape. In 1935, after heavy publicity and an aggressive defense, the Supreme Court ordered a new trial for the "Scottsboro Boys" because they had been denied legal counsel and blacks had been excluded from the jury. Five of the group were again convicted, however, and served long prison terms.

But rising activism signaled changes ahead. The NAACP battled in courts and legislatures against lynching, segregation, and the denial of voting rights. The Urban League campaigned with boycotts and picket lines against businesses in black neighborhoods that employed only whites. In March 1935 hostility toward white-owned businesses in Harlem, fueled by general anger over racism and joblessness, ignited a riot that caused an estimated $200 million in damage and left three blacks dead.

The Communist party publicized lynchings and racial discrimination, and supplied lawyers for the "Scottsboro Boys," as part of a depression-era recruitment effort in the black community. But despite a few notable recruits (including the novelist Richard Wright), few blacks joined the party.

Other minority groups also faced discrimination. California continued its efforts to prevent Japanese-Americans from owning land. In 1934 Congress set an annual limit of fifty on immigrants from the Philippines, still a U.S. possession—lower than that for any other nation. Congress also offered free travel "home" for Filipinos long settled in the United States.

The more than 2 million Hispanic-Americans faced trying times as well. Some were citizens with ancestral roots in the Southwest, but most were recent arrivals from Mexico or Caribbean islands, such as Cuba and Puerto Rico (a U.S. holding whose residents were and are American citizens). Whereas the Caribbean immigrants settled in East Coast cities, most Mexican newcomers worked as migratory agricultural laborers in the Southwest and elsewhere, or in midwestern steel or meatpacking plants.

As the depression deepened, Mexican-born residents faced mounting hostility. The influx of "Okies" fleeing the dust bowl worsened the job crisis, and by 1937 more than half of the cotton workers in Arizona were out-of-staters who supplanted Mexican-born laborers. With their access to migratory work disrupted, Mexican-Americans poured into the barrios (Hispanic neighborhoods) of southwestern cities. Lacking work, half a million Mexicans returned to their native land in the 1930s. Some did so voluntarily, but immigration officials and local authorities expelled thousands. Mexican-American farm workers who remained faced appalling conditions and near-starvation wages. A labor organization called the Confederación de Uniones de Campesinos y Obreros Mexicanos (Confederation of Unions of Mexican Workers and Farm Laborers) emerged from a 1933 strike by grape workers. More strikes erupted in 1935–1936 on farms across the state.

Organizations like the California Fruit Growers Exchange (which marketed it citrus under the Sunkist brand name) fought the unions, sometimes with violence. In one incident in 1933, two workers died when bullets ripped into their striking cotton pickers' union hall. Undeterred, the strikers won a 20 percent pay increase, and others achieved a few successes, too. Their strikes also awakened some Americans to the plight of one of the nation's most exploited groups.

A New Deal for Native Americans

The 1930s also revived attention to the nation's 330,000 Native Americans, most of whom endured poverty, scant education, poor health care, and bleak prospects. The Dawes Act of 1887 (see Chapter 17) had dissolved the tribes as legal entities, allocated some tribal lands to individuals, and sold the rest. By the early 1930s, whites owned about two-thirds of the land that Native Americans had possessed in 1887, including much of the most valuable acreage. That Indians had been granted full citizenship and voting rights in 1924 did little to improve their lot.

In the 1920s a reform movement arose. One reformer, John Collier, who had lived among the Pueblo Indians of New Mexico, founded the American Indian Defense Association in 1923 to preserve the spiritual beauty and harmony that he saw in traditional Indian life. Appointed commissioner of Indian affairs in 1933, Collier cadged funds from New Deal agencies to build schools, hospitals, and irrigation systems on Indian reservations and to preserve sites of cultural importance. The Civilian Conservation Corps employed twelve thousand Indian youths to work on projects on Indian lands.

Pursuing his vision of renewed tribal life, Collier drafted a bill to halt the sale of tribal land, restore the remaining unallocated lands to tribal control, create new reservations, and expand existing ones. It also envisioned tribal councils with broad governing powers and required Indian schools to teach Native American history and handicrafts. The bill sparked opposition. Some Indian leaders criticized it as a plan to transform the reservations into living museums and to treat Native Americans as exotic and backward. Successful Indian property owners and entrepreneurs rejected the bill's tribalist assumptions. The bill did, indeed, reflect the idealism of well-meaning outsiders rather than the views of the nation's diverse Native American groups.

The **Indian Reorganization Act** of 1934, a compromise measure, halted the sale of tribal lands and enabled tribes to regain title to unallocated lands. But Congress scaled back Collier's proposals for tribal self-government and dropped measures to renew tribal culture. A majority of tribes approved the law, as required for it to take effect, but opinion was divided. Still, the restoration of tribes as legal entities laid the groundwork for later tribal business ventures as well as tribal lawsuits seeking to enforce long-violated treaty rights.

Indian Reorganization Act
Effort during the New Deal to restore the sovereignty and viability of Indian tribes

CHECKING IN

- The depression profoundly, and negatively, affected women in the work force.
- Families struggled to cope economically and psychologically.
- Now under government protection, industrial unions like the United Auto Workers organized and grew strong.
- Blacks, often the last hired and first fired, continued to face discrimination, injustice, and even violence.
- Migrant workers were hard hit by the depression as well as by competition from "Okies" and other displaced farmers.

▌THE AMERICAN CULTURAL SCENE IN THE 1930S

What key developments shaped American culture in the 1930s?

Hard times and the New Deal shaped American cultural life in the 1930s. While radio and the movies offered escapist fare, novelists, artists, playwrights, and photographers responded to the crisis as well. As the decade wore on, a more positive and affirmative tone in cultural expressions reflected both the renewed hope of the New Deal and apprehension about events abroad.

Avenues of Escape: Radio and the Movies The standardization of mass culture continued in the 1930s. Each evening millions of Americans gathered around their radios to listen to news, musical programs, and comedy shows. Radio humor flourished when the real world was grim.

So, too, did the fifteen-minute afternoon dramas known as soap operas (because soap companies sponsored them). Despite their assembly-line quality, these daily dollops of romance and melodrama won a devoted audience, mostly house-wives. Identifying with the troubled radio heroines, female listeners gained at least temporary escape from their own difficulties.

The movies were also extremely popular, and most people could still afford the twenty-five-cent admission. In 1939, 65 percent of Americans went to the movies at least once a week. The motion picture, declared one Hollywood executive, had become "as necessary as any other daily commodity."

A few movies dealt realistically with such social issues as labor unrest and the sharecroppers' plight. Two New Deal documentaries, *The Plow That Broke the Plains,* on the origins of the dust bowl, and *The River,* on erosion and floods in the Mississippi Valley, evoked the human and environmental toll of westward expansion. Warner Brothers studio made a series of movies in 1934–1936 celebrating the New Deal. And in *Mr. Deeds Goes to Town* (1936) and *Mr. Smith Goes to Washington* (1939), director Frank Capra, the son of Italian immigrants, offered the idealistic message that "the people" would always triumph over entrenched interests.

Gangster movies, inspired by actual criminals like Al Capone and John Dillinger, served up a different style of film realism. Films like *Little Caesar* (1930) grittily portrayed an urban America of looming skyscrapers and dark, rain-swept streets shredded by the rat-tat-tat of machine guns as rival gangs battled. When civic groups protested the glorification of crime, Hollywood made police and "G-men" (federal law-enforcement agents) the heroes while retaining the violence. The movie gangsters played by Edward G. Robinson and James Cagney were variants of the Horatio Alger hero struggling upward against adversity. Their portrayals appealed to depression-era moviegoers facing equally heavy odds.

Above all, movies offered escape—the chance to briefly forget the depression. Musicals like *Gold Diggers of 1933* (with its theme song, "We're in the Money") offered dancing, music, and cheerful plots involving the triumph of pluck over all obstacles. When color movies arrived in the late 1930s, they seemed an omen of better times ahead.

The Marx Brothers provided the decade's zaniest movie moments. In comedies like *Animal Crackers* (1930), these vaudeville troupers created an anarchic world that satirized authority and demolished all logic. Amid cynicism about the collapse of 1929, the Marx Brothers' mockery matched the American mood.

African-Americans appeared in 1930s' movies, if at all, only as stereotypes. Under the denigrating screen name Stepin Fetchit, black actor Lincoln Perry played the slow-witted buffoon in many movies. In representing women, Hollywood offered mixed messages. While some 1930s' movie heroines found fulfillment in marriage and domesticity, other films chipped away at the stereotype. Katharine Hepburn portrayed autonomous, independent-minded women in such films as *Spitfire* (1934) and *A Woman Rebels* (1936). Mae West, brassy, openly sexual, and fiercely independent, mocked conventional stereotypes in *I'm No Angel* (1933) and other 1930s' hits.

The Later 1930s: Opposing Fascism, Reaffirming Traditional Values

As the 1930s ended, many Americans viewed the nation more favorably. It had survived the depression. The social fabric remained whole; revolution had not come. As other societies collapsed into dictatorships, American democracy endured. Writers, composers, and other cultural creators reflected the changed mood, as despair gave way to a more upbeat and patriotic outlook.

A movement known as the **Popular Front** influenced this shift. In 1935 Russian dictator Joseph Stalin (STAHL-in), fearing attack by Nazi (NAHT-zee) Germany, called for a worldwide alliance, or Popular Front, against Adolf Hitler and his Italian ally in fascism (FASH-ism), Benito Mussolini (ben-EE-toh moos-soh-LEE-nee). Parroting the new Soviet line, U.S. communists who in the early 1930s had attacked FDR and the New Deal now praised Roosevelt and summoned writers and intellectuals to the antifascist cause. Many noncommunists, alarmed by developments in Europe, responded to the call.

The high-water mark of the Popular Front came during the Spanish Civil War of 1936–1939. In July 1936 Spanish fascist general Francisco Franco revolted against Spain's legally elected left-wing government. With military aid from Hitler and Mussolini, Franco won backing from Spanish monarchists, landowners, and industrialists, and from the Roman Catholic hierarchy.

In America, writers, artists, and intellectuals who backed the Popular Front rallied to support the anti-Franco Spanish Loyalists (those loyal to the elected government). The novelist Ernest Hemingway, who visited Spain in 1936–1937, expressed a newfound sense of worthwhile purpose in *For Whom the Bell Tolls* (1940), the story of a young American volunteer who dies while fighting with a Loyalist guerrilla band.

The Popular Front collapsed on August 24, 1939, when the Soviet Union and Nazi Germany signed a nonaggression pact and divided Poland between them. Enthusiasm for cooperating with the communists under the banner of "antifascism" quickly faded.

The New Deal's achievements also contributed to the cultural shift of the later 1930s. The satire and cynicism of the 1920s and early 1930s yielded to a more hopeful view of grass-roots America. In John Steinbeck's best-selling novel *The Grapes of Wrath* (1939), an uprooted dust-bowl family, the Joads, make their difficult way from Oklahoma to California, revealing the strength shown by ordinary people in depression America. As Ma Joad tells her son Tom, "They ain't gonna wipe us out. Why, we're the people—we go on."

In 1936 writer James Agee and photographer Walker Evans spent weeks living with Alabama sharecroppers to research a magazine article. The result was *Let Us Now Praise Famous Men* (1941). Enhanced by Evans's unforgettable photographs, Agee's masterpiece evoked the strength and decency of those living on society's margins.

Composers also reflected this spirit of cultural nationalism. In *Billy the Kid* (1938) and other compositions, Aaron Copland drew upon American legends and folk melodies. George Gershwin adapted a popular 1920s play about black street life in Charleston, South Carolina, for his opera *Porgy and Bess* (1935).

Jazz flourished in the later thirties thanks to swing, a danceable style popularized by the big bands of Benny Goodman, Count Basie, Duke Ellington, and others. Clarinetist Benny Goodman challenged the color line in jazz, including black musicians like pianist Teddy Wilson and vibraphonist Lionel Hampton, along with white performers, in his orchestra. A turning point in the acceptance of jazz came in 1938, when Goodman's band performed at New York's Carnegie Hall.

The later 1930s also saw a heightened interest in regional literature and art. Zora Neale Hurston's novel *Their Eyes Were Watching God* (1937), exploring a black woman's search for fulfillment, was set in rural Florida. In *Absalom, Absalom!* (1936) William Faulkner continued the saga of his mythic Yoknapatawpha County in

Popular Front Coalition of liberal, communist elements against fascism

Mississippi. Painters Thomas Hart Benton of Missouri, John Steuart Curry of Kansas, and Grant Wood of Iowa struck strongly regional notes in their work.

Galleries displayed folk paintings, Amish quilts, and New England weather vanes. A 1938 show at New York's Museum of Modern Art introduced Horace Pippin, a black Philadelphia laborer whose paintings, such as *John Brown Going to His Hanging,* revealed a genuine, if untutored, talent. In 1939 the same museum featured seventy-nine-year-old Anna "Grandma" Moses of Hoosick Falls, New York, whose memory paintings of her farm girlhood enjoyed great popularity.

This cultural nationalism generated a fascination with the nation's past. Americans flocked to historical re-creations, such as Henry Ford's Greenfield Village in Michigan and Colonial Williamsburg in Virginia. In 1936–1939, Texans restored the Alamo in San Antonio, the "Cradle of Texas Liberty." Historical novels like Margaret Mitchell's epic of the Old South, *Gone with the Wind* (1936), became best-sellers. These re-creations and fictions often presented a distorted view of history. Slavery was blurred or sentimentalized at Colonial Williamsburg and in Mitchell's novel. "Texas Liberty" had a different meaning for the state's African-American, Indian, and Hispanic populations than it did for those who turned the Alamo into a tourist shrine.

Streamlining and a World's Fair: Corporate America's Utopian Vision

A design style called streamlining also shaped the visual culture of the late 1930s. This style originated in the 1920s when industrial designers, inspired by the airplane, introduced smoothly flowing curves into the design of commercial products. Streamlining appealed to consumers—a vital business consideration during the depression. When Sears Roebuck streamlined its Coldspot refrigerators, sales surged. As products ranging from house trailers to pencil sharpeners and cigarette lighters emerged in sleek new forms, streamlining helped corporate America rebuild its image and present itself as the benevolent shaper of a better future.

Under the theme "The World of Tomorrow," the 1939 New York World's Fair represented the high point of the streamlining vogue and corporate America's public-relations blitz. Inside the fair's hallmark Perisphere, a giant globe, visitors found "Democracity," a diorama showing a harmonious city of the future.

The hit of the fair was General Motors' Futurama, which gave visitors a vision of the United States in the distant year 1960—a nation of complex multilane highways with stacked interchanges. Futurama built public support for the interstate highway system that would soon become a reality. Also featuring such wonders as television and automatic dishwashers, the World's Fair epitomized corporate capitalism's version of the patriotism and hopefulness that pervaded American culture as the 1930s ended.

The hopefulness was mixed with muted fear. The nation had survived the worst of the depression, but danger loomed overseas. The anxiety triggered by the menacing world situation surfaced on October 31, 1938, when CBS Radio aired an adaptation of H. G. Wells's science-fiction story *War of the Worlds,* directed by Orson Welles. In realistic detail, the broadcast reported

CHECKING IN

- During the depression, radio and the movies offered escapist fare to millions of Americans.
- The Popular Front briefly linked noncommunist and communist intellectuals.
- A positive mood emerged by the late 1930s in works like *The Grapes of Wrath*.
- The success of the New Deal and looming international problems fed into a rising sense of cultural nationalism.
- By 1939 Americans looked to the future with optimism, embodied in the World's Fair, but their optimism was mixed with anxiety about world affairs.

the landing of a spaceship in New Jersey and the advance of aliens with deadly ray guns toward New York. The show sparked a panic as horrified listeners believed the end was at hand. Beneath the terror lay a more rational fear: of approaching war. For although Americans had coped with the depression, the international situation had deteriorated. By October 1938, radio news bulletins warned of an impending war between Germany and England. By the time the New York World's Fair offered its vision of "Tomorrow," the actual world of 1939 was very scary indeed.

Chapter Summary

 DOWNLOAD THE MP3 AUDIO FILE OF THE CHAPTER SUMMARY, AND LISTEN TO IT ON THE GO.

What caused the Great Depression, and how did President Hoover respond? (page 558)

Hoover's emphasis on voluntarism proved inadequate to the magnitude of problems caused by the Great Depression, but he would not move beyond that to extend direct aid to people. Disenchanted Americans sneered at "Hoovervilles" and were appalled by the way the administration responded to the bonus march.

What strategy guided the early New Deal, and what problems and challenges arose in 1934–1935? (page 562)

Initially, Roosevelt welcomed big business in his depression-fighting coalition. The first hundred days of FDR's term saw passage of measures intended to achieve industrial recovery, agricultural recovery, and short-term relief: the Federal Emergency Relief Act, the National Industrial Recovery Act, the Agricultural Adjustment Act, the Tennessee Valley Authority, and the Civilian Conservation Corps. The New Deal also featured reform measures, such as the Securities and Exchange Commission and the Federal Deposit Insurance Corporation.

What key measures and setbacks marked the course of the New Deal from 1935 on? (page 567)

From 1935 on, during the so-called Second New Deal, federal policies became more concerned with social justice and less interested in cooperating with business. Relief projects, such as those of the Works Progress Administration, gave jobs to millions of people, and the National Labor Relations Act opened the way for the success of industrial unionization. The Social Security Act established the framework for the modern social-welfare state. FDR's smashing

KEY TERMS

Reconstruction Finance Corporation *(p. 560)*

Eleanor Roosevelt *(p. 563)*

Frances Perkins *(p. 563)*

Civilian Conservation Corps *(p. 564)*

Federal Emergency Relief Act *(p. 564)*

Agricultural Adjustment Administration *(p. 564)*

National Recovery Administration *(p. 564)*

Tennessee Valley Authority *(p. 565)*

Harry Hopkins *(p. 566)*

Works Progress Administration *(p. 567)*

National Labor Relations Act (Wagner Act) *(p. 569)*

Social Security Act *(p. 569)*

Farm Security Administration *(p. 574)*

Fair Labor Standards Act *(p. 575)*

Congress of Industrial Organizations *(p. 578)*

Indian Reorganization Act *(p. 581)*

Popular Front *(p. 583)*

reelection victory in 1936 solidified the Democratic coalition he had forged, including the white South, farmers, urban ethnics, union members, and African-Americans.

How did the New Deal end? (page 573)

The failure of FDR's "court-packing" scheme and the arrival of a recession in 1937 slowed the momentum of the New Deal, and a congressional coalition of Republicans and conservative Democrats made passage of major legislation virtually impossible. The rise of fascism and Nazism in Europe, and Japanese aggression in Asia, took center stage. By 1938, facing rising conservative opposition and menaces abroad, the New Deal's reformist energies faded.

How did the depression and the New Deal affect specific social groups in the United States? (page 575)

Families struggled economically and psychologically during the depression. Industrial workers, with the backing of the administration, organized unions in previously unassailable sectors, such as automobiles. Women and African-Americans continued to face discrimination, while migrant workers were also hard hit. For Native Americans, New Deal legislation restored tribes' legal status, laying the groundwork for future enterprises and treaty claims.

What key developments shaped American culture in the 1930s? (page 581)

American culture in the 1930s reflected the decade's economic and social realities. While the movies and radio offered diversion, writers, painters, and other cultural creators initially expressed despair and cynicism over capitalism's failure. But as New Deal programs assisted writers and artists, and as foreign threats loomed in the later 1930s, the cultural climate grew more patriotic and affirmative.

CHAPTER 25

Americans and a World in Crisis

1933–1945

Okinawa, 1945

(CL) This icon will direct you to the website where you can Prepare for Class, Improve Your Grade, and Ace the Test: **www.cengage.com/history/boyer/enduringconcise6e**

To most Americans, World War II was "the good war." Unlike the nations of Asia and Europe, the United States suffered no invasion of its homeland, no bombing of its cities, no mass killing of its civilians. The war lifted the United States out of the Great Depression and propelled many into the middle class, and it gave unprecedented opportunities to millions of minorities and women. That "Good War," however, had little to do with E. B. Sledge's experience fighting in the South Pacific.

E. B. Sledge's harrowing wartime experiences drove him to write a memoir of unrelenting horror, *With the Old Breed*. Describing the battles of Peleliu and Okinawa, Sledge depicts a brutal landscape of war without mercy. He once saw a fellow marine use a knife to try to extract the gold teeth of a wounded Japanese soldier, even as the man thrashed in pain. On Okinawa's Half Moon Hill, he dreamed that the decomposed bodies of marines sprawled about him slowly rose, unblinkingly stared at him, and said, "It is over for us who are dead, but you must struggle, and will carry the memories all your life."

The wartime experiences of few Americans matched those of Sledge. Yet World War II fundamentally changed national institutions and transformed individual behavior. It also created a new world order that left the United States at the pinnacle of its power and sowed the seeds of a postwar crisis. It was indeed, in Eleanor Roosevelt's words, "no ordinary time."

THE UNITED STATES IN A MENACING WORLD, 1933–1939

How did the American people and government respond to the international crises of the 1930s?

Apart from improving relations with Latin America, the early administration of President Franklin D. Roosevelt (FDR) remained largely aloof from the crises in the world. Americans reacted ambivalently as Italy, Germany, and Japan grew more aggressive. Millions of Americans, determined not to stumble into war again, supported neutrality. Only a minority wanted the United States to help embattled democracies abroad. All the while, the world slid toward the precipice.

Nationalism and the Good Neighbor

President Roosevelt at first put American economic interests above all else and showed little interest in free trade or international economic cooperation. He did, however, commit himself to an internationalist approach in Latin America, where bitterness over decades of "Yankee imperialism" ran high. In his 1933 inaugural, he had announced a **"Good Neighbor" policy,** renouncing any nation's right to intervene in the affairs of another. Under this policy Roosevelt withdrew the last U.S. troops from Haiti and the Dominican Republic, persuaded American bankers to loosen their grip on Haiti's central banking system, and reduced the U.S. role in Panamanian affairs.

"Good Neighbor" policy
FDR's less interventionist policy toward Latin America

Cuba and Mexico provided major tests of the Good Neighbor policy. In Cuba, an economic crisis in 1933 brought to power a leftist regime that the United States opposed. Instead of sending in the marines, the United States provided indirect aid to a conservative revolt led by Fulgencio Batista in 1934 that overthrew the radical government. American economic assistance would then allow Batista to retain power until his overthrow by Fidel Castro in 1959. In Mexico, a reform government came to power in 1936 and promptly nationalized several oil companies owned by U.S. and British corporations. While insisting on fair compensation, the United States refrained from military intervention.

The Good Neighbor policy did not end U.S. interference in Latin American affairs. But it did substitute economic leverage for heavy-handed intervention and

Chronology

1931–1932	Japan invades Manchuria and creates a puppet government
1933	Adolf Hitler becomes chancellor of Germany and assumes dictatorial powers
1934–1936	Nye Committee investigations
1935–1937	Neutrality Acts
1937	Japan invades China
1938	Germany annexes Austria; Munich Pact gives Sudetenland to Germany; *Kristallnacht,* night of Nazi terror against German and Austrian Jews
1939	Nazi-Soviet Pact; Germany invades Poland; World War II begins
1940	Germany conquers the Netherlands, Belgium, France, Denmark, Norway, and Luxembourg; Germany, Italy, and Japan sign the Tripartite Pact; Selective Service Act; Franklin Roosevelt elected to an unprecedented third term
1941	Lend-Lease Act; Roosevelt establishes the Fair Employment Practices Commission (FEPC); Germany invades the Soviet Union; Japan attacks Pearl Harbor; the United States enters World War II; War Powers Act
1942	Battles of Coral Sea and Midway halt Japanese offensive; Internment of Japanese-Americans; Revenue Act expands graduated income-tax system; Allies invade North Africa (Operation TORCH); First successful atomic chain reaction; CORE founded
1943	Soviet victory in Battle of Stalingrad; Coal miners strike; Smith-Connally War Labor Disputes Act; Detroit and Los Angeles race riots; Allied invasion of Italy; Roosevelt, Churchill, and Stalin meet in Tehran
1944	Allied invasion of France (Operation Overlord); U.S. forces invade the Philippines; Roosevelt wins fourth term; Battle of the Bulge
1945	Yalta Conference; Battles of Iwo Jima and Okinawa; Roosevelt dies; Harry S Truman becomes president; Germany surrenders; Truman, Churchill, and Stalin meet in Potsdam; United States drops atomic bombs on Hiroshima and Nagasaki; Japan surrenders

military occupation. The better relations fostered by FDR would help the United States pursue hemispheric solidarity in World War II, and later in the Cold War.

The Rise of Aggressive States in Europe and Asia

Meanwhile, powerful forces raged across much of the world. As early as 1922, Italy's economic problems and social unrest had opened the way for **Benito Mussolini** and his Fascist party to seize power in Rome. The regime swiftly suppressed dissent and imposed one-party rule.

> **Benito Mussolini** Leader of Italy; founder of fascism

The rise of **Adolf Hitler** in Germany proved more menacing. Hitler's National Socialist, or **Nazi, party** had gained broad support as a result of the depression and German resentment of the harsh Versailles treaty, and Hitler became Germany's chancellor in January 1933. Crushing opponents and rivals, Hitler imposed a brutal dictatorship on Germany and began a program to purify it of Jews—whom he considered an "inferior race" responsible for Germany's defeat in World War I.

> **Adolf Hitler** Dictatorial leader of resurgent, expansionist Germany

> **Nazi party** Hitler's political party; stressed fascism, anti-Semitism

Violating the Versailles treaty, Hitler began rearming Germany in 1935. A year later, German troops reoccupied the Rhineland, a region between the Rhine River

Interactive Map: German and Italian Expansion, 1933–1942

appeasement British policy to avoid war by giving in to German territorial demands for control of Czechoslovakia

and France specifically demilitarized by the Versailles treaty. In 1938, Hitler proclaimed an *Anschluss* (ON-shlooss) (union) between Austria and Germany. Meanwhile, Mussolini, intent on building an empire in Africa, had invaded Ethiopia in 1935. London, Paris, and Washington murmured their disapproval but took no action. An emboldened Hitler then claimed Germany's right to the Sudetenland (soo-DATE-un-land), a part of neighboring Czechoslovakia (check-oh-sloh-VAH-kee-uh) containing 3 million ethnic Germans. British prime minister Neville Chamberlain and his French counterpart, insisting that their countries could not endure another war like that of 1914–1918, yielded to Hitler's demands in return for his assurance that Germany had no further territorial ambitions—a policy dubbed **appeasement**—at a conference in Munich in September 1938.

In Tokyo, meanwhile, nationalistic militarists had gained control of Japan's government and launched a fateful course of expansion. In 1931 Japanese troops invaded the Chinese province of Manchuria, installed a puppet government, and forced China to sign a treaty recognizing Japanese control of the province. In July 1937 Japan launched a full-scale war against China itself.

The American Mood: No More War

The American response reflected a revulsion against war. By the mid-1930s millions of Americans believed that the United States' decision to enter World War I in April 1917 had been a ghastly mistake. In mid-decade a series of books reinforced this conclusion, arguing that banking and corporate interests had dragged the United States into World War I.

Neutrality Acts Laws passed in mid-thirties to keep the United States out of any European wars

Public concern over the "merchants of death" issue led to a special Senate investigation headed by Republican Gerald Nye of North Dakota, which concluded that banking and munitions interests had tricked the United States into war to protect loans and weapon sales to the Allies. A January 1937 poll showed that an astonishing 70 percent of the people believed that the United States should have stayed out of World War I.

By the mid-1930s an overwhelming majority of Americans thought that the "mistake" of intervention should not be repeated. In 1935–1937 a series of **Neutrality Acts** echoed the longing for peace. To prevent a repetition of 1917, these measures outlawed

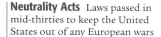

Isolationism vs. Interventionism

In front of the White House in 1941, an American soldier grabs a sign from an isolationist picketing against the United States entering the war in Europe. Isolationists ran the gamut from pacifists who opposed all wars, to progressives who feared the growth of business and centralized power, to ultrarightists who sympathized with fascism or shared Hitler's anti-Semitism.

arms sales and loans to nations at war and forbade Americans to travel on the ships of belligerent powers.

With the public firmly isolationist and American companies like IBM heavily invested in Nazi Germany, confrontation with fascism came solely in sports. At the 1936 Olympics in Berlin, Jesse Owens, an African-American, made a mockery of Nazi theories of racial superiority by winning four gold medals. When the black Joe Louis knocked out German Max Schmeling in the first round of their world heavyweight championship bout, Americans cheered—but still opposed any policy that might involve them in war.

The Gathering Storm: 1938–1939

The interlude of reduced tension that followed the Munich Pact proved tragically brief. "Peace in our time" lasted a mere 5½ months. At 6:00 a.m. on March 15, 1939, Nazi troops thundered across the border into Czechoslovakia. By evening the Nazi flag flew over the Czech capital of Prague (prahg). Five months later, the signing of the Nazi-Soviet Pact gave Hitler a green light to invade Poland.

Although isolationist sentiment remained strong in the United States, opinion began to shift rapidly. After the fall of Czechoslovakia, Roosevelt called for actions "short of war" to demonstrate America's will to check fascism, and he asked Hitler and Mussolini to pledge not to invade thirty-one specific nations. A jeering Hitler ridiculed FDR's message, while in Rome Mussolini mocked Roosevelt's physical disability, joking that the president's paralysis must have reached his brain.

Roosevelt, however, did more than send messages. In October 1938 he asked Congress for a $300 million military appropriation; in November he instructed the Army Air Corps to plan for an annual production of 20,000 planes; in January 1939, he submitted a $1.3 billion defense budget. Hitler and Mussolini, he said, were "two madmen" who "respect force and force alone."

America and the Jewish Refugees

Hitler and the Nazis had translated their hatred of Jews into official policy. The Nuremberg Laws of 1935 stripped Jews of the rights of German citizenship, and increased restrictions on Jews in all spheres of German educational, social, and economic life. This campaign of hatred reached a violent crescendo on November 9–10, 1938, when the Nazis unleashed *Kristallnacht* (Night of the Broken Glass), a frenzy of arson, destruction, and looting against Jews throughout Germany.

No longer could anyone mistake Hitler's malignant intent. Jews, who had been leaving Germany since 1933, streamed out by the tens of thousands, seeking haven. Between 1933 and 1938, 60,000 fled to the United States.

In general the United States proved reluctant to grant sanctuary to the mass of Hitler's Jewish victims. Most Americans, according to public-opinion polls, condemned the Jews' persecution, but only a minority favored admitting more refugees. Congress rejected all efforts to liberalize the immigration law, with its discriminatory quotas. FDR bears some

CHECKING IN

- FDR adopted the Good Neighbor policy toward Latin America.
- Mussolini established a fascist state in Italy in 1922; Hitler and the Nazis took over Germany in 1933 and pursued an expansionist course in Europe; Japan became increasingly militaristic and aggressive in Asia.
- Americans generally remained isolationist; the Neutrality Acts reflected this sentiment.
- When war erupted in Europe, FDR sought increased military funding and ways to evade the Neutrality Acts.
- The American people and government basically ignored the plight of Jews attempting to flee Hitler.

responsibility. While deploring Hitler's persecution of the Jews and helping to establish the Inter-Governmental Committee on Refugees in 1938, he did little else to translate his sympathy for the Jews into political efforts to relax restrictions on immigration.

The consequences of such attitudes became clear in June 1939, when the *St. Louis,* a German liner jammed with 900 Jewish refugees, asked permission to put its passengers ashore at Fort Lauderdale, Florida. Immigration officials refused this request and, according to the *New York Times,* a Coast Guard cutter stood by "to prevent possible attempts by refugees to jump off and swim ashore." The *St. Louis* turned slowly away from the lights of America and sailed back to Germany, where more than 700 of its passengers would die under Nazi brutality.

INTO THE STORM, 1939–1941

What drew the United States into World War II?

After a decade of crises—worldwide depression and regional conflicts—war erupted in Europe in 1939. Following the lightning German victories in western Europe in the spring of 1940, President Roosevelt's policy of neutrality gave way to a policy of economic intervention. He knew that extending aid to those resisting aggression by the so-called Rome-Berlin-Tokyo Axis, as well as his toughening conduct toward Germany and Japan, could, as he said, "push" the United States into the crisis of worldwide war. Japan's attack on the U.S. fleet at Pearl Harbor provided the final push.

The European War

Adolf Hitler precipitated war by demanding that Poland return to Germany the city of Danzig (Gdansk) (dansk), lost after World War I. When Poland refused, Nazi armies poured into Poland at dawn on September 1, 1939, and the Luftwaffe (LOOFT-vah-feh) (German air force) devastated Polish cities. Two days later, Britain and France, honoring commitments to Poland, declared war on Germany. Although FDR invoked the Neutrality Acts, he would not ask Americans to be impartial in thought and deed.

Tailoring his actions to the public mood, which favored both preventing a Nazi victory and staying out of war, FDR persuaded Congress in November to amend the Neutrality Acts to allow the belligerents to purchase weapons from the United States if they paid cash and carried the arms away in their own ships. But "cash-and carry" did not stop the Nazis. In spring 1940 Hitler unleashed blitzkrieg (BLITS-kreeg) (lightning war) against western Europe; the Nazi Wehrmacht (VAIR-mokt) (war machine) swept all the way to the English Channel in a scant two months. In early June the British evacuated most of their army, but none of its equipment, from France. And on June 22 France surrendered.

Hitler then turned his fury against Great Britain, terror-bombing British cities in hopes of forcing a surrender or, failing that, preparing the ground for a cross-channel invasion. With Coventry destroyed and much of London in smoking ruins, Prime Minister **Winston Churchill** pleaded for American aid.

Winston Churchill British wartime Prime Minister; close friend of FDR; staunch ally of the United States

From Isolation to Intervention

In the United States in 1940, news of the "Battle of Britain" competed with speculation about whether FDR would break with tradition and run for an unprecedented third term. Not until the eve of the Democrats' July convention did he reveal that, given the world crisis, he would consent to a "draft" from his party. The Axis threat forced conservative anti-New Deal Democrats to accept both the third term and the nomination of ultraliberal Henry Wallace as vice president. Republicans bowed to the public mood by nominating Wendell Willkie of Indiana, an all-out internationalist who championed greater aid to Britain.

Roosevelt adroitly played the role of a national leader too busy with defense and diplomacy to engage in partisan politics. He appointed Republicans Henry Stimson and Frank Knox as secretaries of war and the navy. Roosevelt approved a peacetime draft and a dramatic increase in defense funding. In September he engineered a "destroyers-for-bases" swap with England, sending fifty vintage American ships to Britain in exchange for leases on British air and naval bases in the Western Hemisphere.

Anti-interventionist critics accused Roosevelt of scheming to entangle the United States in the European conflict. Isolationists organized the Committee to Defend America First, which featured Charles Lindbergh as its most popular speaker and proclaimed that "Fortress America" could stand alone. Most Americans supported Roosevelt's attempt to aid Britain while avoiding war. Heartened by FDR's pledge—"I will never send an American boy to fight in a foreign war"—55 percent of Americans voted him into a third term.

Roosevelt now called on the United States to become "the arsenal of democracy." He proposed a **"lend-lease"** program to supply war materiel to the cash-strapped British. Despite bitter opposition by the isolationists, Congress approved lend-lease in March 1941, and supplies began to flow across the Atlantic. When Hitler's armies invaded the Soviet Union in June 1941, FDR dispatched supplies to the Soviets, despite American hostility toward communism. To defeat Hitler, FDR said, "I would hold hands with the Devil."

"lend lease" Program to "loan" war materiel to allies to avoid Neutrality Acts

To counter the menace of German submarines that threatened to choke the transatlantic supply line, Roosevelt authorized the U.S. Navy to help the British track U-boats. By summer 1941, the U.S. Navy had begun convoying British ships, with orders to destroy enemy ships if necessary. U.S. forces also occupied Greenland and Iceland to keep them out of Nazi hands.

In August, Roosevelt met with Churchill aboard a warship off Newfoundland. They issued a document, the **Atlantic Charter,** that condemned aggression, affirmed national self-determination, and endorsed the principles of collective security and disarmament. After a German submarine fired at an American destroyer in September, Roosevelt authorized naval patrols to shoot on sight all Axis vessels operating in the western Atlantic. On October 31, 1941, a U-boat torpedoed and sank the destroyer *Reuben James*, killing 115 American sailors.

Atlantic Charter World War II equivalent of Wilson's Fourteen Points; signed by FDR and Churchill

Now on a collision course with Germany, Roosevelt persuaded Congress in November to permit the arming of merchant ships and to allow the transport of lend-lease supplies to belligerent ports in war zones. Unprepared for a major war, America was nevertheless fighting a limited one, and full-scale war seemed imminent.

Pearl Harbor and the Coming of War

Hitler's triumphs in western Europe encouraged Japan to expand farther into Asia. The United States opposed Japanese expansion virtually alone. Seeing Germany as America's primary threat, the Roosevelt administration tried to apply enough pressure to deter the Japanese without provoking Tokyo to war before the United States had built the "two-ocean navy" authorized by Congress in 1940.

The Japanese, too, hoped to avoid war, but they would not compromise. Japan's desire to create the Greater East Asia Co-Prosperity Sphere (an empire embracing much of China, Southeast Asia, and the western Pacific) matched America's insistence on the Open Door in China and the status quo in the rest of Asia. Japan saw America's stand as a ploy to block its rise to power, and Americans viewed Japan's talk of legitimate national aspirations as a smoke screen to cloak aggression. Decades of "yellow-peril" propaganda had hardened U.S. attitudes toward Japan, and even those who were isolationist toward Europe tended to be interventionist toward Asia.

The two nations became locked in a deadly dance. In 1940, believing that economic coercion would force the Japanese out of China, the United States ended a long-standing trade treaty with Japan and banned the sale of aviation fuel and scrap metal to it. Tokyo responded by occupying northern Indochina, a French colony, and signing the Tripartite Pact with Germany and Italy in September, creating a military alliance, the Berlin-Rome-Tokyo Axis, that required each government to help the others in the event of a U.S. attack.

When the Japanese then overran the rest of Indochina, Roosevelt in 1941 froze all Japanese assets in the United States and clamped a total embargo on trade with Japan. Tokyo had two choices: submit to the United States to gain a resumption of trade or conquer new lands to obtain vital resources. In October, expansionist war minister General Hideki Tojo (hih-DEH-kee TOH-joh) became Japan's prime minister. Tojo set the first week in December as the deadline for a preemptive strike if the United States did not yield. By late November, U.S. intelligence's deciphering of Japan's top diplomatic code alerted the Roosevelt administration that war was imminent. Negotiators made no concessions during eleventh-hour negotiations under way in Washington. War warnings went out to all commanders in the Pacific, advising that negotiations were deadlocked and that a Japanese attack was imminent. U.S. officials believed that the Japanese would strike British or Dutch possessions or even the Philippines—but the Japanese decided to gamble on a knockout punch. They hoped that a surprise Japanese raid on the American naval base at Pearl Harbor would destroy the U.S. Pacific Fleet and compel Roosevelt, preoccupied with Germany, to seek accommodation with Japan.

Waves of Japanese dive-bombers and torpedo planes thundered across the Hawaiian island of Oahu on the morning of December 7, 1941, bombing ships at anchor in Pearl Harbor and strafing planes parked wingtip to wingtip at nearby air bases. American forces suffered their most devastating loss in history. In less than three hours, 8 battleships, 3 light cruisers, and 2 destroyers had been sunk or crippled, and 360 aircraft destroyed or damaged. The attack killed more than 2,400 Americans and opened the way for Japan's advance to the threshold of Australia in April 1942. Shocked Americans huddled by their radios to hear news of what President Roosevelt called a "date which will live in infamy."

Critics later charged that Roosevelt knew the attack on Pearl Harbor was coming and deliberately left the fleet exposed in order to bring the United States into the war against Germany. There is no conclusive evidence to support this accusation. Roosevelt and his advisers knew that war was close but did not expect an assault on Pearl Harbor. Americans underestimated the resourcefulness, skill, and daring of the Japanese. At the same time, Japanese leaders erred in counting on a paralyzing blow at Pearl Harbor. That miscalculation assured an aroused and united nation determined to avenge the attack.

On December 8, when Roosevelt asked Congress to declare war on Japan, only one dissenting vote was cast. But FDR still hesitated to request a declaration of war against Germany. Hitler resolved the president's dilemma. He went before a cheering Reichstag (RYKH-shtag) on December 11 to declare war on the "half Judaized and the other half Negrified" Americans. Mussolini chimed in with his declaration of war, and Congress reciprocated that same afternoon. America faced a global war that it was not yet ready to fight.

After Pearl Harbor, U-boats wreaked havoc in the North Atlantic and prowled the Caribbean and the East Coast of the United States. Every twenty-four hours, five more Allied vessels went to the bottom. By the end of 1942, U-boat "wolf packs" had destroyed more than a thousand Allied ships, offsetting the pace of American ship production. The United States was losing the battle of the Atlantic.

The war news from Europe and Africa was, as Roosevelt admitted, "all bad." Hitler's rule covered an enormous swath of territory, from the outskirts of Moscow, deep in Russia, to the Pyrenees (PEER-eh-nees) on the French-Spanish border, and from northern Norway to the Libyan (LIB-ee-un) desert. In spring 1942, Nazi armies inflicted more than 250,000 casualties on the Soviet army in Crimea (cry-MEE-uh), and Hitler launched a powerful offensive to seize the Caucasian oil fields. German forces moved relentlessly eastward in North Africa, threatening the Suez (soo-EZ) Canal, Britain's oil lifeline.

The Japanese inflicted defeat after defeat on Allied Pacific forces. Tojo followed Pearl Harbor with a rampage across the Pacific that put Guam, Wake Island, Hong Kong, Singapore, Burma, and the Netherlands East Indies under Japan's control by the end of April 1942. American forces in the Philippines, besieged for months on the island of Bataan, surrendered in May. Japan's rising sun flag blazed over hundreds of islands in the central and western Pacific, and over the entire eastern perimeter of the Asian mainland from the border of Siberia to the border of India.

> ### CHECKING IN
>
> - The war in Europe went badly for a defeated France and a battered Britain.
> - FDR stepped up the American response to the war with cash and carry, lend lease, and naval action against German U-boats.
> - Isolationism remained strong.
> - The Atlantic Charter summed up the Anglo-American vision of a harmonious postwar world.
> - Japanese aggression in Asia increased; it became clear war was imminent.
> - The Japanese attack on Pearl Harbor shocked Americans and drew the United States into the war.

▌ AMERICA MOBILIZES FOR WAR

How did war mobilization transform the American economy and government?

In December 1941 American armed forces numbered only 1.6 million, and war production accounted for just 15 percent of U.S. industrial output. Pearl Harbor changed everything. Within a week of the attack, Congress passed the War Powers

Act, granting the president unprecedented authority. Volunteers and draftees swelled the army and navy. By war's end, 15 million men and nearly 350,000 women had served. The far-reaching domestic changes under way would outlast the war and significantly alter the nation's attitudes, behavior, and institutions.

Organizing for Victory

To direct the military engine, Roosevelt formed the Joint Chiefs of Staff, made up of representatives of the army, navy, and army air force. The changing nature of modern warfare also led to the creation of the Office of Strategic Services (OSS), forerunner of the Central Intelligence Agency, to conduct the espionage required for strategic planning.

War Production Board Government agency that oversaw transition from peacetime to wartime economy

Roosevelt established the **War Production Board** (WPB) to allocate materials, to limit the production of civilian goods, and to distribute contracts. The newly created War Manpower Commission (WMC) supervised the mobilization of men and women for the military, war industry, and agriculture; the National War Labor Board (NWLB) mediated disputes between management and labor; and the **Office of Price Administration** (OPA) imposed strict price controls to check inflation.

Office of Price Administration Government agency that kept inflation down through rationing and strict price controls

In 1942 the United States achieved a miracle of war production. Car makers retooled to produce planes and tanks; a pinball-machine maker converted to armor-piercing shells. By late 1942, 33 percent of the economy was committed to war production. Whole new industries appeared virtually overnight. With almost all of the nation's crude-rubber supply now in Japanese-controlled territory, the government built some fifty new synthetic-rubber plants. By the end of the war, the United States had become the world's largest exporter of synthetic rubber.

America also became the world's greatest weapons manufacturer, producing more war materiel by 1945 than its Axis enemies combined—300,000 military aircraft, 86,000 tanks, 2.6 million machine guns, and 6 million tons of bombs. The United States built more than 5,000 cargo ships and 86,000 warships. Henry J. Kaiser (KYE-zer), who had supervised the construction of the Boulder Dam, introduced prefabrication to cut the time needed to build ships. In 1941 the construction of a Liberty-class merchant ship took six months; in 1943, less than two weeks. By 1945, Kaiser and other shipbuilders were completing a cargo ship every day.

Such breakneck production had costs. The size and powers of the government expanded as defense spending zoomed from 9 percent of gross national product (GNP) in 1940 to 46 percent in 1945; the federal budget soared from $9 billion to $98 billion. Federal civilian employees mushroomed from 1.1 million to 3.8 million. An alliance formed between the defense industry and the military. Because the government sought the maximum production in the shortest time, it encouraged corporate profits. Two-thirds of all war production dollars went to the hundred largest firms, and trends toward economic concentration accelerated.

The War Economy

The United States spent more than $360 billion ($250 million a day) to defeat the Axis, ten times the cost of World War I. Wartime spending and the draft not only vanquished unemployment, but also stimulated an industrial boom that made most

Americans prosper. It doubled U.S. industrial output and the per capita GNP, created 17 million new jobs, increased corporate after-tax profits by 70 percent, and raised the real wages or purchasing power of industrial workers by 50 percent.

The federal government poured $40 billion into the West, making it an economic powerhouse, the center of massive aircraft and shipbuilding industries. California alone secured more than 10 percent of all federal funds; by 1945 nearly half the personal income in the state came from the federal government.

A dynamic Sun Belt, stretching from the coastal Southeast to the coastal Southwest, was the recipient of billions spent on military bases and the needs of the armed forces. Full employment, a longer workweek, larger paychecks, and the increased hiring of minorities, women, and the elderly brought a middle-class standard of living to millions of families. The war years produced the only significant shift toward greater equality in the distribution of income in the twentieth century.

Large-scale commercial farmers prospered, benefiting from higher consumer prices and increased productivity thanks to improved fertilizers and more mechanization. As sharecroppers, tenants, and small farmers left the land for better-paying industrial jobs, the overall agricultural population fell by 17 percent. Farming became "agribusiness," and organized agriculture wielded power equal to organized labor, big government, and big business.

Organized labor grew mightier as union membership rose from 9 million to 14.8 million workers, in part because of the expansion of the labor force. Although the National War Labor Board attempted to limit wage increases to restrain inflation, unions negotiated unprecedented fringe benefits for workers, including paid vacation time and health and pension plans. As most workers honored the "no-strike" pledge that they had given immediately after Pearl Harbor, less than one-tenth of 1 percent of wartime working time was lost to strikes.

Far more than strikes, inflation threatened the wartime economy. The OPA constantly battled inflation, which was fueled by greater spending power combined with a scarcity of goods. Throughout 1942 prices climbed at a 2-percent-per-month clip, but at the year's end, Congress gave the president authority to freeze wages, prices, and rents. As the OPA clamped down, inflation slowed dramatically: consumer prices went up only 8 percent in the war's last two years.

The OPA also instituted rationing to combat inflation and to conserve scarce materials. Under the slogan "Use it up, wear it out, make it do, or do without," the OPA rationed such products as gasoline, sugar, cheese, and meat. Most Americans cheerfully formed car pools, planted victory gardens, and recycled paper, fats, and scrap metal.

Buying war bonds further curtailed inflation by decreasing consumer purchasing power, while giving civilians a sense of involvement in the distant war. Small investors bought $40 billion in "E" bonds, and wealthy individuals and corporations invested nearly twice that amount. Bond sales raised almost half the money needed to finance the war. Roosevelt sought to raise the rest by drastically increasing taxes. Congress refused the president much of what he sought. Still, the Revenue Act of 1942 raised the top income-tax rate from 60 percent to 94 percent and imposed income taxes on middle-and lower-income Americans for the first time. Beginning in 1943, the payroll-deduction system automatically withheld income taxes from wages and salaries.

"A Wizard War"

Recognizing wartime scientific and technological developments, Winston Churchill dubbed World War II "a wizard war." Mathematicians went to work deciphering enemy codes, psychologists devised propaganda, and, as never before, the major combatants mobilized scientists into virtual armies of invention. In 1941 FDR created the Office of Scientific Research and Development (OSRD) for the development of new weapons and medicines. The OSRD spent more than $1 billion to produce improved radar and sonar, rocket weapons, and proximity fuses for mines and artillery shells. It also funded the development of jet aircraft and high-altitude bombsights. Other OSRD research hastened the widespread use of insecticides, contributed to improved blood transfusions, and produced "miracle drugs," such as penicillin.

The demand for greater accuracy in artillery required the kind of rapid, detailed calculations that only computing machines could supply. By 1944 navy personnel in the basement of Harvard's physics laboratory were operating IBM's Mark I, a cumbersome device fifty-one feet long and eight feet high that weighed five tons. A second-generation computer, ENIAC, soon reduced the time to multiply two tenth-place numbers from Mark I's three seconds to less than three-thousandths of a second.

Nothing saved the lives of more wounded servicemen than improvements in battlefield medical care. Military needs led to advances in heart and lung surgery, and to the use of synthetic antimalarial drugs to substitute for scarce quinine. So-called miracle drugs, antibiotics to combat infections, a rarity on the eve of war, would be copiously produced. The use of DDT cleared many islands of malaria-carrying mosquitoes. Along with innovations like the Mobile Auxiliary Surgical Hospital (MASH), science helped save tens of thousands of soldiers' lives and improved the health of the nation as well. Life expectancy rose by three years during the war.

The atomic bomb project began in August 1939 when Albert Einstein, a Jewish refugee and Nobel Prize-winning physicist, warned Roosevelt that Nazi scientists were seeking to use atomic physics to construct an extraordinarily destructive weapon. In 1941 FDR launched a massive Anglo-American secret program—the Soviets were excluded—to construct an atomic bomb. The next year, the participating physicists, both Americans and Europeans, achieved a controlled chain reaction and acquired the basic knowledge necessary to develop the bomb. By July 1945 this program, code-named the **Manhattan Project,** had employed more than 120,000 people and spent nearly $2 billion.

Manhattan Project Code name for program to develop the atomic bomb

Just before dawn on July 16, 1945, a blinding fireball with "the brightness of several suns at midday" rose over the desert at Alamogordo, New Mexico, followed by a billowing mushroom cloud. Equivalent to twenty thousand tons of TNT, the blast from this first atomic explosion was felt a hundred miles away. The atomic age had dawned.

Propaganda and Politics

People as well as science and machinery had to be mobilized. To sustain a spirit of unity, the Roosevelt administration carefully managed public opinion. The Office of Censorship, established in December 1941, examined all letters going overseas and worked with publishers and broadcasters to suppress information that might damage the war effort, such as details of troop movements.

To shape public opinion, FDR created the Office of War Information (OWI) in June 1942. The OWI employed more than four thousand writers, artists, and advertising specialists to explain the war and to counter enemy propaganda. The OWI depicted the war as a moral struggle between good and evil—the enemy had to be destroyed, not merely defeated. Hollywood films highlighted the heroism and unity of the American forces, while inciting hatred of the enemy. Films about the war portrayed the Japanese, in particular, as treacherous and cruel, as beasts in the jungle, as "slant-eyed rats."

While the Roosevelt administration concentrated on the war, Republican critics seized the initiative in domestic politics. Full employment and high wages undermined the Democrats' class appeal, and many of the urban and working-class voters essential to the Roosevelt coalition were serving in the armed forces and did not vote in the 1942 elections. As Republicans gained nine seats in the Senate and forty-six in the House, conservative Republicans and southern Democrats held the power to make or break legislation. Resentful of the wartime expansion of executive authority and determined to curb labor unions and welfare spending, the conservatives abolished the CCC and the WPA, and rebuffed attempts to extend the New Deal.

Despite the strength of the conservative coalition, the war expanded governmental and executive power enormously. As never before, Washington managed the economy, molded public opinion, funded scientific research, and influenced people's daily lives.

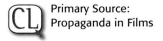

Primary Source: Propaganda in Films

CHECKING IN

- Industrial mobilization was key to Allied victory, and the United States achieved a miracle of war production.
- Wartime spending lifted the U.S. out of the Great Depression.
- Government intervened in the economy to direct production and control inflation.
- Science and technology played a major role in the war effort, with the development of radar, sonar, the first computers, and the atomic bomb.
- The war greatly increased government power in shaping public opinion.

THE BATTLEFRONT, 1942–1944

What were the major aspects of Allied military strategy in Europe and Asia?

America's industrial might and Soviet manpower turned the tide of war. Diplomacy followed the fortunes of war, with Allied unity gradually diminishing as Germany and Japan weakened, and as the United States, Britain, and the Soviet Union each sought wartime strategies and postwar arrangements best suited to its own interests.

Liberating Europe

After Pearl Harbor, British and American officials agreed to concentrate first on defeating Germany and then on smashing Japan. But they differed on where to mount an attack. **Joseph Stalin** demanded a second front, an invasion of western Europe to force Hitler to transfer troops west and thus to relieve pressure on the Russians, who faced the full fury of the Nazi armies. Prime Minister Churchill insisted on clearing the Mediterranean before invading France. He feared that a premature landing in France could mean slaughter, and he wanted American aid in North Africa to protect the Suez Canal, vital to the British. Over Soviet protests, Churchill persuaded Roosevelt to postpone the "second front" in western Europe and to invade North Africa instead. In November 1942, in Operation Torch, American and British troops

Joseph Stalin Dictator of Soviet Union

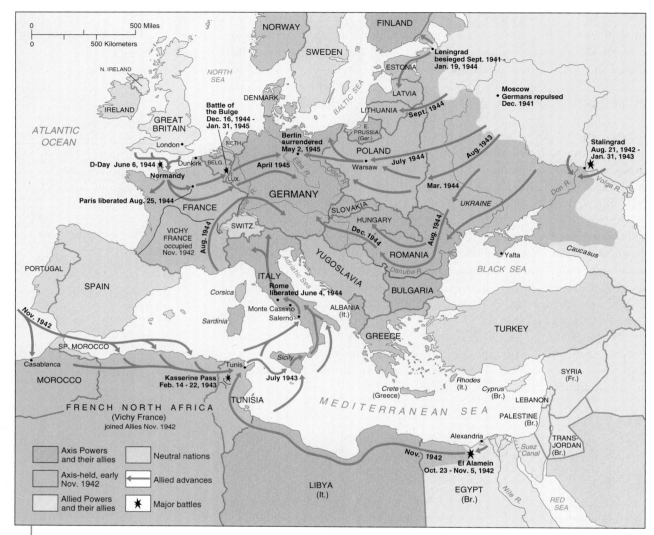

Map 25.1   World War II in Europe and Africa

The momentous German defeats at Stalingrad and in Tunisia early in 1943 marked the turning point in the war against the Axis. By 1945 the Allied conquest of Hitler's "thousand year" Reich was imminent.

under General Dwight D. Eisenhower landed in Morocco and Algeria. Pushing eastward, they trapped the German and Italian armies being driven westward by the British, and in May 1943 some 260,000 German-Italian troops surrendered.

Left alone to face two-thirds of the Nazi force, the Soviet Union hung on and, in the turning point of the European war, defeated Germany in the protracted Battle of Stalingrad (STALL-in-grahd) (August 1942–January 1943). After destroying an entire German army—more than 600,000 men—at Stalingrad, the Red Army went on the offensive along a thousand-mile front (see Map 25.1). Stalingrad cost the Soviet Union more battle deaths in four months than the United States suffered in the entire war.

Although Stalin renewed his plea for a second front, Churchill again objected, and Roosevelt again agreed to a British plan: the invasion of Sicily. In summer 1943 Anglo-American forces gained control of Sicily in less than a month. Italian military leaders deposed Mussolini and surrendered to the Allies on September 8. As Allied forces moved up the Italian peninsula, German troops poured into Italy. Facing elite Nazi divisions in strong defensive positions, the Allies spent eight months inching their way 150 miles to Rome and were still battling through northern Italy when the war in Europe ended.

In 1943 and 1944 the United States and Britain turned the tide in the Atlantic and sent thousands of bombers over Germany. To the east, Soviet troops kept the Nazis in retreat. At the start of 1943, British and American air forces began round-the-clock bombardment, raining thousands of tons of bombs on German cities. In raids on Hamburg (HAHM-boorg) in July 1943, Allied planes dropping incendiary bombs created terrible firestorms, killing at least 35,000 people and leveling the city, much as they had done earlier at Cologne (koh-LOHN) and would do to Dresden in February 1945, where an estimated 60,000 people died.

Meanwhile, in 1943, as the Soviet offensive reclaimed Russian cities and towns from the Nazis, the German armies fell into perpetual retreat. Advancing swiftly, the Red Army drove the Germans out of Soviet territory by mid-1944 and plunged into Poland, where the Soviets set up a puppet government. Late summer and early fall saw Soviet troops seize Romania and Bulgaria and aid communist guerilas under Josip Broz Tito (TEE-toh) in liberating Yugoslavia.

As the Soviets swept across eastern Europe, Allied forces finally opened the long-delayed second front. On June 6, 1944—D-Day—nearly 200,000 Allied troops landed in Normandy in northwestern France, gaining a toehold on French soil. Within six weeks, another million Allied troops had waded ashore. Under General Eisenhower, the Allies liberated Paris in August and reached the German border by the end of summer. However, in the face of supply problems and stiffened German resistance, the Allied offensive ground to a halt.

In mid-December, as the Allies prepared for a full-scale assault on the German heartland, Hitler in a desperate gamble threw his last reserves against American positions. The **Battle of the Bulge**—named for the "bulge" eighty miles long and fifty miles wide that Hitler's troops drove into the Allies' line—raged for nearly a month, and when it ended American troops stood on the banks of the Rhine. It had cost the United States 55,000 soldiers dead or wounded and 18,000 taken prisoner. But the way to Germany lay open, and the end of the European war was in sight.

▌**Battle of the Bulge** Desperate German counteroffensive; launched December 1944; failed to stop the Allied advance into Germany

War in the Pacific

The day after the Philippines fell to Japan in mid-May 1942, U.S. and Japanese fleets confronted each other in the Coral Sea off northeastern Australia, the first naval battle in history fought entirely from aircraft carriers. Both sides took heavy losses, but the Battle of the Coral Sea stopped the Japanese advance on Australia. Less than a month later, a Japanese armada turned toward Midway Island, the crucial American outpost between Hawaii and Japan. Because the U.S. Signal Corps had broken the Japanese naval code, Japan's plans and the locations of her ships were known. American carriers and their planes consequently won a decisive victory, sinking four

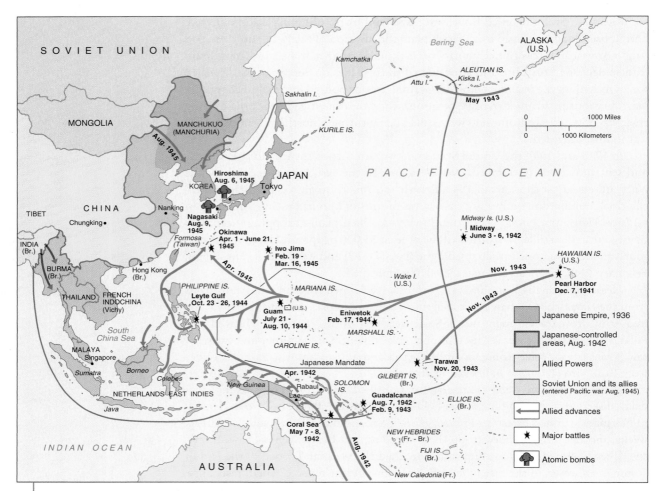

Map 25.2   World War II in the Pacific

American ships and planes stemmed the Japanese offensive at the Battles of the Coral Sea and Midway Island. Thereafter, the Japanese were on the defensive against American amphibious assaults and air strikes.

Japanese carriers and destroying several hundred enemy planes. Suddenly on the defensive, the stunned Japanese could now only try to hold what they had already won.

On the offensive, U.S. marines waded ashore at Guadalcanal in the Solomon Islands in August 1942. Facing fierce resistance as well as tropical diseases like malaria, the Americans needed six months to take the island, a bitter preview of the battles to come. As the British moved from India to retake Burma, the United States began a two-pronged advance toward Japan in 1943. The army, under General Douglas MacArthur, advanced north on the islands between Australia and the Philippines, and the navy and marines, under Admiral Chester Nimitz, "island-hopped" across the central Pacific to seize strategic bases and put Tokyo in range of American bombers. In fall 1944 the navy annihilated what remained of the Japanese fleet at the battles of the Philippine Sea and Leyte Gulf, giving the United States control of Japan's air and shipping lanes and leaving the Japanese home islands open to invasion (see Map 25.2).

The Grand Alliance

Two primary goals underlay Roosevelt's wartime strategies: the total defeat of the Axis at the least possible cost in American lives and the establishment of a world order strong enough to preserve peace, open trade, and ensure national self-determination in the postwar era.

But Churchill and Stalin had other goals. Britain sought to retain its imperial possessions and a balance of power against the Soviet Union in Europe. The Soviet Union wanted a permanently weakened Germany and a sphere of influence in eastern Europe to protect itself against future attacks from the West. To hold together this uneasy alliance, FDR used personal diplomacy to mediate conflicts.

In January 1943 Roosevelt and Churchill met at Casablanca, Morocco's main port, where they resolved to attack Italy before invading France and proclaimed that the war would continue until the Axis accepted "unconditional surrender." In this proclamation they sought to reduce Soviet mistrust of the West, which had deepened because of the postponement of the second front.

In 1943 FDR and Churchill had traveled to Tehran, Iran's capital, to confer with Stalin. Here they had set the invasion of France for June 1944 and agreed to divide Germany into zones of occupation and to impose reparations on the Reich. Most important to Roosevelt, at Tehran Stalin had also pledged to enter the Pacific war after Hitler's defeat.

Roosevelt then turned his attention to domestic politics. Conservative gains in both the Republican and the Democratic parties drove FDR to dump the liberal Henry A. Wallace from the ticket and accept Harry S Truman as his vice presidential candidate. A moderate senator from Missouri, Truman was not strongly opposed by any major Democratic faction and was called "the new Missouri Compromise." He restored a semblance of unity to the party for the 1944 campaign. The Republicans, hoping that unity would carry *them* to victory, nominated moderate New York governor Thomas E. Dewey. The campaign focused more on personalities than on issues, with the Republicans harping on FDR's failing health and FDR touting American military victories.

In November the American electorate handed FDR an unprecedented fourth term, but with his narrowest margin ever—only 53 percent of the popular vote. A weary Roosevelt, secretly suffering from hypertension and heart disease, now directed his waning energies toward defeating the Axis and constructing an international peacekeeping system.

CHECKING IN

- The Anglo-American decision to invade North Africa meant that Russia would remain the only battlefront in Europe, where the Soviet victory at Stalingrad was the turning point in the war.

- On D-Day, June 6, 1944, the Allies launched a cross-channel invasion into France; their offensive stalled until American victory in the Battle of the Bulge in late 1944 opened the path to victory.

- Americans went on the offensive in the Pacific in August 1942, relying primarily on island-hopping and carriers; by late 1944, American forces were poised at the fringe of the Japanese home islands

- Despite their alliance, the United States, Great Britain, and the Soviet Union had very different war goals.

▌WAR AND AMERICAN SOCIETY

What were the major effects of World War II on American society, including minorities and women?

The crisis of war altered the most basic patterns of American life, powerfully affecting those on the home front as well as those who served in the armed forces. Few families were untouched: more than 15 million Americans went to war, an equal number were on the move, and unprecedented numbers of women went to work outside the home. Also, the war opened some doors of opportunity for African-Americans and other minorities, although most remained closed.

The GIs' War

Most Americans in the armed forces griped about regimentation and were more interested in dry socks than in ideology. They knew little of the big strategies and cared less. They wanted to defeat Hitler, avenge Pearl Harbor, and return to a secure, familiar United States.

But the GIs' war dragged on for almost four years, transforming its participants. Millions who had never been far from home traveled to unfamiliar cities and remote lands. Sharing tents and foxholes with fellow Americans of different religions, nationalities, and social backgrounds helped to erase deep-seated prejudices.

Physical misery, chronic exhaustion, and intense combat left psychological as well as physical wounds. In the Pacific, both American and Japanese troops saw the others in racist terms, as animals to be exterminated. Both sides sometimes behaved brutally, machine-gunning pilots parachuting from damaged planes, torturing and killing prisoners, and mutilating enemy dead. Atrocities also occurred in the war against Germany, although on a lesser scale. A battalion of the Second Armored Division calling itself "Roosevelt's Butchers" boasted that it shot all the German soldiers it captured.

The Home Front

Nothing transformed the social topography more than the vast internal migration of an already-mobile people. Americans swarmed to the centers of war production, especially the Pacific coast states, which manufactured half of the nation's wartime ships and airplanes. Six million people left farms to work in cities, and several million southern whites and blacks migrated northward and westward.

Lifestyles became freewheeling as Americans moved far from their hometowns, leaving behind their traditional values. Housing shortages left millions living in converted garages, tent cities, or cars. Overcrowding as well as wartime separations strained family and community life. High rates of divorce, family violence, and juvenile delinquency reflected the disruptions.

Reversing a decade of efforts to exclude women from the labor force, the federal government in 1942 urged women into war production. More than 6 million women entered the labor force during the war, bringing the number of employed women to 19 million. Less than a quarter of the labor force in 1940, women constituted well over a third of all workers in 1945.

Before the war most female wage earners had been young and single. By contrast, 75 percent of the new women workers were married, 60 percent were over thirty-five, and more than 33 percent had children under the age of fourteen. Women tended blast furnaces, operated cranes, drove taxis, and worked in shipyards. **"Rosie the Riveter,"** her muscular arms cradling a gun, symbolized the woman war worker; she was, as a popular song put it, "making history working for victory."

Yet traditional attitudes and gender discrimination existed throughout the war. Women earned only about 65 percent of what men earned for the same work, and they were often denied equal seniority rights. Labor unions often stipulated that women had to give up their jobs to men on their return from military service, and government propaganda portrayed women's war work as a temporary response to an emergency. "A woman is a substitute," asserted a War Department brochure, "like

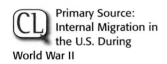

Primary Source: Internal Migration in the U.S. During World War II

"Rosie the Riveter" Symbol of women who assumed what had been "men's work" in war industries

plastic instead of metal." Traditional notions about a woman's place also shaped government resistance to establishing child-care centers for women employed in defense. "A mother's primary duty is to her home and children," the Labor Department's Children's Bureau stated. Funds for federal child-care centers covered few defense workers' children, and the young suffered. New terms, such as *eight-hour orphans* and *latchkey children,* described children forced to fend for themselves. Feeding the fears of those who believed that having women work outside the home would cause the family to disintegrate, juvenile delinquency increased fivefold, and the divorce rate nearly doubled.

The impact of war on women and children was multifaceted and even contradictory. Divorce rates soared, but so did marriage rates and birthrates. Three hundred and fifty thousand women joined the armed forces and for the first time served in positions there other than nurse. Female workers gained unprecedented employment opportunities and public recognition. Although many eagerly gave up their jobs at the end of the war, just as many did not relish losing their income and newfound independence. Overall, the war gave women a new sense of their potential. Most women still hoped to be wives and mothers, but the war had widened women's worlds and challenged traditional notions as nothing before ever had.

The loss of students to the armed services and war production forced colleges to admit large numbers of women and to contract themselves out to the military. Military training programs sent nearly a million servicemen and women to college campuses to acquire skills in engineering, foreign languages, economics, and the sciences. Higher education became more dependent on the federal government, and universities competed for federal contracts and subsidies.

The war profoundly affected American culture. Spending on books and theater entertainment more than doubled. More than 60 million people (in a population of 135 million) attended movies weekly. Hollywood turned out a spate of war films that reinforced the image of Nazis and Japanese as fiends, portrayed GIs as freedom-loving heroes, and intensified Americans' appetite for unconditional victory. But as the war dragged on, people tired of propaganda, and Hollywood reemphasized romance and adventure.

Early in the war, popular music featured patriotic themes. "Goodbye Mama, I'm Off to Yokohama" was the first hit of 1942. As the war continued, themes of lost love and loneliness dominated songs. By 1945 bitterness pervaded the lyrics of bestselling records, and such hits as "Saturday Night Is the Loneliest Night of the Week" revealed an impatience for the war's end.

Rosie the Riveter
Memorialized in song and story, "Rosie the Riveter" symbolized the women war workers who assumed jobs in heavy industry to take up the slack for the absent 15 million men in the armed services. Here a very real Rosie the Riveter is doing her job in April 1943 at the Baltimore manufacturing plant for Martin PMB Mariners.

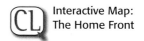 Interactive Map: The Home Front

In bookstores, nonfiction crowded the shelves, and every newsmagazine increased its circulation. Wendell Willkie's *One World* (1943) became the fastest-selling title in publishing history to that time, with 2 million copies snapped up in two years. A vision of a world without military alliances and spheres of influence, this brief volume expressed hope that an international organization would extend peace and democracy through the postwar world.

Americans also stayed glued to their radios during the war. The quest for up-to-date information kept radio audiences at record levels. Networks increased their news programs from 4 percent to nearly 40 percent of their daily schedule. Daytime serials, like those featuring Dick Tracy tracking down Axis spies, reached the height of their popularity; a platoon of new comic book superheroes, including Captain America and Captain Marvel, saw action on the battlefield. Even Bugs Bunny put on a uniform to combat America's foes.

Racism and New Opportunities

Realizing that the government needed the loyalty and work of a united people to win the war, African-American leaders saw new pathways to securing equal rights. In 1942 civil-rights spokesmen insisted that African-American support of the war hinged on the United States' commitment to racial justice. They demanded a double campaign: to gain victory over racial discrimination at home as well as over the Axis abroad.

Membership in the National Association for the Advancement of Colored People multiplied nearly ten times, reaching 500,000 in 1945. The association pressed for anti-poll tax and antilynching legislation, decried discrimination in defense industries and the armed services, and sought to end African-American disfranchisement. The campaign for black voting rights gained momentum when the Supreme Court, in *Smith* v. *Allwright* (1944), ruled Texas's all-white primary unconstitutional. This decision eliminated a barrier that had existed in eight states, although these states promptly resorted to other devices to minimize African-American voting.

A new civil-rights organization, the Congress of Racial Equality (CORE), was founded in 1942. Employing the strategy of nonviolent resistance to challenge Jim Crow, CORE sought to desegregate public facilities in northern cities. Also proposing nonviolent direct action was **A. Philip Randolph,** president of the Brotherhood of Sleeping Car Porters. In 1941 Randolph called for a "thundering march" of 100,000 blacks on Washington "to wake up and shock white America." He had warned Roosevelt that, if the president did not abolish discrimination in the armed services and the defense industry, African-Americans would besiege the nation's capital. FDR agreed to compromise, and in June 1941 issued Executive Order 8802, the first presidential directive on race since Reconstruction. It prohibited discriminatory employment practices by federal agencies and all unions and companies engaged in war-related work and established the Fair Employment Practices Commission (FEPC) to enforce this policy. Although the FEPC did not apply to the armed forces and lacked effective enforcement powers, soaring war production and a shrinking labor pool resulted in the employment of 2 million African-Americans in industry and 200,000 in the federal civil service. African-American membership in labor unions doubled, and the number of skilled and semiskilled African-American work-

A. Philip Randolph Labor leader whose threatened march on Washington led to the creation of the Fair Employment Practices Commission (FEPC)

ers tripled. Average earnings for blacks increased from $457 to $1,976 a year, compared to $2,600 for whites.

About 1 million African-Americans served in the armed forces. Wartime needs forced the military to end policies of excluding blacks from combat units. The all-black 761st Tank Battalion gained distinction fighting in Germany, and the 99th Pursuit Squadron won eighty Distinguished Flying Crosses in combat against the Luftwaffe. Although the army and navy began experiments with integration in 1944, most blacks served in segregated units under white officers. The failure of military authorities to protect African-American servicemen off the post and the use of white military police to keep African-Americans "in their place" sparked conflict on many army bases. At least fifty African-American soldiers died in wartime racial encounters in the United States.

Violence within the military mirrored growing racial tensions at home. As African-Americans militantly protested against discrimination, many whites resisted all efforts by blacks to improve their economic and social status. Numerous clashes occurred. In mid-1943 scores of cities reported pitched battles between whites and African-Americans. The bloodiest race riot exploded in Detroit that June. By its end, twenty-five blacks and nine whites lay dead, more than seven hundred had been injured, and more than $2 million in property had been destroyed.

Yet the war brought significant changes that would eventually result in a successful drive for black civil rights. The migration of over seven hundred thousand blacks from the South turned a southern problem into a national concern. Despite the continuation of racial discrimination, most who left the rural South found a more abundant and hopeful life than the one they had left behind. As the growing numbers of blacks in northern cities began to vote, moreover, African-Americans could hold a balance of power in close elections. This prompted politicians in both major parties to pay more attention to civil-rights issues.

In addition, the horrors of Nazi racism discredited America's own white supremacist attitudes. A former governor of Alabama complained, Nazism has "wrecked the theories of the master race with which we were so contented so long." A pluralist vision of American society now became part of official rhetoric, and of the liberal-left agenda. In a massive study of race problems entitled *An American Dilemma* (1944), Swedish economist Gunnar Myrdal concluded that "not since Reconstruction had there been more reason to anticipate fundamental changes in American race relations." Returning black veterans, and African-Americans who had served the nation on the home front, resolved as never before to gain all the rights enjoyed by whites.

War and Diversity   Wartime winds of change brought new opportunities, and problems, to other American minorities. Twenty-five thousand Native Americans served in the armed forces, including Navajo "code-talkers" who confounded the Japanese by relaying secret messages in an unbreakable code based on their native tongue. Another fifty thousand Indians left reservations to work in defense. For most, it was the first experience of living in a non-Indian world, and after the war some would remain in the cities. Continued discrimination, however, would force a majority back to their reservations, which suffered severely from budget cuts during the war and the immediate postwar years.

braceros "Guest workers"; Mexican laborers legally brought into United States

To relieve agricultural labor shortages, the federal government negotiated an agreement with Mexico to import temporary workers called **braceros** (brah-SARE-ohs). Classified as foreign workers, not immigrants, an estimated 200,000 *braceros* received short-term contracts. Farm owners frequently violated these contracts and also encouraged an influx of illegal immigrants.

Unable to complain about prejudice and the way they were treated without risking deportation, hundreds of thousands of Mexicans were exploited by Anglo planters and ranchers. At the same time, large numbers of Mexicans and Mexican-Americans moved to Los Angeles, Chicago, and other large cities, where they found jobs in garment factories, shipyards, and steel mills. Even as their occupational status and material conditions improved, most Mexican-Americans remained in segregated communities. Much of the hostility toward Mexican-Americans focused on young gang members who wore broad-shouldered jackets called "zoot suits." After a summer of concern about the so-called "Mexican Crime Wave," bands of sailors from nearby bases and soldiers on leave in Los Angeles rampaged through the city in early June 1943, stripping Chicano youth wearing zoot suits, cutting their long hair, and beating them. Military authorities looked the other way. City police intervened only to arrest Mexican-Americans.

In the military itself, Spanish-speaking Americans, like blacks, suffered discrimination. Nevertheless, nearly 350,000 Chicanos served in the armed forces, earning a disproportionate number of citations for distinguished service and Congressional Medals of Honor. And much like black and Indian veterans, Mexican-American veterans organized new groups to press for equal rights.

Thousands of gay men and lesbians who served in the armed forces also found new wartime opportunities. Like other minorities, many gays saw the war as a chance to prove their worth under fire. Yet some suspected of being gay were dishonorably discharged, sent to psychiatric hospitals, or imprisoned in so-called queer stockades. In 1945, gay veterans established the Veteran's Benevolent Association, the first organization in the United States to combat discrimination against homosexuals.

internment of Japanese-Americans Wartime policy to evacuate from West Coast and incarcerate all those with Japanese heritage, U.S. citizens included

The Internment of Japanese-Americans

Far more than any other minority in the United States, Japanese suffered grievously during the war. The internment of 112,000 Japanese-Americans, two-thirds of them native-born U.S. citizens, in relocation centers guarded by military police, was a tragic reminder of the fragility of civil liberties in wartime.

The **internment of Japanese-Americans** policy reflected forty years of anti-Japanese sentiment on the West Coast, rooted in racial prejudice and economic rivalry. Self-serving politicians and farmers who wanted Japanese-American land had long decried the "yellow peril," and after the attack on Pearl Harbor they whipped up the rage and fears of many white Californians. In February 1942 Roosevelt gave in to the pressure and authorized the evacuation of all Japanese-Americans from the West Coast, despite the fact that not a single Japanese-American had been apprehended for espionage or sedition and neither the Federal Bureau of Investigation nor military intelligence had uncovered any disloyal behavior by Japanese-Americans.

Interestingly, only Japanese-Americans on the mainland fell victim to the internment policy. The Hawaiian Islands were home to approximately 160,000 people

A Japanese-American Child Being Evacuated from Los Angeles in April 1942

It did not matter that she, along with some 80,000 other Nisei, were American citizens. "A Jap's a Jap," said General John De Witt, commander of West Coast defenses.

of Japanese ancestry, one-third of the entire population. Nonetheless, despite the potential damage that saboteurs could have inflicted, Hawaiian officials maintained their tradition of interracial harmony. Hawaii's Japanese committed no acts of sabotage; indeed, many became "superpatriots" in order to honor their obligations to the United States.

But on the mainland, Japanese-Americans, forced to sell their lands and homes at whatever prices they could obtain, were herded into barbed-wire-encircled detention camps in desolate areas of the West. The Supreme Court, in *Korematsu* v. *United States* (1944), upheld the constitutionality of the evacuation, stating that it would not question government claims of military necessity during the war. By then, however, the hysteria had subsided, and the government had begun a program of gradual release. In 1982 a special government commission would formally blame the Roosevelt administration's action on "race prejudice, war hysteria, and a failure of political leadership" and would apologize to Japanese-Americans for "a grave injustice." In 1988 Congress voted to pay $20,000 as compensation to each of the nearly 60,000 Japanese-American internees still alive.

CHECKING IN

- War triggered internal migration, as people sought war industry jobs which, like the military, tossed together Americans of widely different backgrounds.
- Women entered the work force in large numbers but were seen as "temporary workers."
- African-Americans made significant gains and set the stage for the civil-rights drive after the war.
- To take advantage of wartime work, Indians left reservations, and Mexicans entered the United States under the *bracero* program.
- Japanese-Americans, interned in camps, were victims of prejudice and war hysteria.

▍TRIUMPH AND TRAGEDY, 1945

What new issues did the U.S. government confront in defeating Germany and Japan in 1945?

Spring and summer 1945 brought stunning changes. In Europe, the collapse of the Nazi Third Reich saw a new balance of power emerge. In Asia, continued Japanese resistance and reluctance to surrender led to the use of the atomic bomb. And in the United States, a new president, Harry Truman, presided over the end of World War II and the beginning of a new, "cold" war.

The Yalta Conference

By the time Roosevelt, Churchill, and Stalin met at the Soviet city of Yalta in February 1945, the military situation favored the Soviet Union. The Red Army had overrun Poland, Romania, and Bulgaria; helped drive the Nazis out of Yugoslavia; penetrated Austria, Hungary, and Czechoslovakia; and was massed only fifty miles from Berlin. American forces, in contrast, were still recovering from the Battle of the Bulge and faced stiff resistance en route to Japan. The Joint Chiefs of Staff, predicting that an invasion of Japan would cost 1 million American casualties, insisted that obtaining Stalin's help in Asia was worth almost any price.

Yalta accords 1945 agreements in which FDR made concessions to Stalin to induce him to join the Pacific war

The **Yalta accords** mirrored these realities. Stalin again promised to declare war on Japan "two or three months" after Germany's surrender, and in return Roosevelt and Churchill promised the Soviet Union concessions in Manchuria and the territories that Russia had lost in the Russo-Japanese War forty years before. Stalin accepted the temporary partitioning of Germany and the postponement of discussions about reparations. On the matter dearest to FDR's heart, Stalin approved plans for a United Nations conference to establish a permanent international organization for collective security.

Stalin, however, proved adamant about Soviet domination in eastern Europe, particularly Poland. Twice in the twentieth century, German troops had used Poland as a pathway for invading Russia. Stalin would not expose his land again, and after the Red Army had captured Warsaw in January 1945, he brutally subdued the noncommunist majority. Roosevelt and Churchill refused to recognize the communist Lublin regime, but they accepted Stalin's pledge to include noncommunist Poles in the new government and to allow free elections. They could do little else. Short of going to war against the Soviet Union while battling Germany and Japan, FDR could only hope that Stalin would keep his word.

Victory in Europe

Meanwhile, Allied armies closed the vise on Germany. In early March 1945, American troops captured Cologne and encircled Germany's industrial heartland. To counter the threat of Soviet power in postwar Europe, Churchill proposed a rapid thrust to Berlin, but Eisenhower, with Roosevelt's backing, overruled the British. Instead, to minimize their casualties and to reassure Stalin, the Americans advanced methodically on a broad front until they met the Russians at the Elbe River at the end of April. By then the Red Army had overrun Vienna and reached the suburbs of Berlin. On April 30 Hitler committed suicide in a bunker under the ruins of Berlin; the city fell to the Soviets on May 2. A hastily assembled German government surrendered unconditionally on May 8.

Jubilant Americans celebrated Victory in Europe (V-E) Day less than a month after they had mourned the death of FDR. On April 12 the exhausted president died of a cerebral hemorrhage. His unprepared successor inherited leadership of the most powerful nation in history—as well as troubles with the Soviet Union that seemed more intractable every day.

Harry S Truman had little familiarity with world affairs. Perhaps sensing his own inadequacies, he adopted a tough pose and counted on American military power to maintain the peace. In office less than two weeks, he lashed out at Soviet

Interactive Map: The Fall of the Third Reich

ambassador V. M. Molotov that the United States was tired of waiting for Moscow to allow free elections in Poland, and he threatened to cut off lend-lease aid if the Soviet Union did not cooperate. The Truman administration then reduced U.S. economic assistance to the Soviets and stalled on their request for a $1 billion reconstruction loan. Stalin consequently broke his Yalta promises and strengthened his control of eastern Europe.

The Truman administration neither conceded the Soviet sphere of influence in eastern Europe nor tried to end it. Truman still sought Stalin's cooperation in establishing the United Nations and in defeating Japan, but Soviet-American relations deteriorated rapidly. By June 1945, when the Allied countries framed the United Nations Charter in San Francisco, hopes for a peaceful new international order had dimmed, and the United Nations emerged as a diplomatic battleground. Truman, Churchill, and Stalin met at Potsdam, Germany, from July 16 to August 2, to complete the postwar arrangements begun at Yalta. Each trying to preserve and enlarge his nation's sphere of influence, the Allies could barely agree even to demilitarize Germany and to punish Nazi war criminals. All the major divisive issues were postponed. Given the diplomatic impasse, military power would determine the contours of the postwar world.

The Holocaust

When news of the **Holocaust** (HAWL-oh-cost)—the term later given to the Nazis' extermination of European Jewry—first leaked out in early 1942, many Americans discounted the reports. Not until November did the State Department admit knowledge of the massacres. A month later, the American broadcaster Edward R. Murrow, listened to nationwide, reported on the systematic killing of millions of Jews, "It is a picture of mass murder and moral depravity unequalled in the history of the world. It is a horror beyond what imagination can grasp. . . . There are no longer 'concentration camps'—we must speak now only of 'extermination camps.'"

Nevertheless, most Americans considered the annihilation of Europe's 6 million Jews beyond belief. There were no photographs to prove it, and, some argued, the atrocities attributed to the Germans in World War I had turned out to be false. So few people took issue with the military's view that the way to liberate those enslaved by Hitler was by speedily winning the war. Pleas by American Jews for the Allies to bomb the death camps and the railroad tracks leading to them fell on deaf ears. In fall 1944, U.S. planes flying over Auschwitz in southern Poland bombed nearby factories but left the gas chambers and crematoria intact, in order, American officials explained, not to divert air power from more vital raids elsewhere.

How much could have been done remains uncertain. Still, the U.S. government never seriously considered rescue schemes or searched for a way to curtail the Nazis' "final solution" to the "Jewish question." Its feeble response was due to its overwhelming focus on winning the war as quickly as possible, congressional and public fears of an influx of destitute Jews into the United States, Britain's wish to placate the Arabs by keeping Jewish settlers out of Palestine, and the fear of some Jewish-American leaders that pressing the issue would increase anti-Semitism at home. The War Refugee Board managed to save the lives of just 200,000 Jews and 20,000 non-Jews, but 6 million other Jews, about 75 percent of the European Jewish population,

Holocaust Extermination of 6 million Jews, 6 million others by Nazis in name of racial purity

Bergen-Belsen Concentration Camp

Entering Germany in 1945, American troops discovered the horrors that the Nazis had perpetrated on European Jews and others. Here, General Eisenhower and U.S. soldiers view the bodies of victims at Bergen-Belsen.

were gassed, shot, or incinerated, as were several million gypsies, communists, homosexuals, Polish Catholics, and others deemed unfit to live in the Third Reich.

"The things I saw beggar description," wrote General Eisenhower after visiting the first death camp liberated by the U.S. Army. He sent immediately for a delegation of congressional leaders and newspaper editors to make sure Americans would never forget the gas chambers and human ovens. Only after viewing the photographs and newsreels of corpses stacked like cordwood and living skeletons with their vacant, sunken eyes staring through barbed wire, did most Americans see that the Holocaust was no myth.

The Atomic Bombs

In the Pacific, the war with Japan ground on. Early in 1945, marines secured the tiny island of Iwo Jima (EE-woh JEE-muh), 700 miles from Japan, at the cost of 25,000 marine casualties. A month later, Americans landed on Okinawa (oh-kee-NAH-wah), a key staging area for the planned invasion of the Japanese home islands, only 350 miles distant. In nearly three months of ferocious combat, U.S. forces sustained 40,000 casualties, whereas more than 110,000 Japanese military died and Japanese civilians took 80,000 casualties.

If the capture of these small islands had entailed such bloodshed, military planners asked, what would the invasion of Japan itself be like? Although a naval blockade had strangled Japan's commerce and its lands lay defenseless to U.S. bombers, the imperial government showed little disposition to surrender. Truman scheduled an invasion of Kyushu (KYOO-shoo), the first of the home islands, for late 1945.

But the successful test of an atomic weapon at Alamogordo in mid-July presented an alternative. While at Potsdam, Truman, on July 25, ordered that an atomic bomb be used if Japan did not surrender before August 3. He publicly warned Japan to surrender unconditionally or face "prompt and utter destruction." When Japan rejected this **Potsdam Declaration,** Truman gave the military the go-ahead. On August 6, a B-29 named *Enola Gay* dropped a uranium bomb on Hiroshima (hee-roh-SHEE-muh), creating "a hell of unspeakable torments." A searing flash of heat, a fireball estimated at 300,000 degrees centigrade, incinerated buildings and vaporized people. Nearly seventy thousand died from the blast and another seventy thousand later died of burns and radiation poisoning. On August 8, as promised, Stalin declared war on Japan. The next day, much of Nagasaki (nah-gah-SAH-kee) disappeared under the mushroom cloud of a plutonium bomb. Finally, on August 14, Japan surrendered, leaving the emperor on the throne but powerless. On September 2, General MacArthur, aboard the battleship *Missouri* in Tokyo Bay, formally accepted the Japanese surrender.

Many have questioned whether the war had to end with the atomic bombings. Some believe that racist American attitudes toward Japan motivated the decision to use the bombs. Yet from the beginning of the Manhattan Project, Germany had been the target; and considering the indiscriminate ferocity of the Allied bombings of Hamburg and Dresden, which killed tens of thousands of civilians, there is little reason to assume that the Allies would not have used atomic bombs against Germany had they been available. Others contend that demonstrating the bomb's destructiveness on an uninhabited island would have moved Japan to surrender. But American policy makers considered a demonstration too risky. Still others argue that Japan was ready to surrender and that an invasion of the home islands was unnecessary. We cannot know for sure. But we do know that, as late as July 28, 1945, Japan rejected a demand for surrender and that not until after the Hiroshima bombing did the Japanese government discuss acceptance of the Potsdam Declaration.

Rapidly worsening relations between the United States and the Soviet Union convinced some that Truman dropped the atomic bomb primarily to intimidate Stalin. The failure of the Americans and Soviets to resolve their differences had led Truman to seek an end to the Pacific war before Stalin could enter. Truman recognized that such an awesome weapon might give the United States leverage to oust the communists from eastern Europe. However, that was not the main reason that the bombs were dropped. Throughout the war Americans had relied on production and technology to win the war with a minimum loss of American life. Every new weapon was used. "Total war" included the terror-bombing of masses of civilians, and within this context the atomic bomb seemed simply one more weapon in an arsenal that had already wreaked enormous destruction on the enemy. No responsible official suggested that the United States accept the deaths of thousands of Americans while not using a weapon developed with 2 billion taxpayer dollars. Indeed, to the vast majority of Americans, the atomic bomb was, in Churchill's words, "a miracle of deliverance" that shortened the war and saved lives.

Potsdam Declaration President Truman's warning to the Japanese, before dropping an atomic bomb on Hiroshima, to surrender or face "utter destruction"

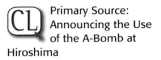
Primary Source: Announcing the Use of the A-Bomb at Hiroshima

CHECKING IN

- Concessions to the Soviets at Yalta and accepting Soviet dominance of eastern Europe reflected military realities of the time.
- Victory over the Nazis in Europe transitioned quickly into a U.S.-Soviet confrontation.
- The end of the war revealed the horrors of the Holocaust.
- After atomic bombs were dropped on Hiroshima and Nagasaki, and the Soviet Union declared war, Japan surrendered.
- The debate continues about whether use of the atomic bombs was necessary.

Chapter Summary

 DOWNLOAD THE MP3 AUDIO FILE OF THE CHAPTER SUMMARY, AND LISTEN TO IT ON THE GO.

How did the American people and government respond to the international crises of the 1930s? (page 588)

As war loomed in Europe, a majority of Americans were determined to avoid becoming involved; the Neutrality Acts were an attempt to prevent involvement. Isolationists formed America First, but FDR sought increased military funding. Americans and the U.S. government turned their backs on Jewish refugees trying to flee Hitler.

What drew the United States into World War II? (page 592)

France had surrendered, and Britain was barely clinging to life by the fall of 1940; despite strong isolationist sentiment, FDR circumvented the Neutrality Acts with cash-and-carry and lend-lease programs for Britain. In Asia, the Japanese became increasingly aggressive but saw the United States as a major obstacle to expansion; their decision to gamble on an all-out attack on American possessions, including Pearl Harbor, precipitated American entry into the war.

How did war mobilization transform the American economy and government? (page 595)

Full mobilization of the industrial economy was the key to Allied victory. U.S. war production boomed as government spending ended the depression. The government established tight control over the economy, the press, and industry. Research and development brought technology to bear on the war, including radar, sonar, the computer, and the atomic bomb.

What were the major aspects of Allied military strategy in Europe and Asia? (page 599)

In Europe, the Soviet Union bore the brunt of the fighting; the battle of Stalingrad was the turning point of the war. The invasion of France on D-Day began the final push to Allied victory. In the Pacific, the United States relied largely on its carrier fleets and island-hopping campaigns. By war's end, however, the U.S.-Great Britain-Soviet Union alliance had seriously eroded because each nation had different war goals.

KEY TERMS

"Good Neighbor" policy (p. 588)
Benito Mussolini (p. 589)
Adolf Hitler (p. 589)
Nazi party (p. 589)
appeasement (p. 590)
Neutrality Acts (p. 590)
Winston Churchill (p. 592)
"lend-lease" (p. 593)
Atlantic Charter (p. 593)
War Production Board (p. 596)
Office of Price Administration (p. 596)
Manhattan Project (p. 598)
Joseph Stalin (p. 599)
Battle of the Bulge (p. 601)
"Rosie the Riveter" (p. 604)
A. Philip Randolph (p. 606)
braceros (p. 608)
internment of Japanese-Americans (p. 608)
Yalta accords (p. 610)
Holocaust (p. 611)
Potsdam Declaration (p. 613)

What were the major effects of World War II on American society, including minorities and women? (page 603)

The Sun Belt prospered as government spending there soared; millions of Americans were caught up in a vast internal migration. People of widely diverse backgrounds came together in war jobs and the military. Large numbers of women entered the industrial work force, as did substantial numbers of African-Americans, Indians, and Mexicans. However, wartime propaganda and longstanding prejudice led to the internment of more than 100,000 Japanese-Americans solely because of their race.

What new issues did the U.S. government confront in defeating Germany and Japan in 1945? (page 609)

The Yalta conference revealed deep divisions among the Allies; FDR made substantial concessions to the Soviet Union because its help would be needed to fight Japan. Victory over Germany quickly turned into U.S.-Soviet. confrontation. The full horrors of the Holocaust became apparent to Americans who had doubted earlier reports. The use of atomic bombs against Japanese cities was a major factor in convincing Japan to surrender, but the necessity of their use is still being debated.

CHAPTER 26

The Cold War Abroad and at Home

1945–1952

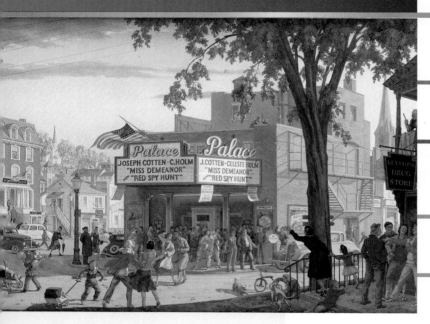

McCarthyism and the Hollywood Witch Hunts, by Thomas Maitland Cleland

CHAPTER PREVIEW

The Postwar Political Setting, 1945–1946
What were the major consequences of the GI Bill of Rights?

Anticommunism and Containment, 1946–1952
How did the policies of the United States and Soviet Union lead to the beginnings of the Cold War?

The Truman Administration at Home, 1945–1952
What effect did the more conservative political climate have on Truman's domestic program?

The Politics of Anticommunism
How did anticommunist sentiment affect American society?

ike no one else, Jackie Robinson personified the accelerating momentum of the struggle against racial discrimination that emerged from the Second World War. While serving in war, Robinson was acquitted of insubordination in a court-martial for refusing to accept segregation on army buses. In 1947, he accepted an offer to play baseball for the Brooklyn Dodgers. The grandson of a slave had become the first African-American to play major league baseball in the twentieth century. He endured racist insults and bean balls, flying spikes and hate mail, even death threats, from fans and other players. But his dazzling play and dignified courage helped the Dodgers win the pennant, and Robinson was named Rookie of the Year.

Robinson became a symbol of progress in race relations and a spur to changes in the United States. In the wake of Robinson's success, professional football and other baseball teams also integrated. The popular press increasingly attacked prejudice; various cities and states passed laws against discrimination; the Supreme

Court chipped away at the judicial foundations of segregation; the Truman administration proposed civil-rights legislation; and antiracism took its place in the agenda of liberalism. A new phase in the struggle to end racism in America had begun.

Meanwhile, a Cold War rapidly emerged as the dominant development of the postwar era. Abandoning its historical aloofness from events outside the Western Hemisphere, the United States now plunged into a global struggle to contain the Soviet Union and stop communism. The nation that only a few years before had no military alliances, a small defense budget, and no troops on foreign soil created a giant military establishment, directly intervened in the affairs of allies and enemies alike, built military bases on every continent, and embarked on a seemingly limitless nuclear-arms race.

Containing communism abroad profoundly changed America at home as well. It transformed the economy, shifted national priorities, expanded the powers of the executive branch, and spawned a second Red Scare. The obsession with subversion and the communist menace silenced the Left, stifled debate, and narrowed the range of what was politically acceptable. The politics of deadlock, inherited from the late 1930s, continued. An anxious yet hopeful people looked to their own prosperity and family life for the joy and blessings denied them by Cold War fears of a nuclear world war.

▌THE POSTWAR POLITICAL SETTING, 1945–1946

What were the major consequences of the GI Bill of Rights?

▌The emerging Cold War profoundly changed the United States for better and for worse. It spurred a quarter-century of economic growth and prosperity, the longest such period in American history. It propelled research in medicine and science that, for the most part, made lives longer and better. And it contributed to a vast expansion of higher education that enabled many Americans to become middle class.

Demobilization and Reconversion When the war ended, GIs and civilians alike wanted all those who had served overseas "home alive in '45." Troops demanding transport ships barraged Congress with threats of "no boats, no votes." On a single day in December 1945, sixty thousand postcards arrived at the White House with the message "Bring the Boys Home by Christmas." Truman bowed to popular demand, and by 1948 American military strength had dropped from 12 million at war's end to just 1.5 million.

Returning veterans faced readjustment problems intensified by a soaring divorce rate and a drastic housing shortage. As war plants closed, moreover, veterans and civilians feared the return of mass unemployment and economic depression. Defense spending plummeted from $76 billion in 1945 to under $20 billion in 1946, and more than a million defense jobs vanished (see Figure 26.1).

By the end of the decade more women were working outside the home than during World War II. They took jobs in traditional women's fields, especially office work and sales, to pay for family needs. Although the postwar economy created new openings

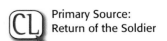

Primary Source:
Return of the Soldier

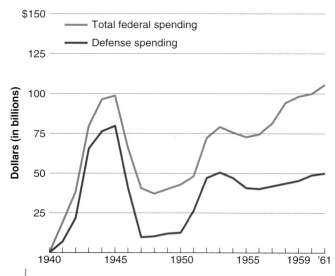

Figure 26.1   National Defense Spending, 1941–1960

In 1950, the defense budget was $13 billion, less than a third of the total federal outlay. In 1961, defense spending reached $47 billion, fully half of the federal budget and almost 10 percent of the gross national product.

Source: From *American Promise*, Vol. 2, 4th ed. By James A. Henretta et al. Reprinted with permission of Bedford/St. Martin's.

GI Bill   Act that allowed for education and home ownership for veterans

for women in the labor market, many public figures urged women to seek fulfillment at home. Popular culture romanticized married bliss and demonized career women as a threat to social stability.

The GI Bill of Rights

The Servicemen's Readjustment Act of 1944, commonly called the GI Bill of Rights or **GI Bill** was designed to forestall the expected recession by easing veterans back into the work force, as well as to reward the "soldier boys" and reduce their fears of female competition. The GI Bill gave veterans priority for many jobs, occupational guidance, and, if need be, fifty-two weeks of unemployment benefits. It also established veterans' hospitals and provided low-interest loans to returning GIs who were starting businesses or buying homes or farms. Almost 4 million veterans bought homes with government loans, fueling a baby boom, suburbanization, and a record demand for new goods and services.

Most vitally in the long run, the government promised to pay millions of veterans for up to four years of further education or job training. Yet some Americans opposed it as opening the door to socialism or to demands by minorities to special entitlements. Many university administrators, fearing the influx of riffraff, echoed the complaint of the University of Chicago president that their learning institutions would become "educational hobo jungles."

In 1946, flush with generous stipends, 1.5 million veterans were attending college, spurring a huge increase in higher education and the creation of many new state and community colleges. Veterans made up over half of all college students in 1947. Often married and the fathers of young children, they were less interested in knowledge than in a degree and a higher-paying job. To accommodate them, colleges featured accelerated programs and more vocational or career-oriented courses.

To make room for the millions of GIs pursuing higher education after the war, many colleges limited the percentage of women admitted or barred students from out of state. The percentage of female college graduates dropped from 40 percent in 1949 to 25 percent in 1950. By then most potential women students were the working wives of the veterans who took advantage of the GI Bill to go to college.

The GI Bill democratized higher education. It allowed many more Americans (most of them the first in their families to attend) to go to college. Later those GIs expected their children to follow suit, and higher education became an accepted part of the American Dream. No longer a citadel of privilege, universities awarded almost half a million degrees in 1950, more than twice as many as in 1940.

The cost was huge, but well spent. The $15 billion that veterans received sent them to school, helped them buy homes, and financed their new businesses. It pro-

Chronology

1944	Servicemen's Readjustment Act (GI Bill)
1945	Postwar strike wave begins. Employment Act; George Kennan's "long telegram"; Winston Churchill's "iron curtain" speech; Coal miners' strike; Inflation soars to more than 18 percent; Republicans win control of Congress
1947	Truman Doctrine; Federal Employee Loyalty Program; Jackie Robinson breaks major league baseball's color line; Taft-Hartley Act; National Security Act; President's Committee on Civil Rights issues *To Secure These Rights*; HUAC holds hearings on Hollywood
1948	Communist coup in Czechoslovakia; State of Israel founded; Berlin airlift; Congress approves Marshall Plan to aid Europe; Truman orders an end to segregation in the armed forces; Communist leaders put on trial under the Smith Act; Truman elected president
1949	North Atlantic Treaty Organization (NATO) established; East and West Germany founded as separate nations; Communist victory in China; People's Republic of China established; Soviet Union detonates an atomic bomb
1950	Soviet spy ring at Los Alamos uncovered; Joseph McCarthy launches anticommunist crusade; Korean War begins; McCarran Internal Security Act; Truman accepts NSC-68; China enters the Korean War
1951	Julius and Ethel Rosenberg convicted of espionage
1952	First hydrogen bomb exploded; Dwight D. Eisenhower elected president; Republicans win control of Congress

pelled millions of veterans into middle-class, heightening the postwar demand for goods and services.

The Economic Boom Begins

In addition to the assistance given to returning servicemen, a 1945 tax cut of $6 billion spurred corporate investment in new factories and equipment, and helped produce an economic boom that began in late 1946. Wartime savings and a pent-up demand for consumer goods further kindled postwar growth and prosperity. The men and women who had endured the Great Depression and the Second World War craved the "good life," and by the end of 1945, they possessed $140 billion in bank accounts and government bonds to purchase it. Advertisements promising "a Ford in your future" and an "all-electric kitchen-of-the-future" became reality as sales of homes, cars, and appliances skyrocketed. New products—televisions, electric clothes dryers, freezers, and hi-fi stereos—emerged as hallmarks of the middle-class lifestyle.

The Bretton Woods agreement (1944) among the Allies had set the stage for the United States to become economic leader of the noncommunist world. In addition to valuing ("pegging") other currencies in relation to the dollar, Bretton Woods created several institutions to oversee international trade and finance: the International Monetary Fund (IMF), the General Agreement on Tariffs and Trade (GATT), and the World Bank.

With many nations in ruins, American firms could import raw materials cheaply; with little competition from other industrial countries, they could increase exports to record levels. Wartime advances in science and technology, which led to revolutionary developments in such industries as electronics and plastics, further bolstered visions of limitless growth and the dawn of "the American century."

Truman's Domestic Program

Americans' hunger for the fruits of affluence left them little appetite for extension of the New Deal. Truman's only major domestic accomplishment in the Seventy-ninth Congress was the Employment Act of 1946. It committed the federal government to ensuring economic growth and established the Council of Economic Advisers to confer with the president and formulate policies for maintaining employment, production, and purchasing power. Congress, however, gutted both the goal of full employment and the enhanced executive powers to achieve that objective.

Congressional eagerness to dismantle wartime controls worsened the nation's chief economic problem: inflation. Consumer demand outran the supply of goods, putting intense pressure on prices. The Office of Price Administration (OPA) continued to set price controls after the war, but food producers, manufacturers, and retailers opposed controls strenuously. Many consumers favored preserving the OPA, but others saw the agency as a symbol of irksome wartime regulation. In June 1946, when Congress passed a bill that extended the OPA's life but removed its powers, Truman vetoed the bill. Within a week, food costs rose 16 percent, and the price of beef doubled.

Congress passed, and Truman signed, a second bill extending price controls in weakened form. Protesting any price controls, however, farmers and meat producers threatened to withhold food from the market. Observing that "meatless voters are opposition voters," Truman lifted controls on food prices just before the November 1946 midterm elections. Democratic candidates fared badly at the polls anyhow. By the time Truman lifted all price controls, shortly after the election, the consumer price index had already jumped nearly 25 percent. Sharp price rises and shrinking paychecks goaded organized labor to demand higher wages. In 1946 alone, more than 4.5 million men and women went on strike. After a United Mine Workers walkout paralyzed the economy for forty days, President Truman ordered government seizure of the mines. A week later the miners returned to work, after Truman had pressured owners to grant most of the demands. Six months later the drama repeated itself.

President Truman with Union Supporters
Following his veto of the Taft-Hartley bill and 1948 election victory, won, in large part, by the strong backing of organized labor, a smiling Truman dons a hard hat with copper miners in Butte, Montana.

In spring 1946 railway engineers and trainmen struck, shutting down the railway system. Truman exploded. "If you think I'm going to sit here and let you tie up this whole country," the president shouted at the heads of the two unions, "you're crazy as hell." In May Truman asked Congress for authority to draft workers who struck in vital industries. Only when the rail workers gave in did the Senate reject Truman's proposals. His threat alienated labor leaders.

By fall 1946 Truman had angered most major interest groups; polls showed that less than one-third of Americans approved of his performance. "To err is Truman," some gibed. Summing up public discontent, Republicans asked, "Had enough?" In the 1946 elections they captured twenty-five governorships and, for the first time since 1928, won control of Congress.

The public mood reflected more than just economic discontent; it also revealed a deep current of fear. An NBC Radio program depicted a nuclear attack on Chicago in which most people died instantly. Schoolchildren wore dog tags in order to be identified after an atomic attack, and practiced crawling under their desks and putting their hands over their heads—"Duck and Cover"—to protect themselves from the bomb. The end of World War II had brought an uneasy peace.

ANTICOMMUNISM AND CONTAINMENT, 1946–1952

How did the policies of the United States and Soviet Union lead to the beginnings of the Cold War?

By the end of 1946, smoldering antagonisms between Moscow and Washington had flared up. With the Nazis defeated, the "shotgun wedding" between the United States and the Soviet Union dissolved into a struggle to fill the power vacuum left by the defeat of Germany and Japan, the exhaustion and bankruptcy of Western Europe, and the crumbling of colonial empires in Asia and Africa. Misperception and misunderstanding proliferated as the two nations sought security, each feeding the other's fears. The Cold War was the result.

Polarization and Cold War

The destiny of Eastern Europe, especially Poland, remained at the heart of U.S.-Soviet contention. Wanting to end the Soviet Union's vulnerability to invasions from the west, Stalin insisted on a demilitarized Germany and a buffer of nations friendly to the Soviet Union along its western flank. He considered a Soviet sphere of influence in Eastern Europe essential to national security, a just reward for the Soviet Union's bearing the brunt of the war against Germany, and no different from the American spheres of influence in Western Europe, Japan, and Latin America. Stalin also believed that, at Yalta, Roosevelt and Churchill had implicitly accepted a Soviet zone in Eastern Europe.

With the Red Army occupying half of Europe at the war's end, Stalin installed pro-Soviet governments in Bulgaria, Hungary, and Romania, while communist governments independent of Moscow came to power in Albania (al-BAY-nee-uh) and Yugoslavia. Ignoring the Yalta Declaration of Liberated Europe, the Soviet Union barred free elections in Poland and brutally suppressed Polish democratic parties.

Interactive Map:
The Global Cold War

Stalin's insistence on dominance in Eastern Europe collided with Truman's unwillingness to concede Soviet supremacy beyond Russia's borders. What Stalin saw as critical to Russian security Truman viewed as a violation of the right of national self-determination, a betrayal of democratic principles, and a cover for communist aggression. Truman and his advisers believed that the appeasement of dictators only fed their appetite for expansion. Only a new world order based on the self-determination of all nations working in good faith within the United Nations could guarantee peace. Truman also thought that accepting the "enforced sovietization" of Eastern Europe would betray American war aims and condemn nations rescued from Hitler's tyranny to another totalitarian dictatorship.

Domestic political considerations also shaped Truman's response to Stalin. Truman understood that the Democratic party would invite political disaster if he reneged on the Yalta agreements. The Democrats counted on winning most of the votes of the 6 million Polish-Americans and millions of other Americans of Eastern European origin, who remained keenly interested in the fates of their homelands. He resolved not to appear "soft on communism."

Combativeness fit the temperament of the feisty Truman. Eager to demonstrate that he was in command, the president matched Stalin's intransigence on Polish elections with his own demands for Polish democracy. Emboldened by America's monopoly of atomic bombs and its undisputed position as the world's economic superpower, the president hoped that the United States could control the terms of postwar settlement.

The Iron Curtain Descends

Truman's assertiveness inflamed Stalin's mistrust of the West and deepened Soviet obsession with their own security. Stalin stepped up his confiscation of materials and factories from occupied territories and forced his satellite nations to close their doors to American trade and influence. In February 1946 he warned that there could be no lasting peace with capitalism and vowed to overcome the American edge in weapons.

George F. Kennan American diplomat in Moscow, architect of the Cold War policy of containment

containment Doctrine of continuous confrontation in order to stop Soviet expansion

Two weeks later, a sixteen-page telegram from **George F. Kennan,** the American chargé d'affaires in Moscow, reached Washington. A leading student of Soviet politics, Kennan warned that the only way to deal with Soviet intransigence was "a long-term, patient but firm and vigilant **containment** of Russian expansive tendencies." Truman, who had already insisted that it was time "to get tough with Russia," accepted the idea of containment, as did many others in Washington who wanted "no compromise" with the communists. Containment soon became gospel.

In early March 1946, Truman accompanied Winston Churchill to Westminster College in Missouri, where the former British prime minister warned of a new threat to democracy. Stalin, he said, had drawn an iron curtain across the eastern half of Europe. Churchill called for an alliance of the English-speaking peoples against the Soviet Union and the maintenance of an Anglo-American monopoly on atomic weapons.

Convinced that American firmness could check Soviet expansionism, Truman in the spring of 1946 threatened to send in American combat troops unless the Soviets withdrew from oil-rich Iran. In June, Truman submitted to the United Nations an atomic-energy control plan requiring the Soviet Union to stop all work on nuclear weapons and to submit to UN inspections before the United States would destroy its own atomic arsenal. As expected, the Soviets rejected the American proposal and offered an alternative plan equally unacceptable to the United States. As mutual hostility escalated, the Soviets and Americans rushed to develop doomsday weapons. In 1946 Congress established the Atomic Energy Commission (AEC) to regulate nuclear development. By 1950, one AEC adviser reckoned, the United States "had a stockpile capable of somewhat more than reproducing World War II in a single day."

Thus, less than a year after American and Soviet soldiers had jubilantly met at the Elbe River to celebrate Hitler's defeat, the Cold War had begun. Economic pressure, nuclear intimidation, propaganda, and subversion, rather than military confrontation, characterized this conflict. Nonetheless, it would affect American life as decisively as any military engagement that the nation had fought.

Containing Communism

In early 1947 America formally stated its commitment to combat Soviet power. On February 21 the British informed the United States that they could no longer afford to assist the governments of Greece and Turkey in their struggles against communist-supplied guerrilla insurgencies and against Soviet pressure for access to the Mediterranean. Britain asked the United States to assume the costs. The harsh European winter, the most severe in memory, heightened the sense of urgency in Washington. The economies of Western Europe had ground to a halt, famine and tuberculosis plagued the Continent, and colonies in Africa and Asia had risen in rebellion. Communist parties in France and Italy appeared ready to topple democratic coalition governments. Truman resolved to meet the Soviet challenge.

He first had to mobilize support for a radical departure from the American tradition of avoiding entangling alliances. In a tense White House meeting on February 27, the new secretary of state, former army chief of staff George C. Marshall, presented the case for massive aid to Greece and Turkey. Congressional leaders balked, more concerned about U.S. inflation than about civil war in Greece. But Dean Acheson, the newly appointed undersecretary of state, seized the moment. The issue, he said, was not one of assisting the repressive Greek oligarchy and Turkey's military dictatorship—it was, rather, a universal struggle of freedom versus tyranny. The fall of Greece or Turkey, he warned, would open Asia, Western Europe, and the oil fields of the Middle East to the Red menace. Shaken, the congressional leaders agreed to support the administration's request—if Truman could "scare hell out of the country."

Truman could and did. On March 12, 1947, addressing a joint session of Congress, he painted global politics as a stark confrontation between liberty and oppression, and asked for military aid for Greece and Turkey. Outlining what became known as the **Truman Doctrine,** the president declared that the United States must support any free people "resisting attempted subjugation by armed minorities or by outside pressures." This unilateral declaration proclaimed the national intention to become a global policeman everywhere on guard against advances by the Soviet Union and its allies. Endorsed by the Republican Congress, the Truman Doctrine laid the foundation for American Cold War policy that would endure for much of the next four decades.

Truman Doctrine Implementation of containment: U.S. would support any government facing communist challenge

To back up the new international initiative, Congress passed the National Security Act of 1947, unifying the armed forces under a single Department of Defense, creating the National Security Council (NSC) to advise the president on strategic matters, and establishing the Central Intelligence Agency (CIA) to gather information abroad and engage in covert activities in support of the nation's security. In June the administration proposed massive U.S. assistance for European recovery. First proposed by the secretary of state and thus called the **Marshall Plan,** such aid would become another weapon in the arsenal against the spread of communism. Truman wanted to end the economic devastation believed to spawn communism. Truman correctly guessed that the Soviet Union and its satellites would refuse to take part in the plan, because of the controls linked to it, and accurately foresaw that Western European economic recovery would expand sales of American goods abroad and promote prosperity in the United States.

Marshall Plan Aid to rebuild Western Europe, including Germany

The Marshall Plan fulfilled its sponsors' hopes. By 1952, industrial production had risen 200 percent in Western Europe, and the economic and social chaos that communists had exploited had been overcome in the sixteen nations that shared the $17 billion in aid. Western Europe revived, prospered, and achieved an unprecedented unity. U.S. business, not coincidentally, boomed.

Confrontation in Germany

The Soviet Union reacted to the Truman Doctrine and the Marshall Plan by tightening its grip on Eastern Europe. Then in 1947–1948 communist coups added Hungary and Czechoslovakia to the Soviet bloc, and Stalin turned his sights on Germany.

The 1945 Potsdam Agreement had divided Germany into four separate zones (administered by France, Great Britain, the Soviet Union, and the United States) and created a joint four-power administration for Germany's capital, Berlin, which lay 110 miles inside the Soviet-occupied eastern zone. As the Cold War intensified, the Western nations began to see a revived Germany as a buffer against Soviet expansion, and they gradually united their zones. In June 1948 Stalin responded by blocking all rail and highway routes through the Soviet zone into Berlin.

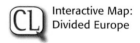

Interactive Map: Divided Europe

Truman resolved neither to abandon Berlin nor to shoot his way into the city—and possibly trigger World War III. Instead, he ordered a massive airlift to provide Berliners with the food and fuel necessary for survival. American cargo planes landed in West Berlin every three minutes around the clock, carrying a mountain of supplies. Then in July 1948 Truman hinted that he would use "the bomb" if necessary and sent a fleet of B-29s, the only planes capable of delivering atomic bombs, to English bases. As tensions rose, Truman confided to his diary that "we are very close to war." The **Berlin airlift** continued for nearly a year.

Berlin airlift Use of cargo planes to supply Berlin, blockaded by Stalin, with supplies in 1948

In May 1949 the Soviets ended the blockade. Stalin's gambit had failed. The airlift highlighted American determination and technological prowess, revealed Stalin's willingness to use innocent citizens as pawns, and dramatically heightened anti-Soviet feeling in the West. In late 1948, U.S. public-opinion polls revealed an overwhelming demand for "firmness and increased 'toughness' in relations with Russia."

Continuing fears of a Soviet attack on Western Europe fostered support for a revitalized West German state and for an Atlantic collective-security alliance. Thus in May 1949 the United States, Britain, and France ended their occupation of Germany and approved the creation of the Federal Republic of Germany (West Ger-

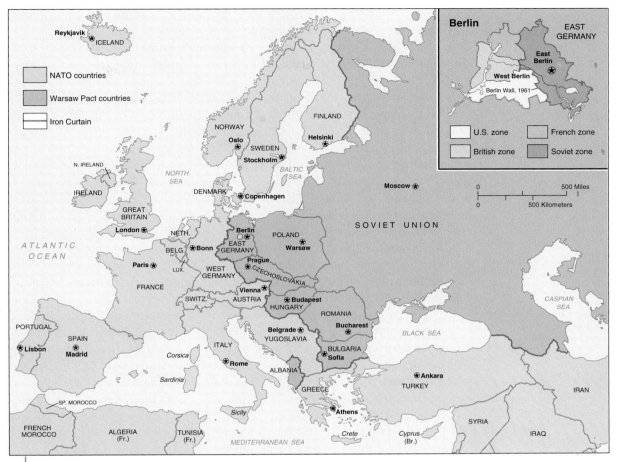

Map 26.1   The Postwar Division of Europe

The wartime dispute between the Soviet Union and the Western Allies over Poland's future hardened after World War II into a Cold War that split Europe into competing American and Soviet spheres of influence. Across an "iron curtain," NATO countries faced the Warsaw Pact nations.

many). A month earlier, ten nations of Western Europe had signed the North Atlantic Treaty, establishing a military alliance with the United States and Canada, and declaring that an attack on any member would be considered an attack against all. For the first time in its history, the United States entered into a peacetime military alliance. After overwhelming Senate approval, the United States officially joined the **North Atlantic Treaty Organization (NATO).**

Truman was convinced that if NATO had been in existence in 1914 and 1939, the world would have been spared two disastrous wars. Accordingly, he spurred Congress to authorize $1.3 billion for military assistance to NATO nations and authorized the stationing of four American army divisions in Europe as the nucleus of the NATO armed force. The Soviet Union responded by creating the German Democratic Republic (East Germany) in 1949, by exploding its own atomic bomb that same year, and by forming an Eastern bloc military alliance, the Warsaw Pact, in 1955. The United States and Soviet Union had divided Europe into two armed camps (see Map 26.1).

North Atlantic Treaty Organization (NATO) U.S.-led political and military alliance against Soviet Union

The Cold War in Asia

Moscow-Washington hostility also carved Asia into contending military and economic camps. The Russians created a sphere of influence in Manchuria, the United States denied Moscow a role in postwar Japan, and the two superpowers partitioned a helpless Korea.

As the head of the U.S. occupation forces in Japan, General Douglas MacArthur oversaw the country's transformation from an empire in ruins into a prosperous democracy. In 1952 the occupation ended, but a military security treaty allowed the United States to retain its Japanese bases on the Soviet-Asian perimeter and brought Japan under the American "nuclear umbrella." Both benefited: Japan could devote most of its resources to economic development, and the United States gained a staunch anticommunist ally. The containment policy in Asia also led the United States to help crush a procommunist guerrilla movement in the Philippines and to aid French efforts to reestablish colonial rule in Indochina—Vietnam, Laos (LAH-oss), and Cambodia (kam-BOH-dee-uh), despite American declarations in favor of national self-determination and against imperialism.

In China, however, U.S. efforts to block communism failed. The Truman administration initially tried to mediate the civil war raging between the Nationalist government of Jiang Jieshi (jyang je-SHIRRS) and the communist forces of **Mao Zedong** (MA-oh zay-DONGS). Between 1945 and 1949 the United States sent nearly $3 billion to the Nationalists. But American dollars could not force Jiang's corrupt government to reform itself and to win the support of the Chinese people, whom it had widely alienated. As Mao's well-disciplined and motivated forces marched south, Jiang's soldiers mutinied and surrendered without a fight. Unable to stem revolutionary sentiment or to build loyalty among the peasants, Jiang's regime collapsed, and he fled to exile on the island of Taiwan (Formosa).

Mao's establishment of the communist People's Republic of China shocked Americans. The most populous nation in the world, seen as a counterforce to Asian communism and a market for American trade, had become "Red China." Although the Truman administration insisted that it could have done little to alter the outcome and placed responsibility for Jiang's defeat on his failure to reform China, most Americans were unconvinced. China's fall to communism particularly embittered those conservatives who believed that America's future lay in Asia, not Europe.

In September 1949, as the "Who lost China" debate raged, the president announced that the Soviet Union had exploded an atomic bomb. The loss of the nuclear monopoly shattered illusions of American invincibility. Combined with Mao's victory, this development would spawn an anticommunist hysteria and lead to irrational searches for scapegoats and subversives to explain American setbacks in world affairs. Ordinary Americans sought safety in civil defense. Public schools held air-raid drills and more than a million purchased or constructed their own family bomb shelters.

In January 1950, stung by charges that he was soft on communism, Truman ordered the development of a fusion-based hydrogen bomb (H-bomb), hundreds of times more powerful than an atomic bomb. In November 1952 the United States exploded its first H-bomb in the Marshall Islands, projecting a radioactive cloud 25 miles into the atmosphere and blasting a canyon a mile long and 175 feet deep in the ocean floor. Nine months later, the Soviets detonated their own hydrogen bomb. The balance of terror escalated.

Mao Zedong Chinese revolutionary whose forces took control of China in 1949

Primary Source: USSR's First Atomic Bomb

In April 1950 a presidentially appointed committee issued a top-secret review of defense policy. The report, **NSC-68,** emphasized the Soviet Union's aggressive intentions and military strength. To counter the Soviets' "design for world domination," NSC-68 called for a vast American military buildup, a large standing army, and a quadrupling of the defense budget to wage a global struggle against communism. By the end of 1950, Truman would order the implementation of NSC-68 and triple the defense budget.

NSC-68 Blueprint for Cold War; called for military buildup, H-bomb, worldwide containment

The Korean War, 1950–1953

After World War II, the Soviet Union and United States temporarily divided Korea at the thirty-eighth parallel for purposes of military occupation. The dividing line had solidified into a political frontier between the Soviet-backed People's Democratic Republic in North Korea and the American-supported Republic of Korea, each claiming the sole right to rule Korea.

On June 24, 1950, North Korean troops swept across the thirty-eighth parallel to attack South Korea. Truman saw the invasion as Soviet-directed aggression. He never doubted that Stalin was testing American will. Mindful of the failure of appeasement at Munich in 1938, Truman said that failure to act would lead to a bloody "third world war." Having been accused of "selling out" Eastern Europe and "losing" China, Truman needed to prove he could stand up to "the Reds."

Without consulting Congress, Truman ordered air and naval forces to Korea from their bases in Japan on June 27. That same day he asked the United Nations to authorize action to repel the invasion. The Soviet delegate was boycotting the Security Council to protest the UN's unwillingness to seat a representative from Mao's China, and Truman gained approval for a UN "police action" to restore South Korea's border. He appointed General Douglas MacArthur to command the UN effort and ordered American ground troops into what now became the **Korean War.** The Cold War had turned hot.

Korean War War with communist North Korea to contain spread of communism in Asia

North Korean forces initially routed the disorganized American and South Korean troops. Then, in mid-September, with UN forces cornered on the southeastern tip of the Korean peninsula, struggling to avoid being pushed into the sea, MacArthur's troops landed at Inchon (in-CHAHN) in a brilliant amphibious maneuver. Within two weeks, U.S. and South Korean forces drove the North Koreans back across the thirty-eighth parallel. Basking in victory, MacArthur persuaded Truman to let him go beyond the UN mandate to repel aggression and to cross the border to liberate all of Korea from communism.

As UN troops approached the Yalu River, the Chinese warned that they would not "stand idly by" if their border was threatened. Ignoring this assertion,

U.S. Marines Battling for Seoul, September 1950

From the start Truman believed that the Soviet Union had orchestrated the North Korean invasion of South Korea. He steadfastly maintained that "if the Russian totalitarian state was intending to follow in the path of the dictatorship of Hitler and Mussolini, they [had to] be met head on in Korea."

Primary Source: MacArthur Outlines His Objectives in Korea

an overconfident MacArthur deployed his forces in a thin line below the river. On November 25 thirty-three Chinese divisions (about 300,000 men) counterattacked, driving stunned UN forces back below the thirty-eighth parallel. By March 1951 the fighting was stabilized at roughly the original dividing line between the two Koreas (see Map 26.2).

Stalemated, Truman reversed course and sought a negotiated peace based on the objective of restoring the integrity of South Korea. MacArthur rocked the boat, however, urging that he be allowed to bomb and blockade China, "unleash" Jiang Jieshi's troops against Mao's regime, and seek a total victory even at the risk of an all-out war with China. Truman refused: "We are trying to prevent a world war—not to start one."

When MacArthur bluntly and repeatedly criticized Truman's limited war—the "appeasement of Communism"—the president fired the general for insubordination on April 10, 1951. To the president, the issue was civilian control of the military, a control that seemed threatened by MacArthur's public insubordination. Public opinion, however, backed the general. The very idea of limited war baffled many Americans, and a mounting casualty list added anger to the mix. It seemed so senseless. Despite warnings from the chairman of the Joint Chiefs of Staff that MacArthur's proposals would result in "the wrong war at the wrong place in the wrong time and with the wrong enemy," a growing number of Americans listened sympathetically to Republican charges that Soviet-directed agents controlled American policy.

Truman, meanwhile, found himself bogged down in Korea, unable to win the war or craft a peace. After two more years of fighting, the two sides reached an armistice in July 1953 that left Korea as divided as it had been at the start of the war. The "limited" conflict cost the United States 54,246 lives (about 33,700 of them direct battlefield deaths) and $54 billion. Following the pattern of World War II, massive U.S. "carpet bombing" killed over 2 million civilians, and left North Korea looking like a moonscape.

The Korean War had significant consequences. It accelerated implementation of NSC-68 and the expansion of containment into a global policy. From 1950 to 1953 defense spending zoomed from one-third to two-thirds of the entire federal budget. The United States acquired new bases around the world, committed itself to rearm West Germany, and joined a mutual-defense pact with Australia and New Zealand. Increased military aid flowed to Jiang Jieshi's troops on Taiwan, and American dollars supported the French army fighting communist insurgents in Indochina. By 1954 the United States was paying three-quarters of French war costs in Vietnam.

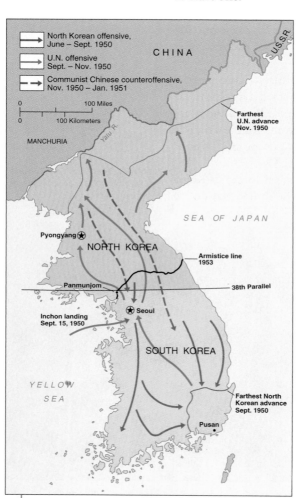

Map 26.2   The Korean War, 1950–1953

The experience of fighting an undeclared and limited war for the limited objective of containing communism confused the generation of Americans who had just fought an all-out war for the total defeat of the Axis.

Truman's intervention in Korea preserved a precarious balance of power in Asia and underscored the administration's commitment to the anticommunist struggle. Containment, originally advanced to justify U.S. aid to Greece and Turkey, had become the ideological foundation for a major war in Korea and, ominously, for a deepening U.S. involvement in Vietnam. Truman's actions enhanced the powers of an already powerful presidency and set the precedent for later undeclared wars. They also helped spark an economic boom, added fuel to a second Red Scare, and fostered Cold War attitudes that lasted long after the war ended.

THE TRUMAN ADMINISTRATION AT HOME, 1945–1952

What effect did the more conservative political climate have on Truman's domestic program?

Since 1929 the nation had known little but the sufferings and short-ages of depression and war. Now Americans wanted to enjoy life. Wide-spread postwar affluence let dreams become reality as Americans flocked to the suburbs, launched a huge baby boom, and rushed to buy stoves, re-frigerators, televisions, and cars. However, not all Americans shared these good times. Poverty remained a stark fact of life for millions. Minorities ex-perienced the grim reality of racism. Yet a major movement by African-Americans for equality gradually emerged from these Cold War years.

Despite these stirrings, family and career, not public issues, preoccupied most Americans. An increasingly conservative temper trumped liberalism. Some second- and third-generation white Americans, whose recent prosperity had dimmed memo-ries of the Great Depression and the New Deal, began to reject liberals at the polls. Although Truman occasionally sought liberal measures, the rise of conservative sen-timents in places like southern California undercut efforts for progressive change.

The Eightieth Congress, 1947–1948

Many Republicans in the Eightieth Congress, which con-vened in January 1947, interpreted the 1946 elections as a mandate to reverse the New Deal. Republican controlled, Congress defeated Democratic bills to raise the minimum wage and to provide fed-eral funds for education and housing.

Truman and the conservatives waged their major battle over the pro-union Wagner Act of 1935 (see Chapter 24). Postwar strikes had whipped up a national consensus for curbing union power. In 1947 Congress passed the **Taft-Hartley Act** (the Labor-Management Relations Act), which barred the closed shop—a workplace where only union members could be hired—and permitted the president to call a sixty-day cooling-off period to delay any strike that might endanger national safety or health. Unions termed the law a "slave labor bill" and demanded a presidential veto.

Truman did veto the measure, and Congress easily overrode the veto. But Tru-man had taken a major step toward regaining organized labor's support. This move

> **CHECKING IN**
>
> - The Soviet Union moved quickly to establish control over Eastern Eu-rope, as Truman and Stalin's mutual distrust grew.
> - The Truman administration adopted containment as the keystone of its foreign policy; the Truman Doctrine in effect made the United States a global policeman.
> - The Marshall Plan helped rebuild Western Europe, including Germany but not the Soviet Union.
> - The Berlin crisis brought the Cold War very close to the boiling point.
> - NSC-68, a top-secret plan, proposed putting the United States on a permanent war footing; it rested on the assumption that negotiation with the Soviets was impossible.
> - The Korean War set the Cold War in concrete, propelled the United States into Asian politics, and in-tensified charges of Soviet influence on American foreign policy.

Taft-Hartley Act Measure that limited power of labor unions

reflected his recognition that his only hope for election in 1948 lay in reforging the New Deal coalition. To this end, he played the role of staunch New Dealer to the hilt, proposing a series of liberal reform bills—federal aid to education, housing, and health insurance; repeal of Taft-Hartley; and high farm-price supports.

Truman courted voters of Eastern European ancestry by emphasizing his opposition to the iron curtain. He overrode the objections of the State Department, which feared alienating the oil-rich Arab world, to extend diplomatic recognition to the new state of Israel immediately after it proclaimed independence. This move reflected both his deep sympathy toward Holocaust survivors who had immigrated to Israel and the strategic importance of Jewish-American voters.

Jackie Robinson First African-American to play major-league baseball

President's Committee on Civil Rights In 1947, it recommended a legal assault on segregation, desegregation of the armed forces, and a permanent FEPC

The Politics of Civil Rights and the Election of 1948

The integration of baseball in 1947, spearheaded by the brilliant **Jackie Robinson,** symbolized a new robustness in the fight against racial segregation in the post-war era. As the head of the NAACP noted in 1945, "World War II has immeasurably magnified the Negro's awareness of the disparity between the American profession and practice of democracy." The war heightened African-American expectations for racial equality, and numerous blacks demanded a permanent Fair Employment Practices Commission (FEPC), the outlawing of lynching, and the right to vote. Voter-registration drives raised the percentage of southern blacks registered to vote from 2 percent in 1940 to 12 percent in 1947.

Fearful of black assertiveness in seeking the vote and of other signs of a bold new spirit among African-Americans, some southern whites reacted brutally. In 1946 in rural Georgia, whites killed several black veterans who had voted that year, and in South Carolina whites blinded a black soldier for failing to sit in the rear of a bus. In Columbia, Tennessee, in 1946, whites rioted against blacks who insisted on their rights. Police arrested seventy blacks and looked the other way as a white mob broke into the jail to murder two African-American prisoners.

In September 1946 Truman met with a delegation of civil-rights leaders. Horrified by their accounts, he vowed to act. Truman believed that every American should enjoy the full rights of citizenship. He also understood the importance of the growing African-American vote, particularly in northern cities. The president realized, too, that white racism damaged U.S. relations with much of the world.

After the 1946 elections, Truman established the **President's Committee on Civil Rights** to investigate race relations. The committee's report, *To Secure These Rights,* published in 1947, called for the eradication of racial discrimination and segregation, and proposed antilynching and anti-poll tax legislation.

Jackie Robinson, 1947
Robinson's brilliant play for the Brooklyn Dodgers did not save him from racial taunts of fans and players or exclusion from restaurants and hotels that catered to his white teammates.

Boldly, Truman in February 1948 sent a special message to Congress urging lawmakers to enact most of the committee's proposals.

When southern segregationists denounced Truman's "stab in the back" and warned of a boycott of the national Democratic ticket, Truman backtracked. He dropped his plans to submit specific civil-rights bills to Congress and endorsed a weak civil-rights plank for the Democratic platform.

At the Democratic convention in July 1948, liberals and urban politicians who needed African-American votes rejected the president's feeble civil-rights plank and committed the party to action on Truman's original proposals. Thirty-five delegates from Mississippi and Alabama responded by stalking out of the convention. They joined other southern segregationists to form the States' Rights Democratic party and nominated Governor Strom Thurmond of South Carolina for the presidency. The Dixiecrats placed their electors on the ballot as the regular Democratic ticket in several states, posing a major roadblock to Truman's chances of victory.

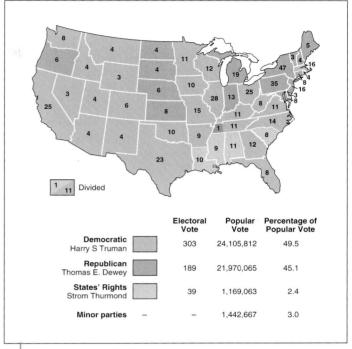

		Electoral Vote	Popular Vote	Percentage of Popular Vote
Democratic Harry S Truman		303	24,105,812	49.5
Republican Thomas E. Dewey		189	21,970,065	45.1
States' Rights Strom Thurmond		39	1,169,063	2.4
Minor parties		–	1,442,667	3.0

Map 26.3   The Election of 1948

Truman's electoral hopes further faded when left-wing Democrats joined with communists to launch a new Progressive party and nominated Henry A. Wallace for president. The Wallace candidacy threatened Truman's chances in northern states, where many urban Democrats saw Wallace as the heir of New Deal liberalism.

To capitalize on Democratic divisions, Republicans tried to play it safe. They nominated the moderate governor of New York, Thomas E. Dewey, and ran a complacent campaign designed to offend the fewest people. Truman, in contrast, campaigned tirelessly. To shouts of "Give 'em hell, Harry," the president hammered away at the "no-good, do-nothing" Republican-controlled Eightieth Congress. Pollsters applauded Truman's spunk but predicted a sure Dewey victory.

A surprised nation awoke the day after the election to learn that the president had won in the biggest electoral upset in U.S. history (see Map 26.3). Ironically, the Progressives and Dixiecrats had helped Truman. Their radicalism had kept both moderate liberals and moderate conservatives safely in the Democratic fold. Moreover, Dixiecrat defections had freed Truman to campaign as a proponent of civil rights.

In July 1948 Truman had issued executive orders barring discrimination in federal employment and creating a committee to ensure "equality of treatment and opportunity" for all persons in the armed services. Truman had also benefited from two Supreme Court decisions. In 1946 the Court had declared segregation in interstate bus transportation unconstitutional (*Morgan v. Virginia,* 1946), and in 1948 it had outlawed restrictive housing covenants that forbade the sale or rental of property to minorities (*Shelley v. Kraemer,* 1948).

The Fair Deal

Fair Deal Truman's unsuccessful proposed extension of New Deal

Despite his narrow victory margin, Truman tried to translate his election into a mandate for liberalism. In his 1949 State of the Union message, he proposed an ambitious social and economic program, the **Fair Deal.** He asked Congress to enlarge New Deal programs in economic security, conservation, and housing, and to go beyond the New Deal in other areas.

The Eighty-first Congress complied with the extension of existing programs but rejected new measures. Lawmakers raised the minimum wage; increased social-security coverage and benefits; expanded appropriations for public power, conservation, and slum clearance; and authorized the construction of nearly a million low-income housing units. They also allowed hundreds of thousands of Holocaust survivors and Europeans displaced by the war, both Jews and non-Jews, to enter the United States. But they rejected federal aid to education, national health insurance, civil-rights legislation, larger farm subsidies, and the repeal of Taft-Hartley.

Congress's rejection of most Fair Deal proposals stemmed from Truman's own lessening commitment to domestic reform in favor of foreign policy, as well as from the strengthening of the congressional conservative coalition. And widespread prosperity sapped public enthusiasm for more reform.

CHECKING IN

- The Republican-controlled Eightieth Congress blocked Truman's proposals and reduced organized labor's power by passing the Taft-Hartley Act.

- Jackie Robinson broke the major-league color barrier by becoming the Brooklyn Dodgers' second baseman; other professional sports also integrated.

- Controversy split the Democratic party in 1948 as Truman moved to enlarge civil-rights protections and segregationist southerners walked out to form the Dixiecrats.

- To the surprise of many, Truman defeated Thomas Dewey to win reelection in 1948.

- The Fair Deal was Truman's attempt to continue and enlarge the New Deal; Congress rejected virtually all of its measures.

THE POLITICS OF ANTICOMMUNISM

How did anticommunist sentiment affect American society?

As the Cold War worsened, some Americans concluded that the roots of the nation's foreign difficulties lay in domestic treason and subversion. How else could the communists have taken China and built an atomic bomb? Millions of fearful Americans would eventually enlist in a crusade that would find scapegoats for the nation's problems and equate dissent with disloyalty.

Similar intolerance had prevailed in the Red Scare of 1919–1920 (see Chapter 22). Since 1938 the House Committee on Un-American Activities—later called the **House Un-American Activities Committee,** or HUAC (HYOO-ack)—had served as a platform for extreme conservatives' denunciation of the New Deal as a communist plot. After World War II, mounting numbers of mainstream Democrats and Republicans climbed aboard the anti-Red bandwagon.

The **Second Red Scare** influenced both governmental and personal actions. Millions of Americans were subjected to loyalty oaths and security investigations after the war. Anticommunist extremism destroyed the Left, undermined labor militancy, and discredited liberalism. It spawned a "silent generation" of college students, and ensured anticommunist foreign-policy rigidity.

House Un-American Activities Committee Called HUAC, "Red-hunting" House committee

Second Red Scare Postwar anticommunist hysteria that cast a cloud of suspicion over government, academia, even Hollywood

Loyalty and Security

The Cold War raised legitimate concerns about American security. The U.S. Communist party had claimed eighty thousand members during World War II, and no one knew how many occupied sensitive government positions. In mid-1945 a raid of the offices of a procommunist magazine revealed that classified documents had been given to the periodical by two State Department employees and a naval intelligence officer. Ten months later, the Canadian government exposed a major spy network that had passed American military information and atomic secrets to the Soviets during the war. Republicans accused the administration of being "soft on communism."

In March 1947 Truman issued Executive Order 9835 establishing the Federal Employee Loyalty Program to root out subversives in the government. The drive for absolute security soon overran concerns about rights, however, as civil servants suspected of disloyalty were allowed neither to face their accusers nor to require investigators to reveal sources.

Mere criticism of American foreign policy could result in an accusation of disloyalty. People could lose their jobs if they liked foreign films, associated with radical friends or family members, or were past members of organizations now declared disloyal. Of the 4.7 million jobholders and applicants who underwent loyalty checks by 1952, 560 were fired or denied jobs on security grounds, several thousand resigned or withdrew their applications, and countless more were intimidated. The probe uncovered no evidence of subversion or espionage, but it did spread fear among government employees.

The Anticommunist Crusade

The very existence of a federal loyalty inquest fed mounting anticommunist hysteria. Federal investigators promoted fears of communist infiltration and legitimized other efforts to expose subversives. Universities banned controversial speakers, and popular magazines ran articles like "Reds Are After Your Child." By the end of Truman's term, thirty-nine states had created loyalty programs, most with virtually no procedural safeguards. Schoolteachers, college professors, and state and city employees throughout the nation signed loyalty oaths or lost their jobs.

In 1947 HUAC began hearings to expose communist influence in American life. HUAC's probes blurred distinctions between dissent and disloyalty, between radicalism and subversion. People who refused to answer HUAC questions often lost their livelihood. Labor unions expelled communist members and avoided progressive causes, concentrating on securing better pay and benefits and becoming bureaucratic special-interest groups. HUAC also left its mark on the entertainment industry. When several prominent film directors and screenwriters refused to cooperate in 1947, HUAC had them cited for contempt and sent to federal prison. Blacklists in Hollywood and in radio broadcasting barred the

The Red Menace, 1949
Although Hollywood generally avoided overtly political films, it released a few dozen explicitly anticommunist films in the postwar era. Depicting American communists as vicious hypocrites, if not hardened criminals, Cold War movies were an effort to protect Hollywood's imperiled public image after HUAC's widely publicized investigation of the movie industry.

employment of anyone with a slightly questionable past, thereby silencing many talented people.

The 1948 presidential campaign fed national anxieties. Truman lambasted Henry Wallace as a Stalinist dupe and accused the Republicans of being "unwittingly the ally of the communists in this country." In turn, the GOP dubbed the Democrats "the party of treason." A rising Republican star, Richard M. Nixon of California, charged that Democrats bore responsibility for "the unimpeded growth of the communist conspiracy in the United States."

To blunt the force of such accusations, the Justice Department prosecuted eleven top leaders of the American Communist party under the Smith Act of 1940, which outlawed any conspiracy advocating the overthrow of the government. In 1951 the Supreme Court upheld the Smith Act's constitutionality, declaring that Congress could curtail freedom of speech if national security demanded such restrictions.

Ironically, the Communist party was fading into obscurity at the very time that politicians were magnifying the threat it posed. By 1950 its membership had shrunk to less than thirty thousand.

**Primary Source:
I'm No Communist**

Alger Hiss and the Rosenbergs

Nothing set off more alarms about the diabolical Red conspiracy in the federal government than the matter of **Alger** (AL-jurr) **Hiss and Whittaker Chambers.** During the 1948 presidential campaign, HUAC conducted a sensational hearing in which Whittaker Chambers, a senior editor at *Time* and a former Soviet agent who had broken with the communists in 1938, identified Hiss as an underground party member in the 1930s.

In the hearing, Chambers appeared a tortured soul crusading to save the West from the Red peril. The elegant and cultured Hiss, in contrast, seemed the very symbol of the liberal establishment; a Harvard Law School graduate, he had served as a presidential adviser on foreign affairs (including the Yalta conference). Hiss denied any communist affiliation and claimed not to know Chambers. Most liberals believed Hiss. They saw him as the victim of conservatives bent on tarnishing New Deal liberalism.

To those suspicious of the Roosevelt liberal tradition, Chambers's persistence intensified fears that the Democratic administration was teeming with communists. Under rigorous questioning by Richard Nixon, Hiss admitted that he had known Chambers but denied having been a communist. Chambers broadened his accusation, claiming that Hiss had committed espionage in the 1930s by giving him secret State Department documents to be sent to the Soviet Union. Hiss protested his innocence but in January 1950 was convicted of perjury, or lying under oath, and received a five-year prison sentence.

Just as the Hiss affair ended, another case shocked Americans. In early February 1950 the British arrested Klaus Fuchs (fooks), a German-born scientist involved in the Manhattan Project, for passing atomic secrets to the Soviets. Fuchs's confession led to the arrest of two Americans, **Ethel and Julius Rosenberg,** as coconspirators. The Rosenbergs insisted that they were victims of anti-Semitism and were being prosecuted for their leftist beliefs. But in March 1951 a jury found them guilty of

Alger Hiss and Whittaker Chambers Hiss was a major figure in Truman administration convicted of perjury for denying communist connections alleged by Chambers

Ethel and Julius Rosenberg Julius Rosenberg spied for the Soviets and was executed, along with this wife, in 1953

conspiring to commit espionage, and on June 19, 1953, the husband and wife were executed, although they maintained their innocence to the end. Soviet documents released in the 1990s implicated both Hiss and Julius Rosenberg.

McCarthyism

At this point, some Americans could not separate fact from fantasy. For them, only conspiracy could explain U.S. weakness and Soviet might. Frustrated by unexpected failure in 1948, Republicans eagerly exploited the fearful mood and accused the "Commiecrats" of selling out America.

Then, in February 1950, Republican senator **Joseph R. McCarthy** of Wisconsin, desperate for an issue on which to run for reelection in 1952, boldly told a West Virginia audience that communists in the State Department had betrayed America. "I have here in my hand a list of 205," McCarthy reported as he waved a laundry list, ". . . a list of names known to the Secretary of State as being members of the Communist party and who nevertheless are still working and shaping policy." Although he could produce no evidence to support his accusations, his senatorial stature and brazen style gave him a national forum. McCarthy soon repeated his charges, though lowering his numbers and toning them down slightly. A Senate committee found McCarthy's accusations "a fraud and a hoax," but he persisted. "McCarthyism" became a synonym for personal attacks on individuals by means of indiscriminate allegations and unsubstantiated charges.

As the Korean War dragged on, McCarthy's efforts to "root out the skunks" escalated. He ridiculed Secretary of State Dean Acheson as the "Red Dean" and called Truman's dismissal of MacArthur "the greatest victory the communists have ever won." Buoyed by the partisan usefulness of McCarthy's onslaught, many Republicans encouraged him. McCarthyism especially appealed to midwestern party members opposed to the welfare state and restrictions on business. For them, anticommunism was a weapon of revenge against liberals and a means to regain the controlling position that conservatism had once held. McCarthy also won a devoted following among blue-collar workers. His attacks appealed to traditionally Catholic ethnics, who wanted to gain acceptance as "100 percent Americans" through a show of anticommunist zeal. Countless Americans also shared McCarthy's scorn for the "bright young men who are born with silver spoons in their mouths." And his conspiracy theory offered a simple answer to the perplexing questions of the Cold War.

McCarthy's political power rested on both the Republican establishment and Democrats fearful of antagonizing him. His GOP support made Democrats' condemnation look like mere partisan criticism. In the 1950 elections, when he helped Republicans defeat Democrats who had denounced him, McCarthy appeared invincible.

Over Truman's veto, Congress in 1950 adopted the **McCarran Internal Security Act,** which required organizations deemed communist by the attorney general to register with the Department of Justice. The McCarran Act authorized the arrest and detention during a national emergency of "any person as to whom there is reason to believe might engage in acts of espionage or sabotage." The McCarran-Walter Immigration and Nationality Act of 1952, also adopted over a presidential veto, maintained the quota system that gave immigrants from northern and western

Joseph R. McCarthy Red-baiting senator from Wisconsin

McCarran Internal Security Act Required all alleged communist organizations to register with the government

Europe 85 percent of available slots, although it did end Asian exclusion. The new law also strengthened the attorney general's authority to exclude or deport aliens suspected of supporting communism.

The Election of 1952

In 1952 public apprehension about the loyalty of government employees combined with frustration over the Korean stalemate to sink Democratic hopes to their lowest level since the 1920s. Both business and labor also resented Truman's freeze on wages and prices during the Korean conflict. Revelations of bribery and influence peddling by some of Truman's old political associates gave Republicans ammunition for charging the Democrats with "plunder at home, and blunder abroad."

With Truman too unpopular to seek reelection, dispirited Democrats drafted Governor Adlai E. Stevenson of Illinois. But Stevenson could not dissociate himself from Truman, and his lofty speeches did not stir the average voter. Above all, Stevenson could not overcome the sentiment that twenty years of Democratic rule was enough.

The GOP nominated the hugely popular war hero Dwight D. Eisenhower. Although essentially apolitical, Eisenhower answered the call of the moderate wing of the Republican party and accepted the nomination. "Ike" chose as his running mate Richard M. Nixon, the former HUAC Red hunter.

Eisenhower and Nixon proved unbeatable. With a captivating grin and an unimpeachable record of public service, Eisenhower projected both personal warmth and the vigorous authority associated with military command. He symbolized the stability for which Americans yearned. At the same time, Nixon kept public apprehensions at the boiling point. Accusing the Democrats of treason, he charged that a Democratic victory would bring "more Alger Hisses, more atomic spies."

The GOP ticket stumbled when newspapers revealed the existence of a "slush fund" that California business leaders had created to keep Nixon in "financial comfort." But Nixon saved himself with a heart-tugging television defense. He explained the resulting gifts, which included a cocker spaniel named Checkers given to his daughters, as intended to benefit his family. His appeal worked. The Republican ticket won 55 percent of the popular vote, cracked the solid South to carry thirty-nine states, and amassed 442 electoral votes. Enough Republicans rode Ike's coattails to give the GOP control of both houses of Congress by small margins.

CHECKING IN

- Truman established the Federal Employee Loyalty Program to enhance security, but at the expense of civil rights.
- HUAC held a series of spectacular hearings to "root out" communism in American life; the hearings catapulted to prominence a young California politician, Richard M. Nixon.
- The cases of Alger Hiss and the Rosenbergs, accused of spying for the Soviets, increased the public's fear of communism at home.
- Senator Joseph R. McCarthy unleashed a reckless anticommunist campaign that made him, for a while, the most feared man in America.
- In the 1952 election, Dwight D. Eisenhower, a war hero and reassuring figure, was the easy victor.

Chapter Summary

 DOWNLOAD THE MP3 AUDIO FILE OF THE CHAPTER SUMMARY, AND LISTEN TO IT ON THE GO.

What were the major consequences of the GI Bill of Rights? (page 617)

Demobilization brought home more than 10 million men and women; the GI Bill sent many of them to college and propelled even more into the middle class. The consumer economy boomed as Americans sought to make up for the deprivations of depression and war. Most of Truman's proposals died in Congress, and in 1946 the Republicans gained control of Congress.

How did the policies of the United States and Soviet Union lead to the beginnings of the Cold War? (page 621)

The Soviet Union moved quickly to consolidate its hold over Eastern Europe. To Stalin, this policy was primarily defensive; to Truman, it was aggression. What was left of the World War II coalition vanished amid clouds of mutual suspicion and distrust. Containment became the bedrock of American foreign policy. The Truman Doctrine proclaimed the United States to be a global policeman, while the Marshall Plan helped rebuild Western Europe. NSC-68 became policy as the Korean War raged, placing the country on a permanent war footing and radically increasing defense spending. The Korean War thrust the United States squarely into Asian politics.

What effect did the more conservative political climate have on Truman's domestic program? (page 629)

The Republican-controlled Eightieth Congress blocked most of Truman's proposals; it clipped labor's wings with the Taft-Hartley Act. Questions of discrimination took center stage when Jackie Robinson integrated major league baseball; in 1948 the civil rights issue split the Democratic party, with segregationist southerners forming their own "Dixiecrat" party. Truman announced the Fair Deal, his attempt to continue and enlarge the New Deal, but virtually none of his new proposals became law.

How did anticommunist sentiment affect American society? (page 632)

Fear of communism permeated American life. Highly-publicized HUAC hearings seemed to reveal communists under every bed, and Truman compounded the fear with his Federal Employee Loyalty Program. The Hiss and Rosenberg cases, alleging betrayal of secret information to the Soviets, intensified the public's jitteriness and set the stage for the emergence of Senator Joseph R. McCarthy and his reckless accusations of communist penetration of the American government. The Republicans would ride "McCarthyism" back to the seat of power in Washington. It would be up to war hero Dwight D. Eisenhower—who easily won the presidency in 1952—to restore unity and renew hopefulness.

KEY TERMS

GI Bill *(p. 618)*

George F. Kennan *(p. 622)*

containment *(p. 622)*

Truman Doctrine *(p. 623)*

Marshall Plan *(p. 624)*

Berlin airlift *(p. 624)*

North Atlantic Treaty Organization (NATO) *(p. 625)*

Mao Zedong *(p. 626)*

NSC-68 *(p. 627)*

Korean War *(p. 627)*

Taft-Hartley Act *(p. 629)*

Jackie Robinson *(p. 630)*

President's Committee on Civil Rights *(p. 630)*

Fair Deal *(p. 632)*

House Un-American Activities Committee *(p. 632)*

Second Red Scare *(p. 632)*

Alger Hiss and Whittaker Chambers *(p. 634)*

Ethel and Julius Rosenberg *(p. 634)*

Joseph R. McCarthy *(p. 635)*

McCarran Internal Security Act *(p. 635)*

America at Mid-Century

1952–1960

The 1950s College Graduate,
by Norman Rockwell

This icon will direct you to the website where you can Prepare for Class, Improve Your Grade, and Ace the Test: **www.cengage.com/history/boyer/enduringconcise6e**

Nostalgia has painted the 1950s as a decade of tranquility, abundance, new homes in the suburbs, family togetherness, and big cars. In movies and television, the fifties are a sunny time when everybody liked Ike, idolized Elvis, and loved Lucy.

First shown in 1951, *I Love Lucy* quickly became the number one show on television. The program's characters mirrored the actual lives of many Americans in the 1950s. Lucille Ball insisted that her real-life husband, Cuban-born bandleader Desi Arnaz, play her on-screen husband, at a time when American minorities gained visibility; that they leave their crowded urban apartment for suburbia just as millions of Americans did so; and that she have a baby, in reality as well as on TV, at the height of the baby boom.

Many Americans in later decades would look back at *I Love Lucy* with nostalgia, seeing it as a symbol of the tranquil "nifty fifties." On the surface, the show depicted a dizzy stay-at home housewife whose husband was master of the house, thus perpetuating a stereotype of female domesticity. Yet, simultaneously, the show skewered the ideology of domesticity. Show after show depicted Lucy's pursuit of a paying job, epitomizing the restless aspirations of a generation of housebound women. *I Love Lucy*—like the 1950s—was filled with contradictions and irony.

Behind the stereotypes lay a reality far more complex, and often far darker. Americans did enjoy the fruits of the decade's consumer culture. Having survived a depression and global war, they reveled in prosperity. They trusted Dwight D. Eisenhower and welcomed the thaw in the Cold War that came after the Korean War.

At the same time, the fifties saw the birth of the space age and of hydrogen bombs. Senator Joseph McCarthy, the Warren Court, and Martin Luther King, Jr. kindled intense political passions. The arrival of an automated society and television's growing power transformed life, as did the baby boom and mass suburbanization. Mid-century America encompassed peace and a widening Cold War, prosperity and persistent poverty, civil-rights triumphs and rampant racism. Although the 1950s were good years for many Americans, like *I Love Lucy* they were hardly placid: both showed us what we were and what we would become.

THE EISENHOWER PRESIDENCY

What domestic policies support the notion of Eisenhower as a centrist or moderate politician?

Rarely in U.S. history has a president better fit the national mood than **Dwight David Eisenhower.** Exhausted by a quarter-century of upheaval—the stock-market crash, the Great Depression, World War II, the Cold War—Americans craved stability and peace. And Eisenhower delivered. Elected in 1952, Eisenhower gave people weary of partisanship a sense of unity, and he inspired confidence.

Dwight David Eisenhower
War hero and thirty-fourth president of the United States whose two-term presidency was marked by moderation and stability; nicknamed "Ike"

"Dynamic Conservatism" The most lauded general of World War II, Eisenhower projected the image of a plain but good man. He expressed complicated issues in simple terms while governing a complex, urban, technological society, and comforting an anxious people.

Born on October 14, 1890, in Denison, Texas, Eisenhower grew up in Abilene, Kansas, in a poor, religious family. More athletic than studious, he graduated from the U.S. Military Academy at West Point in 1915. In directing the Allied invasion of North Africa in 1942 and of western Europe in 1944, he revealed himself to be a brilliant war planner, respected for his managerial ability and talent for conciliation.

Eisenhower's approach to the presidency reflected his wartime leadership style. He concentrated on major matters, delegated authority, and worked to reconcile contending factions. His restrained view of presidential authority stemmed from his respect for the constitutional balance of power and for the dignity of the Oval Office. Eisenhower rarely intervened publicly in the legislative process and assured his cabinet members that he would "stay out of [their] hair." This low-key style, combined with frequent fishing and golfing vacations, led Democrats to scoff at Eisenhower as a leader who "reigned but did not rule."

The image of passivity masked an active and occasionally ruthless politician. Determined to govern the nation on business principles, Eisenhower staffed his administration with corporate executives. "Eight millionaires and a plumber," wrote one journalist. Eisenhower initially worked with the Republican-controlled Congress to reduce the size of government and to slash the federal budget.

For the most part, however, the Eisenhower administration followed a centrist course. More pragmatic than ideological, the president wished to reduce taxes, contain inflation, and govern efficiently. Eisenhower relied heavily on the Council of Economic Advisers (CEA), despite conservative calls for its abolition. When recessions struck in 1953 and 1957, Eisenhower abandoned a balanced budget and increased spending to restore prosperity.

Ike supported extending social-security benefits, raising the minimum wage, adding 4 million workers to those eligible for unemployment benefits, and providing federally financed public housing for low-income families. He also approved construction of the St. Lawrence Seaway, linking the Great Lakes and the Atlantic Ocean, and creation of the Department of Health, Education, and Welfare. In 1956 Eisenhower backed the largest and most expensive public-works program in American history: the Interstate Highway Act, authorizing construction of a 41,000-mile system of expressways. Freeways would soon snake across America, accelerating suburban growth, heightening dependence on cars and trucks, contributing to urban decay and air pollution, and drastically increasing gasoline consumption.

Republicans renominated Ike by acclamation in 1956, and voters gave him a landslide victory over Democrat Adlai Stevenson. With the GOP crowing, "Everything's booming but the guns," the president won by the greatest popular majority since FDR's victory in 1936.

The Downfall of Joseph McCarthy

Although he despised Joseph McCarthy, Eisenhower feared battling the senator. Instead, he allowed McCarthy to grab plenty of rope in hopes that the demagogue would hang himself. He did.

In 1954 McCarthy accused the army of harboring communist spies, and the army charged McCarthy with using his influence to gain preferential treatment for a staff member who had been drafted. The resulting nationally televised Senate investigation, begun in April 1954, brought McCarthy down. A national audience witnessed McCarthy's boorish behavior firsthand on television. His dark scowl, endless interruptions, and disregard for the rights of others repelled many viewers. In June, when McCarthy smeared the reputation of a young lawyer assisting Joseph Welch, the army counsel, Welch struck back: "Until this moment, Senator, I think I really never gauged your cruelty or your recklessness....Have you no sense of decency?" The gallery burst into applause.

The spell of the inquisitor broken, the Senate in December 1954 censured the Wisconsin senator for contemptuous behavior. This powerful rebuke demolished

Chronology

1946	ENIAC, the first electronic computer, begins operation
1947	Levittown, New York, development started
1948	Bell Labs develops the transistor
1950	*Asosiación Nacional México-Americana* established
1952	Dwight D. Eisenhower elected president
1953	Korean War truce signed; Earl Warren appointed chief justice; Operation Wetback begins
1954	Army-McCarthy hearings; *Brown* v. *Board of Education of Topeka;* Fall of Dienbienphu; Geneva Conference.; *Father Knows Best* begins on TV
1955	Salk polio vaccine developed; AFL-CIO merger; first postwar U.S.-Soviet summit meeting; James Dean stars in *Rebel Without a Cause*; Montgomery bus boycott begins
1956	Interstate Highway Act; Suez crisis; Soviet intervention in Poland and Hungary
1957	Eisenhower Doctrine announced; Civil Rights Act (first since Reconstruction); Little Rock school-desegregation crisis; Soviet Union launches *Sputnik*; peak of baby boom (4.3 million births); Southern Christian Leadership Conference founded
1958	National Defense Education Act; United States and Soviet Union halt atomic tests; National Aeronautics and Space Administration (NASA) founded
1959	Fidel Castro comes to power in Cuba; Khrushchev and Eisenhower meet at Camp David.
1960	U-2 incident; Second Civil Rights Act; suburban population almost equals that of central city

McCarthy as a political force. In 1957 he died a broken man. But the fears he exploited lingered. Congress annually funded the House Un-American Activities Committee. State and local governments continued to require loyalty oaths from teachers.

McCarthyism also remained a rallying call of conservatives disenchanted with the postwar consensus. Young conservatives like William F. Buckley, Jr., and the Christian Anti-Communist Crusade continued to claim that domestic communism was a major subversive threat. The John Birch Society denounced Eisenhower as a conscious agent of the communist conspiracy and equated liberalism with treason. Although few saw all the lurking dangers that the John Birch Society did, Barry Goldwater, George Wallace, and Ronald Reagan, among others, used its anticommunist, antigovernment rhetoric to advantage. Stressing victory over communism, rather than its containment, the self-proclaimed "new conservatives" (or radical Right, as their opponents called them) criticized the "creeping socialism" of Eisenhower, advocated a return to traditional moral standards, and condemned the liberal rulings of the Supreme Court.

Jim Crow in Court

Led by a new chief justice, **Earl Warren** (1953), the Supreme Court drew conservatives' wrath for defending the rights of those accused of subversive beliefs. In a 1957 decision, the Court held that the accused had the right to inspect government files used by the prosecution, and that same year the justices overturned convictions of

Earl Warren Chief justice of Supreme Court who broadened constitutional protections for individual rights

Brown v. Board of Education
1954 Supreme Court decision that declared "separate but equal" doctrine unconstitutional; paved way for end of segregation

Southern Manifesto 1956 statement of southern congressmen, opposing the *Brown* decision and defending racial segregation

Communist party officials under the Smith Act. Right-wing opponents plastered "Impeach Earl Warren" posters on highway billboards.

These condemnations paled beside those of segregationists after the ***Brown* v. *Board of Education of Topeka*** (May 1954) ruling. Unanimously reversing *Plessy* v. *Ferguson* and its separate but equal doctrine, the Court held that separating school-children "solely because of their race generates a feeling of inferiority . . . that may affect their hearts and minds in a way unlikely ever to be undone," thereby violating the equal-protection clause of the Fourteenth Amendment. The justices concluded that "separate educational facilities are inherently unequal." A year later the Court ordered the states to desegregate their schools "with all deliberate speed."

The border states complied, but white politicians in the South vowed resistance. Eisenhower refused to force them. Although not a racist, he never publicly endorsed the *Brown* decision, and privately he called his appointment of Earl Warren "the biggest damn fool mistake I ever made."

Polls indicated that 80 percent of white southerners were against the *Brown* decision and, encouraged by Ike's silence, opposition stiffened. White Citizens Councils sprang up, and the Ku Klux Klan revived. Declaring the *Brown* decision "null, void, and of no effect," southern legislatures denied state aid to school systems that desegregated or closed them down. They also permitted school boards to assign black and white children to different schools.

In 1956, more than one hundred members of Congress signed the **Southern Manifesto,** denouncing *Brown* as "a clear abuse of judicial power." An Alabama gubernatorial candidate promised to go to jail to defend segregation, and his opponent promptly vowed to die for it. Segregationists also used violence and economic reprisals against blacks. At the end of 1956, not a single African-American attended school with whites in the Deep South, and few did so in the Upper South.

Little Rock, 1957
Elizabeth Eckford, age 15, one of the nine black students to desegregate Central High School, endures abuse on her way to school, September 4, 1957. Forty years later, the young white woman shouting insults asked for forgiveness.

The Laws of the Land

Southern resistance reached a climax in September 1957 when Arkansas governor Orval Faubus mobilized the state's National Guard to bar nine African-American students from entering Little Rock's Central High School under a federal court order. After another court order forced Faubus to withdraw the guardsmen, jeering whites blocked the black students' entry.

Eisenhower sought to avoid the civil-rights issue, but he believed he had to uphold federal law. He also understood that racism at home hampered American efforts to gain the support of nonwhite Third World nations. The president dispatched federal troops to protect blacks' rights, and soldiers patrolled Central High for the rest of the year. Rather than accept integration, Faubus shut down Little Rock's public high schools for two years. At the end of the decade, fewer than 1 percent of African-American students in the Deep South attended desegregated schools.

Little Rock only strengthened African-Americans' determination to end Jim Crow. The crisis foreshadowed television's vital role in the civil-rights movement by airing images of howling whites abusing resolute black students. A 1957 public-opinion poll showed that 90 percent of whites outside the South approved the use of federal troops in Little Rock.

Most northern whites also favored legislation to enfranchise southern blacks. The Civil Rights Act of 1957, the first civil-rights law since Reconstruction, established a permanent commission on civil rights with broad investigatory powers but did little to guarantee the ballot to blacks. The Civil Rights Act of 1960 only slightly strengthened the first measure. Like the *Brown* decision, however, these laws implied a changing federal attitude about race and encouraged blacks to fight for their rights.

THE COLD WAR CONTINUES

In what ways did Eisenhower continue Truman's foreign policy, and in what ways did he change it?

Eisenhower maintained Truman's containment policy. Stalin's death in 1953 and Eisenhower's resolve to reduce the risk of nuclear war brought a thaw in the Cold War, but the United States and the Soviet Union remained deadlocked. Neither the Cold War nor American determination to check communism ceased. Global fear of a nuclear holocaust mounted in step with both countries' increasingly destructive weapons.

After Stalin's death, the uncertainty in the communist world and Eisenhower's veiled threat to use nuclear weapons broke the stalemate in Korea. The armistice signed in July 1953 set the boundary between North and South Korea once again at the thirty-eighth parallel and established a panel from neutral nations to oversee the return of prisoners of war. Some Americans claimed that communist aggression had been thwarted and containment vindicated; others condemned the truce as peace without honor.

Ike and Dulles

Eager to ease Cold War hostilities, Eisenhower first had to quiet the GOP right wing's clamor to roll back the Red tide. To do so, he chose as his secretary of state **John Foster Dulles** (DULL-us), a rigid, humorless Presbyterian who advocated a holy war against "atheistic communism," backed by the threat of "instant, massive retaliation" with nuclear weapons. Dulles called for "liberation" of the captive peoples of Eastern Europe and for unleashing Jiang Jieshi against Communist China. Believing that the Soviet Union understood only force, Dulles insisted on the necessity of "brinksmanship," the art of never backing down in a crisis, even at the risk of war.

CHECKING IN

- As president, Eisenhower steered a centrist course, which he called dynamic conservatism, with limited expansion of social programs.
- McCarthy self-destructed, revealing his boorishness in the televised Army-McCarthy hearings.
- The radical Right "new conservative" movement grew in spite of McCarthy's demise.
- Although Eisenhower never publicly supported the *Brown* decision, the Little Rock crisis forced his hand; he intervened to enforce integration.
- Even though desegregation made little progress in the South, Congress passed important civil-rights legislation in 1957 and 1960, implying a change in federal attitudes toward race issues.

CL Primary Source: Korea—The War that Could Have Set Off World War III

John Foster Dulles Eisenhower's secretary of state and anticommunist hard-liner

Such saber rattling pleased the Right, but Eisenhower preferred conciliation, partly because he feared a nuclear war—the Soviet Union had tested its own hydrogen bomb in 1953. Eisenhower refused to translate Dulles's rhetoric into action. Aware of the limits of American power, the United States did nothing to check the Soviet interventions that crushed uprisings in East Germany (1953) and Hungary (1956).

As multimegaton thermonuclear weapons replaced atomic bombs in U.S. and Soviet arsenals, Eisenhower worked to reduce the probability of mutual annihilation. He proposed "atoms for peace," whereby both superpowers would contribute fissionable materials to a new UN agency for use in industrial projects. In the absence of a positive Soviet response, the government began construction of an electronic air defense system to provide early warning of a missile attack.

Work also began on commercial nuclear plants in the mid-1950s, promising electricity "too cheap to meter." However, most money continued to go for nuclear research that was military. Radioactive fallout from atomic tests, especially the 1954 U.S. tests that spread strontium 90 over a wide area, heightened world concern about the nuclear-arms race.

In 1955 Eisenhower and Soviet leaders met in Geneva for the first East-West conference since World War II. Discussions produced no concrete plan for arms control, but mutual talk of "peaceful coexistence" led reporters to hail the "spirit of Geneva." In March 1958 Moscow suspended atmospheric tests of nuclear weapons, and the United States followed suit.

But the Cold War continued. Dulles negotiated mutual-defense pacts with forty-three nations. The United States' "New Look" defense program guaranteed "more bang for the buck" by emphasizing nuclear weapons and reducing conventional forces. It spurred the Soviets to seek "more rubble for the ruble" by enlarging their nuclear stockpile.

Meanwhile, the focus of the Cold War shifted from Europe to the Third World, the largely nonwhite developing nations. There the two superpowers waged war by proxy, using local guerrillas and military juntas. There, too, the Central Intelligence Agency (CIA) fought covert wars against those thought to imperil American interests.

CIA Covert Actions

Established in 1947 to conduct foreign intelligence gathering, the CIA soon began to carry out undercover operations to topple regimes friendly to communism. By 1957 half its personnel and 80 percent of its budget were devoted to "covert action." To woo influential foreign thinkers away from communism, the CIA also sponsored intellectual conferences and jazz concerts. It bankrolled anticommunist cultural events, subsidized magazines to publish articles supporting Washington, and recruited college students and businessmen traveling abroad as "fronts" in clandestine CIA activities.

In 1953 the CIA orchestrated a coup to overthrow the government of Iran. Fearing that the prime minister, who had nationalized oil fields, might open oil-rich Iran to the Soviets, the CIA replaced him with pro-American Shah Reza Pahlavi (REH-zah PAH-lah-vee). The United States thus gained a loyal ally on the Soviet border, and American oil companies prospered when the Shah made low-priced oil available to them. But Iranian hatred of America took root—a hostility that would haunt the United States a quarter-century later.

Also in 1953 the CIA intervened in Philippine elections to ensure a pro-American government. In 1954 in Guatemala a CIA-supported band of mercenaries overthrew the elected communist-influenced regime, which had seized land from the American-owned United Fruit Company. The new pro-American government restored United Fruit's properties and trampled political opposition.

The Vietnam Domino

The most extensive CIA covert operations during the 1950s took place in Indochina. The United States viewed Indochina as a Cold War battleground. The Truman administration had provided France with large-scale military assistance to fight the Vietminh (vee-et-MIN), a broad-based Vietnamese nationalist coalition led by the communist Ho Chi Minh (hoe chee min). But the French were losing. In early 1954 the Vietminh besieged twelve thousand French troops in the valley of Dienbienphu (dee-yen-bee-yen-FOO).

France appealed for U.S. intervention, and some American officials toyed with the idea of a nuclear strike, which Eisenhower flatly rejected. In May the French surrendered at Dienbienphu. An international conference in Geneva arranged a cease-fire and divided Vietnam at the seventeenth parallel, pending elections in 1956 to choose the government of a unified nation.

Although unwilling to go to war, Eisenhower would not accept a communist takeover of Vietnam. In what became known as the **domino theory,** Eisenhower warned that, if Vietnam fell to the communists, then Thailand, Burma, Indonesia, and ultimately all of Asia would follow. The United States refused to sign the Geneva Peace Accords and in late 1954 created the Southeast Asia Treaty Organization (SEATO), a military alliance patterned on NATO.

domino theory The belief that if Vietnam fell to the communists, all of Asia would follow

In June 1954 the CIA installed Ngo Dinh Diem (woh din dee-EM), a fiercely anticommunist Catholic, as premier and then president of an independent South Vietnam. CIA agents helped him eliminate political opposition and block the election to reunify Vietnam specified by the Geneva agreements. As Eisenhower later admitted, "possibly 80 percent of the population would have voted for the communist Ho Chi Minh as their leader." Washington pinned its hopes on Diem to maintain a noncommunist South Vietnam with American dollars rather than American lives.

But the autocratic Diem's Catholicism alienated the predominantly Buddhist population, and his refusal to institute land reform and end corruption spurred opposition. In December 1960 opposition to Diem coalesced in the **National Liberation Front.** Backed by North Vietnam, the insurgency attracted broad support and soon controlled half of South Vietnam.

National Liberation Front
Rising communist insurgency in South Vietnam, supported by the government of North Vietnam

Troubles in the Third World

Eisenhower faced his greatest crisis in the Middle East, the **Suez crisis.** In 1954 Gamal Abdel Nasser (gu-MAWL AB-dul NASS-er) came to power in Egypt, determined to modernize his nation. To woo him, the United States offered financing for a dam at Aswan (AS-wahn) to harness the Nile River. But when Nasser purchased arms from

Suez crisis Egypt nationalized the Suez Canal, prompting Britain, France, and Israel to take military action

Czechoslovakia, John Foster Dulles canceled the loan, and Nasser nationalized the British-owned Suez Canal.

Viewing the canal as the lifeline of its empire, Britain planned to take it back by force. Supporting the British were France, which feared Arab nationalism in their Algerian colony, and Israel, which feared the Egyptian arms buildup. The three countries, America's closest allies, coordinated an attack on Egypt in October 1956 without consulting Eisenhower. Ike fumed that the military action would drive the Arab world and its precious oil to the Russians. When Moscow threatened to intervene, Eisenhower forced his allies to withdraw their troops.

The Suez crisis had major consequences. It swelled Third World antiwestern sentiment, and the United States replaced Britain and France as the protector of western interests in the Middle East. Determined to guarantee the flow of oil to the West, in 1957 the president announced the **Eisenhower Doctrine,** a proclamation that the United States would send military aid and, if necessary, troops to any Middle Eastern nation threatened by "Communist aggression."

Such interventions intensified anti-American feelings in Third World nations. Angry crowds in Peru and Venezuela spat at Vice President Nixon and stoned his car in 1958. In 1959 Fidel Castro overturned a dictatorial regime in Cuba and confiscated American properties without compensation. A tougher blow struck on May 1, 1960, two weeks before a scheduled summit conference with Soviet premier Nikita Khrushchev (KROOSH-chef), when the Soviets shot down a U.S. spy plane far inside their border. Khrushchev displayed the captured CIA U-2 pilot and photos taken of Soviet missile sites. Eisenhower refused to apologize, and the summit collapsed.

The Eisenhower Legacy

Just before leaving office, Eisenhower offered Americans a farewell and a warning. The demands of national security, he stated, had produced the "conjunction of an immense military establishment and a large arms industry." Swollen defense budgets had yoked American economic health to military expenditures, and military contracts had become the staff of life for research scholars, politicians, and America's largest corporations. This combination of interests, Eisenhower believed, exerted enormous leverage and threatened the traditional subordination of the military in American life. "We must guard against the acquisition of unwarranted influence . . . by the **military-industrial complex.** The potential for the disastrous rise of misplaced power exists and will persist."

The moderate Eisenhower pleased neither Left nor Right. His acceptance of New Deal social-welfare measures angered the Republican Right, while liberal Democrats faulted his passivity toward McCarthyism and racism. But Ike had given the majority of Americans what they most wanted—prosperity, reassurance, and a breathing spell in which to relish the comforts of life.

Eisenhower Doctrine Committed the United States to policy of intervention in the Middle East (1957)

military-industrial complex Coalition that, according to Eisenhower, was amassing dangerous power

CHECKING IN

- Despite hard-line Dulles rhetoric, Eisenhower pursued a moderate Cold War course and avoided direct confrontation with the Soviet Union.

- The focus of the Cold War shifted to "clients" in the Third World.

- The Central Intelligence Agency conducted covert operations in Iran and Guatemala to overthrow elected governments not friendly enough to the United States.

- While the domino theory led the United States to deeper involvement in South Vietnam, the U.S.-supported regime of Ngo Dinh Diem faced a growing insurgency.

- The Middle East remained a hot spot after the Suez crisis, and the Eisenhower Doctrine committed the United States to intervene there against "Communist aggression."

THE AFFLUENT SOCIETY

What were the main sources, and consequences, of economic prosperity in the 1950s?

In 1958 economist John Kenneth Galbraith published *The Affluent Society,* a study of postwar America. The title reflected the broad-based prosperity that made the 1950s seem the fulfillment of the American dream. By the end of the decade, 60 percent of American families owned homes; 75 percent, cars; and 87 percent, at least one TV. Government spending, a huge upsurge in productivity, and steadily increasing consumer demand pushed the gross national product (GNP) up 50 percent.

Three brief recessions and a rising national debt, almost $290 billion by 1961, evoked concern but did little to stifle economic growth or optimism. The United States had achieved the world's highest living standard ever. By 1960 the average worker's income, adjusted for inflation, was 35 percent higher than in 1945. With just 6 percent of the world's population, the United States produced and consumed nearly 50 percent of everything made and sold on earth.

The New Industrial Society

Federal spending constituted a major source of economic growth, nearly doubling in the 1950s to $180 billion. Federal expenditures, just 1 percent of the GNP in 1929, reached 17 percent by the mid-1950s. These funds built roads and airports, financed home mortgages, supported farm prices, and provided stipends for education. More than half the federal budget—10 percent of the GNP—went to defense spending. The federal government remained the nation's chief sponsor of scientific and technological research and development (R&D).

Particularly for the West, it was as if World War II had never ended. Politicians from both parties labored to keep defense spending flowing westward. By the late 1950s, California alone received half the space budget and a quarter of all major military contracts. Denver had the largest number of federal employees outside Washington, D.C. Government spending transformed the West of rugged individualists into a new West of bureaucrats, defense contractors, and scientists dependent on federal funds.

Government funding and control transformed both the U.S. military and the industrial economy. Financed by the Atomic Energy Commission and using navy scientists, the nation's first nuclear power plant came on line in 1957. The chemical industry continued its wartime surge. As pesticides contaminated ground water supplies and plastics reduced landfill space, Americans—unaware of the hidden perils—marveled at fruits and vegetables covered with Saran Wrap and delighted in their Dacron suits, Acrilan socks, and Teflon-coated pans.

Electronics became the fifth-largest American industry. Electricity consumption tripled in the 1950s as consumers bought all manner of appliances. Cheap oil fueled expansion. Domestic oil production and foreign imports rose steeply, and by 1960 oil had replaced coal as the nation's main energy source. Hardly anyone paid attention when a physicist warned in 1953 that "adding 6 billion tons of carbon dioxide to the atmosphere each year is warming up the Earth."

Production Line at Douglas Aircraft Company

The Cold War stimulated an enormous economic boom in defense spending. By mid-century, more than half the federal budget, about 10 percent of the GNP, went to defense contractors like Douglas Aircraft, which helped the economy of the South and the West to flourish.

Plentiful cheap gasoline fed the growth of the automobile and aircraft industries. Aerospace, the nation's third-largest industry in the 1950s, depended on defense spending and federally funded research. The automobile industry, still the nation's industrial titan, also applied technological R&D. Between 1945 and 1960 automation halved the number of hours and workers needed to produce a car.

The Age of Computers

The computer was a key to technological revolution. In late 1946 the military devised ENIAC, the first electronic computer, to improve artillery accuracy. The unwieldy machine, with eighteen thousand vacuum tubes, could perform five thousand calculations per second. Next came the development of operating instructions, or programs, and the replacement of wires by printed circuits. Then, in 1948, Bell Labs invented tiny, solid-state transistors that ended reliance on radio tubes and initiated the age of computers.

Primary Source: Computers

Sales of electronic computers to industry rose from twenty in 1954 to more than two thousand in 1960. Major manufacturers used them to monitor production lines, track inventory, and ensure quality control. In government, computers were as indispensable to Pentagon strategists playing war games and to the Census Bureau and the Internal Revenue Service. By the mid-1960s more than thirty thousand mainframe computers would be used by banks, hospitals, and universities.

The development of the high-technology complex known as Silicon Valley began in 1951. Stanford University utilized its science and engineering faculties to design products for the Fairchild Semiconductor and Hewlett-Packard companies.

This relationship between universities and corporations became a model followed by other high-tech firms throughout the Santa Clara valley. Similar developments would follow along Massachusetts' Route 128; near Austin, Texas; and in North Carolina's Research Triangle.

The Costs of Bigness

Rapid technological advances accelerated the growth and power of big business. In 1950, twenty-two firms had assets of more than $1 billion; by 1960, fifty did. By then, one-half of 1 percent of corporations earned more than half the total corporate income in the United States. Wealthy firms swallowed weak competitors and became oligopolies. Three television networks monopolized the nation's airwaves; three automobile and three aluminum companies produced 90 percent of America's cars and aluminum; and large corporations controlled the lion's share of assets and sales in steel, petroleum, chemicals, and electrical machinery. Corporations acquired overseas facilities to become "multinational" enterprises. Growth and consolidation meant greater bureaucratization. "Executives" replaced "capitalists." Success required conformity not creativity, teamwork not individuality. According to sociologist David Riesman's *The Lonely Crowd* (1950), the new "company people" were "other-directed," eager to follow the cues from their peers.

Changes in agriculture paralleled those in industry. Farming grew increasingly scientific and mechanized. Between 1945 and 1960, technology halved the work hours necessary to grow crops. Many farm families migrated to cities. Meanwhile, heavily capitalized farm businesses prospered by using more and more machines and chemicals.

Until the publication of Rachel Carson's *Silent Spring* in 1962, few Americans understood the extent to which fertilizers, herbicides, and pesticides poisoned the environment. Carson, a former researcher for the Fish and Wildlife Service, dramatized the problems caused by the use of the insecticide DDT and its spread through the food chain. Her depiction of a "silent spring" caused by the death of songbirds from DDT toxicity led many states to ban its use. The federal government followed suit.

Blue-Collar Blues

Consolidation also transformed the labor movement. In 1955 the AFL and CIO merged, bringing 85 percent of union members into a single unit. Although leaders promised aggressive unionism, organized labor fell victim to its success at the bargaining table. Higher wages, a shorter workweek, paid vacations, health-care coverage, and automatic wage hikes tied to the cost of living led most workers to view themselves as middle class rather than the proletariat.

A decrease in the number of blue-collar workers also sapped labor's momentum. Automation cut membership in the coal, auto, and steelworkers' unions by more than half. Most of the new jobs in the 1950s were in the service sector and in public employment, which banned collective bargaining by labor unions.

In 1956, for the first time in U.S. history, white-collar workers outnumbered blue-collar workers. Although most service jobs were as routinized as any factory job, few unions wooed white-collar workers. The percentage of the labor force in unions dropped from a high of 36 percent in 1953 to 31 percent in 1960, and kept falling.

Prosperity and the Suburbs

As real income (adjusted for inflation) rose, Americans spent less of their income on necessities and more on powered lawn mowers and air conditioners. They heaped their shopping carts with frozen, dehydrated, and fortified foods. When they lacked cash, they borrowed. In 1950, Diners' Club issued the first credit card, and American Express followed in 1958. Installment buying, home mortgages, and auto loans tripled Americans' private indebtedness in the 1950s. In its effort to convince people to buy what they did not need, business spent more on advertising than the nation did on public schools.

Americans purchased 58 million new cars during the 1950s. Manufacturers enticed people to trade in and up by offering flashier models, two-tone color, tail fins, and more powerful engines, such as Pontiac's 1955 "Sensational Strato-Streak V-8," which could go more than twice as fast as any speed limit. The results were increases in highway deaths, air pollution, oil consumption, and "autosclerosis"—clogged urban arteries.

Made for Each Other

The two-tone '55 Chevy Bel Air convertible and a California suburban drive-in. As Americans flocked to the new suburban communities, the number of cars in the country increased by 133 percent between 1945 and 1960; and as Americans raced to buy the latest, flashiest model, almost as many cars were junked each year in the mid-1950s as were manufactured.

Government policy as well as "automania" spurred white Americans' exodus to the suburbs. Federal spending on highways skyrocketed from $79 million in 1946 to $2.6 billion in 1960. Once-remote areas came within "commuting distance" for urban workers. The income-tax code stimulated home sales by allowing deductions for home-mortgage interest payments and for property taxes. The Federal Housing Administration (FHA) and the Veterans Administration (VA) offered low-interest loans; neither promoted housing desegregation.

In 1947 in Long Island, some thirty miles from Manhattan, Alfred and William Levitt used mass-production techniques to construct thousands of look-alike 720-square-foot houses as quickly as possible. With "Levittown" as the ground-breaker, 85 percent of the 13 million new homes built in the 1950s were in the suburbs. In the greatest internal migration in its history, some 20 million Americans moved to the suburbs in the decade—making the suburban population nearly equal to that of the central cities. Although social critics lampooned the "ticky-tacky" houses in "disturbia," suburban life embodied the American dream for many families who longed for their own home, good schools, and neighbors like themselves.

Americans also moved South and West, into the Sunbelt, lured by job opportunities, the climate, and the pace of life. California, where the population went from 9 to 19 million between 1945 and 1964, supplanted New York as the most populous state. Los Angeles boasted the highest per capita ownership of private homes and cars of any city. Initially designed to lure shoppers downtown, the highway system instead had become the road to a home in the suburbs. Orange County, bordering Los Angeles, tripled its population in the 1950s.

Industry also headed South and West, drawn by low taxes, low energy costs, and anti-union right-to-work laws. Senior citizens headed to the easier climate. Both groups brought a conservative outlook. By 1980 the population of the **Sunbelt,** which stretched from the Old Confederacy across Texas to southern California, exceeded that of the North and East. The political power of the Republican party rose accordingly.

CONSENSUS AND CONSERVATISM

How accurate is the image of the 1950s as a period of conservatism and conformity?

Not everyone embraced the conformity of 1950s' consumer culture. Intellectuals found a wide audience for their attack on "organization men" bent on getting ahead by going along and on "status seekers" pursuing external rewards to compensate for inner insecurities. Others took aim at the consumerist middle class: "all items in a national supermarket—categorized, processed, labeled, priced, and readied for merchandising."

This criticism oversimplified reality. It ignored ethnic and class diversity, the acquisitiveness and conformity of earlier generations, and the currents of dissent swirling beneath the surface. But it rightly spotlighted the elevation of comfort over challenge, and of private pleasures over public affairs. It was, in the main, a time of political passivity and preoccupation with personal gain.

Togetherness and the Baby Boom

In 1954 *McCall's* magazine coined the term *togetherness* to celebrate the ideal couple: the man and woman who centered their lives on home and children. Americans in the 1950s tended to marry young, to have babies quickly, and to have more of them. The fertility rate (the number of births per 1,000 women) peaked at 123 in 1957, when an American baby was born every seven seconds.

New antibiotics subdued diphtheria and whooping cough, and the Salk and Sabin vaccines eliminated polio. The plunge in childhood mortality helped to raise American life expectancy from 65.9 years in 1945 to 70.9 years in 1970. Coupled with the **baby boom,** this led to a 19 percent population spurt during the 1950s. By 1960 children under 14 constituted one-third of the population.

Sunbelt States of the southwestern United States; increasingly populous and conservative in the 1950s

baby boom Enormous population spurt from 1946 to 1964

The sheer size of the baby-boom generation (76 million Americans were born between 1946 and 1964) ensured its impact. In the 1950s school construction boomed, as did college enrollments in the 1960s. The 1970s through the 1990s would see peaks in home construction, as the boomers had families, and in retirement investments. In the 1950s the baby boom made child rearing a foremost concern and reinforced the idea that women's place was in the home.

No one did more to emphasize the link between full-time mothers and healthy children than **Dr. Benjamin Spock;** only the Bible outsold his *Baby and Child Care* (1946) in the fifties. Spock urged mothers not to work outside the home, in order to create an atmosphere of warmth and intimacy for their children. Crying babies were to be comforted; breast-feeding came back into vogue.

Dr. Benjamin Spock Physician and author who urged mothers to devote themselves fulltime to the welfare of their children

Domesticity

Popular culture throughout the fifties glorified marriage and parenthood, painting a woman's devotion to life in the home with her children as the most cherished goal. Television mostly pictured women as at-home mothers. Hollywood perpetuated the stereotype of career women as neurotic. As Debbie Reynolds declared in *The Tender Trap* (1955), "A woman isn't a woman until she's been married and had children."

Education reinforced these ideas. Alongside academic subjects, girls studied typing, etiquette, and cooking. Guidance counselors cautioned young women not to miss out on marriage by pursuing higher education. More men than women went to college, and only one-third of college women completed their degrees.

However, profound changes were under way. Increasing numbers of women entered the work force. By 1960, twice as many women worked outside the home as in 1940. In 1960 one-third of the labor force was female, and one out of three married women worked outside the home. Their median wage, however, was less than half that for men.

Most women worked to augment family income, not to challenge stereotypes, and took low-paying, low-prestige jobs. Yet many working women developed a heightened sense of expectations and empowerment. Transmitted to their daughters, that experience would fuel a feminist resurgence in the late 1960s.

Religion and Education

"Today in the U.S.," *Time* claimed in 1954, "the Christian faith is back in the center of things." Religious popularizers—fiery evangelist **Billy Graham,** riveting Roman Catholic bishop Fulton J. Sheen, and "positive-thinking" Protestant minister Norman Vincent Peale—had syndicated newspaper columns, best-selling books, and radio and television programs. Hollywood religious extravaganzas like *The Ten Commandments* (1956) became box-office hits, and TV commercials pronounced that "the family that prays together stays together."

Billy Graham Protestant evangelical preacher and outspoken opponent of homosexuality, communism, and working wives

Millions embraced evangelical fundamentalism and became "born-again" Christians—a trend that would escalate. Billy Graham and Oral Roberts among others developed huge followings by preaching against the hedonism and secularism of modern life; they appealed mainly to Americans alienated by rapid cultural and social change. Despite the aura of religiosity in the fifties, the *intensity* of faith diminished for many people, as mainstream churches downplayed sin and evil, and preached Americanism and fellowship.

Similarly, education swelled in the 1950s yet seemed less rigorous than in earlier decades. The baby boom inflated primary-school enrollment by 10 million. California opened a new school every week throughout the decade and still faced a classroom shortage. The proportion of college-age Americans in higher education climbed from 15 percent in 1940 to more than 40 percent by the 1960s. "Progressive" educators promoted sociability and self-expression—"well-roundedness"—over science, math, and history. Surveys of college students found them conservative, conformist, and careerist, a "silent generation" seeking primarily security and comfort.

The Culture of the Fifties

American culture reflected the spirit of a prosperous era as well as Cold War anxiety. Enjoying more leisure time and bigger paychecks, Americans spent one-seventh of the GNP in 1950 on entertainment. People visited national parks in droves. Spectator sports boomed, new symphony halls opened, and book sales doubled.

New York replaced Paris as the capital of the art world. Like the abstract canvases of Jackson Pollock and the cool jazz trumpet of Miles Davis, the major novels of the fifties displayed introspection and improvisation. John Cheever's *The Wapshot Chronicles* and John Updike's *Rabbit Run* (1960) presented characters vaguely dissatisfied with jobs and home, longing for a more vital and authentic existence but incapable of decisive action.

Southern, African-American, and Jewish-American writers turned out the decade's most vital fiction. William Faulkner continued his dense saga of a family in Yoknapatawpha County, Mississippi, in *The Town* (1957) and *The Mansion* (1960), while Eudora Welty evoked small-town Mississippi life in *The Ponder Heart* (1954). The black experience found memorable expression in James Baldwin's *Go Tell It on the Mountain* (1953) and Ralph Ellison's *Invisible Man* (1951). Philip Roth's *Goodbye, Columbus* (1959) dissected the world of upwardly mobile Jews.

Hollywood reflected the diminished concern with political issues, churning out westerns, musicals, and costume spectacles. Movies about the 1950s portrayed Americans as one happy, white, middle-class family. Minorities and the poor remained invisible, and women appeared largely as "dumb blondes" or cute helpmates. But as TV viewing soared, movie attendance dropped by 50 percent, and 20 percent of the nation's theaters became bowling alleys or supermarkets.

The Television Culture

No cultural medium ever grew so huge so quickly as television. In 1946 one in every eighteen thousand households had a TV set; by 1960, 90 percent of all households owned at least one TV, and more Americans had televisions than had bathrooms.

Business capitalized on the phenomenon. The three main radio networks—ABC, CBS, and NBC—gobbled up virtually every TV station in the country. *TV Guide* soon outsold all other periodicals. First marketed in 1954, the "TV dinner" changed the nation's eating habits. It seemed that TV could sell anything. By the mid-fifties the three major networks *each* had larger advertising revenues than any other communications medium in the world.

Initially, TV showcased talent and creativity. Opera performances appeared in prime time, as did sophisticated comedies and dramas and documentaries like Edward R. Murrow's *See It Now*. Early situation comedies such as *The Life of Riley,* featured ethnic working-class families. As the price of TV sets fell and the chill of McCarthyism spread, the networks' appetite for a mass audience transformed TV into a cautious celebration of conformity and consumerism. Controversy went off the air. Only a few situation comedies, like Jackie Gleason's *The Honeymooners,* set in Brooklyn, did not feature suburban, consumer-oriented, upper-middle-class families. Most portrayed perfectly coiffed moms who loved to vacuum in high heels, frisky yet ultimately obedient kids, and all-knowing dads. Even Lucille Ball and Desi Arnaz in *I Love Lucy*—which no network initially wanted because an all-American redhead was married to a Cuban—had a baby and left New York for suburbia.

Decrying television's mediocrity, in 1961 the head of the Federal Communications Commission called it "a vast wasteland." A steady parade of soaps, unsophisticated comedies, and violent westerns led others to call TV "the idiot box."

Measuring television's impact is difficult. Different people read the "texts" of TV (or of movies or books) in their own way and so receive their own messages from the medium. In the main, television reflected American society and stimulated the desire to be included in that society. It spawned mass fads for Barbie dolls and hula hoops and spread the message of consumerism. It reinforced gender and racial stereotypes, rarely showing African-Americans and Latinos—except in servile roles or prison scenes—and extolling male violence in fighting evil; it portrayed women as zany madcaps or self-effacing moms.

Television also changed political life. Politicians could effectively appeal to the voters over the heads of party leaders, and appearance mattered more than content. At least 20 million watched Senator Joseph McCarthy bully and slander witnesses. Richard Nixon reached 58 million and saved his political career with his appeal in the "Checkers" speech. And Eisenhower's pioneering use of brief "spot advertisements," combined with Stevenson's avoidance of televised appearances, to clinch Ike's smashing presidential victories. In 1960 John F. Kennedy's "telegenic" image would play a significant role in his successful campaign.

All in all, television helped produce a more national culture, diminishing provincialism and regional differences. Its overwhelming portrayal of a contented citizenry reinforced complacency and hid the reality of "the other America."

CHECKING IN

- The baby boom renewed emphasis on the family and "togetherness."
- Motherhood was exalted, although women continued to pursue work outside the home.
- Organized religion and evangelicalism flourished; Billy Graham became a major American figure.
- Americans spent more time and money than ever on entertainment.
- Television became the dominant medium, changing politics as well as enforcing conformity, consumerism, and stereotypes.

THE OTHER AMERICA

In what sense were there two Americas?

"I am an invisible man," declared the African-American narrator of Ralph Ellison's *Invisible Man;* "I am invisible . . . because people refuse to see me." Indeed, few white middle-class Americans of the fifties perceived the extent of social injustice in the United States. "White flight" from cities to suburbs physically separated races and classes. Popular culture focused on affluent white Americans enjoying the "good life." But poverty and racial discrimination were rife and dire, and the struggles for social justice intensified.

Poverty and Urban Blight

Although the percentage of poor families declined from 1947 to 1960, in 1960 some 35 million Americans, one-fifth of the nation, lived below the poverty line. Some 8 million elderly had yearly incomes of less than a thousand dollars.

One-third of the poor lived in depressed rural areas, and 2 million migrant farm workers lived in the most abject poverty. Observing a Texas migratory-labor camp in 1955, a journalist reported that 96 percent of the children had had no milk in the previous six months, eight out of ten adults had eaten no meat, and most slept "on the ground, in a cave, under a tree, or in a chicken house."

The bulk of the poor huddled in decaying inner-city slums. Displaced southern blacks and Appalachian whites, Native Americans forced off reservations, and newly arrived Hispanics strained cities' inadequate facilities. Nearly 200,000 Mexican-Americans herded into San Antonio's Westside barrio; a local newspaper described them as living like cattle in a stockyard. As described by Michael Harrington in *The Other America: Poverty in the United States* (1962), the poor lived trapped in a cycle of want and deprivation. Unable to afford a nutritious diet or doctors, the poor got sick more often and for longer than affluent Americans. Children of the poor started school at a disadvantage and rapidly fell behind; many dropped out. Living with neither hope nor skills, the poor bequeathed a similar legacy to their children.

The pressing need for low-cost housing went unanswered. Slum-clearance and urban-renewal projects shunted the poor from one ghetto to another to make room for parking garages and cultural centers. Bulldozers razed the Los Angeles barrio of Chavez Ravine to make way for Dodger Stadium. Landlords, realtors, and bankers deliberately excluded nonwhites from decent housing. Half of the housing in New York's Harlem predated 1900. There, a dozen people might share a tiny apartment with broken windows, faulty plumbing, and gaping holes in the walls. Harlem's rates of illegitimacy, infant deaths, narcotics use, and crime towered above city and national averages.

North Chicago Slum

Life was not the "nifty fifties" for all Americans. Nearly one in four lived below the poverty line, which was calculated by the federal government to be $2,973 for a family of four in 1959.

Blacks' Struggle for Justice

The collision between the hopes raised by the 1954 *Brown* decision and the indignities of persistent segregation sparked a new phase in the civil-rights movement. African-Americans developed new tactics, founded new organizations, and followed new leaders. They used nonviolent direct-action protest to engage large numbers of blacks in their own freedom fight and to arouse white America's conscience.

Racism touched even the smallest details of daily life. In Montgomery, Alabama, although the city's black bus riders represented more than three-fourths of all passengers, they had to sit in the rear and give up their seats to any standing white riders. In December 1955, when **Rosa Parks,** an officer of the Montgomery NAACP, refused to get up so that a white man could sit, she was arrested. Montgomery's black leaders organized a massive bus boycott. **Martin Luther King, Jr.,** a twenty-seven-year-old minister, articulated the anger of Montgomery blacks. The time had come, he declared, to stop being patient "with anything less than freedom and justice." Accordingly, fifty thousand black Montgomerians boycotted the buses for a year, organizing car pools and often walking miles to work. When city leaders would not budge, blacks filed suit, challenging bus segregation. In November 1956 the Supreme Court affirmed a lower-court decision outlawing such segregation.

The bus boycott demonstrated black strength and determination. It affirmed the possibility of social change. And it vaulted Dr. King, whose oratory simultaneously inspired black activism and touched white consciences, into the national spotlight.

King's philosophy of civil disobedience fused the spirit of Christianity with the strategy of nonviolent resistance. His insistence on nonviolence diminished the threat of bloodshed. Preaching that they must lay their bodies on the line to provoke crises that would force whites to confront their own racism, he urged his followers to love their enemies. The movement's triumphs rested not on its leaders but on the domestic servants who walked instead of riding the buses, the children on the front lines of the battle for school desegregation, and the tens of thousands of ordinary people who marched, rallied, and demonstrated.

Rosa Parks Civil-rights leader whose refusal to give a white man her bus seat triggered the Montgomery bus boycott

Martin Luther King, Jr. African-American minister whose emphasis on nonviolence catapulted him to leadership of civil-rights movement

Latinos and Latinas

Hispanic-Americans initially made less headway in ending discrimination. High unemployment on the Caribbean island brought a steady stream of Puerto Ricans, who, as U.S. citizens, could enter the mainland without restriction. By 1960 nearly a million lived in El Barrio in New York City's East Harlem.

In New York they suffered from inadequate housing and schools, and from police harassment; they were denied decent jobs and political recognition. Family frictions flared in the transition to unaccustomed ways. Parents felt upstaged by children who learned English and obtained jobs that were closed to them. The relationship between husbands and wives changed as women found readier access to jobs than did men.

Mexican-Americans suffered the same indignities. Most were underpaid and segregated from mainstream American life. After World War II, new irrigation systems added 7.5 million acres to the agricultural lands of the Southwest, stimulating demand for cheap Mexican labor. In 1951, to stem the resulting tide of illegal Mexican immigrants, Congress reintroduced the wartime "temporary worker" program that brought in seasonal farm laborers called *braceros*. Many stayed without authorization, joining a growing number of Latinos who entered the country illegally.

During the 1953–1955 recession, the Eisenhower administration's "Operation Wetback" (a term of derision for illegal Mexican immigrants) deported some 3 million allegedly undocumented entrants. Periodic roundups, however, did not stop the millions of Mexicans who continued to cross the poorly guarded border. The **bracero program** itself peaked in 1959, admitting 450,000 workers.

The swelling Mexican-American population became more urban. In Los Angeles County it doubled to more than 600,000, and the *colonias* (ko-lo-NEE-as) of Denver, El Paso, Phoenix, and San Antonio grew proportionately as large. By 1970, 85 percent of Mexican-Americans lived in urban areas. As service in World War II gave Hispanics an increased sense of their own American identity and a claim on their rights as American citizens, urbanization gave them better educational and employment opportunities. Unions like the United Cannery, Agricultural, Packing and Allied Workers of America sought higher wages and better working conditions for their Mexican-American members, and such middle-class organizations as the League of United Latin American Citizens (LULAC) campaigned to desegregate schools and public facilities.

In 1954 the Supreme Court banned the exclusion of Mexican-Americans from Texas jury lists, and in 1958 El Paso elected the first Mexican-American mayor. Latinos also took pride in baseball star Roberto Clemente and their growing numbers in the major leagues, in Nobel Prize winners like biologist Severo Ochoa, and in such Hollywood stars as Anthony Quinn. But the existence of millions of undocumented aliens and the continuation of the *bracero* program stigmatized all people of Spanish descent and depressed their wages. The median income of Hispanics was less than two-thirds that of Anglos. At least a third lived in poverty.

> **bracero program** Guest worker program that brought hundreds of thousands of Mexican laborers to the United States in the 1950s

Native Americans

Native Americans remained the poorest, most ignored minority. Their death rate was three times the national average, and unemployment on reservations ran a staggering 70 to 86 percent for some tribes. Congress again changed course, moving away from efforts to reassert Indian sovereignty and cultural autonomy and back toward the goal of assimilation. Between 1954 and 1962 Congress terminated treaties and withdrew financial support from sixty-one reservations. First applied to the Menominees (meh-NAH-mih-nees) of Wisconsin and the Klamaths (CLAY-muths) of Oregon, who owned valuable timberlands, the policy was disastrous. Further impoverishing the tribes, it transferred more than 500,000 acres of Native American lands to non-Indians.

By 1960 about 60,000 Indians had been relocated to cities. Some became middle class, some ended up in run-down urban shantytowns, and nearly a third eventually returned to their reservations. The National Congress of American Indians vigorously opposed termination, and most tribal politicians advocated Indian sovereignty, treaty rights, and federal trusteeship.

CHECKING IN

- Michael Harrington's *The Other America* called attention to the poverty and deprivation that existed beneath the complacent surface of the 1950s.
- Many of the poor remained trapped in decaying cities.
- With the success of the Montgomery bus boycott, Martin Luther King, Jr., became the dominant figure in the civil-rights movement.
- Poverty and discrimination, often sharpened by illegal immigrant status, continued to dog Mexican-Americans. As their population became more urban, however, Spanish-speakers began to assert their rights.
- Native Americans' welfare slipped even further as government policy veered toward assimilation and termination of treaties.

SEEDS OF DISQUIET

What actions by minorities and youth foretold the movements for social change to come in the 1960s?

Late in the 1950s, apprehension ruffled the placid surface of American life. Questions about the nation's goals and values, periodic recessions, rising unemployment, and the ballooning national debt made Khrushchev's boast that "your grandchildren will live under communist rule" ring in American ears. Third World anticolonialism, especially in Cuba, diminished Americans' national pride. So did the growing alienation of American youth and a technological breakthrough by the Soviet Union.

Sputkik First man-made satellite to orbit the earth; launched by Soviet Union

CL Primary Source: Wonder Why We're Not Keeping Pace?

Sputnik

On October 4, 1957, the Soviet Union launched the first artificial satellite, *Sputnik* ("Little Traveler"). Weighing 184 pounds and only twenty-two inches in diameter, it circled the earth at eighteen thousand miles per hour. When *Sputnik II,* carrying a dog, went into a more distant orbit on November 3, critics said that Eisenhower had allowed a "technological Pearl Harbor."

The Eisenhower administration disparaged the Soviet achievement but behind the scenes pushed to have the American Vanguard missile readied to launch a satellite. On December 6, with millions watching on TV, Vanguard rose six feet into the air and exploded. Newspapers wrote of America's "Flopnik."

Eisenhower didn't laugh. Instead he more than doubled the funds for missile development to $5.3 billion in 1959. He also established the Science Advisory Committee, whose recommendations led to creation of the National Aeronautics and Space Administration (NASA) in July 1958. By decade's end, the United States had launched several space probes and successfully tested the Atlas intercontinental ballistic missile (ICBM).

Spurred by *Sputnik,* Americans embarked on a crash program to improve American education. The National Defense Education Act (1958) for the first time provided direct federal funding to higher education, especially to improve the teaching of the sciences, mathematics, and foreign languages. Far more funds went to university research to ensure national security.

America now banked on higher education to ensure national security. The number of college students skyrocketed from 1.5 million in 1940 to 3.6 million by 1960. That year, the government funneled $1.5 billion to universities, a hundredfold increase over 1940. Linked directly to the Cold War, this hike in educational spending raised unsettling questions. By 1960 nearly a third of scientists and engineers on university faculties worked full time on government research, primarily defense projects. Some observers feared that a military-industrial- *educational* complex was emerging.

A Different Beat

Few adults considered the implications of affluence for the young or the consequences of having a generation of teenagers who could stay in school instead of working. Few thought about the effects of growing up in an age when traditional values, such as thrift, had declining relevance among youth with the leisure and money to shape their own subculture. And despite talk of togetherness, fathers were often too busy to give their children much attention, and mothers sometimes spent more time chauffeuring adolescents than listening to them. Much of what adults knew about teenagers they learned from the mass media, which focused on the sensational and the superficial.

Accounts of juvenile delinquency abounded, portraying high schools as war zones, city streets as jungles, and teenagers as zip-gun-armed hoodlums. In truth, teenage crime barely increased. But male teenagers sporting black-leather motorcycle jackets, their hair slicked into "ducktails," aroused adult alarm.

Too, young Americans embraced rock and roll. In 1952 Cleveland radio host Alan Freed, having observed white teenagers dancing to rhythm-and-blues records by black performers, started a new radio program, "Moondog's Rock and Roll Party," to play "race music." In 1954 Freed took the popular program to New York, creating a national craze for rock and roll.

White performers transformed black rhythm and blues, with its heavy beat and suggestive lyrics, into "Top Ten" rock and roll. In 1954 Bill Haley and the Comets dropped some of the sexual allusions from Joe Turner's "Shake, Rattle, and Roll," added country-and-western guitar riffs, and produced the first major white rock-and-roll hit. When Haley performed "Rock Around the Clock" in *The Blackboard Jungle,* a 1955 film about juvenile delinquency, many parents linked rock and roll with disobedience and crime. Red-hunters saw it as a communist plot to corrupt youth. Segregationists claimed it was a ploy "to mix the races." Psychiatrists feared it was "a communicable disease." Some churches condemned it as "the devil's music."

Elvis Presley confirmed the worst fears. Born in Tupelo, Mississippi, Elvis melded the Pentecostal music of his boyhood with the powerful beat and sexual energy of rhythm and blues. In songs like "Hound Dog" and "All Shook Up" he seemed to proclaim teenage "separateness." Presley's smirking lips and bucking hips shocked white middle-class adults. The more adults condemned rock and roll, the more teenagers loved it. Record sales tripled between 1954 and 1960, and Dick Clark's *American Bandstand* became the decade's biggest TV hit.

"Elvis the Pelvis"
In 1956 Elvis Presley skyrocketed to rock-' n'-roll stardom. His wild, rebellious style captivated young audiences. Girls screamed and fainted, and boys tried to imitate his gyrating hips.

Elvis Presley Mississippi-born rock and roll singer beloved among younger Americans in the 1950s

Portents of Change

In other genres, teens elevated rebellious characters like James Dean in *Rebel Without a Cause* (1955) to cult status for overturning respectable mores. They delighted in *Mad* magazine's ridicule of the phony and pretentious in middle-class America. They

Beats 1950s poets and writers who criticized American materialism

customized their cars to reject Detroit's standards. All were signs of their distinctiveness from the adult world.

Nonconformist writers known as the **Beats** expressed a more fundamental revolt against middle-class society. In works like Allen Ginsberg's *Howl* (1956) and Jack Kerouac's *On the Road* (1957), the Beats scorned the conformity and materialism of "square" America. They romanticized society's outcasts and glorified uninhibited sexuality and spontaneity in the search for "It," the ultimate authentic experience.

The mass media scorned the Beats, as they did all dissenters. But some admiring college youth took up the Beat message. They read poetry and listened to jazz, and some students even protested capital punishment and demonstrated against the continuing investigations of the House Un-American Activities Committee. Others decried the nuclear-arms race. In 1958 and 1959 thousands participated in Youth Marches for Integrated Schools in Washington. Together with the Beats and rock music, this vocal minority of the "silent generation" heralded a youth movement that would explode in the 1960s.

CHECKING IN

- The launch of Russia's *Sputnik* satellite spurred crash programs in space research and education to catch up with the Soviets.
- Vast sums of money were channeled into education; government-funded research threatened to dominate universities.
- Rock and roll took center stage in teen music, widening a growing rift between teenagers and their parents. Elvis Presley became the symbol of teen rebellion and the focus of parental despair.
- Nonconformist writers called "Beats" began to question American culture and society.

Chapter Summary

 DOWNLOAD THE MP3 AUDIO FILE OF THE CHAPTER SUMMARY, AND LISTEN TO IT ON THE GO.

What domestic policies support the notion of Eisenhower as a centrist or moderate politician? (page 639)

Eisenhower refused to descend to McCarthy's level. Instead, he gave the Senator enough rope to hang himself, which he did in the televised Army-McCarthy hearings. The president never publicly supported the *Brown* decision, which declared segregated schools to be unconstitutional. However, resistance to *Brown* in Little Rock forced him to use federal power to achieve integration there. Overall, integration made little progress in the South. Major civil rights legislation emerged from Congress in 1957 and 1960, suggesting a changing federal attitude toward race issues.

In what ways did Eisenhower continue Truman's foreign policy, and in what ways did he change it? (page 643)

Despite the hard-line rhetoric of John Foster Dulles, Eisenhower followed a moderate, nonconfrontational policy in dealing with the Soviet Union. Armed

KEY TERMS

Dwight David Eisenhower *(p. 639)*

Earl Warren *(p. 641)*

Brown v. *Board of Education of Topeka (p. 642)*

Southern Manifesto *(p. 642)*

John Foster Dulles *(p. 643)*

domino theory *(p. 645)*

National Liberation Front (NLF) *(p. 645)*

Suez crisis *(p. 645)*

Eisenhower Doctrine *(p. 646)*

military-industrial complex *(p. 646)*

Sunbelt *(p. 651)*

baby boom *(p. 651)*

Dr. Benjamin Spock *(p. 652)*

conflict shifted to Soviet and American "clients" in the Third World, where the domino theory led the United States to deeper involvement in Vietnam. The Suez Crisis underlined the volatile and dangerous nature of Middle Eastern politics, and the resulting Eisenhower Doctrine committed the United States to resisting Soviet influence in the region.

KEY TERMS continued

Billy Graham *(p. 652)*
Rosa Parks *(p. 656)*
Martin Luther King, Jr. *(p. 656)*
bracero program *(p. 657)*
Sputnik *(p. 658)*
Elvis Presley *(p. 659)*
Beats *(p. 660)*

What were the main sources, and consequences, of economic prosperity in the 1950s? *(page 647)*

A decade of sustained prosperity grew in part from massive federal spending, much of it linked to defense. The computer industry began to develop as business and government took up the new technology. Union membership sagged, owing to prosperity, automation, and the increasing proportion of Americans working in white-collar positions. The suburbs boomed, as did the Sunbelt.

How accurate is the image of the 1950s as a period of conservatism and conformity? *(page 651)*

The baby boom put renewed emphasis on the family and led to the exaltation of motherhood as a woman's principal role; "togetherness" blossomed. Organized religion flourished, as did evangelicalism. Television became the dominant medium, emphasizing conformity and consumerism while changing politics and reinforcing stereotypes.

In what sense were there two Americas? *(page 654)*

Beneath the sheen of the "affluent society" lay poverty and major social problems that Americans generally tried to ignore. Many of the poor remained trapped in decaying cities. Energized by the Montgomery bus boycott, the civil-rights movement gained a dynamic leader in Martin Luther King, Jr. Hispanic-Americans and Native Americans continued to struggle.

What actions by minorities and youth foretold the movements for social change to come in the 1960s? *(page 658)*

The Soviet Union's successful launch of the *Sputnik* satellite shattered American complacency. In response, the government funneled vast sums into the American space program and into education and university research. A new kind of music, rock and roll, emerged to identify a teenage subculture separate from parents; "Elvis the Pelvis" became the symbol of teen rebellion and parental despair. In their nonconformist writings, the Beats openly questioned American materialism and joined rock and roll in laying the foundation for the youth rebellion of the 1960s.

CHAPTER 28

The Liberal Era   1960–1968

Selma to Montgomery March, 1965

CHAPTER PREVIEW

The Kennedy Presidency, 1960–1963
To what extent did the Kennedy administration's domestic record reflect its liberal rhetoric?

The Struggle for Black Equality, 1961–1968
What were the major successes and failures of the civil-rights movement from 1961 to 1968?

Liberalism Ascendant, 1963–1968
How did Lyndon Johnson's Great Society program exemplify the new liberalism of the 1960s?

Voices of Protest
How did 1960s' liberalism affect minorities and women, and vice versa?

The Liberal Crusade in Vietnam, 1961–1968
How did Kennedy and Johnson deepen American involvement in the war in Vietnam?

On February 1, 1960, four African-American students at North Carolina Agricultural and Technical College in Greensboro sat down at the lunch counter at the local Woolworth's and asked for coffee and doughnuts. When the waitress announced, "We don't serve colored here," the students remained seated, staying until the store closed. By the end of the week, hundreds of students had joined the sit-in. By April 1960, sit-ins had spread to seventy-eight southern communities, and by September 1961 some seventy thousand African-American students had targeted segregated restaurants, churches, beaches, libraries, and movie theaters. Greensboro's civic leaders grudgingly allowed blacks to sit down at restaurants and be served.

The sit-ins transformed the struggle for black equality and helped redefine liberalism. In managing the economy, liberals now placed greater emphasis on equalizing opportunity and targeting benefits to those who had been ignored. Liberalism was also redefined by others, including Ralph Nader, who sounded the alarm that many automobiles were "unsafe at any speed"; Betty Friedan, who wrote *The Feminine Mystique* to denounce "the housewife trap"; and students who protested what they saw as an immoral war in Vietnam.

These endeavors symbolized a spirit of new beginnings. The idealism of the young would lead many to embrace John F. Kennedy's New Frontier and to rally behind Lyndon Johnson's Great Society. Both liberal administrations' rhetorical emphasis on social change and activism would generate fervent hopes and lofty expectations. But assassinations of cherished leaders, ongoing racial strife, and a deepening quagmire in Vietnam would dampen optimism, while a reaction by the majority who opposed far-reaching change would curtail reform. A decade that began with bright promise would end in discord and disillusionment.

▌ THE KENNEDY PRESIDENCY, 1960–1963

To what extent did the Kennedy administration's domestic record reflect its liberal rhetoric?

Projecting an image of youth and vigor, **John F. Kennedy** personified the self-confident liberal who believed that an activist state could improve life at home and confront the communist challenge abroad. His wealthy father, Joseph P. Kennedy, seethed with ambition and instilled in his sons a passion to excel and to attain political power. Despite a severe back injury, John Kennedy served in the navy in World War II, and the elder Kennedy persuaded a popular novelist to write articles lauding John's heroism in rescuing his crew after their PT boat had been sunk in the South Pacific.

John F. Kennedy 35th president of the United States; Cold Warrior who projected youthful dynamism

Esteemed as a war hero, John Kennedy used his charm and his father's connections to win election in 1946 to the House of Representatives from a Boston district where he had never lived. Although Kennedy earned little distinction in Congress, Massachusetts voters sent him to the Senate in 1952 and overwhelmingly reelected him in 1958. By then he had a beautiful wife, Jacqueline, and a Pulitzer Prize for *Profiles in Courage* (1956), written largely by a staff member.

Despite the obstacle of his Roman Catholic faith, the popular Kennedy won a first-ballot victory at the 1960 Democratic convention. Just forty-two years old, he sounded the theme of a New Frontier to "get America moving again" by liberal activism at home and abroad.

A New Beginning

"All at once you had something exciting," recalled a University of Nebraska student. "You had a guy who had little kids and who liked to play football on his front lawn. Kennedy was talking about pumping new life into the nation and steering it in new directions." But most voters, middle-aged and middle class, wanted the stability, security, and continuation of Eisenhower's "middle way" that the Republican candidate, Vice President Richard M. Nixon, promised. Although scorned by liberals for his McCarthyism, Nixon was better known and more experienced than Kennedy, identified with the still-popular Ike, and a Protestant.

Nixon fumbled his opportunity, agreeing to meet Kennedy in televised debates. More than 70 million tuned in to the first televised debate between presidential candidates—a broadcast that secured the dominance of television in American politics. Nixon, sweating visibly, appeared haggard and insecure; in striking contrast, the tanned, telegenic Democrat radiated confidence. Radio listeners called the debate a draw, but television viewers declared Kennedy the victor. He shot up in the polls, and Nixon never recovered.

Kennedy also benefited from an economic recession in 1960 and from his choice of a southern Protestant, Senate Majority Leader Lyndon B. Johnson, as his running mate. Still, the election was the closest since 1884. Only 120,000 votes separated the two candidates. Kennedy's religion cost him millions of popular votes, but the Catholic vote in the closely contested midwestern and northeastern states delivered crucial Electoral College votes, enabling him to squeak to victory (see Map 28.1).

Kennedy's inauguration set the tone of a new era: "the torch has been passed to a new generation of Americans." In sharp contrast to the Eisenhower administration's reliance on businessmen (see Chapter 27), Kennedy surrounded himself with liberal intellectuals.

Kennedy seemed more a celebrity than a politician. Aided by his wife, he adorned his presidency with the trappings of culture and excellence, inviting distinguished artists to perform at the White House and studding his speeches with quotations from Emerson. Awed by his grace and wit, the media extolled him as a vibrant leader and adoring husband. The public knew nothing of his fragile health, frequent use of mood-altering drugs to relieve pain, and extramarital affairs.

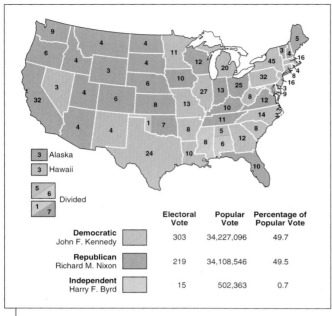

	Electoral Vote	Popular Vote	Percentage of Popular Vote
Democratic John F. Kennedy	303	34,227,096	49.7
Republican Richard M. Nixon	219	34,108,546	49.5
Independent Harry F. Byrd	15	502,363	0.7

Map 28.1   The Election of 1960

Kennedy's Domestic Record

Media images obscured Kennedy's lackluster domestic record. The conservative coalition of Republicans and southern Democrats that had stifled Truman's Fair Deal doomed the New Frontier. Lacking the votes, Kennedy rarely pressed Congress for social legislation.

JFK made stimulating economic growth his domestic priority. To that end, he combined higher defense expenditures with investment incentives for private enterprise. In 1961 he persuaded Congress to boost the defense budget by 20 percent. He vastly increased America's nuclear stockpile and strengthened the military's conventional forces. Kennedy also convinced Congress to finance a "race to the moon,"

Chronology

1960	Sit-ins to protest segregation begin; John F. Kennedy elected president
1961	Peace Corps and Alliance for Progress created; Bay of Pigs invasion; Freedom rides; Berlin Wall erected
1962	Cuban missile crisis
1963	Civil-rights demonstrations in Birmingham; March on Washington; Test-Ban Treaty between the Soviet Union and the United States; Kennedy assassinated; Lyndon B. Johnson becomes president; Betty Friedan, *The Feminine Mystique*
1964	Freedom Summer in Mississippi; California becomes most populous state; Civil Rights Act; Gulf of Tonkin incident and resolution; Economic Opportunity Act initiates "war on poverty"; Johnson elected president
1965	Bombing of North Vietnam and Americanization of the war begin; Assassination of Malcolm X; Civil-rights march from Selma to Montgomery; César Chávez's United Farm Workers strike in California; Teach-ins to question U.S. involvement in war in Vietnam begin; Voting Rights Act; Watts riot in Los Angeles
1966	Stokely Carmichael calls for Black Power; Black Panthers formed; National Organization for Women (NOW) founded
1967	Massive antiwar demonstrations; race riots in Newark, Detroit, and other cities

which Americans would win in 1969 at a cost of more than $25 billion. Most importantly, Kennedy took his liberal advisers' Keynesian advice to call for a huge cut in corporate taxes that would greatly increase the deficit but would presumably provide capital for business to invest, stimulating the economy and thus increasing tax revenues.

When the Kennedy presidency ended tragically in November 1963, the proposed tax cut was bottled up in Congress, but JFK's economic program had doubled the rate of economic growth, decreased unemployment, and held inflation at 1.3 percent a year. The United States was in the midst of its longest uninterrupted economic expansion.

The boom would both cause further ecological damage and provide the affluence that enabled Americans to care about the environment. The fallout scare of the 1950s raised questions about the well-being of the planet. The publication in 1962 of Rachel Carson's *Silent Spring* (see Chapter 27) intensified concern. Additionally, with postwar prosperity, many Americans were concerned less with increased production and more with the quality of life. In 1963 Congress passed a Clean Air Act, regulating automotive and industrial emissions. After decades of heedless pollution, Washington hesitantly began to address environmental problems.

Cold War Activism

In his inaugural address Kennedy proclaimed, "we shall pay any price, bear any burden, . . . oppose any foe to assure the survival and success of liberty." He launched a major military buildup and surrounded himself with Cold Warriors who shared his belief that American security depended on superior force and the willingness to use it. At the same time, he gained congressional backing for economic assistance to Third

World countries to counter the appeal of communism. The Peace Corps, created in 1961, exemplified the New Frontier's liberal anticommunism. By 1963 five thousand Peace Corps volunteers were serving two-year stints as teachers, sanitation engineers, crop specialists, and health workers in more than forty Third World nations.

In early 1961 a crisis flared in Laos, a tiny nation in Southeast Asia, where a civil war between American-supported forces and Pathet Lao rebels seemed headed toward a communist triumph. In July 1962 Kennedy agreed to a face-saving compromise that restored a neutralist government but left communist forces dominant in the countryside.

Spring 1961 brought Kennedy's first major foreign-policy crisis. To eliminate a communist outpost on the United States' doorstep, he approved a CIA plan, drawn up under Eisenhower, to invade Cuba. In mid-April 1961, fifteen hundred anti-Castro exiles landed at Cuba's Bay of Pigs, assuming that their arrival would trigger a general uprising to overthrow Fidel Castro. The invasion was a fiasco. Deprived of air cover because Kennedy wanted to conceal U.S. involvement, the invaders had no chance against Castro's superior forces.

In July 1961, on the heels of the Bay of Pigs failure, Kennedy met in Vienna with Soviet premier Nikita Khrushchev to try to resolve a peace treaty with Germany. When Khrushchev took a hard stance, a shaken Kennedy returned to the United States and declared the defense of West Berlin essential to the free world. He mobilized 150,000 reservists and called for higher defense spending. The threat of nuclear war escalated until mid-August, when Moscow constructed a wall to seal off Soviet-held East Berlin and end the exodus of brains and talent to the West. The Berlin Wall became a concrete symbol of communism's denial of personal freedom until it fell in 1989.

To the Brink of Nuclear War

In mid-October 1962, aerial photographs revealed that the Soviet Union had built bases for intermediate-range nuclear missiles in Cuba, capable of striking most U.S. soil. Smarting from the Bay of Pigs disaster and believing his credibility at stake, Kennedy responded forcefully. In a somber televised address he announced that the United States would "quarantine" Cuba—impose a naval blockade—to prevent delivery of more missiles and would dismantle by force the missiles already in Cuba if the Soviet Union did not do so.

The world held its breath. The two superpowers appeared to be on a collision course toward nuclear war. Soviet technicians worked feverishly to complete the missile launch pads, and Soviet missile-carrying ships steamed toward the blockade; B-52s armed with nuclear weapons took to the air; and nearly 250,000 troops assembled in Florida to invade Cuba. Secretary of State Dean Rusk reported, "We're eyeball to eyeball."

"I think the other fellow just blinked," a relieved Rusk announced on October 25. Kennedy received a message from Khrushchev promising to remove the missiles if the United States pledged never to invade Cuba. As Kennedy prepared to respond positively, a second, more belligerent message arrived from the Soviet leader insisting that American missiles be withdrawn from Turkey as part of the deal. Hours later, an American U-2 reconnaissance plane was shot down over Cuba. Robert Kennedy persuaded his brother to accept the first message and simply ignore the second one. In the early morning hours of October 28, Khrushchev pledged to remove the missiles in return for Kennedy's noninvasion promise. Less publicly, Kennedy later removed U.S. missiles from Turkey.

Only in January 1992 were the full dimensions of the crisis revealed: Soviet forces in Cuba had possessed thirty-six nuclear warheads and nine tactical nuclear weapons for battlefield use. Soviet field commanders had independent authority to use them. Worst of all, Kennedy did not know that the Soviets already had the ability to launch a nuclear strike from Cuba.

Chastened by coming so close to the brink of nuclear war, Kennedy and Khrushchev installed a telephone "hot line" so that the two sides could communicate instantly in future crises and then agreed to a treaty outlawing atmospheric and undersea nuclear testing. These efforts signaled a new phase of the Cold War, later called détente (day-TAHNT), in which the superpowers moved from confrontation to negotiation. Concurrently, the **Cuban missile crisis** escalated the arms race by convincing both sides of the need for nuclear superiority.

Cuban missile crisis Brinksmanship between the United States and Soviet Union over nuclear missiles in Cuba in 1962 that nearly led to nuclear war

The Thousand-Day Presidency

On November 22, 1963, during a trip to Texas to shore up his reelection chances, a smiling JFK rode in an open car along Dallas streets lined with cheering crowds. Shots rang out. The president slumped, dying, his skull and throat shattered. Soon after, aboard Air Force One, Lyndon B. Johnson was sworn in as president.

Grief and disbelief numbed the nation as most Americans spent the next four days in front of their television sets staring at replays of the murder of accused assassin Lee Harvey Oswald; at the somber state funeral, with the small boy saluting his father's casket; at the grieving family lighting an eternal flame at Arlington National Cemetery. Few who watched would forget. Kennedy had helped make TV central to politics; now, in death, it made him the fallen hero-king of Camelot.

The assassination made a martyr of JFK. The public ranked him as one of the very few "great" presidents, associating him with a spirit of energy and innovation. Kennedy loyalists have stressed his intelligence and his ability to change and grow. His detractors, however, point to his unfulfilled liberal rhetoric and the discrepancy between his public image and his private philandering. Kennedy's rhetoric expressed the new liberalism, but he rarely made liberal ideas a reality. Partly because his own personal behavior made him beholden to FBI Director J. Edgar Hoover, JFK allowed the agency to infringe on civil liberties, even as the CIA plotted with the Mafia to assassinate Fidel Castro. He increased the powers of the presidency, and, as never before, a small group of loyal aides secretly dominated policy making.

Internationally, Kennedy left a mixed record. He signed the world's first nuclear-test-ban treaty yet undertook a massive arms buildup. He compromised on Laos but deepened U.S. involvement in Vietnam. He came to question the need for U.S.-Soviet confrontation yet insisted on U.S. global superiority and aggressively prosecuted the Cold War.

Still, JFK inspired Americans to expect greatness, aroused the poor and the powerless, and stimulated the young to activism. Dying during the calm before the storm, he left his successor soaring expectations at home and a deteriorating entanglement in Vietnam.

CHECKING IN

- Kennedy became the first TV president.
- JFK had relatively few successes in domestic legislation, but he promoted tax cuts that stimulated economic growth.
- The Peace Corps symbolized the optimism and idealism of youth who were confident in the New Frontier.
- Kennedy took a hard line in the Cold War and launched a major military buildup; the Cuban missile crisis put the two superpowers at the brink of war, with mixed results.
- After Kennedy's assassination, the Camelot myth stimulated liberal hopes.

THE STRUGGLE FOR BLACK EQUALITY, 1961–1968

What were the major successes and failures of the civil-rights movement from 1961 to 1968?

Following the lunch-counter sit-ins, civil-rights activists tried to convince Kennedy to act on their behalf. He would not do so, fearing it would split the Democratic Party and jeopardize his reelection. He stalled for two years on his promise to outlaw discrimination in federally funded housing by executive order, and then issued a weak order that barely made a dent in segregation. Only action by civil-rights groups that secured public favor held out the possibility of forcing Kennedy's hand.

Nonviolence and Violence

In the spring of 1961, the Congress of Racial Equality (CORE) organized a "freedom ride" through the Deep South to dramatize the flouting of a 1960 Supreme Court edict banning segregation in interstate transportation facilities. It aroused white wrath. Mobs beat the freedom riders in Anniston, Alabama, burned a bus, and mauled the protestors in Birmingham. Yet only after further assaults on the freedom riders in Montgomery did Kennedy deploy federal marshals to restore peace. And only after scores more freedom rides and the arrests of hundreds of protesters did the president prod the Interstate Commerce Commission to enforce the law. Only crisis, not moral suasion, forced Kennedy to act.

Many of the freedom riders were members of the **Student Nonviolent Coordinating Committee** (SNCC), formed in April 1960 by participants in the sit-ins. SNCC stressed both the nonviolent civil disobedience strategy of **Martin Luther King, Jr.,** and the need to stimulate local, grass-roots activism. In fall 1961, it chose Albany, Georgia, as the site of a campaign to desegregate public facilities. Wily local authorities avoided the overt violence that had won the freedom riders national sympathy. In the absence of federal intervention, the Albany movement collapsed. But the lesson had been learned by civil-rights leaders.

It had not been learned by southern whites. An angry mob rioted in fall 1962 when a federal court ordered the University of Mississippi to enroll James Meredith, a black air force veteran. Rallying behind Confederate flags, troublemakers attacked the federal marshals who escorted Meredith to "Ole Miss." The clash left two dead, hundreds injured, and the campus shrouded in tear gas. Federal troops finally restored order and upheld Meredith's right to attend the university of his home state.

Student Nonviolent Coordinating Committee Youth auxiliary of the broader civil rights movement; involved in rallies, sit-ins, and voter registration drives

Martin Luther King, Jr. Baptist minister whose leadership galvanized the modern, grass-roots civil rights movement in the 1960s

 Primary Source: Hosing Down Civil-Rights Demonstrators

The African-American Revolution

As television coverage brought mounting numbers of African-Americans into the struggle for racial equality, civil-rights leaders pressured Kennedy to intervene. Dismantling segregation piecemeal would take generations, they realized; only comprehensive national legislation, backed by the power of the federal government, could guarantee full citizenship for African-Americans. To get this they needed a crisis that would outrage the conscience of the white majority and force the president's hand.

Determined to expose the violent extremism of southern racism, Martin Luther King, Jr., launched nonviolent marches, sit-ins, and pray-ins in Birmingham, Alabama. The most rigidly segregated big city in America, Birmingham's officials had even removed a book from the library that featured white and black rabbits. Few doubted Police Commissioner Eugene "Bull" Connor's pledge that "blood would run in the streets of Birmingham before it would be integrated."

In May, thousands of schoolchildren joined King's crusade. The bigoted Connor lost his temper. He unleashed his men—armed with electric cattle prods, high-pressure water hoses, and snarling attack dogs—on the nonviolent demonstrators. The ferocity of Connor's attacks, caught on camera and television, horrified the world. When jailed for instigating the march, King penned the "Letter from Birmingham Jail." It detailed the humiliations of segregation and justified civil disobedience to protest unjust laws.

"The civil-rights movement should thank God for Bull Connor," JFK remarked. "He's helped it as much as Abraham Lincoln." Kennedy arranged a behind-the-scenes compromise ending the Birmingham demonstrations in return for desegregating stores and upgrading the status of African-American workers. By mid-1963 the rallying cry "Freedom Now!" reverberated across the nation as the protests grew. Increasingly concerned about America's image abroad, Kennedy feared that, if the federal government did not lead the way toward "peaceful and constructive" changes in race relations, blacks would turn to militancy. Accordingly, when Alabama governor George Wallace in June 1963 refused to allow two African-American students to enter the University of Alabama, Kennedy forced Wallace to capitulate to a court desegregation order.

Birmingham, 1963

President Kennedy said this photograph of an African-American being attacked by a police dog during the protest demonstrations in Birmingham made him "sick." It helped galvanize the nation's conscience, leading Kennedy to submit a comprehensive civil-rights bill to Congress.

On June 11, JFK went on television to define civil rights as "a moral issue" and to assert that "race has no place in American life or law." Describing the plight of blacks in Jim Crow America, he asked, "Who among us would be content to have the color of his skin changed and stand in his place? Who among us would then be content with the counsels of patience and delay?" A week later, Kennedy proposed a comprehensive civil-rights measure—which most members of Congress ignored.

The March on Washington, 1963

To compel Congress to act, nearly 250,000 Americans converged on the Capitol on August 28, 1963. There they heard the ringing words of Martin Luther King, Jr., proclaiming that he had a dream of brotherhood, of freedom and justice, a dream that "all of God's children, black men and white men, Jews and Gentiles, Protestants and Catholics, will be able to join hands and sing in the words of the old Negro spiritual, 'Free at last! Free at last! Thank God Almighty, we are free at last!'" King had turned a political rally into a historic event with one of the great speeches of history.

Neither Kennedy's nor King's eloquence could quell the anger of white racists. On the night of the president's address, Medgar Evers, the head of the Mississippi branch of the National Association for the Advancement of Colored People, was murdered by a sniper in Jackson. In September the bombing of a black church in Birmingham killed four girls. And still, southern obstructionism kept the civil-rights bill stymied in Congress, with little hope of passage.

The Civil Rights and Voting Rights Acts

Kennedy's assassination brought to the White House a southerner, Lyndon Johnson, who knew he had to prove himself on the race issue or the liberals "would get me . . . I had to produce a civil rights bill that was even stronger than the one they'd have gotten if Kennedy had lived."

Civil Rights Act Major legislation that created Equal Employment Opportunity Commission

The resulting **Civil Rights Act,** the most significant civil-rights law in U.S. history, banned racial discrimination and segregation in public accommodations. It outlawed bias in federally funded programs, granted the federal government new powers to fight school segregation, and created the Equal Employment Opportunity Commission (EEOC) to enforce a ban on job discrimination on the basis of race, religion, national origin, or gender.

The Civil Rights Act of 1964 did not address the right to vote. So CORE and SNCC activists, believing that the ballot box held the key to power for southern blacks, mounted a major campaign to register black voters. They organized the Mississippi Freedom Summer Project of 1964 to focus on the state most hostile to black rights. One thousand college-student volunteers assisted blacks in registering to vote and in organizing "Freedom Schools" that taught black history and emphasized African-American self-worth. Harassed by Mississippi law enforcement officials and Ku Klux Klansmen, the volunteers endured the firebombing of black churches and civil-rights headquarters as well as arrests and even murders.

The civil-rights workers enrolled nearly sixty thousand disfranchised blacks in the Mississippi Freedom Democratic Party (MFDP). In August 1964, they took their case to the national Democratic convention. But despite stirring testimony from activists like Fannie Lou Hamer, the MFDP was not seated. Rejecting Johnson's offer of two open delegate seats as a "token" gesture, the disillusioned members of the MFDP walked out of the convention.

Determined to win a strong voting-rights law, the SCLC organized mass protests in Selma, Alabama, in March 1965. Blacks were half the population of Dallas County, where Selma was located, but only 1 percent were registered to vote. Selma county sheriff Jim Clark's men attacked black protesters and bystanders indiscriminately and brutally. Showcased on TV, the attacks provoked national outrage and increased support for a voting rights bill.

Voting Rights Act Law that allowed federal government to protect right of blacks to vote; transformed southern politics

Signed by the president in August, the **Voting Rights Act** invalidated the use of any test or device to deny the vote and authorized federal examiners to register voters in states that had disfranchised blacks. The Voting Rights Act of 1965 dramatically expanded black suffrage, boosting the number of registered black voters in the South from 1 million in 1964 to 3.1 million in 1968, and transformed southern politics (see Map 28.2).

The number of blacks holding office in the South swelled from fewer than two dozen to nearly twelve hundred by 1972. That meant jobs for African-Americans,

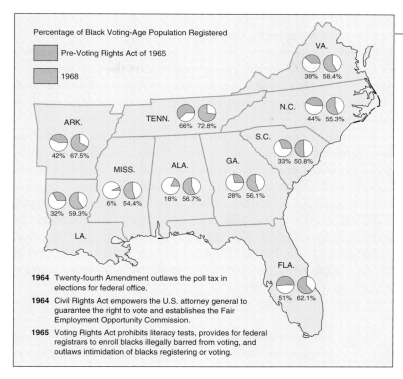

Percentage of Black Voting-Age Population Registered

Pre-Voting Rights Act of 1965

1968

VA. 38% 58.4%

ARK. 42% 67.5%

TENN. 66% 72.8%

N.C. 44% 55.3%

S.C. 33% 50.8%

MISS. 6% 54.4%

ALA. 18% 56.7%

GA. 28% 56.1%

LA. 32% 59.3%

FLA. 51% 62.1%

1964 Twenty-fourth Amendment outlaws the poll tax in elections for federal office.

1964 Civil Rights Act empowers the U.S. attorney general to guarantee the right to vote and establishes the Fair Employment Opportunity Commission.

1965 Voting Rights Act prohibits literacy tests, provides for federal registrars to enroll blacks illegally barred from voting, and outlaws intimidation of blacks registering or voting.

Map 28.2   Voter Registration of African-Americans in the South, 1964-1968

As blacks overwhelmingly registered as Democrats, some former segregationist politicians, among them George Wallace, started to court the African-American vote, and many southern whites began to cast their ballots for Republicans, inaugurating an era of real two-party competition in the South.

 Interactive Map: African Americans and the Southern Vote, 1960–1971

contracts for black businesses, and improvements in facilities and services in black neighborhoods. Most importantly, as Fannie Lou Hamer recalled, when African-Americans could not vote, "white folks would drive past your house in a pickup truck with guns hanging up in the back and give you hate stares. . . . Those same people now call me Mrs. Hamer."

Fire in the Streets

The civil-rights movement changed, but did not revolutionize, race relations. It ended legal segregation and broke the monopoly on political power in the South held by whites. The movement raised hopes for the possibility of greater change. But its inability to transform equality of opportunity into equality of results underscored the limitations of liberal change, especially in the urban ghetto. The movement did not bring African-Americans economic equality or material well-being, and the anger bubbling below the surface soon boiled over.

On August 11, 1965, five days after the Voting Rights Act had been signed, a confrontation between white police and young blacks in Watts, the largest African-American district in Los Angeles, ignited the most destructive race riot in decades. For six days thousands of blacks looted shops, firebombed white-owned businesses, and sniped at police officers and firefighters. When the riot ended, thirty-four people were dead, nine hundred injured, and four thousand arrested.

The violence in 1965 proved to be just a prelude to a succession of "long hot summers." In summer 1966 rioting erupted in more than a score of northern ghettos, forcing whites to heed the squalor of the slums and the savage behavior of police in the ghetto—problems that the civil-rights movement had ignored. The following summer brought nearly 150 racial outbreaks and 40 riots, the most intense and destructive period of racial violence that the United States had ever witnessed. In 1968 riots would flare again in more than one hundred cities after the assassination of Martin Luther King, Jr. The 1964–1968 riot toll would include two hundred dead, seven thousand injured, forty thousand arrested, and at least $500 million worth of property wrecked.

A frightened, bewildered nation asked why such rioting occurred just when blacks were achieving many of their goals. Militant blacks saw the uprisings as revolutionary violence directed at a racist society. Conservatives described them as senseless outbursts by troublemakers. The National Advisory Commission on Civil Disorders (the Kerner Commission) indicted white racism for fostering "an explosive mixture" of poverty, slum housing, poor education, and police brutality. The commission recommended increased federal spending to create new jobs for urban blacks, construct additional public housing, and end de facto school segregation in the North. Aware of a swelling white backlash, LBJ ignored the commission's advice, and most whites approved of his inaction.

Black Power Militant movement for black autonomy and self-respect; rejected the goal of integration

"Black Power"

For many young African-Americans, liberalism's response to racial inequality proved "too little, too late." The demand for **Black Power** that sounded in 1966 paralleled the fury of the urban riots; it expressed the eagerness of militant activists for militant self-defense and rapid social change. Derived from a long tradition of black nationalism, Black Power owed much to the militant rhetoric and vision of Malcolm X.

Black Power

Rejecting the faith long held by African-Americans in the United States and in the professed intentions of white America to remedy injustices, black power advocates insisted on controlling their own movement and institutions, shaping their own agenda and programs, and defining their own demands and destiny.

A former drug addict and street hustler, Malcolm X had converted to the Nation of Islam, or the Black Muslim faith, while in prison. Founded in Detroit in 1931 by Elijah Poole (who took the Islamic name Elijah Muhammad), the Nation of Islam insisted that blacks practice self-discipline and self-respect, and it rejected integration. Malcolm X accordingly urged African-Americans to separate themselves from the "white devil" and to take pride in their African roots and their blackness. Blacks, he claimed, had to rely on armed self-defense and had to seize their freedom "by any means necessary." Malcolm X's assassination by members of the Nation of Islam in February 1965, after he had broken with Elijah Muhammad, did not still his voice. *The Autobiography of Malcolm X* (1965) became the main text for the rising Black Power movement.

Inspired by Malcolm X, many young, urban blacks abandoned reformist strategies and became more militant. In 1966 CORE and SNCC changed from interracial organizations committed to achieving integration to all-black groups advocating racial separatism and Black Power. Even more militant was the Black Panther party, organized that year, which urged black men to overthrow their oppressors by becoming "panthers—smiling, cunning, scientific, striking by night and sparing no one." Violent confrontations with police left some Black Panthers dead and many more in prison.

Black Power advocates had a real impact on African-American life. They helped to organize self-help groups, to establish black studies programs, and to encourage African-Americans to see that "black is beautiful."

CHECKING IN

- JFK avoided dealing with civil rights, but the abuse of blacks seeking their rights in the South and defiance of federal authority at the universities of Alabama and Mississippi forced him to take action.
- The civil-rights movement gained momentum with the founding of CORE, the use of nonviolent protests, and Martin Luther King's "I Have a Dream" speech.
- The Civil Rights Act of 1964 established the Equal Employment Opportunity Commission, and the Voting Rights Act of 1965 transformed southern politics.
- Race riots stunned the nation from 1965 to 1968.
- Radical leaders like Malcolm X and groups like the Black Panthers emerged to proclaim black power and challenge the nonviolent wing of the movement.

LIBERALISM ASCENDANT, 1963–1968

How did Lyndon Johnson's Great Society program exemplify the new liberalism of the 1960s?

Distrusted by liberals as "a Machiavelli in a Stetson," regarded as a usurper by Kennedy loyalists, **Lyndon Baines Johnson** had achieved his highest ambition through the assassination of a popular president in Johnson's home state of Texas. Although just nine years older than Kennedy, he seemed a relic of the past, a backroom wheeler-dealer as crude as his predecessor was smooth.

Yet Johnson had substantial political assets. He had served in Washington almost continuously since 1932, accruing enormous experience and a close association with the Capitol Hill power brokers who helped pass bills. He excelled at wooing allies, neutralizing opponents, forging coalitions, and achieving results.

Johnson's first three years in office demonstrated his determination to prove himself to liberals. He deftly handled the transition of power, won a landslide victory in 1964, and guided through Congress the greatest array of liberal legislation in U.S. history, surpassing the New Deal agenda. Nevertheless, LBJ's swollen yet fragile ego could not abide the sniping of Kennedy loyalists and the press. Wondering aloud, "Why don't people like me?" Johnson pressed to vanquish all foes at home and abroad.

Lyndon Baines Johnson 36th President of the United States; champion of civil rights legislation and the "war on poverty"

Ironically, in seeking consensus and affection, Johnson would divide the nation and leave office repudiated.

The LBJ Treatment

Not content unless he could wholly dominate friend as well as foe, Lyndon Johnson used his body as well as his voice to bend others to his will and gain his objectives.

war on poverty Centerpiece of LBJ's Great Society

Great Society LBJ's dream of an American society of equality and opportunity

Barry Goldwater Arizona Senator and Republican whose loss in the 1964 presidential election unified conservatives

Johnson Takes Over

Calling for early passage of the tax-cut and civil-rights bills as a memorial to Kennedy, Johnson used his legislative skills to good effect, winning passage of the Civil Rights Act of 1964 (discussed earlier) and a $10 billion tax-reduction bill, which produced a surge in capital investment and personal consumption that spurred economic growth and shrank the budget deficit. More boldly, Johnson declared "unconditional **war on poverty** in America."

Largely invisible in an affluent country, according to Michael Harrington's *The Other America* (1962), some 40 million people lived in a "culture of poverty," lacking the education, medical care, and employment opportunities that most Americans took for granted. LBJ championed a campaign to bring these "internal exiles" into the mainstream. Designed to offer a "hand up, not a handout," the Economic Opportunity Act established the Office of Economic Opportunity to fund and coordinate a job corps to train young people in marketable skills; VISTA (Volunteers in Service to America), a domestic peace corps; Project Head Start, to provide compensatory education for preschoolers from disadvantaged families; and an assortment of public-works and training programs.

Summing up his goals in 1964, Johnson offered his vision of the **Great Society.** First must come "an end to poverty and racial injustice." In addition, the Great Society would be a place where all children could enrich their minds, where people could renew their contact with nature, and where all would be "more concerned with the quality of their goals than the quantity of their goods."

The 1964 Election

Johnson's Great Society horrified the "new conservatives," such as William F. Buckley, Jr., and the college students of Young Americans for Freedom. The most persuasive critic was Arizona senator **Barry Goldwater,** an outsider fighting the Washington establishment, a fervent anticommunist, and an advocate of individual freedom. His opposition to big government, deficit spending, racial liberalism, and social-welfare programs found receptive audiences on Sunbelt golf courses and in working-class neighborhoods.

Johnson's advocacy of civil rights frightened southern segregationists and blue-collar workers in northern cities who dreaded the integration of their neighborhoods, schools, and workplaces. Their support of Alabama's segregationist governor

George Wallace in early 1964 presidential primaries heralded a "white backlash" against the civil-rights movement.

Buoyed by this backlash, conservatives in 1964 gained control of the GOP. They nominated Barry Goldwater for the presidency and adopted a platform totally opposed to the new liberalism. Goldwater extolled his opposition to civil-rights legislation and the censure of McCarthy. He denounced the war on poverty and suggested scrapping social security, and he hinted that he might use nuclear weapons against Cuba and North Vietnam. Goldwater's stance appealed to Americans disturbed by the federal government's growing decision-making power. His campaign slogan, "In your heart you know he's right," allowed his liberal opponents to quip, "In your guts, you know he's nuts."

Goldwater's conservative crusade let LBJ run as a liberal reformer but still be the more moderate candidate. LBJ and his running mate, Senator Hubert Humphrey of Minnesota, painted Goldwater as an extremist not to be trusted with the nuclear trigger.

LBJ won a landslide victory, 43 million votes to Goldwater's 27 million. The GOP lost thirty-eight congressional and two senate seats. Many proclaimed the death of conservatism. But Goldwater's coalition of antigovernment westerners, economic and religious conservatives, and anti-integrationist whites presaged conservatism's future triumph. His candidacy transformed the Republicans from a moderate, eastern-dominated party to one decidedly conservative, southern, and western. It built a national base of financial support for conservative candidates and mobilized future leaders of the party, such as Ronald Reagan. But in the short run, the liberals had a working majority.

Triumphant Liberalism

"Hurry, boys, hurry," LBJ urged his aides. "Get that legislation up to the hill and out. Eighteen months from now ol' Landslide Lyndon will be Lame Duck Lyndon." Johnson flooded Congress with liberal proposals, sixty-three in 1965 alone. He got most of what he requested.

The eighty-ninth Congress enlarged the war on poverty and passed another milestone civil-rights act. It enacted **Medicare** to provide health insurance for the aged under social security and a **Medicaid** health plan for the poor. By 1975 the two would serve 47 million people and account for a quarter of the nation's health care expenditures. The legislators appropriated funds for public education and housing and for urban revitalization, and they created new departments of transportation and of housing and urban development, as well as the National Endowments for the Arts and the Humanities.

Of enormous future significance, Congress enacted the **Immigration Act of 1965,** abolishing the national-origins quotas of the 1920s. Annual legal immigration would increase from about 250,000 before the act to well over 1 million, and the vast majority of new immigrants would come from Asia and Latin America. Less than 1 percent of the U.S. population in 1960, Asian-Americans would be nearly 4 percent in 2000, and the Hispanic population would increase from 4.5 percent in 1970 to about 11 percent in 2000. This increasing population diversity vastly expanded the nation's culinary, linguistic, musical, and religious spectrum.

 Primary Source: Medicare

| **Medicare** Government health insurance for the elderly

| **Medicaid** Government health plan for the poor; along with Medicare, a key component in Johnson's Great Society

Immigration Act of 1965
Did away with national-origins quotas and increased legal immigration

The Great Society also sought to protect the environment. In 1964 Congress set aside 9.1 million acres of wilderness. It established Redwood National Park and defeated efforts to dam the Colorado River and flood the lower Grand Canyon; strengthened the Clean Water and Clean Air Acts; and protected endangered species. Responding to the uproar caused by Ralph Nader's revelations about unsafe cars, Congress set the first federal safety standards for automobiles and required states to establish highway safety programs.

The Great Society improved the lives of millions. The poor, 22 percent of the population in 1960, shrank to 13 percent in 1969. African-American family income rose from 54 percent to 61 percent of white family income, and the segment of blacks living below the poverty line plummeted from 40 percent to 20 percent. But in part because Johnson oversold the Great Society and Congress underfunded it, liberal aspirations outdistanced results.

For many in need, the Great Society remained more a dream than a reality. The war against poverty was, in the words of Martin Luther King, Jr., "shot down on the battle-fields of Vietnam." In 1966 Johnson spent twenty times more to wage war in Vietnam than to fight poverty in the United States. Yet the perceived "ungratefulness" of rioting blacks would alienate many middle- and working-class whites. Increasing numbers of Americans feared the growing intrusiveness of the liberal state in their daily lives. The Democrats' loss of forty-seven House seats in 1966 sealed liberalism's fate.

Miranda v. *Arizona* Supreme Court ruling protecting the rights of the accused

CHECKING IN

- LBJ declared war on poverty and enlarged New Frontier social goals.

- The Great Society marked enormous expansion of federal programs for the poor, elderly, and disadvantaged; Head Start, Medicare, the Civil Rights Act, and the Voting Rights Act were just a few of its measures.

- Rules to protect the environment were established.

- The Warren Court continued to pursue a liberal, activist course.

- Increasing involvement in Vietnam doomed the Great Society.

The Warren Court in the Sixties

The Supreme Court did much to promote the liberal agenda. A liberal majority on the Court, led by Chief Justice Earl Warren, acted to expand individual rights to a greater extent than ever before in American history. Kennedy appointed two liberals to the Court, and Johnson two more, including the Court's first black justice, Thurgood Marshall. In the resulting series of landmark cases, the Court prohibited Bible reading and prayer in public schools, limited local power to censor books and films, and overturned state bans on contraceptives. It ordered states to apportion legislatures on the principle of "one person, one vote," increasing the representation of urban minorities.

The Court's upholding of the rights of the accused in criminal cases, at a time of soaring crime rates, particularly incensed many Americans. Criticism of the Supreme Court reached a climax in 1966 when it ruled in *Miranda* v. *Arizona* that police must advise suspects of their right to remain silent and to have counsel during questioning. In 1968, both Richard Nixon and George Wallace would win favor by promising to appoint judges who emphasized "law and order" over individual liberties.

VOICES OF PROTEST

How did 1960s' liberalism affect minorities and women, and vice versa?

The aura of liberalism in the 1960s markedly affected Native Americans, Hispanic-Americans, and women. With younger members pushing radical approaches, each followed the black example in demanding full and equal citizenship rights and in emphasizing group identity and pride.

Native American Activism

In 1961 representatives of sixty-seven tribes drew up a Declaration of Purposes, and in 1964 hundreds of Indians assembled in Washington to lobby for recognition in the war on poverty. Indians suffered the worst poverty, the highest disease and death rates, and the poorest education and housing of any American group. President Johnson established the National Council on Indian Opportunity in 1965. It funneled more federal funds onto reservations than any previous program.

Militant Native Americans, meanwhile, began to organize. By 1968 younger Indian activists, calling themselves "Native Americans," demanded "Red Power." They protested the lack of protection for Indian land and water rights, and the desecration of Indian sacred sites. They established reservation cultural programs to reawaken spiritual beliefs and teach native languages. The Puyallup (pyoo-AL-up) asserted old treaty rights to fish in the Columbia River and Puget Sound. The Navajo and Hopi protested strip-mining in the Southwest.

The most militant group, the **American Indian Movement** (AIM), was founded in 1968 by Chippewas, Sioux, and Ojibwa living in and around Minneapolis. Among its goals was preventing police harassment of Indians in urban "red ghettos." To dramatize the Indian cause, in late 1969 an armed AIM contingent occupied Alcatraz Island in San Francisco Bay, citing a treaty right, and held the island for nineteen months. AIM's militancy aroused other Native-Americans to be proud of their heritage. Many of the eight hundred thousand who identified themselves as Indians in the 1970 census did so for the first time.

American Indian Movement Group that attracted attention to problems facing Native Americans by occupying Alcatraz

Hispanic-Americans and Asian-Americans Organize

The fastest-growing minority, Latinos, or Hispanic-Americans, also grew impatient with their establishment organizations, which had been unable to better the dismal conditions facing most Hispanic-Americans. Turning to the more militant tactics of the civil-rights movement, Latinos found a charismatic leader in **César Estrada Chávez** (SAY-zar SHAH-vez). In 1965 Chávez led a strike by grape pickers of the San Joaquin Valley. Similar efforts had been smashed in the past. But Chávez and United Farm Worker (UFW) cofounder Dolores Huerta organized consumer boycotts of table grapes. They made *La Causa* both a community struggle and part of the larger national movement for civil rights and social justice. Chávez combined religion, labor militancy, and Mexican heritage to stimulate ethnic pride and politicization. For the first time, farm workers gained the right to unionize.

César Estrada Chávez Leader of United Farm Workers

Also in the mid-1960s, young Hispanic activists began using the formerly pejorative terms *Chicano* and *Chicana* to express a militant collective identity. Rejecting assimilation, Chicano student organizations came together in 1967 in *El Movimiento Estudiantil Chicano de Aztlan (MEChA)* to demand bilingual education and more Latino teachers in high schools, as well as Chicano studies programs and organizations at colleges. Concerns about social and political justice led José Angel Gutierrez and others in Texas to create an alternative political party in 1967, *La Raza Unida,* to elect Latinos. Four Mexican-Americans would win seats in Congress in the 1960s.

Chicano* and *Chicana Once pejorative terms for Hispanic men and women, respectively; reclaimed for general use by Hispanic activists

Like the Hispanic Americans of the West, Puerto Ricans in New York City found inspiration in the Black Power movement. The Young Lords, modeled on the Black Panthers, published a newspaper, started drug treatment programs, and even occupied a hospital to demand better medical services in the South Bronx.

Like their counterparts, young activists with roots in the Far East rejected the term *Oriental* and adopted *Asian-American* to signify a new ethnic consciousness. They, too, campaigned for special educational programs and for the election of Asian-Americans. Formed at the University of California in 1968, the Asian American Political Alliance encouraged Asian-American students to claim their own cultural identity. Other Asian-American activists worked to improve housing and working conditions for Asians in garment manufacturing and in hotel and restaurant jobs. The Redress and Reparations Movement agitated to force the government to make restitution for the wartime internment.

Although the fervor of the late sixties would moderate, each of these movements elevated the consciousness and nurtured the confidence of the younger generation. And each contributed to the politics of identity that would continue to grow in importance.

A Second Feminist Wave

The rising tempo of activism in the 1960s also stirred new self-awareness and dissatisfaction among educated women. Several events fanned the embers of discontent into a flame. The 1963 report of the Presidential Commission on the Status of Women, established by Kennedy, documented occupational inequities that were comparable to those endured by minorities. Women received less pay than men for comparable work. And they made up only 7 percent of the nation's doctors and less than 4 percent of its lawyers. The women who served on the presidential commission successfully urged that the Civil Rights Act of 1964 prohibit gender-based as well as racial discrimination in employment.

National Organization for Women (NOW) Leading feminist group

Dismayed by the Equal Employment Opportunity Commission's reluctance to enforce the ban on sex discrimination, these women formed the **National Organization for Women (NOW)** in 1966. A civil-rights group for women, NOW lobbied for equal opportunity, filed lawsuits against gender discrimination, and mobilized public opinion.

NOW's popularity owed much to the publication in 1963 of Betty Friedan's (free-DANS) *The Feminine Mystique.* Calling it "the problem that has no name," Friedan deplored the narrow view that women should seek fulfillment solely as wives and mothers. Suburban domesticity—the "velvet ghetto"—left many women with feelings of emptiness, with no sense of accomplishment, and afraid to ask "the silent question—'Is this all?'" Friedan wanted women to establish "goals that will permit them to find their own identity."

Still another catalyst for feminism came from the involvement of young women in the civil-rights and anti–Vietnam War movements. Women activists gained confidence in their own potential, an ideology to describe oppression, and experience in the strategy and tactics of protest. They also became conscious of their second-class status, as they were sexually exploited and relegated to menial jobs by male activists.

Women's Liberation

In 1968 militant feminists adopted "consciousness-raising" as a recruitment device and a means of transforming women's perceptions of themselves and society. Tens of thousands of women assembled in small groups to share their experiences and air grievances. Women learned from such meetings that their individual, personal problems were in fact shared problems with social causes and political solutions—"the personal is political." This new consciousness begot a sense that "sisterhood is powerful." Radical feminists set up "freedom trash cans" into which women could discard high-heeled shoes, bras, girdles, and other symbols of subjugation. They established health collectives and day-care centers and fought negative portrayals of women in the media, in advertising, and in language. Terms like *male chauvinist pig* entered the American vocabulary, and those like *chicks* exited.

The right to control their own sexuality and decisions whether to have children also became a feminist rallying cry. In 1960 "the Pill" came on the market, giving women greater freedom to be sexually active without the risk of pregnancy. Many women, aware of the dangers of illegal abortions, pushed for their legalization.

In August 1970 feminist factions put aside their differences to join the largest women's rights demonstration ever. Commemorating the fiftieth anniversary of woman suffrage, the Women's Strike for Equality brought out tens of thousands of women across the nation to parade for the right to equal employment and to safe, legal abortions. By then the women's movement had already ended newspapers' practice of listing employment opportunities under "Male" and "Female" headings and forced banks to issue credit to women in their own name. Guidelines that required corporations receiving federal funds to adopt nondiscriminatory hiring and pay practices had been established; and by 1970 more than 40 percent of all women held full-time jobs outside the home.

CHECKING IN

- The American Indian Movement occupied Alcatraz to draw attention to problems of Native Americans.
- Led by César Chávez, Latino farm workers gained the right to unionize.
- Hispanic and Asian groups organized at colleges and universities; they demanded and often obtained courses in their own history and culture.
- *The Feminine Mystique* energized the women's movement and women's liberation became an important force.

THE LIBERAL CRUSADE IN VIETNAM, 1961–1968

How did Kennedy and Johnson deepen American involvement in the war in Vietnam?

The activist liberals who boldly tried to uplift the downtrodden went to war on the other side of the globe to contain communism. Kennedy escalated Eisenhower's efforts in Vietnam to hold "the cornerstone of the Free World in Southeast Asia." Johnson resolved, "I am not going to be the president who saw Southeast Asia go the way China went." The war in Vietnam pursued by liberals ended the era of liberalism. By the time the nation's longest war was over, the United States would be more divided than at any time since the Civil War.

Kennedy and Vietnam

After the compromise in Laos, Kennedy, who was resolved not to give further ground in Southeast Asia, ordered large shipments of weapons to South Vietnam and increased the number of American forces there from less than seven hundred in early 1961 to more than sixteen thousand by late 1963 (see Map 28.3). He accepted Eisenhower's "domino theory" and viewed international communism as a monolithic force, a single global entity controlled by Moscow and Beijing. He wanted to prove that the United States was not the "paper tiger" mocked by Mao Zedong.

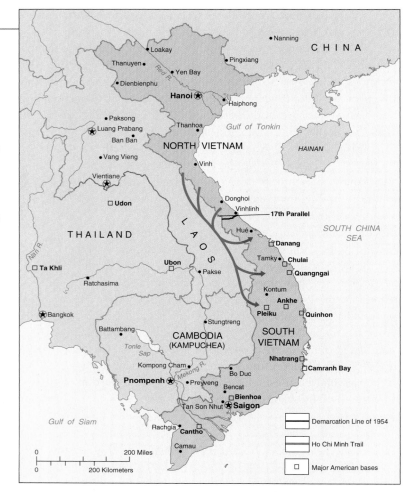

Map 28.3 The Vietnam War, to 1968

Wishing to guarantee an independent, noncommunist government in South Vietnam, Lyndon Johnson remarked in 1965, "We fight because we must fight if we are to live in a world where every country can shape its own destiny. To withdraw from one battlefield means only to prepare for the next."

Interactive Map: The Vietnam War, 1954–1975

To counter communist Vietcong gains in South Vietnam, the United States uprooted Vietnamese peasants and moved them into fortified villages. But South Vietnamese president Diem rejected American pressure to gain popular support through reform measures, instead crushing demonstrations by students and Buddhists. By mid-1963 Buddhist monks were setting themselves on fire to protest Diem's repression, and Diem's own generals were plotting a coup (coo).

Frustrated American policy makers concluded that only a new government could stave off a Vietcong victory and secretly backed the coup efforts. On November 1 military leaders staged their coup, captured Diem and his brother, and shot them. Although the United States promptly recognized the new government, it made little headway against the Vietcong. JFK now faced two unpalatable alternatives: to use American combat forces or to withdraw and seek a negotiated settlement.

What Kennedy would have done remains unknown. Less than a month after Diem's death, John F. Kennedy himself fell to an assassin's bullet. His admirers contend that by late 1963 he was favoring the withdrawal of American forces after the 1964 election. JFK publicly proclaimed in fall 1963 that "it is their war . . . it is their people and their government who have to win or lose the struggle." Skeptics note that the president followed this comment with a ringing restatement of the domino theory and a promise that the United States would not withdraw from the conflict. Virtually all his closest advisers held that an American victory was essential to check communism in Asia. They would counsel Kennedy's successor accordingly.

Escalation of the War

While privately describing Vietnam as "a raggedy-ass fourth-rate country," LBJ feared that an all-out American military effort might lead to World War III. He foresaw that full-scale U.S. engagement in "that bitch of a war" would destroy "the woman I really loved—the Great Society." Yet Johnson thought that only American resolve would prevent a wider war. The president also worried that a pullout would leave him vulnerable to conservative attack and threaten his liberal programs.

Trapped between unacceptable alternatives, Johnson expanded the war, hoping that U.S. firepower would force Ho Chi Minh to the bargaining table. But the North Vietnamese calculated that they could gain more by outlasting the United States than by negotiating.

In 1964 LBJ took bold steps to impress the North Vietnamese with American resolve and to block his opponent, Barry Goldwater, from capitalizing on Vietnam in the presidential campaign. In May his advisers drafted a congressional resolution authorizing an escalation of American military action, and in July LBJ appointed General Maxwell Taylor, an advocate of greater American involvement, as ambassador to Saigon.

In early August, North Vietnamese patrol boats reportedly clashed with two U.S. destroyers patrolling the Gulf of Tonkin (TAWN-kin). Evidence of the attack was unclear. Never admitting that the U.S. destroyers had been aiding the South

LBJ and Vietnam

The Vietnam War spelled Johnson's undoing. Here, peace demonstrators express their feelings about the president's role in the war during a massive antiwar protest at the Pentagon in October 1967.

Vietnamese in clandestine raids against North Vietnam, the president condemned the attacks as unprovoked and called on Congress to pass the previously prepared resolution giving him the authority to "take all necessary measures to repel any armed attack against the forces of the United States and to prevent further aggression." Assured that this power would lead to no "extension of the present conflict," the Senate passed the **Gulf of Tonkin Resolution** by a vote of 98 to 2 and the House, by 416 to 0. Privately, Johnson called the resolution "grandma's nightshirt—it covered everything." He considered it a blank check to commit U.S. forces as he saw fit.

Gulf of Tonkin Resolution
"Blank check" for LBJ to wage war in Vietnam

The Endless War

Early in 1965 Johnson ordered the sustained bombing of North Vietnam. The United States dropped eight hundred tons of bombs daily on North Vietnam from 1965 to 1968, three times the tonnage used by all combatants in World War II. It neither convinced Hanoi to negotiate nor stopped the flow of soldiers and supplies southward from North Vietnam.

Unable to turn the tide by bombing, Johnson committed U.S. combat troops. Adopting a "meat-grinder" or attrition strategy, Johnson sought to inflict unacceptable casualties on the communists to force them to the peace table. Johnson sent 485,000 troops to Vietnam by the end of 1967. But North Vietnam had matched each American troop increase with its own, and there was no end in sight.

Primary Source: Letters Home from Vietnam

Doves Versus Hawks

First on college campuses and then in the wider society, a growing number of Americans began to oppose the Vietnam War. In March 1965, students and faculty at the University of Michigan staged the first teach-in to raise questions about U.S. involvement. Later that spring, 25,000 people, mainly students, rallied in Washington to protest the escalation. In 1966 large-scale campus antiwar protests erupted. Students demonstrated against the draft and university research for the Pentagon.

Intellectuals and clergy joined the chorus of opposition to the war. Some decried the massive bombing of an undeveloped nation; some doubted that the United States could win at any reasonable cost; some feared the demise of liberalism. In 1967 critics, who included Robert Kennedy and Martin Luther King, Jr., spurred hundreds of thousands to participate in antiwar protests.

Critics noted that the war fell especially hard on the poor. Owing to college deferments, the use of influence, and a military-assignment system that shunted the better educated to desk jobs, lower-class youths were twice as likely to be drafted and, when drafted, twice as likely to see combat duty as middle-class youths.

TV coverage of the war further eroded support. Scenes of children maimed by U.S. bombs and of dying Americans, replayed in living rooms night after night, undercut the optimistic reports of government officials. Americans shuddered as they watched napalm (a burning glue that clings to skin and clothing) and defoliants lay waste Vietnam's countryside and leave thousands of civilians dead or mutilated. They saw American troops, sup-

CHECKING IN

- JFK increased the American military presence in Vietnam; the United States supported a military coup against Ngo Dinh Diem.

- The Gulf of Tonkin Resolution, based on shaky evidence of a North Vietnamese attack, seemed to authorize unlimited war at the president's discretion.

- A massive bombing campaign beginning in 1964 failed to alter North Vietnamese resolve; LBJ committed ground combat forces in 1965.

- American troop strength in Vietnam escalated to 475,000 by the start of 1968.

- The United States became increasingly polarized between hawks in favor of total victory and doves favoring negotiation, with college campuses often the site of massive protests.

posedly winning the hearts and minds of the Vietnamese, burn villages and desecrate burial grounds.

Yet most Americans still either supported the war or remained undecided. The desire to get out but not give up became a common sentiment. They were not prepared to accept a communist victory over the United States.

Equally disturbing was how polarized the nation had grown. **"Hawks"** would accept little short of total victory, whereas **"doves"** insisted on negotiating, not fighting. Civility vanished. Demonstrators paraded past the White House chanting, "Hey, hey, LBJ, how many kids did you kill today?" By 1968 the president had become a prisoner in the White House, unable to speak in public without being shouted down. So ended an era of hope and liberalism.

> **"hawks"** Term for those who supported American goals in the Vietnam War
>
> **"doves"** Term for opponents of American military involvement in Vietnam

Chapter Summary

 DOWNLOAD THE MP3 AUDIO FILE OF THE CHAPTER SUMMARY, AND LISTEN TO IT ON THE GO.

To what extent did the Kennedy administration's domestic record reflect its liberal rhetoric? (page 663)

In retrospect, the New Frontier appears to have been more style than substance. JFK got few domestic programs through Congress, although the Peace Corps captured American youth's idealism. JFK took a hard line in the Cold War. The Cuban missile crisis proved a sobering moment and opened the way to détente, as well as to an accelerating arms race.

What were the major successes and failures of the civil-rights movement from 1961 to 1968? (page 668)

JFK tried to avoid dealing with civil rights but was drawn into quelling violence against black protesters and enforcing integration at the universities of Mississippi and Alabama. Martin Luther King continued to lead nonviolent but often dramatic protests, and his "I Have a Dream" speech provided inspiration for millions. The Civil Rights Act of 1964 established the Equal Employment Opportunity Commission, and the Voting Rights Act of 1965 revolutionized southern politics. In the second half of the decade, race riots swept the nation, and radicals like Malcolm X and the Black Panthers emerged to challenge King.

How did Lyndon Johnson's Great Society program exemplify the new liberalism of the 1960s? (page 673)

The Great Society spawned the war on poverty, Medicare, major civil-rights legislation, and increased environmental protection. The Warren Court continued its activist, liberal course. But increased involvement in Vietnam would spell doom for many Great Society programs.

KEY TERMS

John F. Kennedy *(p. 663)*
Cuban missile crisis *(p. 667)*
Student Nonviolent Coordinating Committee (SNCC) *(p. 668)*
Martin Luther King, Jr. *(p. 668)*
Civil Rights Act *(p. 670)*
Voting Rights Act *(p. 670)*
Black Power *(p. 672)*
Lyndon Baines Johnson *(p. 673)*
war on poverty *(p. 674)*
Great Society *(p. 674)*
Barry Goldwater *(p. 674)*
Medicare *(p. 675)*
Medicaid *(p. 675)*
Immigration Act of 1965 *(p. 675)*
Miranda v. *Arizona (p. 676)*
American Indian Movement *(p. 677)*
César Estrada Chávez *(p. 677)*
Chicano and *Chicana (p. 677)*
National Organization for Women (NOW) *(p. 678)*
Gulf of Tonkin Resolution *(p. 682)*
"hawks" *(p. 683)*
"doves" *(p. 683)*

How did 1960s' liberalism affect minorities and women, and vice versa? (page 676)

Native Americans established the American Indian Movement, which dramatized their problems by seizing and occupying Alcatraz. César Chávez organized Latino farm workers, and they gained the right to unionize. Hispanic and Asian students organized and demanded college courses and departments in their own history. Betty Friedan's *The Feminine Mystique* reinvigorated the feminist movement.

How did Kennedy and Johnson deepen American involvement in the war in Vietnam? (page 679)

JFK increased the American military presence in Vietnam, and LBJ felt committed to continuing it. The Gulf of Tonkin Resolution, obtained under suspicious circumstances, freed the president to escalate American involvement, and by 1968 there were 475,000 American combat troops in Vietnam. Opposition to the war mounted, especially on college campuses.

CHAPTER 29

A Time of Upheaval

1968–1974

Bong Son, Vietnam, by Henri Huet, 1966

CL This icon will direct you to the website where you can Prepare for Class, Improve Your Grade, and Ace the Test: **www.cengage.com/history/boyer/ enduringconcise6e**

CHAPTER PREVIEW

The Youth Movement
What were the major landmarks of the youth movement?

The Counterculture
In what ways did the counterculture shape the 1968–1974 period?

1968: The Politics of Upheaval
What were the main causes and consequences of the politics of upheaval in 1968?

Nixon and World Politics
What fundamental changes in American foreign policy were made by President Nixon?

Domestic Problems and Divisions
How did Richard Nixon's political strategy reflect the racial upheavals and radicalism of this era?

The Crisis of the Presidency
What were the main causes of the Watergate scandal?

Dorothy Burlage grew up in southeast Texas, a proper southern belle as well as a self-reliant "frontier woman." Her Southern Baptist parents taught her to conform to the conservative values of her old slaveholding community.

During her college years, Burlage's worldview underwent a dramatic transformation. At the University of Texas she watched with awe as black students her age engaged in a civil-rights struggle she likened to a holy crusade. She left her sorority and joined the Christian Faith-and-Life Community, a group committed to nonviolent radical change. The young activists of the civil rights movement

685

became her political model, their ethos her moral beacon. Burlage attended the founding conference of Students for a Democratic Society (SDS) in 1962. It exhilarated her to be with like-minded idealists, all eager to create a better world.

Commitment and engagement would be characteristic of many of Dorothy's peers. The baby boomers in college spawned a tumultuous student movement and convulsive counterculture that gave the sixties its distinctive aura of upheaval. They exploded the familiar, well-kept world of the 1950s and revived both the Left and Right. Then, disillusioned with the slow pace of change, many became preoccupied with themselves—which again transformed the nation.

Both agent in and beneficiary of the era's realignment, Republican Richard Nixon barely won the presidency in 1968 and then gained an overwhelming reelection victory in 1972. Nixon ended U.S. involvement in Vietnam and inaugurated a period of détente, or reduced tensions, with China and the Soviet Union. In 1974, however, having flouted the very laws he had pledged to uphold, Nixon resigned in disgrace to avoid impeachment. His legacy would be a public disrespect for politics seldom matched in U.S. history.

THE YOUTH MOVEMENT

What were the major landmarks of the youth movement?

By the 1960s the number of American students pursuing higher education had risen from 1 million in 1940 to 8 million. By then, more than half the U.S. population was under age thirty. Their sheer numbers gave the baby boomers a collective identity and guaranteed that their actions would have an impact.

Most baby boomers followed conventional paths in the 1960s. If they went to college—and fewer than half did—they typically took business and other career-oriented degrees. Whether or not they went to college, the vast majority had their eyes fixed on a good salary, a new car, and a traditional family. Many disdained long-haired protesters and displayed "My Country—Right or Wrong" bumper stickers. Tens of thousands of baby boomers mobilized on the Right, idolizing Barry Goldwater, supporting the war in Vietnam, embracing traditional values, and joining organizations like Young Americans for Freedom (YAF).

Toward a New Left

On the other side of the political spectrum, an insurgent minority of liberal arts majors and graduate students at prestigious universities got the lion's share of attention. These students welcomed the idealism of the civil-rights movement, the campaign against nuclear testing, and the rousing call of John F. Kennedy for service to the nation. Determined not to be a "silent generation," they admired such mavericks and outsiders of the 1950s as beat poet Allen Ginsberg and pop-culture rebel James Dean.

In June 1962 sixty students adopted the Port Huron Statement, a broad critique of American society and a call for more genuine human relationships. It announced the formation of a "New Left"—**Students for a Democratic Society (SDS).** Citing the success of civil-rights activists' sit-ins and freedom rides, SDS envisioned a non-

Students for a Democratic Society (SDS) Student group opposed to militarism and racism; called for "participatory democracy"

Chronology

1964	Berkeley Free Speech Movement; the Beatles arrive in the United States
1965	Ken Kesey and Merry Pranksters stage first "acid test"
1966	Abolition of automatic student deferments from the draft
1967	March on the Pentagon; Israeli-Arab Six-Day War
1968	Martin Luther King, Jr., assassinated; race riots sweep nation; students take over buildings at Columbia University; Robert F. Kennedy assassinated; violence mars Democratic convention in Chicago; Vietnam peace talks open in Paris; Richard Nixon elected president
1969	*Apollo 11* lands first Americans on the moon; Nixon begins withdrawal of U.S. troops from Vietnam; Woodstock festival
1970	United States invades Cambodia; students killed at Kent State and Jackson State Universities; Beatles disband; Earth Day first celebrated
1971	United States invades Laos; *Swann* v. *Charlotte-Mecklenburg Board of Education*; *New York Times* publishes Pentagon Papers; Nixon institutes wage-and-price freeze; South Vietnam invades Laos with the help of U.S. air support
1972	Nixon visits China and the Soviet Union; SALT I agreement approved; break-in at Democratic National Committee headquarters in Watergate complex; Nixon reelected president
1973	Vietnam cease-fire agreement signed; Senate establishes special committee to investigate Watergate; President Salvador Allende ousted and murdered in Chile; Vice President Spiro Agnew resigns; Gerald Ford appointed vice president; *Roe* v. *Wade*; Yom Kippur War; OPEC begins embargo of oil to the West; Saturday Night Massacre
1974	House Judiciary Committee votes to impeach Nixon; Nixon resigns; Ford becomes president

violent youth movement transforming the United States into a "participatory democracy" in which individuals would directly control the decisions that affected their lives and could end materialism, militarism, and racism.

Many idealistic students never joined SDS and instead associated themselves with what they vaguely called "the Movement." No matter what the label, a generation of activists found its agenda in the Port Huron Manifesto. Thousands of students became radicalized in the sixties by what they saw as the impersonality and rigidity of campus administrators, the insensitivity of the nation's bureaucratic processes, and mainstream liberalism's inability to achieve deep, swift change.

From Protest to Resistance

The first wave of student protest washed across the campus of the University of California, Berkeley. In fall 1964 civil-rights activists who were veterans of the Mississippi Freedom Summer Project tried to solicit funds and to recruit volunteers near the campus gate, a spot traditionally open to political activities. Prodded by local conservatives, however, the university suddenly banned such enterprises from the area. Organizing as the **Berkeley Free Speech Movement,** a coalition of student groups insisted on the right to campus political activity. The arrest of one student led to the occupation of the university administration building, more arrests, and a strike by nearly 70 percent of the student body. Mario Savio, a philosophy major, tried to

Berkeley Free Speech Movement First major campus protest at University of California, Berkeley

place the Free Speech Movement in a broader context by claiming that the university not only greedily served the interests of corporate America but also treated students as interchangeable robots.

As unrest spread to other campuses, protest took many forms. Students sat in to halt compulsory ROTC (Reserve Officers' Training Corps) programs, rallied to protest dress codes, marched to demand fewer required courses, and threatened to close down universities unless they admitted more minority students and stopped research for the military-industrial complex. The escalation of the Vietnam War in 1965 gave the New Left an opportunity to kindle a mass social movement. When the Johnson administration abolished automatic student deferments for the draft in January 1966, more than two hundred new campus chapters of SDS appeared.

Interactive Map: Disturbances on College and University Campuses, 1967–1969

In 1966 SDS disrupted ROTC classes, organized draft-card burnings, and harassed campus recruiters for the military and for Dow Chemical Company, the chief producer of napalm and Agent Orange, chemicals used in Vietnam to burn villages and defoliate forests. By 1967, SDS leaders were encouraging more provocative acts of defiance, orchestrating civil disobedience at Selective Service centers, and counseling students to flee to Canada or Sweden rather than be drafted. By 1968 SDS claimed one hundred thousand members on three hundred campus chapters.

Spring 1968 saw at least 40,000 students on one hundred campuses demonstrate against war and racism. Most, but not all, stayed peaceful. In April, militant Columbia University students took over the administration building and held a dean captive. The protest expanded, and 1,000 students occupied other campus buildings to protest the war and university military research. Galvanized by the brutality of the police who retook the buildings, the moderate majority of Columbia students joined a general boycott of classes that shut down the university.

August 1969 saw the high point of the movement, with the New Mobilization, a series of huge antiwar demonstrations culminating in mid-November with the March Against Death in Washington, D.C. The 300,000 protesters who descended on the nation's capital marched single file through a cold drizzle, carrying candles and signs with the names of soldiers killed or villages destroyed in Vietnam.

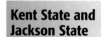

Kent State and Jackson State

A crescendo of violence in spring 1970 marked the effective end of the student movement as a political force. On April 30, 1970, President Richard M. Nixon, Lyndon Johnson's successor, jolted a war-weary nation by announcing that he had ordered U.S. troops to invade Cambodia, a neutral Indochinese nation that had become a staging area for North Vietnamese forces. Nixon had decided to extricate the United States from Vietnam by "Vietnamizing" the ground conflict and intensifying bombing. Students lulled by periodic announcements of troop withdrawals from Vietnam now felt betrayed.

At Kent State University in Ohio, as elsewhere, these frustrations unleashed new turmoil. Radicals broke windows and torched the ROTC building. Nixon lashed out at them as "bums." Ohio governor James Rhodes slapped martial law on the university and ordered three thousand National Guardsmen to Kent. On May 4, the day after the Guard's arrival, six hundred Kent State students demonstrated peacefully against the Cambodian invasion. Suddenly a campus policeman boomed through a

"My God, They're Killing Us"

Following rioting downtown and the firebombing of the ROTC building, Ohio governor James Rhodes called in the National Guard to stop the anti-war protests at Kent State University. On May 4, after retreating from rock-throwing students, nervous guardsmen turned and began to shoot. When the firing stopped, four students lay dead and eleven were wounded.

bullhorn, "This assembly is unlawful! This is an order—disperse immediately!" Students shouted back, "Pigs off campus!" Some threw stones. With bayonets fixed, the guardsmen moved toward the rally and laid down a blanket of tear gas. Hundreds of demonstrators and onlookers, choking and weeping, ran from the advancing troops. Guardsmen in Troop G, poorly trained in crowd control, raised their rifles and fired a volley into the retreating crowd. When the shooting stopped, eleven students lay wounded; four were dead. None was a campus radical.

Ten days later, Mississippi state patrolmen responding to a campus protest fired into a women's dormitory at historically black **Jackson State College,** killing two students and wounding a dozen others. Protests against such senseless violence, the war, and President Nixon thundered across campuses, and more than four hundred colleges and universities shut down as students boycotted classes.

Jackson State College Campus where two students were shot to death by highway patrolmen

The nation was polarized. Although most students blamed Nixon for widening the war and applauded the demonstrators' goals, more Americans blamed the *victims* for the violence and criticized students for undermining U.S. foreign policy. Underlying these attitudes were a deep resentment of privileged college students and an impatience for an end to the social chaos. Many Kent townspeople shared the view of a local merchant who asserted that the guard had "made only one mistake—they should have fired sooner and longer." A local ditty promised, "The score is four, and next time more."

Legacy of Student Frenzy

The campus protests after Kent State and Jackson State represented the final spasm of a fragmenting movement. When a bomb planted by three antiwar radicals destroyed a science building at the University of Wisconsin in summer 1970, killing a graduate student, most students deplored the tactic. With the resumption of classes in the fall, the fad of "streaking"—racing across campus in the nude—more reminiscent of the 1920s than the 1960s, signaled a change in the student mood. By then, Nixon had significantly reduced the number of young men being drafted. Antiwar activists turned to other causes, or to communes, careers, and parenthood. A handful of frustrated radicals went underground, engaging in terrorist acts that justified the government's repression of the remnants of the antiwar movement. The New Left fell victim to government harassment, to its own internal contradictions, and to Nixon's success in winding down the Vietnam War.

The consequences of campus upheavals outlived the New Left. Student radicalism had catalyzed the resentments of millions of people into a rejection of liberalism. Evangelical Protestants, white southerners, and blue-collar workers united in a new conservatism.

Early stirrings of this backlash propelled Ronald Reagan to prominence. In 1966 he won California's governorship, in part because of his opposition to Berkeley demonstrators. The actor-turned-politician won a resounding reelection victory by railing against radicals: "If it takes a bloodbath," he said, "let's get it over with. No more appeasement." Nationwide, other conservatives gained office with similar promises.

The New Left had, however, helped mobilize public opposition to the Vietnam War. It mobilized the campuses into a force that the government could not ignore, and it made continued U.S. involvement in Vietnam difficult. The movement had also aided in liberalizing many facets of campus life and making university governance less authoritarian. Dress codes and curfews virtually disappeared; ROTC became an elective, not a requirement; schools recruited minorities; and students now assisted in shaping their own education.

Some New Left veterans remained active in 1970s causes, especially environmentalism, consumer advocacy, and the antinuclear movement. Female students in the Movement formed the backbone of a women's liberation movement. These involvements, however, fell short of the New Left vision of remaking the social and political order. The generation that the New Left had hoped would be the vanguard of radical change preferred pot to politics, and rock to revolution.

CHECKING IN

- SDS produced a manifesto for change.
- Universities became a major site for protests against social ills and the Vietnam War; the Free Speech movement, sit-ins, and anti-ROTC demonstrations were some of these protests.
- Polarized reactions to the shooting deaths of students at Kent State University and Jackson State College showed how deeply divided the nation had become.
- The New Left movement dissolved in the early 1970s.
- The youth movement left a mixed legacy, including a conservative backlash that would dominate American politics for the rest of the century.

THE COUNTERCULTURE

In what ways did the counterculture shape the 1968–1974 period?

The alienation and hunger for change that drew some youth to politics led others to cultural rebellion. In communes and tribes, these "hippies" denounced individualism and private property, and in urban areas like Chicago's Old Town or Atlanta's Fourteenth Street, "places where you could take a trip without a ticket," they experimented with drugs. Calling them a **counterculture,** historian Theodore Roszack defined them as "a culture so radically disaffiliated from the mainstream assumptions of our society that it scarcely looks to many as a culture at all, but takes on the alarming appearance of a barbarian intrusion."

counterculture Youth movement led by hippies; promoted drugs, lack of social restrictions

Hippies and Drugs

Illustrative of the gap between the two cultures, one saw marijuana as "killer weed," a menace to health and life, and the other thought it a harmless social relaxant. In the absence of scientific evidence that the drug was dangerous, at least half the college students in the late sixties tried marijuana. A minority used mind-altering drugs, especially LSD. The high priest of LSD was Timothy Leary, a former Harvard psychologist fired in 1963 for encouraging students to experiment with drugs—to "tune in, turn on, drop out." Many youths, distancing themselves from middle-class respectability, flaunted outrageous personal styles. They showed disdain for consumerism by wearing surplus military clothing, torn jeans, and tie-dyed T-shirts. Especially galling to adults, young men sported shaggy beards and long hair, the badge of the counterculture.

Musical Revolution

Popular music both echoed and developed a separate generational identity, a distinct youth culture. In the early sixties, college students listened to folk music. In the early 1960s folk songs protesting war and racism mirrored the early decade's optimistic idealism. Bob Dylan sang hopefully of changes "blowin' in the wind" that would transform society. Then in 1964 Beatlemania swept the United States. Moving beyond their early romantic songs, the Beatles gloried in the youth culture's drugs ("I'd love to turn you on"), sex ("Why don't we do it in the road?"), and radicalism ("You say you want a revolution"). They would soon be joined by the Rolling Stones, the Motown rhythm-and-blues black performers, and eardrum-shattering acid rockers—each extolling "sex, drugs, and rock-and-roll" for a generation at war.

In August 1969, 400,000 young people gathered for the **Woodstock festival** in New York's Catskill Mountains to celebrate their vision of freedom and harmony. For three days and nights they reveled in the music of dozens of rock stars and openly shared drugs, sexual partners, and contempt for the Establishment. The counterculture heralded Woodstock as the dawning of an era of love, peace, and sharing—the Age of Aquarius.

In fact, the counterculture was disintegrating. Pilgrimages of "flower children" to San Francisco's Haight-Ashbury district and to New York's East Village in the mid-sixties had brought in their wake a train of muggers, rapists, and dope peddlers. In December 1969, hippie Charles Manson and his "family" of runaways ritually murdered a pregnant movie actress and four of her friends. Then a Rolling Stones concert at the Altamont Raceway near San Francisco deteriorated into a violent melee in which four concertgoers died. In July 1970 the Beatles disbanded. John Lennon sang, "The dream is over. What can I say?"

Woodstock festival Outdoor concert in upstate New York that attracted half a million or more young people to celebrate "sex, drugs, and rock and roll"

CL Primary Source: Arnold Skolnick, Woodstock, 3 Days of Peace, Music,…

The Sexual Revolution

The counterculture's "if it feels good, do it" approach to sex fit into an overall atmosphere of greater permissiveness. These shifts in attitude and behavior unleashed a sexual revolution that would flourish until the mid-1980s, when the AIDS epidemic and the "graying" of the youth movement chilled the ardor of heedless promiscuity.

Many commentators linked the sexual revolution to waning fears of unwanted pregnancy. In 1960 oral contraceptives reached the market, and by 1970, 12 million women were taking "the Pill." Still other women used the intrauterine device (IUD, later banned as unsafe) or the diaphragm. Some states legalized abortion. In 1970 in New York State, one fetus was legally aborted for every two babies born. The Supreme Court's *Roe v. Wade* (1973) struck down all remaining state laws infringing on a woman's right to abortion during the first three months of pregnancy.

Roe v. Wade Supreme Court decision that a woman's right to abortion is constitutionally protected

The Court also threw out most laws restricting "sexually explicit" art with "redeeming social importance." Mass culture quickly exploited the new permissiveness. *Playboy* magazine featured ever-more-explicit erotica, and women's periodicals encouraged their readers to enjoy recreational sex. Hollywood filled movie screens with scenes of explicit sex; Broadway presented plays featuring frontal nudity and mock orgies; and even television presented frank discussions of once-forbidden subjects.

Attitudinal changes brought behavioral changes, and vice versa. Cohabitation—living together without marriage—became thinkable to average middle-class Americans. The use of contraceptives spread to women of all religious backgrounds—including Roman Catholics, despite the Catholic Church's stand against "artificial" birth control.

Gay Liberation

Stimulated by the other protest movements in the sixties, gay liberation emerged publicly in late June 1969. During a routine raid by New York City police, the homosexual patrons of the Stonewall Inn, a gay bar in Greenwich Village, unexpectedly fought back. The furor triggered a surge of "gay pride," a new sense of identity and self-acceptance, and widespread activism. The **gay liberation** movement that emerged asserted, "We are going to be who we are."

gay liberation Organized attempt to end discrimination against homosexuals

By 1973 eight hundred openly gay groups campaigned for equal rights for homosexuals, for incorporating lesbianism into the women's movement, and for removing the stigmas of immorality and depravity attached to being gay. That year the American Psychiatric Association officially ended its classification of homosexuality as a mental disorder.

Simultaneously, several cities and states began to broaden their civil-rights statutes to include "sexual orientation" as a protected status, and in 1975 the U.S. Civil Service Commission officially ended its ban on the employment of homosexuals. Millions of gays had "come out," demanding public acceptance of their sexual identity.

The baby boomers transformed sexual relations as much as gender and racial relations. The institutions of marriage and family were fundamentally altered. But what some hailed as sexual liberation others bemoaned as moral decay. Offended by "topless" bars, X-rated theaters, and "adult" bookstores, many Americans applauded politicians who promised a war on immorality. The public association of the counterculture, the sexual revolution, and gay liberation with student radicalism and ghetto riots swelled the tide of conservatism as the sixties ended.

CHECKING IN

- Hippies denounced materialism and selfishness and created a counter-culture on communes and in urban centers like Haight-Ashbury in San Francisco.
- Alienated young people openly experimented with drugs like marijuana and LSD.
- Folk music, the Beatles, and acid rock symbolized the counter-culture, culminating in the 1969 festival at Woodstock.
- The Pill and the legalization of abortion helped launch the sexual revolution that swept from the counterculture into the mainstream.
- The Gay Liberation movement became more assertive.

1968: THE POLITICS OF UPHEAVAL

What were the main causes and consequences of the politics of upheaval in 1968?

The social and cultural turmoil of the 1960s unfolded against a backdrop of frustration with the Vietnam War and disillusionment with liberalism. The stormy events of 1968 would culminate in a tempest of a political campaign and a turbulent realignment in American politics, the first since the New Deal.

The Tet Offensive in Vietnam

In January 1968 liberal Democratic senator **Eugene McCarthy** of Minnesota, a Vietnam War critic, announced that he would challenge Lyndon B. Johnson for the presidential nomination. Pundits scoffed that McCarthy had no chance of unseating Johnson, who had won the presidency in 1964 by the largest margin in U.S. history. But McCarthy persisted, determined that at least one Democrat enter the primaries on an antiwar platform.

Suddenly, America's hopes for victory in Vietnam sank, and with them LBJ's political fortunes. On January 31, the first day of **Tet offensive,** the Vietnamese New Year, National Liberation Front (NLF) and North Vietnamese forces mounted a huge offensive, attacking more than one hundred towns in South Vietnam and even the U.S. Embassy in Saigon. U.S. troops repulsed the offensive after a month of ferocious fighting, inflicting a major military defeat on the communists (see Map 29.1).

Victory, however, came at an enormous psychological cost. The dramatic initial reports of the media, highlighting the number of American casualties, undercut Johnson's and General Westmoreland's claims of imminent victory. The Tet offensive deepened the growing mood of gloom about the war and intensified doubts that the United States could win at an acceptable cost. Public approval of the president's conduct of the war fell to just 26 percent in the immediate aftermath of Tet.

After Tet, McCarthy's criticism of the war won many new sympathizers. *Time, Newsweek,* and the *Wall Street Journal* published editorials urging a negotiated settlement. The nation's most respected newscaster, Walter Cronkite of CBS, observed that "it seems now more certain than ever that the bloody experience of Vietnam is to end in a

Eugene McCarthy Minnesota senator opposed to Vietnam War who challenged LBJ in 1968 primaries

Tet offensive Coordinated attack by North Vietnamese that convinced many Americans that the war could not be won

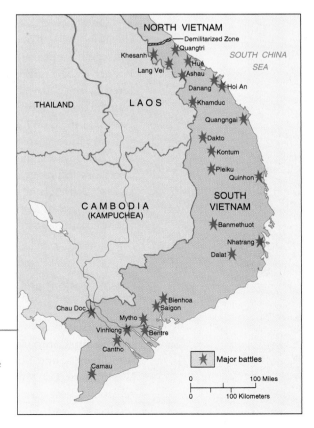

Map 29.1 The Tet Offensive, January–February 1968

Although the Tet offensive proved a major tactical defeat for the communists, it effectively undermined American public support for the war.

stalemate." "If I've lost Walter," LBJ sighed, "then it's over. I've lost Mr. Average Citizen." The number of Americans who described themselves as prowar "hawks" slipped from 62 percent in January to 41 percent in March, whereas the antiwar "doves" jumped from 22 percent to 42 percent.

A Shaken President

Beleaguered, Johnson pondered a change in American policy. When the Joint Chiefs of Staff sought an additional 206,000 men for Vietnam, he turned to old friends for advice. The former secretary of state and a venerable Cold Warrior Dean Acheson told him, "the Joint Chiefs of Staff don't know what they're talking about."

Meanwhile, nearly five thousand college students swarmed to New Hampshire to stuff envelopes and ring doorbells for Eugene McCarthy in the nation's first primary contest. McCarthy astonished the experts by winning nearly half the popular vote in the primary contest of a state usually regarded as conservative.

After this upset, twice as many students converged on Wisconsin to canvass its more liberal voters. Expecting Johnson to lose, Senator **Robert Kennedy,** also promising to end the war, entered the Democratic contest. Projecting the familiar Kennedy glamour and magnetism, Kennedy was the one candidate whom Johnson feared could deny him renomination. Indeed, millions viewed Kennedy as the rightful heir to the White House. Appealing to minorities, the poor, and working-class ethnic whites, Kennedy became, according to one columnist, "our first politician for the pariahs, our great national outsider."

On March 31, Johnson surprised a television audience by announcing a halt to the bombing in North Vietnam. Saying that he wanted to devote all of his efforts to the search for peace, Johnson then startlingly announced, "I shall not seek, and I will not accept, the nomination of my party for another term as your president." Embittered by the personal abuse that he had endured, and reluctant to polarize the nation further, the president called it quits. Two days later, McCarthy trounced the president in the Wisconsin primary.

All but forgotten in retirement, Johnson died of a heart attack in January 1973. In many ways a tragic figure, he had carried out Vietnam policies shaped by his predecessors and received little acclaim for his domestic achievements, especially in civil rights. Although he often displayed high idealism and generosity of spirit, the enduring image of LBJ is that of a crude, overbearing politician with an outsized ego that masked deep insecurities.

Assassinations and Turmoil

On April 4, three days after the Wisconsin primary, Martin Luther King, Jr., was killed in Memphis, Tennessee, where he had gone to support striking sanitation workers. The assassin was James Earl Ray, a white escaped convict. As the news spread, black ghettos burst into violence in 125 cities. Twenty blocks of Chicago's West Side went up in flames, and Mayor Richard Daley ordered police to shoot to kill arsonists. In Washington, D.C., under night skies illuminated by seven hundred fires, army units set up machine-gun emplacements outside the Capitol and White House. The rioting left 46 dead, 3,000 injured, and nearly 27,000 in jail.

Robert Kennedy Brother of John F. Kennedy and former Attorney General

Entering the race as the favorite of the party bosses and labor chieftains, LBJ's vice president, **Hubert Humphrey,** turned the contest for the nomination into a three-cornered scramble. McCarthy remained the candidate of the "new politics"—a moral crusade against war and injustice directed to affluent and educated liberals. And Kennedy campaigned as the tribune of the less privileged, the only candidate who appealed to white ethnics and the minority poor. But in early June, after his victory in the California primary, the brother of the murdered president was himself assassinated by a Palestinian refugee, Sirhan Sirhan, who loathed Kennedy's pro-Israel views.

The deaths of King and Kennedy further estranged young activists, convinced others of the futility of nonviolence, and devastated the already beleaguered forces of liberalism. The dream of peace and racial justice turned to despair. "I won't vote," one youth said. "Every good man we get they kill." Kennedy's death cleared the way for Humphrey's nomination, but Democrats were far from united.

While Kennedy's death cleared the way for Humphrey's nomination, increasing numbers of Democrats turned to third-party candidate George Wallace's thinly veiled appeal for white supremacy or to the GOP nominee Richard M. Nixon. Nixon promised to end the war in Vietnam with honor, to restore "law and order," and to heed "the voice of the great majority of Americans, the forgotten Americans, the nonshouters, the non-demonstrators, those who do not break the law, people who pay their taxes and go to work, who send their children to school, who go to their churches,…who love this country." George Wallace tapped into the same wellspring of angry reaction as Nixon. Wallace pitched his message to blue-collar workers and southern whites fed up with antiwar protesters, black militants, hippies, and liberal intellectuals.

In August 1968, violence outside the Democratic National Convention in Chicago reinforced the appeal of both Wallace and Nixon. Thousands descended on the city to protest the Vietnam War. Some radicals, however, wanted to provoke a confrontation to discredit the Democrats. A handful of anarchistic **"Yippies"** (the Youth International Party) sought to ridicule the political system by threatening to dump LSD in Chicago's water system and to release greased pigs in the city's crowded Loop area.

Determined to avoid the rioting that had wracked Chicago after the assassination of Martin Luther King, Jr., Mayor Richard Daley gave police a green light to attack "the hippies, the Yippies, and the flippies." The result was a police riot, televised live to a huge national audience. As protesters chanted, "The whole world is watching," Chicago police clubbed demonstrators and bystanders alike. The brutality on the streets overshadowed Humphrey's nomination, tore the Democrats further apart, and created an enduring image of them as the party of dissent and disorder. The real victor in Chicago was conservatism.

Conservative Resurgence

Nixon capitalized on the tumult. His TV campaign commercials flashed images of campus and ghetto uprisings. He portrayed himself as the representative of the Silent Majority, "the working Americans who

Hubert Humphrey LJB's vice president who ran for president against Richard Nixon in 1968

"Yippies" The Youth International Party, protest group led by counterculture guru Abbie Hoffman

CHECKING IN

- The Tet offensive, which cost tremendous U.S. casualties, undermined American belief in the Vietnam War.

- Shaken by Tet and opposition from Eugene McCarthy and Robert Kennedy, LBJ announced that he would not run for reelection.

- The assassinations of Martin Luther King and Robert Kennedy sparked riots, including one at the Democratic National Convention.

- Richard Nixon and George Wallace stoked and rode the conservative backlash.

- With Nixon's election as president, Republicans emerged as the new majority party.

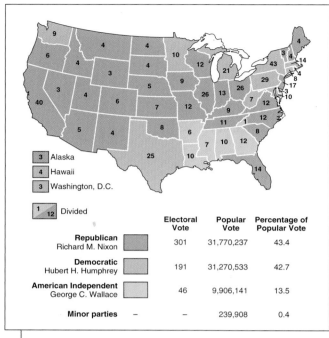

	Electoral Vote	Popular Vote	Percentage of Popular Vote
Republican Richard M. Nixon	301	31,770,237	43.4
Democratic Hubert H. Humphrey	191	31,270,533	42.7
American Independent George C. Wallace	46	9,906,141	13.5
Minor parties	–	–	239,908	0.4

3 Alaska
4 Hawaii
3 Washington, D.C.
1 / 12 Divided

Map 29.2   The Election of 1968

have become forgotten Americans." He castigated the Supreme Court for safeguarding criminals at the expense of law-abiding citizens and told white southerners that "our schools are for education—not integration."

Also appealing to the reaction against liberalism, George Wallace stoked the fury of the working class against "bearded anarchists, smart-aleck editorial writers, and pointy-headed professors looking down their noses at us." Promising to keep peace, he vowed that "if any demonstrator ever lays down in front of my car, it'll be the last car he'll ever lie down in front of." Nearly 14 percent of the electorate voted for Wallace in November.

Nixon and Humphrey split the rest of the vote almost evenly (see Map 29.2). Nixon garnered only 301 electoral votes. But, with Humphrey receiving just 38 percent of the white vote and not even close to half the labor vote, the long-dominant New Deal coalition was shattered and the liberal era ended.

The 57 percent of the electorate who chose Nixon or Wallace would dominate American politics for the rest of the century. While the national Democratic party fractured into a welter of contending groups, the Republicans attracted a new majority who lived in the suburbs and the Sun Belt, regarded the federal government as wasteful, blamed student protestors and hippies for a perceived decline in morality, and objected to special efforts to assist minorities and those on welfare.

NIXON AND WORLD POLITICS

What fundamental changes in American foreign policy were made by President Nixon?

A Californian of Quaker roots, Richard Milhous Nixon was elected to Congress as a navy veteran in 1946. He won prominence for his role in the HUAC investigation of Alger Hiss (see Chapter 26) and advanced to the Senate in 1950 by accusing his Democratic opponent of disloyalty. He served two terms as Eisenhower's vice president, but lost the presidency to Kennedy in 1960 and the California governorship in 1962. Ignoring what seemed a political death sentence, Nixon campaigned vigorously for GOP candidates in 1966 and won his party's nomination and the presidency in 1968.

In office, Nixon focused mainly on foreign affairs. Considering himself a master of *realpolitik* (ray-ALL-pol-i-teek)—a pragmatic approach stressing national interest rather than ethical goals—he sought to check Soviet expansionism and to reduce superpower conflict, to limit the nuclear-arms race, and to enhance the United States' economic well-being. He planned to move the United States out of Vietnam and into an era of détente—reduced tensions—with the communist world. To manage diplomacy, Nixon chose **Henry Kissinger,** a refugee from Hitler's Germany and a professor of international relations, who shared Nixon's penchant for secrecy and for the concentration of decision-making power in the White House.

Henry Kissinger Harvard professor chosen to be Nixon's top foreign-policy advisor

Vietnamization

Nixon's grand design hinged on ending the Vietnam War. The war was sapping American military strength, worsening inflation, and thwarting détente. In August 1969 the president unveiled what became known as the Nixon Doctrine, in which he redefined the United States' role in the Third World as that of a helpful partner rather than a military protector.

The Nixon Doctrine reflected the president's recognition of the war weariness of both the electorate and the U.S. troops in Vietnam. Johnson's decision to negotiate rather than to escalate had left American troops with the sense that little mattered except survival. Morale plummeted. Discipline collapsed. Army desertions rocketed from 27,000 in 1967 to 76,000 in 1970. Racial conflict became commonplace, and drug use soared. The army reported hundreds of cases of "fragging"—enlisted men killing officers.

The toll of atrocities against the Vietnamese mounted. In March 1968 an army unit led by an inexperienced lieutenant, William Calley, massacred several hundred defenseless civilians in **My Lai** (mee lie). Soldiers gang-raped girls, lined up women and children in ditches and shot them, and then burned the village. Revelations of such incidents, and the rising number of returned soldiers who joined Vietnam Veterans Against the War, undercut the already-diminished support for the war.

My Lai Vietnamese village where American troops massacred more than four hundred civilians

The My Lai Massacre

Under the command of First Lieutenant William Calley, the men of Charlie Company entered the small village of My Lai in March 1968 to attack the Vietcong believed to be there. Instead, they found unarmed civilians, mostly women and children, and massacred them. The military kept the incident secret for a year, but when news of the incident surfaced in 1969, it became symbolic of the war's brutality and the futility of the U.S. effort in the Vietnam War.

Despite pressure to end the war, Nixon would not sacrifice America's prestige. Seeking "peace with honor," he acted on three fronts. First was "Vietnamization," replacing American troops with South Vietnamese. By 1972 U.S. forces in Vietnam had dropped from half a million to thirty thousand. Second, Nixon bypassed South Vietnamese leaders by sending Kissinger to negotiate secretly with North Vietnam's foreign minister, Le Duc Tho (lay duck tow). Third, to force the communists to compromise despite the U.S. troop withdrawal, Nixon escalated the bombing of North Vietnam and secretly ordered air strikes on North Vietnamese supply routes in Cambodia and Laos.

LBJ's War Becomes Nixon's War

The secret B-52 raids against Cambodia neither made Hanoi beg for peace nor disrupted communist supply bases. They did, however, undermine the stability of that tiny republic. In early 1970 North Vietnam increased its infiltration of troops into Cambodia, both to aid the Cambodian communists, the Khmer Rouge (kmair rooj), and to escalate its war in South Vietnam. Nixon ordered a joint U.S.–South Vietnamese incursion into Cambodia at the end of April 1970. The invaders seized large caches of arms and bought time for Vietnamization. But the costs were high. The invasion ended Cambodia's neutrality, widened the war throughout Indochina, and provoked massive American protests, culminating in the student deaths at Kent State and Jackson State.

In February 1971, Nixon had South Vietnamese troops invade Laos to destroy communist bases there. The South Vietnamese were routed. Emboldened, North Vietnam mounted a major campaign in April 1972—the Easter Offensive—their largest since 1968. Nixon retaliated by mining North Vietnam's harbors and unleashing B-52s on its major cities. He vowed: "The bastards have never been bombed like they are going to be bombed this time."

America's Longest War Ends

On October 26, just days before the 1972 presidential election, Kissinger announced that "peace is at hand." The cease-fire agreement that he had secretly negotiated required the withdrawal of all American troops, provided for the return of U.S. prisoners of war, and allowed North Vietnamese troops to remain in South Vietnam.

Kissinger's negotiations had sealed Nixon's reelection, but South Vietnam's President Thieu (tyoo) refused to sign a cease-fire agreement permitting North Vietnamese troops to remain in the South. An angry Le Duc Tho then pressed Kissinger for additional concessions. President Nixon again resorted to B-52 raids. The 1972 Christmas bombings of Hanoi and Haiphong, the most destructive of the war, roused fierce opposition domestically and globally but broke the deadlock.

The Paris Accords signed in late January 1973, essentially restated the terms of the October truce. The agreement ended hostilities between the United States and North Vietnam but left unresolved the differences between North and South Vietnam, guaranteeing that Vietnam's future would yet be settled on the battlefield.

The war in Vietnam would continue despite 58,000 American deaths, 300,000 wounded, and the expenditure of at least $150 billion. Virtually all who survived, wrote one marine, returned "as immigrants to a new world. For the culture we had known dissolved while we were in Vietnam . . . made us aliens when we returned." Beyond media attention on the psychological difficulties of readjusting to civilian life, which principally fostered an image of them as disturbed and dangerous, the nation paid little heed to its Vietnam veterans—reminders of a war that Americans wished to forget.

Few Americans gave much thought to the 2 million Vietnamese casualties or the price paid by Cambodia. In 1975, the fanatical Khmer Rouge (Cambodian communists), led by Pol Pot, took power and turned Cambodia into a genocidal "killing field," murdering some 2 million, an estimated third of the population.

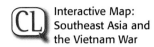 Interactive Map: Southeast Asia and the Vietnam War

Détente

Disengagement from Vietnam helped Nixon to achieve a turnabout in Chinese-American relations and **détente** with the communist superpowers. These developments, the most significant shift in U.S. foreign policy since the start of the Cold War, created a new relationship among the United States, China, and the Soviet Union.

détente Effort to reduce tensions between the U.S. and the communist nations

Presidents from Truman to Johnson had refused to recognize the People's Republic of China in 1949. The United States had vetoed the admission of "Red China" to the United Nations and pressured American allies to restrict trade with the communist giant. But by 1969 a widening Sino-Soviet split made the prospect of improved relations attractive to both Mao Zedong and Nixon. China wanted to end its isolation; the United States wanted to play one communist power against the other; and both wanted to thwart Soviet expansionism in Asia.

In June 1971, Kissinger began secret negotiations with Beijing, laying the groundwork for Nixon's historic February 1972 trip to China "to seek the normalization of relations." The first visit ever by a sitting American president to the largest nation in the world, it ended more than twenty years of Chinese-American hostility. Full diplomatic recognition followed in 1979.

Equally significant, Nixon went to Moscow in May 1972 to sign agreements with the Soviets on trade and technological cooperation. The Strategic Arms Limitation Talks (SALT I) froze each side's offensive nuclear missiles for five years and committed both superpowers to strategic equality rather than nuclear superiority. Although it did not end the arms race, SALT I moved both countries toward "peaceful coexistence" and, in an election year, enhanced Nixon's stature.

Nixon in China

One of the great triumphs of his administration was the rapprochement with the People's Republic of China. Planned in total secrecy, Nixon's trip to China in February 1972 stunned the world and gave the president the aura of a bold, imaginative statesman.

Shuttle Diplomacy

Not even better relations with China and the Soviet Union ensured global stability. In 1967 Israel, fearing that a massive Arab attack was imminent, launched a preemptive strike on its Arab neighbors, routing them in six days. Israel occupied the Egyptian-controlled Sinai (SIE-nie) and Gaza (GAH-zuh) Strip, the Jordanian-ruled West Bank and East Jerusalem, and Syria's Golan (go-LAHN) Heights. Israel promised to give up most of the occupied lands in exchange for a negotiated peace, but the Arab states refused to negotiate with Israel or to recognize its right to exist. Palestinians, many of them refugees, turned to the Palestine Liberation Organization (PLO), which called for Israel's destruction.

War exploded again in 1973 when Egypt and Syria launched surprise attacks against Israel on the Jewish high holy day of Yom Kippur (yawm kip-POOR). Only massive shipments of military supplies from the United States enabled a reeling Israel to stop the assault. In retaliation, the Arab states embargoed shipments of crude oil to the United States and its allies. The five-month embargo dramatized U.S. dependence on foreign energy sources. Acute oil shortages and soaring costs fed inflation and spurred the use of nuclear power.

The dual shocks of the energy crisis at home and renewed Soviet influence among Arab hardliners spurred Nixon and Kissinger to pursue "shuttle diplomacy." Flying from one Middle East capital to another for two years, Kissinger negotiated a ceasefire, pressed Israel to cede additional captured Arab territory, and persuaded the Arabs to end the oil embargo. Although shuttle diplomacy left the Palestinian issue still festering, it successfully excluded the Soviets from a major role in Middle Eastern affairs.

Nixon-Kissinger *realpolitik* based American aid on a nation's willingness to oppose the Soviet Union, not on the nature of its government. Thus the Nixon administration liberally supplied arms to the shah of Iran, to President Ferdinand Marcos in the Philippines, and to the white supremacist regime of South Africa, as well as to antidemocratic regimes in Brazil and South Korea and to Portuguese colonial authorities in Angola.

When Chileans elected a Marxist, Salvador Allende (ah-YEN-day), president in 1970, Nixon secretly funded the CIA to support opponents of the leftist regime. The United States also cut off economic aid to Chile. In 1973 a military junta overthrew the Chilean government and killed Allende. Nixon quickly recognized the dictatorship, and economic aid and investment again flowed to Chile.

Although committed to containing communist influence, Nixon understood the limits of U.S. power and the changed realities of world affairs. Discarding the vision of a bipolar world that had shaped American foreign policy since 1945, Nixon took advantage of the Chinese-Soviet split to improve American relations with both nations. His administration also improved the U.S. position in the Middle East and ended American involvement in Vietnam. The politician who had built his reputation as a staunch Cold Warrior initiated a new era of détente.

CHECKING IN

- Nixon and Kissinger considered themselves masters of *realpolitik*, stressing national interest rather than theoretical or ethical goals.

- The Nixon Doctrine called for decreasing the American role in Vietnam; however, Nixon then stepped up bombing and expanded the war into Cambodia and Laos.

- The Paris Accords ended American involvement in Vietnam in January 1973.

- Nixon pursued détente with an opening to China and limiting of strategic arms.

- Kissinger's shuttle diplomacy guaranteed the United States a pre-eminent role in the Middle East and helped ease some Israeli-Arab tensions.

DOMESTIC PROBLEMS AND DIVISIONS

How did Richard Nixon's political strategy reflect the racial upheavals and radicalism of this era?

Although Richard M. Nixon yearned to be remembered as an international statesman, domestic affairs kept intruding. He tried to reform the welfare system and solve complex economic problems. But the underside of Nixon's personality appealed to the darker recesses of national character and intensified the fears and divisions among Americans.

The Nixon Presidency
Richard Nixon the politician was highly intelligent but also displayed the rigid self-control of a man monitoring his own every move. When the private Nixon emerged, he was suspicious, insecure, and filled with anger. Nixon's conviction that enemies lurked everywhere, waiting to destroy him, verged on paranoia. He sought to annihilate his partisan enemies, especially the "eastern liberal establishment" that had long opposed him.

Some observers viewed Nixon as the classic outsider: reared in pinched surroundings, physically awkward, unable to relate easily to others. Although at the height of national power, Nixon remained fearful that he would never be accepted. In the early Nixon years, the president's strengths were most apparent. Nixon spoke of national reconciliation, took bold initiatives internationally, and dealt with domestic problems responsibly. But the darker side ultimately prevailed and drove him from office in disgrace.

Symbolic of this positive start, the nation joined the new president in celebrating the first successful manned mission to the moon. On July 20, 1969, astronaut **Neil Armstrong** descended from the lunar lander *Eagle* to the surface of the Sea of Tranquility, and announced to enthralled television audiences back on earth, "That's one small step for man, one giant leap for mankind." Five more lunar expeditions followed, but in 1975 the space race essentially ended with the United States and Soviet Union engaging in cooperative efforts to explore the rest of the universe.

The first newly elected president since 1849 whose party controlled neither house of Congress, Nixon cooperated with the Democrats to increase social-security benefits, build subsidized housing, expand the Job Corps, and grant the vote to eighteen-year-olds. Responding to the growing environmental movement, which brought out 20 million Americans for the first Earth Day in 1970, the president approved new laws limiting pesticide use, protecting endangered species and marine mammals, safeguarding coastal lands, and controlling strip-mining. Nixon also signed bills creating the Occupational Safety and Health Administration (OSHA), to enforce health and safety standards in the workplace, and the Environmental Protection Agency (EPA), requiring federal agencies to prepare an environmental-impact analysis of all proposed projects.

Conservatives grumbled as government grew larger and more intrusive and as race-conscious employment policies, including quotas, were mandated for all federal contractors. Conservatives grew still angrier when Nixon unveiled the Family

Neil Armstrong First man to set foot on the moon

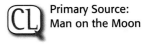
Primary Source:
Man on the Moon

Assistance Plan (FAP) in 1969. A bold effort to overhaul the welfare system, FAP proposed a guaranteed minimum annual income for all Americans. Caught between liberals who thought the income inadequate and conservatives who disliked it on principle, FAP died in the Senate.

A Troubled Economy

Nixon inherited the fiscal consequences of Lyndon B. Johnson's effort to wage the Vietnam War and finance the Great Society by deficit financing, to have both "guns and butter." Facing a large budget deficit of $25 billion in 1969 and an inflation rate of 5 percent, Nixon cut government spending and encouraged the Federal Reserve Board to raise interest rates. The result was a combination of inflation and recession that economists called "stagflation" and Democrats termed "Nixonomics."

Accelerating inflation lowered the standard of living for many families and sparked a wave of strikes as workers sought wage hikes to keep up with the cost of living. It also encouraged the wealthy to invest in art and real estate instead of technology and factories. More plants shut down, industrial jobs dwindled, and millions of displaced workers lost their savings, their health and pension benefits, and their homes.

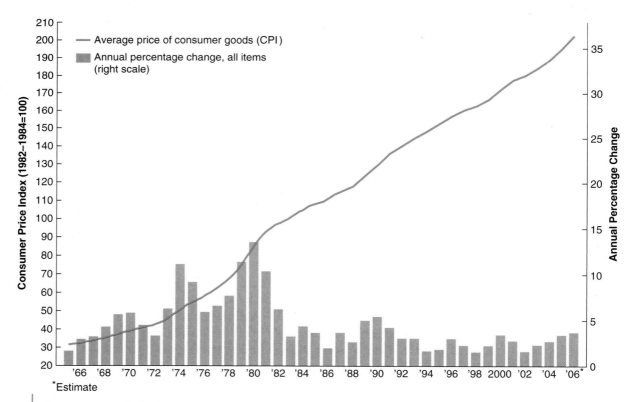

Figure 29.1   Inflation, 1965–2006

Inflation, which had been moderate during the two decades following the Second World War, began to soar with the escalation of the war in Vietnam in the mid-1960s. In 1979 and 1980 the nation experienced double-digit inflation in two consecutive years for the first time since World War I.

Throughout 1971 Nixon lurched from policy to policy. Declaring, "I am now a Keynesian," he increased deficit spending to stimulate the private sector. It resulted in the largest budget deficit since World War II. Then Nixon devalued the dollar to correct the balance-of-payment deficit. Finally, he froze wages, prices, and rents for ninety days, a Band-Aid that worked until after the 1972 election. Then Nixon again reversed course, replacing controls with voluntary—and ineffective—guidelines. Inflation and sluggish growth would dog the U.S. economy throughout the decade.

Law and Order

Despite his public appeals for unity, Nixon hoped to divide the American people in ways that would bring about a realignment in politics and create a new Republican majority coalition. His "southern strategy" sought to attract Dixie's white Democrats into the GOP fold, while his stands on crime, drugs, antiwar protestors, and black militants wooed blue-collar laborers and suburbanites—voters whom political strategist Kevin Phillips vividly described as "in motion between a Democratic past and a Republican future."

To combat the militants he despised, Nixon used full federal government resources. The Internal Revenue Service (IRS) audited their tax returns; the Small Business Administration denied them loans; and the FBI illegally wiretapped them. The FBI worked with local officials to disrupt and immobilize Black Panthers. The CIA illegally investigated and compiled dossiers on thousands of American citizens. The Department of Justice prosecuted antiwar activists and militant blacks in highly publicized trials. Nixon himself drew up an "enemies list" of adversaries to be harassed by the government.

In 1970 Nixon widened his offensive against the antiwar movement by approving the Huston Plan, which would use the CIA and FBI in various illegal missions. The plan called for extensive wiretapping and electronic surveillance, break-ins to find or plant evidence of illegal activity, and a new agency to centralize domestic covert operations under White House supervision. But FBI chief J. Edgar Hoover opposed the Huston Plan as a threat to the FBI's independence. Blocked, Nixon secretly created his own White House unit to discredit his opposition and to ensure executive security. Nicknamed "the **plumbers**" because of their assignment to plug government leaks, the team was headed by ex-FBI agent G. Gordon Liddy and former CIA operative E. Howard Hunt.

plumbers Group set up by Nixon White House to carry out dirty tricks and undermine opposition to the president

The plumbers first targeted Daniel Ellsberg, a former Defense Department analyst who had turned over to the press the **Pentagon Papers,** a secret documentary history of U.S. involvement in Vietnam. On June 13, 1971, the *New York Times* began publishing the Pentagon Papers, which revealed a long history of White House lies to foreign leaders, Congress, and the American people. Although the papers contained nothing damaging about his administration, Nixon feared that they would undermine public trust in government and establish a precedent for publishing classified material. The Supreme Court ultimately ruled that the documents' publication was protected under the First Amendment. Livid, Nixon directed the Justice Department to indict Ellsberg for theft and ordered the plumbers to break into the office of Ellsberg's psychiatrist in search of information against the man who had become an instant hero to the antiwar movement.

Pentagon Papers Secret chronicle of presidential lies regarding U.S. involvement in Vietnam published by the *New York Times*

Driving Southward and Backward

To outflank George Wallace and win the votes of both southern whites and blue-collar workers from the North, Nixon's "southern strategy" included delaying school desegregation plans and strong opposition to busing children to achieve racial balance in the schools.

CHECKING IN

- Despite his enormous political skills, Nixon was a deeply flawed man—a classic outsider who worried about "enemies."

- Early in his presidency Nixon accepted some moderate social and environmental-protection measures.

- Economic "stagflation," inherited from the years of funding the Vietnam War and the Great Society, led Nixon to attempt a variety of unsuccessful cures.

- Nixon ordered a secret and frequently illegal campaign against his opponents, using the FBI, IRS, CIA, and White House "plumbers."

- Nixon's "southern strategy" courted white conservatives by opposing busing and other desegregation measures and promoting law and order; the southern strategy governed Nixon's Supreme Court nominations.

The Southern Strategy

Nixon especially courted whites upset by the drive for racial equality. The administration opposed extension of the Voting Rights Act of 1965, sought to cripple enforcement of the Fair Housing Act of 1968, pleaded for the postponement of desegregation in Mississippi schools, and filed suits to prohibit busing children to desegregate schools.

The strategy of wooing white southerners dictated Nixon's Supreme Court nominations. To reverse the Warren court's liberalism, he sought strict constructionists, judges who would not "meddle" in social issues or be "soft" on criminals. In 1969 he appointed Warren Burger as chief justice. Nixon then tried to appoint a Deep South conservative, but the Senate rejected both of his nominees. However, by 1972 Nixon had succeeded in appointing to the Supreme Court three justices with reputations as strict constructionists: Harry Blackmun of Minnesota, Lewis Powell of Virginia, and William Rehnquist of Arizona. The Nixon appointees would steer the court in a moderate direction. Although ruling liberally in cases involving abortion, desegregation, and the death penalty, the Burger court would shift to the right in rulings on civil liberties, community censorship, and police power.

As the 1970 congressional elections neared, Nixon's vice president, Spiro T. Agnew, assailed the Democrats as "sniveling hand-wringers" and the news media as "nattering nabobs of negativism." Liberals deplored Agnew's alarming alliterative allegations. The 1970 elections were a draw, with the GOP losing nine House seats and winning two Senate seats.

THE CRISIS OF THE PRESIDENCY

What were the main causes of the Watergate scandal?

In his second inaugural, Nixon pledged to make the next four years "the best four years in American history." Ironically, they would rank among its sorriest. His vice president would resign in disgrace, his closest confidants would go to jail, and he would serve barely a year and a half of his second term before resigning to avoid impeachment.

The Election of 1972

Nixon's reelection appeared certain. He counted on his diplomatic successes and his winding down of the Vietnam War to win over moderate voters. He expected his southern strategy and law-and-order posture to attract Wallace voters. Continuing Democratic divisions boosted Nixon's optimism. His only major worry, another third-party candidacy by George Wallace, vanished on May 15, 1972 when Wallace was shot during a campaign stop and paralyzed from the waist down. He withdrew from the race, leaving Nixon a monopoly on the white backlash.

The Senate's most outspoken dove, **George McGovern** of South Dakota, capitalizing on the antiwar sentiment, blitzed the Democratic primaries. New party rules requiring broader inclusion of minority, female, and youthful delegates in state delegations aided the liberal McGovern. A disapproving labor leader complained about "too much hair and not enough cigars at this convention," but McGovern won the nomination on the first ballot.

Perceptions of McGovern as inept and radical drove away all but the most committed supporters. McGovern dropped his vice-presidential running mate, Thomas Eagleton, when it became known that Eagleton had received electric-shock therapy for depression. Subsequently, several prominent Democrats publicly declined to run with him. McGovern's endorsement of decriminalization of marijuana, immediate withdrawal from Vietnam, and pardons for those who had fled the United States to avoid the draft exposed him to GOP ridicule as the candidate of the radical fringe.

Remembering his narrow loss to Kennedy in 1960 and too-slim victory in 1968, Nixon left no stone unturned. To do whatever was necessary to win, he appointed his attorney general, John Mitchell, to head the Committee to Re-Elect the President (CREEP). Millions in contributions financed a series of "dirty tricks" against Democrats and paid for a special espionage unit, led by Liddy and Hunt of the White House plumbers, to spy on the opposition. Early one morning in June 1972, the Republican undercover team, with Mitchell's approval, attempted to wiretap telephones at the Democratic National Committee headquarters in Washington's Watergate complex. A security guard foiled the break-in. Arrested were James McCord, the security coordinator of CREEP, and several other Liddy and Hunt associates.

A White House cover-up began immediately. Nixon announced that "no one in this administration, presently employed, was involved in this bizarre incident." He then ordered staff members to expunge Hunt's name from the White House telephone directory, to buy the silence of those arrested with $400,000 in hush money and hints of a presidential pardon, and to direct the CIA to halt the FBI's investigation of the Watergate break-in on the pretext that the inquiry would damage national security.

With the McGovern campaign a shambles and Watergate seemingly contained, Nixon won the election overwhelmingly, amassing nearly 61 percent of the popular vote and 520 electoral votes. Strongly supported only by minorities and low-income voters, McGovern carried just Massachusetts and the District of Columbia. The election solidified the 1968 realignment.

However, the GOP gained only twelve seats in the House and lost two in the Senate. The outcome demonstrated the growing difficulty of unseating incumbents, the rise of ticket-splitting, and the decline of both party loyalty and voter turnout. Only 55.7 percent of eligible voters went to the polls, down from 63.8 percent in 1960.

George McGovern Liberal Senator from South Dakota and Democratic candidate for president in 1972

The Watergate Upheaval

The scheme to conceal links between the White House and the accused Watergate burglars had succeeded during the 1972 campaign. But after the election, federal judge John Sirica (sir-RICK-uh) refused to accept the defendants' claim that they had acted

"Deep Throat" Source for much of journalists Woodward and Bernstein's exposure of Watergate crimes

on their own. Threatening severe prison sentences, Sirica coerced James McCord of CREEP into confessing that highly placed White House aides knew in advance of the break-in and that the defendants had committed perjury during the trial. Two *Washington Post* reporters, Carl Bernstein and Bob Woodward, following clues furnished by **"Deep Throat,"** an unnamed informant, wrote a succession of front-page stories tying the break-in to illegal contributions and "dirty tricks" by CREEP. (In 2005 Mark Felt, former second-in-command of the FBI, revealed that he had been Deep Throat.)

In February 1973 the Senate established the Special Committee on Presidential Campaign Activities to investigate. As the trail of revelations led closer to the Oval Office, Nixon fired his special counsel, John Dean, who refused to be a scapegoat, and announced the resignations of his principal aides, H. R. Haldeman and John Ehrlichman. Pledging to get to the bottom of the scandal, he appointed Secretary of Defense Elliott Richardson, a Boston patrician of unassailable integrity, as his new attorney general and, bowing to Senate demands, instructed Richardson to appoint a special Watergate prosecutor with broad powers of investigation and subpoena. Richardson selected Archibald Cox, a Harvard law professor and Democrat.

In May the special Senate committee began a televised investigation. Chaired by Sam Ervin of North Carolina, an expert on constitutional law, the hearings revealed the existence of the "enemies list," the president's use of governmental agencies to harass his opponents, and administration favors in return for illegal campaign donations. Most damaging to Nixon, the hearings exposed the White House's active involvement in the Watergate cover-up. But the Senate still lacked concrete evidence of the president's criminality, the "smoking gun" that would prove Nixon's guilt.

Then another presidential aide revealed that Nixon had installed a secret taping system that recorded all conversations in the Oval Office. The Ervin committee and Cox insisted on access to the tapes, but Nixon refused, claiming executive privilege. In October, when Cox sought a court order to obtain the tapes, Nixon ordered Attorney General Richardson to fire him. Richardson resigned in protest, as did the deputy attorney general, leaving the third-ranking official in the Department of Justice, Solicitor General Robert Bork, to dump Cox. The furor raised by the "Saturday Night Massacre" sent Nixon's public-approval rating plunging downward. As Nixon named a new special prosecutor, Leon Jaworski, the House Judiciary Committee began impeachment proceedings.

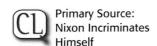 Primary Source: Nixon Incriminates Himself

A President Disgraced

Adding to Nixon's woes that October, Vice President Agnew, charged with income-tax evasion and acceptance of bribes, pleaded no contest—"the full equivalent of a plea of guilty," according to the trial judge. Agnew left office with a three-year suspended sentence and a $10,000 fine. House minority leader Gerald R. Ford replaced Agnew.

In March 1974 Jaworski and the House Judiciary Committee subpoenaed the president for the tape recordings of Oval Office conversations after the Watergate break-in. Nixon released edited transcripts of the tapes, filled with gaps and the phrase "expletive deleted." Despite the excisions, the president emerged as petty and vindictive.

Nixon's sanitized version of the tapes satisfied neither Jaworski nor the House Judiciary Committee. Both pressed for unedited tapes. In late July the Supreme Court rebuffed the president's claim of executive privilege. Chief Justice Burger cited the president's obligation to provide evidence necessary for the due process of law and ordered Nixon to release the unexpurgated tapes.

In late July the House Judiciary Committee adopted three articles of impeachment, accusing the president of obstruction of justice for impeding the Watergate investigation; abuse of power, especially his partisan use of the FBI and IRS; and of contempt of Congress for refusing to obey a congressional subpoena for the tapes.

Checkmated, Nixon conceded in a televised address on August 5 that he had withheld relevant evidence. He then surrendered the tapes, which contained the smoking gun proving that the president had ordered the cover-up, obstructed justice, subverted one government agency to prevent another from investigating a crime, and lied about his role for more than two years.

Impeachment and conviction were now certain. On August 9, 1974, Richard M. Nixon became the first American president to resign. Gerald Ford took office as the nation's first chief executive who had not been elected either president or vice president.

CHECKING IN

- Nixon's reelection strategy involved wiretapping and "dirty tricks," including breaking into Democratic party headquarters at the Watergate building to bug telephones.

- Investigative reporters Carl Bernstein and Bob Woodward uncovered links between the Watergate burglars and the White House.

- A series of House and Senate hearings revealed the extent of illegal activities and the involvement of the president and his chief aides.

- The Supreme Court ruled that Nixon must release taped conversations that incriminated him in the cover-up.

- Rather than be impeached, Nixon resigned the presidency in August 1974.

Chapter Summary

 DOWNLOAD THE MP3 AUDIO FILE OF THE CHAPTER SUMMARY, AND LISTEN TO IT ON THE GO.

What were the major landmarks of the youth movement? (page 686)

Longing for meaning in their lives, as well as personal liberty, campus-based activist groups like SDS and the Free Speech Movement sought a more humane democracy, a less racist and materialist society, and an end to the war in Vietnam. The New Left movement began to dissipate after the shooting deaths of students at Kent State and Jackson State, leaving a legacy of conservative backlash.

In what ways did the counterculture shape the 1968–1974 period? (page 690)

The dissatisfaction with the status quo that engendered protest pushed some young people into cultural rebellion. Denouncing materialism and selfishness, hippies "turned on and dropped out," seeking fulfillment in sex, drugs,

KEY TERMS

Students for a Democratic Society (SDS) *(p. 686)*

Berkeley Free Speech Movement *(p. 687)*

Jackson State College *(p. 689)*

counterculture *(p. 690)*

Woodstock festival *(p. 691)*

Roe v. *Wade (p. 692)*

gay liberation *(p. 692)*

Eugene McCarthy *(p. 693)*

Tet offensive *(p. 693)*

Robert Kennedy *(p. 694)*

Hubert Humphrey *(p. 695)*

"Yippies" *(p. 695)*

and rock and roll. Woodstock represented the high point of the counterculture. The sexual revolution and gay liberation both flourished.

What were the main causes and consequences of the politics of upheaval in 1968? (page 693)

Shaken by the Tet offensive, the American people began to question whether Vietnam was worth the price. LBJ encountered serious opposition in the primaries and dropped out of the presidential race. The assassinations of Martin Luther King and Robert Kennedy spawned riots, including one at the Democratic National Convention. Richard Nixon and George Wallace capitalized on the conservative backlash, and with Nixon's election as president the Republicans emerged as the new majority party.

What fundamental changes in American foreign policy were made by President Nixon? (page 696)

Nixon and Kissinger, his chief adviser, considered themselves masters of *realpolitik*. In addition to finally ending American involvement in Vietnam, they forged an opening to China, enlarged détente with the Soviet Union, and tried to mediate Middle Eastern politics.

How did Richard Nixon's political strategy reflect the racial upheavals and radicalism of this era? (page 701)

Nixon was politically skilled, deeply flawed, and convinced that he was surrounded by enemies. He endorsed secret campaigns against his opposition, using the FBI, IRS, CIA, and White House plumbers. Nixon courted white southern conservatives by opposing school busing and other desegregation measures.

What were the main causes of the Watergate scandal? (page 704)

Nixon's 1972 reelection strategy included wiretapping, "dirty tricks," and a break-in to tap phones at the Democratic party headquarters in the Watergate building. Investigative reporters began to uncover the extent of illegality, and House and Senate committees revealed how deeply the president and his closest aides were involved. Ultimately Nixon resigned the presidency rather than be impeached. The deepening public disenchantment with politicians and disillusionment with government would last into the next century.

KEY TERMS continued

Henry Kissinger *(p. 697)*
My Lai *(p. 697)*
détente *(p. 699)*
Neil Armstrong *(p. 701)*
plumbers *(p. 703)*
Pentagon Papers *(p. 703)*
George McGovern *(p. 705)*
"Deep Throat" *(p. 706)*

CHAPTER 30

Conservative Resurgence, Economic Woes, Foreign Challenges

1974–1989

Vietnamese-American Family in Austin, Texas, Learning the Basics of Baseball

CHAPTER PREVIEW

Cultural Changes
What issues and trends helped spark a growing conservative movement in the 1970s?

Economic and Social Changes in Post-1960s America
What social and economic developments most affected American life between 1974 and 1989?

Years of Malaise: Post-Watergate Politics and Diplomacy, 1974–1981
What were the major achievements and failures of the Ford and Carter presidencies?

The Reagan Revolution, 1981–1984
What core beliefs most shaped Ronald Reagan's presidency?

Reagan's Second Term, 1985–1989
What key domestic and international developments marked Reagan's second term?

Discount chains like Wal-Mart changed mass marketing in the United States after 1960. During the 1970s high unemployment and high inflation eroded consumer buying power in conventional stores, and Wal-Mart's rock-bottom prices were a boon to low-income families. One hundred shares of stock bought for $1,650 in 1970 soared to a value of $3 million by 1990. By 2008, with more than 2 million employees and some 7,300 discount stores, Sam's Clubs, and Super Centers worldwide, Wal-Mart boasted annual revenues of more than $378 billion and was the world's largest retailer of general merchandise.

Wal-Mart also faced heavy criticism. For example, Wal-Mart fought off unionization of its low-paid employees by establishing a profit-sharing plan. Its most vociferous critics were small-town merchants driven out of business by Wal-Mart's aggressive high-volume, price-slashing approach to marketing.

The Wal-Mart phenomenon was part of a transformation of the American economy in the 1970s and 1980s. The service sector grew rapidly as discount stores and fast-food outlets spread, and high-tech industries prospered. But the "old economy"—steel mills, auto plants, and factories in the industrial heartland—grew weaker, battered by imports. For many dependent on the industrial economy, the American dream seemed to fade.

This chapter, which traces American history from the Nixon resignation to the end of the second Reagan administration, 1974–1989, focuses on three key themes: the continuing impact of the 1960s on U.S. culture and politics, as reflected in the growing strength of conservatism; the rise and fall of the economy and long-term changes in the labor market; and the continuing importance of events abroad despite the end of the Vietnam War. Worsening Cold War tensions, Middle East crises, and terrorist attacks all underscored that America's future could not be separated from unfolding world events.

CULTURAL CHANGES

What issues and trends helped spark a growing conservative movement in the 1970s?

As personal pursuits and leisure diversions shaped 1970s' American culture, women in large numbers entered the work force. The sexual revolution continued, but the shadow of AIDS introduced a sobering note. Although antiwar and Black Power protests faded, some activist causes rooted in the 1960s gained momentum, notably environmentalism, the women's movement, and gay rights. A conservative turn; a revival of evangelical religion; and sharp divisions over abortion, homosexuality, and other issues also shaped 1970s' culture.

Personal Pursuits and Diversions

The Vietnam War shattered the early-1960s' liberal consensus, and the radical New Left movement soon fragmented as well, creating political turmoil on the Left. The Watergate crisis, in turn, temporarily disoriented conservatives. With politics in disarray, personal preoccupations beckoned.

Some young people practiced Transcendental Meditation or joined the Reverend Sun Myung Moon's Unification Church. Others embraced the International Society for Krishna Consciousness. Several thousand rural communes arose as some counterculture veterans sought to escape the urban-corporate world and live in harmony with nature. Most of these ventures proved short-lived.

By the early 1980s, journalists discovered the "Yuppie" (young urban professional), preoccupied with physical fitness and consumer goods. The stereotype had some basis in fact. Physical well-being became a middle-class obsession. Yuppies jogged and exercised, ate pesticide-free natural foods, and stopped smoking when medical evidence linked cigarettes to lung cancer, heart disease, and other ills. The

Chronology

1974	Richard Nixon resigns presidency; Gerald Ford sworn in; Indian Self-Determination Act
1975	South Vietnamese government falls; *Mayagüez* incident
1976	Jimmy Carter elected president
1977	Panama Canal treaties ratified; introduction of Apple II computer; Gay Pride parades in New York and San Francisco
1978	Carter authorizes federal funds to relocate Love Canal residents
1979	Menachem Begin and Anwar el-Sadat sign peace treaty at White House; second round of OPEC price increases; accident at Three Mile Island nuclear plant; Carter establishes full diplomatic relations with the People's Republic of China
1980	Alaska Lands Act; Soviet invasion of Afghanistan; Iran hostage crisis; Ronald Reagan elected president
1981	Major cuts in taxes and domestic spending, coupled with large increases in military budget; AIDS first diagnosed
1982	Equal Rights Amendment dies; CIA funds contra war against Nicaragua's Sandinistas; Central Park rally for nuclear-weapons freeze
1983	239 U.S. marines die in Beirut terrorist attack; U.S. deploys Pershing II and cruise missiles in Europe; Reagan proposes Strategic Defense Initiative (Star Wars); U.S. invasion of Grenada
1984	Reagan defeats Walter Mondale to win second term
1984–1986	Congress bars military aid to contras
1985	Rash of airline hijackings and other terrorist acts
1986	Congress passes South African sanctions; Immigration Reform and Control Act
1987	Congressional hearings on Iran-contra scandal; stock-market crash
1988	Reagan trip to Moscow

actress Jane Fonda, earlier an antiwar activist, promoted a series of exercise videos beginning in 1982.

In the cultural arena, the politically engaged songs of the 1960s gave way to disco, suitable for dancing but carrying little cultural weight. Blockbuster movies like *Jaws* (1975), *Rocky* (1976), *Star Wars* (1977), and *E.T.* (1982) offered escapist fare. *Happy Days,* the top TV show of 1976–1977, evoked nostalgia for the 1950s. The TV series *Dallas,* chronicling the steamy affairs of a Texas oil family, captivated millions in the early 1980s. Football's Super Bowl and other sports extravaganzas attracted vast TV audiences.

Cable TV, introduced in the early 1970s, broadened viewers' options. By 1988, over half of U.S. homes had cable. Innovations in consumer electronics also shaped the era. By the early 1990s, 70 percent of U.S. households had VCRs (videocassette recorders), enabling users to tape TV shows for later viewing and to rent movies on cassette. In the music field, the compact disc (CD), introduced in 1983, offered high-quality sound.

And the personal computer arrived. In the late 1970s, two young Californians, Steven Jobs and Stephen Wozniak, reduced computers from room size to desk-top size and marketed the phenomenally successful Apple computer. As Apple sales shot

The Rise of the Yuppie

In 1984, *Newsweek* magazine proclaimed "the Year of the Yuppie," or young urban professional, a rapidly growing group in the 1980s.

up, computer manufacturers multiplied, especially in California's Silicon Valley. In 1981 IBM launched its PC (personal computer) and quickly grabbed 40 percent of the market, but computer entrepreneurs continued to proliferate. By 1997, 44 percent of American households owned personal computers. American culture in these years was not all escapism and technological novelties, however. Bruce Springsteen's "Born in the USA" (1984) told of a young man "sent . . . to a foreign land to go and kill the yellow man" who now finds himself with "[n]owhere to run . . . nowhere to go." The 1970s also saw the rise of punk rock, an aggressively anti-establishment genre promoted by such groups as the Sex Pistols, the Ramones, and the Clash; of Tejano music (*Tejanos* is Spanish for "Texans of Hispanic descent"); and of rap or hip-hop. Rap, beginning in the 1970s in poor black New York City neighborhoods, and involving free-form improvised recitations, gained a broad following in the 1980s and beyond.

Along with escapist fare, directors also produced some brilliant films exploring the darker side of American life in the 1970s. Robert Altman's *Nashville* (1975) offered a disturbing vision of cynical mass-culture producers, manipulative politicians, and lonely, alienated drifters. Roman Polanski's *Chinatown* (1974) probed the personal and political corruption beneath the sunny surface of Southern California life.

Changing Gender Roles and Sexual Behavior

Many women's lives changed dramatically in these years. Spurred by a resurgent women's movement as well as by inflation pressures, the number of women working outside the home leaped from under 20 million in 1960 to nearly 60 million by 1990 (see Figure 30.1).

Women's wages still lagged behind those of men, however, and the workplace remained gender-segregated. Women were concentrated in such fields as nursing, teaching, retail sales, and secretarial work, while men dominated management positions and the professions. But even this changed as women entered the ranks of management. (Top management remained a male preserve, however, a phenomenon known as the "glass ceiling.")

As women pursued higher education or careers, their median age at first marriage rose from twenty in 1960 to twenty-four in 1990. The birthrate fell as well, and by 1980 the statistically average U.S. family had 1.6 children, far below earlier levels. In the wake of the landmark *Roe* v. *Wade* decision of 1973 (see Chapter 29), the number of abortions rose from about 750,000 in 1973 to more than 1.5 million in 1980 and then leveled off.

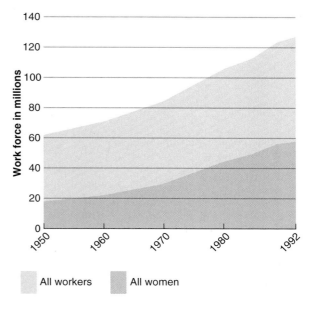

Figure 30.1   Women in the Work Force, 1950-1992

After 1960 the proportion of American women who were gainfully employed surged upward. As a result, young women coming of age in the 1990s had far different expectations about their lives than had their grandmothers or even their mothers.

Sources: *Statistical Abstract of the United States,* 1988 (Washington, D.C.: U.S. Government Printing Office, 1987), 373; *World Almanac and Book of Facts,* 1989 (New York: Pharos Books, 1988), 152; *Statistical Abstract of the United States,* 1993 (Washington D.C.: U.S. Government Printing Office, 1993), 400, 401

The freer attitude toward sex received a setback with the spread of the deadly viral infection **AIDS** (acquired immune deficiency syndrome), first diagnosed in 1981. AIDS spread mainly among sexually active homosexuals and bisexuals, intravenous drug users sharing needles, and persons having sexual intercourse with these high-risk individuals. Though the worst lay ahead, more than thirty-one thousand Americans had died of AIDS by the end of the 1980s.

Medical authorities warned against unprotected sex. The message was driven home when film star Rock Hudson died of AIDS in 1985, and basketball superstar Earvin ("Magic") Johnson announced that he carried the HIV virus, a precursor of AIDS. While the epidemic emboldened some Americans to express their hatred of homosexuality, it also stimulated medical research and an outpouring of concern. Under the shadow of AIDS, many Americans grew more cautious in their sexual behavior. The exuberant 1960s slogan "Make Love, Not War" gave way to a more somber message: "Safer Sex."

AIDS Acquired immune deficiency syndrome; first diagnosed in 1981

The Persistence of Social Activism

The environmental-protection movement, a legacy of the 1960s, grew stronger in the 1970s. Older organizations such as the Sierra Club and the Wilderness Society, as well as new ones such as Greenpeace, won fresh recruits. Greenpeace worked to preserve old-growth forests and protect the world's oceans. By 2000, it had 250,000 U.S. members. The Save the Whales campaign, launched in 1971, opposed the slaughter of the world's largest mammals.

Environmentalists also targeted the nuclear-power industry. Adopting techniques from the civil-rights and antiwar campaigns, activists protested at planned nuclear-power plants. The movement crested in 1979 when a partial meltdown crippled the **Three Mile Island** nuclear-power plant in Pennsylvania. A Jane Fonda movie released at the same time, *China Syndrome,* portrayed a fictional but plausible nuclear-power disaster caused by a California earthquake. The Three Mile Island accident deepened public concerns about nuclear power.

Of the 1960s' many legacies, the revitalized women's movement (see Chapter 28) proved most enduring: The National Organization for Women (NOW), founded in

Three Mile Island Nuclear-power plant in Pennsylvania where disaster nearly struck in 1979

1966, boasted nearly fifty thousand members by 1975. Although NOW remained mainly white and middle class, African-American, Latina, and Asian women organized as well. Women workers agitated for better wages and working conditions.

With the movement's growth came political clout. The National Women's Political Caucus (1971) promoted a feminist agenda. By 1972, many states had liberalized their abortion laws and outlawed gender bias in hiring. That same year Congress passed an **Equal Rights Amendment** (ERA) to the Constitution barring discrimination on the basis of sex. Twenty-eight states quickly ratified it, and ultimate adoption seemed likely.

Equal Rights Amendment
A proposed amendment to the U.S. Constitution barring discrimination on the basis of sex

Conservatives worried that women's changing roles would weaken the family. Women themselves conceded the stresses of balancing career and family, but few pined for the era when child care, housework, and volunteerism had defined "women's sphere." As the 1980s ended, many American women enjoyed unprecedented opportunities, but barriers persisted, and complex issues remained.

As we saw in Chapter 29, many gay men and lesbians came out of the closet in the 1970s, openly avowing their sexual orientation and protesting job discrimination and harassment. In 1977, Gay Pride parades drew seventy-five thousand marchers in New York City and three hundred thousand in San Francisco, a center of gay activism. Two years later, a national gay and lesbian civil-rights parade attracted one hundred thousand marchers to Washington, D.C. In 1987 Massachusetts congressman Barney Frank acknowledged his homosexuality.

Organizations like the National Gay Task Force, founded in 1973 (and later renamed the National Gay and Lesbian Task Force), demanded the repeal of anti-gay laws and passage of legislation protecting homosexuals' civil rights. Responding to the pressure, many states and cities repealed laws against same-sex relations between consenting adults and barring job discrimination on the basis of sexual orientation.

Grass-Roots Conservatism

But a backlash was building, rooted in the 1960s and earlier. The sixties was a polarizing decade. Many Americans, especially blue-collar whites, deplored what they viewed as the decade's radical excesses. As we saw in Chapter 29, Richard Nixon exploited this disaffection to win the White House in 1968.

The conservative resurgence had even deeper roots. **William F. Buckley** had launched the conservative *National Review* magazine in 1955 and founded Young Americans for Freedom in 1960. Barry Goldwater's 1964 presidential campaign alerted conservatives to the importance of broadening their appeal beyond hardcore conservative loyalists.

William F. Buckley Author, editor, and commentator who helped shape the modern conservative movement

The career of Phyllis Schlafly, devout Roman Catholic, law-school graduate, mother of six, and tireless activist, illustrates the movement's post-1960 evolution. Her *Phyllis Schlafly Report,* begun in 1967, attacked the New Left and the counterculture. In the 1970s, Schlafly and her organization, The Eagle Forum, focused on hot-button cultural issues such as abortion; gay rights; and the Equal Rights Amendment, which she fiercely opposed.

In local communities, especially in the fast-growing South and West (see Chapter 27), conservatives found each other and mobilized politically. This process was especially evident in southern California's Orange County, where conservatives were intensely anticommunist, dismayed by 1960s' radicals, and suspicious of the "liberal intellectuals" dominating the media and national politics. Foreshadowing changes ahead nationally, Orange County helped elect **Ronald Reagan** governor of California in 1966 and in 1978 helped pass Proposition 13, a state referendum calling for deep cuts in property taxes.

As Schlafly's campaigns illustrate, 1970s' conservatives mobilized around specific issues, especially abortion. In the wake of *Roe* v. *Wade,* a "Right to Life" or "Pro-life" movement led by Roman Catholic and conservative Protestant activists rallied, signed petitions, and picketed abortion clinics and pregnancy-counseling centers.

Responding to the pressure, Congress in 1976 ended Medicaid funding for most abortions, in effect denying this procedure to the poor. Most feminists, by contrast, adopted a "pro-choice" stance, arguing that women and their physicians, not the government, should make reproductive decisions. Opinion polls reflected deep divisions, although a majority favored the pro-choice" position. The Equal Rights Amendment, denounced by Schlafly and other conservatives, died in 1982, three states short of the three-fourths required for ratification.

Gay and lesbian activism particularly inflamed conservatives, who saw it as evidence of society's moral collapse. TV evangelist Jerry Falwell thundered, "God . . . destroyed the cities of Sodom and Gomorrah because of this terrible sin." In 1977, singer Anita Bryant led a campaign against a Miami ordinance protecting homosexuals' civil rights. Thanks in part to Bryant's efforts, voters repealed the ordinance. Other cities, too, reversed earlier measures favoring gay rights. In 1978, as the backlash intensified, a member of the San Francisco board of supervisors fatally shot gay board-member Harvey Milk and Milk's ally, Mayor George Moscone. When the killer received a light sentence, riots erupted in the city.

Ronald Reagan Fortieth president of the United States; his two terms were marked by patriotic rhetoric, tax cuts, and militant anticommunism

Evangelical Protestants Mobilize

The conservative movement also found expression in the rapid growth of evangelical Protestantism, with its emphasis on strict morality, biblical inerrancy, and a personal "born again" conversion experience. Evangelical denominations such as the Assemblies of God and the Southern Baptist Convention grew explosively in the 1970s and 1980s, as did independent suburban megachurches. Meanwhile, liberal denominations such as the Methodists, Congregationalists, and Unitarians lost members.

Many evangelicals plunged into politics. As one observed in 1985, "I always thought that churches should stay out of politics. Now it seems almost a sin not to get involved." Jerry Falwell's Moral Majority, founded in 1979 as a "pro-life, pro-family, pro-moral, and pro-America" crusade, actively supported conservative candidates. Pat Robertson, head of the Christian Broadcasting Network and host of its popular *700 Club,* mounted an unsuccessful presidential bid in 1988.

While battling abortion, homosexuality, and pornography, often in alliance with conservative Catholics, evangelicals also attacked the Supreme Court's 1962 ***Engel*** v. ***Vitale*** decision banning organized prayer in public schools as a violation of the First Amendment. While pushing to reverse this ruling, evangelicals also advocated home schooling and private Christian schools, to shield children from what they saw as the secularist (nonreligious) values.

Engel v. ***Vitale*** Supreme Court's 1962 decision prohibiting organized prayer in public schools

For many evangelicals, Bible prophecy reinforced their political mobilization. Hal Lindsey's *The Late Great Planet Earth* (1970), a popularization of one system of prophetic interpretation, was *the* nonfiction best seller of the 1970s. Lindsey found the Soviet Union, communist China, the Arab-Israeli conflict, the United Nations, and growing domestic wickedness all foretold in the Bible. He urged true believers to rally on the side of righteousness as the End approached.

Christian bookstores, radio stations, and TV evangelists fueled the revival. Along with Falwell's *Old Time Gospel Hour,* popular broadcasts included Jim and Tammy Bakker's *PTL* (Praise the Lord) program and Jimmy Swaggart's telecasts from Louisiana. The so-called electronic church suffered after 1987 amid sexual and financial scandals, but the evangelical resurgence continued. In a world of change, evangelicals found certitude, reassurance, and a sense of community in their shared faith. In the process, they profoundly influenced late-twentieth-century American life.

ECONOMIC AND SOCIAL CHANGES IN POST-1960s AMERICA

What social and economic developments most affected American life between 1974 and 1989?

Inflation, industrial decline, and other economic problems offered a troubling counterpoint to the developments of these years. Many white-collar professionals and people involved with the emerging information-based economy prospered. Others, however, including displaced factory workers, did not. Although many African-Americans successfully pursued the academic and professional avenues opened by the civil-rights movement, others remained in poverty. Although Native Americans faced adversities, the 1970s brought brighter economic prospects and a new assertiveness in pursuing treaty rights. Shifting patterns of immigration, meanwhile, changed the nation's ethnic and demographic profile, with major implications for the future.

A Changing Economy   Disturbing economic developments influenced U.S. politics and shadowed the lives of millions of Americans in the 1970s. Largely owing to surging oil prices, the inflation rate spiked to around 11 percent in 1973, dipped a bit, and then soared to almost 14 percent by 1980. Overall, consumer prices more than doubled from 1970 to 1980. This grinding rate of inflation battered American families and turned hard-pressed taxpayers against the welfare programs adopted during past Democratic administrations.

The family farm, historically revered as the backbone of America, continued its long decline in these years. In 1960 about 6 percent of the U.S. labor force worked on farms; by 1994 the figure was 2.5 percent. The farm population was aging, as young people sought opportunities in the cities. The small-farm operators who still hung on often held second jobs to make ends meet. Overall farm production increased, however. As big operators bought failing farms, average farm size grew from 375 to 430 acres between 1970 and 1990. Federal subsidy programs encouraged the rise of giant agribusinesses. Industrial stagnation, or **deindustrialization,** worsened the era's economic woes. The steel and automobile industries were especially hard hit. As soaring gasoline prices boosted sales of more fuel-efficient foreign imports, U.S. car makers suffered. U.S. purchases of foreign cars, mainly from Japan, grew from 2 million in 1970 to 4 million in 1989. Facing severe production cutbacks, GM, Ford, and Chrysler laid off more than 225,000 workers.

> **deindustrialization** Devastating post-war decline of heavy industry in urban northeast and Midwest

Longer-term sources of industrial decline included aging machinery, inefficient production methods, and fierce competition from foreign companies paying lower wages. The unemployment rate reached 8.5 percent in 1975. In one five-year period, 1979–1983, 11.5 million U.S. workers lost jobs because of plant closings and cutbacks.

As industrial workers lost jobs, the union movement weakened. In 1960, 31 percent of U.S. workers belonged to unions; in 1985, the figure stood at 18 percent, with further declines ahead. Some workers did join unions in these years, mainly teachers, public employees, and service workers, many of whom were female. However, service-sector unionization only slowed, but did not reverse, the overall decline of union membership.

The Two Worlds of Black America

Millions of blacks experienced significant upward mobility in these years, thanks to the civil-rights movement. In 1965, black students accounted for under 5 percent of total college enrollment; by 1990 the figure had risen to 12 percent, close to their proportion in the general population. TV's *Cosby Show,* a late-1980s comedy in which Bill Cosby played a doctor married to a lawyer, portrayed this upwardly mobile world.

Outside this world lay the inner-city slums, inhabited by perhaps a third of the black population. Here, up to half the young people never finished high school, and the jobless rate soared as high as 60 percent. Cocaine and other drugs pervaded the inner cities. Some black children recruited as lookouts for drug dealers eventually became dealers themselves. With drugs also came violence. In the 1980s, a young black male was six times as likely to be murdered as a young white male. Drug abuse affected all social levels, including yuppies and show-business celebrities. But drug use and trafficking particularly devastated the inner cities.

To compensate for past racial discrimination, some cities set aside a percentage of building contracts for minority businesses. Some educational institutions reserved slots for minority applicants. These so-called **affirmative-action** programs faced court challenges, however. In *Bakke* v. *University of California* (1978), the Supreme Court declared strict racial quotas unconstitutional. The court, did, however, uphold programs to encourage minority businesses or minority-student enrollment in higher education, so long as they did not involve specific quotas.

> **affirmative action** Programs that promote opportunities for minorities

Brightening Prospects for Native Americans

Building on their occupation of Alcatraz Island in San Francisco Bay (see Chapter 28), members of the militant American Indian Movement briefly occupied the Bureau of Indian Affairs in Washington in 1972. In response to spreading protests, the **Indian**

Indian Self-Determination Act
1974 law giving some control of federal programs to tribes

Self-Determination Act of 1974 granted tribes control of federal aid programs on the reservations and oversight of their own schools.

The 1990 census recorded more than 1.7 million persons as American Indians, in contrast to some eight hundred thousand in 1970. This upsurge reflected not only natural increase and ethnic pride, but also economic advantages associated with tribal membership. Under a 1961 law permitting them to buy or develop land for commercial projects, tribes launched business ventures ranging from resorts and gambling casinos to mining and logging operations.

Indian tribes also reasserted long-ignored treaty rights through the Indian Claims Commission, a federal agency set up in 1946. In 1971, the Native peoples of Alaska won 40 million acres and nearly $1 billion in settlement of treaty claims. In 1980, the Sioux were awarded $107 million for South Dakota lands taken from them illegally.

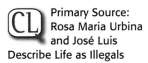

Primary Source: Rosa Maria Urbina and José Luis Describe Life as Illegals

High rates of joblessness, alcoholism, and disease persisted among Indians. But the renewed pride, economic ventures, and progress in asserting treaty rights offered hope. In the popular culture, movies like *Little Big Man* (1970) and *Dances with Wolves* (1990), while idealizing Indians, represented an improvement over the negative stereotypes of earlier films.

Immigration Reform and Control Act Provided path to citizenship for some aliens

New Patterns of Immigration

These years saw a steady influx of immigrants, both legal and illegal. Whereas most immigrants once arrived from Europe, some 45 percent now came from the Western Hemisphere and 30 percent from Asia. As in the past, economic need drew these newcomers. In oil-rich Mexico, for example, falling oil prices in the 1980s worsened the nation's chronic poverty, spurring many to seek jobs in the north. But life in the United States was often harsh. In 1980, some 26 percent of persons of Hispanic origin in the United States lived in poverty, twice the national rate. Despite adversity, Hispanic newcomers preserved their language and traditions, influencing U.S. culture in the process.

Millions of Hispanic immigrants lacked official documentation. Many sweated in the garment trades, cleaned houses, held low-paying service-sector jobs, and labored in agricultural fields. The **Immigration Reform and Control Act** of 1986, an update of the 1965 Immigration Act (see Chapter 28), outlawed the hiring of undocumented immigrants, but offered legal status to aliens who had lived in the United States for five years.

Immigration from Asia climbed as newcomers arrived from South Korea, Vietnam, and the Philippines. The motive, again, was primarily economic, though many Hmong (mong), the indigenous people of Indochina who had supported the United States in the Vietnam War, came for political reasons. Valuing education, many Asian immigrants advanced academically and economically.

CHECKING IN

- Family farmers became an endangered species as agribusiness boomed.
- Some African-Americans made great gains in education and economics, but many remained trapped in poverty in inner-city slums plagued by drugs and blight.
- Native Americans continued to push for their rights and succeeded in gaining the enforcement of some treaties.
- A major shift in immigration patterns brought an influx of Hispanic and Asian newcomers.
- A swelling number of illegal immigrants arrived from Mexico and Central America and frequently faced hardship and exploitation.

Years of Malaise: Post-Watergate Politics and Diplomacy, 1974–1981

What were the major achievements and failures of the Ford and Carter presidencies?

In the aftermath of the Vietnam failure and Richard Nixon's disgrace, Presidents **Gerald Ford** and Jimmy Carter grappled with domestic and foreign problems. Amid inflation and industrial stagnation, unease gripped the nation. Globally, the later 1970s brought mostly humiliations, from the final Vietnam withdrawal to a maddening hostage crisis.

Gerald Ford Thirty-eighth President of the United States; his one term in office overshadowed by his pardon of Nixon and an economic recession

The confident 1950s and early 1960s, when prosperous America had savored its role as the Free World's leader, now seemed remote. A nation long convinced that it was immune to the historical forces that constrained other societies seemed prey to forces beyond its control. But events made clear that America could not evade global involvement.

The Caretaker Presidency of Gerald Ford, 1974–1977

Gerald Ford became president on August 9, 1974, after Richard M. Nixon's resignation. A Michigan congressman who had served as Republican minority leader before becoming vice president, Ford displayed a likeable decency. Most Americans found him a welcome relief after Nixon. The honeymoon soon ended, however, when Ford pardoned Richard Nixon for "any and all crimes" committed while in office. Ford said he wanted to help heal the body politic, but many Americans reacted with outrage.

More conservative than Nixon on domestic issues, Ford vetoed environmental, social-welfare, and public-interest measures, but the heavily Democratic Congress overrode most of the vetoes. Economic problems dogged Ford's presidency. In 1973, oil prices had shot up as a result of an Arab oil embargo and price hikes by the **Organization of Petroleum Exporting Countries** (OPEC), a marketing consortium formed in 1960. The United States, heavily dependent on imported oil, felt the shock as surging prices of gasoline, heating oil, and other petroleum-based products worsened the inflationary spiral and produced long lines of angry drivers at gas stations.

Organization of Petroleum Exporting Countries Oil-exporting nations whose embargo caused fuel prices to spike in 1973

In October 1974, Ford unveiled a program of voluntary price restraint dubbed "Whip Inflation Now" (WIN), but prices continued to zoom. When the Federal Reserve Board tried to cool the economy by raising interest rates, a severe recession resulted. Unemployment approached 11 percent by 1975. Americans for the first time since World War II struggled to curb energy consumption. Congress set fuel-efficiency standards for automobiles in 1975 and imposed a national speed limit of fifty-five miles per hour.

National morale sank further in April 1975 when the South Vietnamese government fell, ending two decades of U.S. effort in Vietnam. The TV networks chronicled desperate helicopter evacuations from the U.S. embassy in Saigon (soon renamed Ho Chi Minh City) as North Vietnamese troops closed in. A few weeks later, Cambodia seized a U.S. merchant ship, the *Mayagüez*. A military rescue ordered by Ford freed the thirty-nine *Mayagüez* crew members but cost the lives of forty-one U.S. servicemen. As the nation entered the election year 1976—also the bicentennial of the Declaration of Independence—Americans found little reason for optimism.

Jimmy Carter Thirty-ninth President of the United States; his one-term presidency identified key issues but was plagued by multiple problems

The Outsider as Insider: President Jimmy Carter, 1977–1981

Gerald Ford won the 1976 Republican nomination. **Jimmy Carter,** a Georgia peanut grower and former governor, swept the Democratic primaries by stressing themes that appealed to post-Watergate America: his honesty, his status as a Washington outsider, his Christian faith.

Carter won by a narrow margin. The vote broke along class lines: the well-to-do went for Ford; the poor, overwhelmingly for Carter. Despite the rising conservative tide, popular revulsion against Nixon and Watergate temporarily interrupted the Republican advance. In office, Carter rejected the trappings of Nixon's "imperial presidency." On inauguration day, he walked from the Capitol to the White House.

Despite the populist symbolism, Carter never framed a clear political philosophy. Liberals and conservatives both claimed him. He and Congress fought the recession with a tax cut and a modest public-works program, and the jobless rate fell to around 5 percent by late 1978. But with public opinion turning against "big government," he offered few proposals to deal with inner-city poverty, industrial decline, and other major problems.

Environmental issues loomed large for Carter. In 1980, Congress passed the Alaska Lands Act, which set aside more than 100 million acres of public land in Alaska for parks, wildlife refuges, and national forests. Energy companies hoping to tap Alaska's oil fields protested, and laid plans to carry on the battle.

Carter confronted an environmental crisis in Niagara Falls, New York. In a district called Love Canal, schools, homes, and apartments had been built on the site of a former chemical dump. In the 1970s, when residents complained of odors and strange substances oozing from the soil, tests confirmed that toxic chemicals were seeping into basements and polluting the air and water. Medical researchers found elevated levels of cancer, miscarriages, and birth defects among Love Canal residents. In 1978 President Carter authorized federal funds to relocate Love Canal families. In late 1980, as his term ended, Carter signed legislation creating a federal "Superfund" to clean up the nation's most polluted industrial sites.

Overall, Carter's domestic record proved thin. Congress ignored his proposals for government administrative reforms. His calls for a national health-insurance program, overhaul of the welfare system, and reform of the income-tax laws fell flat. "Carter couldn't get the Pledge of Allegiance through Congress," groused one legislator.

Carter's foreign-policy record proved similarly mixed. As a candidate he had urged more emphasis on protecting human rights worldwide, in contrast to Henry Kissinger's single-minded focus on U.S. national interests. His secretary of state, Cyrus Vance, worked to combat abuses in Chile, Argentina, South Africa, and elsewhere. In Latin America, the president completed negotiations on treaties transferring the Canal Zone to Panama by 1999. In a rare success for Carter, the Senate ratified the treaties.

In dealing with America's Cold War adversaries China and the Soviet Union, Carter pursued the Nixon-Kissinger strategy of seeking better relations. When Mao

Zedong's successor, Deng Xiaoping, expressed interest in closer ties, Carter responded by restoring full diplomatic relations with Beijing in 1979. Toward the Soviet Union, Carter first showed conciliation, but toughness ultimately won out. In 1979, Carter and the Soviet leader Leonid Brezhnev signed the SALT II treaty, limiting each side's nuclear arsenals. The conciliatory approach dissolved in January 1980 when Russia invaded Afghanistan. As U.S.-Soviet relations soured, Carter withdrew SALT II from the Senate and adopted a series of anti-Soviet measures, including a boycott of the 1980 Summer Olympics in Moscow.

The Middle East: Peace Accords and Hostages

Carter's proudest achievement and his most bitter setback both came in the Middle East. In September 1978 he hosted Egyptian leader Anwar el-Sadat (AN-wahr el-sah-DAHT) and Israeli leader Menachem Begin (meh-NAKH-em BAY-gin) at Camp David, where they agreed on a peace framework. The resulting **Camp David Accords** set a timetable for giving more autonomy to the Palestinians in the West Bank and Gaza, occupied by Israel since the 1967 war. In March 1979, the two leaders signed a formal peace treaty at the White House. The president's hopes for a comprehensive Middle East settlement collapsed as the Israeli government continued to build Jewish settlements in the occupied territories and Islamic fundamentalists assassinated Sadat in 1981. Nonetheless, Camp David was the high point of Carter's presidency.

Camp David Accords Agreement brokered by Jimmy Carter that started a peace process in the Middle East

The low point of his presidency also came in the Middle East. Protests against the repressive regime headed by the shah of Iran, a longtime American client and ally, swelled throughout 1978 and climaxed in January 1979 as the shah left Iran. Ayatollah Ruhollah Khomeini (eye-uh-TOLL-uh roo-HOLL-ah ho-MAY-nee), who had orchestrated the antishah movement from exile in Paris, returned triumphantly to Tehran to impose strict Islamic rule and preach hatred of "the great Satan," the United States.

Iran Hostage Crisis, 1979
As the Iranians staged scenes like this at the U.S. embassy in Tehran for the TV cameras, American frustration soared and President Carter's political fortunes plunged.

When Carter allowed the shah to enter the United States for cancer treatment, Khomeini supporters stormed the American embassy in Tehran and seized more than fifty American hostages. For the next 444 days the Carter administration was virtually paralyzed as appalled Americans watched TV images of blindfolded hostages, anti-American mobs, and burning U.S. flags. Not until January 20, 1981, the day Carter left office, did the Iranian authorities release the hostages.

Troubles and Frustration as Carter's Term Ends

Inflation reached horrendous levels as Carter's term wore on. As OPEC boosted oil prices, U.S. gasoline prices edged toward the then-unheard-of level of $1 a gallon. The national mood soured as inflation surged and as lines of fuming motorists again surrounded gas stations. As the Federal Reserve Board battled inflation by raising interest rates, mortgages and business loans became prohibitively expensive. Economic activity stalled, worsening so-called **stagflation,** the combination of business stagnation and price inflation that characterized the U.S. economy through much of the 1970s.

stagflation Combination of economic stagnation and rising prices

For Carter, the lesson of the crisis was clear: the cheap, unlimited energy that for decades had fueled U.S. economic growth could no longer be counted on, and energy conservation demanded high priority. As early as 1977 Carter had created a new Department of Energy and proposed higher oil and gasoline taxes, tax credits for conservation measures, and research on alternative energy sources. However, he failed to resolve either the hostage crisis abroad or the energy crisis at home.

Americans turned against the remote figure in the White House. Carter's approval rating plummeted to 26 percent in summer 1979. The president delivered a televised address discussing "national malaise" and "loss of confidence," but the speech only deepened the spreading suspicion that Carter himself was a large part of the problem. The Democrats glumly renominated Jimmy Carter in 1980, but defeat in November loomed.

Carter's sudden emergence in 1976 illustrated how, in the TV era, a relative unknown could bypass party power brokers and win a national following. Voters longing to see integrity restored to the presidency had embraced him. Keenly analytical, Carter identified many emerging issues, including environmental protection; energy conservation; and reform of the nation's tax, welfare, and health care systems. But he lacked the political skills to build a consensus around his proposed solutions. A post-presidential career of public service restored Carter's reputation, and brought him the Nobel Peace Prize in 2002. But when he left office in January 1981, few expressed regrets.

CHECKING IN

- The Ford administration struggled with continued inflation, an oil crisis, and the collapse of South Vietnam.
- Carter was elected as an outsider but found it impossible to govern that way.
- The Carter administration enjoyed few domestic successes but several foreign policy achievements, including the SALT II arms limitation treaty, the Panama Canal treaties, and recognition of the People's Republic of China.
- Carter's greatest achievement came with the Camp David Accords between Egypt and Israel.
- The Iran hostage crisis undermined and ultimately destroyed Carter's presidency.

THE REAGAN REVOLUTION, 1981–1984

What core beliefs most shaped Ronald Reagan's presidency?

In 1980, with Carter's popularity abysmally low, Ronald Reagan, a Republican who promised a break with the past, won the presidency (see Map 30.1). The Reagan era saw mixed economic developments. It began with a recession, and ended with a stock-market crash. In between, however, inflation eased, business activity picked up, and the stock market surged. While Reagan's program of tax cuts, military spending, and business deregulation provided some economic stimulus, these policies also gave rise to mounting federal deficits.

An avid Cold Warrior, Reagan in his first term blasted the Soviets rhetorically, pursued a costly military buildup, and financed guerrillas seeking to overthrow leftist regimes in Latin America. Like other presidents before and since, he also grappled with crises in the Middle East.

Roots of the Reagan Revolution

Ronald Reagan grew up in Dixon, Illinois, the son of an alcoholic father and a churchgoing evangelical mother. He first came to the public eye as a Hollywood actor and president of the Screen Actors' Guild. A New Dealer in the 1930s, Reagan had moved to the right in the 1950s, and in 1954 had become the General Electric Company's corporate spokesperson. As governor of California (1967–1975), he popularized conservative ideas and denounced campus demonstrators.

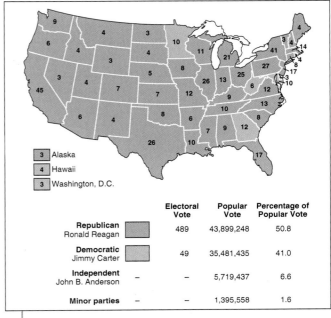

		Electoral Vote	Popular Vote	Percentage of Popular Vote
Republican Ronald Reagan		489	43,899,248	50.8
Democratic Jimmy Carter		49	35,481,435	41.0
Independent John B. Anderson		–	5,719,437	6.6
Minor parties		–	1,395,558	1.6

3 Alaska
4 Hawaii
3 Washington, D.C.

Map 30.1   The Election of 1980

Jimmy Carter's unpopularity and Ronald Reagan's telegenic appeal combined to give Reagan a crushing electoral victory.

In the 1980 Republican primaries, Reagan easily bested his principal opponent, George H. W. Bush (father of the later President George W. Bush), whom he then chose as his vice-presidential running mate. He faced a weakened Jimmy Carter in the general election. Benefiting from the erosion of Democratic strength in the South fostered by George Wallace and by Richard Nixon's southern strategy, Reagan carried every southern state except Carter's own Georgia. Over half of white blue-collar workers, once solidly Democratic, voted Republican. Of FDR's New Deal coalition, only black voters remained firmly Democratic. Republicans gained eleven Senate seats, giving them a majority for the first time since 1955.

Jerry Falwell and other politicized evangelicals helped Reagan's cause. Falwell's pro-Reagan Moral Majority registered an estimated 2 million new voters in 1980 and 1984. Population changes also contributed to Reagan's success. While Democratic strongholds in the urban Northeast and Midwest had lost population in the 1970s, Texas, California, Florida, and other more conservative Sunbelt states had grown rapidly.

Primary Source: First Success of the Religious Right

What underlay Reagan's appeal? First, voters frightened by stagflation welcomed his seemingly painless panacea: a big tax cut that would stimulate the economy. Moreover, Reagan's praise of private initiative struck many voters as preferable to the liberal ideology of "government handouts." Reagan also embraced the cultural values of the emerging conservative movement. Many Americans at all socioeconomic levels, disturbed by the excesses of the 1960s, longed for a return to a partly imagined time when traditional values prevailed.

Reagan, a seasoned actor, wove these essentially negative themes into an appealing positive message of support for "traditional values." His unabashed patriotism, calls for military strength, and praise of America's greatness soothed the battered psyche of a nation traumatized by Vietnam and Watergate. Some thought Reagan glib and superficial and his ideology fundamentally mean-spirited. But in 1980, a majority of voters found his upbeat message inspiring.

Reaganomics

Reagan's economic program, called Reaganomics by the media, boiled down to the belief that American capitalism, freed of heavy taxes and government regulation, would achieve wonders of productivity. Reagan's first budget message proposed a 30 percent reduction in federal income taxes over three years. Trimming the proposal slightly, Congress in May 1981 voted a 25 percent income-tax cut over three years.

To make up for the lost revenues, Reagan proposed cuts in such programs as school lunches, student loans, job training, and urban mass transit. Congress cut less than Reagan wanted, but it did slash more than $40 billion from domestic spending in 1981. Conservative Democrats supported the reductions. Although mainstream economists warned that the tax cut would produce catastrophic federal deficits, Reagan insisted that lower tax rates would stimulate economic growth, pushing up tax revenues.

Reaganomics also involved less government regulation of business. Deregulation had begun under Carter, but Reagan extended it into new areas such as banking, the savings-and-loan industry, transportation, and communications. The Federal Communications Commission cut federal rules governing the broadcast industry. The secretary of transportation cut regulations aimed at reducing air pollution and improving vehicle efficiency and safety.

Secretary of the Interior James Watt of Wyoming opened federal wilderness areas and coastal waters to oil, gas, and timber companies, and cut back on endangered-species laws. Before coming to Washington, Watt had spearheaded the so-called Sagebrush Rebellion, a movement of ranchers, farmers, and mine owners aimed at shifting federal lands in the West to state and county control. After petitions demanding his ouster garnered more than a million signatures, and a series of public-relations gaffes, Watt resigned in 1983.

Strongly pro-business, Reagan took a tough line against organized labor. In 1981, when the Professional Air Traffic Controllers Organization (PATCO) went on strike, Reagan invoked the 1948 Taft-Hartley law against strikes by federal employees, and ordered them back to work. When more than 11,000 PATCO members defied the order, Reagan fired them and barred them permanently from federal employment.

While implementing Reaganomics, the administration also faced the immediate problem of inflation. The Federal Reserve Board led the charge, pushing interest rates ever higher. This harsh medicine, coupled with a drop in oil prices, did its job. Inflation fell to around 4 percent in 1983 and held steady thereafter.

The Fed's high interest rates soon brought on a recession, however. By late 1982, unemployment stood at 10 percent. The Fed's policy also hurt U.S. exports. As foreign investors bought dollars to earn high U.S. interest rates, the dollar rose in value vis-à-vis foreign currencies, making U.S. goods more expensive abroad. With exports declining and U.S. consumers buying cars, TVs, and stereo systems made in Japan and elsewhere, the U.S. annual trade deficit shot up, reaching a whopping $111 billion in 1984.

Soaring federal deficits added to the economic muddle. Reagan's tax cuts reduced federal revenues without immediately producing the predicted business boom, while increased military appropriations far exceeded domestic spending cuts. With the budget and trade deficits mounting, Reagan in 1982–1983 accepted a reduced rate of military spending, less drastic cuts in social programs, emergency job programs, and various tax increases disguised as "revenue-enhancement measures."

The economy remained worrisome through 1982. Like other recent presidents, Reagan appeared headed for failure. In the 1982 midterm elections, the Democrats regained twenty-six House seats. But 1983 brought an economic rebound. Encouraged by tax cuts, falling interest rates, and evidence that inflation had been tamed at last, consumers went on a buying binge, and a booming stock market evoked memories of the 1920s. Corporate mergers proliferated. Chevron bought Gulf for $13 billion; GE acquired RCA (and its NBC subsidiary) for $6.3 billion. Banks and savings-and-loan companies, newly deregulated, ladled out billions to developers planning shopping malls, luxury apartments, condominiums, and retirement villages. Through it all, the stock market roared on.

The Wall Street frenzy had an unsavory underside. Ivan Boesky went to prison after a 1986 conviction for insider trading. On October 19, 1987, the stock market crashed, reducing the paper value of the nation's stocks by 20 percent overnight. The market recovered, but the collapse had a sobering effect on giddy investors.

Even during the great bull market, economic problems persisted. The trade gap widened; the deficit passed $200 billion in 1986; and many farmers, inner city poor, recent immigrants, and displaced industrial workers suffered through the boom times. But by 1988—just in time for another election campaign—the overall economic picture looked brighter than it had in years.

The "Evil Empire" and Crises in the Middle East

Unleashing blasts of anti-Soviet rhetoric, Reagan described the Soviet Union as an "evil empire" and "the focus of evil in the modern world." Anti-Soviet sentiment crested in September 1983 when the Soviets shot down a Korean passenger plane that had strayed into their airspace, killing 269.

Obsession with the Soviets also influenced Reagan policy in El Salvador and Nicaragua, two poor Central American nations caught up in revolutionary turmoil. The Reagan White House backed the Salvadoran military junta in its brutal suppression of a leftist insurgency supported by Fidel Castro's Cuba. A U.S.-backed moderate won El Salvador's 1984 presidential election, but the killing of the regime's opponents went on.

In Nicaragua, the Carter administration had initially granted aid to the Sandinista revolutionaries who overthrew dictator Anastasio Somoza (ahn-ah-STAHSS-ee-oh soh-MOH-zuh) in 1979. Reagan reversed this policy, claiming that the Sandinistas were turning Nicaragua into a procommunist state like Cuba. In 1982, the CIA organized and financed an anti-Sandinista guerrilla army, called the contras, based in neighboring Honduras and Costa Rica. The contras, with links to the

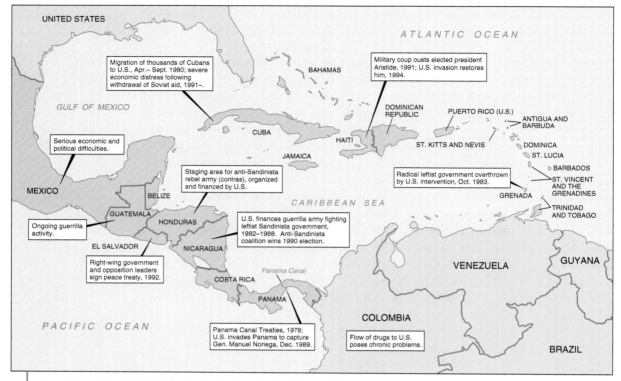

Map 30.2   The United States in Latin America and the Caribbean

Plagued by poverty, population pressures, repressive regimes, and drug trafficking, Latin America saw turmoil and conflict—but also some hopeful developments—in the 1980s and 1990s.

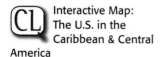

Interactive Map: The U.S. in the Caribbean & Central America

hated Somoza regime, conducted raids, planted mines, and carried out sabotage inside Nicaragua that took a heavy toll of civilian lives.

For Reagan, the campaign to overthrow the Sandinistas and to control events in Latin America became an obsession (see Map 30.2). "The national security of all the Americas is at stake," he somberly told a joint session of Congress in May 1983. Fearing another Vietnam, Americans grew alarmed as details of this U.S.-run war leaked out. Congress voted a yearlong halt in U.S. military aid to the contras in December 1982 and imposed a two-year ban in 1984. Despite these prohibitions, the White House continued to funnel money contributed by foreign governments and right-wing groups in the United States to the contras.

Reagan's one unqualified success in Latin America involved the tiny West Indian island of Grenada, where a 1983 coup had installed a radical pro-Castro government. In October 1983, two thousand U.S. troops invaded Grenada and set up a pro-U.S. government. Democrats grumbled, but most Grenadians, as well as other West Indian governments, approved.

The Middle East, so frustrating to earlier administrations, also bedeviled President Reagan. Late in 1980, Iraq under strongman Saddam Hussein invaded its neighbor Iran. The incoming Reagan administration, hoping to slow the spread of Islamic fundamentalism as represented by Iran's anti-American Ayatollah Khomeini, backed Iraq in this bloody eight-year war. (Two decades later, under very different circumstances, the United States would invade Iraq to overthrow Saddam Hussein [see Chapter 32].)

Meanwhile, the conflict among Israel, the Palestinians, and Israel's Arab foes dragged on. Many Americans felt a strong bond with Israel, and the United States gave Israel large annual grants in military aid and other assistance. Many Bible-prophecy believers saw Israel's fate as connected to God's end-time plan. At the same time, the United States also gave extensive aid to Egypt and relied heavily on oil from Saudi Arabia and other Arab states that were strongly anti-Israel. Whipsawed by conflicting pressures, Reagan enjoyed no more success than other U.S. presidents in achieving peace in the region.

In 1981 Israel and the Palestine Liberation Organization (PLO) concluded a cease-fire. But the PLO continued building up forces at its base in southern Lebanon. In June 1982, Israeli troops under General Ariel Sharon, Israel's defense minister, invaded Lebanon, defeated the PLO, and forced its leaders, including chairman Yasir Arafat, to evacuate Lebanon.

This invasion deepened tensions among Lebanon's various Christian and Muslim factions. With Sharon's approval, a Lebanese Christian militia force entered two Palestinian refugee camps near Beirut to root out armed gunmen. Instead, in revenge for the earlier assassination of Lebanon's Christian president, they massacred hundreds of camp residents, including women and children.

After these events, Reagan ordered two thousand marines to Lebanon as part of a multinational peacekeeping force. The Muslims accused the Americans of favoring Israel and the Christian side, and in October 1983 a Shiite Muslim on a suicide mission crashed an explosive-laden truck into a poorly guarded U.S. barracks, killing 239 marines. Reagan had never clearly explained how the deployment served U.S. interests, and the disaster further discredited his policy. In early 1984 he withdrew the surviving marines. Reagan's efforts to promote a wider Middle East peace settlement proved equally ineffective. In September 1982, he tried to restart Arab-Israeli peace talks based on the 1978 Camp David Accords, but the effort failed.

Military Buildup and Antinuclear Protest

Convinced that the United States had grown dangerously weak militarily, Reagan launched a massive military expansion. The Pentagon's budget nearly doubled, reaching more than $300 billion by 1985. The buildup included nuclear weapons. In 1983 the administration deployed 572 nuclear-armed missiles in Western Europe, counterbalancing Soviet missiles in Eastern Europe.

On the domestic front, the Federal Emergency Management Agency designed an elaborate nuclear-war defense plan whereby city residents would flee to nearby small towns. A Defense Department official claimed that backyard shelters would save millions of people in a nuclear holocaust. "With enough shovels," he asserted, "everybody's going to make it."

Such talk, coupled with the military buildup and Reagan's anti-Soviet rhetoric, alarmed many Americans. A campaign for a verifiable multinational freeze on the manufacture and deployment of nuclear weapons won strong support. Antinuclear

Strategic Defense Initiative
Costly "Star Wars" program to build a missile defense system

protesters packed New York's Central Park in June 1982. That November, voters in nine states approved nuclear-freeze resolutions.

To counter the freeze campaign, Reagan in March 1983 proposed the **Strategic Defense Initiative** (SDI), a computerized anti-missile system involving space-based lasers and other high-tech components. Critics quickly dubbed the scheme "Star Wars," and experts warned of its monumental technical hurdles and the danger that it would further escalate the nuclear-arms race. Nevertheless, Reagan prevailed. A costly SDI research program began, and the freeze campaign faded.

Reagan Reelected

The 1984 Republican convention enthusiastically renominated Reagan. To his admirers, the president had fulfilled his promise to revitalize the free-enterprise system, rebuild U.S. military might, and make America again "stand tall" in the world. They applauded his tax cuts, his attacks on big government, and his tough stance toward the Soviets. The booming economy further strengthened his popularity.

Reagan's 1981 selection of Sandra Day O'Connor as the first woman justice on the U.S. Supreme Court had won widespread praise. So had his jaunty response in March 1981 when a ricocheting bullet fired by a deranged young man struck him in the chest. Rushed to the hospital, Reagan had insisted on walking in. "Please tell me you're all Republicans," he had quipped to physicians.

Jesse Jackson Civil-rights leader whose "rainbow coalition" campaign for president in 1984 garnered 3.5 million votes

The field of Democratic hopefuls included **Jesse Jackson,** an African-American civil-rights leader and former aide to Martin Luther King, Jr., who proposed a "rainbow coalition" of African-Americans, Hispanics, displaced workers, and other groups hard-hit economically. Jackson garnered 3.5 million votes and won in five southern states. But former vice president Walter Mondale came in first overall. His vice-presidential choice, New York congresswoman Geraldine Ferraro, became the first woman to run on a major-party presidential ticket. Democratic campaigners criticized Reagan for runaway military spending, massive budget deficits, cuts in social programs, and assaults on the government's regulatory powers.

Reagan and Vice-President Bush won 59 percent of the popular vote and carried every state but Mondale's Minnesota plus the District of Columbia. Many white working-class voters again defected to Reagan. Reagan's ideological appeal and his mastery of TV, combined with prosperity, had carried the day. The Democrats still controlled the House of Representatives, but the Republicans' post-1968 dominance of the White House—interrupted only by Jimmy Carter's single term—continued.

Some frustrated Democrats sought to reverse their image as a "big government" and "tax-and-spend" party dominated by special interests. In 1985 Arkansas governor Bill Clinton, Senator Al Gore of Tennessee, and other moderates formed the Democratic Leadership Council (DLC) to stake out a more centrist party position. In the early 1990s Clinton would use the DLC as a springboard for a presidential bid.

CHECKING IN

- Reagan entered office stressing optimism, patriotism, tax cuts, and cultural conservatism.
- "Reaganomics" led to sharp tax cuts, an even sharper rise in the federal deficit, and reduced federal regulation of business and industry.
- A severe recession early in the administration gave way to boom times and a soaring stock market.
- Reagan depicted the Soviet Union as the ultimate source of evil in the world.
- Despite a congressional ban, the Reagan administration gave aid to the contras fighting the Sandinista government in Nicaragua.
- The administration nearly doubled military spending, built up the nuclear arsenal, and promoted the controversial "Star Wars" missile defense system.

REAGAN'S SECOND TERM, 1985–1989

What key domestic and international developments marked Reagan's second term?

Economic problems persisted in Reagan's second term, and the president made two Supreme Court appointments. But events abroad—and a major scandal related to the administration's foreign policy—dominated these years. An unexpected easing of Cold War tensions signaled the approaching end of that long conflict. Continued tensions in the Middle East and a wave of terrorist attacks made clear, however, that even a post–Cold War world would remain dangerous.

Supreme Court Appointments, Budget Deficits, the Iran-Contra Scandal

Reagan's second term brought some legislative achievements, including the Immigration Reform and Control Act and a tax-reform law that spared some 6 million low-income Americans from paying any income taxes. Reagan reshaped the Supreme Court in 1986 by elevating William Rehnquist, a Nixon appointee, to the chief justiceship upon the retirement of Warren Burger, and appointing Antonin Scalia to replace him. Scalia would prove one of the Court's most outspokenly conservative members.

When another vacancy opened in 1987, Reagan nominated Robert Bork, a judge and legal scholar whose abrasive personality and rigid views led the Senate to reject him. A second nomination also failed, but Reagan's third choice, Anthony Kennedy, a conservative California jurist, won quick confirmation.

Federal budget deficits—a byproduct of Reagan's tax cuts and military spending increases—surpassed $200 billion in 1985 and 1986, and hovered at about $150 billion for the next two years. This, coupled with the yawning trade gap and a savings-and-loan industry scandal related to deregulation (see Chapter 31), were Reagan's principal economic legacies.

The worst crisis of Reagan's presidency, the so-called **Iran-contra scandal,** began obscurely late in 1986 when a Beirut newspaper reported that in 1985 the United States had shipped, via Israel, 508 antitank missiles to Iran, America's avowed enemy. Admitting the sale, Reagan claimed that the goal had been to encourage "moderate elements" in Tehran and to gain the release of U.S. hostages held in Lebanon by pro-Iranian groups. In February 1987 a presidentially appointed investigative panel blamed Reagan's chief of staff, Donald Regan, who resigned.

More details soon emerged, including the revelation that Lieutenant Colonel **Oliver North,** a National Security Council aide in the White House, had secretly diverted profits from the Iran arms sales to the Nicaraguan contras at a time when Congress had forbidden such aid. To hide this crime, North and his secretary had altered and deleted sensitive computer files and destroyed incriminating documents.

In May 1987 a joint House-Senate investigative committee opened hearings on the scandal. The nation watched in fascination as North, resplendent in his marine uniform, boasted of his patriotism, and as National Security Adviser John Poindexter testified that he had deliberately concealed the fund-diversion scheme from Reagan.

Iran-contra scandal Scandal in which Reagan administration sold weapons to Iran to illegally finance contras

Oliver North Marine colonel at heart of illegal aid to contras

Primary Source: Oliver North Testimony

The committee found no positive proof of Reagan's knowledge of illegalities, but roundly criticized the lax management style and contempt for the law that had pervaded the Reagan White House. In 1989, North was convicted of obstructing a congressional inquiry and destroying and falsifying official documents. (The conviction was later reversed on a technicality.) Although ultimately less damaging to the presidency than the Watergate scandal, the Iran-contra affair dogged the Reagan administration's final years as a serious abuse of executive power.

Other scandals plagued Reagan's second term, including allegations of bribery in military-procurement contracts. Attorney General Edwin Meese resigned in 1988 amid charges that he had used his influence to promote ventures in which he had a financial interest. In 1989 came revelations that former interior secretary James Watt and other prominent Republicans had been paid hundreds of thousands of dollars for using their influence on behalf of housing developers seeking federal subsidies.

Reagan's popularity seemed unaffected by all this dirty linen. The veteran actor possessed an uncanny ability to convey warmth and sincerity and to shrug off damaging revelations with a disarming joke. Some dubbed him the Teflon president—nothing seemed to stick to him. Moreover, a surprising turn of events in Russia would end his presidency on a high note.

Intermediate-range Nuclear Forces (INF) Treaty Title of first treaty to ban an entire class of nuclear weapons; major U.S.-Soviet agreement

President Reagan Visits Red Square

As the Cold War crumbled, President Reagan flew to Moscow in 1988 to celebrate a nuclear-arms reduction treaty with Soviet premier Mikhail Gorbachev.

Reagan's Mission to Moscow

A dramatic warming in Soviet-American relations began early in Reagan's second term. At meetings in Europe in 1985 and 1986, Reagan and the new Soviet leader, Mikhail Gorbachev, revived the stalled arms-control process. Gorbachev worked to reduce superpower tensions to gain breathing space as he struggled with mounting crises at home. His ambitious program involved nothing less than democratizing the Russian government and economy, ending the Communist Party's absolute power, and loosening Moscow's grip on the satellite nations of Eastern Europe.

In June 1987, speaking near the Berlin Wall, President Reagan dramatically declared: "Mr. Gorbachev, tear down this wall!" That December, in Washington, the two leaders signed the **Intermediate-range Nuclear Forces (INF) Treaty,** eliminating 2,500 U.S. and Soviet missiles from Europe. This treaty, in turn, led to Reagan's historic visit to Moscow in May 1988, where the two leaders strolled and chatted in Red Square.

The INF treaty and Reagan's trip to Moscow marked the beginning of the end of the Cold War. Historians still debate the relative importance of Reagan's military buildup versus the Soviet Union's own internal weaknesses in bringing about this outcome. Whatever history's judgment, the fact that one of America's most dedicated Cold Warriors presided over the early stages of its demise remains one of the ironies of recent American history.

The Middle East: Tensions and Terrorism

As relations with Moscow improved in Reagan's second term, conditions in the Middle East worsened. In 1987 Palestinians in Gaza and the West Bank rose up against Israeli occupation. U.S. Secretary of State George Shultz attempted to bring Jordan and the Palestinians into negotiations with Israel over a plan for Palestinian autonomy. But the Israeli government refused to negotiate until the uprising ended; and the Palestinians rejected Shultz's proposals for not going far enough toward creating a Palestinian state. Israel continued to build Jewish settlements in the disputed West Bank.

A deadly byproduct of the Middle East conflict was a series of bombings, assassinations, hijackings, and hostage-takings. In April 1986, after terrorists bombed a Berlin nightclub popular with American GIs, President Reagan ordered a retaliatory air attack on Libya, which had been implicated in the bombing. In the worst of the terrorist incidents, a bomb exploded aboard a Pan Am jet over Scotland in December 1988, killing all 259 aboard, including many Americans. In 1991 the U.S. and British governments formally charged two Libyan officials in the attack. In 2001, a special Scottish court sitting in the Netherlands acquitted one of the men but convicted the other of murder and imposed a life sentence.

This cycle of terrorism reflected profound divisions in the Middle East. Hatred of Israel gripped parts of the Arab world, particularly among a growing Islamic fundamentalist movement sparked by clerical calls for *jihad* (holy war in defense of Islam) against a secular West. The stationing of U.S. troops in Saudi Arabia, as well as expanding Jewish settlements in the Palestinian territories, also fed the anger that fueled terrorist attacks.

Assessing the Reagan Years

After Nixon's disgrace, Ford's caretaker presidency, and Carter's rocky tenure, Reagan's two full terms helped restore a sense of stability to American politics. Reagan's domestic record was mixed: inflation eased, and the economy turned upward, but federal deficits soared, and the administration ignored festering social issues, environmental concerns, and long-term economic problems.

Reagan's critics dismissed his presidency as a time when self-interest trumped the public good. Apart from anticommunism and flag-waving patriotism, they contended, Reagan offered few goals around which all Americans could rally. Reaganism offered little to the poor beyond the hopes that have always been associated with free-enterprise capitalism. Building on Richard Nixon's strategy (see Chapter 29), Reagan exploited the anxieties and resentments of middle-class white voters.

To his admirers, such criticism was beside the point. They credited Reagan for reasserting traditional values of self-reliance and free enterprise; criticizing governmental excesses; and restoring national pride with his infectious optimism and patriotism. Reagan's militant anticommunism contributed mightily to America's victory in the Cold War. Ronald Reagan died of Alzheimer's disease in 2004, at ninety-three. But ideas underlying "the Reagan revolution" lived on, and still influence American politics.

CHECKING IN

- Reagan won legislative victories with tax reform and a new immigration law, but federal deficits and the trade gap continued to soar; the United States became a debtor nation.

- Illegal aid to the Nicaraguan contras, paid for by secret U.S. arms sales to Iran, was the most spectacular of several scandals that beset Reagan's second term; the president nonetheless remained personally popular.

- Despite his often-heated anti-Soviet rhetoric, Reagan eventually met with the new Soviet leader, Mikhail Gorbachev, and reached arms-control agreements that began to wind down the Cold War.

- Major problems flared in the Middle East as the Intifada (uprising) erupted among Palestinians.

- Terrorism surfaced as a major threat with the hijacking of planes, bombings, and kidnappings.

Chapter Summary

 DOWNLOAD THE MP3 AUDIO FILE OF THE CHAPTER SUMMARY, AND LISTEN TO IT ON THE GO.

What issues and trends helped spark a growing conservative movement in the 1970s? (page 710)

Many of the issues that had dominated the sixties continued to reverberate through American life. Environmentalism, especially concerns about nuclear power, expanded. Feminism advanced, but women found themselves bumping up against the "glass ceiling" that kept the cooperate elite a male preserve. AIDS short-circuited the sexual revolution. The conservative backlash strengthened, with Christian fundamentalists as a standard-bearer.

What social and economic developments most affected American life between 1974 and 1989? (page 716)

Family farms continued to diminish in importance and number, displaced by agribusiness. Some African-Americans made great gains, but many languished in poverty, especially in inner cities plagued by drugs and decay. A major shift in immigration patterns brought an influx of Hispanic and Asian newcomers, but illegal immigration increased, especially from Mexico and Central America.

What were the major achievements and failures of the Ford and Carter presidencies? (page 719)

Neither administration was able to contain inflation, made worse by OPEC-created oil crises in 1973 and 1979. The Carter administration did enjoy some foreign-policy successes, notably the Camp David Accords that the president brokered between Egypt and Israel. However, the nagging Iran hostage crisis gravely weakened the Carter administration.

What core beliefs most shaped Ronald Reagan's presidency? (page 722)

Under Reagan's economic policies, dubbed "Reaganomics," sharp tax cuts led to steep deficits, and deregulation reduced government oversight of business, with mixed results. Calling the Soviet Union an "evil empire," Reagan supplied arms and other aid to the contras, anti-Sandinista guerrillas fighting in Nicaragua, despite a congressional ban. Military spending soared, including funding for the Strategic Defense Initiative ("Star Wars"), Reagan's controversial missile-defense scheme.

KEY TERMS

AIDS *(p. 713)*

Three Mile Island *(p. 713)*

Equal Rights Amendment *(p. 714)*

William F. Buckley *(p. 714)*

Ronald Reagan *(p. 715)*

Engel v. *Vitale (p. 715)*

deindustrialization *(p. 717)*

affirmative action *(p. 717)*

Indian Self-Determination Act *(p. 718)*

Immigration Reform and Control Act *(p. 718)*

Gerald Ford *(p. 719)*

Organization of Petroleum Exporting Countries *(p. 719)*

Jimmy Carter *(p. 720)*

Camp David Accords *(p. 721)*

stagflation *(p. 722)*

Strategic Defense Initiative *(p. 728)*

Jesse Jackson *(p. 728)*

Iran-contra scandal *(p. 729)*

Oliver North *(p. 729)*

Intermediate-range Nuclear Forces (INF) Treaty *(p. 730)*

What key domestic and international developments marked Reagan's second term? (page 729)

As the federal deficit and trade gap soared, the United States became a debtor nation. Despite second-term scandals, including Iran-contra, Reagan remained popular. Muting his "evil empire" rhetoric, Reagan met with Mikhail Gorbachev as the Cold War wound down. Conditions in the Middle East deteriorated, however, as violence between Palestinians and Israel increased, and a surge in terrorist attacks threatened America and other Western nations.

Beyond the Cold War: Charting a New Course

CHAPTER 31

1988–2000

Bill and Hillary Clinton on the Campaign Trail in Texas, August 1992

CL This icon will direct you to the website where you can Prepare for Class, Improve Your Grade, and Ace the Test: **www.cengage.com/history/boyer/ enduringconcise6e**

O f all the physical reminders of the Cold War, the most notorious was the Berlin Wall, built by the Russians in 1961. Snaking around the city, this concrete and barbed-wire barrier with its watchtowers and armed guards had stood as a stark emblem of Cold War divisions. Nearly two hundred people had been shot trying to escape across the Wall.

On October 18, 1989, East Germany's communist regime collapsed. When East Berliners rushed to the Wall, guards opened the gates. As people joyously poured through, West Berliners greeted them with flowers, tears, and shouts of welcome. Giddy young people danced on the Wall itself. By November, the wall had practically disappeared. A hated Cold War symbol had faded into history.

Americans sighed in relief as the Soviet Union collapsed, but dangers remained. While U.S. leaders struggled with post–Cold War disorders, an immediate crisis arose in the Middle East as Saddam Hussein's Iraq invaded oil-rich Kuwait, forcing Reagan's successor, President George Bush, to respond.

When Bill Clinton replaced George Bush in the White House in 1993, domestic issues took center stage. As his term ended in scandal and impeachment, the Supreme Court intervened to resolve the disputed 2000 presidential election. Ostentatious consumption, undercurrents of violence, and deep cultural conflicts shaped American life as the century ended.

THE BUSH YEARS: GLOBAL RESOLVE, DOMESTIC DRIFT, 1988–1993

What foreign and domestic issues loomed largest during the Bush administration, 1989–1993?

Ronald Reagan's vice president, **George H. W. Bush,** elected president in 1988, was a patrician in politics. The son of a powerful Connecticut senator, he had fought in World War II and attended Yale before entering the Texas oil business. He had served in Congress, directed the Central Intelligence Agency (CIA), and fought for the 1980 Republican nomination before being tapped as Ronald Reagan's running mate in 1980.

As president, Bush compiled a curiously uneven record. Internationally, he reacted decisively when Iraq invaded Kuwait, and he worked to ease Israeli-Palestinian tensions. His domestic record was thin, however, as he typically substituted platitudes for policy.

George H. W. Bush Forty-first President; successes abroad overshadowed by a mixed record at home

The Election of 1988

Vice President Bush easily won the 1988 Republican presidential nomination. As his running mate he selected Senator Dan Quayle of Indiana, son of a newspaper publisher. The field of Democratic contenders eventually narrowed to Massachusetts governor Michael Dukakis (doo-KAH-kiss), who ran with Texas senator Lloyd Bentsen.

In the campaign, Bush stressed Reagan's achievements. He pointed to better Soviet relations, low inflation, and the 14 million new jobs created during the 1980s. A TV commercial aired by Bush supporters, playing on racist stereotypes, featured a black convict who committed rape and murder after his release under a Massachusetts prisoner-furlough program.

Dukakis emphasized his managerial skills. "This election is not about ideology, it's about competence," he insisted. But Dukakis seemed wooden, and his dismissal of ideology made it difficult for him to define his political vision. Both candidates relied on TV-oriented "photo opportunities," vague slogans, and sound bites. Bush visited flag factories and military plants. Dukakis proved his toughness on defense by posing in a tank. Bush won, carrying forty states and garnering 54 percent of the vote. The Democrats, however, retained control of Congress and most state legislatures.

The Cold War Ends

Soviet power collapsed with breathtaking speed. In May 1989 Soviet President Mikhail Gorbachev announced that Moscow would no longer use its power to prop up Eastern Europe's unpopular communist regimes. One by one, these governments fell. New democratic governments sprang up behind what had been the iron curtain. In November 1989 exuberant Germans celebrated the opening of the Berlin Wall, and within a year Germany was reunited for the first time since 1945. The Baltic republics—Latvia, Lithuania, and Estonia—forcibly annexed by the Soviet Union on the eve of World War II, declared their independence. Other Soviet republics followed. Gorbachev, overwhelmed by forces he himself had unleashed, resigned. In Moscow, Boris Yeltsin filled the power vacuum.

Secretary of State James Baker, a longtime Bush ally, proceeded cautiously as these events unfolded. Baker worked to ensure the security of the twenty-seven thousand nuclear weapons based in Russia and in newly independent Ukraine (you-CRANE), Belarus (bell-ah-ROOS), and Kazakhstan (ka-ZAHK-stan), and to prevent rogue states or terrorist groups from acquiring nuclear materials or know-how from these countries.

For decades, the superpowers had backed their client states and rebel insurgencies in the Third World. As the Cold War faded, prospects brightened for resolving some local disputes. Despite some progress in Nicaragua, where the U.S.-funded contra war finally ended, poverty and economic exploitation still plagued Latin America. In 1989, Bush ordered a U.S. invasion of Panama to capture the nation's ruler, General Manuel Noriega (MAN-wel no-ree-AY-guh). Formerly on the CIA payroll, Noriega had accepted bribes to permit drugs to pass through Panama. Convicted of drug trafficking, he received a life prison term.

U.S. relations with the Philippines, a former colony and longtime ally, shifted as well. In 1991 the Philippines legislature ended an agreement permitting two U.S. naval bases in the islands. With the Cold War over, the Bush administration agreed to close the bases.

Meanwhile, South Africa's policy of racial segregation, called apartheid, provoked growing protests by U.S. black leaders and campus activists. In 1986, over a Reagan veto, Congress had imposed economic sanctions against white-ruled South Africa, including a ban on U.S. corporate investment. The South African government in 1990 released black leader Nelson Mandela (man-DELL-uh) after years in prison. When South Africa scrapped its apartheid policy in 1991, President Bush lifted the sanctions. In 1994, underscoring the new political order in South Africa, Mandela was elected president.

In 1989, Chinese troops brutally crushed a pro-democracy demonstration in Beijing's Tiananmen (tee-yehn-ahn-men) Square, killing several hundred unarmed students and workers. A wave of arrests and public executions followed. The Bush administration curtailed diplomatic contacts and urged banks to postpone loans to China. But Bush, committed to U.S. trade expansion, did not break diplomatic relations or cancel trade agreements with Beijing.

CL Interactive Map: The End of the Cold War Changes the Map of Europe

Chronology

1988	George Bush elected president
1989	Massive Alaskan oil spill by *Exxon Valdez*; Supreme Court, in several 5-to-4 decisions, restricts civil-rights laws; U.S. invasion of Panama; Manuel Noriega overthrown; China's rulers crush prodemocracy movement; Berlin Wall is opened
1990	Federal Clean Air Act strengthened; Americans with Disabilities Act passed; Iraq invades Kuwait; Recession (1990–1993); Germany reunified; Soviet troops start withdrawal from Eastern Europe
1991	Persian Gulf War (Operation Desert Storm); hearings on Clarence Thomas's Supreme Court nomination; collapse of Soviet Union
1992	Supreme Court in *Planned Parenthood* v. *Casey* approves abortion restrictions but upholds *Roe* v. *Wade*; President Bush commits U.S. troops in Somalia; Bill Clinton elected president
1993	Congress approves NAFTA treaty; economy expands, stock market surges (1993–2000); Clinton health care reform plan fails (1993–1994); some eighty Branch Davidians die in fire as federal agents raid compound in Waco, Texas; World Trade Center bombing kills six
1994	Christian Coalition gains control of Republican party in several states; Yasir Arafat and Yitzhak Rabin sign Oslo Accords at White House; Clinton withdraws U.S. forces from Somalia; United States joins the World Trade Organization (WTO); Republicans proclaim "Contract with America"; win control of House and Senate; Newt Gingrich becomes Speaker
1995	Oklahoma City federal building bombed; Dayton Accords achieve cease-fire in Bosnia; Clinton commits U.S. troops to enforce agreement
1996	Welfare Reform Act; Clinton defeats Bob Dole to win second term
1997	Congressional battle over tobacco-industry regulation
1998	Clinton impeached by House of Representatives in sex scandal
1999	Senate dismisses impeachment charges; Columbine High School shootings; U.S. and NATO forces intervene in Kosovo
2000	George W. Bush wins presidency when Supreme Court ends Florida election dispute

As the Cold War faded, trade issues loomed large. America's trade deficit with Japan stirred special concern. Early in 1992, facing a recession and rising unemployment in an election year, President Bush turned an Asian trip into a trade mission. Joined by U.S. business leaders, he urged the Japanese to buy more U.S. products. The trade gap continued, however.

The Persian Gulf War, 1991

One foreign crisis brought a forceful response. On August 2, 1990, Iraq invaded its neighbor Kuwait. Iraq's dictator, Saddam Hussein, viewed Kuwait's (koo-WAITs) ruling sheiks as Western puppets and asserted Iraq's historic claims to Kuwait's vast oil fields.

Under Saddam, Iraq had pursued chemical- and nuclear-weapons programs and threatened not only Kuwait but also other Arab nations and Israel. During the Iraq-Iran war (1980–1988), however, the United States had favored Iraq, and even assisted Saddam's military buildup (see Chapter 30). Now, however, confronted by Iraq's invasion of Kuwait, Washington protested vigorously.

Kuwait, 1991
Burning oilfields, set ablaze by retreating Iraqis, provide an eerie backdrop to motorized U.S. troops participating in Operation Desert Storm, the high point of the Bush presidency.

Avoiding Lyndon Johnson's mistakes in Vietnam, Bush built a consensus in Congress, at the United Nations, and among the American people for a clear objective: Iraq's withdrawal from Kuwait. Bush built a coalition of thirty-four nations and deployed more than 500,000 U.S. troops to achieve that goal.

The UN imposed economic sanctions against Iraq and insisted that Saddam withdraw from Kuwait by January 15, 1991. On January 12, the Senate and the House endorsed military action. Most Democrats voted against war, favoring continued economic sanctions.

The air war began on January 16. For six weeks B-52 and F-16 bombers pounded Iraqi troops, supply depots, and command centers in Iraq's capital, Baghdad. In retaliation, Saddam fired Soviet-made Scud missiles against Tel Aviv and other Israeli cities, as well as against the Saudi capital, Riyadh. On February 23 two hundred thousand U.S. troops under General H. Norman Schwarzkopf moved across the desert toward Kuwait (see Map 31.1). Iraqi soldiers fled or surrendered en masse. U.S. forces destroyed thirty-seven hundred Iraqi tanks while losing only three. With Iraqi resistance crushed, President Bush declared a cease-fire, and Kuwait's ruling family returned to power. U.S. casualties numbered 148 dead—including 35 killed inadvertently by U.S. firepower—and 467 wounded. Iraqi military casualties were estimated to be 25,000 to 65,000.

Persian Gulf War A U.S.-led coalition army ousted Saddam Hussein's Iraq army from Kuwait in 1991

For President Bush, the **Persian Gulf War** proved that Americans were again ready to use military might to pursue national interests. "By God, we've kicked the Vietnam syndrome once and for all," he declared. Some had urged President Bush to invade Iraq and overthrow Saddam Hussein. Bush rejected this course. Invading Iraq, he reasoned, could involve an extended occupation and unleash sectarian conflict. Saddam granted UN inspectors access to his weapons-production facilities. The UN also imposed "no-fly zones" on Iraqi aircraft, but Saddam's army brutally suppressed uprisings by Shiite Muslims in the south and ethnic Kurds in the north.

Interactive Map: Operation Desert Storm: The Ground War

Home-Front Problems and Domestic Policies

In the early 1990s the impact of Reagan-era tax cuts and deregulation began to hit home. First came the collapse of the savings-and-loan (S&L) industry, provider of home loans and a modest but secure return to depositors. As interest rates had risen in the late 1970s because of inflation, the S&Ls had offered higher interest to attract deposits. Money freed up by the Reagan tax cuts flowed into S&Ls with their high rates of return. Meanwhile, in the deregulation fervor, Congress eased the rules governing S&Ls, enabling them to make loans on risky real-estate ventures. As recession hit, many of these investments went bad. In 1988–1990, nearly six hundred S&Ls failed, wiping out many depositors' savings.

Because the government insures S&L deposits, the Bush administration in 1989 set up a program to repay depositors and sell off depreciated properties. Estimates of the bailout's cost topped $400 billion.

The federal deficit, a byproduct of Reagan's tax cuts and military spending, continued to mount. In 1990, Congress and Bush agreed on a deficit-reduction plan involving spending cuts and tax increases. Bush's retreat from his 1988 "no new taxes" pledge angered many voters. Despite the agreement, the deficit reached $290 billion in 1992. The Gulf War, the S&L bailout, and soaring welfare and Medicare/Medicaid payments sank the budget-balancing effort.

Making matters worse, recession struck in 1990. Retail sales slumped; housing starts fell. The auto industry, battered by Japanese imports, fared disastrously. GM cut its work force by more than seventy thousand. By 1992 the jobless rate exceeded 7 percent. If 1984 was "morning in America," wrote a columnist, quoting a Reagan campaign slogan, this was "the morning after."

Map 31.1   The Mideast Crises, 1980–2000

With terrorist attacks, the Iran-Iraq War, the Persian Gulf War, and the ongoing struggle between Israel and the Palestinians, the Middle East was the site of almost unending violence, conflict, and tension in these years.

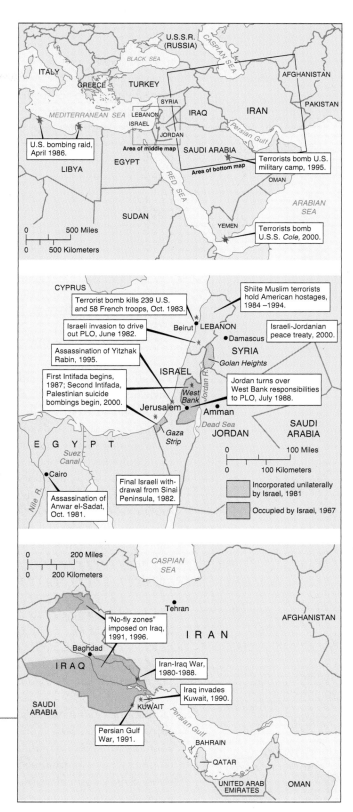

The recession worsened inner-city joblessness and despair. In April 1992, an outbreak of arson and looting erupted in a poor black district of Los Angeles. The immediate cause was black outrage over a jury's acquittal of four white police officers whose beating of a black motorist had been captured on videotape. The riots left some forty persons dead and millions in property damage, underscoring the desperate conditions in the inner cities.

Bush's greatest domestic success came in 1990, with the passage of the **Americans with Disabilities Act,** barring discrimination against disabled persons in hiring or education. In an echo of the earlier African-American civil-rights campaign, Congress passed this law following demonstrations and lobbying by the disabled and organizations representing them. Thanks to this law, job opportunities for handicapped persons increased, and the number of physically or cognitively impaired children attending public schools rose significantly.

Environmental concerns surged in 1989 when a giant oil tanker, the *Exxon Valdez,* ran aground in Alaska's Prince William Sound, spilling more than 10 million gallons of oil. The accident fouled coastal habitats and jeopardized Alaska's fishing industry. A 1991 Environmental Protection Agency study found that pollutants were seriously depleting the atmosphere's ozone layer, which reduces cancer-causing solar radiation.

Bush compiled a mixed environmental record. In a bipartisan effort, the White House and the Democratic Congress agreed on a toughened Clean Air Act in 1990. The government also began the costly task of disposing of radioactive wastes from nuclear facilities. On the other hand, the administration scuttled treaties on global warming, backed oil exploration in Alaskan wilderness preserves, and proposed to open protected wetlands to developers.

President Bush made two Supreme Court nominations. David Souter, a New Hampshire judge of moderate views, won easy confirmation in 1990. With **Clarence Thomas,** however, Bush continued Reagan's effort to shift the court sharply to the right. Bush nominated Thomas in 1991 to replace Thurgood Marshall, who had fought segregation as an NAACP lawyer. Thomas, also an African-American, supported right-wing causes and opposed affirmative-action programs. Noting his weak qualifications, critics charged Bush with playing racial politics.

In the Senate Judiciary Committee hearings, a former Thomas associate at the Equal Employment Opportunity Commission, Anita Hill, accused him of sexual harassment. Thomas narrowly won confirmation, but Republican efforts to discredit Hill's testimony alienated many women. When women candidates did very well in the 1992 elections, many observers concluded that resentment over the Thomas hearings had played a role.

On the Court, Thomas allied with Justice Antonin Scalia in upholding executive power, interpreting the Constitution narrowly, and championing conservative social issues. In 1990–1991, the Court narrowed the rights of arrested persons and upheld regulations barring physicians in federally funded clinics from discussing abortion with their patients. In *Planned Parenthood* v. *Casey,* a five-to-four decision in 1992, the Court affirmed *Roe* v. *Wade* but upheld a Pennsylvania law restricting abortion rights by imposing a twenty-four-hour waiting period and other requirements. Conservative activism was replacing liberal activism on the high court.

Americans with Disabilities Act Law that bars discrimination against handicapped in jobs and education

Clarence Thomas Ultraconservative Bush appointee to the Supreme Court, challenged on grounds of alleged sexual harassment

Primary Source:
Webster v.
Reproductive Health Services

1992: Clinton Versus Bush, and a Third-Party Challenge

George Bush's approval ratings soared after the Persian Gulf War, only to fall below 50 percent as the recession hit. Intimidated by Bush's post–Gulf War popularity, top Democrats stayed out of the 1992 presidential race. But Governor Bill Clinton of Arkansas took the plunge. Fending off reports of marital infidelity, Clinton defeated other hopefuls in the primaries and won the nomination. As his running mate, he chose Senator **Albert Gore, Jr.,** of Tennessee. In his acceptance speech, Clinton pledged action on environmental, health care, and economic issues.

President Bush quashed a primary challenge by conservative columnist Pat Buchanan, but at the Republican party convention Buchanan and evangelist Pat Robertson gave divisive speeches staking out deeply conservative positions on contested cultural issues. Delegates from Robertson's Christian Coalition cheered, but moderate Republicans deplored the party's rightward turn.

Political outsider **H. Ross Perot** (pair-OH), founder of a Texas data-processing firm, also entered the race. The nation's economic problems were simple, Perot insisted on TV talk shows; only party politics stood in the way of solving them. At his peak of popularity, nearly 40 percent of the voters supported Perot. His eccentricities and thin-skinned response to critics cost him support, but he remained a wild card in the election.

Bush attacked Clinton's character and charged that he had evaded the Vietnam-era draft. Clinton, meanwhile, focused on the economy and pledged to work for a national health care system, welfare reform, and programs to promote economic growth and new technologies. Clinton won 43 percent of the vote to Bush's 38 percent. Perot amassed 19 percent—the best showing for a third-party candidate since Teddy Roosevelt in 1912. Clinton carried big industrial states; lured back many blue-collar "Reagan Democrats"; and did well in the South. In the congressional races, thirty-eight African-Americans and seventeen Hispanics won seats. Overall, the new Congress included fifty-three women. Magazines hailed "The Year of the Woman." With Democrats in control of Congress and the executive branch, an end to the much-deplored Washington "gridlock" seemed possible.

Albert Gore, Jr. Tennessee senator and noted expert on environmental issues who served as Clinton's vice president

H. Ross Perot Texas billionaire who ran for president as third-party candidate in 1992, 1996

CHECKING IN

- The Cold War ended suddenly with the collapse of the Soviet Union in late 1991.
- When Saddam Hussein invaded Kuwait, Bush forged a coalition to drive him out; although driven from Kuwait, Saddam retained power in Iraq.
- Despite foreign-policy successes, the Bush administration accomplished little domestically; recession struck, environmental concerns accelerated, and racial tensions exploded into riots.
- Bush attempted to move the Supreme Court to the right with the appointment of the controversial, conservative Clarence Thomas.
- Arkansas governor Bill Clinton defeated Republican George H. W. Bush and third-party candidate Ross Perot to win the presidency in 1992.

THE CLINTON ERA BEGINS: DEBATING DOMESTIC POLICY, 1993–1996

What domestic policy issues, political events, and economic trends most shaped Clinton's first term?

In contrast to George Bush, a member of the World War II generation, **William Jefferson (Bill) Clinton** was the first president from the baby-boom generation. Born in Arkansas in 1946, he admired Elvis Presley and played the saxophone. He attended Georgetown University, Oxford University (as a Rhodes Scholar), and Yale Law School, where he met his future wife, Hillary Rodham. He returned to Arkansas after graduation and won the governorship in 1979, at age thirty-two.

William Jefferson (Bill) Clinton Forty-second President; controversial two-term presidency marked by a surging economy at home

Clinton's presidency began energetically but soon encountered setbacks. When disgruntled voters gave the Republicans a stunning victory in the 1994 midterm election, Clinton moved to the right.

Shaping a Domestic Agenda

In contrast to Republican predecessors like Nixon and Bush, Clinton preferred domestic issues to foreign policy. Of course, like all presidents, Clinton confronted serious diplomatic challenges. For the most part, however, domestic policy dominated his attention.

Clinton and Vice President Al Gore were leaders of the New Democratic Coalition, a group of moderates unhappy with the party's ultra-liberal, "tax and spend" reputation. To win back middle-class and blue-collar voters, Clinton's campaign stressed Middle America's concerns: jobs, health care, soaring welfare costs. As he steered the party toward the middle, traditional liberals and black leaders expressed uneasiness. Seeking middle ground on abortion, he said it should be "safe, legal, and rare." Clinton and Gore firmly endorsed environmental protection, a popular cause with voters.

Lending symbolic support to the women's movement, Clinton named women to head several cabinet positions and other high offices. To fill a Supreme Court vacancy in 1993, he nominated Judge Ruth Bader Ginsberg. In 1997 he named **Madeleine K. Albright** as secretary of state—the highest U.S. government office ever held by a woman. More controversial was Clinton's early effort to fulfill a campaign pledge to end homosexuals' exclusion from military services. Forced to retreat from his initial plan for full inclusion, Clinton agreed to a compromise summed up in the phrase "Don't ask, don't tell." According to this policy, so long as homosexual soldiers do not openly reveal their sexual orientation, commanders may not investigate it.

On the economic front, Clinton proposed military spending cuts and tax increases to ease the budget deficit. To combat the recession, he recommended programs to stimulate job creation and economic growth. In August 1993, Congress adopted Clinton's spending cuts and tax increases, but the economic-stimulus package fell by the wayside.

Clinton also urged ratification of the **North American Free Trade Agreement (NAFTA)** negotiated by the Bush administration. This pact admitted Mexico to the free-trade zone created earlier by the United States and Canada. While critics warned that U.S. jobs would flee to Mexico, NAFTA backers, including most economists, predicted a net gain in jobs as Mexican markets opened to U.S. products. Congress approved NAFTA in 1993, handing Clinton a welcome victory.

With Medicare and Medicaid costs exploding, health care reform stood high on Clinton's "to do" list. From 1980 to 1992, government payments for these programs ballooned from 8 percent to 14 percent of the federal budget. Clinton appointed his wife Hillary to head a health care task force. This body, working mainly in secret, devised a sweeping plan for universal health insurance, including caps on premiums and a national board to monitor costs. Lobbyists for doctors, the insurance industry, tobacco companies, and other groups ganged up to oppose the plan. Critics attacked the secretive way it had been formulated. By fall 1994, the Clintons' bill had died, and health care reform was stalled.

Madeleine K. Albright Clinton's secretary of state; then the highest government office ever held by a woman

North American Free Trade Agreement (NAFTA) Agreement to create a free trade community including the United States, Canada, and Mexico

Crime and welfare reform also ranked high among voter concerns. In 1994, Clinton pushed through Congress an anticrime bill including a ban on assault weapons and funds for more prisons and police officers. That same year, Clinton offered a welfare-reform bill. It required able-bodied welfare recipients to go to work after two years. The bill included job training and child-care provisions, as well as measures to force absent fathers ("deadbeat dads") to support their offspring. It also permitted states to deny additional payments to welfare mothers who had more children. Congress delayed welfare reform until 1995, however, when Republican majorities in both houses shaped their own bill.

By 1994, Clinton's popularity was sagging. Exploiting the "character issue," critics publicized the Clintons' earlier involvement in a shady Arkansas real-estate speculation, the Whitewater Development Company. The 1993 suicide of assistant White House counsel Vincent Foster, the Clintons' close friend, attracted conspiracy theorists. In 1994, Paula Jones, an Arkansas state employee, filed a lawsuit claiming that Clinton when governor had solicited sexual favors.

Favorable economic news helped Clinton weather the setbacks. By 1994, the unemployment rate had fallen to the lowest level in four years, and inflation remained well under control. The federal deficit dropped each year from 1993 to 1997. Nevertheless, by mid-1994 Clinton's approval ratings had sunk to 42 percent.

Sensing Clinton's vulnerability, the opposition grew bolder. Radio commentator Rush Limbaugh won fans for his jeering attacks on liberals. By 1994, Pat Robertson's **Christian Coalition** controlled several state Republican parties. With its passion and organizational energy, the religious Right represented an increasingly potent political force.

Christian Coalition Conservative evangelical lobbying group with growing influence over Republican party in 1990s

A Sharp Right Turn: 1994–1996

Clinton had won in 1992 as a "New Democrat," but by 1994 many voters saw him as an old Democrat of the "tax-and-spend" variety. To critics, Clinton's failed health care plan embodied all the flaws of the New Deal/Great Society style of top-down reform.

Meanwhile, a network of organizations, including the Christian Coalition, the Heritage Foundation, and the National Rifle Association, built on the conservative movement dating to the 1970s (see Chapter 30) to orchestrate a sharp rightward swing in the body politic. An endless drumbeat of conservative radio commentary denounced the "liberal elite" and inflamed differences over such hot-button issues as obscenity, abortion, gun control, gay rights, school prayer, "radical feminism," sex education, and an alleged erosion of "family values."

Primary Source: Teenagers Against Abortion

Republican congressman **Newt Gingrich** (GING-rich) of Georgia mobilized the discontent. In a September 1994 ceremony on the Capitol steps, some three hundred Republican congressional candidates signed Gingrich's "Contract with America" pledging to propose tax cuts, tougher crime laws, antipornography measures, and other reforms. In November, voters gave the GOP control of both houses of Congress for the first time since 1954. The outcome signaled a significant rightward shift. Evangelical Christians, energized by politicized preachers like Falwell and Robertson, turned out in large numbers, mostly to vote Republican.

Newt Gingrich Republican congressman from Georgia who helped bring his party to power; elected Speaker in 1994

Republicans hailed the election as a further step in a conservative resurgence launched by Barry Goldwater in 1964. In the House of Representatives, a jubilant horde of 230 Republicans, 73 of them newly elected, chose Newt Gingrich as Speaker and set about enacting the Contract with America. A constitutional amendment requiring a balanced federal budget passed the House but narrowly failed in the Senate. Fulfilling pledges to combat pornography, Congress passed a Communications Decency Act strengthening the government's censorship powers. (In 1997, the Supreme Court ruled the law unconstitutional.)

The torrent of bills, hearings, and press releases recalled the heady days of the early New Deal and Lyndon Johnson's Great Society. Now, however, the activist energy came from the conservative side of the political spectrum.

The architect of this revolution, Newt Gingrich, stumbled in 1995 when he first accepted, and then turned down, a $4.5 million advance from a publishing house owned by Rupert Murdoch, a media tycoon with interests in federal legislation. Journalists also focused on Gingrich's network of political action groups. The 1994 election also signaled a go-it-alone view of America's world role. The Contract with America largely ignored foreign policy. Republican leaders denounced the United Nations and refused to pay $1 billion in past UN dues.

Savoring their electoral triumph, conservatives renewed the battle for welfare reform. They offered two arguments. The first was economic. AFDC, with 14.2 million women and children on its rolls, cost about $125 billion in 1994, a sharp jump since 1989 (see Figure 31.1). Though dwarfed by the other benefits enjoyed by the middle class, this was still a heavy budgetary drain. The second argument was ideological: the belief that welfare had become a "lifelong entitlement" that encouraged irresponsible behavior and trapped recipients in a cycle of dependence. Though partially based on stereotypes rather than empirical data, such views were widely held.

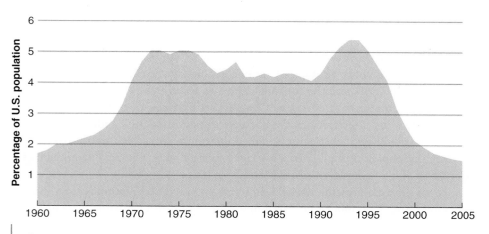

Figure 31.1   Percentage of U.S. Population on Welfare, 1960–2005

From just 1.7 percent in 1960, the percentage of Americans on welfare crept steadily upward until 1994, when it peaked at 5.5 percent, representing more than 14 million people. The percentage declined sharply thereafter, reflecting both the booming economy and the impact of the Welfare Reform Act of 1996.

Sources: Administration for Children and Families, Department of Health and Human Services; House Committee on Ways and Means, Subcommittee on Human Resources Report, Feb. 28, 2006.

President Clinton's welfare reform proposal favored federally funded child care and job-training programs to ease the transition from welfare to work. However, Republicans argued that businesses, the states, and private agencies could best provide these services. After vetoing two earlier welfare bills, in August Clinton signed the landmark **Welfare Reform Act of 1996.** Reversing sixty years of welfare policy, the law ended the largest federal program, AFDC. Instead, states would now receive block grants to develop their own programs within strict guidelines limiting most recipients to two years of continuous coverage.

Critics warned of the effects on inner-city welfare mothers lacking education or job skills. Traditional Democratic liberals such as Massachusetts senator Edward Kennedy argued that Clinton had not fought strongly enough to protect welfare recipients in negotiating with congressional Republicans.

The direst predictions did not materialize. From 1996 to 2005 the number of families on welfare fell by 57 percent, and the birthrate among unmarried women leveled off. The percentage of unmarried mothers in the work force rose from around 48 percent in 1996 to around 65 percent in 2000, although many held low-paying, unskilled jobs, and changed jobs frequently. On balance, however, most observers rated welfare reform at least a qualified success.

| **Welfare Reform Act of 1996** |
| Clinton joined Republicans to end AFDC and move thousands off welfare rolls |

CHECKING IN

- Clinton was a fiscally moderate "New Democrat" determined to focus on domestic issues.
- The Clinton administration passed a successful economic reform package but failed miserably on health care reform.
- Amid an investigation of the Clintons' financial dealings in Arkansas, the political climate turned poisonous, with the Republican Right vilifying Clinton and other liberals.
- The 1994 elections brought conservative Republicans led by Newt Gingrich to control of Congress, armed with a "Contract with America."
- Clinton worked with the Republicans for a far-reaching overhaul of welfare.

THE ECONOMIC BOOM OF THE 1990S

What groups benefited from the economic boom of the 1990s, and what groups did not?

The 1990s saw one of the longest periods of sustained economic growth in U.S. history. Productivity increased, unemployment fell, and inflation remained low. Federal deficits dropped as tax revenues increased. In 1998, for the first time since 1969, the federal budget actually showed a surplus.

For some, the surging stock market stimulated the urge to get rich quick, acquire more possessions, and enjoy the good times. But real wages lagged behind the stock market, and workers who lacked the skills required by the emerging knowledge-based economy faced difficulties.

An Uneven Prosperity

The economic boom of the 1990s had various sources, but the new business opportunities associated with the personal computer and the information revolution were certainly crucial (see Chapter 32). Rising international trade, a low inflation rate, and low interest rates all helped sustain the boom. Unemployment, which stood at 7.5 percent in 1992, fell to 4 percent by 2000. Corporate earnings soared. The gross domestic product, a key economic indicator, rose nearly 80 percent in the decade.

Wall Street boomed as stock prices far outran many companies' actual value or earnings prospects. From under 3,000 in 1991, the Dow Jones Industrial Average edged toward 12,000 by early 2001. New investors flocked into the market. By 1998, nearly 50 percent of U.S. families owned stock directly or through their pension plans. As early as 1996 Federal Reserve Board chairman Alan Greenspan warned of "irrational exuberance" in the stock market, but with little effect.

Information-technology (IT) stocks proved especially popular. The NASDAQ composite index, loaded with technology stocks, soared from under 500 in 1991 to over 5,000 by early 2000. Some stock offerings by IT start-up companies hit fantastic levels, turning young entrepreneurs into paper millionaires. Corporate mergers multiplied as companies sought to improve their profitability. In the biggest merger of all, the Internet company America Online (AOL) acquired Time-Warner (itself the product of earlier mergers) for $182 billion.

The prosperity was very unevenly distributed, however. From 1979 to 1996 the portion of total income going to the wealthiest 20 percent of Americans increased by 13 percent, while the share going to the poorest 20 percent *dropped* by 22 percent. Adjusted for inflation, the buying power of the average worker's paycheck fell or remained flat through much of the period from 1986 to 2000. As corporations maintained profits by "downsizing" and cost cutting, job worries gnawed at many Americans.

While many service workers, teachers, and other white-collar groups belonged to unions, only 13.5 percent of the total labor force was unionized in 2000, weakening this means by which workers had historically bettered their wages and job conditions. Unions' political clout diminished as well. Congress ratified the 1993 NAFTA treaty, for example, despite protests from organized labor.

Job-market success increasingly required special training and skills, posing problems for high-school graduates, displaced industrial workers, and welfare recipients entering the labor force. Overall employment statistics also obscured racial and ethnic variables. In 2000, the jobless rate for blacks and Hispanics, despite having dropped, remained significantly higher than the rate for whites. In short, while the economic boom benefited many, a wide gap separated those who prospered and those who experienced minimal gains or none at all.

globalization The removal of barriers to flow of capital, goods, and ideas across national borders

CHECKING IN

- The 1990s saw low inflation, rising stock markets, and a booming information-technology industry.

- Income inequalities widened, as globalization chiefly benefited those with education and technological skills.

- Job cuts in manufacturing fed worries about economic security while labor unions continued their decline.

- Clinton promoted NAFTA and other free trade agreements, even with countries with poor human rights records.

America and the Global Economy

As the NAFTA agreement made plain, foreign trade ranked high on Clinton's agenda. When the U.S. trade deficit hit $133 billion in 1993, including a $59 billion trade gap with Japan, Clinton, like his predecessor, pressured the Japanese to buy more U.S. goods.

Clinton also preserved trading ties with China despite Beijing's human-rights abuses and one-party rule. Clinton welcomed Chinese president Jiang Zemin for a state visit in 1997 and visited China in 1998. This reflected economic realities. China had become America's fourth-largest trading partner, after Canada, Mexico, and Japan. In 2000, when U.S. imports from China surpassed $100 billion, Congress granted China the same status as America's other trading partners, rather than making trade with China dependent on year-by-year agreements.

Economic **globalization** increasingly shaped U.S. policy. When the Mexican peso collapsed in 1995, jeopardizing U.S.-Mexican trade and threatening to increase illegal migration northward, Clinton quickly granted Mexico $40 billion in loan guarantees.

In 1997–1998, when political corruption and other factors weakened the economies of Thailand, South Korea, Indonesia, and other Asian nations, the Clinton administration worked to promote stability in the region. As the Asian economic crisis spread, Japan's banks faltered, the Tokyo stock market fell, and the yen lost value. When Brazil and Argentina also sank into recession, analysts questioned how long the U.S. boom could continue. All these developments underscored how deeply the United States had become enmeshed in a complex global economy.

CLINTON'S FOREIGN POLICY: DEFINING AMERICA'S ROLE IN A POST–COLD WAR WORLD

How did the Clinton administration respond to political and economic developments abroad?

Bill Clinton preferred domestic issues to foreign policy. Yet America could not withdraw from the world. When Clinton's attention turned abroad, he faced four key challenges: protecting U.S. trade; using American power wisely in the post-Soviet era; promoting peace between Israel and the Palestinians; and responding to security threats, including nuclear proliferation and terrorism.

The Balkans, Russia, and Eastern Europe in the Post-Soviet Era

The aftershocks of the Soviet collapse unsettled the region of southeastern Europe known as the Balkans (BALL-kuns). In Yugoslavia, an unstable nation comprised of Serbia, Bosnia, Croatia, and other enclaves, the ruling communist party gave up power in 1990. In 1991–1992, as Yugoslavia broke apart, Serbian forces launched a campaign of "ethnic cleansing" in neighboring Bosnia. This meant supporting Bosnia's ethnic Serbs while killing or driving out Muslims and Croats. Serbian troops overran UN-designated "safe havens" and slaughtered Muslims. When a UN peacekeeping force failed to stop the killing, a joint U.S. and NATO operation launched air strikes against Bosnian Serb targets in August 1995.

Later in 1995, the Clinton administration flew the leaders of Bosnia's warring factions to Dayton, Ohio, for talks. The resulting Dayton Accords imposed a cease-fire and created a framework for governing the region. Clinton committed twenty thousand U.S. troops to a NATO force in Bosnia to enforce the cease-fire.

In 1998, Serbian forces attacked Muslims in Serbia's southern province, **Kosovo.** Early in 1999, NATO, under U.S. leadership, bombed Serbian facilities in Kosovo and in Serbia itself, including Belgrade, the capital. This reliance on air power, with minimal risk of U.S. casualties, became Clinton's preferred form of military engagement. Haunted by Vietnam, American public opinion wavered as well, appalled by the suffering and refugee crisis in the Balkans as well as in the African nation of Rwanda, but wary of expanding U.S. involvement. In June 1999, however, U.S. troops

Kosovo Province of former Yugoslavia victimized by a Serbian ethnic-cleansing campaign

joined a NATO occupying force in Kosovo that maintained peace and allowed refugees to trickle back.

U.S. diplomacy also continued to focus on the safe disposal of nuclear weapons in the former Soviet Union. In the 1993 Strategic Arms Reduction Treaty (START II), the United States and Russia agreed to cut their long-range nuclear arsenals by half. This left many deactivated nuclear weapons in Russia, Ukraine, Kazakhstan, and Belarus. Both the Bush and Clinton administrations used diplomacy, economic aid, and technical assistance to assure the secure destruction of these weapons.

Despite U.S. disapproval of Russia's brutal war against rebels in the breakaway republic of Chechnya (CHECH-nee-uh) and concern over Boris Yeltsin's alcoholism and increasingly erratic behavior, Clinton continued to support the Russian president. In 1999, however, over Russia's protests, NATO with U.S. support admitted three new members from the former Soviet bloc—Hungary, Poland, and the Czech Republic. With Yeltsin's resignation in December 1999, Prime Minister Vladimir Putin (VLAH-dee-meer POO-tun), a former agent of the KGB, the Soviet secret police, succeeded him as president.

The Middle East: Seeking an Elusive Peace, Combating a Wily Foe

After hopeful beginnings, Clinton's pursuit of peace in the Middle East failed. The 1987 Palestinian uprising, or Intifada, against Israel's military occupation of the West Bank and Gaza (see Chapter 30) continued into the 1990s. Prospects for peace brightened in 1993, after Israeli and Palestinian negotiators meeting in Norway agreed on a six-year timetable for peace. The so-called Oslo Accords provided for a Palestinian state in exchange for Israeli concessions. In 1994, President Clinton presided as Israeli prime minister Yitzhak Rabin (YEET-shahk rah-BEEN) and Yasir Arafat (YAH-seer AHR-uh-faht), head of the Palestine Liberation Organization, signed the agreement at the White House.

The bloodshed continued, however, and in 1995 a young Israeli opposed to the Oslo Accords assassinated Rabin. Israel's next election brought Benjamin Netanyahu (net-ahn-YA-hoo) of the hard-line Likud (li-KOOD) party to power. Suicide bombings by Palestinian extremists in 1996–1997 killed some eighty Israelis, triggering retaliatory attacks. Jewish settlements, with accompanying highways, checkpoints, and infrastructure, spread across Palestinian territory.

Clinton brought Israel's next prime minister, Ehud Barak (EH-hood buh-RAHK), to Camp David in July 2000 to meet with Arafat and to try to broker a new peace. Barak made major concessions; but Arafat rejected Barak's offer, and the summit failed. Palestinians launched a new Intifada against Israel in 2000. As Clinton left office, the Israeli-Palestinian conflict raged on (see Chapter 32).

Iraq also demanded Clinton's attention. After the Persian Gulf War, the United Nations had imposed strict sanctions on Iraqi oil exports and set up an inspection system to prevent Iraq from building chemical or nuclear weapons. In 1997, when Saddam Hussein barred UN inspectors from certain sites, Clinton dispatched thirty thousand troops to the Persian Gulf. He drew back after the UN secretary general, Kofi Annan (KOH-fee AHN-nahn), secured Saddam's agreement to open inspections. Saddam soon reneged, however, and the crisis continued (see Chapter 32).

Nuclear Proliferation, Terrorism, and Peacekeeping Challenges

Nations that signed the 1968 Nuclear Nonproliferation Treaty pledged not to develop nuclear weapons. India and Pakistan, long at odds over the disputed border region of Kashmir (KAHSH-meer), did not sign, however, and in 1988 India tested a nuclear bomb. Despite urgent pleas from the United States and other powers, Pakistan followed suit. Both the Bush and Clinton administrations imposed sanctions on the two countries, but the spread of nuclear weapons in this region deepened proliferation fears.

Communist North Korea also roused concern. Despite having signed the Non-proliferation Treaty, North Korea began a program of nuclear-weapons development and missile testing. In 1994, facing UN economic sanctions, North Korea pledged to halt its nuclear-weapons program; five years later, confronting famine and economic crisis, it suspended long-range missile testing in return for an easing of U.S. trade and travel restrictions. The country's nuclear intentions remained worrisome, however.

Attacks by anti-American Islamic extremists continued. In February 1993, a powerful bomb exploded in a parking garage beneath one of the towers of New York's World Trade Center. Six persons died in the blast and hundreds were injured. Five Islamic militants were arrested and three given life sentences.

In 1992, President Bush had committed some twenty-six thousand U.S. troops to a UN humanitarian mission to Somalia (soh-MAH-lee-uh), an East African nation afflicted by civil war and famine. As the warring factions battled, forty-four Americans were killed, including eighteen murdered in Mogadishu, Somalia's capital. President Clinton withdrew the U.S. force in 1994, and the UN mission ended a year later. Later evidence implicated anti-American Islamic extremists loyal to **Osama bin Laden** (oh-SAHM-uh bin LAH-dun) in the Mogadishu killings. A wealthy Saudi Arabian and Islamic fundamentalist militant, bin Laden had been expelled from Saudi Arabia in 1991 and taken refuge in Sudan, where he planned anti-Western terrorist activities.

Osama bin Laden Radical Islamic terrorist who masterminded murderous attacks against U.S. military and civilians

Two bombings at U.S. military installations in Saudi Arabia in 1995–1996 killed twenty-four Americans. On August 7, 1998, simultaneous bomb blasts at the U.S. embassies in Kenya and Tanzania (tan-zuh-NEE-uh) killed 220, including Americans and many local people. U.S. intelligence again pinpointed Osama bin Laden as the mastermind of the attacks. Expelled from Sudan in 1996, bin Laden had shifted his base of operations to Afghanistan, where he organized terrorist training camps. Clinton ordered cruise missile strikes on one of bin Laden's Afghan camps as well as on a suspected chemical-weapons factory in Sudan allegedly financed by bin Laden. On October 12, 2000, a bomb aboard a small boat in the harbor of Aden (AH-den), Yemen (YEH-mun), ripped a gaping hole in the U.S. destroyer *Cole,* killing seventeen sailors.

Closer home, in Haiti, a Caribbean island-nation wracked by poverty and disease, a military junta overthrew President Jean-Bertrand Aristide (shawn bear-TRAHN ah-ree-STEED) in September 1991 and terrorized his supporters. The Clinton administration supported a 1994 UN resolution authorizing military action against the junta. With a U.S.-led invasion flotilla anchored offshore, the junta's leaders went into exile, and Aristide, backed by a U.S. occupation force, resumed the presidency.

A New World Order Painfully Emerges

The peaceful post–Cold War era that many had anticipated seemed an ever-receding mirage as Americans of the 1990s confronted international issues of maddening complexity. The Soviet adversary had collapsed, and the threat of global thermonuclear war receded, but crises still flared around the world. Like firefighters battling many small blazes rather than a single conflagration, policy makers now wrestled with a baffling tangle of issues.

Confronting such complexities, some citizens simply gave up. In a 1997 poll, only 20 percent of Americans said that they followed foreign news, down sharply from the 1980s. Seeking to clarify the confusing world situation, analysts noted at least four large-scale trends in the post–Cold War era:

- First, economic considerations played an ever-greater role in international affairs. Multinational networks of trade and finance increasingly shaped America's foreign-policy interests.
- Second, a growing chasm divided the prosperous, stable industrialized world from societies marked by poverty, disease, and explosive population growth. This vast gulf helped spawn resentment and even terrorism.
- Third, despite and partially because of a globalizing economy and mass culture, ethnic divisions and religious fundamentalisms intensified. As many as a million people perished in genocidal violence in the African nation of Rwanda (ruh-WAN-duh) in 1994. Traumatized by the Somalia fiasco, President Clinton failed to intervene.
- Finally, the United Nations worked to define its role in the new era. By 2000 more than forty thousand UN peacekeeping forces and civilian personnel were serving in fifteen world trouble spots.

Despite the countertrends, opinion polls indicated that most Americans supported internationalist approaches to world problems and viewed the UN favorably, despite its flaws. With the Cold War over, America's position as simply one player—albeit a major player—in a truly global order became inescapably clear.

CHECKING IN

- As the Balkans exploded in ethnic conflict, Clinton committed U.S. troops and air power to a NATO peacekeeping effort.
- African conflicts persisted; Clinton expressed concern but withdrew American forces from Somalia and did not intervene in the Rwanda genocide.
- The United States helped negotiate the Oslo Accords, providing for a Palestinian state, but Palestinians rejected a later "land-for-peace" deal, and progress stalled.
- Nuclear proliferation remained a concern as India and Pakistan tested nuclear weapons, and North Korea undertook development programs.
- As terrorism directed at Americans and the West increased, the outlines of a "new world order" became clear.

THE CLINTON ERA ENDS: DOMESTIC POLITICS, IMPEACHMENT, DISPUTED ELECTION, 1996–2000

Why did political differences become sharper from 1996 to 2000?

Straddling the political center, Bill Clinton won reelection in 1996. His second term saw various battles over domestic and foreign policy. It is mainly remembered, however, for a sex scandal that led to Clinton's impeachment—a crisis that further poisoned a contentious political climate. A disputed presidential election in 2000 did little to heal the nation's divisions.

Campaign 1996 and After: Battling Big Tobacco; Balancing the Budget

Bill Clinton had won the nickname "the Comeback Kid" after a long-shot victory in the 1992 New Hampshire primary, and after the 1994 Republican landslide he again hit the comeback trail. In 1996, Clinton got another lucky break: a weak Republican opponent. Bob Dole, a partially disabled World War II hero and widely-respected senator from Kansas, won the nomination. Dole ran a lackluster campaign, and Clinton won with 49 percent of the vote, to Dole's 41 percent. (The Texas maverick H. Ross Perot garnered 8 percent.)

Tobacco regulation, a major public-health issue, loomed large in Clinton's second term. In 1997, facing lawsuits by former smokers and by states saddled with medical costs linked to smoking-related diseases, the tobacco industry agreed to pay some $368 billion in settlements. The agreement limited tobacco advertising, especially when directed at young people.

Since the agreement required government approval, the debate now shifted to Washington. Southern legislators close to the tobacco companies defended the industry, but the Clinton administration backed a bill imposing tougher penalties, higher cigarette taxes, and stronger antismoking measures. The industry struck back with a $40 million lobbying campaign and heavy contributions to key legislators, killing the bill. The Republican party, commented John McCain, Arizona's maverick Republican senator, appeared to be "in the pocket of the tobacco companies." In 1998, the tobacco industry reached a new settlement, scaled back to $206 billion, with forty-six states.

Hoping to appeal to progressives without alienating moderates, Clinton in his January 1998 State of the Union address offered some initiatives to help the poor, such as enrolling the nation's 3 million uninsured children in Medicaid. But he also introduced proposals attractive to the middle class (college-tuition tax credits; extending Medicare to early retirees) and to fiscal conservatives (reducing the national debt; shoring up social security). Some liberals dismissed the speech as "Progressivism Lite," but it had political appeal, and under normal conditions would have certified Clinton's political comeback.

Scandal Grips the White House

But conditions were not normal. Even as Clinton spoke, scandal swirled around the White House. Adultery charges had long clung to Clinton, and now he faced the Paula Jones sexual-harassment suit, dating from his days as Arkansas governor.

Seeking to show a pattern of sexual harassment, Jones's lawyers subpoenaed Clinton and quizzed him about reports linking him to a young White House intern, **Monica Lewinsky.** The president denied everything, as did Lewinsky. As the rumors became public (via an Internet website devoted to political gossip), Clinton denounced them as false. Hillary Clinton blamed "a vast right-wing conspiracy." In fact, political conservatives *were* digging for damaging information on Clinton. Clinton settled Paula Jones's suit, but more problems awaited. In secretly taped telephone conversations, Monica Lewinsky had described an affair with Clinton from 1995 through early 1997. In January 1998, the tapes were passed to Kenneth Starr, an independent counsel appointed to investigate the Clintons' murky real-estate dealings in Arkansas.

Monica Lewinsky White House intern whose brief liaison with Bill Clinton was discovered by Whitewater investigators

The Comeback Kid Comes Back

Political cartoonists enjoyed a field day with the impeachment of Bill Clinton, which, in the short run at least, did more damage to the Republicans than it did to Clinton, whose approval ratings remained high.

Starr's investigation now shifted to whether Clinton had committed perjury in his Paula Jones testimony. In August, after jail threats and a promise of immunity, Lewinsky admitted the affair before Starr's grand jury. Soon after, in videotaped testimony, Clinton admitted "conduct that was wrong" with Lewinsky but denied a "sexual relationship" under his narrow definition of the term.

Other presidents had pursued extramarital affairs, but by the 1990s changing standards, sexual-harassment laws, and the glare of media publicity had made such behavior more objectionable and harder to conceal. Unsurprisingly, the scandal unfolded in tabloid headlines, late-night television jokes, Internet humor, and conservative radio talk shows.

In a September 1998 report to the House Judiciary Committee, Kenneth Starr narrated the Clinton-Lewinsky affair in lurid detail. He recommended impeachment on the grounds that Clinton had committed perjury and obstructed justice.

The Judiciary Committee, on a party-line vote, forwarded four articles of impeachment to the House of Representatives. In a similarly partisan vote, the House approved and sent to the Senate two articles of impeachment: perjury and obstruction of justice. Clinton thus became the first president since Andrew Johnson to be impeached (though Nixon came close).

Opinion polls sent the Republicans an ominous message: most Americans opposed impeachment. In the 1998 midterm elections, as the impeachment process unfolded, the Democrats gained five House seats.

In January 1999 the trial began. As Chief Justice William Rehnquist presided, House Republicans presented their case while White House lawyers challenged what one called a "witches' brew of speculation." Through it all, Clinton's approval ratings soared. While people deplored his behavior, few believed that it met the Constitution's "high crimes and misdemeanors" standard for removal from office. With the economy booming, the public appeared willing to tolerate his personal flaws. On February 12, the Senate rejected the impeachment charges and ended the trial. In January 2001, as he left office, Clinton admitted to perjury, paid a $25,000 fine, and lost his law license for five years.

While escaping the worst, Clinton had suffered grievous damage, mostly self-inflicted. He remained active in his final two years in office, committing U.S. forces to Kosovo and working to resolve the Israeli-Palestinian dispute, for example, but the scandal unquestionably tarnished his presidency. The Republican party suffered as well. In 1999 Newt Gingrich, closely identified with the impeachment effort, and embroiled in ethical controversies and issues involving his marital life, resigned as Speaker and left Congress.

Election 2000: Bush Versus Gore

As the 2000 campaign got under way, the Democrats, bouncing back from the impeachment crisis, confidently nominated Vice President Al Gore for the top job. As his running mate, Gore chose Connecticut senator Joseph Lieberman, making him the first Jewish-American candidate on a major party ticket. The Republican contest narrowed to Arizona senator John McCain and Texas governor **George W. Bush,** son of the former president. Bush, with powerful backers and a folksy manner, won the nomination. The Green party nominated consumer advocate Ralph Nader.

George W. Bush 43rd President; son of former president, promised to restore dignity to the White House

Both Gore and Bush courted the center while trying to hold their bases. For Bush, this meant corporate interests, religious conservatives, and the so-called Reagan Democrats. Gore's base included liberals, academics and professionals, union members, and African-Americans. Gore pointed to the nation's prosperity and pledged to extend health care coverage and protect social security. In televised debates Gore was far more articulate and displayed greater mastery of detail than Bush. But many voters found the vice president pompous and arrogant.

Bush, with an easygoing manner but little national or foreign-policy experience, was widely seen as a lightweight wholly dependent on family influence. He promised to restore dignity to the White House. Polls showed that most voters agreed with Gore on the issues and preferred his economic policies. Ominously for Gore, however, they preferred Bush as a person. The election seemed a toss-up.

The resulting disputed election (see Map 31.2) worsened the partisan rancor of these years. Gore won the popular vote by more than 500,000, but the Electoral College remained up for grabs. The struggle narrowed to Florida, whose twenty-five electoral votes would determine the outcome.

Flaws in Florida's electoral process quickly became apparent. In Palm Beach County, a poorly designed ballot led several thousand Gore supporters to vote for the wrong candidate. In other counties with many poor and African-American voters, antiquated voting machines rejected thousands of ballots in which the paper tabs, called "chads," were not fully punched out. When Gore supporters demanded a hand count of these rejected ballots, Bush's lawyers sued to stop the recounts. Florida's secretary of state, Katherine Harris (the co chair of Bush's Florida campaign), refused to extend the deadline for certifying the vote.

On November 21 the Florida Supreme Court, with a preponderance of Democrats, unanimously ruled that a hand recount should constitute the official result. Meanwhile, on November 26, Katherine Harris had certified the Florida vote, awarding Bush the state. But on December 8, ten days before the scheduled

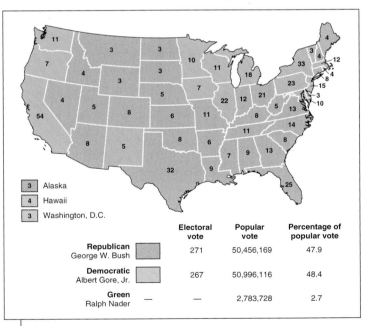

	Electoral vote	Popular vote	Percentage of popular vote
Republican George W. Bush	271	50,456,169	47.9
Democratic Albert Gore, Jr.	267	50,996,116	48.4
Green Ralph Nader	—	—	2,783,728	2.7

Map 31.2   The Election of 2000

For the first time since 1888, the winner of the popular vote, Al Gore, failed to win the presidency. The electoral-college system and the Supreme Court's intervention in the disputed Florida vote put George W. Bush in the White House.

Electoral College vote, the Florida Supreme Court ordered an immediate recount of all suspect ballots. The U.S. Supreme Court heard an appeal, and on December 12, by a 5-to-4 vote, halted the recount. Gore conceded the next day. Five Supreme Court justices (all Republican appointees) had made George W. Bush president.

The election produced an evenly divided Senate. Each party had fifty senators, giving Vice President Cheney the deciding vote. (The Republicans narrowly held the House of Representatives.) As he left office, Bill Clinton issued presidential pardons to 167 people, including his half-brother, in trouble on drug charges; persons caught up in Clinton-related scandals; and white-collar offenders who were big Democratic contributors. Despite Clinton's political skills and good intentions, few expressed regret as he left Washington.

Would George W. Bush heal the nation's divisions and pursue a wise foreign-policy course? Americans waited hopefully.

CULTURAL TRENDS AT CENTURY'S END

What cultural developments marked the 1990s?

American life in the 1990s reflected both the decade's prosperity and its cultural conflicts. While the newly rich flaunted their wealth and Americans pursued leisure diversions, undercurrents of violence also marked the decade. As cultural disagreements deepened, the values of openness and tolerance for diversity seemed under threat.

Affluence and a Search for Heroes

The economic boom of the 1990s produced instant fortunes for some and an orgy of consumption that set the decade's tone. Wall Street and Silicon Valley spawned thousands of youthful millionaires. Elegant restaurants offered obscenely expensive cigars and rare wines, and exclusive shops sold $13,000 handbags.

The economic boom also encouraged a hard-edged "winner-take-all" mentality like that of the Gilded Age, when the rich turned their backs on the larger society. In *Bowling Alone: The Collapse and Revival of American Community* (2000), political scientist Robert Putnam sharply criticized American public life. Putnam found diminished civic engagement and weakened interest in public issues, as evidenced by declines in voter participation, political activism, and civic participation. He even found less informal socializing, from dinner with friends to card parties and bowling leagues, as Americans pursued purely personal goals.

With the stock market surging, the Cold War over, and other threats only beginning to come into focus, many Americans set out to enjoy themselves. Attendance at the Disney theme parks in Florida and California neared 30 million in 2000. The sales of massive sport-utility vehicles (SUVs), like GM's gargantuan Hummer (based on the military Humvee), soared, despite environmentalists' laments about their fuel inefficiency.

The Hummer (b. 1992; d. 2006)
A civilian version of the Humvee, a military vehicle used in the Persian Gulf War, these massive gas-guzzling behemoths became a status symbol during the economic boom of the 1990s. GM stopped production of the largest model in 2006.

As in the 1980s, the mass media offered escapist fare. The 1997 blockbuster film *Titanic,* with spectacular special effects, grossed $600 million. The top-rated TV show of 1999–2000, *Who Wants to Be a Millionaire?* unabashedly celebrated greed. So-called reality TV shows like *Survivor,* popular as the decade ended, offered viewers a risk-free taste of the hazards that American life itself (at least for the affluent) conspicuously lacked.

Millions avidly followed TV coverage of the 1995 murder trial of O. J. Simpson, a former football star accused of killing his former wife and her friend. The Clinton sex scandals often seemed little more than another media diversion in a sensation-hungry decade.

Again, as was true of the 1980s, other evidence from the popular culture suggests a more complex picture. Some critics interpreted *Titanic,* which sided with its working-class hero in steerage against the rich snobs in first class, as a comment on America's widening class differences. The Clint Eastwood western *Unforgiven* (1992) seemed to express nostalgia for an earlier era when life presented rugged challenges and hard moral choices. The decade also reveled in the heroic era of World War II, featuring it in a series of TV specials, books like Tom Brokaw's *The Greatest Generation* (1998), and movies like *Saving Private Ryan* (1998) and *Pearl Harbor* (2001).

Outbursts of Violence Stir Concern
A popular 1999 film, *American Beauty,* and TV's *The Sopranos,* an HBO series about a mobster and his family, which debuted in 1999, explored dark impulses and violent undercurrents in American life. The violence was not limited to pop-culture fantasy.

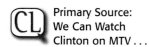

Primary Source:
We Can Watch
Clinton on MTV . . .

Oklahoma City bombing
April 1995 bombing of a federal building that killed 168 people by home-grown terrorist Timothy McVeigh

True, the overall crime rate fell nearly 20 percent between 1992 and 2000. But bursts of violence punctuated the decade. The annual toll of gun deaths exceeded twenty-eight thousand in 2000. In 1999, two students at Columbine High School near Denver fatally shot twelve students and a teacher before committing suicide. After the Columbine massacre President Clinton again called for stricter gun-control laws, but the firearms lobby fought such efforts.

The violence sometimes reflected the intensity of the nation's culture wars. In 1998, two youths tortured and murdered a gay student at the University of Wyoming, Matthew Shepard, because of his sexual orientation. As the abortion controversy raged, some "pro-life" advocates turned violent. In 1997 bombers struck abortion clinics in Tulsa and Atlanta. The following year, a Buffalo physician who performed abortions was shot dead.

On April 19, 1995, in the decade's most horrifying burst of mass violence, a rental truck packed with explosives demolished the nine-story Murrah Federal Building in Oklahoma City, Oklahoma. The blast killed 168 people, including 19 children in the building's day-care center. Police soon arrested Timothy McVeigh, a Gulf War veteran with vague links to secretive antigovernment militia groups obsessed with conspiracy theories. McVeigh, convicted of murder, was executed in 2001.

The **Oklahoma City bombing** came precisely two years after a government raid on the Waco, Texas, compound of the Branch Davidians, an apocalyptic religious sect led by David Koresh, charged with firearms violations. The raid ended tragically when fires probably set by Koresh and others erupted inside the compound as federal tanks moved in, leaving some eighty Branch Davidians dead. Timothy McVeigh claimed that his Oklahoma City attack was in retaliation for the deaths at Waco.

CHECKING IN

- Mass culture in the 1990s was marked by gaudy commercialism, a fixation with scandal, and a decline in civic participation.
- Although crime declined, outbursts of violence such as the Columbine massacre and the Oklahoma City bombing prompted anxieties about public safety.
- In 1993, a government raid on the Waco, Texas, compound of the Branch Davidians, an apocalyptic religious sect, resulted in some eighty deaths.
- Conservatives, through organizations like the Christian Coalition, gained ground in the "culture wars" in the 1990s and built a mass cultural and political movement.
- Well-organized evangelical groups espoused an interpretation of current events based in biblical prophecy and called for the nation to restore "traditional values."

Culture Wars: A Broader View

Fortunately, the decade's culture wars typically involved words and symbolic gestures, not bullets and bombs. For example, the Smithsonian Institution canceled a 1995 exhibit marking the fiftieth anniversary of the atomic bombing of Japan when politicians and veterans' organizations attacked it for documenting the bombs' human toll and for presenting differing views of President Truman's decision.

But if the culture wars, whose origins lay in the 1960s, did not often descend into violence, they did involve fierce contests that some viewed as nothing less than a struggle for the nation's soul. The Christian Coalition's attempted takeover of the Republican party was part of a larger campaign to reverse what conservatives saw as America's moral decay. The struggle unfolded on many fronts, from televangelists' programs and radio talk shows to school-board protests and boycotts of TV shows deemed immoral.

As gays and lesbians grew more vocal and visible, conservative politicians continued to mobilize against their demands for equality. The Southern Baptist Convention, America's largest Protestant denomination, urged a boycott of Disney World because it had unofficially sponsored "Gay Pride" days.

The fast-growing evangelical and charismatic churches, including suburban megachurches with thousands of members, denounced society's wickedness and the government's complicity in the nation's alleged moral decline. In 1997 some seven hundred thousand men representing a conservative Protestant movement called Promise Keepers rallied in Washington, D.C., for a day of prayer, hymn singing, and pledges to reclaim moral leadership of their households. President Clinton's sexual misdeeds underscored for conservatives the moral rot they saw eating away at America.

Pat Robertson's *The New World Order* (1991) saw much of world history as a vast conspiracy that will soon end in the rule of the Antichrist. The best-selling *Left Behind* series of novels (1995–2004), coauthored by the conservative activist Tim LaHaye and loosely based on certain biblical prophecies, described an End Time apocalypse in which Jesus Christ and an army of true believers will destroy the sinister forces of evil increasingly dominating the modern world.

In *One Nation After All* (1998), sociologist Alan Wolfe reported on his interviews with middle-class Americans, whom he found accepting of diversity and suspicious of extremist positions. The virtues of tolerance and live-and-let-live, Wolfe suggested, still prevailed in Middle America. In its optimism and moderate tone, such a perspective captured a deep-seated pragmatic approach to cultural differences, and struck a cautiously encouraging note amid the clash of contending viewpoints as the twentieth century ended.

Chapter Summary

 DOWNLOAD THE MP3 AUDIO FILE OF THE CHAPTER SUMMARY, AND LISTEN TO IT ON THE GO.

What foreign and domestic issues loomed largest during the Bush administration, 1989–1993? (page 735)

The collapse of the Soviet Union ended the Cold War, but new problems quickly replaced old ones. Saddam Hussein's invasion of Kuwait provoked a coordinated response by the United States and its allies, driving him out of Kuwait but allowing him to remain in power, and up to mischief, in Iraq. The Bush administration tended to ignore domestic policy; recession struck hard, environmental concerns accelerated, and racial tensions exploded into riots. Bush paid the penalty for his neglect of domestic issues when Americans elected Bill Clinton president in 1992.

What domestic policy issues, political events, and economic trends most shaped Clinton's first term? (page 741)

A baby boomer and fiscally moderate "New Democrat," Clinton preferred to focus on domestic issues; he pushed a major economic reform package through Congress but failed dismally in attempts to achieve health care reform. As conservative evangelists and talk-radio hosts denounced Clinton, the political climate turned poisonous. Conservative Republicans gained control of Congress

KEY TERMS

George H. W. Bush *(p. 735)*

Persian Gulf War *(p. 738)*

Americans with Disabilities Act *(p. 740)*

Clarence Thomas *(p. 740)*

Albert Gore, Jr. *(p. 741)*

H. Ross Perot *(p. 741)*

William Jefferson (Bill) Clinton *(p. 741)*

Madeleine K. Albright *(p. 742)*

North American Free Trade Agreement (NAFTA) *(p. 742)*

Christian Coalition *(p. 743)*

Newt Gingrich *(p. 743)*

Welfare Reform Act of 1996 *(p. 745)*

globalization *(p. 746)*

Kosovo *(p. 747)*

in 1994; led by Newt Gingrich, they promised radical change but achieved little. Adapting to a more conservative climate, Clinton managed to achieve welfare reform, but his administration would soon be overtaken by myriad scandals.

What groups benefited from the economic boom of the 1990s and what groups did not? (page 745)

The stock market soared, largely on the wings of technology stocks, unemployment fell, and the gross domestic product nearly doubled. Nonetheless, income inequality actually increased, and more and more people worried about job security as corporations "downsized" to improve profits. Labor unions, their membership numbers depleted, were powerless to stop the exportation of manufacturing jobs and the passage NAFTA, which Clinton signed into law in 1993.

How did the Clinton administration respond to political and economic developments abroad? (page 747)

Clinton committed American forces to the Balkans as peacekeepers. He expressed concern about conflicts in Africa but did not intervene. His attempts at forging an Israeli-Palestinian peace faltered, as had so many others. Clinton continued to pursue the dismantling of Cold War nuclear arsenals and nonproliferation of nuclear weapons. As terrorism directed at Americans and the West increased, some features of a post-Cold War world order began to emerge: emphasis on trade and globalization, a growing gap between rich and poor nations, and the rise of anti-Western religious fundamentalism.

Why did political differences become sharper from 1996 to 2000? (page 750)

Once reelected, Clinton moved even more to the center, supporting tax cuts and a balanced budget, and actually achieving a budget surplus. However, the Monica Lewinsky scandal and independent counsel Kenneth Starr's expansion of the Whitewater investigation undermined these successes and nearly undid his presidency. Based on a lurid report by Starr, a partisan House impeached Clinton, but Republicans could not muster enough votes in the Senate to convict him. In the face of the scandal, Clinton's personal popularity remained high. In the disputed 2000 presidential election, finally resolved by the Supreme Court, George W. Bush, son of the former president Bush, defeated Vice President Al Gore.

What cultural developments marked the 1990s? (page 754)

The proliferation of electronic media, notably 24-hours news television and the rise of the Internet, provided the context for a fragmented cultural scene in the 1990s. Scandal (including Clinton's impeachment drama) and violence (school shootings and terrorist attacks) filled the airwaves while Americans filled their garages with expensive SUVs and their homes with other consumer goods. Against this seeming debauchery arose an opposition movement, rooted in evangelical Christianity. The Religious Right rejected secularism and liberal politics; viewed current events through the lens of biblical prophecy; and called for the nation to restore traditional family values. This movement's well-organized political arm, led by the Christian Coalition, became a powerful voting bloc in the Republican party and helped to elect George W. Bush in 2000.

CHAPTER 32

Global Dangers, Global Challenges

2001 to the Present

Cell Phone Users at a New York City Subway Entrance

CHAPTER PREVIEW

America Under Attack: September 11, 2001, and Its Aftermath
How did the Bush administration respond to the September 11 attacks, internationally and domestically?

Politics and the Economy in Bush's First Term, 2001–2005
Beyond security concerns, what economic and social issues did Bush address in his first term?

Foreign Policy in a Threatening Era
What challenges faced the United States in the Middle East and elsewhere in the world after 2000?

Social and Cultural Trends in Contemporary America
What demographic and economic trends have most shaped contemporary America?

Domestic Policy Since 2004
What were the most pressing domestic issues after 2004?

(CL) This icon will direct you to the website where you can Prepare for Class, Improve Your Grade, and Ace the Test:
www.cengage.com/history/boyer/enduringconcise6e

Bao Xiong (bough shong), a Hmong-American born in 1977, spent her first two years in a refugee camp in Thailand. The Hmong (mong) are an Asian ethnic group that originated in northern China and later migrated to the mountainous regions of Laos and Vietnam. During the Vietnam War, the U.S. Central Intelligence Agency recruited many Laotian Hmong to fight the communists. Facing deadly reprisals after the U.S. withdrawal from Vietnam, more than 200,000 Hmong, including Bao Xiong's family, fled to refugee camps in Thailand. Here they endured terrible conditions.

In 1979, two-year-old Bao came with her family to America. They settled first in East Moline, Illinois, where her father learned

759

English, enrolled in college, and tried—without success—to resume his teaching career. In 1991, the family moved to Milwaukee, where Bao's mother and father started a laundry while also working in factories. Despite their hard life, Bao Xiong's parents inspired her with their love of learning.

After high school, Bao enrolled in college and majored in elementary education. While pursuing her college degree, she also raised three daughters and taught thirty hours a week in a local ESL (English as a Second Language) program. Bao graduated in 2004 and continued her career as a teacher in the Milwaukee school system. "I want to be a role model for my Hmong students," she said; "I very much want to be an influence in their education and their lives."

The Hmong experience is only one chapter in the larger story of immigration in the contemporary United States. American history from the beginning has been shaped by immigration, voluntary and involuntary, from the British Isles, Africa, Europe, Asia, and Latin America, and this remains true in the early twenty-first century.

This final chapter of *The Enduring Vision* looks at the events and trends shaping U.S. history today. While Americans adapted to unsettling social and economic changes, a conservative administration in Washington pursued its vision of the nation's future. Looming over the period were the shocking terrorist attacks of September 11, 2001, and the administration's response, including a bitterly divisive conflict in Iraq. In troubling times, the nation's capacity for overcoming adversity offered promise for the future. Bao Xiong is one of millions of newcomers who will help shape that future.

AMERICA UNDER ATTACK: SEPTEMBER 11, 2001, AND ITS AFTERMATH

How did the Bush administration respond to the September 11 attacks, internationally and domestically?

Although George W. Bush had campaigned as a centrist, his early decisions suggested a hard-line conservative approach. On September 11, 2001, a horrific attack by airplane hijackers on U.S. buildings and citizens riveted the nation's attention. Targeting the mastermind of the attack, Bush mobilized a multinational coalition to invade Osama bin Laden's stronghold in Afghanistan. He also secured new laws and reorganized federal agencies to tighten homeland security. Then, insisting that Iraq's dictator Saddam Hussein had conspired in the 9/11 attacks and possessed weapons of mass destruction, Bush launched an invasion of Iraq as well.

The Bush Administration Begins

George W. Bush, who turned fifty-five in 2001, was a president's son and a senator's grandson. After earning an MBA at Harvard, Bush entered the oil business in Texas. He was known for partying and drinking, but a religious conversion and marriage to Laura Welch stabilized his life. Business and family connections helped him win the Texas governorship in 1994 and the Republican presidential nomination in 2000. **Richard (Dick) Cheney** became his running mate.

Richard (Dick) Cheney
George W. Bush's neoconservative vice president; shaped energy policy and advocated for expanded executive powers

Chronology

2001	Bush administration repudiates Kyoto protocol on emission standards; Congress passes $1.35 trillion tax cut bill; stock market falls; Enron Corporation collapses; wave of corporate bankruptcies and scandals; Congress passes No Child Left Behind Act; U.S. withdraws from ABM (Anti-Ballistic Missile) Treaty and deployed missile defense system; terrorist attacks on World Trade Center, Pentagon (September 11); U.S. and allied forces overthrow Taliban regime in Afghanistan; captured Taliban fighters and others imprisoned at Guantánamo Bay, Cuba; USA-Patriot Act passed
2002	Bipartisan Campaign Reform Act (McCain-Feingold law); Department of Homeland Security created; Sarbanes-Oxley Act tightens business accounting regulations; Bush secretly authorizes National Security Administration to spy without warrants; Republicans gain in midterm elections
2003	U.S. and coalition forces invade Iraq (March 21); North Korea withdraws from Nuclear Non-Proliferation Treaty; prescription-drug benefits added to Medicare
2004	Revelation of abuses at Baghdad's Abu Ghraib prison; George W. Bush wins second term, defeating John Kerry
2005	Congress passes Energy Act; Bush signs bill barring "cruel, inhuman, and degrading" treatment of prisoners; trade deficit and budget deficit hit record levels; Bush names John Roberts and Samuel Alito to Supreme Court; Hurricane Katrina devastates New Orleans; lobbyist Jack Abramoff indicted on multiple criminal charges
2006	Tom Delay resigns House seat; congressional report documents government failures in Hurricane Katrina response; radical Hamas organization wins Palestinian elections; Iran resumes nuclear enrichment program; U.S. sells India nuclear fuel and reactor parts; GM and Ford announce major layoffs; Congress debates immigration-law changes; Hispanic immigrants march in major cities; Democrats gain control of both houses in midterm elections; resignation of Defense Secretary Donald Rumsfeld

Bush named **Colin Powell,** former head of the Joint Chiefs of Staff, as secretary of state, making him the highest-ranking African-American to serve in a presidential administration. Condoleezza Rice of Stanford University, also African-American, became national security adviser. Other Bush appointees were, like Vice President Cheney, veterans of earlier Republican administrations with corporate ties. Secretary of Defense **Donald Rumsfeld** had held the same post under President Ford and later headed a pharmaceutical company.

> **Colin Powell** Commander of U.S. forces in Persian Gulf War; served as Bush's secretary of state

> **Donald Rumsfeld** Secretary of defense under Bush until 2006

On issue after issue, Bush proposed measures that reflected the interests of the wealthy; corporate America; and the religious right. Bush's conservative appointments and domestic policies troubled many moderate Republicans, including Vermont senator James Jeffords, who in May 2001 left the Republican Party to become an independent. By the summer of 2001, Bush's approval rating had fallen to about 50 percent. But all this faded as the administration and the nation faced an awesome crisis.

Day of Horror: September 11, 2001

On the morning of **September 11, 2001,** three commercial airplanes hijacked by terrorists slammed into the Pentagon outside Washington, D.C., and the twin towers of New York's World Trade Center. As Americans watched in horror, the blazing towers collapsed, carrying more than 2,800 men and women to their deaths. The Pentagon

> **September 11, 2001** Date, emblazoned in national memory, of the terrorist attacks on New York City and Washington, D.C.

America Under Attack

Rescuers remove a flag-draped body from the ruins of the World Trade Center.

attack left 245 dead on the ground. A fourth plane crashed in Pennsylvania when heroic passengers prevented terrorists from hitting another target, possibly the White House. At the World Trade Center, nearly 350 firefighters and 23 police officers perished.

The hijackers deliberately targeted symbols of U.S. economic and military power. The government soon identified the hijackers, all Muslims from the Middle East, and traced their movements before September 11.

Terrorism was familiar elsewhere, and had taken many American lives, civilian and military, in the 1980s and 1990s. But not since the War of 1812 had foreign enemies attacked major cities on the U.S. mainland. As the nation mourned, political divisions faded. Flags appeared everywhere. The World War II anthem "God Bless America" enjoyed renewed popularity. When the damaged New York Stock Exchange reopened after six days, stock prices plunged. They soon recovered, but consumer confidence remained fragile.

In October, an editor at the *National Enquirer* died of anthrax, a rare bacterial disease, contracted from spores mailed in a letter. Letters containing anthrax spores next appeared in the offices of NBC news and two senators. Four other persons died from anthrax-tainted mail. As panic spread, scientists traced the spores to a U.S. research laboratory, and investigators focused on finding a domestic perpetrator rather than a foreign terrorist.

Confronting the Enemy in Afghanistan

President Bush on September 12 declared the attacks an "act of war." On September 14, the Senate unanimously authorized Bush to use "all necessary and appropriate force" to retaliate and to prevent future acts of terrorism. On September 20 a somber Bush blamed the attack on a terrorist network called **al Qaeda** (al KYE-duh) ("the base") headed by Osama bin Laden in Afghanistan. Bin Laden, the renegade son of a wealthy Saudi Arabian contractor, had long denounced America for supporting Israel and for stationing "infidel" troops on Saudi soil. (Ironically, the United States

al Qaeda Terrorist organization directed by Osama bin Laden

had backed bin Laden in the 1980s, when he was fighting Russian forces in Afghanistan.) Though bin Laden claimed to be defending Islam, most Islamic leaders repudiated him. Among the poor in some Arab cities and Palestinian refugee camps, however, the attacks produced celebratory demonstrations.

Bush announced his determination to uproot al Qaeda. He also targeted al Qaeda's protectors, the Taliban, a Pakistan-based movement of strict and militant Muslims, which had controlled Afghanistan since 1996. This phase of America's antiterrorist effort enjoyed broad international backing. On October 7, U.S., British, Canadian, Pakistani, and other forces launched the attack. For the first time, NATO forces fought in defense of a member nation. A coalition of anti-Taliban groups within Afghanistan, called the Northern Alliance, assisted in the campaign as well.

The Taliban soon surrendered Kabul, the Afghan capital, and other strongholds. By mid-December, despite sporadic resistance, the United States and its allies claimed victory. Hundreds of captured al Qaeda fighters were sent to the U.S. base in **Guantánamo Bay,** Cuba. In June 2002, with U.S. support, Afghan tribal leaders established a new government and named an interim prime minister, Hamid Karzai. Osama bin Laden remained at large, however, and many al Qaeda loyalists retreated to mountainous eastern Afghanistan and prepared to fight on.

Guantánamo Bay Naval base in Cuba; site of controversial prison holding hundreds of alleged terrorists

Tightening Home-Front Security

Bush's September 20 speech also signaled a broader response to the attacks. America would target not only al Qaeda, he said, but "every terrorist group of global reach." He also said that Americans must "give law enforcement the additional tools it needs to track down terror here at home."

In one step to shore up domestic security, Congress late in 2001 created the Transportation Security Administration and federalized the nation's 28,000 airport security personnel. But other aspects of the open-ended antiterrorism campaign hinted at by Bush proved more controversial. The Justice Department detained hundreds of Middle Easterners living in the United States, some for minor visa violations, and held them without filing charges or even revealing their names.

The **USA-Patriot Act,** the administration's sweeping antiterrorist bill passed by Congress in October 2001, extended the government's powers to monitor telephone and e-mail communications and library patrons' Internet searches. Civil-liberties organizations protested. Even some conservatives, traditionally suspicious of big government, questioned this expansion of federal power. In November 2001, Bush signed an executive order empowering the government to try noncitizens accused of fomenting terrorism in secret military tribunals rather than in civil courts. In 2002, news media reported disturbing evidence of missed clues before the 9/11 attack. Administration officials also acknowledged that through the summer of 2001, President Bush's daily security briefings had included warnings of an al Qaeda plot to hijack a U.S. airliner.

USA-Patriot Act Antiterrorism bill passed after 9/11 attacks expanding government's powers of investigation and surveillance

To coordinate antiterrorism efforts, Congress created a new cabinet-level **Department of Homeland Security** in November 2002. The new department absorbed the Coast Guard, the Customs Service, the Federal Emergency Management Agency (FEMA), the Immigration and Naturalization Service, and other agencies. The FBI and the CIA remained independent.

Department of Homeland Security New cabinet-level agency created after 9/11 charged with domestic security responsibilities

In 2003 Bush named a blue-ribbon commission, headed by Republican Thomas Kean, a former New Jersey governor, and Democrat Lee Hamilton, a former congressman, to examine pre-9/11 intelligence failures. The commission's 2004 report pinpointed a lack of communication between the FBI, the CIA, and other agencies, and called for a restructuring of U.S. intelligence operations. To the dismay of critics, some of the commission's recommendations were ignored. Most incoming shipping containers continued to go unchecked, for example, and U.S. chemical plants remained vulnerable.

The Campaign in Iraq, 2003–2004

Although Afghanistan remained unstable and Osama bin Laden uncaptured, the administration's attention shifted elsewhere. In his January 2002 State of the Union address, President Bush identified Iran, Iraq, and North Korea as an "axis of evil." Of the three, Iraq loomed largest. Iraq's ruler, Saddam Hussein, had been a thorn in America's flesh since the Persian Gulf War, which had left him weakened but still in power. In a barrage of speeches, Bush, Vice President Cheney, Defense Secretary Rumsfeld, and National Security Adviser Rice accused Saddam of complicity in the 9/11 attacks and of stockpiling or developing nuclear, chemical, and biological weapons.

This shift of focus to Iraq was orchestrated by a close-knit group of Republicans who subscribed to a political philosophy called **Neoconservatism.** This group advocated an aggressive foreign policy dedicated to spreading democracy in the Arab world and beyond. Skeptical of multilateral approaches, neoconservatives believed that the United States, as the world's superpower, should act alone to pursue its goals. Such a policy, they believed, would advance freedom and create a safer environment for Israel, America's ally in the Middle East. For neoconservatives, democratizing Iraq was a first step in their ambitious agenda.

The call for invading Iraq proved controversial from the start. Critics challenged the administration to prove its claims. A preemptive war would not only violate U.S. principles, they charged, but could also drag on for years, unleash anger across the Arab world, and undermine the larger antiterrorist campaign. Great Britain's Tony Blair backed the administration, but other NATO allies, as well as Russia and most Arab leaders, objected. To counter the rush to war, they called for a UN resolution demanding that Iraq readmit UN weapons inspectors, who had departed in 1998 when Iraq blocked their access to some sites.

In October 2002, Congress passed a resolution sponsored by the administration authorizing President Bush to "defend the national security of the United States against the continuing threat posed by Iraq." While Republicans overwhelmingly supported the resolution, Democrats were divided, fearful of opposing Bush on an issue he called vital to American security. President Bush would later use this resolution as the legal basis for invading Iraq.

As the November 2002 midterm elections approached, President Bush, enjoying post-9/11 approval ratings close to 70 percent, campaigned tirelessly, stressing his leadership in the war on terror. Democrats hammered at the recession, corporate scandals, and Bush's environmental record. With 9/11 memories still raw, Bush's talk of terrorism hit home. Republicans regained control of the Senate and increased their House majority. Political reshuffling after the defeat led to a notable first:

Neoconservatism Political school of thought, ascendant in Bush administration, espousing enlarged executive powers and unilateral approach to foreign policy

Democrat Nancy Pelosi of California became the first woman of either party to hold the position of House minority leader.

Bolstered by the election, the administration pushed its Iraq invasion plans. In November 2002 Baghdad agreed to let in UN inspectors. They soon withdrew, however, as U.S. and British forces assembled in the Persian Gulf. In a February 2003 UN speech, Secretary of State Colin Powell, relying on evidence supplied by the CIA, insisted that Saddam Hussein was developing weapons of mass destruction (WMDs).

The war began on March 19, 2003, as U.S. cruise missiles rained down on Baghdad. The land invasion commenced two days later. Securing the oil fields around Basra, U.S. and British troops moved north, encountering unexpected guerrilla resistance as they approached Baghdad. In early April, U.S. troops occupied Baghdad and toppled a large statue of Saddam. As the regime fell and Saddam fled, widespread looting erupted.

On May 1, after a navy jet had brought him to the aircraft carrier *Abraham Lincoln* off San Diego, President Bush declared major combat operations over. A banner behind him proclaimed "Mission Accomplished." Bush named L. Paul Bremer, a career Foreign Service officer, to administer civil affairs in Iraq. Saddam was captured in December, and later put on trial.

But conditions in Iraq deteriorated. Iraq's Sunni Muslims, though a minority, had long dominated Iraqi politics and resented Bremer's decision to disband the Iraqi army and dismiss all government officials who had served under Saddam. The resulting power vacuum sparked sectarian violence. Conditions worsened through 2004 as bombings, kidnappings, and deadly highway blasts caused by improvised explosive devices (IEDs) occurred daily. In September, the toll of U.S. dead in Iraq passed 1,000. Vice President Cheney had predicted that the Iraqis would welcome the Americans as liberators. Now reality blasted such wishful thinking.

CHECKING IN

- The September 11 terrorist attacks were comparable to Pearl Harbor in their effect on Americans; a wave of patriotism swept the country.

- Bush proclaimed war on terrorism; a U.S.-led coalition invaded Afghanistan, routed the pro–Al Qaeda Taliban government, and established a pro-American democracy.

- The administration created a new, cabinet-level Department of Homeland Security, and Congress passed the Patriot Act despite serious concerns about civil liberties.

- In 2002, reflecting the influence of neoconservatives, Bush and his advisors made the case for preemptive war against Iraq; Congress passed a resolution authorizing the use of force.

- The U.S. military operation that toppled Saddam's regime began in March 2003 and was over by April; but administrative missteps and other factors sparked a violent insurgency that by 2004 threatened all U.S. goals in Iraq.

POLITICS AND THE ECONOMY IN BUSH'S FIRST TERM, 2001–2005

Beyond security concerns, what economic and social issues did Bush address in his first term?

Although the 9/11 attacks and their aftermath dominated Bush's first term, the administration also proposed a series of economic and social initiatives. Debate over these measures unfolded amid a sharp recession and a cascade of corporate bankruptcies and scandals.

Economic Reverses and Corporate Scandals

The prosperity and stock-market boom of the 1990s (see Chapter 31) barely outlasted the decade. In March 2001, the stock market recorded its worst week since 1989, falling by 6 percent. The high flying Silicon Valley information-technology companies, which had led the boom of the later 1990s, were especially hard hit. As the market value of the surviving companies plummeted, instant millionaires watched their portfolios shrivel.

Few shed tears when luxury boutiques and pricey restaurants suffered reverses. But the recession that began in Silicon Valley and Wall Street soon spread. Industrial production dropped, and every state lost jobs. By June 2003, with the unemployment rate at 6.4 percent, 2.6 million workers had lost their jobs.

The longest economic boom in American history had ended with a thud. The Bush administration, having inherited a budget surplus, now projected years of deficits. To stimulate the economy, the Federal Reserve Board cut interest rates eleven times in 2001. A wave of corporate bankruptcies and scandals further eroded investor confidence. Business deregulation, a culture of greed, and overly complex corporate structures had created a situation that invited fraudulent practices.

Houston's Enron Corporation, with close ties to the administration, was an early casualty. A marketer of electric power, Enron flourished in the 1990s and claimed revenues of $101 billion by 2000. The end came abruptly. Late in 2001 Enron filed for bankruptcy and admitted to falsifying profit reports. More than five thousand Enron workers lost both their jobs and their retirement funds. Shortly before the collapse, Enron founder Kenneth Lay and other top officials had sold their Enron stock, profiting handsomely. In 2006, a Houston jury convicted Lay and former Enron CEO Jeffrey Skilling on multiple counts of fraud and conspiracy. The company's logo, a crooked "E," seemed all too appropriate.

The parade continued. In 2002 WorldCom, America's second-largest telecommunications company, admitting that it had overstated profits by billions, filed for bankruptcy. CEO Bernard Ebbers, convicted of securities fraud in 2005, received a twenty-five-year prison sentence. John T. Rigas, head of Adelphia Corporation, the nation's sixth-largest cable company, received a fifteen-year prison term for fraud. Dennis Kozlowski, the CEO of Tyco, an industrial products and service company, was indicted for looting the company of $600 million. Kozlowski's trial included testimony about a $6,000 shower curtain for his New York apartment. Kozlowski received a long prison sentence and was fined $70 million. Finally, top mutual-fund managers faced charges of increasing their bonuses by advising investors to buy stocks at inflated prices. The Wall Street investment firm Merrill Lynch paid $200 million in fines.

Despite some positive economic news, the stock market fell through much of 2002 and early 2003, as traumatized investors remained wary. Executives who had been celebrities in the 1990s now faced public hostility. Declared the chairman of Goldman Sachs, a Wall Street investment bank, "I cannot think of a time when business . . . has been held in less repute." Politicians responded to mounting public anger. In July 2002 Congress passed the Sarbanes-Oxley Act, which imposed stricter financial reporting rules and toughened criminal penalties for business fraud.

The U.S. economy grew by 4.2 percent in 2004. But job growth and middle-class wages lagged. While the real income of the nation's richest 1 percent increased by more than 12 percent in 2004, the average real income of the remaining 99 percent grew by only 1.5 percent. "[I]t's a great economy if you're a high-level corporate executive," wrote economist Paul Krugman. "For most other Americans, economic growth is a spectator sport." By mid-2006, even this uneven recovery faltered.

The Republican Domestic Agenda

In February 2001, fulfilling a campaign promise, President Bush proposed a $1.6 trillion cut in income taxes over a ten-year period. Though the measure reduced all rates, wealthy taxpayers received the highest percentage reduction. As the recession began, Bush argued that the cuts would stimulate investment and speed recovery. In May Congress passed a $1.35 trillion tax cut—lower than Bush's proposal and somewhat less slanted toward the rich. Mounting budget deficits predictably followed, erasing the surplus Clinton had achieved.

The administration's 2001 energy bill proposed incentives to expand coal, oil, and natural-gas production and called for drilling in Alaska's **Arctic National Wildlife Refuge** (ANWR). President Bush defended the bill as a way to reduce U.S. dependence on foreign oil. The energy bill finally passed by Congress in August 2005 rejected the provision for drilling in ANWR. It did, however, exempt energy companies from some environmental regulations and grant $14.5 billion in tax breaks to oil, natural gas, coal, and nuclear-power companies. It did not tighten vehicle fuel-efficiency requirements, even on gas-guzzling trucks and SUVs.

Arctic National Wildlife Refuge Bush called for oil exploration in this vast wildlife area in Alaska

On education, Bush pushed a program he labeled **"No Child Left Behind."** Bush's plan called for standardized national tests in grades four and eight to measure reading and math skills, with penalties for schools that fell short. In 2001, Congress mandated annual testing. Some schools, focusing on raising test scores, cut back art, music, history, and other subjects. The massive federal intrusion in public education, historically a local matter, troubled some conservatives.

"No Child Left Behind" Label for Bush law mandating standardized testing in reading and math in grades four and eight

Christian conservatives ranked among Bush's strongest supporters in 2000. Moving quickly to reward them, Bush in 2001 created an Office of Faith-Based and Community Initiatives to funnel federal grants to churches for social programs. Under this initiative, grants went to anti-abortion groups and prison ministries run by evangelicals. Operation Blessing, a charity operated by televangelist Pat Robertson, received $22 million in direct grants and food surpluses.

Bush's education plan also included a voucher system by which children could attend private or religious schools at taxpayers' expense. Congress rejected this proposal, but some states introduced their own voucher plans. By 2006 some 4,000 private and church-sponsored schools were partially supported by student vouchers. Some did well; others showed no better results than the public schools; and some 400 had closed for various reasons.

President Bush also sought favor with Christian conservatives, who overwhelmingly oppose abortion, by restricting stem-cell research. Stem cells are valuable for medical research. But because they are harvested from human embryos (from the "surplus" embryos stored at fertility clinics), some anti-abortion groups opposed stem-cell research. In a 2001 presidential directive, Bush barred funding for research on all but a handful of existing stem-cell lines. Medical researchers warned that this restriction could inhibit their work.

Campaign Finance Reform and the Election of 2004

As political campaign costs soared, reformers worked to curb the endless fundraising the system required. They especially targeted so-called soft money contributions to political parties that then flowed on to specific candidates. In the 2000 election, soft-money contributions reached $400 million.

In 2002 President Bush signed a reform bill co-sponsored by Arizona Republican John McCain and Wisconsin Democrat Russell Feingold. It banned soft-money contributions; barred fake TV "issue ads" designed to influence elections; and included other provisions to reduce the power of money in politics. As lobbying organizations sought loopholes and challenged the law on free-speech grounds, its ultimate impact remained unclear.

As the 2004 election approached, Howard Dean, a physician and former Vermont governor, emerged as the early frontrunner for the Democratic presidential nomination. But while Dean's candor and antiwar position energized the Democratic base, it also alienated many voters. In the campaign's first test, the Iowa primary, he came in a disappointing third. His candidacy quickly faded. Nevertheless, Dean had bluntly criticized the Iraq War and demonstrated the Internet's potential for fundraising and rallying support.

John Kerry Senator from Massachusetts and Vietnam War veteran; Democratic nominee for president in 2004

Senator **John Kerry** of Massachusetts, a decorated Vietnam War veteran, won the nomination. Bush began his reelection campaign with a massive war chest of some $150 million from corporate sources and wealthy donors called "Pioneers." Bypassing the McCain-Feingold restrictions on organizational contributions, the Pioneers raised money from friends and colleagues. Of 246 "Pioneers," 104 later received appointments in the Bush administration.

In the campaign, Kerry criticized the administration's response to 9/11. Although he had supported a Senate resolution approving the use of force in Iraq as a last resort, Kerry now accused Bush of misleading the nation about Saddam Hussein. President Bush defended both the Iraq conflict and the Patriot Act as crucial to the war on terrorism. Citing Kerry's changing positions, Republicans accused him of "flip-flopping" indecisiveness.

Highlighting Bush's less than distinguished military record, Kerry played up his tour in Vietnam. (Anti-Kerry TV commercials questioned his Vietnam record and emphasized his 1971 antiwar activities.) Kerry, a Catholic, sought to counter Bush's edge with evangelical Christians. The candidates' positions on cultural issues reflected national divisions. Kerry opposed the death penalty; Bush supported it. Kerry supported *Roe* v. *Wade;* Bush favored a ban on all abortions except in rare circumstances. Kerry backed stricter gun control; Bush opposed it.

The divisive issue of same-sex marriage loomed large during the campaign. As some cities and states began experimenting with the legalization of same-sex marriage, opinion polls found 63 percent of Americans opposed. (By 2006 that figure had dropped to 51 percent.) While Kerry favored leaving this issue to the states, Bush endorsed a constitutional amendment banning gay marriage. With eleven states adding referenda banning same-sex marriage to the fall ballot, the issue energized religious conservatives. The referenda passed by lopsided margins in all eleven states, and Bush won in nine of the eleven, including closely contested Ohio.

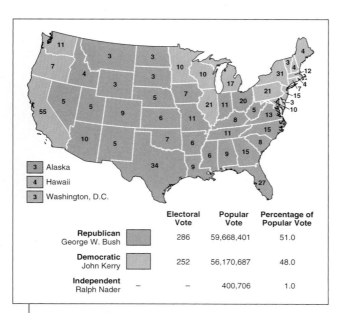

	Electoral Vote	Popular Vote	Percentage of Popular Vote
Republican George W. Bush	286	59,668,401	51.0
Democratic John Kerry	252	56,170,687	48.0
Independent Ralph Nader	–	–	400,706	1.0

Map 32.1   The Election of 2004

On election day, Bush garnered 51 percent of the popular vote to Kerry's 48 percent (see Map 32.1). Kerry won states in the Northeast, the Upper Midwest, and the coastal states of the West. In the rest of the nation, the majority went for Bush. Bush narrowly won the Electoral College vote, with Ohio the pivotal state. Republicans gained a net of four Senate seats and four House seats. A tax-cutting president seen as a leader in the "war on terror" and a defender of embattled conservative cultural values had eked out a narrow victory.

Kerry had won the two largest states, California and New York, and 55 percent of voters under thirty voted Democratic. In Illinois a charismatic young Democrat, Barak Obama, won election to the Senate.

The election highlighted the political role of new technologies. Internet-based initiatives like *MoveOn.org* raised funds in support of liberal causes. Hundreds of bloggers (independent website operators) sustained a freewheeling flow of political commentary. While conservative organizations had long mobilized their supporters via direct mail, radio, and TV, liberals appeared to have the edge in the new arena of Internet-based activism. Indeed, the popular culture offered many challenges to conservative ideology. Michael Moore's 2004 documentary *Fahrenheit 9/11* mounted a witty critique of the administration's response to 9/11.

The 2004 election again underscored the political role of organized groups. Conservative organizations remained active. Pat Robertson's Christian Coalition and James Dobson's Focus on the Family mobilized Bush's base of religious and cultural conservatives. Among evangelical Christians, however, support for Bush was not unanimous. Jim Wallis, founder of the evangelical Sojourners movement, sharply criticized the religious right in his book *God's Politics: Why the Right Gets It Wrong and the Left Doesn't Get It* (2005).

▰CHECKING IN

- The September 11 attacks and the bursting of the technology-stock bubble brought the free-wheeling prosperity of the 1990s to an end.

- A spate of corporate scandals, some involving jail terms for disgraced CEOs of major companies, undermined confidence in corporate America.

- Bush and Congressional Republicans passed huge tax cuts, an education bill mandating standardized testing, and an energy bill laden with incentives for big oil companies.

- Cultural and religious concerns drove Republican opposition to stem-cell research and same-sex marriage.

- Stressing national security and moral issues, Bush defeated Kerry in the 2004 elections; the Republicans increased their margin of control in both houses of Congress.

FOREIGN POLICY IN A THREATENING ERA

What challenges faced the United States in the Middle East and elsewhere in the world after 2000?

By 2005, two years into the Iraq War, insurgent violence and sectarian conflict raged unabated. Home-front support eroded amid accusations of prisoner abuse, illegal spying in the name of security, and deceptions in the administration's case for invading Iraq. The continuing Israeli-Palestinian struggle, threats of nuclear proliferation, and rising international concern about environmental hazards further challenged U.S. policy makers.

The Continuing Struggle in Iraq; Sagging Home-Front Support

In his second inaugural address in January 2005, Bush described the Iraq War as part of a global campaign to spread democracy, "with the ultimate goal of ending tyranny in our world." The speech echoed Woodrow Wilson's 1917 war message proclaiming America's mission to make the world "safe for democracy" (see Chapter 22).

U.S. Ground Troops in Iraq

U.S. ground troops, like those seen here, faced threats of insurgent attacks and anticoalition violence through 2008.

In Iraq the conflict dragged on. Determined to prevent a government of Shiites (who comprised the majority of the population) allied with the Kurds of northern Iraq, Sunnis organized a campaign of disruption and violence. A November 2004 operation in Fallujah, involving more than 10,000 U.S. and Iraqi forces, left 38 Americans dead. Typically, however, the insurgents returned once the troops withdrew. In January 2007, General David Petraeus took over the command of U.S. forces in Iraq and was given 20,000 additional troops to improve the security conditions. The "surge" of American troops into Baghdad, combined with the strategy of arming sectarian militia groups in the provinces, tamped down the violence somewhat in 2007 and early 2008.

Amid the turmoil, U.S. attempts to train an Iraqi army faltered, as did the reconstruction effort. In Baghdad and other cities, electricity and other basic services remained unpredictable. Oil exports, Iraq's major income source, remained below prewar levels.

Bringing democracy to Iraq proved equally difficult. Sunnis boycotted a January 2005 election to choose a National Assembly. The result was an assembly and government dominated by Shiites. Sunnis accused Shiite militias and even rogue Interior Ministry "death squads" of targeting Sunni leaders and detonating car bombs in Sunni neighborhoods. Sunnis participated in a second round of parliamentary voting in December 2005, but the vote followed sectarian lines. In February 2006, suicide bombers destroyed a revered Shiite shrine, the golden-domed Al-Askariya Mosque in Samarrah, triggering anti-Sunni reprisal attacks. (The Kurds in northern Iraq mostly remained aloof from the carnage.)

Historically a patchwork of ethnic and religious groups ruled by successive Persian, Greek, and Arab invaders, Iraq was governed by British colonial administrators after World War I and became an independent nation only in 1932. Whether it could avoid fragmenting into separate Sunni, Shiite, and Kurdish enclaves amid the chaos that followed Saddam's overthrow remained deeply problematic.

Over 160,000 U.S. troops were in Iraq by 2007. They fought few open battles, but casualties continued. By March 2008 more than 4,000 GIs had been killed in Iraq and more than 30,000 wounded. Combined with operations in Afghanistan, the war's cost stood at around $440 billion, with billions more in prospect. (Some economists predicted that the final toll of the Afghanistan and Iraq wars would be measured in the trillions.) As other nations in the coalition withdrew their forces, the burden fell more heavily on the United States.

Opposition to the Iraq war moved from the margins to the political center. In November 2005, Pennsylvania congressman Jack Murtha, a Vietnam veteran with a hawkish record on military matters, urged immediate withdrawal from Iraq. A Senate Intelligence Committee report along with tell-all books by former administration officials reached the same conclusion: the evidence supporting the case for war back in 2002–2003 had been trumped up or even fabricated. The Pentagon's decision to go in with a minimum number of troops and lack of planning for post-invasion reconstruction also faced intense criticism.

Another sign of the "mainstreaming" of antiwar sentiment, at least for Democrats, came during the presidential primary contests of 2008. Senator Barack Obama's early opposition to the war gave him the edge over his chief Democratic rival, Senator Hillary Clinton, who had voted for the October 2002 resolution authorizing the use of force against Iraq. Even some Republicans had turned against the war. Between 2006 and mid-2008, Bush's national approval ratings by most polls hovered at or below 30 percent.

Evidence of prisoner mistreatment deepened home-front uneasiness and damaged U.S. prestige in Arab nations. In April 2004, revolting photographs surfaced showing the abuse and sexual humiliation of Iraqis held by U.S. forces at Baghdad's Abu Ghraib prison. The army demoted the general in command of the prison and court-martialed some participants.

Further allegations soon surfaced charging prisoner abuse in Afghanistan, in Iraq, and at Guantánamo Bay, where more than 500 men seized in Afghanistan were held as "enemy combatants." In 2004, the International Committee of the Red Cross described interrogation methods at Guantánamo as "tantamount to torture." Evidence also surfaced that the CIA had secretly transported detainees to an uncertain fate in Egyptian and Eastern European prisons. UN agencies and officials in Great Britain, Spain, and other countries called upon the United States to close the Guantánamo facility.

In 2005, defying the White House, Congress passed an amendment proposed by Senator John McCain (himself a victim of torture while imprisoned during the Vietnam War) to a military appropriations bill. McCain's amendment outlawed "cruel, inhuman, and degrading" treatment of prisoners. Bush signed the bill, but in an increasingly common practice he issued a "signing statement" asserting, in effect, that he was not bound to obey the McCain amendment.

Deepening civil-liberties concerns, Americans learned in 2005 that President Bush in 2002 had secretly authorized the National Security Agency (NSA) to tap U.S. citizens' overseas phone calls and e-mails without securing a warrant. Bush and

Attorney General Gonzales defended the spying as vital to catching terrorists. A CBS News opinion poll found that most Americans thought that Bush had exceeded his authority in approving warrantless NSA spying on U.S. citizens. Even many Republicans, traditionally suspicious of governmental excesses, found Bush's actions disturbing.

In June 2006, the U.S. Supreme Court rejected the administration's claims that it could set up special military tribunals to try the Guantánamo prisoners. Such tribunals, the Court held, violated both federal law and the Geneva Conventions governing the treatment of prisoners of war. In a broader sense, the Court rejected the Bush administration's claim that it could pursue the war on terrorism with little regard for Congress, the Constitution, or international law.

Adding to the accumulation of disturbing developments, *Time* magazine in March 2006 reported that in November 2005, U.S. marines had killed twenty-four unarmed Iraqi men, women, and children in the town of Haditha in Iraq's Anbar Province after a roadside IED had killed a member of their unit. As military criminal-justice teams investigated these alleged incidents, and subsequent cover-ups, memories of the Vietnam-era massacre at My Lai stirred uneasily.

Central to America's relationships with the Muslim world was U.S. support for Israel and for a "two state" solution recognizing Palestinian interests. On this front, prospects seemed bleak. When Palestinian leader Yasir Arafat rejected the Camp David peace plan and a second Palestinian Intifada began in 2000 (see Chapter 31), violence in the region escalated. Ariel Sharon, elected Israel's prime minister in February 2001, demanded an end to violence before talks could resume. Israel also began building a security barrier, partially extending into the West Bank, to control access and prevent suicide attacks. The prospects of a U.S.-sponsored "road map to peace," proposed in 2003, briefly brightened in November 2004 when Arafat died and Mahmoud Abbas, a moderate, replaced him. In August 2005 Israel withdrew all Jewish settlements from Gaza.

But in this conflict, one step forward always seems to be followed by two steps back. In January 2006, Palestinian elections gave victory to the radical Hamas organization, which had perpetrated many attacks on Israeli civilians and even denied Israel's right to exist. When Hamas refused to renounce violence, the United States, the European Union, Russia, and the UN halted its regular grants to the Palestinian Authority.

After Sharon suffered a stroke in January 2006, his deputy Ehud Olmert succeeded him. Olmert asserted Israel's unilateral right to keep settlements in disputed territories; set its borders with the West Bank; extend the intrusive security barrier; and determine the future of Jerusalem, a highly sensitive issue. All Palestinian groups rejected these principles.

Violence exploded in June 2006 as Palestinian militants in Gaza killed two Israeli soldiers on the border and kidnapped a third. Israel retaliated with heavy bombing in Gaza. Tensions escalated as Hezbollah, a militant organization supported by Iran and Syria and based in southern Lebanon, killed three Israeli soldiers and lobbed scores of rockets into northern Israel. Israel bombed not only Hezbollah bases but also the Beirut airport and bridges and highways throughout Lebanon, resulting in heavy property damage and loss of life. As in Iraq, America's influence in mediating this deepening conflict seemed steadily to diminish.

Nuclear Proliferation Threats

Although the end of the Cold War had reduced fears of global thermonuclear war, nuclear-related issues remained. President Reagan's antimissile "Star Wars" initiative (see Chapter 30) was revived by George W. Bush. A missile-defense system, defenders argued, could protect America against a missile attack from North Korea or other "rogue states." Russian president Vladimir Putin, eager for U.S. investment and NATO membership, agreed to abandon the 1972 Anti-Ballistic Missile (ABM) Treaty if both sides further reduced their nuclear arsenals. The Bush administration agreed. Soon after, NATO granted Russia a consultative relationship, though not full membership.

Meanwhile, the administration joined with other nations to address the specter of nuclear proliferation, especially in North Korea and Iran. Isolated and impoverished North Korea, ruled by an eccentric dictator, Kim Jong Il, displayed an almost paranoid suspicion of outsiders.

Claiming to fear attack from the 30,000 U.S. troops in South Korea, North Korea boasted of its nuclear-weapons program (see Chapter 31) and in 2003 withdrew from the Nuclear Non-Proliferation Treaty. A North Korean long-range missile test in 2006, although unsuccessful, deepened concern about its intentions. Six-nation negotiations led by China initially got nowhere, but in June 2008 North Korea pledged to halt its nuclear-weapons program and disabled a key uranium-enrichment facility. U.S. officials welcomed this development, but called for strict inspection and verification procedures.

Dissidents in Iran, meanwhile, revealed in 2002 the existence of uranium-enrichment laboratories essential for building nuclear weapons. Iran's president Mahmoud Ahmadinejad (AH-mu-din-a-JOD), a fiery nationalist and Islamic fundamentalist, taunted America and said Israel "should be wiped off the map." He denied that Iran sought nuclear weapons, but insisted on its sovereign right to develop nuclear power. In 2005 and 2006, the United States and Iran jousted on this issue and there was even talk of possible U.S. military action. Tensions subsided somewhat in December 2007, when a U.S. National Intelligence Estimate report concluded with "high confidence" that Iran's nuclear weapons program ended four years earlier.

A Widening Trade Gap and China's Growing Power

As the pace of globalization increased, the most immediate impact for the United States was a surging trade deficit, which hit a record $794 billion in 2007. This massive imbalance mainly reflected rising prices on imported oil; surging foreign car sales; and a yawning trade gap with China. With China's admission to the **World Trade Organization** in 2001, its exports boomed. In 2007, the U.S. trade deficit with China topped $256 billion.

As imports grew, so did protectionist pressures. U.S. manufacturers complained that China artificially manipulated its currency, the yuan, to make Chinese exports cheaper. The situation was complex, however. Cheap Chinese imports helped U.S. retailers keep their prices low. When U.S. textile manufacturers pressured Bush to impose quotas on clothing imported from China, Wal-Mart and other discount chains fought the effort. Also, many Chinese imports were produced for U.S. companies that reaped the profits when these goods were sold.

| **World Trade Organization**
World body governing international trade

With a GDP exceeding $2 trillion in 2005, China was quickly overtaking Japan and Germany for the title of the world's second-largest economy, behind the United States. Some economists predicted it would be first in twenty years. On a 2005 visit to Beijing, President Bush acknowledged China's centrality in the global marketplace and in the U.S. economy while criticizing the regime's repressiveness and its restraints on religious freedom. Others attacked China's poor environmental record, including massive greenhouse-gas emissions. With 40 percent of its 1.3 billion people living at the subsistence level, China urgently needs continued economic development, and for this, the U.S. market is crucial.

Environmental Hazards Become a Global Concern

Three Mile Island, Love Canal, and the *Exxon Valdez* disaster (see Chapters 30 and 31) all underscored modern technology's environmental risks. With the Cold War over, the United States helped Russia, Ukraine, and Kazakhstan dispose of their nuclear-weapons materials (see Chapter 31). America also faced the task of disposing of its own radioactive waste from nuclear-weapons facilities. In 2002, over protests by local politicians, President Bush designated Yucca Mountain in the Nevada desert as the nation's nuclear-waste disposal site. Controversy and technical snags delayed the project, and the facility is not scheduled to open until well into the 2010s.

Other environmental hazards threatened as well. Acid rain carrying sulfur dioxide and other pollutants from U.S. factories and vehicle exhaust damaged Appalachian forests and Canadian lakes. As fluorocarbons depleted the atmosphere's ozone layer, more solar radiation reached the earth's surface, increasing skin-cancer risks. Above all, **global warming** posed a long-range hazard.

global warming Worldwide surge in average temperatures most scientists attribute to greenhouse-gas emissions

The fact of global warming is beyond dispute. The Earth's average temperature rose by one degree Fahrenheit in the twentieth century, and the rate of increase shot up after 1970. Nearly all scientists also agree that carbon dioxide, methane, and other gases from fossil-fuel combustion in factories, homes, and motor vehicles contribute significantly to global warming. Scientists predict a 40 percent increase in carbon dioxide emissions by 2020, with a corresponding surge in global warming. If this happens, scientists foresee not only hotter temperatures, but also still higher sea levels from melting polar ice, disrupted climatic conditions affecting crops, and ferocious tropical storms.

The United States, with other industrialized and developing nations, was deeply implicated in these global environmental trends. With under 5 percent of the world's population, America accounts for 25 percent of global energy consumption. And this energy comes heavily from the fossil fuels that figure prominently in global-warming discussions. A 2005 EPA study found that U.S. motor vehicles were, on average, significantly less fuel efficient than they had been in the late 1980s.

The Bush administration's environmental record was mixed at best. On taking office, Bush halted the EPA's implementation of measures to reduce carbon dioxide emissions from power plants. Government scientists who questioned administration policies were marginalized. Rejecting calls for

CHECKING IN

- Violence in Iraq increased between 2004 and 2006 into a melee of violence, slowing political and economic progress.

- The "surge" of troops in 2007 improved security conditions somewhat, but American opinion had turned against the war, and Bush's approval ratings plummeted.

- The abuse of prisoners and denial of basic rights to "enemy combatants" prompted mounting criticism, as did revelations about a warrantless domestic spying program.

- Israel-Palestinian relations remained tense; in 2006 Israel invaded Lebanon in an effort to root out Hezbollah.

- Nuclear proliferation became a focus of the administration's attention, while the trade deficit with China widened and global warming concerns intensified.

stricter emission laws and fuel-efficiency standards, the administration instead touted distant and uncertain alternative energy sources, such as hydrogen-powered fuel cells.

A UN-sponsored conference on global warming, held in Kyoto, Japan, in 1997, drafted a protocol setting strict emission targets for industrialized nations. President Clinton signed it but did not submit it for Senate ratification, fearing defeat. President Bush repudiated the protocol entirely, charging that it would jeopardize America's standard of living. The **Kyoto Accords,** as revised in 2001, went into effect in 2005, with only the United States, Australia, India, and China refusing to cooperate.

Kyoto Accords Most industrial nations, with the exception of the U.S. and several others, agreed to carbon-reduction goals set by this agreement

SOCIAL AND CULTURAL TRENDS IN CONTEMPORARY AMERICA

What demographic and economic trends have most shaped contemporary America?

In the late twentieth and early twenty-first centuries the long-term migration from the Northeast, Midwest, and Plains states to the South and West continued, as did the flow of immigrants from Asia and Latin America. Fundamental economic changes affected millions of Americans, benefiting some but creating difficulties for others, including displaced industrial workers and inner-city residents.

An Increasingly Diverse People

The rapid growth, geographic mobility, and ethnic diversity long characteristic of U.S. society continued in these years, as did the historic shift to the South and West, reflecting both internal migration and immigration patterns. The West added 10.4 million residents in the 1990s, with California alone increasing by more than 4 million.

Household arrangements continue to evolve. The proportion of "traditional" families headed by a married heterosexual couple fell from 74 percent in 1960 to 50 percent in 2004. People living alone made up 26 percent of households in 2004, while 4.2 percent of households were maintained by unmarried partners.

The graying of the baby-boom generation (those born between 1946 and 1964) pushed the median age from around 33 in 1990 to 36 in 2004, the highest in American history. On the public-health front, average life expectancy at birth rose from seventy-four to seventy-seven between 1980 and 2002.

America is becoming increasingly diverse and multicultural. Growing immigration from Asia and Latin America in recent decades reversed a long decline in the proportion of foreign-born persons in the population. The population of some 305 million (as of 2008) is about 13 percent Hispanic, 12 percent black, 4 percent Asian, and 1 percent American Indian. Some 6 million Muslims, mainly from the Middle East and North Africa, add to the ethno-religious mix. The nation's Hispanics are nearly 60 percent of Mexican origin, with Puerto Ricans, Cubans, and Salvadorans comprising most of the balance. With their high birthrate, Hispanics are predicted to comprise 25 percent of the population by 2050.

Americanization, Twenty-First Century Style
Recent immigrants from Afghanistan join a fitness class in Fremont, California, in 2001.

Upward Mobility and Social Problems in a Multiethnic Society

While these groups faced problems, opportunity beckoned. For African-Americans, median family income in 2003 approached $30,000. While well below the median for non-Hispanic white families ($47,777), this was 14 percent higher, in constant dollars, than the 1990 figure. College-educated blacks enjoyed significantly higher earnings, while the number of black-owned businesses reached 1.2 million in 2002. The substantial black middle and professional classes, in short, are growing and thriving.

But blacks in the inner cities, where the unskilled have few job prospects, school dropout rates soar, and drug trafficking is pervasive, face a different reality. By age thirty-five, nearly a third of black males lacking a college education have served prison time. Inner-city black women face risks as well. In 1970, unmarried women accounted for 37 percent of black births; in 2002, the figure stood at 68 percent. Many of these births were to teenage girls, reducing their prospects for education and employment.

But the inner cities present hopeful trends as well, as church leaders and community activists work to provide opportunities and break the cycle of self-destructive behavior. Battling urban violence, several cities sued gun manufacturers for injuries or deaths caused by unregistered firearms.

Among Native Americans, renewed tribal pride and activism continued. Citing Article VI of the Constitution, which describes all U.S. treaties as "the supreme law of the land," tribes sued to enforce the 331 Indian treaties ratified between 1778 and 1871. Indian gambling casinos, approved by Congress in 1988, proliferated. Connecticut's giant Foxwoods Casino, run by the Mashantucket Pequots, earned $6 billion annually. Many citizens deplored the spread of gambling. But casino income did enable tribes to support schools, museums, job training, and substance-abuse programs.

The Hispanic population, too, resisted sweeping generalizations. Many Hispanics were well educated, prosperous, and upwardly mobile. Hispanic households' median income rose to $33,000 by 2003, and unemployment among Hispanics dropped from 9 percent in 1995 to 5.5 percent in early 2006.

In 2004, 22 percent of Hispanics were living in poverty, many in inner-city neighborhoods plagued by gangs, alcohol and drug addiction, teen pregnancy, and erratic school attendance. Religion and family loom large in Hispanic culture, but stressful social conditions took their toll. Many unskilled Hispanic newcomers took poorly paid jobs as gardeners, maids, day laborers, and migrant farm workers.

Hispanics, like other immigrant groups, mobilized to promote their interests. In 2005, more than five thousand Hispanics held elective public office, including Los Angeles mayor Antonio Villaraigosa, the city's first Hispanic mayor since 1872. Though Hispanics have tended to vote at lower rates than non-Hispanic whites, 7.6 million cast ballots in 2004, making them an increasingly important constituency.

Of the nation's 13 million Asian-Americans in 2004, 75 percent had arrived since 1980. This group, too, presents a variegated picture, though with certain commonalities. Prizing education and supported by family networks, many followed a trajectory of academic achievement and upward mobility. In 2004 nearly 50 percent of adult Asian-Americans held college degrees.

After passage of the Immigration Reform Act of 1965, many Indian doctors, engineers, and academics emigrated to America, often joined later by parents and other family members. As the story of Bao Xiong illustrates (see opening vignette), the Hmong comprise yet another distinct Asian immigrant group contributing a new strand to American life.

By 2050, demographers calculate, no single ethno-racial group will be a majority in America. Non-Hispanic whites, in other words, while still a plurality, will simply be another minority. Many Americans of mixed origins, like the golfer Tiger Woods and politician Barack Obama, resist being pigeonholed. From 1960 to 2000, the number of interracial married couples in the United States rose from 149,000 to 1.5 million. Recognizing these realities, in 2000 the Census Bureau permitted citizens to check more than one racial category, or none at all.

Not everyone welcomed the new diversity, and the phenomenon of "white flight" continued. Between 1990 and 1995 both Los Angeles and New York lost more than 1 million native-born inhabitants, approximately equal to the new arrivals from Asia and Latin America. Language became a major battleground. While some campaigned to make English America's "official language," others called for school instruction in children's native tongue, or at least bilingual classes.

In an increasingly diverse nation, some observers foresaw a society divided psychologically if not physically along lines of race, ethnicity, religion, or national origin. The 2005 movie *Crash*, winner of the Academy Award for best picture, portrayed a society seething with racial and ethnic hostility. Many people clearly seek the reassurance of a clear-cut group identity, while others retreat into enclaves defined by wealth, profession, or social status. The persistence of the culture wars and abusive political rhetoric (see Chapter 31) deepens the divisions.

In such a situation, what does it mean to be "American"? In his 1908 play *The Melting Pot*, Israel Zangwill, a Jewish immigrant from England, foresaw the blending of immigrants into a common national identity. A century later, Zangwill's metaphor has faded, in part because its advocates usually assumed that entering the "melting pot" meant abandoning one's ethnic roots and cultural traditions and conforming to an Anglo or northwestern European model. If the "melting pot" model doesn't work, what will unite this diverse society? Americans share a common identity as consumers of goods and mass-culture entertainment. Is this enough? Can the nation's civic culture match its commercial and leisure culture? The answer remains unclear.

The "New Economy" and the Old Economy

In *The Coming of Post-Industrial Society: A Venture in Social Forecasting* (1973), sociologist Daniel Bell offered a remarkably accurate prediction of changes in the U.S. economy. In the late nineteenth and early twentieth centuries, America's mainly farm economy gave way to one driven by industrial production. As the twentieth century ended, an equally profound transformation occurred: the decline of industry and the rise of a professional and service-based economy. Farming and manufacturing continued, of course, but not as major sources of employment.

A snapshot of the U.S. labor force in 2004 tells the story. In a work force of 140 million, 62 percent held white-collar jobs, ranging from business and financial management and professions such as medicine, the law, teaching, engineering, telecommunications, and computer programming to sales, office work, and careers in the entertainment and leisure fields (see Figure 32.1). Lower-paid service-sector workers in health care, personal services, and food-related occupations comprised another 16 percent. A mere 23 percent worked in manufacturing, farming, construction, and transportation. Daniel Bell's "post-industrial society" has become a reality.

The rewards of the new economy were unevenly distributed. Some young people with the necessary education, skills, and contacts found exciting challenges and good salaries in the new electronics, programming, and telecommunications fields. For less-privileged youths, supermarkets, car washes, fast-food outlets, and discount superstores provided entry-level jobs, but few long-term career prospects. For displaced industrial workers, the impact could be devastating.

Globalization contributed to the transformation of the U.S. economy. The availability of cheap imported products hastened the decline of U.S. manufacturing, from toys and textiles to steel and automobiles. As VW, Toyota, Honda, Subaru, and other foreign automakers grabbed more U.S. sales, America's automakers, in trouble since the 1970s (see Chapter 30), faced a crisis. Ford's market share fell from 25 percent in 2000 to 17 percent in 2005. In 2006 and 2007, the "Big Three" auto makers an-

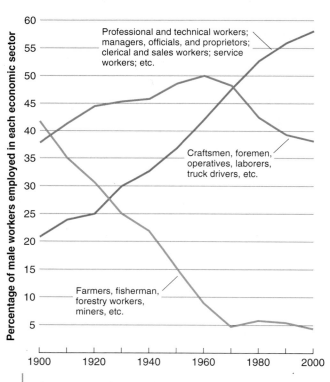

Figure 32.1 Changing Patterns of Work, 1900-2000

This chart illustrates the sweeping changes in the male U.S. labor force in the twentieth century. Farming, fish, forestry, and mining industry participation fell dramatically while the number of workers in the service, technical, managerial, sales, clerical, and professional categories rose steadily.

Source: Historical Statistics of the United States, Colonial Times to 1970 (1975); Statistical Abstract of the United States, 2002; Caplow, Hicks, and Wattenberg, The First Measured Century: An Illustrated Guide to Trends in America (Washington D.C.: The AEI Press, 2001).

nounced major restructuring plans, including closing scores of factories and cutting tens of thousands of jobs. As gas prices hit $4 a gallon in 2008, sales of SUVs and light trucks, moneymakers for U.S. automakers in the 1990s, plummeted, worsening the crisis.

General Motors, an icon of America's industrial might, having lost $10.6 billion in 2005 and watched its stock price tumble by 50 percent, announced plans to lay off 30,000 of its 113,000 factory workers. Workers willing to quit were offered buyouts of up to $140,000. Said one GM engineer: "This once was the premier company. . . . Today, you know this company is crumbling around you." One wit described GM as a health-care company that also makes cars. In other countries with national health-insurance plans paid for by taxes, governments rather than individual companies cover these costs.

In these circumstances, the long decline in union membership continued, sinking to only 12 percent of the work force in 2006. As unions grew weaker, workers had less bargaining power to resist wage cuts and other concessions demanded by management. As if to rub salt in the wound, Toyota, poised to overtake GM as the world's largest carmaker, was celebrating record sales and *hiring* workers for its nine manufacturing plants in seven states. In auto making, as throughout the U.S. economy, globalization's effects are complicated. One thing is clear, however: the economic order familiar to the parents and grandparents of today's youth is gone forever.

CHECKING IN

- Overall life expectancy increased; the Sun Belt continued to grow; and immigration led to growing diversity.
- Racial problems continued, especially in urban ghettos; Native Americans asserted their treaty rights and built casinos; Hispanic and Asian communities grew dramatically.
- Widespread acceptance of mixed-race sports heroes and public figures and increasing incidence of interracial marriage hinted at a movement away from fixed notions of race.
- As the population grew increasingly diverse ethnically, the "melting pot" metaphor suggesting sameness and uniformity faded.
- The service economy expanded rapidly, pushing many into low-paying jobs but creating lucrative jobs for the educated; the industrial economy and labor unions shrank.

DOMESTIC POLICY SINCE 2004

What were the most pressing domestic issues after 2004?

President Bush called for social-security reform and expanded prescription-drug benefits for seniors, but his domestic policies did little to lift his approval ratings. The administration's slow response to the devastation of Hurricane Katrina in 2005 brought new charges of incompetence. Bush sought to preserve his conservative legacy through two Supreme Court appointments, but a mushrooming federal deficit, lobbying scandals, blatant congressional spending on pet projects, and soaring gasoline prices as oil companies reported record profits further soured the public mood, affecting the 2006 midterm elections and the 2008 presidential and congressional races.

Funding Social Security and Health Care as the Federal Deficit Soars

Since social security was introduced in 1935, conservative Republicans have argued for its abolition or privatization. Launching his second term, Bush called for a partial privatization of social security, enabling workers to shift some of their social-security funds to private investment accounts. Bush pushed this proposal heavily, but the public remained cool, and Democrats criticized it as a dangerous experiment.

In 2003, the Republican Congress expanded the 1965 Medicare program (see Chapter 28) to cover part of seniors' prescription-drug expenses beginning in 2006. Drug costs worried older Americans, but the plan proved extremely complicated. "I have a Ph.D., and it's too complicated to suit me," said one. Because retirees vote in large numbers, their frustration worried GOP strategists.

The prescription-drug benefit further burdened an already costly program. In 2004, Medicare and Medicaid cost $600 billion, more than double the 1990 figure. These costs, along with social-security benefits, will soar even higher as baby boomers retire. These entitlement programs, plus Iraq War costs and interest payments on the $9 trillion national debt, produced explosive federal deficits. The deficit, $319 billion in 2005, was projected to surpass $480 billion in 2009.

Despite such numbers, Bush insisted that his tax cuts be made permanent. This action, budget experts predicted, would drive the deficit over $500 billion by 2015. As Washington issued bonds to cover the growing debt, China and other foreign governments awash in dollars because of the U.S. trade deficit snapped them up. But economists warned that this method of funding the debt would eventually dry up, leaving the tab to future generations of Americans.

Worsening the deficit crisis, Congress members continued the long-standing practice of quietly inserting into spending bills special provisions known as "earmarks" that benefited their districts. A 2005 highway bill included 6,000 earmarks promoting pet projects, including two "bridges to nowhere" proposed by Alaska senator Ted Stevens.

Hurricane Katrina Worst natural disaster in U.S. history; destroyed much of New Orleans and Gulf Coast in August 2005

Hurricane Katrina Tests the Bush Administration

In August 2005, **Hurricane Katrina** struck the Gulf Coast, taking as many as 1,400 lives. Coastal areas of Alabama, Mississippi, and Louisiana suffered massive damage. Disrupted shipping on the Mississippi River hurt corn and soybean growers far to the north. Katrina and a subsequent hurricane smashed oil refineries and offshore oil rigs.

The most catastrophic damage hit New Orleans, the legendary "Big Easy" at the mouth of the Mississippi. Much of the city lies below sea level, protected by levees from the Gulf of Mexico and Lake Pontchartrain. As levees burst under Katrina's storm surge, rampaging water flooded New Orleans's lower sections, populated mainly by poor blacks. Many residents drowned or died awaiting rescue. Thousands poured into New Orleans's Superdome, which soon became a squalid disaster zone. Some died of heat prostration as they waited along highways for rescue. Public schools, churches, and hospitals closed their doors. In May 2006, New Orleans's population was only about 40 percent of its pre-storm level.

As New Orleans endured the worst natural disaster in recent U.S. history, the government response at all levels was appallingly inadequate. FEMA head Michael Brown, a political appointee with no disaster experience, proved hopelessly ineffectual. Though initially praised by Bush ("Heck of a job, Brownie"), he soon resigned. President Bush made token visits and delivered a TV speech in the city's historic district, but the administration's performance did not match the president's rhetoric.

The distribution of emergency relief funds involved massive fraud. FEMA spent $900 million on 26,000 mobile homes, many of which sat empty and unused. Worse,

New Orleans in the Aftermath of Hurricane Katrina, September 1, 2005
Four days after the city's levees burst and flood waters devastated their homes, New Orleans residents await evacuation to the Superdome, which quickly becomes a scene of nightmarish conditions as thousands of desperate people crowded in.

by summer 2006 no coherent plan had emerged for reconstructing New Orleans's destroyed districts or bringing back the city's scattered residents. The levees were hastily repaired, yet no one knew how they would withstand future hurricanes. Recovery in the hardest-hit parts of the city remained stalled. As streets stood silent and empty, with no electricity and rows of shattered and abandoned houses, sections of New Orleans resembled a ghost town.

Extending Republican Influence: From the Supreme Court to K Street

When Supreme Court justice Sandra Day O'Connor, a Reagan appointee, announced her retirement in July 2005, Bush nominated as her replacement federal appeals-court judge John G. Roberts, Jr., who had held posts in the Reagan Justice Department and White House. When Chief Justice William Rehnquist died in September, Bush nominated Roberts as chief justice. He won easy Senate confirmation while revealing little about his judicial philosophy.

To fill the second vacancy, Bush nominated Samuel Alito, Jr., a federal appeals-court judge enthusiastically supported by conservatives. As a Justice Department lawyer in the Reagan administration, and later as a judge, Alito had espoused a very broad view of the powers of the executive branch—a view embraced by the Bush administration to justify its actions at home and abroad after 9/11. Alito, too, won confirmation, though on a much closer vote than Roberts. The Court now had five Roman Catholic justices, something unthinkable in earlier eras of anti-Catholic prejudice.

On the subject of *Roe* v. *Wade,* public opinion remained remarkably consistent, with most leading polls showing about 55 percent of Americans supporting legal abortions with certain restrictions, 24 percent favoring no restrictions at all, and 20 percent believing that all abortion should be banned.

As Supreme Court politics drew the nation's attention, so did the growing influence of Washington lobbyists. Lobbying has been a part of American politics from the beginning. Today, many Washington lobbyists, often ex-legislators or legislative aides, have offices on K Street, near the White House. Lobbyists' influence grew enormously during the ascendancy of Congressman Tom DeLay of Texas, the Republican majority whip (1995–2003) and majority leader (2003–2005). The ranks of registered lobbyists expanded from around 15,000 in 2000 to nearly 33,000 in 2005.

A series of high-visibility cases in 2005 focused attention on lobbyists and the role of money in politics. In September, DeLay resigned as majority leader after his indictment by a Texas grand jury for violating state election laws. In December, a federal grand jury indicted Jack Abramoff, a high-flying Washington lobbyist with close ties to DeLay. The indictments of Abramoff and a top aide alleged that they had obtained millions of dollars from corporations interested in influencing legislation. Much of this money went as bribes or campaign donations to Congress members— mostly Republicans but also some prominent Democrats. Pleading guilty at his hearing early in 2006, Abramoff admitted "a multitude of mistakes."

DeLay and Abramoff emerged as symbols of a corrupt system by which lobbyists influenced legislation through contributions, gifts, lavish dinners, expensive golf junkets, and hiring politicians' relatives. As public disgust mounted, politicians scrambled to return Abramoff's contributions, distance themselves from lobbyists, and regulate lobbyists' behavior more strictly. Whether the flurry of reform would reduce the power of money in government in the long run remained unclear.

Debating Immigration   The thorny issue of immigration reform surged to prominence in 2006. Attention focused on the estimated 11 million illegal immigrants, 78 percent of them from Mexico or elsewhere in Latin America, up from 3.9 million in 1992. Many worked for low wages in a "shadow economy" as migrant agricultural laborers, motel cleaners, janitors, gardeners, fast-food employees, and nursing-home attendants, or in food-processing plants.

In 2001, President Bush had proposed a "guest worker" program by which short-term immigrants would receive temporary work visas requiring them to return to their own country when the permit expired. When the administration introduced an immigration-reform bill late in 2005, debate about this program again seized public attention.

Emotions ran high. Some invoked America's tradition of welcoming newcomers, symbolized by the Statue of Liberty, and argued that the undocumented immigrants did the hard but necessary work that few others would do. Others argued that if undocumented immigrants working for low wages were excluded, the law of supply-and-demand would push up the wages for these jobs and U.S. citizens would take them, increasing opportunities for the unemployed.

As the debate went on, private citizens in the Southwest organized the Minuteman Project in 2005 to monitor the U.S.-Mexican border and report illegal entries to the Border Patrol. Late in 2005, the House of Representatives passed a tough immigration bill introduced by Wisconsin's James Sensenbrenner. This bill required the deportation of illegal aliens, called for the construction of a 700-mile barrier along the U.S.-Mexican border, and made it a felony for anyone to help undocumented immigrants.

Reaction to the Sensenbrenner bill was swift. Catholic bishops denounced the criminalizing of aid to illegal immigrants and advised priests to disobey such a law. In March and April 2006, immigrant advocates organized protest demonstrations. Over half a million marched in Los Angeles; 100,000 in Chicago. Spanish-language radio stations and TV channels—an increasingly important segment of the mass media—supported the demonstrations.

A backlash quickly erupted. "My first thought is anger, folks," declared right-wing radio pundit Rush Limbaugh. In the Senate, meanwhile, a bipartisan bill provided for beefed-up border control, but also established procedures by which undocumented immigrants could eventually secure citizenship. With opponents lining up to denounce this as a covert form of "amnesty" for illegal immigrants, the bill failed. By mid-2008, the legislative outcome of immigration reform remained uncertain.

The Elections of 2006 and 2008

Mid-term elections often focus on local issues. In 2006, however, the voters rendered a stinging judgment on the Iraq War, the Republican Congress, and the Bush administration. Even President Bush admitted that his party had taken a "thumping." In the House of Representatives, the Democrats won at least 29 seats, to regain the majority. They also won control of the Senate, by the barest of margins, 51–49. The number of women in the Senate inched upward, from 14 to 16, a record high.

The results made clear voters' discontent over the nation's direction, and especially over the Iraq War, from the deceptions with which it was launched to the disastrous way it was conducted. Facing this reality, President Bush the day after the election announced the resignation of Defense Secretary Donald Rumsfeld, a chief architect of the war.

Other issues influencing the outcome were massive federal budget deficits and a constant stream of corruption and personal scandals that dominated the news in the months before the election. Facing all these negatives, the Republicans could not capitalize on favorable economic news, such as a rising stock market, lower gas prices, and falling unemployment. In addition, new technologies loomed large in the campaign, including computerized phone banks, video cameras and blogs that publicized candidates' embarrassing gaffes, and even the personal websites on YouTube.

The Democratic victories meant new Congressional leadership in 2007: Harry Reid of Nevada as Senate Majority Leader, and Nancy Pelosi of San Francisco as Speaker of the House of Representatives, the first woman to hold that post. At a victory party in Washington, D.C., Pelosi told her fellow Democrats: "Today we have made history. Now let us make progress." The Democratic victory in 2006 did not translate into rapid progress, however. Republican opposition and presidential vetoes handed the Democrats a series of legislative defeats. Voter disgruntlement reached new heights in 2007 and early 2008. Surveys showed that most Americans had lost faith in both the president and Congress, and that they wanted the troops back from Iraq.

Economic woes added to the dismay. In 2007, it was revealed that billions of dollars of securities backed by so-called subprime loans, given by mortgage companies to homeowners with poor credit, were practically worthless. The resulting credit crisis spooked the financial markets and popped the housing bubble. Rising housing prices had subsidized the American consumer's spending habits since 2001. Now, reports of flat or falling home prices stoked fears of a recession. Worse still, a combination of geopolitical fears and oil speculation drove gas prices above $4 per gallon, the highest ever and more than double the price when George Bush and Dick Cheney—two former oil company executives—took office.

Frustration with the status quo boiled over in the early stages of the 2008 presidential election. Out of a crowded field of contenders, voters in the Republican primaries and caucuses selected Senator John McCain of Arizona to run in the November general election. McCain's plainspoken directness and reputation as a maverick were well-suited to a restless electorate. McCain had also criticized Bush's handling of the war in Iraq and advocated sending more U.S. troops into the conflict.

The antiestablishment sentiment was even stronger on the Democratic side. In a hotly contested race, Democratic primary voters rejected two well-known names—Senator John Edwards, who ran for vice president in 2004, and Senator Hillary Clinton, wife of former president Bill Clinton—in favor of a relatively unknown, forty-six-year old, African-American senator from Illinois, Barack Obama. Although little separated the three candidates on the issues, Obama's opposition to the Iraq war, spellbinding oratory, and calls for change jibed well with the mood of Democratic voters.

The nominees for president formed a study in contrasts. On one side was the energetic and patriotic McCain, seventy-two years of age, a Navy veteran with twenty-six years of experience in Congress. Against him stood the cool and unflappable Obama, a former community organizer and law professor. McCain took a risk in selecting the folksy Sarah Palin, Governor of Alaska, as his vice presidential running mate. Obama made a comparatively safe choice and partnered with the seasoned Joe Biden, senator from Delaware. On the campaign trail, Palin hammered away at Obama's past contact with a 1960s-era radical named Bill Ayers (they were once on a charitable foundation together); McCain painted Obama as dangerously untested and even naïve. Unfazed, Obama repeatedly tied

Obama and Biden.
President-elect Barack Obama, left, with Joseph Biden at his election night party in Chicago's Grant Park, November 4, 2008. "At this defining moment," said Obama, "change has come to America."

McCain's voting record and policies to the deeply unpopular President George W. Bush. Obama's soaring speeches were laced with calls for common purpose and hope for a better day. Chants of "Yes we can!" resounded at his huge rallies.

Pollsters initially predicted a tight race. But then, an economic calamity transformed the election and paved the way for a decisive and historic result. Ever since the collapse of brokerage house Bear Stearns in March 2008, a worried Wall Street struggled to contain the damage from the subprime loan crisis. In early September, anxiety gave way to panic. Saddled with billions in worthless mortgage-backed securities, Fannie Mae and Freddie Mac—holding about half of the nation's mortgage debt—were placed under government control. Later that month came the bankruptcies of Lehman Brothers and Washington Mutual; the fire-sale acquisition of Merrill Lynch; and the government bailout of insurance giant AIG. The news on Main Street was just as dire. The Dow Jones Industrial average, a bellwether for retirement accounts, fell 35 percent; global markets sank; the job market tightened; consumer confidence plunged; and millions of homeowners faced foreclosure. Some economists warned darkly of a "second Great Depression."

President Bush tried to ease the global credit crisis with a $700 billion financial rescue package. But conservative Republicans in Congress opposed it and many voters saw it as a boondoggle for corporate malefactors. In a moment of high political drama, John McCain abruptly left the campaign trail and went to Washington to save the imperiled rescue package. In the end, both McCain and Obama voted for the bill, which passed. But the incident exposed McCain to attacks that he was "erratic" and linked him more closely to the unpopular George W. Bush. Obama's poll numbers shot up. On Election Day, Obama took 53% of the popular vote and made deep inroads into Republican strongholds, winning North Carolina, Virginia, Florida, and Indiana. Democrats gained eighteen seats in the House and six in the Senate, padding their lead in both chambers. While Republicans lamented their bad luck, Democrats hailed the outcome as a repudiation of Republican policies and a final verdict on the Bush years.

Beyond partisan politics lay deeper meanings. Significantly, the topic of race rarely appeared on the campaign trail. Fears that white Americans would refuse to vote for a black president proved largely unfounded. A majority of whites under the age of thirty and about two-thirds of all Hispanics voted for Obama. It was no doubt too early to conclude that America had entered a "post-racial" age. But it was also clear that something remarkable had happened. Barack Obama—son of an immigrant from Kenya and a white woman from Kansas—had been chosen to lead the world's most powerful nation. Facing looming problems at home and abroad, and with hope intermixed with fear, America prepared to inaugurate its first black president on January 20, 2009—almost exactly one hundred years after the founding of the NAACP.

Conclusion

In 2001, accepting the Nobel Peace Prize a few weeks after 9/11, UN Secretary General Kofi Annan said: "We have entered the third millennium through a gate of fire." But Annan went on to evoke the vision that had inspired the UN's founders in 1945. Despite the hatred and inequalities

CHECKING IN

- Bush's plan to privatize social security faltered; a new Medicare drug benefit program, added to the costs of the military operation in Iraq, resulted in ballooning budget deficits.

- Hurricane Katrina obliterated much of New Orleans and the Gulf Coast; the federal response was widely viewed as inadequate.

- Bush appointed two conservatives, John Roberts and Samuel Alito, Jr., to the U.S. Supreme Court; a series of high-profile political scandals disgusted voters.

- Various proposals to reform immigration policy failed, leaving the issue unresolved; Democrats reclaimed the House and Senate in the 2006 midterm elections.

- Falling housing values and rising gas prices deepened the electorate's petulant mood; a yearning for change manifested in the 2008 presidential primaries, when voters showed a preference for anti-establishment candidates.

dividing nations and peoples, he insisted, the fate of all Earth's inhabitants is interconnected. The task of the twenty-first century, he said, is to achieve "a new, more profound awareness of the sanctity and dignity of every human life, regardless of race or religion. . . . Humanity is indivisible."

As we conclude this history of America and its people, what is the "enduring vision" of our title? There is, of course, no single vision, but many. That is part of America's meaning. Nor is this a vision of a foreordained national destiny unfolding effortlessly, but rather of successive generations' laborious, often frustrating struggle to define what their common life as a people should be. For all the failures, setbacks, and wrong turns, the shared visions, at their best, are rooted in hope, not fear. In 1980, Jesse de la Cruz, a Mexican-American woman who fought for years to improve conditions for California's migrant workers, summed up the philosophy that kept her going: "Is America progressing toward the better? . . . We're the ones that are gonna do it. We have to keep on struggling. . . . With us, there's a saying: *La esperanza muere al ultimo.* Hope dies last. You can't lose hope. If you lose hope, that's losing everything."

Chapter Summary

 DOWNLOAD THE MP3 AUDIO FILE OF THE CHAPTER SUMMARY, AND LISTEN TO IT ON THE GO.

How did the Bush administration respond to the September 11 attacks, internationally and domestically? (page 760)

The 9/11 attacks catapulted the United States into a shadowy war on terrorism. An American-led coalition invaded Afghanistan to drive out al Qaeda and overthrow the Islamic Taliban government. At home, a new, cabinet-level agency, the Department of Homeland Security, was created; Congress enacted the controversial Patriot Act, which the administration said was necessary to combat terrorism but which critics considered a danger to civil liberties. Bush identified Iraq as part of an "Axis of Evil" that also included North Korea and Iran. The administration claimed that Saddam Hussein was linked to al Qaeda and that he was building weapons of mass destruction (neither turned out to be accurate). With little global support, Bush invaded Iraq and routed Saddam Hussein; a major insurgency followed, fueled largely by sectarian conflicts among the Iraqi people.

Beyond security concerns, what economic and social issues did Bush address in his first term? (page 765)

The collapse of the technology sector of the stock market triggered a recession. The spectacular bankruptcy of the Enron Corporation was only the first of a succession of corporate scandals involving misconduct by top management. On the domestic front, Bush pursued a conservative agenda, including massive tax cuts (which enlarged the budget deficit), education reform labeled "No Child Left Behind," an energy bill that provided tax breaks to energy companies, and opposition to stem-cell research. Bush won reelection in 2004 by stressing national security and moral issues. Republicans increased their control in Congress.

What challenges faced the United States in the Middle East and elsewhere in the world after 2000? (page 769)

Domestic support for the war eroded amid worsening sectarian violence in Iraq, revelations of abuses by the U.S. military and domestic spying in the name of security, and skepticism about the administration's case for invading Iraq. Other troubling world developments included worsening Israeli-Palestinian relations; nuclear programs in North Korea and Iran; and China's growing economic and military power. As global warming and other environmental hazards roused concern, the Bush administration downplayed the threat and rejected international efforts to address the problem.

What demographic and economic trends have most shaped contemporary America? (page 775)

Major social trends in these years included continuing migration to the South and West, chronic inner-city problems, and increasing ethnic diversity as the Hispanic and Asian populations grew. Increased immigration, especially from Latin America and Asia, ignited a debate about whether such an influx could be assimilated and whether American diversity would be a melting pot or a salad bowl in which ethnic identities remained strong. On the economic front, the long-term shift from industrial production to an information-based and service economy proceeded, and a massive tide of foreign imports stirred uneasiness, especially in the troubled domestic auto industry.

What were the most pressing domestic issues after 2004? (page 779)

In his troubled second term, Bush persuaded Congress to pass a costly prescription-drug benefit for Medicare recipients and appointed two conservative jurists to the Supreme Court. But he failed, however, in his efforts to partially privatize Social Security and reform immigration policy. The administration's much-criticized response to Hurricane Katrina prompted questions about its competence and further drove down Bush's approval ratings. Riding a wave of voter discontent, Democrats reclaimed control of Congress in the 2006 midterm elections. As the Iraq War dragged on, the housing market collapsed, and gas prices spiked, the dominant theme in the early stages of the 2008 presidential campaign was "change." As Republican primary and caucus voters chose as their candidate Arizona senator John McCain, a Vietnam POW with a reputation as a maverick, the Democrats opted for a young and charismatic African-American senator from Illinois, Barack Obama. Obama won a decisive victory in the general election.

Appendix

DECLARATION OF INDEPENDENCE

IN CONGRESS, JULY 4, 1776

The Unanimous Declaration of the Thirteen United States of America

When, in the course of human events, it becomes necessary for one people to dissolve the political bands which have connected them with another, and to assume, among the powers of the earth, the separate and equal station to which the laws of nature and of nature's God entitle them, a decent respect to the opinions of mankind requires that they should declare the causes which impel them to the separation.

We hold these truths to be self-evident: That all men are created equal; that they are endowed by their Creator with certain unalienable rights; that among these are life, liberty, and the pursuit of happiness; that, to secure these rights, governments are instituted among men, deriving their just powers from the consent of the governed; that whenever any form of government becomes destructive of these ends, it is the right of the people to alter or to abolish it, and to institute new government, laying its foundation on such principles, and organizing its powers in such form, as to them shall seem most likely to effect their safety and happiness. Prudence, indeed, will dictate that governments long established should not be changed for light and transient causes; and accordingly all experience hath shown that mankind are more disposed to suffer, while evils are sufferable, than to right themselves by abolishing the forms to which they are accustomed. But when a long train of abuses and usurpations, pursuing invariably the same object, evinces a design to reduce them under absolute despotism, it is their right, it is their duty, to throw off such government, and to provide new guards for their future security. Such has been the patient sufferance of these colonies; and such is now the necessity which constrains them to alter their former systems of government. The history of the present King of Great Britain is a history of repeated injuries and usurpations, all having in direct object the establishment of an absolute tyranny over these states. To prove this, let facts be submitted to a candid world.

He has refused his assent to laws, the most wholesome and necessary for the public good.

He has forbidden his governors to pass laws of immediate and pressing importance, unless suspended in their operation till his assent should be obtained; and, when so suspended, he has utterly neglected to attend to them.

He has refused to pass other laws for the accommodation of large districts of people, unless those people would relinquish the right of representation in the legislature, a right inestimable to them, and formidable to tyrants only.

He has called together legislative bodies at places unusual, uncomfortable, and distant from the depository of their public records, for the sole purpose of fatiguing them into compliance with his measures.

He has dissolved representative houses repeatedly, for opposing, with manly firmness, his invasions on the rights of the people.

He has refused for a long time, after such dissolutions, to cause others to be elected; whereby the legislative powers, incapable of annihilation, have returned to the people at large for their exercise; the state remaining, in the mean time, exposed to all the dangers of invasions from without and convulsions within.

He has endeavored to prevent the population of these states; for that purpose obstructing the laws of naturalization of foreigners; refusing to pass others to encourage their migration hither, and raising the conditions of new appropriation of lands.

He has obstructed the administration of justice, by refusing his assent to laws for establishing judiciary powers.

He has made judges dependent on his will alone, for the tenure of their offices, and the amount and payment of their salaries.

He has erected a multitude of new offices, and sent hither swarms of officers to harass our people and eat out their substance.

He has kept among us, in times of peace, standing armies, without the consent of our legislatures.

He has affected to render the military independent of, and superior to, the civil power.

He has combined with others to subject us to a jurisdiction foreign to our constitution, and unacknowledged by our laws, giving his assent to their acts of pretended legislation:

For quartering large bodies of armed troops among us;

For protecting them, by a mock trial, from punishment for any murders which they should commit on the inhabitants of these states;

For cutting off our trade with all parts of the world;

For imposing taxes on us without our consent;

For depriving us, in many cases, of the benefits of trial by jury;

For transporting us beyond seas, to be tried for pretended offenses;

For abolishing the free system of English laws in a neighboring province, establishing therein an arbitrary government, and enlarging its boundaries, so as to render it at once an example and fit instrument for introducing the same absolute rule into these colonies;

For taking away our charters, abolishing our most valuable laws, and altering fundamentally the forms of our governments;

For suspending our own legislatures, and declaring themselves invested with power to legislate for us in all cases whatsoever.

He has abdicated government here, by declaring us out of his protection and waging war against us.

He has plundered our seas, ravaged our coasts, burned our towns, and destroyed the lives of our people.

He is at this time transporting large armies of foreign mercenaries to complete the works of death, desolation, and tyranny already begun with circumstances of cruelty and perfidy scarcely paralleled in the most barbarous ages, and totally unworthy of the head of a civilized nation.

He has constrained our fellow-citizens, taken captive on the high seas, to bear arms against their country, to become the executioners of their friends and brethren, or to fall themselves by their hands.

He has excited domestic insurrection among us, and has endeavored to bring on the inhabitants of our frontiers the merciless Indian savages, whose known rule of warfare is an undistinguished destruction of all ages, sexes, and conditions.

In every stage of these oppressions we have petitioned for redress in the most humble terms; our repeated petitions have been answered only by repeated injury. A prince, whose character is thus marked by every act which may define a tyrant, is unfit to be the ruler of a free people.

Nor have we been wanting in our attentions to our British brethren. We have warned them, from time to time, of attempts by their legislature to extend an unwarrantable jurisdiction over us. We have reminded them of the circumstances of our emigration and settlement here. We have appealed to their native justice and magnanimity; and we have conjured them by the ties of our common kindred, to disavow these usurpations, which would inevitably interrupt our connections and correspondence. They, too, have been deaf to the voice of justice and of consanguinity. We must, therefore, acquiesce in the necessity which denounces our separation, and hold them, as we hold the rest of mankind, enemies in war, in peace friends.

We, therefore, the representatives of the United States of America, in General Congress assembled, appealing to the Supreme Judge of the world for the rectitude of our intentions, do, in the name and by the authority of the good people of these colonies, solemnly publish and declare, that these United Colonies are, and of right ought to be, FREE AND INDEPENDENT STATES; that they are absolved from all allegiance to the British crown, and that all political connection between them and the state of Great Britain is, and ought to be, totally dissolved; and that, as free and independent states, they have full power to levy war, conclude peace, contract alliances, establish commerce, and do all other acts and things which independent states may of right do. And for the support of this declaration, with a firm reliance on the protection of Divine Providence, we mutually pledge to each other our lives, our fortunes, and our sacred honor.

JOHN HANCOCK [*President*]
[*and fifty-five others*]

CONSTITUTION OF THE UNITED STATES OF AMERICA

PREAMBLE

We the people of the United States, in order to form a more perfect union, establish justice, insure domestic tranquility, provide for the common defense, promote the general welfare, and secure the blessings of liberty to ourselves and our posterity, do ordain and establish this CONSTITUTION for the United States of America.

ARTICLE I

Section 1.   All legislative powers herein granted shall be vested in a Congress of the United States, which shall consist of a Senate and a House of Representatives.

Section 2.   The House of Representatives shall be composed of members chosen every second year by the people of the several States, and the electors in each State shall have the qualifications requisite for electors of the most numerous branch of the State Legislature.

No person shall be a Representative who shall not have attained to the age of twenty-five years, and been seven years a citizen of the United States, and who shall not, when elected, be an inhabitant of that State in which he shall be chosen.

Representatives and direct taxes shall be apportioned among the several States which may be included within this Union, according to their respective numbers, *which shall be determined by adding to the whole number of free persons, including those bound to service for a term of years and excluding Indians not taxed, three-fifths of all other persons.* The actual enumeration shall be made within three years after the first meeting of the Congress of the United States, and within every subsequent term of ten years, in such manner as they shall by law direct. The number of Representatives shall not exceed one for every thirty thousand, but each State shall have at least one Representative; *and until such enumeration shall be made, the State of New Hampshire shall be entitled to choose three, Massachusetts eight, Rhode Island and Providence Plantations one, Connecticut five, New York six, New Jersey four, Pennsylvania eight, Delaware one, Maryland six, Virginia ten, North Carolina five, South Carolina five, and Georgia three.*

When vacancies happen in the representation from any State, the Executive authority thereof shall issue writs of election to fill such vacancies.

Note: Passages no longer in effect are printed in italic type.

The House of Representatives shall choose their Speaker and other officers; and shall have the sole power of impeachment.

Section 3.   The Senate of the United States shall be composed of two Senators from each State, *chosen by the legislature thereof,* for six years; and each Senator shall have one vote.

Immediately after they shall be assembled in consequence of the first election, they shall be divided as equally as may be into three classes. The seats of the Senators of the first class shall be vacated at the expiration of the second year, of the second class at the expiration of the fourth year, and of the third class at the expiration of the sixth year, so that one-third may be chosen every second year; and if vacancies happen by resignation or otherwise, during the recess of the legislature of any State, the Executive thereof may make temporary appointments until the next meeting of the legislature, which shall then fill such vacancies.

No person shall be a Senator who shall not have attained to the age of thirty years, and been nine years a citizen of the United States, and who shall not, when elected, be an inhabitant of that State for which he shall be chosen.

The Vice President of the United States shall be President of the Senate, but shall have no vote, unless they be equally divided.

The Senate shall choose their other officers, and also a President *pro tempore,* in the absence of the Vice President, or when he shall exercise the office of the President of the United States.

The Senate shall have the sole power to try all impeachments. When sitting for that purpose, they shall be on oath or affirmation. When the President of the United States is tried, the Chief Justice shall preside: and no person shall be convicted without the concurrence of two-thirds of the members present.

Judgment in cases of impeachment shall not extend further than to removal from the office, and disqualification to hold and enjoy any office of honor, trust or profit under the United States; but the party convicted shall nevertheless be liable and subject to indictment, trial, judgment and punishment, according to law.

Section 4. The times, places and manner of holding elections for Senators and Representatives shall be prescribed in each State by the legislature thereof; but the Congress may at any time by law make or alter such regulations, except as to the places of choosing Senators.

The Congress shall assemble at least once in every year, and such meeting *shall be on the first Monday in December, unless they shall by law appoint a different day.*

Section 5. Each house shall be the judge of the elections, returns and qualifications of its own members, and a majority of each shall constitute a quorum to do business; but a smaller number may adjourn from day to day, and may be authorized to compel the attendance of absent members, in such manner, and under such penalties, as each house may provide.

Each house may determine the rules of its proceedings, punish its members for disorderly behavior, and with the concurrence of two-thirds, expel a member.

Each house shall keep a journal of its proceedings, and from time to time publish the same, excepting such parts as may in their judgment require secrecy; and the yeas and nays of the members of either house on any question shall, at the desire of one-fifth of those present, be entered on the journal.

Neither house, during the session of Congress, shall, without the consent of the other, adjourn for more than three days, nor to any other place than that in which the two houses shall be sitting.

Section 6. The Senators and Representatives shall receive a compensation for their services, to be ascertained by law and paid out of the treasury of the United States. They shall in all cases except treason, felony and breach of the peace, be privileged from arrest during their attendance at the session of their respective houses, and in going to and returning from the same; and for any speech or debate in either house, they shall not be questioned in any other place.

No Senator or Representative shall, during the time for which he was elected, be appointed to any civil office under the authority of the United States, which shall have been created, or the emoluments whereof shall have been increased, during such time; and no person holding any office under the United States shall be a member of either house during his continuance in office.

Section 7. All bills for raising revenue shall originate in the House of Representatives; but the Senate may propose or concur with amendments as on other bills.

Every bill which shall have passed the House of Representatives and the Senate, shall, before it become a law, be presented to the President of the United States; if he approve he shall sign it, but if not he shall return it with objections to that house in which it originated, who shall enter the objections at large on their journal, and proceed to reconsider it. If after such reconsideration two-thirds of that house shall agree to pass the bill, it shall be sent, together with the objections, to the other house, by which it shall likewise be reconsidered, and, if approved by two-thirds of that house, it shall become a law. But in all such cases the votes of both houses shall be determined by yeas and nays, and the names of the persons voting for and against the bill shall be entered on the journal of each house respectively. If any bill shall not be returned by the President within ten days (Sundays excepted) after it shall have been presented to him, the same shall be a law, in like manner as if he had signed it, unless the Congress by their adjournment prevent its return, in which case it shall not be a law.

Every order, resolution, or vote to which the concurrence of the Senate and House of Representatives may be necessary (except on a question of adjournment) shall be presented to the President of the United States; and before the same shall take effect, shall be approved by him, or being disapproved by him, shall be repassed by two-thirds of the Senate and House of Representatives, according to the rules and limitations prescribed in the case of a bill.

Section 8. The Congress shall have power

To lay and collect taxes, duties, imposts, and excises, to pay the debts and provide for the common defense and general welfare of the United States; but all duties, imposts and excises shall be uniform throughout the United States;

To borrow money on the credit of the United States;

To regulate commerce with foreign nations, and among the several States, and with the Indian tribes;

To establish an uniform rule of naturalization, and uniform laws on the subject of bankruptcies throughout the United States;

To coin money, regulate the value thereof, and of foreign coin, and fix the standard of weights and measures;

To provide for the punishment of counterfeiting the securities and current coin of the United States;

To establish post offices and post roads;

To promote the progress of science and useful arts by securing for limited times to authors and inventors the exclusive right to their respective writings and discoveries;

To constitute tribunals inferior to the Supreme Court;

To define and punish piracies and felonies committed on the high seas and offenses against the law of nations;

To declare war, grant letters of marque and reprisal, and make rules concerning captures on land and water;

To raise and support armies, but no appropriation of money to that use shall be for a longer term than two years;

To provide and maintain a navy;

To make rules for the government and regulation of the land and naval forces;

To provide for calling forth the militia to execute the laws of the Union, suppress insurrections, and repel invasions;

To provide for organizing, arming, and disciplining the militia, and for governing such part of them as may be employed in the service of the United States, reserving to the States respectively the appointment of the officers, and the authority of training the militia according to the discipline prescribed by Congress;

To exercise exclusive legislation in all cases whatsoever, over such district (not exceeding ten miles square) as may, by cession of particular States, and the acceptance of Congress, become the seat of government of the United States, and to exercise like authority over all places purchased by the consent of the legislature of the State, in which the same shall be, for erection of forts, magazines, arsenals, dock-yards, and other needful buildings;—and

To make all laws which shall be necessary and proper for carrying into execution the foregoing powers, and all other powers vested by this Constitution in the government of the United States, or in any department or officer thereof.

Section 9. *The migration or importation of such persons as any of the States now existing shall think proper to admit shall not be prohibited by the Congress prior to the year 1808; but a tax or duty may be imposed on such importation, not exceeding $10 for each person.*

The privilege of the writ of habeas corpus shall not be suspended, unless when in cases of rebellion or invasion the public safety may require it.

No bill of attainder or ex post facto law shall be passed.

No capitation, or other direct, tax shall be laid, unless in proportion to the census or enumeration herein before directed to be taken.

No tax or duty shall be laid on articles exported from any State.

No preference shall be given by any regulation of commerce or revenue to the ports of one State over those of another; nor shall vessels bound to, or from, one State, be obliged to enter, clear, or pay duties in another.

No money shall be drawn from the treasury, but in consequence of appropriations made by law; and a regular statement and account of the receipts and expenditures of all public money shall be published from time to time.

No title of nobility shall be granted by the United States: and no person holding any office of profit or trust under them, shall, without the consent of the Congress, accept of any present, emolument, office, or title, of any kind whatever, from any king, prince, or foreign state.

Section 10. No State shall enter into any treaty, alliance, or confederation; grant letters of marque and reprisal; coin money; emit bills of credit; make anything but gold and silver coin a tender in payment of debts; pass any bill of attainder, ex post facto law, or law impairing the obligation of contracts, or grant any title of nobility.

No State shall, without the consent of Congress, lay any imposts or duties on imports or exports, except what may be absolutely necessary for executing its inspection laws: and the net produce of all duties and imposts, laid by any State on imports or exports, shall be for the use of the treasury of the United States; and all such laws shall be subject to the revision and control of the Congress.

No State shall, without the consent of Congress, lay any duty of tonnage, keep troops or ships of war in time of peace, enter into any agreement or compact with another State, or with a foreign power, or engage in war, unless actually invaded, or in such imminent danger as will not admit of delay.

ARTICLE II

Section 1. The executive power shall be vested in a President of the United States of America. He shall hold his office during the term of four years, and, together with the Vice President, chosen for the same term, be elected as follows:

Each state shall appoint, in such manner as the legislature thereof may direct, a number of electors, equal to the whole number of Senators and Representatives to which the State may be entitled in the Congress; but no Senator or Representative, or person holding an office of trust or profit under the United States, shall be appointed an elector.

The electors shall meet in their respective States, and vote by ballot for two persons, of whom one at least shall not be an inhabitant of the same State with themselves. And they shall make a list of all the persons voted for, and of the number of votes for each; which list they shall sign and certify, and transmit sealed to the seat of government of the United States, directed to the President of the Senate. The President of the Senate shall, in the presence of the Senate and the House of Representatives, open all the certificates, and the votes shall then be counted. The person having the greatest number of votes shall be the President, if such number be a majority of the whole number of electors appointed; and if there be more than one who have such majority, and have an equal number of votes, then the House of Representatives shall immediately choose by ballot one of them for President; and if no person have a majority, then from the five highest on the list said house shall in like manner choose the President. But in choosing the President the votes shall be taken by States, the representation from each State having one vote; a quorum for this purpose shall consist of a member or members from two-thirds of the States, and a majority of all the States shall be necessary to a choice. In every case, after the choice of the President, the person having the greatest number of votes of the electors shall be the Vice President. But if there should remain two or more who have equal votes, the Senate shall choose from them by ballot the Vice President.

The Congress may determine the time of choosing the electors and the day on which they shall give their votes; which day shall be the same throughout the United States.

No person except a natural-born citizen, *or a citizen of the United States at the time of the adoption of this Constitution*, shall be eligible to the office of President; neither shall any person be eligible to that office who shall not have attained to the age of thirty-five years, and been fourteen years a resident within the United States.

In case of the removal of the President from office or of his death, resignation, or inability to discharge the powers and duties of the said office, the same shall devolve on the Vice President, and the Congress may by law provide for the case of removal, death, resignation, or inability, both of the President and Vice President, declaring what officer shall then act as President, and such officer shall act accordingly, until the disability be removed, or a President shall be elected.

The President shall, at stated times, receive for his services a compensation, which shall neither be increased nor diminished during the period for which he shall have been elected, and he shall not receive within that period any other emolument from the United States, or any of them.

Before he enter on the execution of his office, he shall take the following oath or affirmation:—"I do solemnly swear (or affirm) that I will faithfully execute the office of the President of the United States, and will to the best of my ability preserve, protect and defend the Constitution of the United States."

Section 2. The President shall be commander in chief of the army and navy of the United States, and of the militia of the several States, when called into the actual service of the United States; he may require the opinion, in writing, of the principal officer in each of the executive departments, upon any subject relating to the duties of their respective offices, and he shall have power to grant reprieves and pardons for offenses against the United States, except in cases of impeachment.

He shall have power, by and with the advice and consent of the Senate, to make treaties, provided two-thirds of the Senators present concur; and he shall nominate, and by and with the advice and consent of the Senate, shall appoint ambassadors, other public ministers and consuls, judges of the Supreme Court, and all other officers of the United States, whose appointments are not herein otherwise provided for, and which shall be established by law: but Congress may by law vest the appointment of such inferior officers, as they think proper, in the President alone, in the courts of law, or in the heads of departments.

The President shall have power to fill up all vacancies that may happen during the recess of the Senate, by granting commissions which shall expire at the end of their next session.

Section 3. He shall from time to time give to the Congress information of the state of the Union, and recommend to their consideration such measures as he shall judge necessary and expedient; he may, on extraordinary occasions, convene both houses, or either of them, and in case of disagreement between them, with respect to the time of adjournment, he may adjourn them to such time as he shall think proper; he shall receive ambassadors and other public ministers; he shall take care that the laws be faithfully executed, and shall commission all the officers of the United States.

Section 4. The President, Vice President and all civil officers of the United States shall be removed from office on impeachment for, and on conviction of, treason, bribery, or other high crimes and misdemeanors.

ARTICLE III

Section 1. The judicial power of the United States shall be vested in one Supreme Court, and in such inferior courts as the Congress may from time to time ordain and establish. The judges, both of the Supreme and inferior courts, shall hold their offices during good behavior, and shall, at stated times, receive for their services a compensation which shall not be diminished during their continuance in office.

Section 2. The judicial power shall extend to all cases, in law and equity, arising under this Constitution, the laws of the United States, and treaties made, or which shall be made, under their authority;—to all cases affecting ambassadors, other public ministers and consuls;—to all cases of admiralty and maritime jurisdiction;—to controversies to which the United States shall be a party;—to controversies between two or more States;—*between a State and citizens of another State;*—between citizens of different States;—between citizens of the same State claiming lands under grants of different States, and between a State, or the citizens thereof, and foreign states, citizens or subjects.

In all cases affecting ambassadors, other public ministers and consuls, and those in which a State shall be party, the Supreme Court shall have original jurisdiction. In all the other cases before mentioned, the Supreme Court shall have appellate jurisdiction, both as to law and fact, with such exceptions, and under such regulations, as the Congress shall make.

The trial of all crimes, except in cases of impeachment, shall be by jury; and such trial shall be held in the State where said crimes shall have been committed; but when not committed within any State, the trial shall be at such place or places as the Congress may by law have directed.

Section 3. Treason against the United States shall consist only in levying war against them, or in adhering to their enemies, giving them aid and comfort. No person shall be convicted of treason unless on the testimony of two witnesses to the same overt act, or on confession in open court.

The Congress shall have power to declare the punishment of treason, but no attainder of treason shall work corruption of blood, or forfeiture except during the life of the person attainted.

ARTICLE IV

Section 1. Full faith and credit shall be given in each State to the public acts, records, and judicial proceedings of every other State. And the Congress may by general laws prescribe the manner in which such acts, records, and proceedings shall be proved, and the effect thereof.

Section 2.   The citizens of each State shall be entitled to all privileges and immunities of citizens in the several States.

A person charged in any State with treason, felony, or other crime, who shall flee from justice, and be found in another State, shall on demand of the executive authority of the State from which he fled, be delivered up, to be removed to the State having jurisdiction of the crime.

No person held to service or labor in one State, under the laws thereof, escaping into another, shall, in consequence of any law or regulation therein, be discharged from such service or labor, but shall be delivered up on claim of the party to whom such service or labor may be due.

Section 3.   New States may be admitted by the Congress into this Union; but no new State shall be formed or erected within the jurisdiction of any other State; nor any State be formed by the junction of two or more States, or parts of States, without the consent of the legislatures of the States concerned as well as of the Congress.

The Congress shall have power to dispose of and make all needful rules and regulations respecting the territory or other property belonging to the United States; and nothing in this Constitution shall be so construed as to prejudice any claims of the United States, or of any particular State.

Section 4.   The United States shall guarantee to every State in this Union a republican form of government, and shall protect each of them against invasion; and on application of the legislature, or of the executive (when the legislature cannot be convened); against domestic violence.

ARTICLE V

The Congress, whenever two-thirds of both houses shall deem it necessary, shall propose amendments to this Constitution, or, on the application of the legislatures of two-thirds of the several States, shall call a convention for proposing amendments, which, in either case, shall be valid to all intents and purposes, as part of this Constitution, when ratified by the legislatures of three-fourths of the several States, or by conventions in three-fourths thereof, as the one or the other mode of ratification may be proposed by the Congress; provided *that no amendments which may be made prior to the year one thousand eight hundred and eight shall in any manner affect the first and fourth clauses in the ninth section of the first article;* and that no State, without its consent, shall be deprived of its equal suffrage in the Senate.

ARTICLE VI

All debts contracted and engagements entered into, before the adoption of this Constitution, shall be as valid against the United States under this Constitution, as under the Confederation.

This Constitution, and the laws of the United States which shall be made in pursuance thereof; and all treaties made, or which shall be made, under the authority of the United States, shall be the supreme law of the land; and the judges in every State shall be bound thereby, anything in the Constitution or laws of any State to the contrary notwithstanding.

The Senators and Representatives before mentioned, and the members of the several State legislatures, and all executive and judicial officers, both of the United States and of the several States, shall be bound by oath or affirmation to support this Constitution; but no religious test shall ever be required as a qualification to any office or public trust under the United States.

ARTICLE VII

The ratification of the conventions of nine States shall be sufficient for the establishment of this Constitution between the States so ratifying the same.

Done in Convention by the unanimous consent of the States present, the seventeenth day of September in the year of our Lord one thousand seven hundred and eighty-seven and of the Independence of the United States of America the twelfth. In witness whereof we have hereunto subscribed our names.

[Signed by]
G° WASHINGTON
Presidt and Deputy from Virginia
[*and thirty-eight others*]

AMENDMENTS TO THE CONSTITUTION

AMENDMENT I*

Congress shall make no law respecting an establishment of religion, or prohibiting the free exercise thereof; or abridging the freedom of speech, or of the press; or the right of the people peaceably to assemble, and to petition the government for a redress of grievances.

AMENDMENT II

A well-regulated militia being necessary to the security of a free State, the right of the people to keep and bear arms shall not be infringed.

AMENDMENT III

No soldier shall, in time of peace, be quartered in any house without the consent of the owner, nor in time of war, but in a manner to be prescribed by law.

AMENDMENT IV

The right of the people to be secure in their persons, houses, papers, and effects, against unreasonable searches and seizures, shall not be violated, and no warrants shall issue but upon probable cause, supported by oath or affirmation, and particularly describing the place to be searched, and the persons or things to be seized.

AMENDMENT V

No person shall be held to answer for a capital, or otherwise infamous crime, unless on a presentment or indictment of a grand jury, except in cases arising in the land or naval forces, or in the militia, when in actual service in time of war or public danger; nor shall any person be subject for the same offense to be twice put in jeopardy of life or limb; nor shall be compelled in any criminal case to be a witness against himself, nor be deprived of life, liberty, or property, without due process of law; nor shall private property be taken for public use without just compensation.

AMENDMENT VI

In all criminal prosecutions, the accused shall enjoy the right to a speedy and public trial, by an impartial jury of the State and district wherein the crime shall have been committed, which district shall have been previously ascertained by law, and to be informed of the nature and cause of the accusation; to be confronted with the witnesses against him; to have compulsory process for obtaining witnesses in his favor, and to have the assistance of counsel for his defense.

AMENDMENT VII

In suits at common law, where the value in controversy shall exceed twenty dollars, the right of trial by jury shall be preserved, and no fact tried by a jury shall be otherwise reexamined in any court of the United States, than according to the rules of the common law.

AMENDMENT VIII

Excessive bail shall not be required, nor excessive fines imposed, nor cruel and unusual punishments inflicted.

AMENDMENT IX

The enumeration in the Constitution, of certain rights, shall not be construed to deny or disparage others retained by the people.

AMENDMENT X

The powers not delegated to the United States by the Constitution, not prohibited by it to the States, are reserved to the States respectively, or to the people.

AMENDMENT XI   [*Adopted 1798*]

The judicial power of the United States shall not be construed to extend to any suit in law or equity, commenced or prosecuted against one of the United States by citizens of another State, or by citizens or subjects of any foreign state.

AMENDMENT XII   [*Adopted 1804*]

The electors shall meet in their respective States, and vote by ballot for President and Vice President, one of

---

* The first ten Amendments (Bill of Rights) were adopted in 1791.

whom, at least, shall not be an inhabitant of the same State with themselves; they shall name in their ballots the person voted for as President, and in distinct ballots the person voted for as Vice President, and they shall make distinct lists of all persons voted for as President, and of all persons voted for as Vice President, and of the number of votes for each, which lists they shall sign and certify, and transmit sealed to the seat of government of the United States, directed to the President of the Senate;—the President of the Senate shall, in the presence of the Senate and House of Representatives, open all the certificates and the votes shall then be counted;—the person having the greatest number of votes for President shall be the President, if such number be a majority of the whole number of electors appointed; and if no person have such majority, then from the persons having the highest numbers not exceeding three on the list of those voted for as President, the House of Representatives shall choose immediately, by ballot, the President. But in choosing the President, the votes shall be taken by States, the representation from each State having one vote; a quorum for this purpose shall consist of a member or members from two-thirds of the States, and a majority of all the States shall be necessary to a choice. And if the House of Representatives shall not choose a President whenever the right of choice shall devolve upon them, before *the fourth day of March* next following, then the Vice President shall act as President, as in the case of the death or other constitutional disability of the President.

The person having the greatest number of votes as Vice President shall be the Vice President, if such a number be a majority of the whole number of electors appointed; and if no person have a majority, then from the two highest numbers on the list the Senate shall choose the Vice President; a quorum for the purpose shall consist of two-thirds of the whole number of Senators, and a majority of the whole number shall be necessary to a choice. But no person constitutionally ineligible to the office of President shall be eligible to that of Vice President of the United States.

AMENDMENT XIII   [*Adopted 1865*]

Section 1.   Neither slavery nor involuntary servitude, except as a punishment for crime whereof the party shall have been duly convicted, shall exist within the United States, or any place subject to their jurisdiction.

Section 2.   Congress shall have power to enforce this article by appropriate legislation.

AMENDMENT XIV   [*Adopted 1868*]

Section 1.   All persons born or naturalized in the United States, and subject to the jurisdiction thereof, are citizens of the United States and of the State wherein they reside. No State shall make or enforce any law which shall abridge the privileges or immunities of citizens of the United States; nor shall any State deprive any person of life, liberty, or property, without due process of law; nor deny to any person within its jurisdiction the equal protection of the laws.

Section 2.   Representatives shall be apportioned among the several States according to their respective numbers, counting the whole number of persons in each State, excluding Indians not taxed. But when the right to vote at any election for the choice of Electors for President and Vice President of the United States, Representatives in Congress, the executive and judicial officers of a State, or the members of the legislature thereof, is denied to any of the male inhabitants of such State, being twenty-one years of age and citizens of the United States, or in any way abridged, except for participation in rebellion, or other crime, the basis of representation therein shall be reduced in the proportion which the number of such male citizens shall bear to the whole number of male citizens twenty-one years of age in such State.

Section 3.   No person shall be a Senator or Representative in Congress or Elector of President and Vice President, or hold any office, civil or military, under the United States, or under any State, who, having previously taken an oath, as a member of Congress, or as an officer of the United States, or as a member of any State legislature, or as an executive or judicial officer of any State, to support the Constitution of the United States, shall have engaged in insurrection or rebellion against the same, or given aid and comfort to the enemies thereof. Congress may, by a vote of two-thirds of each house, remove such disability.

Section 4.   The validity of the public debt of the United States, authorized by law, including debts incurred for payment of pensions and bounties for services in suppressing insurrection or rebellion, shall not be questioned. But neither the United States nor any State shall assume or pay any debt or obligation incurred in aid of insurrection or rebellion against the United States, or any claim for the loss or emancipation of any slave; but all such debts, obligations, and claims shall be held illegal and void.

Section 5. The Congress shall have the power to enforce, by appropriate legislation, the provisions of this article.

AMENDMENT XV   [Adopted 1870]

Section 1. The right of citizens of the United States to vote shall not be denied or abridged by the United States or by any State on account of race, color, or previous condition of servitude.

Section 2. The Congress shall have power to enforce this article by appropriate legislation.

AMENDMENT XVI   [Adopted 1913]

The Congress shall have power to lay and collect taxes on incomes, from whatever source derived, without apportionment among the several States, and without regard to any census or enumeration.

AMENDMENT XVII   [Adopted 1913]

Section 1. The Senate of the United States shall be composed of two Senators from each State, elected by the people thereof, for six years; and each Senator shall have one vote. The electors in each State shall have the qualifications requisite for electors of [voters for] the most numerous branch of the State legislatures.

Section 2. When vacancies happen in the representation of any State in the Senate, the executive authority of such State shall issue writs of election to fill such vacancies: Provided, that the Legislature of any State may empower the executive thereof to make temporary appointments until the people fill the vacancies by election as the Legislature may direct.

Section 3. This amendment shall not be so construed as to affect the election or term of any Senator chosen before it becomes valid as part of the Constitution.

AMENDMENT XVIII   [Adopted 1919l repealed 1933]

Section 1.   *After one year from the ratification of this article the manufacture, sale, or transportation of intoxicating liquors within, the importation thereof into, or the exportation thereof from the United States and all territory subject to the jurisdiction thereof, for beverage purposes, is hereby prohibited.*

Section 2.   *The Congress and the several States shall have concurrent power to enforce this article by appropriate legislation.*

Section 3.   *This article shall be inoperative unless it shall have been ratified as an amendment to the Constitution by the legislatures of the several States, as provided by the Constitution, within seven years from the date of the submission thereof to the States by the Congress.*

AMENDMENT XIX   [Adopted 1920]

Section 1. The right of citizens of the United States to vote shall not be denied or abridged by the United States or by any State on account of sex.

Section 2. The Congress shall have the power to enforce this article by appropriate legislation.

AMENDMENT XX   [Adopted 1933]

Section 1. The terms of the President and Vice President shall end at noon on the 20th day of January, and the terms of Senators and Representatives at noon on the 3d day of January, of the years in which such terms would have ended if this article had not been ratified; and the terms of their successors shall then begin.

Section 2. The Congress shall assemble at least once in every year, and such meeting shall begin at noon on the 3d day of January, unless they shall by law appoint a different day.

Section 3. If, at the time fixed for the beginning of the term of the President, the President-elect shall have died, the Vice President-elect shall become President. If a President shall not have been chosen before the time fixed for the beginning of his term, or if the President-elect shall have failed to qualify, then the Vice President-elect shall act as President until a President shall have qualified; and the Congress may by law provide for the case wherein neither a President-elect nor a Vice President-elect shall have qualified, declaring who shall then act as President, or the manner in which one who is to act shall be selected, and such persons shall act accordingly until a President or Vice President shall have qualified.

Section 4.   The Congress may by law provide for the case of the death of any of the persons from whom the House of Representatives may choose a President whenever the right of choice shall have devolved upon them, and for the case of the death of any of the persons from whom the Senate may choose a Vice President whenever the right of choice shall have devolved upon them.

Section 5.   Sections 1 and 2 shall take effect on the 15th day of October following the ratification of this article.

Section 6.   This article shall be inoperative unless it shall have been ratified as an amendment to the Constitution by the Legislatures of three-fourths of the several States within seven years from the date of its submission.

AMENDMENT XXI   [*Adopted 1933*]

Section 1.   The eighteenth article of amendment to the Constitution of the United States is hereby repealed.

Section 2.   The transportation or importation into any State, Territory, or Possession of the United States for delivery or use therein of intoxicating liquors, in violation of the laws thereof, is hereby prohibited.

Section 3.   This article shall be inoperative unless it shall have been ratified as an amendment to the Constitution by conventions in the several States, as provided in the Constitution, within seven years from the date of submission thereof to the States by the Congress.

AMENDMENT XXII   [*Adopted 1951*]

Section 1.   No person shall be elected to the office of President more than twice, and no person who has held

the office of President, or acted as President, for more than two years of a term to which some other person was elected President shall be elected to the office of President more than once. But this article shall not apply to any person holding the office of President when this article was proposed by the Congress, and shall not prevent any person who may be holding the office of President, or acting as President, during the term within which this article becomes operative from holding the office of President or acting as President during the remainder of such term.

Section 2.   This article shall be inoperative unless it shall have been ratified as an amendment to the Constitution by the legislatures of three-fourths of the several States within seven years from the date of its submission to the States by the Congress.

AMENDMENT XXIII   [*Adopted 1961*]

Section 1.   The District constituting the seat of Government of the United States shall appoint in such manner as the Congress may direct:

A number of electors of President and Vice President equal to the whole number of Senators and Representatives in Congress to which the District would be entitled if it were a State, but in no event more than the least populous State; they shall be in addition to those appointed by the States, but they shall be considered for the purposes of the election of President and Vice President, to be electors appointed by a State; and they shall meet in the District and perform such duties as provided by the twelfth article of amendment.

Section 2.   The Congress shall have the power to enforce this article by appropriate legislation.

AMENDMENT XXIV   [*Adopted 1964*]

Section 1.   The right of citizens of the United States to vote in any primary or other election for President or Vice President, for electors for President or Vice President, or for Senator or Representative in Congress, shall not be denied or abridged by the United States or any State by reason of failure to pay any poll tax or other tax.

Section 2.   The Congress shall have the power to enforce this article by appropriate legislation.

AMENDMENT XXV   [*Adopted 1967*]

Section 1.   In case of the removal of the President from office or of his death or resignation, the Vice President shall become President.

Section 2.   Whenever there is a vacancy in the office of the Vice President, the President shall nominate a Vice President who shall take office upon confirmation by a majority vote of both Houses of Congress.

Section 3.   Whenever the President transmits to the President pro tempore of the Senate and the Speaker of the House of Representatives his written declaration that he is unable to discharge the powers and duties of his office, and until he transmits to them a written declaration to the contrary, such powers and duties shall be discharged by the Vice President as Acting President.

Section 4.   Whenever the Vice President and a majority of either the principal officers of the executive departments or of such other body as Congress may by law provide, transmit to the President pro tempore of the Senate and the Speaker of the House of Representatives their written declaration that the President is unable to discharge the powers and duties of his office, the Vice President shall immediately assume the powers and duties of the office as Acting President.

Thereafter, when the President transmits to the President pro tempore of the Senate and the Speaker of the House of Representatives his written declaration that no inability exists, he shall resume the powers and duties of his office unless the Vice President and a majority of either the principal officers of the executive department[s] or of such other body as Congress may by law provide, transmit within four days to the President pro tempore of the Senate and the Speaker of the House of Representatives their written declaration that the President is unable to discharge the powers and duties of his office. Thereupon Congress shall decide the issue, assembling within forty-eight hours for that purpose if not in session. If the Congress, within twenty-one days after receipt of the latter written declaration, or, if Congress is not in session, within twenty-one days after Congress is required to assemble, determines by two-thirds vote of both Houses that the President is unable to discharge the powers and duties of his office, the Vice President shall continue to discharge the same as Acting President; otherwise, the President shall resume the powers and duties of his office.

AMENDMENT XXVI   [*Adopted 1971*]

Section 1.   The right of citizens of the United States, who are eighteen years of age or older, to vote shall not be denied or abridged by the United States or by any State on account of age.

Section 2.   The Congress shall have power to enforce this article by appropriate legislation.

AMENDMENT XXVII*   [*Adopted 1992*]

No law, varying the compensation for services of the Senators and Representatives, shall take effect, until an election of Representatives shall have intervened.

---

* Originally proposed in 1789 by James Madison, this amendment failed to win ratification along with the other parts of what became the Bill of Rights. However, the proposed amendment contained no deadline for ratification, and over the years other state legislatures voted to add it to the Constitution; many such ratifications occurred during the 1980s and early 1990s as public frustration with Congress's performance mounted. In May 1992 the Archivist of the United States certified that, with the Michigan legislature's ratification, the article had been approved by three-fourths of the states and thus automatically became part of the Constitution. But congressional leaders and constitutional specialists questioned whether an amendment that took 202 years to win ratification was valid, and the issue had not been resolved by the time this book went to press.

PRESIDENTIAL ELECTIONS, 1789–2008

Year	States in the Union	Candidates	Parties	Electoral Vote	Popular Vote	Percentage of Popular Vote
1789	11	GEORGE WASHINGTON	No party designations	69		
		John Adams		34		
		Minor candidates		35		
1792	15	GEORGE WASHINGTON	No party designations	132		
		John Adams		77		
		George Clinton		50		
		Minor candidates		5		
1796	16	JOHN ADAMS	Federalist	71		
		Thomas Jefferson	Democratic-Republican	68		
		Thomas Pinckney	Federalist	59		
		Aaron Burr	Democratic-Republican	30		
		Minor candidates		48		
1800	16	THOMAS JEFFERSON	Democratic-Republican	73		
		Aaron Burr	Democratic-Republican	73		
		John Adams	Federalist	65		
		Charles C. Pinckney	Federalist	64		
		John Jay	Federalist	1		
1804	17	THOMAS JEFFERSON	Democratic-Republican	162		
		Charles C. Pinckney	Federalist	14		
1808	17	JAMES MADISON	Democratic-Republican	122		
		Charles C. Pinckney	Federalist	47		
		George Clinton	Democratic-Republican	6		
1812	18	JAMES MADISON	Democratic-Republican	128		
		DeWitt Clinton	Federalist	89		
1816	19	JAMES MONROE	Democratic-Republican	183		
		Rufus King	Federalist	34		
1820	24	JAMES MONROE	Democratic-Republican	231		
		John Quincy Adams	Independent Republican	1		
1824	24	JOHN QUINCY ADAMS	Democratic-Republican	84	108,740	30.5
		Andrew Jackson	Democratic-Republican	99	153,544	43.1
		William H. Crawford	Democratic-Republican	41	46,618	13.1
		Henry Clay	Democratic-Republican	37	47,136	13.2
1828	24	ANDREW JACKSON	Democratic	178	642,553	56.0
		John Quincy Adams	National Republican	83	500,897	44.0
1832	24	ANDREW JACKSON	Democratic	219	687,502	55.0
		Henry Clay	National Republican	49	530,189	42.4
		William Wirt	Anti-Masonic	7	33,108	2.6
		John Floyd	National Republican	11		

Because candidates receiving less than 1 percent of the popular vote are omitted, the percentage of popular vote may not total 100 percent.

Before the Twelfth Amendment was passed in 1804, the electoral college voted for two presidential candidates; the runner-up became vice president.

PRESIDENTIAL ELECTIONS, 1789–2004 (*continued*)

Year	States in the Union	Candidates	Parties	Electoral Vote	Popular Vote	Percentage of Popular Vote
1836	26	MARTIN VAN BUREN	Democratic	170	765,483	50.9
		William H. Harrison	Whig	73		
		Hugh L. White	Whig	26	739,795	49.1
		Daniel Webster	Whig	14		
		W. P. Mangum	Whig	11		
1840	26	WILLIAM H. HARRISON	Whig	234	1,274,624	53.1
		Martin Van Buren	Democratic	60	1,127,781	46.9
1844	26	JAMES K. POLK	Democratic	170	1,338,464	49.6
		Henry Clay	Whig	105	1,300,097	48.1
		James G. Birney	Liberty		62,300	2.3
1848	30	ZACHARY TAYLOR	Whig	163	1,360,967	47.4
		Lewis Cass	Democratic	127	1,222,342	42.5
		Martin Van Buren	Free Soil		291,263	10.1
1852	31	FRANKLIN PIERCE	Democratic	254	1,601,117	50.9
		Winfield Scott	Whig	42	1,385,453	44.1
		John P. Hale	Free Soil		155,825	5.0
1856	31	JAMES BUCHANAN	Democratic	174	1,832,955	45.3
		John C. Frémont	Republican	114	1,339,932	33.1
		Millard Fillmore	American	8	871,731	21.6
1860	33	ABRAHAM LINCOLN	Republican	180	1,865,593	39.8
		Stephen A. Douglas	Democratic	12	1,382,713	29.5
		John C. Breckinridge	Democratic	72	848,356	18.1
		John Bell	Constitutional Union	39	592,906	12.6
1864	36	ABRAHAM LINCOLN	Republican	212	2,206,938	55.0
		George B. McClellan	Democratic	21	1,803,787	45.0
1868	37	ULYSSES S. GRANT	Republican	214	3,013,421	52.7
		Horatio Seymour	Democratic	80	2,706,829	47.3
1872	37	ULYSSES S. GRANT	Republican	286	3,596,745	55.6
		Horace Greeley	Democratic	*	2,843,446	43.9
1876	38	RUTHERFORD B. HAYES	Republican	185	4,034,311	48.0
		Samuel J. Tilden	Democratic	184	4,288,546	51.0
		Peter Cooper	Greenback		75,973	1.0
1880	38	JAMES A. GARFIELD	Republican	214	4,453,295	48.5
		Winfield S. Hancock	Democratic	155	4,414,082	48.1
		James B. Weaver	Greenback-Labor		308,578	3.4
1884	38	GROVER CLEVELAND	Democratic	219	4,879,507	48.5
		James G. Blaine	Republican	182	4,850,293	48.2
		Benjamin F. Butler	Greenback-Labor		175,370	1.8
		John P. St. John	Prohibition		150,369	1.5

*When Greeley died shortly after the election, his supporters divided their votes among the minor candidates.

Because candidates receiving less than 1 percent of the popular vote are omitted, the percentage of popular vote may not total 100 percent.

PRESIDENTIAL ELECTIONS, 1789–2004 (continued)

Year	States in the Union	Candidates	Parties	Electoral Vote	Popular Vote	Percentage of Popular Vote
1888	38	BENJAMIN HARRISON	Republican	233	5,477,129	47.9
		Grover Cleveland	Democratic	168	5,537,857	48.6
		Clinton B. Fisk	Prohibition		249,506	2.2
		Anson J. Streeter	Union Labor		146,935	1.3
1892	44	GROVER CLEVELAND	Democratic	277	5,555,426	46.1
		Benjamin Harrison	Republican	145	5,182,690	43.0
		James B. Weaver	People's	22	1,029,846	8.5
		John Bidwell	Prohibition		264,133	2.2
1896	45	WILLIAM McKINLEY	Republican	271	7,102,246	51.1
		William J. Bryan	Democratic	176	6,492,559	47.7
1900	45	WILLIAM McKINLEY	Republican	292	7,218,491	51.7
		William J. Bryan	Democratic; Populist	155	6,356,734	45.5
		John C. Wooley	Prohibition		208,914	1.5
1904	45	THEODORE ROOSEVELT	Republican	336	7,628,461	57.4
		Alton B. Parker	Democratic	140	5,084,223	37.6
		Eugene V. Debs	Socialist		402,283	3.0
		Silas C. Swallow	Prohibition		258,536	1.9
1908	46	WILLIAM H. TAFT	Republican	321	7,675,320	51.6
		William J. Bryan	Democratic	162	6,412,294	43.1
		Eugene V. Debs	Socialist		420,793	2.8
		Eugene W. Chafin	Prohibition		253,840	1.7
1912	48	WOODROW WILSON	Democratic	435	6,296,547	41.9
		Theodore Roosevelt	Progressive	88	4,118,571	27.4
		William H. Taft	Republican	8	3,486,720	23.2
		Eugene V. Debs	Socialist		900,672	6.0
		Eugene W. Chafin	Prohibition		206,275	1.4
1916	48	WOODROW WILSON	Democratic	277	9,127,695	49.4
		Charles E. Hughes	Republican	254	8,533,507	46.2
		A. L. Benson	Socialist		585,113	3.2
		J. Frank Hanly	Prohibition		220,506	1.2
1920	48	WARREN G. HARDING	Republican	404	16,143,407	60.4
		James N. Cox	Democratic	127	9,130,328	34.2
		Eugene V. Debs	Socialist		919,799	3.4
		P. P. Christensen	Farmer-Labor		265,411	1.0
1924	48	CALVIN COOLIDGE	Republican	382	15,718,211	54.0
		John W. Davis	Democratic	136	8,385,283	28.8
		Robert M. La Follette	Progressive	13	4,831,289	16.6
1928	48	HERBERT C. HOOVER	Republican	444	21,391,993	58.2
		Alfred E. Smith	Democratic	87	15,016,169	40.9
1932	48	FRANKLIN D. ROOSEVELT	Democratic	472	22,809,638	57.4
		Herbert C. Hoover	Republican	59	15,758,901	39.7
		Norman Thomas	Socialist		881,951	2.2

Because candidates receiving less than 1 percent of the popular vote are omitted, the percentage of popular vote may not total 100 percent.

PRESIDENTIAL ELECTIONS, 1789–2004 (*continued*)

Year	States in the Union	Candidates	Parties	Electoral Vote	Popular Vote	Percentage of Popular Vote
1936	48	FRANKLIN D. ROOSEVELT	Democratic	523	27,752,869	60.8
		Alfred M. Landon	Republican	8	16,674,665	36.5
		William Lemke	Union		882,479	1.9
1940	48	FRANKLIN D. ROOSEVELT	Democratic	449	27,307,819	54.8
		Wendell L. Willkie	Republican	82	22,321,018	44.8
1944	48	FRANKLIN D. ROOSEVELT	Democratic	432	25,606,585	53.5
		Thomas E. Dewey	Republican	99	22,014,745	46.0
1948	48	HARRY S TRUMAN	Democratic	303	24,105,812	49.5
		Thomas E. Dewey	Republican	189	21,970,065	45.1
		Strom Thurmond	States' Rights	39	1,169,063	2.4
		Henry A. Wallace	Progressive		1,157,172	2.4
1952	48	DWIGHT D. EISENHOWER	Republican	442	33,936,234	55.1
		Adlai E. Stevenson	Democratic	89	27,314,992	44.4
1956	48	DWIGHT D. EISENHOWER	Republican	457	35,590,472	57.6
		Adlai E. Stevenson	Democratic	73	26,022,752	42.1
1960	50	JOHN F. KENNEDY	Democratic	303	34,227,096	49.7
		Richard M. Nixon	Republican	219	34,108,546	49.5
		Harry F. Byrd	Independent	15	502,363	.7
1964	50	LYNDON B. JOHNSON	Democratic	486	43,126,506	61.1
		Barry M. Goldwater	Republican	52	27,176,799	38.5
1968	50	RICHARD M. NIXON	Republican	301	31,770,237	43.4
		Hubert H. Humphrey	Democratic	191	31,270,533	42.7
		George C. Wallace	American Independent	46	9,906,141	13.5
1972	50	RICHARD M. NIXON	Republican	520	47,169,911	60.7
		George S. McGovern	Democratic	17	29,170,383	37.5
1976	50	JIMMY CARTER	Democratic	297	40,827,394	49.9
		Gerald R. Ford	Republican	240	39,145,977	47.9
1980	50	RONALD W. REAGAN	Republican	489	43,899,248	50.8
		Jimmy Carter	Democratic	49	35,481,435	41.0
		John B. Anderson	Independent		5,719,437	6.6
		Ed Clark	Libertarian		920,859	1.0
1984	50	RONALD W. REAGAN	Republican	525	54,451,521	58.8
		Walter F. Mondale	Democratic	13	37,565,334	40.5
1988	50	GEORGE H. W. BUSH	Republican	426	47,946,422	54.0
		Michael S. Dukakis	Democratic	112	41,016,429	46.0
1992	50	WILLIAM J. CLINTON	Democratic	370	43,728,275	43.2
		George H. W. Bush	Republican	168	38,167,416	37.7
		H. Ross Perot	Independent		19,237,247	19.0

Because candidates receiving less than 1 percent of the popular vote are omitted, the percentage of popular vote may not total 100 percent.

PRESIDENTIAL ELECTIONS, 1789–2008 *(continued)*

YEAR	STATES IN THE UNION	CANDIDATES	PARTIES	ELECTORAL VOTE	POPULAR VOTE	PERCENTAGE OF POPULAR VOTE
1996	50	WILLIAM J. CLINTON	Democratic	379	47,401,185	49.2
		Robert Dole	Republican	159	39,197,469	40.7
		H. Ross Perot	Reform		8,085,294	8.4
2000	50	GEORGE W. BUSH	Republican	271	50,456,141	47.9
		Albert Gore Jr.	Democratic	266	50,996,039	48.4
		Ralph Nader	Green		2,882,807	2.7
2004	50	GEORGE W. BUSH	Republican	286	60,608,582	51.0
		John Kerry	Democratic	252	57,288,974	48.0
		Ralph Nader	Independent		406,924	1.0
2008	50	BARACK OBAMA	Democratic	365	66,050,000*	53*
		John McCain	Republican	173	58,010,000*	46*

*Approximations of popular vote and percentages based on available information as volume went to press.

Because candidates receiving less than 1 percent of the popular vote are omitted, the percentage of popular vote may not total 100 percent.

Photograph Credits